INTERNATIONAL ART TRADE AND LAW

LE COMMERCE INTERNATIONAL DE L'ART ET LE DROIT

Freedom of Museums to Sell, Trade or Otherwise Dispose of Objects of Art in their Collections/Liberté des musées de procéder à des transactions d'objets d'art

Freedom of Collectors to Sell or Give Away All or Part of their Collections/ Liberté du collectionneur de disposer de tout ou partie de sa collection

Rights of Artists and their Heirs/Droits des créateurs et de leurs héritiers

Auction Sales and Conditions/Les conditions de vente aux enchères

International Temporary Exhibitions and Insurance/L'assurance des expositions temporaires internationales

Volume III in the series: *International Sales of Works of Art.*

Cet ouvrage constitue le Volume III de la série des publications: *La Vente Internationale d'Oeuvres d'Art.*

III

International Sales of Works of Art
La Vente Internationale d'Oeuvres d'Art

International Art Trade and Law
Le Commerce International de l'Art et le Droit

Martine Briat
Judith A. Freedberg

Editors

Institute of International Business Law and Practice
International Chamber of Commerce

Springer Science+Business Media, LLC

Kluwer Law and Taxation Publishers
P.O. Box 23 Tel.: 31-5700-47261
7400 GA Deventer Telex: 49295
The Netherlands Fax: 31-5700-22244

ICC Publishing S.A.
38, Cours Albert 1er Tel.: 33-1-49532828
75008 Paris Telex: 650770
France Fax: 33-1-42253623
Telegrams: Incomerc Paris

Cover design: Jacqueline de Jong

ICC Publication 484

ISBN 978-90-6544-546-9 ISBN 978-94-017-1925-4 (eBook)
DOI 10.1007/978-94-017-1925-4

Originally published by Kluwer Academic Publishers in 1991

Introduction

The Programme for the third Symposium on the International Art Trade and Law was developed by the Institute for International Business Law and Practice of the International Chamber of Commerce and its Chairman, Prof. Pierre Lalive who has also provided the Preface to this Volume. Under the auspices of the Institute, a Questionnaire was formulated and circulated. The collected materials were reproduced and distributed at the Symposium by the Amsterdam Chamber of Commerce.

Reporters from thirteen countries responded to the Questionnaire. On the basis of these National Reports, General Reports were prepared and presented at the Symposium.

Part One of this Volume includes:

- Questionnaire covering Topics 1–5
- General information on a number of countries taken from the National Reports.

Part Two is divided into five Sections, corresponding with the five Topics addressed in the Questionnaire:

Topic 1. Freedom of museums to sell, trade or otherwise dispose of objects of art in their collection
Topic 2. Freedom of collectors to sell or give away all or part of their collections
Topic 3. Rights of artists and their heirs
Topic 4. Auction sales and conditions
Topic 5. International temporary exhibitions and insurance

followed by
Concluding Remarks by Prof. John H. Merryman.

Each Topic is dealt with in Part Two in its own Section which is set up as follows:

- Introduction
- General Report(s) (to be read in conjunction with the Questionnaire on that Topic)

- National Reports (to be read in conjunction with the Questionnaire on that Topic)
- Papers on Specific Aspects.

The lively discussions at the Symposium – due to limitation of space – are reported in the form of a brief summary incorporated in the Introduction to each Topic. This summary is followed by a list of the names of the participants who took part in the discussions.

Part One is preceded by the *Addresses*, and Part Two is followed by Annexes comprised of:

- Committees
- Sponsors.

Not all material received from the National Reporters could be reproduced in this Volume. This applies, in particular, to *legislation, court decisions,* and *auction sales conditions* which were annexed to the Reports, the original German language versions of the *National Reports: F.R. Germany* by Messrs. L. Bischop, M. Lange and U. Lohaus, prepared under the supervision of O. Sandrock, and the *'Communication from the [European] Commission to the Council on the Protection of National Treasures Possessing Artistic Historic or Archaeological Value: Needs Arising from the Abolition of Frontiers in 1992'*.

Copies of Reports, with annexes, as well as the 'Communication' can be obtained at cost price from the ICC Institute of International Business Law and Practice, 38 Cours Albert 1er, 75008 Paris.

The editors express their thanks to Dr. Jaap van der Tas for his assistance in reporting the discussions, and, in particular, to Prof. Pieter Sanders for his advice and support in preparing this publication.

Table of Contents

* Editor's note: Report in French.

Préface

De tout temps, l'"oeuvre d'art' semble avoir été considérée à la fois comme l'occasion d'une expérience esthétique et comme un objet de commerce. Jamais pourtant plus qu'aujourd'hui le second aspect n'avait-il pris le pas sur le premier.

L'évolution actuelle peut s'expliquer par deux ordres de raisons au moins, qu'il suffit d'esquisser ici et dont le premier est moins visible que le second. La notion même d'"art' s'est élargie et diversifiée jusqu'à la dilution, et il en est de même du concept d'expérience esthétique; comme l'écrit Yves Michaud:[1] '*Les valeurs du sentir esthétique sont devenues aussi incertaines que l'art où elles sont supposées se manifester*'. Aussi est-il inévitable qu'un public désorienté privilégie toujours davantage, voire exclusivement, ces critères plus saisissables que sont les valeurs monétaires, établies par un marché de l'art où la passion de l'amateur et du collectionneur apparaît souvent secondaire face au goût de l'épargne et de l'investissement ou aux appétits spéculatifs.

On arrive ici au second ordre de raisons, qui sont bien connues: l'importance économique considérable du marché de l'art – qu'une médiatisation à outrance tend du reste à faire peut-être surestimer – un marché de plus en plus international ou internationalisé, au demeurant, comme l'ensemble des relations sociales contemporaines.

La destinée de Vincent Van Gogh, dont le centenaire de la mort vient d'être célébré avec éclat aux Pays-Bas (notamment par la splendide exposition qu'ont visité les nombreux participants au Colloque d'Amsterdam de juin 1990), illustre cette évolution de façon saisissante, plus que celle d'aucun autre peintre sans doute.

On dit que, de son vivant, Van Gogh n'aurait vendu qu'une seule toile, et il pouvait écrire à son frère Théo: 'C'est une perspective assez triste de devoir se dire que jamais peut-être la peinture que je fais n'aura une valeur quelconque'.[2]

1. Dans un récent ouvrage, brillant et 'dérangeant': *L'Artiste et les Commissaires – Quatre essais non pas sur l'art contemporain mais sur ceux qui s'en occupent* (Editions Jacqueline Chambon, Nîmes 1989) p. 25.
2. *Lettres à son frère Théo* (Editions Gallimard, 1988) p. 396 (524 F.).

Quel contraste avec les prix 'records', même gonflés par l'effet souvent méconnu d'un environnement ou d'artifices juridiques ou fiscaux particuliers, de tableaux tels que les Tournesols, les Iris et le Portrait du Dr. Gachet, vendus au cours de ces dernières années aux prix respectivement de 39,6, 53,9 et 82,5 millions de dollars! Ici encore, on peut citer Vincent qui écrivait, plus justement cette fois: '*Moi qui n'ai pas le sou... je dis toujours que l'argent est une monnaie et la peinture en est une autre.*'[3]

Nul aujourd'hui n'ignore donc plus l'importance du commerce international de l'art, importance d'ordre économique et financier certes mais aussi, on le sait moins, d'ordre social, culturel, politique et par conséquent juridique. Il s'en faut de beaucoup, cependant, pour que le public ou les milieux intéressés eux-mêmes mesurent clairement l'impact et la complexité du contexte juridique qui entoure et modèle à la fois cette évolution. Songeons par exemple aux courants, en partie contradictoires, tendant d'une part à la protection du 'patrimoine culturel' des nations et d'autre part à la libéralisation des échanges, notamment dans la perspective du grand marché unique européen de 1993. Que de problèmes, anciens ou nouveaux, se posent et se poseront aux artistes, aux marchands, aux musées, aux Etats, aux organisations internationales, aux associations professionnelles, à l'amateur d'art, bref à 'Monsieur Tout-le-Monde'!

En 1985 et en 1988, l'Institut du Droit et des Pratiques des Affaires Internationales a organisé à Genève, avec le concours de la Faculté de Droit de l'Université, un premier puis un deuxième Colloque international sur les 'Aspects juridiques du commerce international des oeuvres d'art'. Réunissant pour la première fois praticiens et universitaires, de nationalités et de spécialités diverses, ces rencontres interdisciplinaires ont obtenu un succès considérable et donné lieu à deux substantielles publications, sous le titre général *La Vente Internationale d'Oeuvres d'Art*, ouvrages dont il est permis de dire, sans manquer à l'objectivité, qu'ils constituent une mine de renseignements et de réflexions (quelque 1500 pages au total) sur les multiples aspects actuels, juridiques et non-juridiques, du commerce international de l'art.[4]

Fort de la réussite de ces deux expériences et des sollicitations reçues à cet égard, l'Institut du Droit et des Pratiques des Affaires Internationales pouvait dès lors, sans grand risque, se dire 'jamais deux sans trois' et préparer l'organisation d'un troisième Colloque international, lui aussi interdisciplinaire au sens le plus large de ce terme, comparatiste et international.

Après Genève, c'est une autre 'ville-refuge', de vieille tradition, qui a été choisie pour accueillir cette manifestation: Amsterdam, grande cité commerçante en même temps que centre du 'siècle d'or' néerlandais et siège d'admirables musées. Grâce à la collaboration et à l'appui de divers milieux

3. *Op. cit.*, p. 467 (576 F.).
4. A la suite de nombreuses demandes, l'Institut compte faire préparer un *Index général* à la série de publications sur 'La Vente Internationale d'Oeuvres d'Art' pour en faciliter la consultation.

néerlandais, et en particulier de la Chambre de Commerce d'Amsterdam, ainsi que d'une organisation locale efficace et accueillante, la *Stichting Art Trade and Law* que préside M. Jan M. Boll, ce troisième Colloque s'est déroulé de façon parfaite. Il convient ici de renouveler l'expression de notre vive gratitude à tous les artisans de cette manifestation, au Maire de la Ville d'Amsterdam, à M. Jan M. Boll et aux membres de son Comité et de son Conseil; cela sans oublier notre collègue le Professeur Pieter Sanders, qui fait partie aussi du Conseil de l'Institut: c'est à lui et à Madame Judith Freedberg, que les lecteurs du présent ouvrage doivent de recevoir les actes du Colloque, dans un délai si rapide.

A l'heure des remerciements il est impossible d'omettre ces principaux artisans du succès que sont les nombreux rapporteurs et auteurs – on en trouvera plus loin les travaux – et surtout à Madame Martine Briat, directeur de l'Institut, qui a assumé avec une compétence et un dynamisme sans faille la lourde tâche de diriger la préparation, pendant de nombreux mois, de ce troisième Colloque. Le profane n'imagine guère l'importance et les difficultés d'une telle préparation, qui comporte d'abord celle du choix des sujets.

Parmi les divers thèmes possibles d'analyses et de discussions, entre professionnels ou non-professionnels, juristes ou non-juristes, nos consultations nous ont conduit à privilégier quatre grands thèmes d'actualité, ainsi qu'on le verra à la table des matières du présent ouvrage. L'un d'entre eux s'imposait plus que d'autres, car il concernait directement ce que l'on pourrait appeler les 'grands absents' des deux précédents Colloques, les artistes, dont deux représentants n'ont pas hésité à venir exprimer leurs préoccupations, avec talent et clarté, à une assistance aussi nombreuse qu'intéressée. La protection des droits des artistes, et notamment le fameux et controversé 'droit de suite', les droits de leurs héritiers face aux galeries d'art, aux collectionneurs ou aux musées ont fait l'objet de communications et interventions importantes, dont l'intérêt est tel qu'une poursuite de la discussion paraît déjà s'imposer.

On peut en dire autant des autres thèmes du Colloque, découlant eux aussi de l'actualité, qui concernent ces autres 'acteurs' du marché de l'art que sont les musées, les amateurs et collectionneurs, et les marchands, 'auctioneers' ou commissaires-priseurs. Pour les premiers, l'Institut avait choisi de mettre l'accent, plutôt que sur des thèmes 'généraux' déjà discutés précédemment tels que celui de l'acquisition de bonne foi d'une oeuvre d'art, sur deux questions particulières: celle du droit, contesté dans certains pays, de vendre des objets de leurs collections, et celle des expositions temporaires internationales (avec leurs aspects d'assurance, de transport, de douane et de garanties diverses). Pour les derniers, plusieurs communications ont été consacrées à l'évolution, en fait et en droit, des conditions de vente aux enchères, aux tendances actuelles du marché, aux obligations des maisons de vente et à l'éventuelle harmonisation internationale de ces conditions – par exemple dans le cadre du 'marché unique européen'.

Le choix des sujets traités, dans une publication ou dans un Colloque, ne dépend pas seulement – est-il besoin de le dire? – de l'actualité ou d'un dosage 'rationnel' entre les diverses expériences nationales ou les aspects divers d'un domaine interdisciplinaire tel que celui du commerce de l'art. Il dépend aussi, et beaucoup, de considérations d'opportunité ou, simplement, de la disponibilité des auteurs et intervenants. Il est donc inévitable que soient constatés et peut-être regrettés quelques déséquilibres ou quelques 'lacunes', susceptibles du reste d'encourager l'Institut, ainsi qu'aiment à dire les sportifs, à 'faire mieux la prochaine fois'! Quoi qu'il en soit, la présente publication devrait intéresser un vaste public, quand bien même elle ne saurait donner, par la nature même des choses, une idée complète de la diversité et de la richesse des discussions qui se sont poursuivies au cours de ce troisième Colloque international. L'utilité de ce genre de manifestation tient en effet aussi, on le sait, à cet élément essentiel que sont les contacts personnels et les conversations de couloir ou de 'pauses café' entre participants de diverses spécialités et divers pays.

On peut lire dans la correspondance de Berlioz: 'L'Art et le Commerce s'exècrent terriblement'. Assez typique de l'époque romantique, cette observation excessive du génial auteur de la 'Symphonie fantastique' ne se situe-t-elle pas aux antipodes de notre époque, où il serait banal d'affirmer que le commerce aime l'art, avec excès, et où la réciproque elle-même peut paraître manifeste à beaucoup?

Pierre Lalive

Addresses

Welcoming Address

DRS. HEDY D'ANCONA, MINISTER FOR WELFARE, HEALTH AND CULTURAL AFFAIRS, THE NETHERLANDS

read by Drs. J. Riezenkamp, Director General for Cultural Affairs

Mr. Mayor, Ladies and Gentlemen,

I am very grateful to be able to address a few words to you on this occasion, the opening ceremony of the ICC international symposium devoted to art trade and law. During the next two days you will be discussing several problems and concepts which are directly related to international political issues on the one hand, and Dutch cultural policy on the other.

First of all, it is very likely that the free movement rules of 1992 will open up a whole new art market, with both positive and negative effects for international art trade and national protection of each country's cultural heritage. Holland in particular, famous for both its mercantile and artistic traditions, may find itself torn between two opposite concepts.

In the private sphere, the Dutch legal rules relating to the art trade are liberal – there is the 'Conservation of Cultural Heritage Act' which can prevent the sale of art to foreign countries, but this Act covers only a very limited number of artifacts (for instance, only thirty to forty single paintings, that is, not part of a collection). Within the public domain – that part of the Dutch cultural heritage for which the Government is responsible – the protection and conservation of our national art treasures is a prime consideration. We have, however, no formal legislation in this respect, where we act in accordance with the International Council of Museums Code of Professional Ethics.[1] The feeling is that official rules and regulations should be kept to a minimum, and state concern for artworks within its responsibility is self-evident.

This whole problem of free trade versus protection is open to discussion at this symposium. The crux of the matter is how to protect the interests of the individual countries without making the system so impractical that it hinders trade or the legitimate interests of owners. I am looking forward to your conclusions.

Another matter on your agenda is the evolution of the international art

1. Editor's note: excerpts from this Code of Professional Ethics are reproduced *infra* pp. 87–91.

market. There is a flux of new investors with new reasons for buying and collecting art. Prices are soaring. As the writer, Joseph Heller, put it: '*There are people willing to pay a great deal to own the most expensive painting in the world. They will not pay as much for one that costs less.*' Dutch museums (and their foreign counterparts) are finding it increasingly difficult to finance new acquisitions for their collections.

In Holland we have a system of semi-public foundations such as the *Rembrandt Vereniging* which with generous support from the *Prins Bernhard Fonds*, annually spend one and a half to two million guilders on acquisition subsidies, and public funding in the form of direct government subsidies. We do what we can. At this moment, state subsidizing is mainly focussed on the acquisition of contemporary Dutch art, although a policy change is in preparation with a view to a united Europe in 1992.

However, it is in the interests of the art trade itself to keep prices within reasonable boundaries. Museum collections represent cultural history. As such, museum art reflects the cultural value of artworks, and determines more or less the 'gold-standard' of art. If museums cannot collect at this representative level, history may become distorted, and the historical value of art could decline. In the long run, this could have a negative effect on art trading. Let's keep in mind that 'the most expensive painting in the world' is a relative concept.

Because of the extreme prices being paid for works of art, insurance premiums are also fetching records. It is becoming increasingly difficult, financially, to organize comprehensive review exhibitions such as we are experiencing this summer, with Velasquez in Madrid and Van Gogh and Frans Hals here in the Netherlands.

Here we have our State Indemnity Rule to help cope with these problems. A Dutch State-owned museum organizing a top exhibition can apply for a government guarantee for incurred losses or damages during transport or the exhibition itself, to the museum's artworks or those on loan from other museums or private collectors. Museums applying for government support of this kind have to meet certain requirements. Other countries have comparable indemnity rules. It would seem a good idea to harmonize these varying national indemnity rules to allow important exhibitions to travel smoothly from one country to the next. I hope this symposium will be able to prepare some preliminary spadework in this field.

Visits to the Van Gogh and Frans Hals exhibitions have been programmed for the social part of this symposium. Both exhibitions would have been impossible without major government support in insurance matters. I sincerely hope you enjoy the shows. They may well be the last of their kind.

Another item on your work program are the rights of the artist, one such right being the right of remuneration on resale of his work. This applies in various European countries, but not in the Netherlands (which is perhaps one of the reasons for Holland's popularity within the art trade). Your suggestions on this problem could be valuable for Dutch government policy in this respect.

All in all, this promises to be a very interesting symposium. During the next two days you will be putting the learned heads together, or crossing the learned swords, on a large number of issues still open to public, and therefore political, discussion. The results of this symposium could pave the way for government action towards smoother international relationships with a view to the art trade. The solutions to these issues may not be readily available. However, I am confident you will be able to clarify these problems, and am sincerely interested in your conclusions.

I wish you the best of success in the coming days.

Opening Address

THE RIGHT HONOURABLE THE LORD CARRINGTON, K.G.,
CHAIRMAN OF CHRISTIE'S

Ladies and gentlemen, I fully understand that the pressures of Parliament have meant that the Minister was not able to be present and I want to thank the Director General for giving such an interesting speech in her absence.

I apologize for addressing your conference in English. Unfortunately, I do not share the linguistic ability of the famous German General von Moltke, who had the reputation of being able to be silent in seven different languages.

On the face of it, it may seem paradoxical that a conference devoted to the art trade should be opened in one of the world's great public museums. For occasionally one hears criticism of the art market from those involved in the museum world, complaining that auction houses and dealers are responsible for the escalating prices that prevent them from adding to museum collections. While it is inevitable that museums, often dependent on public funds, may find it difficult to compete with the vast sums of money sometimes spent on works of art, it is worth remembering that it was the collections of rich private patrons of the past that formed the basis of many of our great public museums throughout the world. It is as true now as it ever was that the private collections of today often become the museums of tomorrow.

The encouragement and support of serious private collectors is by no means, therefore, detrimental to the future of our great museums and galleries. The art market provides the means by which collectors, both private and public, can buy and sell works of art and it is the international aspect of this market that I want to emphasize.

The international art market is nothing new. Many of you in Amsterdam will remember the great sale of the Nanking cargo. Although sold only four years ago, it had originally left the Far East to satisfy the enormous demand for oriental porcelain in mid-eighteenth century Europe. The disaster that befell the Dutch East Indiaman, the 'GELDERMALSEN', in the South China Sea in 1751 delayed the sale of her cargo by two hundred years. However, it received the same enthusiastic welcome that no doubt it would have done had the unfortunate ship arrived on time.

Culture has never been a respecter of national frontiers: the art of Holland was enriched by its trading contacts with the Far East. It is difficult to imagine the development of European porcelain, for example, divorced from the influence of porcelain making in China and Japan. One of the great glories of Britain is her country houses filled with works of art acquired on the Grand Tour or through our international trade and our Empire.

Naturally, there is now a desire to see these collections preserved in the country where they now are and most countries have regulations to control the export of national treasures. Very few would dispute the desirability of some sort of control, but we must be careful to avoid systems of export regulation that are confiscatory to the private owner and, by their rigidity, merely have the effect of encouraging smuggling. We must also be careful of cultural nationalism that incarcerates art within national frontiers and prevents the cross-fertilization of ideas on which the development of art and taste so clearly depends.

Here in Europe, the impending completion of the single market in 1992, bringing with it the removal of frontier restrictions within the Community, has brought this debate to a head. A way must be found of reconciling, on the one hand, the anxieties of some Member States that their national heritage will be threatened with, on the other hand, the spirit of liberalism upon which the European Community is based. Above all, a solution must be found that is practical and workable.

It is interesting that the founders of the European Community recognized this problem when they incorporated in the Treaty of Rome the right of Member States to protect their national treasures from export. With the advent of the Single Market, no doubt there will be a need for some sort of definition of what is meant by 'national treasures'.

However, the same article of the Treaty of Rome goes on to rule that the right to restrict export must not be used as an artificial means of inhibiting free trade. The European Community is based on the desire to facilitate trade within Europe and between Europe and the outside world. The art market is part of this and is now hugely valuable. Last year, for example, works of art to the value of £ 1,670 million were imported into Great Britain alone and the value of exports was £ 1,864 million. The economic benefits in terms of invisible earnings and taxation revenue are considerable.

In our discussions about the free movement of works of art within the European Community, we must not forget the rest of the world. Both economically and culturally a 'fortress Europe' mentality, which substitutes one form of nationalism for another, must be resisted.

Your conference will, no doubt, consider many of the problems that the international trade encounters. I have already mentioned the need to reconcile the rights of private owners to buy and sell works of art with the desire of nations to preserve what they see as their national heritage. Another consideration is the varying laws that surround the change of title of ownership of works of art. Under English law, for instance, except in rare circumstances of a sale through market overt, title to stolen property can never pass to a subsequent buyer, however innocent. In some jurisdictions, title to previously stolen property can pass to an innocent buyer. This problem can only get worse with the creation of the Single Market.

Tracing and policing the illegal market in stolen works of art is another consideration. More than one independent organization is developing an international scheme to record on computer and disseminate information on stolen works of art. To be effective such a service has to be up to date, easy to refer to and not too expensive. These problems are being addressed and developments will be watched with interest by the art trade, museums, collectors and policing agencies alike.

Certainly the experience of Christie's demonstrates the strength and variety of the international art market. Here in Amsterdam, for example, we held our first sale ever entirely devoted to the Cobra group of post war artists. In Hong Kong in March we sold Oriental works of art, including a modern Chinese painting for over three and one-half million Hong Kong dollars.

Auction sales have taken place in Geneva, Rome, Monaco and London and, as many of you will have read, in New York a painting by Van Gogh of Dr. Gachet, sold for a world record price of $82.5 million. Only twenty years or so ago, virtually all Christie's sales took place in London and only a small proportion of things sold came from outside of the United Kingdom. Now, auction sales are held in most major centres throughout the world, and I hope that all the European capitals in particular will soon be opened up to international competition. I have mentioned the high points, but every day thousands of works of art change hands for much lower values throughout the world.

A growing and prospering market such as this of course produces new and more complex problems, and I see from the agenda of your meeting that many distinguished speakers will be addressing you on a range of topics which are of great concern to all of us involved in the international art market. May I wish you well in your discussions.

CHENUE
EMBALLEUR
RIJKSMUSEUM
A4004 1641-B2
LORENZO MONACO
Kop van een Madonna
K896
4004
Inventaris A

The Adventures of a Madonna Painting

PROF. DR. HENK W. VAN OS, DIRECTOR-GENERAL OF THE RIJKSMUSEUM

This small Madonna painting can be found in the department of Foreign Paintings of the Rijksmuseum. Although it has been attributed to the fourteenth century Florentine painter Lorenzo Monaco, modern expert opinion tends to favour an unknown artist from his circle.

On this occasion, however, our attention is not focused on the front of the painting, but on the back, from which its history – one might say its complete *Art Trade* provenance – can be deduced.

The left-hand bottom corner shows an Italian inscription, probably dating from the eighteenth century. Although some of the words are no longer legible, the content is clear: the portrait, having fallen into the sea and floated around for three days, was miraculously washed ashore and retrieved.

Such stories about Madonna portraits have been circulated before, and were often devised to promote the unique and holy aspects of the portraits of the Virgin Mary.

From the inscription on a photograph from 1903, it appears that the panel was in the Carthusian monastery in Galluzo, Italy, at that time – and may already have been there much earlier. The oval label in the left-hand top corner of the Paris transport firm Chenue proves the panel to have been the property of a certain Braner in 1910, as it reads: Braner 5/7/10.

In 1934 it was in the Otto Lanz collection in Amsterdam and consequently on show in the famous *Italiaansche kunst in Nederlands bezit* exhibition in the Amsterdam Stedelijk Museum in that same year. Otto Lanz was a Swiss surgeon, who had been living on the Museumplein in Amsterdam since 1902. He had an extensive collection of early Italian art, and 122 of the 1293 entries in the Stedelijk Museum exhibition were borrowed from his collection. He died in 1935 and shortly afterwards his whole collection was entrusted for safe-keeping to the Rijksmuseum, because of the financial situation of the estate.

After long negotiations, the collection was purchased in 1941 for the museum of Adolf Hitler – the *Führersmuseum* – in Linz. Shortly afterwards it was transferred to Germany and housed in the Kremsmünster monastery in Austria. For security reasons it was stored with thousands of other works of art in the salt mines of Alt Aussee in 1944. The central black crayon number on the back of the panel testifies to this. Plans to blow up the whole art collection when capitulation was imminent, were thwarted by sabotage. And so an essential part of European cultural property was saved thanks to the dedication of a number of courageous Austrians.

After the war, all the paintings, including our Madonna, were sent to the Central Collecting Point of the Allied Powers in München. And this is where *Art Trade* ends and *Law* begins: the restitution of the works of art to their rightful owners. This meant restitutions to countries, not to private individuals. Purchases by the Nazis were considered to have taken place under duress, so that the objects in question were considered spoils of war that had to be returned. Consequently, the Lanz collection was not transferred to the heirs, but to the kingdom of the Netherlands, in this case to the *Stichting Nederlands Kunstbezit*, founded for this purpose, and subsequently called the *Dienst voor 's Rijks Verspreide Kunstvoorwerpen*, the present *Rijksdienst Beeldende Kunst* (Netherlands Office for Fine Arts.)

Thus the Madonna found herself in our museum, together with a number of other paintings. It was given on loan to the Rijksmuseum in 1948 (cf. the label to the left: 1430, *Inventaris* C). In 1960, the loan was turned into ownership (cf. the label to the right: 4004 *Inventaris* A). And so the recuperation of art bought by the Nazis resulted in an important enrichment of the Dutch public art collection.

Part One: General

QUESTIONNAIRE ON TOPICS 1–5

TOPIC 1. FREEDOM OF MUSEUMS TO SELL, TRADE OR OTHERWISE DISPOSE OF OBJECTS OF ART IN THEIR COLLECTIONS

1. May a museum sell, trade or otherwise dispose of an object or objects of art in its collection?

2. What kinds of objects of art held by a museum may be sold? Under which procedures?

3. What kinds of museums can sell objects of art?

4. Is a museum authorized to sell an object of art which was part of a gift from a private person? If yes, is there a period prior to which such a sale cannot be made?

5. When an object of art is part of a public collection, is it possible to transfer or export it? Under which procedures?

6. Are you aware of any cases in which an object of art held by a museum or belonging to a nation's cultural patrimony was exported, sold or otherwise disposed of? If yes, please describe any judicial actions (or other action) which resulted.

7. Please indicate any acts, decrees or regulations or decisions which could be used as a basis for judicial action in the following situations:

a. A museum has sold an object of art belonging to a nation's 'cultural patrimony'.
b. A museum has sold an object of art *not* classified or *not* registered as a 'national cultural good'
- to a private person
- to another museum.

c. A museum has exchanged an object of art
- classified or registered as a 'national cultural good'
- *not* classified or *not* registered as 'national cultural good'

with another museum
- located in your country
- located in another country.

d. A museum has sold an object of art to a private person or another museum because its aesthetic value was lower at the time of the sale than at the time of its acquisition because of an error in the appraisal of its authenticity.

TOPIC 2. FREEDOM OF COLLECTORS TO SELL OR GIVE AWAY ALL OR PART OF THEIR COLLECTIONS

1. Can a private collector sell or give as a gift all or part of a collection belonging to him but classified as a 'national cultural good'

- to a private person of his choice
- to an auction house
- to a museum of his choice
- to a private foundation (charity)
- to any foreign person, auction house, museum or foundation in any country?

2. Under each of the above-mentioned circumstances, how would the price be determined in case of a sale?

3. Can a private collector sell or give as a gift an object of art belonging to him which is not classified as a 'national cultural good'

- to a private person of his choice
- to an auction house
- to any foreign person, auction house, museum or foundation in any country?

4. Under which conditions may a private collector choose freely the country in which the object of art belonging to him will be situated? May a collector with residence in several countries send all or part of his collection from one residence to another?

TOPIC 3. RIGHTS OF ARTISTS AND THEIR HEIRS

1. What are the rights held by artists on their work? What can they prohibit? What requires their consent? How can they commercially exploit their work?

2. What are the conditions required for the exercise of the following rights by artists or their heirs, particularly in relation to *a.* galleries; and *b.* museums:

- right to disclose a work
- right to reproduce a work
- right to perform a work
- right to use a work
- right to receive royalties and resale proceeds from a work
- right to exhibit a work even if it is owned by a private person and whether or not it is held in a private or public place

- right to withdraw an authorization given by the artist to reproduce, disclose or perform a work
- right to destroy a work
- right to oppose the exhibition of a work whether or not it has been exhibited previously
- right to object to any substantial alteration or relocation of a work which threatens its integrity
- right to be recognized as the creator of a work?

Please describe all other rights accruing to an artist as well as the conditions necessary to their exercise.

3. Is it possible to assign any of the above-mentioned rights to the heirs of an artist? If yes, which rights, to which heirs, and how must they be assigned?

TOPIC 4. AUCTION SALES AND CONDITIONS

1. Are auction sales conditions regulated in your countries? If yes, by whom? How?

2. Can you provide us with the text of standard auction sales conditions?

3. What are the risks involved in auctioning works of art of unclear origin or ownership? How do auction sales conditions deal with these problems? What other commercial realities have a bearing on these problems; please give examples.

4. Will auction sales conditions be harmonized in 1992? If yes, how?

TOPIC 5. INTERNATIONAL TEMPORARY EXHIBITIONS AND INSURANCE

1. What are the main difficulties faced by the principal organizer of an international temporary exhibition?

2. What other difficulties arise from the organization of an international temporary exhibition?

3. How are the liabilities shared among the bodies (institutions or other persons) organizing an international temporary exhibition?

4. Please list the international treaties which govern international temporary exhibitions.

GENERAL INFORMATION BY COUNTRY

(TAKEN FROM NATIONAL REPORTS)

Austria: Introduction*

Ignaz Seidl-Hohenveldern**

I. PRELIMINARY REMARKS

The notion of 'museum' is not defined by law. Art. 31 of the Federal Law of 1 July 1981 in the version of *Bundesgesetzblatt* (henceforth BGBl) 1989/663 on the Organization of Research describes the tasks of the Federal Museums to be collecting, safeguarding, presenting to the public and taking inventory of objects of art, undertaking research and advising other museums. There are two strands controlling the activities of museums mentioned in Topic 1 of the Questionnaire:

(1) the right of control of the State (i.e., the Federation, and its regional sub-entities, i.e., the *Länder* and towns) as owner of the museum concerned,
(2) the right of control of the State acting *jure imperii* to protect objects of art as national monuments and to prevent their export.

These strands overlap in most cases.

II. RIGHT OF CONTROL AS OWNER

Most of the Austrian art collections and certainly the best-known ones are Federal Museums. Here, I shall only indicate the rights of control resulting from the ownership of the Federation. We must keep in mind, however, that the situation is more or less similar in respect of museums owned by the *Länder* or municipalities, the Federal Laws and officers mentioned *infra* being replaced by the corresponding *Land* or municipal laws or officers, e.g., the Federal Minister by *Land* or City Councillor. In general, a museum does not enjoy full legal personality separate from the territorial entity owning it. Federal Museums enjoy a semi-autonomy in financial matters,

* Editor's note: *see* 'National Report on Topic 1' *infra* p. 97, 'National Report on Topic 2' *infra* p. 169, 'National Report on Topic 3' *infra* p. 223, 'National Report on topic 4' *infra* p. 365 and 'National Report on Topic 5' *infra* p. 433.

** Professor, Institut für Völkerrecht und Internationale Beziehungen, Vienna.

e.g., they can freely accept gifts or dispose of the profits from the museum cafeteria. At the end of the fiscal year, these sums may be carried over and are not absorbed in the general Federal budget. However, this right of relative financial autonomy does not include an autonomous right of disposal concerning objects in the museum's collection (Art. 31a(1) under *1* of the above-mentioned Federal Law).

According to Art. 63 of the Federal Budget Law, BGBl 1986/213, the Federal Minister of Finance may sell, exchange or give away Federal assets, if such disposal serves the fulfillment of a Federal task, or if the object is no longer needed and if the value of the assets does not exceed a maximum amount of 10 million Schilling (1.4 million DM) for a single item or 150 million Schilling for all component parts of a bulk transaction. In all other cases such disposal requires the enactment of a Federal Law pursuant to Art. 42(5) of the Federal Constitution.

According to a General Notice published in the *Official Journal* of the Austrian Finance Administration (*Amtsblatt der Osterr. Finanzverwaltung*) No. 1 of 2 January 1986, the sale or exchange of movables by the competent authority (in the case of museum, the Federal Minister of Research) requires the agreement of the Federal Minister of Finance only if the value of the individual item exceeds 150,000 Schilling (21,000 DM) or 1.5 million Schilling (210,000 DM) for a bulk transaction.

The right to dispose of property belonging to entities of the Roman Catholic Church is governed by Art. XIII(2) of the Austrian Concordat of 5 June 1933, BGBl 1934 II/2 according to which Church property is administered in accordance with Canon law. Disposal of Church property requires the agreement of the superior religious authority competent under Canon law.[1]

III. RIGHT TO CONTROL THE DISPOSAL OF MONUMENTS *JURE IMPERII*

The Federal Monuments Office (*Bundesdenkmalamt*) exercises *jure imperii* control rights,

(1) over all monuments in Austria pursuant to the Federal Law on the Protection of Monuments (FLPM) as last amended by Federal Law BGBl 1978/167,[2] and
(2) over the export of such monuments pursuant to the Federal Law Prohibiting the Export of Cultural Property (FLPECP) as last amended by Federal Law BGBl 1986/391.[3]

Unlike many other countries, Austria has not established any list of objects

1. Supreme Court, 28 May 1980, 32 Österr. Zeitschrift f. öff. Recht u. Völkerrecht (1982) pp. 294 *et seq.*, 110 Clunet (1983) p. 633.
2. Cf. N. HELFGOTT, *Die Rechtsvorschriften für den Denkmalschutz* (Vienna, Manz 1979).
3. Cf. N. HELFGOTT, *Ausfuhrverbotsgesetz für Kulturgut* (Vienna, Manz 1987).

belonging to Austria's 'cultural patrimony' or to Austria's 'national cultural goods'.

Austrian law assumes that any object of historic, artistic or otherwise cultural significance owned by a public or religious entity is a protected object (monument), unless the Federal Monuments Office, upon request by the owner, certifies that a given object belonging to that category is not a monument.[4]

The Federal Monuments Office may declare any other significant object to be a monument, if this is in the public interest. Such declaration must be notified to the owner by an individual administration act.[5]

The Federal Monuments Office may declare any collection not owned by a public or religious entity to constitute a single monument, whose continued existence as a unit lies in the public interest.[6] A similar declaration in respect to collections owned by public or religious entities is redundant in view of the general assumption of Art. 2(1) FLPM.

There are only very few private collections in Austria. The more important ones have been declared to constitute a single monument pursuant to Art. 4(3) and Art. 6(5) FLPM, e.g., the Leopold collection and the Harrach collection. Individual items in other private collections not declared to constitute a single monument may yet be declared individually to constitute a monument pursuant to Art. 3(1) FLPM.

1. Transfer inside Austria

Monuments owned exclusively or predominantly by public or religious entities may be sold, given away or exchanged only with the written consent of the Federal Monuments Office (Art. 6(1) and Art. 4(2) FLPM).

The Federal Monuments Office will give such consent only if it is informed of the name of the new owner. The Office then will put the new owner on notice that the object acquired by him is a protected monument. Such notice is redundant if the object is acquired by another public or religious entity.

A disposal without the consent of the Federal Monuments Office is not void in such a case, but the object concerned retains its quality as a monument pursuant to Art. 2, i.e., the new owner cannot export it.[7]

Any sale, gift or exchange of a monument owned by a private person must be announced forthwith to the Federal Monuments Office, indicating the name of the new owner. The former owner, moreover, has to inform the new owner of the fact that the latter has acquired a monument.[8]

---

4. Art. 2(1) FLPM, HELFGOTT, *Die Rechtsvorschriften für den Denkmalschutz*, p. 47.
5. Art. 3(1) FLPM, HELFGOTT, *Die Rechtsvorschriften für den Denkmalschutz*, p. 53.
6. Arts. 4(3) and 6(5) FLPM, HELFGOTT, *Die Rechtsvorschriften für den Denkmalschutz*, pp. 56 and 70.
7. HELFGOTT, *Die Rechtsvorschriften für den Denkmalschutz*, p. 72.
8. Art. 6(4) FLPM, HELFGOTT, *Die Rechtsvorschriften für den Denkmalschutz*, p. 70.

The voluntary sale, gift, exchange or mortgaging of individual objects from private collections which, as a unit, have been declared to constitute a monument, requires the written consent of the Federal Monuments Office. Such a sale without the written consent is null and void pursuant to Art. 879 ABGB (Austrian General Civil Code). An object sold without such consent may be declared forfeited.[9]

A forcible auction of individual objects from such a collection shall be stopped at the request of the Federal Monuments Office. However, such a collection may be put on auction if it is sold as a single unit.[10]

Any sale or purchase without the consent of the Federal Monuments Office or any non-observance of the obligation to inform this Office may be punished by up to six weeks arrest and/or by the corresponding fine. Each day of arrest may be converted into a sum of money to be paid as fine. This sum varies in accordance with the income of the person concerned (Art. 14(1) FLPM).

In addition thereto, the offender may have to pay the sum required to purchase an object of similar quality if the object concerned has been lost to Austria owing to his activities (replacement fine) (Art. 14(2) FLPM). The statute of limitations begins to run only from the moment when the facts became known to the Federal Monuments Office (Art. 14(5) FLPM).

2. *Export from Austria*

Any export of monuments from Austria requires permission by the Federal Monuments Office pursuant to the Federal Law Prohibiting the Export of Cultural Property (Art. 2(1) FLPECP). The work of living artists and of artists having died less than twenty years ago shall be held to be monuments only if they have become part of a collection owned by public or religious entities (Art. 2(5) FLPECP).

I refer to my report to the Second ICC Symposium on the International Trade in Art as to the circumstances which govern the policy of the Federal Monuments Office for granting individual or even general export permission.[11] In case of a risk of export of even a single monument of particularly high value belonging to a private collection not constituting a monument as a unit, such monument may be placed under supervision. Any change in the existence, in the place or custody and in the person of the holder shall be notified forthwith to the Federal Monuments Office.[12]

---

9. Art. 14(2) FLPM, HELFGOTT, *Die Rechtsvorschriften für den Denkmalschutz*, p. 85.
10. Art. 6(5) FLPM, HELFGOTT, *Die Rechtsvorschriften für den Denkmalschutz*, p. 70.
11. As reported in B. KNAPP, 'General Report – Restriction to the Importation and Exportation in the Art Trade' in ICC Institute, ed., *International Sales of Works of Art/La Vente Internationale d'Oeuvres d'Art* (Paris/Deventer, ICC Publishing/Kluwer 1990) p. 15 at p. 29.
12. Art. 4(2) FLPECP, HELFGOTT, *Ausfuhrverbotsgesetz für Kulturgut*, p. 94.

A violation of the general export prohibition shall constitute an offence to be punished by arrest for up to six months and/or the corresponding fine.[13] To any such fine will be added the replacement fine (Art. 12(2) FLPECP). Otherwise, the object concerned may be forfeited.[14]

13. Art. 12(1) FLPECP, HELFGOTT, *Ausfuhrverbotsgesetz für Kulturgut*, p. 44.
14. Art. 12(4) FLPECP, HELFGOTT, *Ausfuhrverbotsgesetz für Kulturgut*, p. 44.

Belgique: Introduction

Francis Haumont*

Le présent rapport rédigé dans le cadre du colloque qui s'est tenu en juin 1990 à Amsterdam sur certains aspects juridiques du commerce international de l'art porte sur la disponibilité des objets d'art en droit belge.

Il nous est apparu indispensable de procéder en deux étapes.

Dans une première partie, nous exposerons les différentes mesures en droit belge prises dans le cadre de la politique de protection du patrimoine culturel mobilier et tendant à limiter la disponibilité de l'objet d'art.

Dans la seconde partie du rapport, nous apporterons les réponses les plus complètes possibles au Questionnaire en nous basant sur l'exposé de la première partie.[1]

I. LES LIMITATIONS A LA LIBRE DISPOSITION DES OBJETS D'ART EN DROIT BELGE

1. Introduction institutionnelle

Avant de procéder à l'examen des mesures juridiques tendant à limiter la disponibilité d'une oeuvre d'art par son propriétaire, il est indispensable de donner un rapide aperçu de l'organisation institutionnelle complexe de la Belgique.

En effet, les compétences qui jadis appartenaient au seul Etat central, sont aujourd'hui, avec la fédéralisation de la Belgique, réparties entre différentes institutions à savoir l'Etat, les Régions et les Communautés.

La Belgique comporte trois Régions: la Région wallonne, la Région flamande et la Région de Bruxelles-capitale. Elle comporte également trois Communautés: la Communauté française, la Communauté flamande et la Communauté germanophone. Une des principales difficultés de compréhension du système institutionnel belge réside dans le fait que les territoires des Régions et des Communautés se superposent sans coïncider.

---

* Chargé de cours à l'Université Catholique de Louvain; Avocat au Barreau de Bruxelles.

1. Note d'Editeur: *v.* pour le 'Rapport National sur le sujet 1' *infra* p. 99 et pour le 'Rapport National sur le sujet 2' *infra* p. 171.

En matière de protection du patrimoine culturel, les compétences se partagent entre les Régions et les Communautés: le patrimoine culturel immobilier (monuments et sites) est de la compétence des Régions, tandis que la protection du patrimoine culturel mobilier dépend des Communautés. Ceci explique que nous mentionnons des décrets communautaires qui régissent ces questions. Cependant, certaines dispositions nationales restent d'application faute d'avoir été remplacées par des décrets communautaires.

2. *Les instruments de limitation de la disponibilité*

A côté des mesures radicales que constituent les appropriations des objets d'art par les pouvoirs publics, il existe d'autres instruments d'intervention auxquels ceux-ci peuvent recourir, plus limités à première vue, mais qui peuvent s'avérer particulièrement efficaces: les mesures limitant la disponibilité de l'objet d'art.

a. Le classement

La loi du 7 août 1931 sur la conservation des monuments et des sites permet de classer les monuments et les édifices dont la conservation est d'intérêt national (aujourd'hui, on parlera d'intérêt communautaire ou régional). Ce classement a pour effet de placer lesdits monuments et édifices sous la protection des autorités chargées de la protection du patrimoine culturel.[2]

En ce qui concerne les objets d'art, ce classement ne sera efficace que dans la mesure où certains de ces objets peuvent être considérés comme des immeubles par incorporation ou par destination.[3] Dans cette hypothèse, le classement de l'immeuble frappera également ces objets d'art considérés comme des immeubles. Cela est d'ailleurs expressément prévu par le décret du 3 mars 1976 applicable en Communauté flamande[4] et par le décret du 17 juillet 1987 applicable en Communauté française.[5]

Ce régime du classement d'immeuble ne touche donc qu'indirectement les objets d'art et, dans la pratique, ne semble réellement efficace du point de vue de la protection du patrimoine culturel mobilier que pour le mobilier d'églises classées.

De plus, l'effet du classement de l'immeuble proprement dit sur les objets d'art devenus immeubles est limité. On constate effectivement que, dans le cadre de la loi du 7 août 1931 précitée, le propriétaire d'un monument ou d'un édifice classé ne peut y apporter aucun changement définitif qui en modifie l'aspect, avant d'y avoir été autorisé par les autorités compétentes.[6]

2. Art. 1er. Ce mécanisme a été repris par le décret du 3 mars 1976 applicable en Communauté flamande et par le décret du 17 juillet 1987 applicable en Communauté française.
3. Cf. art. 517 Code civil.
4. Art. 2, 2.
5. Art. 1er, a) 1°.
6. Art. 3, al. 1er. *V. aussi* décret du 3 mars 1976 (Communauté flamande), art. 11, §1er.

Si des transformations sont apportées aux bâtiments, elles seront, sauf exceptions, aisément percevables et donc contrôlables. En revanche, l'enlèvement d'un tableau ou d'une statuette passera plus inaperçu, particulièrement lorsque l'inventaire des objets d'art devenus immeubles par incorporation ou par destination n'a pas été établi.

Les objets d'art peuvent, en tant qu'éléments du patrimoine culturel mobilier, faire également l'objet d'un classement.

C'est ainsi que les arts. 17 à 20 de la loi du 7 août 1931 précitée prévoient l'établissement d'un inventaire des objets mobiliers appartenant aux différentes autorités publiques dont la conservation est d'intérêt national ou communautaire. Ce régime n'est cependant pas applicable aux musées de l'Etat (et aujourd'hui des Communautés) et des provinces.

Le fait d'être repris dans cet inventaire entraîne le classement d'un objet.[7]

Un tel classement aura pour effet de soumettre toute restauration, réparation ou aliénation de l'objet à autorisation préalable.[8] Toute aliénation faite sans cette autorisation préalable sera nulle et l'action en nullité imprescriptible.[9]

Bien qu'en vigueur depuis près de 60 ans, ce texte n'a donné lieu à aucune application, les autorités chargées de dresser de tels inventaires ne s'estimant pas équipées pour cette tâche.

Ce mécanisme de classement d'objets mobiliers s'apparente, en fait, à celui de l'affectation d'objets d'art au domaine public. En effet, ce classement n'est applicable qu'aux objets mobiliers appartenant aux pouvoirs publics et ces derniers peuvent garantir à ce patrimoine culturel mobilier une protection similaire par leur seule affectation au domaine public. Nous y reviendrons.[10]

La Communauté flamande s'est manifestement davantage souciée de la protection des objets d'art. Un décret du Conseil flamand du 17 novembre 1982 portant protection du patrimoine culturel mobilier instaure un mécanisme de protection proche de celui prévu aux arts. 17 et suivants de la loi du 7 août 1931. Les modalités de mise en oeuvre et de fonctionnement de ce régime de protection sont cependant nettement plus précises.

Il revient à l'Exécutif flamand de dresser des projets de liste d'objets ou de collections qui font partie du patrimoine culturel mobilier appartenant aux autorités publiques. Ces projets de liste peuvent devenir des listes établies par l'Exécutif suite à une procédure d'enquête et de consultation.[11] Le fait d'être classé dans ces listes assure à l'objet d'art ou à la collection une protection renforcée: obligation de maintenir les objets et collections classés *in situ*,[12] interdiction d'aliénation et d'exportation sans autorisation

7. Loi du 7 août 1931, art. 18.
8. Art. 19, al. 1er.
9. Art. 20.
10. *V. infra.*
11. Arts. 4–6.
12. Art. 8, §1er.

préable,[13] obligation de maintenir les objets classés en bon état et d'informer immédiatement l'Exécutif de toute destruction et endommagement.[14]

Par ailleurs, le classement ouvre au propriétaire de l'objet ou la collection classés la possibiltié de se voir allouer par l'Exécutif flamand des subventions pour l'exécution de travaux de réparation et de restauration du patrimoine culturel mobilier protégé.[15]

Ce régime de protection s'applique aux objets et collections appartenant à des personnes morales de droit public à l'exception toutefois des musées, des bibliothèques et des archives du Royaume ou de la Communauté flamande.[16] A cet égard, la même observation que celle déjà émise à propos des dipositions de la loi du 7 août 1931 peut être formulée, à savoir que ce régime se rapproche singulièrement de celui de la domanialité publique.

Il est toutefois possible d'étendre l'application de ce régime au patrimoine culturel mobilier appartenant à des personnes privées.

Toutefois, cette extension ne sera possible que si la personne privée propriétaire des objets ou des collections à protéger le demande expressément.[17]

Il s'agit là d'un comportement à première vue peu banal dans le chef d'un tel propriétaire. Il se comprend mieux lorsque l'on sait que, dans cette hypothèse, le propriétaire qui a demandé que tout ou partie de son patrimoine culturel mobilier soit classé et protégé, peut bénéficier de l'allocation de subventions en vue de réparer ou restaurer ces objets ou ces collections.[18]

b. L'affectation au domaine public

Les biens appartenant aux pouvoirs publics sont répartis entre leur domaine public et leur domaine privé.

Sans entrer dans l'exposé des controverses quant aux définitions de la notion de domaine public,[19] retenons, pour notre part, que fait partie du domaine public, 'tout bien appartenant à une personne administrative qui, soit à raison de sa configuration, soit à raison d'un aménagement spécial, soit à raison de son importance historique ou scientifique, est nécessaire à un service public ou à la satisfaction d'un besoin public et ne saurait être remplacé par un autre'.[20]

Si l'essentiel du domaine public des autorités administratives est constitué de biens immeubles, le régime de la domanialité publique peut également

13. Art. 8, §2.
14. Art. 8, §3.
15. Art. 14 *et seq.*
16. Art. 2, 6°.
17. Art. 32.
18. Art. 14, §1er.
19. *V.* sur cette question, J. DEMBOUR, *Droit administratif* (Université de Liège 1978) pp. 362 *et seq.*
20. M. WALINE, *Manuel élémentaire de droit administratif* (Sirey, Paris 1946) p. 432.

s'appliquer à des biens meubles. Cette extension du domaine public résulte d'une construction jurisprudentielle et doctrinale.[21]

La jurisprudence soumet l'application du régime de la domanialité publique aux biens meubles à deux conditions. La première est qu'une décision de l'autorité compétente ait donné aux biens une destination qui les soumet à l'usage du public. Il faut, en outre, que cette décision ait été exécutée, c'est-à-dire que l'objet soit concrétement affecté à cet usage.[22]

C'est ainsi qu'appartiennent au domaine public, au même titre d'ailleurs que les bâtiments qui les abritent, les objets des collections réunies par les différentes autorités publiques dans leurs musées ou bibliothèques et mises à la disposition du public en vue de son instruction scientifique, artistique ou professionnelle.[23]

Il est important de souligner que les collections des musées et des bibliothèques ne font pas partie de plein droit du domaine public. Comme nous l'avons relevé précédemment, la Cour de cassation considère que des objets mobiliers qualifiés 'd'antiquités' et appartenant aux pouvoirs publics, dussent-ils intéresser l'histoire et la géologie, ne sont pas, de leur nature, affectés à l'usage de tous. Ils ne sont du domaine public que lorsqu'un acte leur a donné une destination qui les soumet à l'usage du public et que cette destination a été réalisée. Un simple arrêté se bornant à prescrire le transfert à des dépôts spéciaux, des objets qui intéressent la géologie, la minéralogie et l'histoire n'implique pas le transfert réel et effectif à l'usage de tous.[24]

Les objets servant à l'exercice du culte, tels vases et ornements sacrés de même que les accessoires indispensables à la célébration du culte font partie du domaine public. La Cour de cassation a même considéré que les objets d'art comme les tableaux, tapisseries et boiseries exposés en vue de la simple ornementation des églises font partie également du domaine public, en raison du fait qu''étant destinés à exciter la piété des fidèles, ils doivent être considérés comme affectés directement à l'usage de tous'.[25]

Le fait de faire partie du domaine public d'une autorité administrative garantit à l'objet d'art ainsi affecté une protection contre les éventuelles emprises des particuliers de même que contre les agissements des pouvoirs publics. En effet, les biens du domaine public sont soumis à un régime juridique spécial qui consacre leur indisponibilité par le biais des règles d'inaliénabilité, d'imprescriptibilité et d'insaisissabilité.

Concrètement, cela implique qu'il ne sera pas possible au pouvoir public propriétaire d'un objet d'art affecté au domaine public de le vendre ou de le céder. De même, un particulier ne pourra pas se prévaloir des régles de la prescription acquisitive pour en réclamer la propriété. La seule manière

21. Cette construction est implicitement admise par la loi du 7 août 1931 et par le décret flamand du 17 novembre 1982 (*V. infra*).
22. Cass., 17 novembre 1927, Pas., 1928, I, p. 17.
23. Cass., 2 octobre 1924, Pas., 1924, I. p. 530.
24. Cass., 17 novembre 1927, Pas., 1928, I, p. 17.
25. Cass., 11 novembre 1886, Pas., 1886, I, p. 410.

pour cette autorité de pouvoir céder un tel bien sera de mettre préalablement en oeuvre une procédure de désaffectation. Ce ne sera qu'au moment où ce bien sera intégré dans le domaine privé de l'administration que celle-ci pourra l'aliéner.[26]

L'affectation d'objet d'art au domaine public est certainement un moyen efficace d'assurer la protection du patrimoine culturel mobilier appartenant aux autorités administratives. Cependant, elle ne peut, par définition, que concerner les biens des pouvoirs publics et jamais le patrimoine culturel mobilier privé.

Ce régime est très proche de celui instauré par les mesures de classement telles que nous les avons exposées précédemment. En effet, le classement entraîne, en principe, l'interdiction d'aliéner l'objet d'art classé. Cependant, ce classement ne va pas nécessairement jusqu'à l'affectation de l'objet classé au domaine public. C'est ce qui permet, notamment, aux autorités compétentes d'autoriser l'aliénation de l'objet classé. Par ailleurs, autre différence importante entre les deux régimes, le classement peut concerner, comme nous l'avons vu, le patrimoine culturel mobilier appartenant à des personnes privées. Ce qui n'est pas le cas du régime de la domanialité publique.

On peut se poser la question de savoir dans quelle mesure les biens mobiliers appartenant aux pouvoirs publics peuvent à la fois être affectés au domaine public et faire l'objet d'un arrêté de classement dans le cadre de la législation sur la protection du patrimoine culturel mobilier.

Les deux régimes peuvent se combiner. Le classement, comme nous l'avons vu, ne suffit pas à affecter le bien classé au domaine public. L'application des deux régimes à un même objet est évidemment de nature à renforcer sa protection. Il est à signaler que ce cumul n'est cependant pas envisageable pour les biens du patrimoine culturel mobilier des musées, bibliothèques et archives du Royaume et des Communautés. Ces biens ne peuvent, en effet, faire l'objet d'un arrêté de classement.[27]

c. L'inexportabilité

Un autre moyen de protéger les biens culturels mobiliers consiste à les frapper d'inexportabilité ou, à tout le moins, de soumettre les exportations d'objets d'art au contrôle strict des autorités administratives.

Par définition, les biens mobiliers affectés au domaine public sont inexportables puisqu'inaliénables.[28]

Selon la loi du 7 août 1931, le patrimoine culturel mobilier classé ne peut être aliéné sans autorisation préalable. Comme nous l'avons vu, l'autorisation peut réserver un droit de préemption 'au profit des collections publiques du

26. Sous réserve, bien entendu, du respect des dispositions régissant les aliénations des biens appartenant aux pouvoirs publics.
27. Loi du 7 août 1931, art. 17, al. 2. Décret flamand du 17 novembre 1982, art. 2, 6°.
28. Ceci vise bien entendu l'exportation par le biais de l'aliénation et non le prêt d'oeuvres classées dans le cadre d'échanges culturels internationaux.

royaume'.[29] Quant au décret flamand sur la protection du patrimoine culturel mobilier, il soumet à l'autorisation préalable toute aliénation des biens classés appartenant aux pouvoirs publics.[30] En ce qui concerne les exportations d'objet faisant partie du patrimoine culturel mobilier classé, elles sont également soumises à autorisation préalable que ces objets classés fassent partie du patrimoine culturel mobilier public ou du patrimoine culturel mobilier privé.[31]

Les interdictions ou le contrôle des exportations d'objets d'art découlant du régime de la domanialité public ou de celui du classement ne vise que deux catégories bien déterminées d'objets d'art. En revanche, le mécanisme de contrôle instauré par la loi du 16 mai 1960 relative au patrimoine culturel de la nation vise un ensemble beaucoup plus large d'oeuvres d'art.

En effet, l'art. ler de cette loi permet à l'autorité compétente de réglementer, et notamment de subordonner à une autorisation, l'exportation des oeuvres énumérées ci-après qui ont plus de cent ans d'âge ou dont les auteurs sont décédés depuis plus de cinquante ans:

i. les peintures, sculptures, estampes et dessins, quelles qu'en soient la nature, l'origine ou la technique d'exécution;
ii. les produits des arts décoratifs tels que tapisseries, orfèvrerie, dinanderie et autres métaux ouvragés, céramiques, émaux et vitraux;
iii. les lettres, autographes, manuscrits, incunables et pièces d'archives.

Cette protection apparaît cependant toute relative à la lecture de l'art. 2 de la loi qui dispose que 'l'autorisation ne peut être refusée que dans les cas exceptionnels où l'exportation sollicitée est de nature à causer un dommage grave au patrimoine culturel de la nation'.

En fait, cette protection est inexistante. En effet, seuls des arrêtés d'exécution pourraient lui permettre d'entrer en vigueur. Or, nous les attendons toujours depuis près de 30 ans.[31]

Les mesures d'inexportabilité ou de contrôle des exportations des objets d'art sont donc limitées en droit belge. Ceci ne rencontre que partiellement les objectifs poursuivis par la Convention de l'Unesco concernant les mesures à prendre pour interdire et empêcher l'importation, l'exportation et le transfert de propriété illicites des biens culturels adoptée à Paris le 14 novembre 1970. Lorsque l'on examine les législations d'autres pays, on constate que les mesures adoptées par ces derniers sont souvent plus drastiques que chez nous.[32] C'est ainsi que, par exemple, l'Italie soumet les exportations d'objets du patrimoine culturel mobilier à l'obtention d'une

---

29. Loi du 7 août 1931, art. 19, al. 1er.
30. Décret flamand du 17 novembre 1982, art. 8 §4.
31. Il semblerait que les autorités douanières ne se montrent guère enclinés à l'entrée en vigeur d'un tel régime.
32. Sur cette question, *v.* R. GOY, 'La protection internationale des biens culturels et le droit public interne' in *La protection juridique internationale des biens culturels*, Actes du 13ème colloque de droit européen, Delphes, 20–22 septembre 1983 (Conseil d'Europe, Strasbourg 1984, pp. 68 *et seq.*)

autorisation préalable, mais également, conditionnait jusqu'il y a peu, ces exportations au paiement d'une taxe à l'exportation.[33]

Les interdictions d'exportation d'oeuvres d'art et la taxation de telles exportations posent problèmes au regard des dispositions du Traité instituant la Communauté économique européenne.

En effet, l'art. 34 du Traité interdit les restrictions quantitatives à l'exportation entre les Etats-membres ainsi que toutes mesures d'effet équivalent. En refusant l'autorisation d'exportation d'un objet d'art ou en taxant une telle exportation, l'Etat-membre ne contrevient-il pas à l'art. 34 du Traité de Rome?

L'art. 36 du Traité précise notamment que les dispositions de l'art. 34 ne font pas obstacle aux interdictions ou restrictions d'exportation justifiées pour des raisons de protection des trésors nationaux ayant une valeur artistique, historique ou archéologique.

Dès lors le refus d'autorisation d'exportation d'un objet d'art présentant un tel intérêt n'est pas contraire aux stipulations de l'art. 34 du Traité.[34]

En revanche, le fait de taxer l'exportation vers les autres Etats-membres de la Communauté d'objets présentant un intérêt artistique, historique, archéologique ou ethnographique est contraire au Traité et ne peut se justifier sur base de l'article 36. En effet, ce type de taxe ne permet pas d'atteindre l'objectif visé par cet article, qui est de protéger le patrimoine artistique, historique ou archéologique, mais n'a, pour conséquence, que de rendre plus onéreuse l'exportation des produits en cause.[35]

33. Sur cette question, *v.* R. GOY, 'La taxation des exportations des objets d'art dans les Etats de la Communauté économique européenne' in *Etudes de finances publiques* (Economica, Paris 1984) pp. 845–854.

34. Sur cette question, *v.* C.E. fr., 7 octobre 1987 et note d'obs. J. LAVEISSIERE, Rec. Dalloz Sirey (1988) pp. 269–272.

35. Cour de justice de la Communité européenne 10 décembre 1968, *Commission c. République italienne*, 7/68, Rec. CJCE, p. 617; *v.* égal. P. PESCATORE, 'Le commerce d'art et le Marché commun', Rev. trim. dr. europ. (1986) pp. 451–462.

Grèce: Introduction

Antonias Dimolitsa*

Le régime juridique grec concernant le commerce de l'art se verrait formé d'un mélange de dispositions tirées du droit des antiquités, du droit de la propriété littéraire et artistique et du Code Civil et s'avèrerait nécessairement incomplet dans la complexité et spécificité des problèmes surgissant dans ce domaine. La présentation qui suit est basée sur le Questionnaire préparé par les organisateurs du colloque et ne peut – dans le cadre de la multiplicité des questions soulevées – qu'avoir un but d'information et non pas de dissertation.[1]

Il est évident que, pour la Grèce, les dispositions du droit des antiquités, dispositions homogènes, empreintes d'un esprit de protection fort étendue et stricte du patrimoine culturel, constituent un trait particulier de ce régime et influent considérablement sur la liberté du commerce de l'art. Il serait par conséquent utile, en vue des questions soulevées mais avant d'essayer d'y répondre concrètement, de donner quelques indications générales sur les restrictions du droit de propriété par rapport aux antiquités et aux oeuvres assimilées à celles-ci.

1. Il serait de prime abord nécessaire de préciser que selon une jurisprudence et doctrine plutôt établies, doivent être considérés comme antiquités, jouissant de la protection de la loi codifiée 5351/1932 sur les antiquités, non seulement les biens archéologiques datés jusqu'à 1453, mais aussi toutes les oeuvres d'art créées jusqu'à 1830, tant meubles qu'immeubles (la controverse doctrinale qui existait à la suite de la décision de la Cour de Cassation 407/1972 – Chroniques Pénales k' 524 – sur les biens meubles créés entre 1453 et 1830 est actuellement estompée). Les oeuvres créées jusqu'à 1830 sont ainsi directement protégées par la loi sur les antiquités. Par contre, conformément à la loi 1469/1950, les oeuvres d'art postérieures à 1830 peuvent être déclarées dignes d'une 'protection étatique spéciale' par un acte administratif émis suivant avis du Conseil Archéologique. Ce fut

---

* Avocat, Athènes.

1. Note d'Editeur: *v.* pour le 'Rapport National sur le le sujet 1' *infra* p. 113, pour le 'Rapport National sur le sujet 2' *infra* p. 175 et pour le 'Rapport National sur le sujet 3' *infra* p. 265.

notamment le cas pour toutes les icônes créées jusqu'à la fin du 19ème siècle (décision YA 4411/29.2/16.3.1968 du Ministre auprès de la Présidence du Conseil). Cette 'protection étatique spéciale' équivaut d'ailleurs à une application par analogie de certaines dispositions de la loi 5351/1932.

2. L'Etat jouit d'un droit de propriété absolue et permanente sur les antiquités. Les particuliers peuvent détenir ou vendre des antiquités en possession desquelles ils se sont trouvés 'de bonne foi' ou 'par hasard', sous la condition de les avoir déclarées aux autorités compétentes (art. 5 loi 5351/1932); ce droit de détention va de pair avec l'obligation de prendre soin de la sauvegarde des antiquités détenues, sous le contrôle de l'Etat. Tout transfert (vente – donation) d'une antiquité sans déclaration préalable y afférente est, d'ailleurs, déclaré nul par la loi (art. 13 loi 5351/1932). La déclaration aux autorités de toutes antiquités dès la mise en possession de celles-ci étant nécessaire dans tous les cas, il se peut qu'une antiquité soit jugée d'une importance scientifique minime et d'une valeur vénale négligeable: c'est seulement dans ce cas que l'usage par la personne qui la détient devient libre. Si, au contraire, l'antiquité a une grande valeur et que la personne qui la détient est un antiquaire, l'autorité compétente peut procéder à l'achat obligatoire de l'oeuvre au prix convenu si non, à un prix fixé suivant une procédure arbitrale.

3. L'exportation d'une antiquité n'est permise qu'à la suite d'une licence spéciale émise par l'autorité compétente. L'autorité compétente a le pouvoir discrétionnaire d'accorder ou pas la licence, mais elle est obligée, en cas de refus et sur demande de la personne qui désire l'exportation, d'acheter l'oeuvre à la moitié de sa valeur déclarée. Seules sont librement exportées les antiquités importées et déclarées à leur importation (art. 18 loi 5351/1932).

4. Une dernière indication générale sur le droit des antiquités serait, enfin, que toutes les dispositions de la loi 5351/1932 sont assorties de sanctions pénales.

Italie: Introduction*

Tommaso Alibrandi**

En réponse aux questions formulées dans le Questionnaire, je fais observer que la réglementation italienne actuellement en vigueur (Loi n° 1089/39) est sous-tendue en ligne générale par des critères restrictifs. L'optique juridique nettement différente de la conception italienne, que l'on peut déduire des questions de ce Questionnaire, implique au contraire une législation en matière de protection du patrimoine artistique et historique qui attribue aux directeurs des musées une espèce d'autonomie de gestion, qui ne fait pas partie des compétences institutionnelles des conservateurs des musées italiens.

Du point de vue de l'appartenance, dans le système italien, les musées (galeries, etc.) peuvent relever de la compétence:

(a) de l'Etat et des collectivités territoriales (régions, provinces, communes);
(b) d'organismes publics non territoriaux;
(c) de personnes privées.

Dans le premier cas, le régime juridique des musées est celui de la domanialité. A cet égard, les arts. 5 et 6 du décret royal du 30 janvier 1913, n° 363, prévoient l'obligation de tenir un inventaire régulier des biens contenus dans les musées (et dans les galeries) de l'Etat, et ce, selon les règles établies par le règlement général pour la comptabilité et l'administration du patrimoine de l'Etat. Ces biens, sous la responsabilité personnelle des dirigeants des institutions, doivent être fixés au lieu de leur destination de la façon la plus adaptée pour en garantir la conservation et la garde.

Dans le cas des musées appartenant à des organismes publics non territoriaux, l'art. 4 de la loi du ler juin 1939, n° 1089, prévoit l'application du régime spécial de protection réglementé par la loi ci-dessus mentionnée. L'on peut en dire autant – par le mécanisme (et subordonné à la notification) de la contrainte – pour les musées appartenant à des personnes privées. Le propriétaire privé d'un musée (galerie ou pinacothèque) peut donc également, si aucune contrainte de droit public n'est intervenue par suite de

* Note d'Editeur: *v.* pour le 'Rapport National sur le sujet 1' *infra* p. 117, et pour le 'Rapport National sur le sujet 2' *infra* p. 177.

** Professeur, Libera Università Internazionale degli Studi Sociali, Facoltà di Scienze Politiche, Rome.

l'application de la loi de 1939, démembrer sa collection, en enlever ou en vendre des pièces à son gré.

Une fois assujetties au régime de la loi spéciale, les collections des musées (galeries, etc.) ne peuvent, quel qu'en soit le motif, faire l'objet d'un démembrement sans l'autorisation du Ministre des biens culturels. Le Ministre peut également en interdire l'aliénation lorsqu'il en dérive un préjudice à leur conservation ou que la jouissance publique en soit affectée (art. 34 de la loi).

Enfin, aux termes des arts. 52 et 63 de la loi, les collections sont soumises à l'usage et à la jouissance publique, qui se manifestent essentiellement dans l'obligation pour le propriétaire d'ouvrir les collections au public à des fins culturelles.

Japan: Introduction*

Norihiko Hadano** and Jun Norisugi**

For purposes of understanding the responses to the questions posed in the subsequent sections, a brief overview of the regulatory classification of objects of art in Japan is necessary.

The most important law in this area is the Law for the Protection of Cultural Properties (Law No. 215, enacted 30 May 1950) (the 'Law'). The stated purpose of the Law is to 'preserve and utilize cultural properties, so that the culture of the Japanese people may be furthered and a contribution be made to the evolution of world culture' (Art. 1). 'Cultural Properties' within the meaning of the Law are divided into four categories: (i) 'Tangible Cultural Properties' (objects), (ii) 'Intangible Cultural Properties' (art and skill employed in drama, music and the applied arts), (iii) 'Folk-cultural Properties' (manners and custom related to food, clothing, religious faiths, festivals, etc.) and (iv) 'Monuments' (Art. 2).

If an object fits within the class of Tangible Cultural Property, the degree to which its disposition is regulated depends on whether it is further classified as an Important Cultural Property. If so, it is registered and its possession, repair, alteration, sale, export and transfer are strictly regulated by the Law. Finally, an additional and even stricter set of regulations is imposed upon those Important Cultural Properties that are further designated as 'National Treasures'. There are currently 8694 objects in Japan that have been designated as Important Cultural Properties. Of those, 827 have been designated as National Treasures.

Although the applicability of the regulatory regime imposed by the Law depends on whether an object falls within any or all of the above classifications, the Law itself provides only the most general guidance as to which criteria are to be utilized for purposes of classification. For example, an object is a Cultural Property if 'it possesses a high and/or artistic value in and for [Japan]'. Moreover, for purpose of determining which Cultural Properties are to be designated Important Cultural Property, the Law gives the Ministry of Education and the Agency for Cultural Affairs (ACA) (both

* Editor's note: *see* 'National Report on Topic 1' *infra* p. 119.

** Attorney at Law, Masuda & Ejiri, Tokyo.

of which are responsible for interpreting, administering and enforcing the Law) great discretion in designating which objects shall fall within their jurisdiction and, as is the case with most public agencies, they take a broad interpretation of the definition of Cultural Properties. The fact that these agencies have not adopted internal guidelines regarding designation criteria makes the process somewhat unpredictable.

For purposes of understanding the responses to questions posed in Topic 1, it should be noted that museums are organized as *Zaidan* (foundations). Under Japanese law, *Zaidan* are juridical persons that are established and operated on a not-for-profit basis. In Japan, there are both public and private museums. Although the latter may receive subsidies from the national or local government, they are funded principally on a private basis. While, for purposes of the Law, private and public museums are treated in the same way, public museums have enacted internal regulations which prohibit them from selling objects which have been classified as Important Cultural Properties.

The Netherlands: Introduction

Anton A. Quaedvlieg*

I. INTRODUCTION

Traditionally, the Netherlands has a great reputation in the visual arts. In the field of trade that reputation is no less great, and quite solid even when taken as prejudice. It should be no surprise that there is plenty of activity also at the point of contact between these two: in the international art trade Amsterdam is still a household word.

Where love of art and mercantile spirit are both part of the national character, one may well wonder which of these attributes is paramount in the legal rules relating to the art trade. The mercantile spirit would advocate a liberal rule; the love of art on the other hand might impose restrictions on the freedom of transactions, particularly with a view to regulating or barring export.

In the *private* sphere the Dutch legal rules relating to the arts should no doubt be described as liberal. There is the 'Conservation of Cultural Heritage Act' (*Wet tot Behoud van Cultuurbezit*) which can, *inter alia*, prevent the sale of art to foreign countries, but it covers only a very limited number of works of art. In addition there are copyright rules which safeguard certain rights for the artist or his estate also after a work of visual art has been sold or assigned. However, these rules as such have no direct financial consequences for the owner of the work: for example, there is no *droit de suite*, no right for the author to claim proceeds of resale.

There is an entirely different picture in the sphere of *public law*, or more precisely: with respect to property of cultural value that has been entrusted to the care of the government. Here the protection and conservation of the national art treasures is the prime consideration. Any government agency toying with the idea of selling off works of art left in their trust – particularly when objects of great cultural-historical value are involved – can count on opposition from their superiors in government, and public disapproval as

---

* Professor, Catholic University Nijmegen. The author gratefully acknowledges the assistance of the law firm Trenité Van Doorne, Amsterdam with which he was associated during the writing of this Report. Report translated by F. C. Compton.

well. As yet there is no formal legislation, although this seems to be in the making.

It is these observations which may serve as a guideline in the following – more detailed – overviews and in the answers to the Questionnaire.[1]

II. RULES APPLICABLE IN THE NETHERLANDS ON THE SUBJECT OF ART

1. *Introduction*

A brief reply to the points raised in the Questionnaire under 1 and 2, without too many digressions and side remarks, is extremely difficult if one cannot see the answers against the background of the existing laws and regulations as a whole. For this reason we will give the reader the briefest possible outline of those laws and regulations.

2. *Private Art Collections: Conservation of Cultural Heritage Act*[2]

a. List of protected objects in private ownership

The Conservation of Cultural Heritage Act ('the Act') makes it possible for objects of art or art collections to be placed on a list of 'protected objects' ('the List') by order of the Minister of Welfare, Health and Cultural Affairs. On this point the Explanatory Memorandum on the Act notes that publicly owned objects should preferably not be put on the List, because the government may be expected to have a sufficient sense of responsibility to prevent the disappearance of really important art treasures owned by the government itself.

b. How objects are placed on the List; appeal against listing

In urgent cases objects can be listed by an emergency procedure (for example, when an object or a collection is about to be sold by auction), but in most cases objects are placed on the List solely on the basis of the criteria mentioned below, and apart from any intention to sell that the owner may have. The advantage of this system is that it offers some degree of legal security, also to gallery owners and auction houses, for the List is public and so gives anyone the opportunity of checking whether an object or a collection is or is not protected. For reasons of privacy the public version of the List obviously does not give the owners' names or addresses.

---

1. Editor's note: *see* 'National Report on Topic 1' *infra* p. 123, 'National Report on Topic 2' *infra* p. 179 and 'National Report on topic 3' *infra* p. 269 and p. 277.
2. Act of 1 February 1984, *Staatsblad* No. 49.

Prior to making a listing order – emergency cases excepted – the Minister will consult the State Commission for the Museums (*Rijkscommissie voor de Musea*). The State Commission may also give advice on its own initiative. The owner may appeal against the listing order; this is possible under an Act – called *Wet Administratieve Rechtspraak Overheidsbeschikkingen* (*AROB*) – which provides for appeal against government orders to the Justice Division of the Council of State. The Minister, for his part, has the power to take the object or collection off the List again.

c. Objects eligible for listing

A 'protected object' is defined as 'a movable object of cultural-historical or scientific significance which by itself or as part of a collection of the Dutch cultural good should be preserved and for that purpose has been placed on the List of protected objects or is a part of a collection placed on said List' (Art. 1a of the Act). This definition is accentuated in the Decree of 13 March 1985,[3] Art. 2(1) of which says:

> 'If an object can be classified as irreplaceable and essential it is of such cultural-historical or scientific significance that it should be preserved for the Dutch cultural heritage and to that end should be placed on the List.'

The next two paragraphs (2 and 3) elaborate further on the concepts of 'irreplaceable' and 'essential'. A striking detail is that in the definition of what is 'essential' the historical value of the object or its value for the purposes of research or gaining of knowledge are mentioned in particular. Value in terms of money plays no part in the decision to place an object on the List. Only a very limited number of objects on the List is of very great monetary value. In practice, however, one will often find that the commercial value of an object rises *as a result* of its being placed on the List. Neither does the aesthetic value as such count as a criterion for placing an object on the List. The works placed on the List may be included in the following categories: visual art, history and natural history.[4]

d. Some additional remarks concerning the objects placed on the List

Not very many works of art qualify as 'protected objects', which is what was specifically intended by the lawmakers. What they envisaged was no more but that 'the public may receive an impression of the surviving expressions of the cultural history of the Netherlands, from at least a few good examples in each field'.[5]

3. Decree of 13 March 1985, *Staatsblad* 262, containing an administrative order for the enforcement of Arts. 3(3) and 21 of the Conservation of Cultural Heritage Act.
4. Classification since the Decree of 30 January 1987, *Staatsblad* 196, amending the Administrative Order on the Conservation of Cultural Heritage Act.
5. P.J.J. VAN BUUREN and S.C.H. KONING, 'Wet tot Behoud van Cultuurbezit'. *Ars Aequi* (1985) p. 84.

The most effective measure to prevent overspending is that only a very limited provisional budget (approx. 250,000 guilders) is available each year to enable the government to fund purchases which it is in some (urgent) cases required to make under the Act.

For example, there are only thirty to forty paintings on the List, including one *Rembrandt* and one *Frans Hals*. On the other hand, many historical objects and former church possessions do fall under the List.

Contemporary works are very rarely placed on the List; the most recent ones date from before the Second World War. The underlying reason is that listing a contemporary work might wrongly be taken as a judgment or mark of appreciation. Moreover, so the authorities say, the State has itself already acquired a substantial volume of cultural works from more recent date.

The latter argument is true. The State does pursue an active and generous policy of acquisition and subsidizing. Apart from numerous other schemes we would mention the so-called one percent scheme, which makes it mandatory for the government to spend one percent of the construction cost of public projects on purchasing works of living Dutch artists to decorate the buildings.

Listing of works from a *foreign* origin is not ruled out, provided that such works are of sufficient significance to the development of culture in the Netherlands.

e. Instances in which listing is not possible or possible only with permission

Art. 5 of the Act provides that the owner's permission is required for listing if the object is (a) the property of the author or the author's heirs, or (b) the property of the person who imported it into the Netherlands or of the person who acquired it within five years after it was imported into the Netherlands, or their heirs. This provision is expressly intended as a gesture to the art trade. The returning of objects that have been abroad for a brief period (e.g., in connection with an exhibition, or for restoration, or as a result of theft) does not come under the definition of 'importation into the Netherlands'.

The term 'heirs' here also includes heirs who have acquired the object in some other way than by succession (by gift, for example). However, permission from the heirs is only required up to thirty years after the testator's death.

Art. 5 of the Act also contains elements that may be important to the art trade. Suffice is to quote this article, which will speak for itself.

> '1. If an object, a collection or a part of a collection (a) is held by a person who temporarily moves his residence to the Netherlands; or (b) is loaned by a non-resident for exhibition in the Netherlands; or (c) by reason of comparable circumstances, in the Minister's opinion reached in consultation with the State Commission, does not belong in the Netherlands, the Minister if so requested or of his own accord will give an undertaking that it will not be placed on the List.
> 2. The Minister will revoke such undertaking if and when the circumstances by reason of which it was given no longer exist. In such cases the Minister will not

enforce this Act within one year after the date of revocation. The owner will be notified of revocation immediately, such notice to specify the effective date of revocation.'

f. Consequence of listing

A full description of the detailed rules on the consequence of listing would exceed the scope of this paper. For this reason, suffice it to mention the most important consequences:

i. Anyone who intends to auction, sell, trade, assign, encumber, hire out or lend protected objects, or intends to assign protected objects to non-residents at the division of joint property, or intends to change the place where protected objects are located, has the mandatory *duty to report* this and to await subsequent *permission*. If within a certain period of time no express objection has been made this will be taken as implied permission.
ii. If the acts listed above are intended to take the protected object *outside the Netherlands*, permission from the *Minister* is required.
iii. If the Minister objects to sale or to assignment to a non-resident or to relocation to the owner's habitual residence outside the Netherlands, such objection will at the same time constitute an *offer to purchase*, on the same terms and conditions (including the price) as those laid down in the agreement of sale, or, if such terms and conditions had not yet been determined, on the terms and conditions to be agreed with the Minister. If the negotiations with the Minister fail, the purchase price will be determined by the District Court at The Hague.
iv. When eventually the Unesco Paris Convention of 14 November 1970 is ratified by the Netherlands, the listing of an object will have the same force as 'specific designation' within the meaning of that Convention.

3. Public Ownership of Art: Conservation and Protection a Priority of Government Policy

a. Government policy and legal consequences

Since the government and the government-controlled museums are expected 'to possess sufficient sense of responsibility to counter the disappearance of really important works of art they themselves hold',[6] those drafting the Act proceeded on the principle that State-owned objects of art should preferably not be placed on the List of Protected Objects. This is still the ruling principle today. The result is that there is (as yet) no such thing as a 'Conservation of *Public* Treasures Act', although in government *policy* such conservation is indeed pursued.

6. Report of Parliamentary Proceedings 16.749, *Explanatory Memorandum*, p. 10.

Having said this, there do exist legal means to try and prevent an undesirable sell-off of objects or collections. The most obvious remedy is spontaneous rescission or suspension by the Crown of the public authority's decision on which the intended sale is based, or appeal against that decision under the *AROB* Act. The public authority will do wise not to proceed to sale until the terms for appeal have expired. If the agreement of sale has already been concluded, it is generally assumed today that subsequent appeal or subsequent rescission or suspension by the Crown leaves the sale intact. (*See*, Topic 1 at p. 125)

b. *Res extra commercium?*

The question, however, is whether a national cultural good held by a government agency or government-controlled museum should, by virtue of its designation as public property, be classified as *res extra commercium* (property outside the realm of trade) and what the consequences of this would be. Such a classification would definitely be conceivable with respect to objects that meet the criteria for being placed on the List. Art. 1368 of the Civil Code says that property outside the realm of trade cannot be the subject matter of a contract. Does this make sale impossible? Boll[7] believes it does, in support of which he cites the 'Royal Decree of Franeker' to be quoted later (see footnote 13) and the judgment of the Appeal Court at The Hague (see footnote 17). Beekhuis[8] believes that sale of such property is not inconceivable, provided that its public destination remains intact. The position of the *bona fide* purchaser is a controversial point. Meijers[9] believes that Art. 2014 of the Civil Code does not apply to archival documents and museum pieces: the third party-acquirer would therefore not be protected. Scholten[10] and Beekhuis[11] dispute this opinion.

c. Case law

Incidents about the sale of national cultural goods are rare in the Netherlands, but when they do occur they can raise a lot of dust. In 1881, the Crown rescinded a Council resolution of the city of Veere to sell a goblet which Maximilian of Burgundy had given to that city in 1547.[12] In 1897, the same thing happened to the Council resolution of the city of Franeker to sell a globe-shaped bowl which was given to that city in 1607.[13]

7. J. M. BOLL, '"Composition with two lines" or "The curious character of the right of ownership of government bodies to objects of art" and the "Cultural Heritage Act"' (translanted), *Rechtsgeleerd Magazijn Themis* (1989) p. 134.
8. ASSER/BEEKHUIS I *Zakenrecht* 12th edn. (Zwolle 1985) No. 135, p. 94.
9. E. M. MEIJERS, *Verzamelde Privaatrechtelijke Opstellen II* (Leiden 1954–1955) p. 110; also V. J. Ph. SUYLING, *Inleiding tot het burgerlijk recht*, 5th edn. (Haarlem 1940).
10. P. SCHOLTEN, *Asser-Scholten (Zakenrecht)* 8th edn. (1945) p. 142.
11. ASSER/BEEKHUIS I (*Zakenrecht*) No. 141, p. 98.
12. Royal Decree of 9 September 1881, *Staatsblad* 154.
13. Royal Decree of 24 February 1897, *Staatsblad* 68.

The next incident did not happen until nearly a hundred years later. In 1987, the Council of the city of Hilversum decided to sell a Mondriaan painting called *Composition with two lines* which the Dutch Arts League had given to that city in 1932.[14] The Crown suspended the Council resolution.[15] A striking detail is that the Royal Decree remarks explicitly that the painting 'is of such great importance to the Dutch cultural heritage that it satisfies the criteria which the Conservation of Cultural Heritage Act imposes on the placing of objects on the List'. The injunction proceedings which the city of Hilversum subsequently filed against the State in the civil court[16] – which decided it did have jurisdiction – did not produce the desired result, also on appeal.[17] The suspension continued in force. In the end the issue was resolved by an amicable arrangement when the painting was bought by the city of Amsterdam.

Finally, we would mention a plan on the part of the Municipal Museum at The Hague to sell a few paintings from its collection (two *Picassos* and one early *Monet*) in order to fund some other purchases which the Museum felt were better suited to its particular style. Apparently the initial reactions were not encouraging, for the plan never made it to the City Council.

d. Guidelines; expert committee

At the moment there are signs indicating that the Minister will soon draft clearer guidelines on this subject for the public authorities, although at the time of writing of this paper there was no concrete information available yet. However, if we presume that the Minister will base her views (partly) on the advice previously given by the State Commission for the Museums[18] and a memorandum written by the Directors of the State Museums, we may expect that sale of objects of art will not be totally prohibited, at least insofar as such objects do *not* fall within the criteria of the Conservation of Cultural Heritage Act. On the other hand, it is quite likely that a series of subsidiary requirements will be imposed. All in all, the State Commission for the Museums takes the position that the sale or trade of objects from State-owned collections is acceptable only in very exceptional cases.

An important detail is that the State Commission for the Museums has suggested that plans to sell should be presented for testing and advice to an expert committee of the Council for Cultural Matters (*Raad voor het Cultuurbeheer*): this would indicate a realistic promise for greater clarity as to whether or not in actual cases the sale or trade of objects from State-owned collections is advisable and permitted.

14. In detail on this: J. M. BOLL, *loc. cit.*, R. M. Themis (1989, No. 3), p. 125 *et seq.*
15. Royal Decree of 17 June 1989, *Staatsblad* 344.
16. *See* BOLL's reflections on the question of jurisdiction of the civil courts in this matter in his paper cited in footnote 7.
17. President District Court The Hague, 14 July 1987, KG 1987, 315; Appeal Court The Hague, 26 November 1987, KG 1988, 72.
18. Advice of the State Commission for the Museums, 21 November 1989, ref. MR/III-89-482.

4. UNESCO Convention of Paris of 14 November 1970 on the Means of Prohibiting and Preventing the Illicit Import, Export and Transfer of Ownership of Cultural Property[19]

The Netherlands has not yet ratified the Paris Convention of 14 November 1970 but intends to do so in the near future. The Convention could have been ratified sooner if it had not been for the fact that the rules relating to seizure and surrender of stolen cultural property, at least insofar as the position of the *bona fide* third party-acquirer is concerned, necessitates an adjustment of the Dutch civil law. The matter is now being studied by the Minister of Justice.

Art. 6 of the Conservation of Cultural Heritage Act already serves as a prelude to the ratification of the Paris Convention, inasmuch as the placing of an object on the List of objects protected under the Act also serves as a specific designation within the meaning of Art. 1 of the Convention.

19. *Traktatenblad* 1983, 66: English and French text in *Traktatenblad* 1972, 50. Editor's note: also reproduced in ICC Institute, ed., *International Sales of Works of Art/La Vente Internationale d'Oeuvres d'Art* (ICC Publishing/Kluwer, Paris/Deventer 1990) in French, pp. 171–185 and in English, pp. 187–200.

Spain: Introduction*

Bernardo Cremades**

The Spanish Government has recently enacted legislation which has as its aim the protection and development of the 'Spanish Historic Patrimony'. The principal legislation can be found in Law 16/1985 of 25 June, on the Spanish Historic Patrimony, and Royal Decree 111/1986 of 10 January, on the partial development of the Law and the new fiscal legislation. The Law and the corresponding Royal Decree establish distinct levels of protection which correspond to different legal categories.

Thus, in order to adequately answer the questions presented by the Symposium, we must first describe the classifications made by the new legislation and the consequences which follow.

I. CLASSIFICATIONS

The Law of 1985 defines three categories of goods: goods making up the Spanish Historic Patrimony, goods of singular relevancy and goods of Cultural Interest.

The first category, goods making up the *Spanish Historic Patrimony*, is quite wide. The Law of 1985 declares that the following goods make up the Spanish Historic Patrimony:

> 'The movable or immovable objects of artistic, historic, palaeontological, archeological, ethnographic, scientific or technical interest. Also forming a part of the same are the Documentary and Bibliographic Patrimony, the archeological deposits and zones, as well as natural sites, gardens and parks which have artistic, historic or anthropological value.'

* Editor's note: *see also* by M. VIRGOS SORIANO, 'National Report on Topic 1' *infra* p. 127, 'National Report on Topic 2' *infra* p. 181, 'National Report on Topic 3' *infra* p. 277 and 'National Report on Topic 4' *infra* p. 401.

** Attorney at Law, J. y B. Cremades y Asociados, Madrid.

The Documentary and Bibliographic Patrimony is made up of:

- The documents of any era generated, retained or collected by any organ or entity of a public character, by legal persons in which the State has a majority participation, other physical or legal public entities and private persons who are administrators of public services in relation to the administration of such services in the exercise of their duties.
- Documents with an age greater than forty years, generated, retained or collected by entities and associations of political, syndicated or educational character, and educational and cultural foundations and associations of private character, in the exercise of their functions.
- Documents with an age greater than one hundred years, generated, retained, or collected by any other individual entity or physical person.
- Libraries or bibliographic collections of public ownership and the historic, scientific or artistic literary works in written or printed form of which there are not at least three specimens in the public libraries or services.
- Cinematographic films, records, photographs, audiovisual materials and other materials of which there are not at least three specimens (samples) in the public services, or one specimen in the case of cinematographic films.

The Law also specifically declares that the Spanish Historical Patrimony includes the archeological patrimony, i.e., movable and immovable goods of a historical character susceptible of being studied in an archeological method (these goods are declared to be public property and are inalienable), and geological and palaeontological elements related to the history of man, his origins and antecedents. The last category of goods forming a part of the Spanish Historic Patrimony are the goods which are or have been a relevant expression of the traditional culture of the Spanish people in their material, social or spiritual characteristics.

Public administrators are expressly prohibited from alienating movable goods making up the Spanish Historical Patrimony. These goods may only be alienated or transferred between public institutions. Prohibited alienations are null, and the Attorney General is to bring a civil action of nullity.

The second category provided for by the Law are those goods not declared to be of cultural interest but which, nevertheless, because of their *singular relevancy* or their notable historic, artistic, technical or cultural value, must be entered into the General Inventory of movable goods.

In order to facilitate the elaboration of the General Inventory, the proprietors or possessors of goods which make up the Spanish Historical Patrimony must inform the competent organ charged with the protection of the Spanish Historical Patrimony of the Autonomous Community in whose territory the good is situated of the sale or transfer to third parties, including the price and conditions of sale, of the movable goods indicated in Art. 26 of the Royal Decree of 1986. The Royal Decree covers:

a. Goods for which proceedings have begun for their inclusion in the General Inventory.

b. Goods which form a part of the Spanish Historical Patrimony whose economic value is equal to or greater than:

- 7,000,000 pesetas for pictorial or sculptural works of less than 100 years of age.
- 5,000,000 pesetas for pictorial works of more than 100 years of age.
- 4,000,000 pesetas for sculptural works, reliefs or bas-reliefs of more than 100 years of age.
- 3,000,000 pesetas for tapestries, rugs or historic textiles, engravings, collections of documents in any base, printed books and historical musical instruments.
- 2,000,000 pesetas for furniture.
- 1,000,000 pesetas for antique ceramic, porcelain or crystal objects, unitary documents in any base and manuscripts.
- 500,000 pesetas for archeological objects.
- 100,000 pesetas for ethnological objects.

c. Goods that the Government determines by Royal Decreee at the proposal of the Ministry of Culture.

Persons or entities who habitually engage in the commerce of goods making up the Spanish Historical Patrimony must formalize a register book of the transactions effectuated regarding the goods referred to above before the competent organ of the corresponding Autonomous Community.

Based on the notification of alienation between individuals or merchants (obligatory in the case of inventoried goods, Goods of Cultural Interest, goods of a value equal to or superior to those mentioned above), the State or relevant Autonomous Community may, within a period of two months of the notification, make use of the right of pre-emption to purchase the goods for itself, for a beneficent entity, or for an entity of public law, at the price agreed upon between the parties. The decision to exercise the right of preferential purchase must be communicated within the two month period and payment must be made within a period of two years.

When the intention of alienation has not been correctly notified, the State Administration, through the Ministry of Culture, may exercise the right of repurchase, under the same terms provided for the right of pre-emption, within a period of six months from the date in which it obtained reliable knowledge of the alienation.

Ecclesiastical institutions are prohibited from transferring or ceding to individuals or mercantile entities the inventoried goods which are in their possession. Such an alienation will be null and void. In such cases, the Attorney General is to bring a civil action of nullity.

The goods included in the General Inventory as goods making up the Spanish Historical Patrimony must be preserved, maintained and kept in custody by their proprietors or by the owners on record of real rights over the goods or possessors of such goods. The use of such goods must not put in danger the value which counsels their preservation. Any changes in their use must be authorized by the organs competent for the execution of the Law.

The third category provided for by the new legislation is that of *Goods of Cultural Interest*. Goods of Cultural Interest are those movable or immovable goods which require the singular protection and guardianship of the Law, and must be entered into the General Register.

Goods of Cultural Interest are subject to all of the rules provided for goods of 'singular relevancy'. In addition, such goods are expressly declared to be unexportable.

The work of a living author may not be declared to be of Cultural Interest, unless there exists the express authorization of its owner or it is acquired by the Administration.

II. EXPORTATION

For the purposes of exportation, the legislation distinguishes between:

- Goods expressly declared to be unexportable, as a precautionary measure until the good is included in the General Inventory or is declared to be of Cultural Interest.
- Goods declared to be of Cultural Interest, or for which proceedings for this declaration have been opened. Their permanent exportation is prohibited and their temporary exportation requires the previous and express permission of the Ministry of Culture.
- Goods included in the General Inventory, or for which proceedings for their inclusion have been opened. Express and previous authorization is required for the permanent or temporary exportation of these goods.
- Goods making up the Spanish Historical Patrimony of more than one hundred years of age. Their permanent or temporary incorporation requires the previous and express permission of the Ministry of Culture.

The State Administration has a period of two months to grant or deny permission to permanently export the good. If permission is granted, the inscription of a good in the General Inventory will be cancelled. If permission is denied, the Autonomous Community must include the good in one of the categories of protection, if it was not already so included.

The declaration of value of goods which are the object of a request for permission for exportation is to be considered as an irrevocable offer of sale in favour of the State Administration. If permission for exportation is not granted, the State Administration, through the Ministry of Culture, has a period of six months to accept the offer of sale, and one year to effectuate payment.

If permission for temporary exportation is granted, the permission must contain conditions of return and other guarantees deemed necessary for the preservation of the exported good. When dealing with Goods of Cultural Interest or those declared unexportable, the resolution must always be express and requires in all cases the previous opinion of the Council of Assessment, Valuation and Exportation of Goods of the Spanish Historical Patrimony.

The movable goods whose importation has been legally realized and is duly documented may not be declared to be of cultural interest for a period of ten years from the date of their importation. Such goods may be exported after license by the Administration. The licence is to be granted automatically if the request complies with the requisites required by the legislation in force, and the Administration may not exercise any right of preferred acquisition respecting such goods. After ten years, such goods will be included in the general regimen of the Law of 1985.

The exportation of goods making up the Spanish Historical Patrimony which is accomplished without the required authorization constitutes a crime or, if such is the case, an infraction of contraband. Those persons who have taken part in the exportation of the good and those others who, by their fraudulent or negligent acts or omissions, have facilitated or made possible such exportation, will be jointly liable.

In the case of temporary exportation, the nonfulfilment of the conditions of return will be considered an illegal exportation.

Part Two: Topics 1–5

TOPIC 1. FREEDOM OF MUSEUMS TO SELL, TRADE OR OTHERWISE DISPOSE OF OBJECTS OF ART IN THEIR COLLECTIONS

LIBERTE DES MUSEES DE PROCEDER A DES TRANSACTIONS D'OBJETS D'ART

Introduction: Topics 1 and 2

TOPICS 1 AND 2: FREE CIRCULATION OF WORKS OF ART AND THE RIGHTS OF MUSEUMS AND PRIVATE COLLECTORS

The first session of the Symposium, chaired by *Prof. Julio Gonzalez Campos*, had two objectives: 1. to examine the policies of museums regarding the management of their collection (Topic 1) and 2. to determine the problems which private collectors face when they want to purchase new items for their collections or move their collections from one place to another (Topic 2).

Basing his discussion on the replies from twelve countries to the Questionnaire, *Mr. Philip C. Jessup, Jr.*, described various practices and policies that have been adopted by museums, as well as their rights concerning the disposal of works of art belonging to their collections. He emphasized the financial dilemma which many museums face when working out their collection management and purchase policies (*see infra*, pp. 67–72). *Mr. Ashton Hawkins* described the guidelines followed by museums in order to help them deal with such dilemmas. After having pointed out that private collections frequently form the basis of public collections, *Mr. Hans Koenig* examined the various national laws which restrict collectors' freedom (*see infra*, pp. 157–166). *Mr. Geoffrey Lewis* described the major instruments of international co-operation developed for the protection of 'cultural patrimony' (*see infra*, pp. 73–85). He recounted the historical evolution of the concept of cultural patrimony and related concepts, which in turn evoked many questions during the general discussion.

Questions were raised about the real content of the concept of cultural patrimony and about its application on the international level. The participants in the general discussion generally emphasized the difficulties in exporting and enforcing the concept of 'inalienability' in countries where this is an unfamiliar concept. Questions were also raised regarding the justification of conditions imposed in some cases on museums by donors and about the continued application of such conditions after the death of the donor. The discussion concluded with a lively debate – including an exposition of the International Council of Museums Code of Professional Ethics (*see* for excerpt, *infra*, pp. 87–91) regarding the approach museums should take in order to resolve their financial difficulties which, in particular, hinder the enrichment of their collections. In many cases, they must also seek to compensate for the reduction in the number of gifts due to the revokation in certain countries of the tax benefits relating to gifts to museums.

List of Participants in Discussion

Ignaz Seidl-Hohenveldern (Austria)
Kurt Siehr (F. R. Germany)
Jean Chatelain (France)
Anthony Brown (United Kingdom)
Patrick O'Keefe (Australia)
Marina Schneider (UNIDROIT)

General Reports

General Report

TOPIC 1. FREEDOM OF MUSEUMS TO SELL, TRADE OR OTHERWISE DISPOSE OF OBJECTS OF ART IN THEIR COLLECTIONS

Philip C. Jessup, Jr.*

In response to a detailed Questionnaire sent out by the Institute of International Business Law and Practice of the International Chamber of Commerce in Paris, replies have been received from legal experts in Austria, Belgium, France, Germany, Greece, Italy, the Netherlands, Spain, Sweden, Switzerland, United Kingdom and the United States.[1] As was predictable, the legal situation respecting this question varies from country to country. In almost every jurisdiction, however, whether by national law or otherwise, there appears to be a general policy favouring the maintenance of museum collections for the benefit of the public for whom they are organized and operated. As stated recently by an American art critic: 'When museums put treasured works up for auction, they cast into doubt their role as guardians of cultural patrimony.'[2] In almost every regime under study, the freedom of art museums to dispose of objects from their collections is either barred or else it is subject to severe restrictions.

I. TYPE OF MUSEUM

One important factor in answering the question as to whether or not a particular museum is legally free to dispose of a work of art in its collection is the manner in which the museum is organized under the laws of its jurisdiction. Where most of the museums in a nation are established by the national government, it is natural that national law will determine the rules respecting the disposal of museum objects. In France, for example, the guiding rule is *inaliénabilité* or the impossibility to sell and dispose of public collections and, as our reporter notes:

> 'It is clearly established that museum collections belong to the public domain if the museums are either State museums or museums owned by public local entities or by public legal bodies.'[3]

---

* Secretary and General Counsel, National Gallery of Art, Washington, D.C.

1. Editor's note: *see* the 'National Reports' following this 'General Report'.
2. Michael KIMMELMAN, *New York Times*, 1 April 1990.
3. *See* J. CHATELAIN, 'France: National Report on Topic 1' *infra* p. 109.

In the few French museums which are not public, the 'inalienability' principle has been imposed by agreement with the local government. Even if this is not the case, such museums consider that their collections cannot be sold.

A similar ban against museum sales from their collections exists in Belgium and in Spain for public museums, but Spanish ecclesiastic and private museums may de-accession if permitted by their individual charters. The Prado has a special status as an autonomous institution but it does not have the capacity to sell or exchange works of art in its collection. Even removal from the facilities requires authorization of the Ministry of Culture. In Belgium, 'municipal museums' may dispose of their objects, although the law is not clear on this point. Certain Belgian museums, such as the museum of Liège, would require the authorization of its control authority, the Minister of Internal Affairs.

In Austria, most museums are either Federal, *Länder* or city owned. Governmental procedures exist in each case for the possible disposal of museum assets. The same is true in Sweden for museums owned by the state or a municipality where special permission to sell is required from the Government. But it is interesting to note that the Swedish budget for 1990/91 proposes to give state owned museums the right to sell items that are 'useless and not required for the activities of the museums'.

In Germany most museums are owned by public local authorities which have the power to authorize the sale of works of art by the museum, although certain local authorities have prohibited such sales in specific cases such as in the case of the Cologne Museum, *die Staatsgalerie* of Stuttgart and the Bavarian National Museum.

In Greece public museums are not prohibited from exchanging or even selling works of art except for antiquities which can be disposed of only if declared as not being useful by the Archeological Council. Antiquities have been defined by court decisions in Greece as archeological goods dated until 1453 and all other works of art created until 1830, whether they are movable or immovable. Private museums in Greece, which are governed by individual statutes, are generally prohibited from selling their works of art.

A distinction is made in Italy where public museums are prohibited from disposing of works of art unless, under limited conditions, they are given permission to do so by the Ministry of Cultural Property. Privately owned museums in Italy may sell works of art after informing the Ministry but the Ministry then has a right of first refusal on the same terms.

In the Netherlands, a proposed sale by a public museum, particularly of an object of great historical value, will generate opposition from governmental superiors, as well as the public, it is reported. No formal legislation has been enacted yet but it is in the process at the moment.

Procedures for de-accessioning exist for certain public museums in Switzerland depending on the law of their establishment but these may be limited to cases of similar objects or works deemed 'superfluous' by the museum committee. Private museums in Switzerland are governed by their founding charters which may or may not permit disposals of works of art.

This is similar to the situation in the United Kingdom where each public museum is established under a separate statute. Certain museums are prohibited from disposals while others may do so under limited circumstances. Local museums in the United Kingdom are discouraged from disposing of works of art by the Museum Association code of practice. Certain museums in the United Kingdom are established by private gifts or bequests, and may be restricted by their founding instrument in respect of disposals. This is true, for example, of the Wallace Collection in London and the Burrell Collection in Glasgow.

The same is true in the United States as in the case of the Isabella Stewart Gardner Museum in Boston and the Freer Gallery of Art in Washington which are barred by their founding charters from disposing of collection objects or, as in the case of the National Gallery of Art in Washington, where the trustees adopted from the beginning a policy against de-accessioning. On the other hand, there are no Federal or State laws in the United States prohibiting de-accessioning by museums.

II. NATIONAL CULTURAL PATRIMONY

Many of the countries under review have some form of legislation establishing and controlling a national cultural patrimony. These laws often impose additional restrictions on the sale of art, particularly where the sale is for export. In Austria, for example, the Federal Monuments Office may declare a significant object to be a monument which may be disposed of, whether by sale, gift or exchange, only with written permission of the office. Without the written consent of the Federal Monuments Office, such sale is null and void and the object may be declared forfeited. The seller is subject to arrest or fine. Exports of these objects also require permission and are otherwise prohibited. Violations are punished by imprisonment or fine.

The national cultural patrimony law in Germany regulates the export of German cultural goods but applies to exports of art only by private museums or other private persons, while the public museums, as noted above, are controlled by their respective governing authority, rather than by a single national law.

As noted before in the case of Greece, a special regime is maintained for archaeological treasures found in Greece and their export is prohibited, whether by a museum or a private owner, unless a special license is obtained from the government. If the license is refused, however, the licensing authority may be required to purchase the work of art which has been classified as part of the national cultural heritage.

In the Netherlands, there is a 'Conservation of Cultural Heritage Act' which would apply to privately owned museums and controls the sale abroad of listed works of art. Objects of art or art collections are placed on the list as 'protected objects' by order of the Minister of Welfare, Health and Cultural Affairs, but the list is very limited containing, for example, only thirty to forty paintings including one *Rembrandt* and one *Frans Hals*. In the case of proposed exports, objection by the Minister constitutes an offer to purchase the work of art on the same terms as the proposed sale.

According to the *Explanatory Memorandum* on the Dutch Act, 'publicly owned objects should preferably not be put on the list, because the government may be expected to have a sufficient sense of responsibility to prevent the disappearance of really important art treasures owned by the government itself.' Nevertheless, the Minister is reported to be drafting guidelines for public authorities which may follow the conclusion of the recent Royal Commission for the Museums in November 1989 which takes the position 'that the sale or trade of objects from State-owned collections is acceptable only in very exceptional circumstances'.

Spain also has special rules for the protection of cultural property, the Spanish Historical Patrimony Act. Limitation on sales depends on the type of organization owning the work of art. Public entities, for example, cannot sell such objects while religious institutions may not transfer movable cultural property to private persons or commercial entities until 1995. The Swedish law of 'cultural patrimony' regulates certain qualified objects but they are subject to special export permission while no such regime of cultural patrimony is reported to exist either in Switzerland or the United States.

As for the United Kingdom, a concept of national cultural patrimony exists in the operation of the export licensing regulations. Such licences are required if an object is over fifty years in age, regardless of origin, and is in excess of a specific value. Normally a licence is granted if the work of art has been in the country for less than fifty years. Otherwise it is referred to an expert to determine its importance. If so, the licence is delayed pending possible purchase by a public museum at the fair market value.

III. PRIVATE GIFTS

Another form of restriction on the freedom of a museum to dispose of a work of art from its collection may arise where a donor of an object to the museum has specified that the museum shall not de-accession the gift and the museum has accepted this restriction. In most of the legal regimes reported on, such restrictions are recognized and enforced. This is the case in Austria, for example, where the gift is by bequest in a will. And in Belgium, the museums and competent authorities having accepted a donation, cannot dispose of the works of art which have entered their collections.

In Germany, if a public museum breaches a condition subsequent in a gift, the gift is considered to be null and void and the donor can prosecute the public authorities concerned, and if the museum has sold the gift the donor can be reimbursed the value of the object at the time of the gift. In Greece and Italy, a clearly stated restriction against sale will also be binding on the donee museum.

Under Dutch law, the stipulation in a deed of gift to a museum against disposal will prevent the museum from making an authorized sale, but a purchaser from the museum will obtain good title unless he acted in bad faith. In Spain, such a restriction – if clearly stated – will be enforced and a subsequent sale may be revoked by the donor unless, once again, the purchaser acts in good faith. But such prohibitions on disposal are limited by law in Spain to thirty years.

In Sweden, where the donor has prohibited sale, even the government will have difficulties in allowing a sale. Under such circumstances, very special reasons are required for the government to break through those regulations.

In the United Kingdom and the United States, a private restriction accepted by a donee museum is also recognized by the law.

IV. CASES OF MUSEUM SALES

A case of the limited circumstances under which Austrian museums have sold works of art from their collections is reported from the 'hunger period' following World War I when second copies of prints were sold by the Federal Prints Museum (the Albertina).

Our German reporter states that the policy restricting sales by local public museums was

> 'instigated following a bad experience in recent years of sales involving certain objects of art that were sold by the museums and which reached very high prices at a subsequent auction sale.'[4]

An earlier example of government intervention was seen in the Netherlands in 1881 when the Crown rescinded a Council resolution of the city of Veere to sell a goblet which Maximillian of Burgundy had given to that city in 1547. Nearly a hundred years later, in 1987, the Crown suspended a proposed sale by the Council of the city of Hilversum of a painting by Mondriaan called *Composition with two lines* given to the city by the Dutch Arts League in 1932. The Royal Decree stated that the painting

> 'If an object can be classified as irreplaceable and essential it is of such cultural-historical or scientific significance that it should be preserved for the Dutch cultural heritage and to that end should be placed on the List.'[5]

A Swedish case of government control occurred in 1976 when a set of jewels donated to the National Museum was no longer considered important to the collections. The museum asked for permission to sell them but permission was not granted because it was a donation.

A different form of transfer is noted in the United Kingdom where public collections exchange objects of greater relevance to the receiving museum. Two years ago, for example, the Tate Gallery and the Victoria and Albert

---

4. *See* L. BISCHOP, 'F.R. Germany: National Report on Topic 1' *infra* pp. 105–107.
5. *See* A.A. QUAEDVLIEG, 'The Netherlands: Introduction' *supra* pp. 45–52 and 'The Netherlands: National Report on Topic 1' *infra* pp. 123–125.

Museum swapped their respective examples of post-baroque sculpture so that the Tate held all the pre-Rodin sculpture and the Victoria and Albert held all the post-Rodin examples.

Finally, two examples from the United States regarding sales by museums of objects given to them by private individuals, which happens to be the method by which the bulk of public art collections in the United States has been acquired. In the early 1970's, the Attorney General of the State of New York launched an investigation of the practices of New York museums in the disposal of works of art. According to the press, the key event leading up to this was the sale by the Metropolitan Museum of Art of works of art received from the estate of a Miss Adelaide Milton de Groot under a nonbinding request that the museum not sell the works. Eventually guidelines were agreed to and since then continued efforts have taken place to reach a consensus on museum de-accessioning policy in the United States. Policy statements have been adopted both by individual museums, such as the Metropolitan, and by the Association of Art Museum Directors in 1987. It is interesting to note, for example, that as reported in the press, when the Museum of Modern Art recently sold and exchanged seven works from its collection in order to acquire Van Gogh's portrait of Joseph Roulin, it first obtained the approval of the works' original donors or their heirs. The price has been estimated at US$ 45 million.

General Report Topic 1

INTERNATIONAL ISSUES CONCERNING MUSEUM COLLECTIONS

Geoffrey Lewis*

I. INTRODUCTION

This paper is concerned with those aspects of the museum operation involving the free circulation of cultural property at an international level. The subject has been well treated in recent texts, not least in the third volume of *Law and the Cultural Heritage* on the movement of cultural property (O'KEEFE and PROTT 1989).[1] However, the intention here is to review the international movement of heritage material against:

(a) the international legislative and regulatory framework on cultural property and its significance to museums;
(b) the national legislation in Europe, as revealed in the Questionnaire returns,[2] which will have to be considered in any regional action within the Continent, particularly in the context of Art. 36 of the Treaty of Rome.

For this purpose the terms *cultural property* and *museum collection* are taken to include material from the arts, humanities and sciences as is the case in most of the international legislation on cultural property. The emphasis, however, is on art and historical material.

The museum operation is complex and the subject of perpetual conflict in that it is concerned with both preservation and usage. The movement of

---

* Former Director of the Department of Museum Studies, University of Leicester; former President of the International Council of Museums (ICOM).

1. Editor's note: references between parentheses in the text refer to Appendix B, 'Bibliography and References'.
2. Responses to the Questionnaire relating to this subject were received from the following countries: Austria (Ignaz Seidl-Hohenveldern); Belgium (Francis Bauduin and Francis Haumont); France (Jean Chatelain); Federal Republic of Germany (Ludger Bischop); Greece (Antonias C. Dimolitsa); Italy (Tommaso Alibrandi and Geraldo Aversa); Japan (Norihiko Hadano and Jun Norisugi); The Netherlands (Anton A. Quaedvlieg); Spain (Bernardo M. Cremades, Fernando Pombo and Miguel Virgós Soriano); Sweden (Christian Wegenius); Switzerland (Blaise Knapp); United Kingdom (Adrian Barr-Smith); United States (Philip C. Jessup, Jr. and Stephen E. Weil). Sections of this paper owe much to the information provided through the Questionnaire, which I gladly and gratefully acknowledge here.

cultural property epitomizes this and occurs in many museum activities, more particularly in the acquisition and disposal of collections, the transportation of objects and specimens for conservation purposes or for study and scholarship and the assembling and distribution of travelling exhibitions. That this occurs on an international scale is, in part, because of the nature of the material. Neither the natural nor human heritage is necessarily peculiar to the present-day administrative and political area where it is housed. It has, therefore a significance elsewhere as well. Even if it is peculiar to that area it may well assume an importance as a medium in communicating knowledge about that area. In either case there is a supra-national interest in it, as shown below.

II. INTERNATIONAL LEGISLATION AND REGULATION

The development of legislation relating to cultural property has been treated elsewhere (e.g., WILLIAMS 1978). It should be noted that the notion of the special nature of cultural property is of considerable antiquity. By the early nineteenth century, however, it is beginning to take on a more familiar form; for example, when the British Parliament considered the purchase of the Earl of Elgin's collection of marbles from the Parthenon, such issues as the propriety of ambassadorial collecting and the significance of a nation's cultural heritage were considered in the debate (HOUSE OF COMMONS 1816). But for much of the last two centuries the notion of cultural property has developed in the context of protection in the context of armed conflict. The decision of the Vienna Congress of 1815 requiring the restitution of the works of art removed during the Napoleonic Wars to their countries of origin is well known and a clear recognition of the special nature of cultural property. Its identification with public property, and yet distinctive from it, follows on later in the nineteenth century: this occurs in the Lieber Code, developed in 1863 for use during the American Civil War and at the Brussels Conference of 1874 which in turn influenced the Hague Conventions of 1899 and 1907. The Code allowed the appropriation of all public property by the victorious forces but required that works of art, libraries, collections, etc. should be protected and eventual ownership determined by peace treaty. In similar vein the Hague Convention 1907 states:

> 'the property of institutions dedicated to educators, the arts and sciences, even when State property, shall be treated as private property.'

The ineffectiveness of this Hague Convention led to further examination of the issues by the International Museums Office and others but it was not until 1954 that a new Convention[3] was approved. By this time the notion of

3. Unesco *Final Act of the Intergovernmental Conference on the Protection of Cultural Property in the Event of Armed Conflict*, The Hague, 1954.

cultural property had taken on a clear international aspect as the 1954 Convention reflected: 'cultural property belonging to any person whatsoever shall be recognized as the cultural heritage of all mankind'. This is emphasized elsewhere in the Convention by suggesting that it is an 'international responsibility of all nations to protect their own and other peoples' heritage'.

It is against this philosophy of the distinctive nature of cultural property and the global character of the material that the first international instrument concerned with peacetime protection and usage of cultural property appeared in 1960. This expressed a further notion that it promotes 'mutual understanding among nations'. This theme, combined with that of promoting cultural identity within nations, continues to this day. In the twenty years from 1960 no less than twelve Conventions or Recommendations were passed by the Unesco General Conference on the importance of cultural property in this regard;[4] some of the reasons for this have been discussed elsewhere (LEWIS 1987). There is similar activity at a regional level under the aegis of the Council of Europe commencing with the European Cultural Convention 1954 from which developed in due course Conventions on the archaeological, underwater and architectural heritage with the most recent concerned with offences on cultural property. For that matter the European Communities have also involved themselves in cultural affairs for some years, promoting the idea of *European Rooms* in museums of the Member States whom they have also encouraged to ratify international agreements on the protection of cultural property and seeking freedom of trade in cultural goods (Commission of the European Communities 1977). In this there is a consistency of approach in the most recent statement by the Commission.[5]

In the context of international agreements this paper is concerned particularly with museum collections, their protection and free movement and therefore attention is drawn to the Unesco Convention of 1970[6] and that

4. The Unesco legislation of this period includes: Recommendation concerning the most effective means of rendering museums accessible to everyone, Paris, 1960; Recommendation on the means of prohibiting and preventing the illicit export, import and transfer of ownership of cultural property, Paris, 1962; Recommendation concerning the preservation of cultural property endangered by public and private works, Paris, 1968; Convention on the means of prohibiting and preventing the illicit import, export and transfer of ownership of cultural property, Paris, 1970; Convention concerning the protection of the world cultural and natural heritage, Paris, 1972; Recommendation concerning the protection, at national level, of the cultural and natural heritage, Paris, 1972; Recommendation concerning the international exchange of cultural property, Nairobi, 1976; Recommendation concerning the safeguarding and contemporary role of historic areas, Nairobi, 1976; Recommendation for the protection of movable cultural property, Paris, 1978; Recommendation for the safeguarding and preservation of moving images, Belgrade, 1980.
5. Commission of the European Communities: Communication to the Council on the Protection of National Treasures possessing Artistic, Historic or Archaeological Value: Needs arising from the Abolition of the Frontiers in 1992, Brussels, 22 November 1989 [Doc. COM (89) 594 final].
6. Unesco: Convention on the means of prohibiting and preventing the illicit import, export and transfer of ownership of cultural property, 1970. (Editor's note: reproduced in ICC Institute, ed., *International Sale of Works of Art/La Vente Internationale d'Oeuvres d'Art* (ICC Publishing/Kluwer, Paris/Deventer 1990) pp. 171–185 (French) and 187–200 (English).

passed by the Council of Europe on the archaeological heritage in 1969.[7] Both are concerned with counteracting illicit transfers between countries as a safeguard to the heritage of the country of origin and particularly the scientific integrity of the material. Sixteen European States[8] have ratified the legislation on the archaeological heritage but only five Member States of the Council of Europe[9] have endorsed Unesco's 1970 Convention. To the curator this is a startling difference of approach to fundamentally the same principle. The variations, broadly, are geographical (one is European and the other global) and subject (one is concerned with archaeological discoveries and the other with cultural property at large). It is not intended to examine the reasons for this except to say that it is widely believed among curators that there is a strong lobby from the art trade against the 1970 Convention.

For the curator this is a major issue. It may be the aesthetics or the rarity of the object that makes it a desirable acquisition but the essence of cultural property is the information that it carries with it: provenance, context, association, etc.; the Director-General of the Rijksmuseum demonstrated this eloquently in his opening address.[10] Illicit trade, moral and legal considerations apart, suppresses information to the detriment of scholarship and the better understanding of the piece. In the absence of ratification of the 1970 Unesco Convention by the governments of some of the major nations in Europe, the museum profession has paid particular attention to codify its position in the matter. As early as 1972 the British Museum, the Museums Association and other national bodies in the United Kingdom issued a statement[11] clarifying their position in the matter.

The International Council of Museums (1970) issued a statement on the ethics of acquisition at the time of the Convention but this has now been superseded by a much fuller statement in its *Code of Professional Ethics* (ICOM 1987). This code suggests, *inter alia*, that each museum authority should publish, and regularly review, its collecting policy; ensure that it acquiries valid title to all acquisitions; respect wildlife protection and conservation legislation in collecting for the natural sciences and refuse to purchase material illicitly removed from archaeological sites. There is a general presumption of the permanence of museum collections, that in the event of disposal other museums should have first refusal and that any moneys resulting from a sale should be used solely to supplement the

---

7. Council of Europe: European Convention on the protection of the archaeological heritage, 1969.
8. Austria, Belgium, Cyprus, Denmark, France, Federal Republic of Germany, Greece, Italy, Liechtenstein, Luxembourg, Malta, Portugal, Spain, Sweden, Switzerland and the United Kingdom.
9. Cyprus, Greece, Italy, Portugal and Spain.
10. Editor's note: *see supra* pp. 10–14.
11. The statement included the following: 'That it is and will continue to be the practice of museums and galleries in the United Kingdom that they do not and will not knowingly acquire any antiquities or other cultural material which they have reason to believe has been exported in contravention of the current laws of the country of origin.'

collections. In the event of a request for the return of cultural property to its country of origin dialogue based on scientific and professional principles should be initiated between the parties. An extract from the relevant parts of the ICOM *Code of Professional Ethics* forms Appendix A (*see infra* pp. 87–91).

III. SOME EUROPEAN ISSUES

Philip Jessup (see *supra* pp. 67–71) has summarized the issues as far as the national legislation permits museums to dispose of objects in their collections. In Europe there is a strong presumption against disposal but the circumstances and practice in the United States are markedly different[12] and it is necessary to be wary of transferring practice across the Atlantic without being aware of the major differences that exist in museum philosophy and organization. It is clear that the free circulation of cultural material on a world basis, means that the international community has to negotiate within a great diversity of national legislations, developed from a number of different principles. This will now be examined from the small sample of legislation in the Questionnaire returns. This fits broadly into a tripartite classification embracing the notions of 'public property', 'cultural property' and 'museum property'; the latter term is a convenience and has no legal meaning.

1. Public Property

Legislation relating to public property arises mainly through the law of the public domain as part of the Roman law system. This, normally, provides for the inalienability of all such property. Thus, the inclusion of public museums within the terms of public domain legislation provides very strong protection for State museum collections. This is the position in France[13] where the principle has been extended also to local government and other public bodies,[14] thus securing the collections held by these museums also. This means that only private collections and museums do not have this protection. Although there are powers to declassify inalienable material in France, they have never been extended to cultural goods.

Similar principles apply in Italy,[15] Spain and Switzerland. As in France, so in Italy and Switzerland the legislation applies to all public authorities to District level. In Italy the non-territorial public bodies are the subject of other legislation.[16] For Spain the legislation with its concept of inalienability

12. *See*, for example, WEIL (1990) pp. 105–126.
13. France: Code on the Public Domain, Art. 52.
14. France: Law 88–13 of 5 January 1988, Art. 13(1).
15. Italy: Royal Decree 363 of 30 January 1913.
16. Italy: Law 1089 of 1 June 1939.

has been developed to include all archaeological discoveries[17] and the property of the Royal Crown.[18] This also applies to all objects recognized as part of the Spanish National Patrimony in State ownership; these may be transferred within the State but not to a third party[19] and may be exchanged with other States for items of similar cultural value.[20] Public property which is no longer in public use or service may be alienated;[21] this is known as patrimonial property but cultural material deemed to be part of the national patrimony remains fully protected. Such material in the possession of religious institutions is also closely controlled and may only be transferred to the State, other public bodies or to other religious institutions.[22] Different circumstances prevail in Belgium where a Court of Appeal ruled that ecclesiastical material formed part of the public domain, as do certain monuments and edifices and their contents. Other cultural property, such as that in public museums, is not classified in this way in Belgium.[23]

It is clear that the transfer of ownership of cultural property is extremely unlikely if it is protected under public domain legislation. The transfer between public sector institutions within the same administration may take place but this can hardly be considered a change of ownership. Spain with its powers to exchange items of similar cultural value with other States[24] appears to be unique.

2. *Cultural Property*

In many ways this is no more than a sub-set of public property legislation in that it recognizes the public significance of a certain type of material and seeks its preservation. But it arises under a different legal system and with the majority of respondents to the Questionnaire reporting specific legislation relating to cultural property in their countries, there is ample justification for treating it separately.

The form of the cultural property legislation varies considerably. It can relate to the whole artistic, historic and scientific heritage or only to a narrow subject area within one of these fields; it may be concerned with all heritage material or only to specified material of excellence within it; it may relate to named material only. In addition different principles may be applied to different types of owner or only be invoked in a certain set of circumstances such as export or death. In some cases cultural property law operates in parallel with public property legislation.

17. Spain: Law on Historical Patrimony 1985, Art. 44.
18. Spain: Law on National Patrimony 1982, Art. 6(2).
19. Spain: Law on Historical Patrimony 1985, Art 28(2).
20. Spain: Law on Historical Patrimony 1985, Art. 34.
21. Spain: Law on the State Patrimony 1964, Art. 95.
22. Spain: Law on Historical Patrimony 1985, Art. 28(2).
23. Belgium: Cour de Cassation, 11 November 1886: Pas., 1886, I, p. 410.
24. Spain: Law on National Patrimony 1982, Art. 34.

Of the eleven European countries responding to the Questionnaire, six have general cultural property legislation which protects the artistic and historic heritage and in some cases extends to the natural sciences as well. In the case of Greece the legislation[25] is specific and protects the excavated archaeological heritage and works of art made prior to 1830. In Sweden and the United Kingdom, legal protection of cultural property applies only in the event of export. Taxation relief in respect of the transfer of heritage material to the public sector in the United Kingdom (LEWIS 1990) may also be regarded as a protective measure.

Those countries with general protective legislation will normally classify the material concerned and this presupposes some form of listing or registration. It should be noted here that one of the requirements of the 1970 Unesco Convention is the establishment of a list of important public and private cultural property whose export would constitute 'an appreciable impoverishment of the national heritage'.[26] The idea of a register of national treasures is also mooted in the recent communication from the Commission of the European Communities. Current practice in Europe, however, is inconsistent and far from comprehensive. For example, in the Federal Republic of Germany, the registered works of art number only 501; in the Netherlands there are about forty paintings on the national list although a number of historical and ecclesiastical items are included. The Dutch list, however, relates only to privately owned cultural property and this is also the case under the Belgian scheme. In the Roman law countries, an inventory of the public domain property is maintained although in Spain there is a specific requirement for notable cultural property and material of 'singular relevancy' to be entered in the General Inventory. This, of course, relates only to public property. Most museums have their own inventories but rarely give any status in this context to the objects recorded.

The 1970 Unesco Convention requires cultural property of importance to be 'specifically designated'[27] by the State. At a national level, however, there is considerable variation of intent and meaning in the terminology used in different European countries. In Austria these are known as 'monuments'; other terms include 'cultural goods' in the Federal Republic of Germany;[28] 'national property' in Italy;[29] 'protected objects' in the Netherlands[30] and 'national patrimony' in Spain.[31] These arrangements are normally organized at a national level but in Germany and Switzerland this is the responsibility of the *Land* and Cantons respectively while in Belgium[32]

25. Greece: Antiquities Law 5351/1932.
26. Art. 5(b).
27. Art. 1.
28. Federal Republic of Germany: Law of 6 August 1955.
29. Italy: Law 1089 of 1 June 1939.
30. The Netherlands: Conservation of Cultural Heritage Act: Act of 1 February 1984, *Staatsblad* No. 49.
31. Spain: Law on National Patrimony, 1982.
32. Belgium: Flemish Decree of 17 November 1982.

the matter of cultural objects may be dealt with at Community level. The administration of the schemes fall under a variety of government offices: Internal Affairs (Belgium and Federal Republic of Germany); Monuments (Austria); Cultural Property (Italy); Culture and an Archaeological Council (Greece); Cultural Affairs (The Netherlands); Trade and Industry (United Kingdom). It should be noted that the government department concerned with the protection of cultural property is not necessarily that with responsibility for museums.

The ownership of cultural property can affect the way it is treated. For example, any object of historic, artistic or other cultural significance owned by a public or religious body in Austria is automatically regarded as a 'monument' unless declared otherwise. In the Federal Republic of Germany, however, the law protecting the national patrimony applies only to private persons, including private museums,[33] and similarly the list of 'protected objects' in the Netherlands does not include publicly owned material.[34] As already seen, ecclesiastical establishments in Belgium[35] and Spain[36] are treated separately.

The transfer of ownership of cultural property within the country concerned is normally governed by the protective legislation described above and in all cases notification, if not the authorization of the government department concerned is required. Permission to export listed or registered items on a permanent basis is most unlikely to be granted. Attention is drawn to the study on the export of works of art undertaken at the second Symposium 1990 in Geneva (KNAPP 1990).

In certain countries separate statutes relating to the export of cultural property may be relevant. Such legislation relating to temporary export for scholarly or exhibition purposes applies in Greece,[37] Italy[38] and Spain.[39] In each case the authority of the appropriate Minister – in Greece, the Council of Ministers – is necessary before significant cultural property can be temporarily exported, normally for exhibition purposes. Elsewhere more general legislation may govern temporary export with the decision to proceed resting either with the Minister concerned or the governing board of the museum. Another variation is the period that cultural material is permitted temporarily to be abroad. In Spain items declared to be of cultural interest will receive an export permit for a maximum of ten years; in Austria this may be for nine years but in Belgium appears only to be for one year. An increasingly important aspect of temporary exports, particularly for inter-

33. Federal Republic of Germany: Law of 6 August 1955.
34. The Netherlands: Conservation of Cultural Heritage Act: Act of 1 February 1984.
35. Belgium: Cour de Cassation, 11 November 1886: Pas., 1886, I, p. 410.
36. Spain: Law on Historical Patrimony 1985, Art. 28(2).
37. Greece: Law 654/1977.
38. Italy: Law 328 of 2 April 1950.
39. Spain: Royal Decree 111/1986, Art. 56. Temporary imports are specifically governed by a Ministerial Order of 28 November 1986 on the procedure of application of the EEC Regulations on temporary imports (Council Regulation 3599/82, *Official Journal* 31 December 1982 and Commission Regulation 1751/84, *Official Journal* 29 June 1984).

national exhibition work, concerns the insurance of the works and State indemnity is provided through Spanish law,[40] in Britain[41] and Sweden.

The criteria for controlling permanent exports is often determined by age and monetary value. Sweden[42] is a case in point. Other examples include Greece, which freely exports contemporary art but an antiquity has to be determined 'not useful' before export can take place.[43] Austria has a similar provision and allows the work of artists who died less than twenty years ago to be exported unless the item formed part of the public collection.[44] Belgium protects works of fine and decorative art as well as archives which are more than a century old, or the works of an author deceased over fifty years ago.[45] Spain also uses one hundred years as the baseline for preventing the export of its historic patrimony.[46] In the United Kingdom an export licence is required for any item more than fifty years old which exceeds a certain value; this is currently £40,000 for oil and tempera paintings, other than portraits, with a graded scale for other types of material.[47] An anomaly has been discovered in the British system recently, regarding the export of palaeontological specimens; a reptile fossil found in Scotland and sold to the Stuttgart Museum for £207,000 has been ruled outside the export control procedure for cultural property.[48] This issue is currently under review.

The appearance of an important item on the market for internal or external transfer may result in the use of pre-emptive powers to acquire the item for the State. In Switzerland a number of public authorities[49] have the right of pre-emption in certain circumstances while in the Netherlands objection to export constitutes an offer by the Dutch government to purchase the item on appropriate terms and conditions.[50] In the United Kingdom the export licence of an outstanding heritage item may be withheld for a period to allow the public collections in Britain the opportunity to acquire the item at the current market price. A recent ministerial statement that the facility to maintain important heritage material in Britain may be extended to the private sector is the subject of some controversy.[51]

---

40. Spain: Law on Historical Patrimony 1985 as supplemented by Budget Act 37/1988 (*see Disposicion adicional primera*).
41. United Kingdom: National Heritage Act 1980.
42. Sweden: Law SOU 1988:950, regulating the export of cultural property.
43. Greece: Royal Decree 13 of 20 May 1919 and Presidential Decree 22 of 28 October 1931.
44. Austria: Federal Law Prohibiting the Export of Cultural Property, Art. 2(5) (*Bundesgesetzblatt* 1986/391).
45. Belgium: Law of 16 May 1962.
46. Spain: Law on Historical Patrimony 1985.
47. United Kingdom: Import, Export and Customs Powers (Defence) Act 1939 with ministerial announcement on the open general export licence, 7 July 1989.
48. *The Times*, 31 January 1990.
49. The Cantons of Berne, Jura, Ticino and Vaud can all exercise powers of pre-emption on cultural property.
50. The Netherlands: Conservation of Cultural Heritage Act: Act of 1 February 1984.
51. *The Times*, 21 March 1990.

3. *Museum Property*

Museum legislation, as well as established custom and practice, are important factors influencing transfers from museum collections. This is perhaps surprising for an institution whose function does not appear to be well defined in law. In Austria,[52] France and the United Kingdom,[53] for example, the notion of a 'museum' – which may be a private or public sector institution – does not find expression in museum legislation. The view among museum professionals in Europe and the general tenor of national museum legislation, where it exists, is that museums are responsible for the collection and preservation of the nation's movable cultural heritage. There is therefore a presumption against transfers from their collections but that if there are, they should normally be between museums. The legal position of the non-national museums is less clear, although the same principles are normally followed in the public sector. Where transfers occur, they will only be with the approval of the governing board of the museum if it is within their competence to authorize it; a gift with conditions may require higher authorization.

In some cases museums do not have separate legal identity from the government that established or authorized their existence. Other countries, however, appear to be giving their national museums greater autonomy. In Spain, the Prado now has separate legal identity[54] with stronger powers than other museums in Spain; these include powers to collect but prevent the sale or exchange of works of art from its collection. The *Centro de Arte Reina Sofia* in Madrid will soon have a similar status. The United Kingdom government has also given greater autonomy and powers to a number of its national museums over the last ten years; these include the Victoria and Albert Museum, the National Museum of Science and Industry (the Science Museum), the Royal Armouries[55] and the Royal Museums of Scotland[56] all of which are now governed by Statute.

Today all of the major national museums in the United Kingdom have separate legal identity through Statute or, in a few cases, an Order in Council, a Royal Charter or a Deed of Gift. Typically the Trustees of national museums are empowered to dispose of items only if they are duplicates, are unsuitable to be retained in the collection (having regard to student usage) or have become unsuitable by reason of damage, deteriora-

---

52. Under Art. 31 of Austrian Federal Law of 1 July 1981 on the organization of research, the tasks of museums are described as: collecting, safeguarding, presenting to the public and inventorying art objects, undertaking research and advising other museums (*Bundesgesetzblatt* 1989/663).
53. In the United Kingdom the term 'museum' – in the specialized context of taxation relief – is defined as 'any institution which exists wholly or mainly for the purpose of preserving for the public benefit a collection of scientific, historic or artistic interest' (Inheritance Tax Act 1984, Schedule 3).
54. Spain: Royal Decree 1432/1985.
55. United Kingdom: National Heritage Act 1983.
56. United Kingdom: National Heritage (Scotland) Act 1985.

tion, etc. The National Gallery, however, has been prevented by Statute from disposing of any of its collections since 1954.[57] The transfer of items between certain national museums is authorized under the same legislation.[58] The position of non-national museums is less clear legally and there is no case law. However, the general position taken – and required as policy for a museum to be registered to receive government grant – is that there is a strong presumption against disposal but that in such an event other museums should first have the opportunity to acquire the material. This conforms with the code of practice adopted by the Museums Association[59] which in turn is based on the ruling of a Government-appointed Committee of Enquiry[60] which reported in 1964 that:

> 'The basic principle upon which the law rests is that when private persons give property for public purposes the Crown undertakes to see that it is devoted to the purposes intended by the donor, and to no others. When a work of art is given to a museum or gallery for general exhibition, the public thereby acquires rights in the object concerned and these rights cannot be set aside. The authorities of the museum or gallery are not the owners of such an object in the ordinary sense of the word: they are merely responsible, under the authority of the Courts, for carrying out the intentions of the donor....
>
> 'These general principles must be taken in conjunction with the following specific points:
>
> '(a) where a work of art is given to a charitable institution, one of whose principle purposes is the exhibition of such objects to the public, a natural presumption arises that it has been given for this purpose; and unless this presumption is displaced by evidence to the contrary it cannot be sold without special authority;
>
> '(b) if a work of art is part of the general property of an exhibiting institution such as a museum or gallery, as is the case when it has been bought out of general funds, it cannot be sold unless the governing instrument of the institution ... clearly permits such a course.'

The British Government has recently undertaken a study on the disposal of museum collections[61] and is expected to issue a statement shortly with a possible recommendation for additional legislation; this is not expected to support the view expressed above. In Sweden a new policy has been introduced following the announcement in the State Budget for 1990–91 that items 'useless and not required for the activities of the museum' may be sold.[62] The National Swiss Museum is permitted to sell works of art from its

---

57. United Kingdom: National Gallery and Tate Gallery Act 1954.
58. *Ibid.*
59. 'Code of Practice for Museum Authorities', in Museums Association, *Museums Yearbook 1990–91*, p. 3.
60. COTTISLOE, Lord, *Report of the Committee of Enquiry into the Sale of Works of Art by Public Bodies*, HMSO, 1964.
61. United Kingdom: 'Powers of Disposal from Museum and Gallery Collections: a consultative paper', issued by the Office of Arts and Libraries, August 1988 (typewritten report).
62. Sweden: State Budget, 1990–91.

collection, provided two similar works remain, or if they are surplus to requirements.[63] However, the constitutions of a number of Swiss private museums prohibit sales from their collections.

IV. SOME CONCLUDING REMARKS

The extent and nature of the international legislation on cultural property provides a clear indication of the subject's importance in the international community. The notions which have been associated with it over the last two centuries help to identify its special significance. It is a special class of property and society considers that it needs to be protected. Further, although it may be publicly owned it is to be treated separately from public property and the notions normally associated with this, an aspect which comes particularly into focus in times of armed conflict. It is viewed, simultaneously, as the 'cultural heritage of all mankind' but also as the means of promoting national identity; the latter has a particular bearing on the issues concerning the prohibition of illicit transfers of cultural property and on requests from nations for the return and restitution of material where the heritage has been particularly denuded.

At the same time the legislation also recognizes the scientific value of the material – and the site or context from which it may be derived – and that it may well be the primary evidence contributing information and understanding to different disciplines. Its contribution to knowledge and its ability to promote cultural understanding together make it a medium for exhibition of considerable educational and political force. Because of these factors there is close control on transfers of ownership of cultural property both internationally and regionally but at the same time temporary transfers for exhibition purposes are encouraged.

At the operational level in the nations of Europe, there appears to be strong support for the protection of the archaeological heritage, which, although not discussed here, is paralleled for the natural heritage. This is not reflected, however, in recognition of the broader protection of cultural property which could be offered through ratifying the 1970 Unesco Convention. The national legislation in Europe, with the possible exception of Switzerland and Sweden, does provide some protection but is diverse in character and varying in the protection it affords.

Those countries operating with public domain legislation provide strong protection – inalienability – to cultural property in national collections. Some countries may provide supplementary legislation to meet particular requirements. There are, however, certain disadvantages, one of which is the generality of a Code for public property and the lack of flexibility that this brings when the special requirements of cultural property have to be met.

63. Switzerland: Federal Law of 27 June 1890: The Swiss National Museum.

These may be for the temporary transfer of exhibition work or for more permanent dealings, say with other countries. In addition public domain legislation only offers protection to cultural property in the public sector (which may or may not extend to non-national government). Separate arrangements are necessary for the private sector unless all cultural property is vested in the government.

A number of European States have specific legislation controlling cultural property within that country. This, in theory, will normally cover relevant material held in both the public and private sectors and provide an opportunity for a unified and consistent approach to the matter. In practice, however, certain nations apply such legislation to the private sector only. An advantage of this approach is the possibility of linking more directly with international legislation. Most countries adopting this approach classify the material and list key items; there appear to be considerable differences of standard between countries. However, the transfer of ownership of a key piece outside the country would be most unusual. Other countries exercise control only if there is a request to export an item, some having powers of pre-emption. The administration of cultural property legislation of this nature is mainly at national level.

Legislation governing the administration of museums and their collections is normally subsidiary to national laws governing cultural property. The concept of a museum does not appear to be well defined in law, although notwithstanding this, the legislation, where it exists, normally accentuates the dual role of preservation and presentation. At least two countries have recently given some of their national museums separate legal identity and increased autonomy through new enabling legislation. Where such legislation exists there will normally be strong protection for the collections, in some cases preventing the disposal of any item in the collection. This strong presumption for the permanence of museum collections has, however, been challenged by politicians in certain countries. However, at present, the collections of museums without governing legislation can be regarded as at greater risk.

The present position then is a diversity of legislation giving varying degrees of protection to museum collections with some opportunity for the circulation of material, mainly between museums and for exhibition purposes. The changing social role of museums, however, with its increasing emphasis on collection utilization may be bringing false perceptions of them as preservation agencies. A full examination of the cultural property and museum legislation in Europe would seem to be a necessary prerequisite in the preparations for 1992. With this should also come a further re-examination of the 1970 Unesco Convention in an attempt to provide protective legislation acceptable to the major European States. The preliminary draft of the Unidroit Convention on Stolen or Illegally Exported Cultural Objects would no doubt be one aspect of such discussions.

Appendix A

EXTRACTS FROM THE INTERNATIONAL COUNCIL OF MUSEUMS CODE OF PROFESSIONAL ETHICS

3. *Acquisitions to Museum Collections*

3.1 Collecting Policies

Each museum authority should adopt and publish a written statement of its collecting policy. This policy should be reviewed from time to time, and at least once every five years. Objects acquired should be relevant to the purpose and activities of the museum, and be accompanied by evidence of valid legal title. Any conditions or limitations relating to an acquisition should be clearly described in an instrument of conveyance or other written documentation. Museums should not, except in very exceptional circumstances, acquire material that the museum is unlikely to be able to catalogue, conserve, store or exhibit, as appropriate, in a proper manner. Acquisitions outside the current stated policy of the museum should only be made in very exceptional circumstances, and then only after proper consideration by the governing body of the museum itself, having regard to the interests of the objects under consideration, the national or other cultural heritage and the special interests of other museums.

3.2 Acquisition of Illicit Material

The illicit trade in objects destined for public and private collections encourages the destruction of historic sites, local ethnic cultures, theft at both national and international levels, places at risk endangered species of flora and fauna, and contravenes the spirit of national and international patrimony. Museums should recognize the relationship between the marketplace and the initial and often destructive taking of an object for the commercial market, and must recognize that it is highly unethical for a museum to support in any way, whether directly or indirectly, that illicit market.

A museum should not acquire, whether by purchase, gift, bequest or exchange, any object unless the governing body and responsible officer are satisfied that the museum can acquire valid title to the specimen or object in question and that in particular it has not been acquired in, or exported from, its country of origin and/or any intermediate country in which it may have been legally owned (including the museum's own country) in violation of that country's laws.

So far as biological and geological material is concerned, a museum should not acquire by any direct or indirect means any specimen that has been collected, sold or otherwise transferred in contravention of any national or international wildlife protection or natural history conservation law or treaty of the museum's own country or any other country except with the express consent of an appropriate outside legal or governmental authority.

So far as excavated material is concerned, in addition to the safeguards set out above, the museum should not acquire by purchase objects in any case where the governing body or responsible officer has reasonable cause to believe that their recovery involved the recent unscientific or intentional destruction or damage of ancient monuments or archaeological sites, or involved a failure to disclose the finds to the owner or occupier of the land, or to the proper legal or governmental authorities.

If appropriate and feasible, the same tests as are outlined in the above four paragraphs should be applied in determining whether or not to accept loans for exhibition or other purposes.

3.3 Field Study and Collecting

Museums should assume a position of leadership in the effort to halt the continuing degradation of the world's natural history, archaeological, ethnographic, historic and artistic resources. Each museum should develop policies that allow it to conduct its activities within appropriate national and international laws and treaty obligations, and with a reasonable certainty that its approach is consistent with the spirit and intent of both national and international efforts to protect and enhance the cultural heritage.

Field exploration, collecting and excavation by museum workers present ethical problems that are both complex and critical. All planning for field studies and field collecting must be preceded by investigation, disclosure and consultation with both the proper authorities and any interested museums or academic institutions in the country or area of the proposed study sufficient to ascertain if the proposed activity is both legal and justifiable on academic and scientific grounds. Any field programme must be executed in such a way that all participants act legally and responsibly in acquiring specimens and data, and that they discourage by all practical means unethical, illegal and destructive practices.

3.4 Co-operation between Museums and Collecting Policies

Each museum should recognize the need for co-operation and consultation between all museums with similar or overlapping interests and collecting policies, and should seek to consult with such other institutions both on specific acquisitions where a conflict of interest is thought possible and, more generally, on defining areas of specialization. Museums should respect the boundaries of the recognized collecting areas of other museums and should avoid acquiring material with special local connections or of special local interest from the collecting area of another museum without due notification of intent.

3.5 Conditional Acquisitions and Other Special Factors

Gifts, bequests and loans should only be accepted if they conform to the stated collecting and exhibition policies of the museum. Offers that are subject to special conditions may have to be rejected if the conditions proposed are judged to be contrary to the long-term interests of the museum and its public.

3.6 Loans to Museums

Both individual loans of objects and the mounting or borrowing of loan exhibitions can have an important role in enhancing the interest and quality of a museum and its services. However, the ethical principles outlined in paras. 3.1 to 3.5 above must apply to the consideration of proposed loans and loan exhibitions as to the acceptance or rejection of items offered to the permanent collections: loans should not be accepted or exhibitions mounted if they do not have a valid educational, scientific or academic purpose.

3.7 Conflicts of Interest

The Collecting policy or regulations of the museum should include provisions to ensure that no person involved in the policy or management of the museum, such as a trustee or other member of a governing body, or a member of the museum staff, may compete with the museum for objects or may take advantage of privileged information received because of his or her position, and that should a conflict of interest develop between the needs of the individual and the museum, those of the museum will prevail. Special care is also required in considering any offer of an item either for sale or as a tax-benefit-gift, from members of governing bodies, members of staff, or the families or close associates of these.

4. Disposal of Collections

4.1 General Presumption of Permanence of Collections

By definition one of the key functions of almost every kind of museum is to acquire objects and keep them for posterity. Consequently there must always be a strong presumption against the disposal of specimens to which a museum has assumed formal title. Any form of disposal, whether by donation, exchange, sale or destruction requires the exercise of a high order of curatorial judgement and should be approved by the governing body only after full expert and legal advice has been taken.

Special considerations may apply in the case of certain kinds of specialized institutions such as 'living' or 'working' museums, and some teaching and other educational museums, together with museums and other institutions displaying living specimens, such as botanical and zoological gardens and aquaria, which may find it necessary to regard at least part of their collections as 'fungible' (i.e. replaceable and renewable). However, even here there is a clear ethical obligation to ensure that the activities of the institution are not detrimental to the long-term survival of examples of the material studied, displayed or used.

4.2 Legal or Other Powers of Disposal

The laws relating to the protection and permanence of museum collections, and to the power of museums to dispose of items from their collections vary greatly from country to country, and often from one museum to another within the same country. In some cases no disposals of any kind are permitted, except in the case of items that have been seriously damaged by natural or accidental deterioration. Elsewhere, there may be no explicit restriction on disposals under general law.

Where the museum has legal powers permitting disposals, or has acquired objects subject to conditions of disposal, the legal or other requirements must be fully complied with. Even where legal powers of disposal exist, a museum may not be completely free to dispose of items acquired: where financial assistance has been obtained from an outside source (e.g. public or private grants, donations from a Friends of the Museum organization, or private benefactor), disposal would normally require the consent of all parties who had contributed to the original purchase.

Where the original acquisition was subject to mandatory restrictions these must be observed unless it can be clearly shown that adherence to such restrictions is impossible or substantially detrimental to the institution. Even in these circumstances the museum can only be relieved from such restrictions through appropriate legal procedures.

4.3 De-accessioning Policies and Procedures

Where a museum has the necessary legal powers to dispose of an object the decision to sell or otherwise dispose of material from the collections should only be taken after due consideration, and such material should be offered first, by exchange, gift or private treaty sale, to other museums before sale by public auction or other means is considered.

A decision to dispose of a specimen or work of art, whether by exchange, sale or destruction (in the case of an item too badly damaged or deteriorated to be restorable) should be the responsibility of the governing body of the museum, not the curator of the collection concerned acting alone. Full records should be kept of all such decisions and the objects involved, and proper arrangements made for the preservation and/or transfer, as appropriate, of the documentation relating to the object concerned, including photographic records where practicable.

Neither members of staff, nor members of the governing bodies, or members of their families or close associates, should ever be permitted to purchase objects that have been de-accessioned from a collection. Similarly, no such person should be permitted to appropriate in any other way items from the museum collections, even temporarily, to any personal collection or for any kind of personal use.

4.4 Return and Restitution of Cultural Property

If a museum should come into the possession of an object that can be demonstrated to have been exported or otherwise transferred in violation of the principles of the Unesco *Convention on the Means of Prohibiting and Preventing the Illicit Import, Export and Transfer of Ownership of Cultural Property (1970)* and the country of origin seeks its return and demonstrates that it is part of the country's cultural heritage, the museum should, if legally free to do so, take responsible steps to co-operate in the return of the object to the country of origin.

In the case of requests for the return of cultural property to the country of origin, museums should be prepared to initiate dialogues with an open-minded attitude on the basis of scientific and professional principles, (in preference to action at governmental or political level). The possibility of developing bilateral or multilateral co-operation schemes to assist museums in countries which are considered to have lost a significant part of their cultural heritage in the development of adequate museums and museum resources should be explored.

Museums should also respect fully the terms of the *Convention for the Protection of Cultural Property in the Event of Armed Conflict* (The Hague Convention, 1954), and in support of this *Convention*, should in particular abstain from purchasing or otherwise appropriating or acquiring cultural objects from any occupied country, as these will in most cases have been illegally exported or illicitly removed.

4.5 Income from Disposal of Collections

Any moneys received by a governing body from the disposal of specimens or works of art should be applied solely for the purchase of additions to the museum collections.

Appendix B

BIBLIOGRAPHY AND REFERENCES

BATOR, Paul M., *The International Trade in Art* (University of Chicago Press 1983 and Medway Reprints 1988).

BYRNE-SUTTON, Quentin, *Le trafic international des biens culturels sous l'angle de leur revendication par l'Etat d'origine* (Schulthess Polygraphischer Verlag AG, Zurich 1988).

CHATELAIN, Jean, *Administration et Gestion des Musées* (La Documentation Française, Paris 1984).

COUNCIL OF EUROPE, *The Art Trade: Report of the Committee on Culture and Education* (Strasbourg 1988).

COMMISSION OF THE EUROPEAN COMMUNITIES, 'Community action in the cultural sector', *Bulletin of the European Communities* (Supplement 6/77, Luxembourg).

HOUSE OF COMMONS, 'Report of the Select Committee appointed to inquire into the expediency of purchasing the Collection mentioned in the Earl of Elgin's Petition to the House, etc.', III *Parliamentary Papers* (1816) 49.

INTERNATIONAL COUNCIL OF MUSEUMS, *Ethics of Acquisition* (ICOM, Paris 1970).

INTERNATIONAL COUNCIL OF MUSEUMS, *Statutes [&] Code of Professional Ethics* (ICOM, Paris 1987).

KNAPP, Blaise, 'Restrictions on Importation and Exportation in the Art Trade' in ICC Institute, ed., *International Sales of Works of Art/La Vente Internationale d'Oeuvres d'Art* (ICC Publishing/Kluwer, Paris/Deventer 1990) pp. 11–47.

LEWIS, Geoffrey, 'The return of cultural property', 129 *Journal of the Royal Society of Arts* (London 1981) pp. 435–453.

LEWIS, Geoffrey, 'Museums: International and National Self-Regulation' in P. Lalive, ed., *International Sales of Works of Art/La Vente Internationale d'Oeuvres d'Art* (Institute of International Business Law and Practice – International Chamber of Commerce/Faculté de Droit, Université de Genève 1988) pp. 559–566.

LEWIS, Geoffrey, 'Heritage Giving Through Taxation in the U.K.' in ICC Institute, ed., *International Sales of Works of Art/La Vente Internationale d'Oeuvres d'Art* (ICC Publishing/Kluwer, Paris/Deventer 1990) pp. 589–599.

LYSTER, Simon, *International Wildlife Law* (Grotius, Cambridge 1985).

MERRYMAN, John H., 'Thinking about the Elgin Marbles', 83 *Michigan Law Review* (Michigan Law Review Association 1985, No. 8) pp. 1881–1923.

MERRYMAN, John H., 'The retention of cultural property', 21 *U. C. Davis Law Review* (University of California 1988, No. 3) pp. 477–513.

MERRYMAN, John H. & ELSEN, Albert E., *Law, Ethics and the Visual Arts* 1 & 2 (Second Edition) (University of Pennsylvania Press 1987).

O'KEEFE, P. J. & PROTT, L. V., *Law and the Cultural Heritage* 1: Discovery and Excavation (Professional Books/Butterworths 1984).

O'KEEFE, P. J. & PROTT, L. V., *Law and the Cultural Heritage* 3: Movement (Butterworths, London 1989).

UNESCO, *A Guide to the Operation of the Agreement on the Importation of Educational, Scientific and Cultural Material* (Unesco, Paris 1958).

UNESCO, *The Protection of Movable Cultural Property. Compendium of Legislative Texts*, I & II, (Unesco, Paris 1984).

WEIL, Stephen E., *Rethinking the Museum and other meditations* (Smithsonian Institution Press, Washington 1990).

WILLIAMS, Sharon A., *The International and National Protection of Movable Cultural Property* (Oceana, Dobbs Ferry, NY 1978).

WILSON, David M., *The British Museum: Purpose and Politics* (Trustees of the British Museum, London 1990).

National Reports

Austria

NATIONAL REPORT ON TOPIC 1. FREEDOM OF MUSEUMS TO SELL, TRADE OR OTHERWISE DISPOSE OF OBJECTS OF ART IN THEIR COLLECTIONS

Ignaz Seidl-Hohenveldern*

1.–3. Under the conditions set out in the Introduction,[1] museums may sell, exchange or give away objects they hold. Thus, Federal Museums have given monuments of particular value for a *Land* to the *Land* museum concerned and vice versa. It is not the policy of Austrian museums to sell objects, not even objects from the study collections inaccessible to the public. In the hunger period after World War I, second copies of prints from the Albertine (Federal Prints Museum) were sold, a sale still much regretted by Austrian Experts. I recall, however, two instances, in 1938 and 1952, when objects of considerable value were sold in order to acquire objects of the highest cultural significance to Austria.

4. A museum is not authorized to sell an object of art which was part of a gift from a private person, if the donor stipulated that the object should remain in the museum. A request has to be respected. Julius v. Benda left his collection of old masters to the Kunsthistorisches Museum on condition that the paintings should remain together as they were in his house. During Nazi rule, the paintings were placed in different sectors of the museum. The will of v. Benda was disregarded in view of the Jewish origin of the donor. After 1945, the museum asked the heirs of v. Benda whether they wished to see the paintings re-assembled or whether they would be satisfied with a plaque on each painting stating its origin. The heirs agreed to the latter solution.

5. As to the possibility to transfer or export an object of art which is part of a public collection, *see* my 'Introduction' in Part One, pp. 25–29.

6. The sale of an Art Déco wardrobe from an Austrian Federal Museum to United States Ambassador Lauder, in 1988, caused an uproar in the press and questions were asked in Parliament. The case was exacerbated further by Lauder's request to export a Schiele painting bought in Vienna from a

* Professor, Institut für Völkerrecht und Internationale Beziehungen, Vienna.
1. Editor's note: *see also* 'Austria: Introduction' in Part One.

private party.[2] While Ambassador Lauder was in Vienna, the wardrobe had been loaned to him. Loans from museums to Austrian missions abroad and to foreign missions in Vienna are permitted pursuant to Art. 7(4) of the Federal Law Prohibiting the Export of Cultural Property.[3] On leaving Vienna, Ambassador Lauder wanted to purchase the borrowed wardrobe. Apparently, the approval of the Ministries concerned had been obtained for the sale of the wardrobe. The museum envisaged purchasing other coveted objects with the proceeds from this sale. Ambassador Lauder has requested but not yet obtained the permission to export the wardrobe.

7. *a.* If a museum has sold an object of art belonging to the nation's 'cultural patrimony', it is an offence unless covered by a sales licence and, in case of export, by an export permit.
b. If a museum has sold an object of art not classified or not registered as a 'national cultural good' to either a private person or to another museum, the situation is as described as under *a., supra,* unless the museum is a private collection not held to be a monument as a unit.
c. If a museum has exchanged an object of art, regardless of whether it is classified as a 'national cultural good', with another museum in Austria or elsewhere, the situation is as described under *b., supra* except that even such a private collection cannot export monuments without permission.
d. The fact that a museum has sold or exchanged an object of art, whether it belongs to the nation's cultural heritage or not, to a private person or to another museum makes no difference as to the possibility of judicial action in respect to the situations described in *a. – c., supra.* I am not aware of any relevant case law in regard to this question in general.

2. *Die Presse*, Viennese newspaper, 21 January 1988; *International Herald Tribune* 23 January 1988.
3. Cf. N. HELFGOTT, *Ausfuhrverbotsgesetz für Kulturgut* (Vienna, Manz 1987) p. 32.

Belgique

RAPPORT NATIONAL SUR LE SUJET 1. LIBERTE DES MUSEES DE PROCEDER A DES TRANSACTIONS D'OBJETS D'ART*

Francis Haumont**

1. Les musées peuvent disposer librement d'objets d'art ou d'une collection pour autant que celui ou celle-ci n'ait pas fait l'objet d'une mesure administrative en limitant la libre disposition.

2. Seuls les objets d'art ne faisant pas l'objet d'une mesure de classement ou n'étant pas repris dans les biens faisant partie du domaine public peuvent être vendus.

En ce qui concerne ces objets non classés ou non affectés au domaine public, aucune procédure particulière ne doit être appliquée pour la vente, si ce ne sont les procédures traditionnelles dites de tutelle. C'est ainsi que, par exemple, un musée municipal ne pourra opérer une transaction sur un objet d'art seulement si les autorités de tutelle l'autorisent.

En revanche, si l'objet d'art devant faire l'objet de la transaction est un bien du patrimoine culturel classé ou affecté au domaine public, il conviendra, avant d'opérer la transaction, soit d'obtenir les autorisations requises ou le déclassement, soit de procéder préalablement à sa désaffectation. Ces mesures de déclassement ou de désaffectation suivent, dans les grandes lignes, les règles applicables à la procédure de classement et d'affectation. Nous y reviendrons à l'occasion de l'examen de la question 5.

3. A priori, il n'existe pas de différence entre les différents musées en ce qui concerne les habilitations à vendre.

Cependant, les objets d'art ne font pas tous uniformément l'objet des mêmes mesures administratives tendant à en limiter la disponibilité. C'est ainsi que le régime du classement n'est pas applicable aux objets d'art des musées dépendant de l'Etat central ou des Communautés. On pourrait donc considérer que ces musées, par le fait de l'absence de classement, bénéficient d'une plus grande liberté de transaction.

De même, les musées privés voient rarement certains de leurs biens culturels mobiliers faire l'objet d'une mesure de classement.

De plus, les biens de ces musées ne dépendant pas des autorités administratives, ne sont jamais affectés au domaine public et, par voie de

---

* Note d'Editeur: *v.* pour 'Introduction au Rapport' *supra* p. 31.

** Chargé de cours à l'Université Catholique de Louvain, Avocat au Barreau de Bruxelles.

conséquence, leur disponibilité n'est nullement altérée par une affectation au domaine public.

De ce fait, on pourrait dire que les musées privés sont plus à même de disposer librement des objets leur appartenant, non pas en vertu d'une habilitation particulière par rapport aux musées du secteur public, mais en raison de la quasi-absence de mesures administratives frappant leur patrimoine.

4. Il n'existe aucune disposition légale interdisant aux musées la vente d'un objet d'art non classé et non affecté au domaine public dont ils seraient devenus propriétaire par donation.

En revanche, le musée pourrait être lié, dans la libre disposition de l'objet reçu, par les éventuelles clauses du don.

Il faut néanmoins observer qu'une condition d'inaliénabilité absolue dans l'objet et dans le temps est contraire à l'ordre public et doit être réputée non écrite.

Par ailleurs, eu égard au fait que les donations aux musées doivent être autorisées (nous y reviendrons), l'autorisation est en pratique presque toujours refusée si la condition d'inaliénabilité dépasse 10 ans. Notons, cependant que le donateur peut exiger que l'oeuvre ne soit pas vendue de son vivant.

Notons également que la dation d'oeuvres d'art en paiement des droits de succession, qui bien entendu n'est pas assimilable comme telle à une donation, n'est assortie, en droit belge, d'aucune limitation quant à la libre disposition de l'oeuvre par l'Etat, même si la ratio legis de la loi instaurant la dation en paiement est de maintenir ces oeuvres dans le patrimoine culturel public.[1]

5. La notion de 'collection publique' n'est pas comme telle d'application en Belgique.

Comme nous l'avons exposé dans la première partie du présent rapport,[2] un objet d'art peut être classé ou affecté au domaine public.

Si le bien est classé, il peut faire l'objet d'une aliénation ou d'un échange moyennant une autorisation de l'Exécutif de la Communauté sur avis préalable de la Commission royale des monuments et des sites. Il est à noter qu'aucune disposition légale ne prévoit que l'autorisation d'aliéner et l'aliénation valent déclassement du bien. Celui-ci reste donc classé[3] et peut d'ailleurs faire l'objet d'un droit de préemption au profit des autorités publiques.[4]

Notons que si le bien classé par la Communauté flamande appartient à

1. Sur cette question, *v.* 'Le régime belge et la dation d'oeuvre d'art en paiement de droits de succession', *Revue de droit intellectuel* (1988) pp. 105 *et seq*. Note d'Editeur, *v. aussi* ICC Institute, ed., *International Sales of Works of Art/La Vente Internationale d'Oeuvres d'Art* ICC Publishing/Kluwer, Paris/Deventer 1990) pp. 561–584.
2. Note d'Editeur: *v.* 'Introduction au Rapport' *supra* pp. 000.
3. Décret flamand du 17 novembre 1982, art. 12.
4. Loi du 7 août 1931, art. 19.

une personne privée, son aliénation n'est pas subordonnée à une autorisation préalable,[5] mais, comme nous le verrons, le déplacement de l'oeuvre d'art l'est.[6]

L'autre formule permettant l'aliénation d'un bien faisant partie du patrimoine mobilier classé est de le déclasser. Aucune disposition nationale ou comunautaire ne prévoit comme tel le déclassement. Il est cependant de pratique administrative. La procédure n'en est donc pas déterminée.

En ce qui concerne les biens faisant partie du domaine public, ils sont, par application du régime même de la domanialité publique, inaliénalables. Ils ne peuvent donc ni être vendus, ni exportés (sauf, bien entendu, à titre de prêt dans le cadre d'une exposition à l'étranger).

La seule possibilité pour pouvoir procéder à une telle aliénation est de désaffecter le bien en question.

La procédure de désaffectation est similaire à celle de l'affectation. Elle se limite le plus souvent à la désinscription de l'oeuvre d'art du registre ou du catalogue du musée. Il va de soi que cette désinscription ne peut être faite que par l'autorité habilitée à le faire.

Enfin, rappelons ce que nous avons relevé dans la première partie de ce rapport en ce qui concerne les limitations à l'exportation d'oeuvres d'art.

Les exportations définitives d'objets classés sont soumises à autorisation.[7] Par ailleurs, la loi du 16 mai 1960 relative au patrimoine culturel de la Nation soumet une série d'objets[8] à autorisation préalable. Cette loi n'est cependant toujours pas d'application faute d'arrêtés d'éxécution que l'on attend depuis trente ans!

6. Les décisions des cours et tribunaux sont peu nombreuses dans cette matière [les cas où des objets d'art détenus par un musée ou faisant partie du patrimoine culturel national ont été soit exportés soit donnés, soit aliénés, soit échangés]. Elles portent essentiellement sur la question de savoir si tel ou tel objet d'art qui a été aliéné fait partie du domaine public et, à ce titre, ne pouvait être vendu.

Cette question a donné lieu à des décisions concernant des 'antiquités' trouvées dans le lit de cours d'eau ou des oeuvres d'art sises dans des églises. Il n'y a pas eu, à notre connaissance, de décision concernant des aliénations de biens dont le vendeur connaissait l'appartenance au patrimoine culturel mobilier classé ou affecté au domaine public.

Récemment, la ville de Liège a marqué son intention de vendre une toile de Picasso dans le cadre des difficultés financières que connaît la ville. Le processus n'est pas allé jusqu'à son terme à savoir la désaffectation du tableau et sa vente, et ce en raison du tollé assez général que cette annonce a provoqué.

---

5. Décret flamand du 17 novembre 1982, art. 8, §4.
6. Décret flamand du 17 novembre 1982, art. 8, §1er; Loi du 7 août 1931, art. 19.
7. Décret flamand du 17 novembre 1982, art. 12.
8. *V*. 'Introduction au Rapport' *supra* (2.c. L'inexportabilité, p. 36).

7.*a*. Un musée a vendu un objet d'art appartenant au patrimoine culturel national

Plusieurs hypothèses doivent être envisagées pour répondre à ce cas.

En Communautés germanophone ou française, si l'objet d'art a fait l'objet d'une mesure de classement sur base de la loi du 7 août 1931, il ne pourrait y avoir de poursuites judiciaires que dans la mesure où la vente n' a pas été autorisée par l'Exécutif de la Communauté française ou de la Communauté germanophone. Cette vente sera nulle et, selon l'art. 20 de la loi du 7 août 1931, l'action en nullité et l'action en revendication de l'objet vendu sont imprescriptibles. Cependant, à notre connaissance, il n'y a pas eu de décisions judiciaires appliquant cette disposition.

En Communauté flamande, si l'objet d'art a fait l'objet d'une mesure de classement sur base du décret flamand du 17 novembre 1982, il ne pourrait y avoir de poursuites judiciaires que dans la mesure où le bien appartient à une autorité publique et où cette vente n'a pas été autorisée par l'Exécutif communautaire sur avis de la commission royale des monuments et des sites. Dans cette hypothèse, sur base des arts. 28 et 30 du décret, outre les peines d'emprisonnement et les amendes qui peuvent être prononcées, le jugement de condamnation peut être accompagné d'un ordre contraignant de restitution. La question étant de savoir dans quelle mesure un tel jugement pourrait contraindre l'acquéreur de bonne foi.

Dans l'hypothèse où l'appartenance de l'objet d'art au patrimoine culturel national découle de son affectation au domaine public, la vente non précédée d'une désaffectation de l'objet vendu sera nulle. L'action en nullité et l'action en restitution sont imprescriptibles en raison précisément du fait que les biens du domaine public sont inaliénables et imprescriptibles.

7.*b*. Un musée a vendu un objet d'art qui n'est pas classé ou qui ne figure pas sur le registre du patrimoine culturel national à une personne privée, ou à un autre musée

A priori, la vente est parfaite dès l'instant où aucune disposition légale n'interdit cette transaction. Ceci vaut même pour les ventes à l'exportation de biens non classés ou non affectés, mais repris dans la liste des biens énumérés dans la loi du 16 mai 1960 relative au patrimoine culturel de la Nation dans la mesure où, comme nous l'avons vu, cette loi, faute d'arrêtés d'exécution, n'est pas d'application.

Il convient, toutefois, de mentionner les régles de tutelle qui, le cas échéant, conditionnent la vente à l'accord des autorités de tutelle. C'est ainsi que, par exemple, une vente par une commune d'une oeuvre d'art non classée et non affectée au domaine public, ne sera effective que moyennant la non-opposition de la Députation permanente du conseil provincial.[9] Il s'agit d'une clause suspensive qui sera reprise systématiquement dans les contrats de vente.

---

9. *V.* p. ex., art. 13 du Décret du 20 juillet 1989 organisant la tutelle sur les communes, les provinces et les intercommunales de la Région wallonne.

7.*c*. Un musée a échangé un objet d'art

i. Classé ou figurant sur le registre du patrimoine culturel national avec un musée belge ou étranger

En fait, l'échange est une des formes de l'aliénation. Il s'ensuit que ce que nous avons dit à propos de la vente sous 7.*a*. est également d'application en cas d'échange.

ii. Non classé et ne figurant pas au registre du patrimoine culturel national avec un musée belge ou étranger

Comme nous venons de le voir, l'échange est une des formes de l'aliénation. Dés lors, ce que nous avons exposé à l'occasion de la réponse au 7.*b*. est applicable à l'hypothèse présente.

7.*d*. Un musée a vendu un objet d'art à une personne privée ou à un autre musée, car sa valeur esthétique ou économique était plus basse au moment de le vendre qu'au moment de l'acquisition

En soi, cette opération n'est pas soumise à des règles autres que celles que nous avons évoquées précédemment.

On ne peut envisager cette opération que pour autant qu'elle réponde aux conditions émises à la vente proprement dite, indépendamment de la question du prix.

En ce qui concerne le prix, il se peut que l'autorité de tutelle suspende ou annule une vente en raison de la perte financière qu'elle entraîne. Il conviendrait, dans l'hypothèse d'une erreur d'expertise au moment de l'acquisition, de convaincre cette autorité de tutelle de l'intérêt de la vente même à perte. Le cas n'a donné lieu, à notre connaisance, à aucune décision judiciaire.

F. R. Germany

NATIONAL REPORT ON TOPIC 1. FREEDOM OF MUSEUMS TO SELL, TRADE OR OTHERWISE DISPOSE OF OBJECTS OF ART IN THEIR COLLECTIONS*

Ludger Bischop**

Generally in the Federal Republic of Germany, the museums are only 'purchasers' of works of art. They very rarely sell works of art belonging to their collections, because the possibilities for selling works of art are very limited.

Three kinds of limitations for the sale of works of art by museums can be described:

I. Limitations due to the 'public' character of museums
II. Limitations due to gifts made to the museums
III. Limitations due to the character of 'cultural goods'.

I. THE FIRST LIMITATION

In order to describe this limitation, it is necessary to explain how museums are organized in the Federal Republic of Germany. In Germany, ninety to ninety-five percent of the museums are owned by public entities (communes, states (*Länder*) and the Federal State) and managed in accordance with the 'public administrative rules'. Among the different public entities, the communes (local public authorities) are the responsible bodies for most of the museums.

A work of art that belongs to a museum owned by a public local authority is considered to be part of the local 'patrimony' (it is owned by the local authority). Therefore, when a director of a local museum wants to sell an object of art, the authorities of the communes must authorize this sale. This approval of the sale can be rendered void by a higher authority (e.g., by the Ministry of Internal Affairs of the State).

In addition to these limitations based on general public administrative rules determining the sale of public property, some local public authorities

* Editor's note: this Report is an English language summary of the German language National Report on Topic 1.

** Research Assistant, Institute for International Business Law, Westfälischen Wilhelms-Universität Münster.

have laid down special regulations. According to these special rules, a museum is not entitled to sell works of art and the director of the museum concerned is obliged not to sell any part of the museum collections. This is the case, e.g., for the Cologne Museums, the Staatsgalerie of Stuttgart and also the Bavarian National Museum.

This policy was instigated following a bad experience in recent years of sales involving certain objects of art that were sold by the museums and which reached very high prices at a subsequent auction sale. Moreover, the sale of objects by museums from their collections is foreign to the spirit in which public museums have been created. Following the tradition of the French revolution, the main tasks of a museum are the conservation, control and research of works of art. The trade aspects are very unfamiliar to European museums.

II. THE SECOND LIMITATION

The second limitation concerns works of art that have been donated to museums as gifts.

In considering the legal aspects of a gift, one has to take into account that according to German private law, a gift contract consists of two different contracts: first there is the contract which obliges the donor to transfer something to the donee as a gift; secondly, there is the contract of transfer of property which is the fulfilment of the first contract. Both contracts can be subject to a subsequent condition.

A donor can make both contracts subject to the condition that the work of art given as a gift must stay in the museum and may not be sold to a third person.

If only the first contract is subject to this subsequent condition and the donee has not complied with this condition, the promise of the donor becomes null and void. Then the donor can claim the restitution of the work of art on the basis of an action for unjust enrichment (Sect. 812(1) 1st sentence, 1st alternative BGB). Where the museum has already transferred the ownership of the work of art concerned to the purchaser, the donor is entitled to claim compensation for his lost property; the amount of the compensation depends upon the value of the work of art.

Where both contracts are subject to the subsequent condition described above, the sale of the object of art contrary to the condition would annul the transfer. Then the donor could be entitled to a *replevin* of his property on the basis of Sect. 985(1) BGB. If the museum has already transferred ownership to a good faith purchaser, the museum is liable *vis-à-vis* the donor for the purchase price, on the basis of Sect. 816(1) 1st sentence, BGB.

Even if there was not a subsequent condition to the gift, the museum must respect a 'moral' and factual condition before taking the decision to sell the work of art, subject to the gift. Namely, the fact that a museum can sell a work of art donated as a gift by private persons may discourage other persons from providing gifts to museums. Therefore, there is a trend in the policy of museums not to sell a work of art that originates as a private gift.

In connection with the ambiguity of a gift made to a museum, the same question can arise in regard to the loan of works of art by private persons to a museum. In Germany, works of art that are on loan are exempted from tax for the loaner; loans to a museum have also other advantages, e.g., the guarantee that a work of art will be well-conserved.

III. THE THIRD LIMITATION

The third limitation is due to the fact that the work of art belongs to the national cultural patrimony of Germany. In this case, the law on the protection of the national cultural patrimony applies (Law of 6 August 1955). This law regulating the export of German cultural goods can only apply to the sale of a work of art (which is considered as a 'cultural good') by a *private* museum, as this law applies only to the exportation of 'cultural goods' owned by private persons. Therefore, this law is of limited interest due to the fact that ninety percent of German museums are 'public-owned'. This situation can be explained by the fact that the public authorities exercise considerable control over the management of the 'public' museums.

France

RAPPORT NATIONAL SUR LE SUJET 1. LIBERTE DES MUSEES DE PROCEDER A DES TRANSACTIONS D'OBJETS D'ART

Jean Chatelain*

I. L'INALIENABILITE

La réponse à toutes les questions figurant à cette rubrique du questionnaire général est commandée par un principe: l'inaliénabilité des collections publiques.

1. La source de ce principe

La source de ce principe est la théorie du Domaine public qui est née en France dans la première partie du XIXe siècle de l'effort combiné de la jurisprudence des tribunaux et de sa mise en formule par la doctrine des principaux théoriciens du Droit.

La théorie a ensuite été confirmée par des textes formels: ainsi l'art L.52 du code du domaine de l'Etat: 'les biens du domaine public sont inaliénables et imprescriptibles' et, pour les biens des collectivités locales, l'art 13.1 de la loi 88–13 du 5 janvier 1988: 'les biens du domaine public des collectivités territoriales, de leurs établissements publics et de leurs groupements sont inaliénables et imprescriptibles'.

2. Champ d'application de la domanialité publique

Il a été peu à peu défini par la jurisprudence publique et la doctrine. Pour le sujet ici traité, il est acquis sans aucune contestation que les objets des collections des musées publics (ceux appartenant à l'Etat, aux collectivités territoriales et à leurs établissements publics) sont rangés dans le domaine public.

Les objets des musées privés qui restent rares en France ne sont pas soumis en théorie à ce régime qui est propre au patrimoine public. Mais, la plupart des musées privés importants sont des musées d'associations ou de

* Professeur, Université de Paris I Panthéon – Sorbonne, Paris.

fondations liées à des collectivités publiques par des accords précis qui visent notamment à établir l'inaliénabilité de leurs collections. Par exemple, les collections de l'Union Centrale des arts décoratifs à Paris qui est une association reconnue d'utilité publique sont formellement déclarées 'propriété de l'Etat' par les accords successifs conclus depuis plus de 70 ans entre l'association et l'Etat.

Quant aux musées purement privés – et notamment ceux qui pourraient appartenir à des sociétés commerciales ou à des personnes physiques privées, ils ne sont pas considérés par les autorités publiques compétentes comme étant de véritables musées et ils en portent seulement le nom parce que la loi française ne fait pas du mot 'musée' une appellation réglementée. En total, 95% des musées français sont sans équivoque des institutions publiques ou semi-publiques et pratiquent eux aussi, le système de l'intangibilité de leurs collections.

On s'en tiendra pour la suite au cas normal qui est celui des collections publiques proprement dites.

3. Contenu du régime de la domanialité publique

Il tient pour l'essentiel à deux règles: l'inaliénabilité (a) et l'imprescriptibilité (b).

a. L'inaliénabilité

L'inaliénabilité signifie qu'on ne peut pas aliéner volontairement un bien du domaine public sans lui faire perdre auparavant ce caractère.

Si, donc on voulait aliéner un tel objet, il faudrait commencer par le 'déclasser', (ou le 'désaffecter' les deux mots ayant ici le même sens) par une première décision. L'objet en question continuerait à faire partie du patrimoine public, mais il serait désormais rangé dans la partie domaine privé de ce patrimoine.[1]

Cette opération de déclassement est pratiquée régulièrement pour certains biens du domaine public ayant une fonction utilitaire et qu'il faut donc remplacer quand ils sont hors d'usage ou démodés (p. ex. les matériels militaires). Elle est ignorée dans le cas des biens culturels, car ceux-là, au contraire des premiers, prennent de plus en plus d'importance et d'intérêt avec le temps. Les cas de déclassement formel d'objets de collections des musées sont donc tout à fait exceptionnels et dans la pratique inexistants. Les collections des musées sont donc en fait inaliénables à perpétuité ou tout au moins aussi longtemps qu'on maintiendra la conception des musées en

1. On peut pour synthéser, écrire, patrimoine public (d'une collectivité publique) = domaine public (soumis à un régime juridique spécialement protecteur) + domaine privé (soumis au droit commun) – la partie domaine publique étant constituée par les biens essentiels pour la bonne gestion des services; le domaine privé regroupant les autres.

vigueur depuis deux siècles qu'ils sont apparus en France.[2] Il en résulte que la plupart des questions posées au questionnaire ne se posent pas en France.

Au cas où, par extraordinaire, un objet en principe inaliénable viendrait à être cédé par un agent du musée, cette cession serait nulle de nullité absolue. L'action en nullitée pourrait être intentée pendant 30 ans par toute personne publique compétente (le représentant de la collectivité, le préfet du départment, le Ministre de la culture), et même, par une personne privée ayant intérêt pour agir. Mais, on n'en connaît pratiquement presque pas d'exemple.

Si par contre, l'objet venait à être déclassé; il deviendrait alors aliénable en tant que bien du domaine privé. Il faudrait cependant à la collectivité propriétaire respecter les régles d'aliénation posées par son statut (par exemple, la disposition du Code des communes pour les collections municipales) ou encore veiller au respect de dispositions limitatives qui pourraient résulter par exemple des clauses des libéralités d'où proviendraient certains objets. Mais il ne s'agit plus alors du droit des musées, mais de règles qui lui sont étrangères.[3]

b. L'imprescriptibilité

Celle-ci a pour but de protéger les pièces du musée contre les aliénations involontaires qui résulteraient d'une perte ou d'un vol. Elle est alors très simple: elle signifie qu'un objet perdu ou volé peut toujours être revendiqué entre les mains d'un possesseur même de bonne foi; sans aucune limite de temps et sans indemnité, c'est donc une règle très protectrice du patrimoine public en même temps que trés rigoureuse pour les acquéreurs éventuels. Elle est toujours incontestée, mais les applications en restent assez rares pour les raisons suivantes:

i. Il faut bien entendu commencer par retrouver l'objet. Il faut ensuite démontrer que cet objet appartenait bien aux collections de tel ou tel musée – ce qui exige des inventaires bien tenus, et très détaillés, (accompagnés autant que possible d'une bonne photo). D'où l'importance des inventaires et des marques aussi indélibiles que possible portées sur les objets de musée.
ii. Les Etats qui connaissent la domanialité publique l'appliquent chez eux à leur propre profit et non pas à celui des Etats étrangers. La théorie de la

2. L'affirmation, toute absolue qu'il paraisse, est incontestée dans les musées d'art, d'histoire et d'archéologie. Elle est un peu moins strictement respectée dans les musées d'histoire naturelle ou de techniques qui peuvent plus aisément posséder des pièces rigoureusement identiques en double, en triple, etc. Mais même dans leur cas, le principe de base est celui de l'intangibilité.
3. En sens inverse, les dispositions du Code civil relatives aux donations pourraient amener à battre en brèche dans certains cas, le principe de l'inaliénabilité du domaine public, par exemple si l'objet y était entré pour une donation dont la nullité serait constatée par un tribunal. Dans un tel cas, l'objet ne serait pas véritablement entré dans le patrimoine public et donc dans le domaine public.

domanialité publique existe par exemple en France comme en Italie. Un objet volé dans un musée français et retrouvé en France pourra être revendiqué au nom de la domanialité – mais s'il est retrouvé en Italie, l'Etat français revendiquant sera considéré comme un simple particulier soumis au droit commun; et bien entendu il en serait de même dans le cas d'un objet volé en Italie et revendiqué en France par l'Etat italien. Or, la plupart des objets volés sont transportés très vite au delà des frontières.

Il serait donc très souhaitable que des accords de réciprocité soient conclus entre Etats qui connaissent le système de la domanialité publique pour qu'ils étendent de l'un à l'autre les effets de la théorie.

II. BIBLIOGRAPHIE

J. CHATELAIN, *Oeuvres d'art et objets de collection en Droit français* (Paris, Berger Sevrault 1982) (2e édition à paraître en 1990).

J. CHATELAIN, *Administration et gestion des musées.* (Paris, La documentation française 1987).

G. WOLKOWITSCH, *Archives-Bibliothèques – Musées: statuts des collections accessibles au public* (Paris, Economica 1986).

Grèce

RAPPORT NATIONAL SUR LE SUJET 1. LIBERTE DES MUSEES DE PROCEDER A DES TRANSACTIONS D'OBJETS D'ART*

Antonias Dimolitsa**

Indépendamment de la forme juridique des musées – personnes morales de droit public ou personnes morales de droit privé, en l'occurrence fondations – il faut surtout se référer aux objets même de leurs collections et distinguer entre antiquités (I.) et oeuvres d'art récentes, non spécialement protégées (II.), afin de circonscrire cette liberté.

I. ANTIQUITES

Selon l'art. 53 de la loi 5351/1932, des antiquités qui sont jugées 'inutiles' pour les musées ou les autres collections de l'Etat peuvent être échangées contre des antiquités, se trouvant en Grèce ou à l'étranger, considérées comme 'utiles' pour ceux-ci, ou même être vendues. C'est le Conseil Archéologique qui juge définitivement sur l' 'inutilité' par voix unanime. Si un consensus n'y est pas atteint et si la majorité est contre l' 'inutilité', la décision du Conseil est définitive. Si, en revanche, la majorité est pour l''inutilité', le Ministre de la Culture est obligé d'inviter trois éphores d'antiquités en vue de leur participation à une nouvelle session du Conseil: l''inutilité' est alors décidée s'il y a neuf voix en sa faveur.

Des dispositions parallèles se rencontrent dans deux décrets (Décret Royal 13/20.5.1919 'sur la vente d'antiquités inutiles' et Décret Présidentiel 22/28.10.1931 'sur la vente d'antiquités') considérés comme toujours en vigueur, qui réglementent la procédure à suivre depuis la liste des antiquités 'inutiles' dressée par les Directeurs des musées jusqu'à la vente simple ou aux enchères et le placement du produit des ventes.

Il paraît pourtant, qu'au moins en ce qui concerne la vente d'antiquités, ces dispositions légales ne se virent jamais appliquées, car elles furent dès le début vivement critiquées par les archéologues pour employer cette notion de base qu'est l''inutilité' des antiquités. On en trouve seulement quelques rares applications en matière d'échange d'antiquités avec des musées étrangers.

---

* Note d'Editeur: *v.* pour 'l'Introduction au Rapport' *supra* p. 39.

** Avocat, Athènes.

II. OEUVRES D'ART RECENTES

Si on passe maintenant aux oeuvres récentes non spécialement protégées par la loi, celles-ci peuvent se trouver dans des musées nationaux ou privés. Comme oeuvres récentes, non spécialement protégées par la loi, doivent être considérées toutes les oeuvres d'art ultérieures à 1830 ainsi que les icônes ultérieures à 1900.[1] Ces oeuvres, jouissant d'un régime de liberté de vente ou d'exportation quand elles se trouvent dans les mains de particuliers, cela ne semble pas être le cas, au moins en pratique, quand elles font partie d'une collection de musées nationaux (1) ou privés (2).

1. Musées nationaux

A part la loi constitutive du Musée de la Guerre (Décret-Loi 132/1969, art. 2(3)) dans laquelle apparaît une mention claire et précise interdisant toute vente ou donation d'objets de sa collection, dans aucune des autres lois constitutives de musées n'apparaît pareille mention. En revanche, tant l'achat que l'acceptation de donations ou de legs y sont spécialement réglementés. Faut-il voir dans ce silence des lois, une interdiction pure et simple de toute vente? La question acquiert un intérêt particulier pour la Pinacothèque Nationale (loi constitutive 1079/1980), dans laquelle sont rassemblées la plupart des oeuvres d'art récentes, produits de legs, d'achats ou de donations. Sur proposition du Comité Artistique, le Conseil d'Administration de la Pinacothèque accepte des donations ou des legs (art. 9). Ce qui se passe parfois en pratique est que des legs ou donations se voient acceptés pour la seule raison de l'existence de quelques – ou même d'une seule – oeuvres intéressantes dans ceux-ci. Les autres oeuvres sont alors mises en dépôt, bien qu'elles eussent pu être vendues à des collectionneurs ou des particuliers suivant une procédure de vente simple ou aux enchères, en devenant ainsi une source de revenus qui pourraient être utilisés à l'achat d'oeuvres d'art effectivement intéressantes pour les collections de la Pinacothèque. Il n'en est rien, aucune oeuvre n'a jamais été mise en vente par la Pinacothèque jusqu'à présent. Pourtant, la possibilité d'une application par analogie de la loi 2039/1939 'sur la liquidation et l'administration des héritages, legs et donations laissés à l'Etat à des fins d'utilité publique', suivant laquelle l'Etat a le droit de disposer de ces biens s'il le juge utile, ne serait pas, à notre avis, à exclure théoriquement. Il suffirait de suivre la procédure y prévue sur recommandation du Comité Artistique et décision du Conseil d'Administration de la Pinacothèque au moins dans les cas où le défunt ou le donateur n'auraient pas exprimé leur volonté dans le sens de l'interdiction de la vente. En conclusion, l'interprétation du silence des lois constitutives des musées nationaux dans le sens de la possibilité de vente d'objets de leur collections, sous certaines conditions

1. *V.* 'l'Introduction' *supra* p. 39.

et suivant la procédure de la loi 2039/1939, nous paraît imposée par la notion d'utilité publique. Il est d'ailleurs évident qu'une réglementation spéciale y afférente serait souhaitable.

2. *Musées privés*

Les musées privés ont la forme de fondations dont les statuts sont approuvés par un décret présidentiel (arts. 108–110 du C.C.) sur proposition du Ministère de la Culture et avis conforme du Conseil National des Legs (loi 2039/1939); ils fonctionnent sous la supervision et le contrôle des Ministères des Finances et de la Culture. La possibilité ou pas de vente d'oeuvres d'art de leurs collections dépend des prévisions de leurs statuts. La vente est d'habitude interdite par une formule générale (voir p. ex. Décret Présidentiel du 14.6.1983 approuvant la constitution du 'Vorres-Museum', J.O. 406/14.7.83, art. 3(3) al. 2). Si ceci est raisonnable par rapport à la collection du fondateur, on pourrait se douter de son utilité par rapport à des donations ou legs ultérieurs provenant de tierces personnes, pour les mêmes raisons que ci-dessus.

Italie

RAPPORT NATIONAL SUR LE SUJET 1. LIBERTE DES MUSEES DE PROCEDER A DES TRANSACTIONS D'OBJETS D'ART

Tommaso Alibrandi*

1. Comme cela a été précité dans l'introduction,[1] les musées appartenant à l'Etat et aux collectivités territoriales ne peuvent pas échanger ou disposer d'autres manières d'objets d'art parce qu'il s'agit, aux termes des arts. 822 *et seq.* et suivants du Code civil de biens domaniaux et musées de propriété privé, peuvent au contraire démembrer les collections et vendre des biens particuliers à condition qu'ils n'aient pas déjà fait l'objet de contraintes prévues par la loi n° 1089/1939.

2. Aucun type d'objets d'art ne peut être vendu par les musées.

3. Il n'existe pas des catégories de musées qui seraient habilités plus que d'autres à vendre des objets d'art.

4. Un musée ne peut pas être autorisé à vendre un objet d'art qui faisait partie d'une donation effectuée par une personne privée.

5. Il n'est pas possible d'exporter un objet d'art qui fait partie d'une collection publique parce qu'il est assujetti à l'art. 4 de la loi n° 1089/1939. S'il fait partie d'une collection, l'on applique l'art. 5 de la loi n° 1089/1939. Les échanges pour des expositions temporaires sont possibles, mais seulement de toutes les oeuvres du musée, et non pas d'un objet particulier; pour ce faire l'avis des directeurs (*Sopintendenti*) compétents et du Comité de secteur (*Comitato di Settore*) est nécessaire, ainsi que la licence d'exportation temporaire d'une durée de six mois.

6. Officiellement, on ne connaît pas de cas où des objets d'art détenus par un musée ou faisant partie du 'patrimoine culturel national' ont été soit exportés, soit donnés, soit aliénés, soit échangés. Les suites judiciaires qui en découleraient, seraient toutefois les sanctions prévues par la loi n° 1089/1939.

---

* Professeur, Libera Università Internazionale degli Studi Sociali, Facoltà di Scienze Politiche, Rome.

1. Note d'Editeur: *v.* pour l' 'Introduction au Rapport' *supra* p. 41.

7. La loi qui sert de fondement à des poursuites judiciaires est la loi n° 1089/1939.
a. Il n'est pas possible qu'un musée vende un objet d'art appartenant au 'patrimoine culturel national'.
b. Si un musée a vendu un objet d'art qui n'est pas classé ou qui ne figure pas sur le registre du 'patrimoine culturel national' à une personne privée ou à un autre musée, et cela est connu officiellement, l'on applique les sanctions prévues par la loi n° 1089/1939.
c. Le bien faisant l'objet d'une contrainte peut être échangé avec un autre musée situé en Italie.
d. Il n'est pas possible pour un musée de vendre un objet d'art à une personne privée ou à un autre musée, car sa valeur esthétique ou économique serait en ce cas plus basse au moment de la vente qu'au moment de l'acquisition (à cause p. ex. d'une erreur d'expertise sur l'attribution de l'oeuvre).

Japan

NATIONAL REPORT ON TOPIC 1. FREEDOM OF MUSEUMS TO SELL, TRADE OR OTHERWISE DISPOSE OF OBJECTS OF ART IN THEIR COLLECTIONS*

Norihiko Hadano** and Jun Norisugi**

1. A museum may sell, trade or otherwise dispose of an object in its collection, depending on its classification under the Law.

2. Under the Law for the Protection of Cultural Property, all objects may be sold by a museum. However, if the sale involves the export of an object which falls under the category of a Cultural Property, the exporter will have to demonstrate that the Cultural Property is not an Important Cultural Property and obtain written confirmation of that fact from the Agency for Cultural Affairs (ACA) since Art. 44 prohibits the exportation of Important Cultural Properties. Since the ACA has detailed registration records of those Cultural Properties which have been designated as Important Cultural Properties, this confirmation procedure is fairly straightforward (taking between ten and thirty days) and merely requires presentation of the object in question to the ACA in Tokyo. The ACA provides written confirmation to the effect that the object is not an Important Cultural Property and this document is presented to customs prior to export.

As stated in the Introduction, however, the problem lies not in the approval process itself but rather in the determination as to whether the object is a Cultural Property. If it is not, there is no requirement to provide evidence of it not being an Important Cultural Property. As a practical matter, if the seller is a museum, the object will most probably be of significant value and the customs officers will make an assumption that it constitutes Cultural Property, thus requiring evidence that it is not Important Cultural Property.

3. As stated in the Introduction, the internal regulations of *public* museums usually prohibit them from selling objects which are classified as Important Cultural Properties. They may, however, sell Cultural Properties provided that, if the Cultural Properties are to be exported, the approval process under 2., *supra* is adhered to.

---

* Editor's note: *see also* 'Japan: Introduction' in Part One.

** Attorney at Law, Masuda & Ejiri, Tokyo.

Private museums may sell objects classified as Important Cultural Properties provided that: (i) the sale does not involve exportation or such exportation is permitted pursuant to special permission given by the ACA (*see* 5., *infra*), (ii) the notification procedures set forth in Art. 46 of the Law are adhered to. The procedure set forth in Art. 46 regarding the domestic sale of Important Cultural Properties is as follows:

- the seller or donor must complete a form to be submitted to the ACA in which he/she specifies: (i) the registration number of the Important Cultural Property and the date on which it was designated as such, (ii) current location of the object, (iii) name and address of current owner, (iv) name and address of current holder (if different), (v) name and address of prospective buyer and (vi) if the transaction involves a sale, the proposed selling price.
- Once notified, the ACA has the authority to intervene if it determines either: (i) that the object is of such importance that it should be purchased by the State or (ii) that the proposed buyer is not in a position to adequately protect and preserve the object in question. If the ACA does determine to intervene, its only recourse is to offer to purchase the object. If it declines to do so, the transaction will proceed upon the terms set forth in the notification submitted by the seller or donor. If the ACA offers to purchase the object, the seller or donor may decline but may not attempt to sell the object to a third party again without submitting a new notification.

It should be noted that this notification/offer procedure is the primary means by which the State actually acquires Important Cultural Property.

4. There is no public law which addresses if a museum is authorized to sell an object of art which was part of a gift from a private person. Nor do public or private museums have internal regulations that are of relevance. A museum's obligations would therefore be defined by the agreement, whether explicit or implicit, which it had reached with the donor in question. To the extent that the museum breached these obligations, it could be subject to a claim by the donor in contract; such a claim would only be for monetary damages and the donor could not challenge the buyer's title to the object unless the donor explicitly reserved title when it donated the object to the museum.

5. As stated under 3., *supra*, if the object in question is classified as an Important Cultural Property, the general rule is that it may not be exported, regardless of whether or not it is part of a public collection. Art. 44 of the Law provides an exception in those cases where the ACA has given permission of export 'in recognition of its special necessity from the viewpoint of international exchange of culture or from other considerations'. This permission must be obtained even if the export is in connection with a temporary transfer (e.g., an exhibition).

As stated under 2., *supra*, Cultural Properties may be exported provided that confirmation is obtained to the effect that they are not Important Cultural Properties. This rule applies even if the exportation does not involve transfer of ownership.

6. We are aware of only one judicial action in which an object of art belonging to Japan's national cultural patrimony was sold.

On 6 March 1975, a decision was rendered by the Japanese Supreme Court in which a temple was prosecuted under Art. 46 of the Law for selling an Important Cultural Property in violation of the Law. Although the Temple was required to pay a fine, the court did not render the sale void or require the buyer to give up the object in question.

7. To the extent that the museum is *public*, the sale of an Important Cultural Property would violate its own internal regulations.

If the museum is *private* and the sale of an Important Cultural Property does not take place in conformity with the procedure outlined under 3., *supra*, the sale will be in violation of Art. 46 of the Law and the seller shall be subject to a fine of 50,000 Yen under Art. 110 of the Law. The Law does not provide, however, that the actual sale will be voided and the judicial precedent discussed under 6., *supra*, confirms this fact.

If either a public or private museum *exports* an Important Cultural Property, such export will be in violation of Art. 44, absent specific approval from the ACA (*see* Sections 2. and 6., *supra*). The seller (or, if the seller is a museum, the responsible officers of the museum) shall be subject to a fine of 500,000 Yen and up to five years imprisonment under Arts. 106 and 107(5) of the Law.

As stated under 2., *supra*, the sale by an museum of an object which is *not classified* as an Important Cultural Property is not restricted; provided, however, that if: (i) the sale involves an export and (ii) the object is a Cultural Property, approval by the ACA will be required (*see* under 2., *supra*).

An *exchange* will be treated as a sale under the Law and therefore the above responses regarding sale and export will be applicable.

In regard to the sale by a museum of an object of art to a private person or another museum because its aesthetic value was lower at the time of the sale than at the time of its acquisition because of an error in the appraisal of its authenticity, although the officials we have spoken with believe that such an occurrence would not occur, they have informed us that it would be acceptable.

The Netherlands

NATIONAL REPORT ON TOPIC 1. FREEDOM OF MUSEUMS TO SELL, TRADE OR OTHERWISE DISPOSE OF OBJECTS OF ART IN THEIR COLLECTIONS*

Anton A. Quaedvlieg**

1. In principle it is possible for a museum to sell, trade or dispose of an object or objects in its collection but subject to restrictions to be mentioned below.

2. As to the question of whether or not objects of art held by a museum may be sold, it is not relevant what *kind* of objects they are. What is relevant is their *significance* to the Dutch cultural heritage: by reason of that significance they may, pursuant to the Conservation of Cultural Heritage Act, be placed on the List of Protected Objects, at least insofar as they are privately owned objects. When it concerns objects in public collections, not only their significance to the Dutch cultural heritage is important but also the acquisition policy of the museum concerned and its co-ordination with the acquisition policy and collections of other Dutch museums will play a part. As yet there exist no formal rules governing the sale of objects in public collections, but the authorities intend to introduce such rules in the not too distant future.

a. Procedures

Private museums have the duty of prior reporting and securing permission if they intend to sell objects that are listed by virtue of the Conservation of Cultural Heritage Act.

No standard procedures are prescribed for public (State-owned) museums, but such procedures may be introduced in the near future. However, public museums do require permission to sell from the government authority controlling them.

3. What *kind* of museum intends to sell objects in its collection is, as such, never an impediment preventing the sale of objects of art, although it has to

* Editor's note: *see also* 'The Netherlands: Introduction in Part One.

** Professor, Catholic University of Nijmegen. The author gratefully acknowledges the assistance of the law firm Trenité Van Doorne, Amsterdam with which he was associated during the writing of this Report. Report translated by F. C. Compton.

be remembered that a sale by a public museum is subject to more restrictions than a sale by a private museum. This is connected with the duty of the government 'to ensure that objects of art belonging to the national cultural good are saved for the Dutch cultural heritage'.[1] Furthermore, public museums need permission for the sale from the government authority to whom they are responsible.

4. *a.* If the donor does *not* stipulate in the deed of gift that the object may not be sold or otherwise disposed of, the museum is authorized to sell the object. Even so, however, museums – particularly public museums (because of their mission to save and preserve cultural good) – will follow a cautious policy. There is no period prior to which a sale cannot be made.
4. *b.* If the donor *does* stipulate in the deed of gift that the object may not be sold or otherwise disposed of, the museum is not authorized to sell the object. If the gift is sold despite this, such transaction will not, however, affect the third party-acquirer's title of ownership. There might be an exception to this in special circumstances. If the third party-acquirer acted in bad faith and if an accusation of inducing a breach of contract can be upheld against him, such act – as being actionable in tort – might result in an obligation to give the object back.

5. The possibility of transfer and/or export of an object which is part of a public collection is not excluded. On this subject there are (as yet) no prescribed procedures, except that permission is required from the government authority to whom the museum is responsible. For the rest the decision to transfer or export an object is a matter of policy. That policy has not (yet) been formalized in set rules, but the tendency is towards a restrictive policy. Some criteria that could be applied to the decision are described below.

a. Export

It is safe to assume that export of objects which are irreplaceable or essential to the Dutch cultural heritage – or in other words: come under the criteria of the Conservation of Cultural Heritage Act – is ruled out.

Export of objects not covered by criteria of the Act will be judged against the merits of such sale, seen in the light of the museum's own and the national policy, and the possible wish of other national museums to acquire the objects. Sale to foreign museums will be preferred to sale to foreign private collectors.

1. Royal Decree of 17 June 1987, *Staatsblad* 344, as cited by J. M. BOLL, '"Composition with two lines" or "The curious character of the right of ownership of government bodies to objects of art" and the "Cultural Heritage Act"' (translated), *Rechtsgeleerd Magazijn Themis* (1989) p. 132.

b. Transfer

Transfer of objects to individuals or corporations who are reasonably presumed to want to export the objects in the course of time will probably be judged against roughly the same rules of policy.

In the case of transfer of objects within the Netherlands, the merits of such transfer would be judged against the museum's own policy and the policy and collections of other museums. Transfer to another museum will be preferred to transfer to private collectors.

6. As far as we know there have been three cases in which an object of art held by a museum or belonging to the nation's cultural patrimony was sold or otherwise disposed of which resulted in some form of legal or administrative action. These are described in the Introduction, pp. 50–51.

7. There are bases for judicial action in several situations.

If the government authority who is responsible for a public museum has sold an object of art to a bona fide purchaser, then, according to the current trend in case law and doctrine, the authority – save for exceptional circumstances – shall be bound to perform the contract.[2] The museum cannot evade its contractual obligations on the mere ground that the sale of the object is in conflict with the criteria of conservation of the nation's cultural heritage or in conflict with the guidelines that govern the policy of the museum which sold the object. Under Dutch law, this applies regardless of the new owner's status or identity (museum/private person). The same applies in cases of barter. As for *private* museums, *see* Topic 2, paragraph 1.

Ratification of the Unesco Paris Convention of 1970 will of course enable the Netherlands to avail itself of the possibilities which that Convention offers to restore certain property to the national cultural heritage.[3]

2. On contracts of sale made with the government, *see* N. S. G. KOEMÀN, *Bestemmingsplan en privaatrecht*, 3rd edn. (Deventer 1989) pp. 44–52; G. SPIER, 'Overeenkomsten met Overheidslichamen' in A. R. BLOEMBERGEN and W. M. KLEIN, eds., *Contractenrecht* (Kluwer) VIII, No. 37 and No. 50; Supreme Court 27 January 1989, *Nederlandse Jurisprudentie* 1990, 89, annotated by CBHB, in *Verboom v. the Crown*.
3. Reproduced in ICC Institute, ed., *International Sales of Works of Art/La Vente Internationale d'Oeuvres d'Art* (ICC Publishing/Kluwer, Paris/Deventer 1990) in French, pp. 171–185 and in English, pp. 187–200.

Spain

NATIONAL REPORT ON TOPIC 1. FREEDOM OF MUSEUMS TO SELL, TRADE OR OTHERWISE DISPOSE OF OBJECTS OF ART IN THEIR COLLECTIONS*

Miguel Virgós Soriano**

1.[1] In Spain there are three basic types of museums: public, ecclesiastic, and private; each of them with its peculiar legal status.

Public museums belong to the State, Autonomous Communities (political regions), and local governments. The regulations of all of them follow similar patterns. Acquisition, collection, preservation and presentation of objects of cultural value are their purposes and fundamental philosophy; trading is not. They cannot sell or otherwise dispose of objects from their collection.

The only two possibilities are deposit of some of those objects in another place, or loans (short or long-term). Even for that purpose, it has to be taken into account that public museums are not the owners of their collections. They may also have in deposit private objects for their exhibition. Authorization will have to be obtained, as a general rule.

The *basic regulation* of State museums (the most important one) is to be found in the 1985 Spanish Historical Patrimony Act (*Ley del Patrimonio Histórico Español* (1985 LPH), Arts. 59–66) and in the Royal Decree 620/1987 (*Reglamento de Museos de Titularidad Estatal y del Sistema Español de Museos*). To co-ordinate their policies, public museums (and some private ones) are integrated into the Spanish system of museums (*see* Arts. 26–27 Royal Decree 620/1987). A Council of Museums has consultative functions (*Junta Superior de Museos*, *see* Order of 12 June 1987). Other aspects of the State organization may be of interest (*see* Art. 4 Royal Decree 565/1985 and Arts. 1–10 Royal Decree 111/1986). For other museums, the regional law must be consulted.[2]

The *Museo del Prado* has a special status as an autonomous institution (*organismo autónomo*) within the State. Although under public control, it enjoys more powers and autonomy than other public museums (see the Royal Decree 1432/1985). *El Prado* is a legal person and it has capacity to acquire but not to sell or exchange works of art in its collection. The

* Editor's note: *see also* 'Spain: Introduction' by B. CREMADES in Part One.

** Associate Professor, Facultad de Derecho, Universidad Autónoma de Madrid.

1. Editor's note: Section 1 is in response to questions 1 and 3 of the Questionnaire.
2. *See Legislación sobre el Patrimonio Histórico* (Madrid 1987) ed. Tecnos.

authorization of the Ministry of Culture is necessary to remove any work from the museums facilities. The *Centro de Arte Reina Sofía* will soon receive the same legal status (as *organismo autónomo*).

Ecclesiastic museums are regulated by their own charters. The 1979 Agreement between Spain and the Holy See opens the way to canonic law. With the limitation that we will see under 3. *infra*, they may dispose of objects from their collections when admitted by those specific rules. Immovables, not chattels comprise the fundamental wealth of the Church in Spain.

Private museums are also regulated by their own charters. Autonomy is the basic principle. They may dispose of objects according to the said charters. Generally they will adopt the form of (or be an instrumentality of) a foundation (a *fundación* in Spanish Law is only possible for a non profit public-interest purpose, but with it the founder achieves a permanent assignment of the goods). Foundations are under public control. (*See* Decree 2930/1972 on *Fundaciones culturales privadas y entidades análogas*. For foreign foundations operating in Spain, *see* Arts. 57–58.)

Both ecclesiastic and private museums with relevant collections may integrate themselves into the Spanish system of museums (*Sistema Español de Museos*) through agreement with the Ministry of Culture (*see* Art. 26 Royal Decree 620/1987).

2. Ownership of the objects (the *proprietary* question) and cultural value of the object itself (the *property* question) determine the answer to the question as to what kinds of objects of art held by a museum may be sold, and under which procedures.

Therefore, two sets of rules must be taken into account, the general rules on property and the special rules for the protection of cultural property (basically the 1985 LPH).[3]

Private property may always be disposed of by its owner. A limitation arises in case of foundations, as already said (*see* under 1. *supra*). The 1985 LPH subjects export to special limitations (*see* Report 2nd Symposium).

In regard to cultural objects in possession of *religious institutions*, the 1985 LPH imposes a very important limitation on the freedom to dispose of cultural property. Any transfer of movable cultural property part of the 'Spanish Historical Patrimony' to private persons or commercial entities is forbidden for ten years from 1985. They may only be transferred to the State, public law entities, or other religious institutions within Spain. After that period, the prohibition will only affect classified cultural property (registered as 'of cultural interest' or recorded in the Inventory, *see* Art. 28(1) and *disposición transitoria 5a* LPH 1985).

---

3. For the concept and content of the 'Spanish Historical Patrimony', *see* J. D. GONZALES CAMPOS and M. VIRGOS SORIANO, 'Law and Practice of International Art Trade in Spain' (Report to the 2nd Symposium, Geneva 1988) in ICC Institute, ed., *International Sales of Works of Art/La Vente Internationale d'Oeuvres d'Art* (ICC Publishing/Kluwer, Paris/Deventer 1990) pp. 103–126, hereafter 'Report 2nd Symposium'.

In regard to *public property*, the 1985 LPH contains a special regulation for cultural property. According to it, public administrations may transfer movable cultural property, that is part of the 'Spanish Historical Patrimony' only among themselves, but not to third parties (Art. 28(2) LPH). They cannot sell those objects. *Preservation* is the basic policy. As all the objects of art integrated in the collections of public museums fall in that broad category, no item of cultural property protected by the 1985 LPH may be sold. However, the government may exchange movables of similar cultural value with other States (Art. 34 LPH, which also encompasses property in 'public domain').

The 1985 LPH imposes a negative answer to question 2. However, it may be of interest to remember the two basic categories relating to public property.

- Property in the *public domain* is designated with a public use or service or has been declared such by law (for instance, all cultural property which is the product of archaeological discoveries, Art. 44 LPH). This property is as such inalienable.
- Property not designated with a public use or service but belonging to the public administrations (State, regional, local) is designated as *patrimonial property*. It may be alienated, normally through public auction (*see*, for State property, Art. 95 of the 1964 Law on the State Patrimony). As already analyzed, the special regulation for cultural property severely limits this possibility (Art. 28(1) LPH).

Property devoted to the Royal Crown forms a special category. It constitutes the so-called *National Patrimony*, regulated by a 1982 Act (*Ley del Patrimonio Nacional* (LPN)). A number of works of art belong to it. This property is inalienable (Art. 6(2) LPN).

4. In regard to the authorization of a museum to sell an object of art which was part of a gift from a private person, the work of art, once its property is transferred, shares the legal regime of the rest of the collection in which it is integrated. The above-mentioned rules are applicable. If the donee is a public administration, public institution, or ecclesiastic institution the general limitations referred to above will be applied. Consequently, inalienability will be the rule.

If the donee is a private institution, it must be taken into account that free circulation of private property is a fundamental principle of Spanish Law. The general rule will be that the donee becomes absolute owner. If the donor wishes to limit the donee's freedom to dispose of the work of art, he must clearly state the limitation. A *modal gift* (the donor wants the object to be kept and exhibited by the museum) may be revoked in case of infringement, but the revocation cannot be effective against good faith purchasers (Art. 647 II Civil Code, *a contrario sensu*, and Art. 1124, IV Civil Code). *Prohibitions to dispose* are admitted only on a temporary basis (legal persons, thirty years, Arts. 781, 785 and 789, which are also applicable to gifts *inter vivos*, and Art. 515 Civil Code by analogy). Usually, the donee will be a foundation (which allows the permanent designation of a patrimony with a public interest). The charter must be then consulted because the object will fall under its specific regulations.

5. In regard to the question of whether it is possible to transfer or export an object of art which is part of a public collection, as already said, *inalienability* is the rule. The answer is therefore negative. Deposit, short or long-term loans, and exchange are the alternatives.

International trade and protection of the Spanish Historical Patrimony are matters of State competence. The central government may approve international exchanges (*see* Art. 34 1985 LPH.). For loans or international exhibitions abroad, two procedures must be complied with. First, the general regulations for public museums, which require the authorization of the Ministry of Culture (or regional authority in the case of regional museums). Second, a temporary export permit is always necessary. The longest period of time that the law allows an object of cultural property to remain abroad is ten years for those declared 'of cultural interest' and twenty years for others (*see* Art. 56 Royal Decree 111/1986). The Ministry of Culture, through the General Direction for Fine Arts and Archives, is the competent authority for this permit. Because of the decentralized political structure of Spain, it is necessary to take into account that some Autonomous Communities have competence over the *procedure* of application (*see* Art. 47 Royal Decree 111/1986 and Report 2nd Symposium).

6. There are a number of cases in which an object of art held by a museum or belonging to the Spanish national cultural patrimony have been exported. Every time an illegally exported object of art is detected abroad, judicial actions (criminal or civil) are initiated. The last well known case involved the painting by Goya *La Marquesa de Santa Cruz*, put up to auction at Christie's after being removed from the country without permit. A settlement was reached and the painting belongs now to the *Museo del Prado* collection. The whole history can be traced through the newspaper *El País* February 1986).

7. Apart from the general rules already mentioned on museums (*see* under 1. *supra*) and public property (*see* under 2. *supra*), here we will only indicate the special cultural property regulations which could be used as a basis for judicial action in the situations mentioned below. The broad concept of cultural property encompassed by the 1985 Act on the Spanish Historical Patrimony must also be taken into account.

a. A museum has sold an object belonging to a nation's 'cultural patrimony': Art. 28 of the 1985 Act on the Spanish Historical Patrimony (BOE 29–6–85) and Art. 4 Royal Decree 111/1986 (BOE 28–1–86), which implements the Law.

b. A museum has sold an object not classified as a 'national cultural good': Art. 28 and transitory rule n. 5 (*disposición transitoria 5a*) of the 1985 Act; Art. 44 Royal Decree 111/1986.

c. A museum has exchanged an object of art with another museum:

- located in Spain: Art. 28 of the 1985 Act on the Spanish Historical Patrimony;
- located in another country: Art. 34, Art. 5 and Art. 29 of the 1985 Act; Arts. 46–57 Royal Decree 111/1986.

d. A museum has sold an object of art because its value was lower than thought; there is no specific rule. The general rules already seen will be applied (Art. 28 and transitory rule n. 5 1985 LPH).

Sweden

NATIONAL REPORT ON TOPIC 1. FREEDOM OF MUSEUMS TO SELL, TRADE OR OTHERWISE DISPOSE OF OBJECTS OF ART IN THEIR COLLECTIONS

Christian Wegenius*

1. State owned museums are not allowed to sell items from their collections without a special permission from the government.

In the case of municipal museums, the municipality takes the decision whether a sale is permitted or not.

If the object has been donated and the donor has prohibited sale and other dispositions, even the government will have difficulties in allowing a sale. Under such circumstances very special reasons are required for the government to break through those regulations.

In the Swedish state budget for 1990/91, the minister proposes to give state owned museums the right to sell items that are 'useless and not required for the activities of the museum'. This is thus a new exception from the main rule stated above.

Many Swedish museums today have extensive collections of objects from which they can only expose smaller parts at a time. It is considered to be a problem that the museums have insufficient capacity to take care of all their objects in a proper way. This new liberalization would then be a way of partly solving this problem at the same time as it is a way to strengthen the financial position of the museums. This, in turn, is beneficial both for their economy in general and also for their capacity to acquire new objects.

2. In regard to question 5, when an object of art is part of a public collection, it is possible to transfer or export it under acceptable agreements assuring the safety of the object. The purpose must also be of a suitable nature, e.g., for taking part in public exhibition.

3. In regard to question 6, a set of jewels donated to the National Museum was no longer considered important in the collections and in 1976 the Museum asked permission from the government to sell it. The permission was not granted since it was a donation.

Some years later the set was stolen from the National Museum and sold at a public auction in Stockholm. The theft was revealed after the jewels were

* Executive Vice President, Beijers Auktioner AB, Stockholm.

sold. The government then bought back the jewels for the Museum, using in part the money deriving from the auction.

4. In regard to question 7, in Sweden there is only one law which regulates what is considered to be part of our 'cultural patrimony' in the case of objects. This is Law SOU 1988:950 which regulates the export limitation of cultural objects. The law stipulates that certain qualified objects, of certain value and age, are subject to special permission for exportation. The purpose of the law is to prevent objects that are considered to be of special value to the cultural patrimony from leaving the country.

In Sweden otherwise the prohibition for museums to sell their objects derives from an old practice saying that state bodies are not allowed to sell their property without consent in law or from the government.

Suisse

RAPPORT NATIONAL SUR LE SUJET 1. LIBERTE DES MUSEES DE PROCEDER A DES TRANSACTIONS D'OBJETS D'ART

Blaise Knapp*

I. LA LIBERTE DES MUSEES DE PROCEDER A DES TRANSACTIONS D'OBJETS D'ART

Dans le cadre de la présente étude, nous entendrons uniquement par 'objets d'art', des biens mobiliers en faisant abstraction des objets immobiliers, même si ceux-ci peuvent être des objets d'art et peuvent faire l'objet de transactions.

A notre sens, l'étude doit être divisée en deux parties; la première sera consacrée aux musées propriété de collectivités publiques et la seconde aux musées privés.

1. Les musées publics

Bien que nous soyons adressé à de nombreux musées cantonaux et municipaux, seuls le Musée cantonal des Beaux-Arts du canton de Vaud, le Musée de l'Elysée de Lausanne, le Musée d'Histoire de Berne, le Musée d'Art et d'histoire de Neuchâtel, le Musée du Rietberg de Zurich et le Kunsthaus de Zurich nous ont fourni une documentation nous permettant de répondre aux questions soulevées dans le questionnaire reçu. En outre, nous avons disposé des statuts du Musée national.

a. Les structures juridiques

Les musées ici analysés peuvent en ce qui concerne leur structure juridique, se diviser en deux catégories.

On distingue en effet, les musées qui sont des services dépendant d'une administration communale, cantonale ou fédérale et ceux qui sont indépendants d'une telle administration. Si l'on préfère, certains musées sont des établissements autonomes sans personnalité juridique, intégrés, sous réserve de l'autonomie qui leur est accordée quant à leur organisation interne, à

* Professeur, Université de Genève, Faculté de Droit, Genève.

leurs activités et leurs budget, dans l'organisation de l'administration centrale alors que d'autres sont des établissements publics dotés non seulement de l'autonomie mais encore de la personnalité juridique, sous réserve des pouvoirs de surveillance dont dispose une autorité de l'administration centrale.

Ainsi, le Musée cantonal des Beaux-Arts du canton de Vaud est régi par la loi vaudoise sur les activités culturelles du 19 septembre 1978, qui instaure ce musée ainsi qu'un Fonds du Musée cantonal alimenté par une subvention annuelle du canton, inscrite au budget du Département de l'Instruction publique et des cultes et par des dons et legs privés. Ce Fonds est géré par le Département cantonal des Finances. Le Musée n'a pas la personnalité juridique; ses agents sont des fonctionnaires du canton; ses activités sont soumises à la surveillance du Département vaudois de l'Instruction publique et des cultes.

La situation est identique en ce qui concerne le musée de l'Elysée de Lausanne, un musée pour la photographie. Le musée bénéficie, en outre, depuis 1988, de l'appui d'une fondation de droit privé la 'Fondation de l'Elysée, une fondation pour la photographie' dont le but est 'constituer, par des achats ou des commandes originales, une collection montrant l'histoire de la photographie, depuis les origines, déposer la collection au Musée de l'Elysée à Lausanne et permettre une consultation publique et des expositions'.

Le Musée d'art et d'histoire de Neuchâtel relève quant à lui de la Ville de Neuchâtel.

Le Musée du Rietberg est un service de la Ville de Zurich, directement rattaché au Président de la Ville. Il bénéficie de l'appui d'une association de droit privé qui a pour fin de promouvoir le musée et son développement.

Ces quatre musées sont ainsi des établissements autonomes sans personnalité juridique, insérés dans les administrations dont ils relèvent.

Le Kunsthaus de Zurich est régi par une convention du 29 mai 1953, conclu entre la Ville de Zurich et la *Züricher Kunstgesellschaft* (une association de droit privé) créant une fondation pour l'administration du Musée dit Kunsthaus. Cette convention a ainsi créé une personne de droit public. Elle a été complétée par la convention du 2 mars 1988 entre la Ville et la *Züricher Kunstgesellschaft* déterminant les devoirs des deux partenaires. On en retiendra que la *Züricher Kunstgesellschaft* a notamment le devoir de conserver et développer les collections du Musée, d'organiser des expositions temporaires et qu'elle doit soumettre son budget et ses comptes au Conseil de Ville pour approbation. La Ville verse une subvention annuelle à la société. Enfin, on notera que la Ville de Zurich (et le canton et les communes) désignent 9 des 17 membres du comité directeur de la *Kunstgesellschaft* et doivent approuver au préalable les propositions de modifications des statuts de cette société présentées à l'assemblée générale de celle-ci. En outre, une *Vereinigung Züricher Kunstfreunde* a été créée, sous la forme d'une pure association de droit privé, dont le but est notamment de contribuer au développement des collections du Musée par des prêts.

Le Musée historique de Berne est le fruit d'une convention du 20 février 1889 entre le canton de Berne, la commune bourgeoise de Berne et la Ville de Berne créant une fondation de droit public destinée à bâtir un musée et à y conserver des biens historiques bernois. La Fondation a la personnalité juridique de droit public. La Fondation est dirigée par une Commission de surveillance dont les membres sont désignés par les partenaires à la convention.

Le Musée national suisse est un musée de la Confédération. Il a été créé par la loi fédérale concernant la création d'un musée national suisse du 27 juin 1890. Ce musée a donc un statut de droit public. Il est destiné à recevoir les antiquités nationales importantes en matière historique et de Beaux-Arts. Le Musée est financé par la Confédération, par des dons et legs privés et par le produit des entrées. Depuis le ler novembre 1989, date de l'entrée en vigueur de la modification de l'Ordonnance règlant les tâches des départements, des groupements et des offices, l'Office fédéral de la culture du Département fédéral de l'intérieur est chargé d'administrer le Musée national. Sa gestion est surveillée par une commission extérieure à l'administration sous la haute surveillance du Conseil fédéral. Les agents du Musée sont des agents de la Confédération soumis au régime commun et à un réglement spécifique du 30 décembre 1930, concernant le commerce des oeuvres d'art par les fonctionnaires du Musée, leurs expertises et leurs acquisitions d'objets susceptibles d'intéresser le Musée. Il résulte de ces éléments que le Musée national est un service de l'administration centrale qui bénéficie de fonds séparés et d'une autonomie limitée.

b. Le régime des biens

On aura ainsi pu constater une grande variété dans les structures juridiques mises en place. La distinction entre les musées dépourvus de la personnalité juridique et ceux qui l'ont, prendra notamment toute son importance lorsqu'il faudra constater quel est l'organe compétent pour gérer le musée, pour décider des acquisitions et d'éventuelles aliénations, pour intervenir lorsqu'une aliénation illégale aura eu lieu, lorsqu'un prêt se révélera équivalent à une aliénation, lorsqu'il faudra mener des procès contre des vendeurs malhonnêtes ou poursuivre des détenteurs illégitimes d'oeuvres volées. En revanche, en ce qui concerne la propriété des biens, il ne nous paraît pas qu'il soit nécessaire de faire une distinction entre les biens des établissements (ou fondations) selon que ceux-ci ont ou non la personnalité juridique. La distinction essentielle concerne les biens propres des musées et les biens exposés non-propriété du musée.

i. Les biens propres des musées

Dans tous les cas, les objets destinés à figurer à l'inventaire du Musée sont acquis par la collectivité publique dont le musée dépend ou par ces institutions de droit public que sont les musées. Ils font partie des propriétés de la collectivité ou des institutions acheteuses, donataires ou légataires qui, même non-dotées de la personnalité juridique, peuvent néanmoins avoir un patrimoine propre.

Il s'agit dès lors de déterminer le régime de la propriété applicable à des biens mobiliers appartenant à des collectivités ou établissements publics.

A cet égard, en droit suisse, une distinction est faite entre les biens dont la collectivité est propriétaire afin d'en tirer un revenu comme n'importe quelle personne privée (patrimoine financier) et ceux dont elle est propriétaire afin d'accomplir les tâches d'intérêt public que la législation lui impose de poursuivre (patrimoine administratif).[1]

Les premiers sont à la libre disposition de l'autorité, sauf règle contraire; les seconds ne peuvent être aliénés, sauf désaffection préalable (c'est-à-dire sauf s'ils ne servent plus à l'accomplissement de la tâche d'intérêt public à laquelle ils étaient affectés) ou sauf règle expresse contraire.

Il convient, donc, d'abord, de dire si les musées et les objets qui les composent font partie du patrimoine administratif ou du patrimoine financier des collectivités et établissements dont ils relèvent.

Il ne nous paraît pas douteux que les musées ont un but culturel ainsi que cela résulte clairement des actes de fondation des musées ici envisagés. Il est partout question de développer la culture et l'histoire. Ce ne sont pas là des buts de nature commerciale. En outre, les droits payés par les visiteurs sont généralement modestes, précisément, pour attirer les visiteurs et les instruire. Dès lors, on doit constater que les biens appartenant aux musées font partie du patrimoine administratif.

En tant que tels, ils devraient être inaliénables.

Néanmoins, d'une part, il faut réserver la possibilité de désaffecter selon une procédure réglée par une loi, des biens et, partant, d'en faire des biens du patrimoine financier, donc, librement aliénables, d'autre part, des règles qui doivent, par définition, être expressés dès lors qu'elles dérogent au principe d'inaliénabilité, peuvent autoriser des aliénations;[2] ainsi, la loi sur le Musée national suisse, à son art. 9, permet l'aliénation de 'doublets ou autres objets pouvant être distraits des collections', sous réserve d'un droit de préemption des collections publiques cantonales 'en tenant compte de leurs ressources et aux conditions les plus modérées'. Le règlement sur l'administration du Musée national suisse du 14 novembre 1979, précise que les ventes et échanges d'objets appartenant au Musée national ne peuvent avoir lieu que si la Commission donne son accord au Directeur, et si, soit il existe plusieurs exemplaires d'un même objet dans les collections, soit l'objet est 'devenu superflu'.

L'art. 436 du règlement du Musée historique de Berne prévoit la possibilité de vendre des objets 'pour améliorer les collections' si ces objets se trouvent en dehors des centres d'intérêt du Musée. Il faut alors obtenir le consente-

1. *V.* B. KNAPP, *Précis de droit administratif*, 3e ed. (1988) n° 2890 *et seq*.
2. Note d'Editeur: le Kunsthaus de Zurich a usé de cette procédure en vendant le 26 octobre 1990, deux peintures de Renoir – 'Paysage de printemps' et 'Nature morte aux poissons' – afin de pouvoir acquérir un panneau mural de Georg Basalitz. C'est la première fois qu'un musée suisse vend des oeuvres faisant partie de ses collections.

ment unanime des responsables de l'administration de la collection et l'accord d'une majorité des deux tiers de la Commission de surveillance.

Les autres musées ici envisagés ne connaissent apparemment ni règles ni pratiques analogues cohérentes. Ils paraissent s'inspirer des méthodes pratiques indiquées par M. Cl. Lapaire dans son *Manuel de Muséologie* paru en 1983.

Encore faut-il se demander ce qu'il convient d'entendre par 'aliénation'. En effet, on peut se demander si un dépôt, une exposition ou un prêt dans un autre musée ne doivent pas être tenus pour une aliénation s'ils sont de longue durée. Par exemple, le Musée cantonal des Beaux-Arts du canton de Vaud possède un règlement sur les prêts; mais les prêts visés ne concernent que d'autres services de l'administration cantonale et sont précaires. Il ne peut donc pas s'agir d'aliénations déguisées.

Les textes régissant les musées de l'Elysée et du Rietberg n'envisagent même pas de prêts.

Le Kunsthaus de Zurich conclut des contrats de prêt de ses oeuvres à des fins d'exposition à des conditions précises imposant les mesures de conservation nécessaires et des conditions d'assurance imposées au bénéficiaire du prêt. La durée du prêt peut être indéterminée, mais le contrat peut, généralement, être dénoncé avec un préavis d'un mois. Les arts. 437 *et seq.* du règlement du Musée historique de Berne prévoit une procédure particulière pour l'autorisation de prêts en général; des prêts à des particuliers ne sont admis que si le Musée y a un intérêt spécial et si la sécurité des objets est garantie. Tout prêt peut être interdit si l'objet est particulièrement précieux ou délicat; en tout état de cause, un prêt ne peut dépasser 5 ans.

L'art. 12 du règlement sur l'administration du Musée national prévoit simplement que le directeur peut prêter des objets 'avec l'accord de la commission'.

La loi sur le Musée national prévoit, enfin, à ses arts. 6 et 7, un régime particulier pour les objets prêtés au Musée mais appartenant à des villes ou à des cantons suisses différent de celui applicable à des objets appartenant à des personnes privées. En effet, seuls les propriétaires privés peuvent librement disposer de leurs biens, les proprétaires 'publics' ne peuvent pas les retirer du Musée national.

ii. Les biens exposés non-propriété du Musée

La situation est différente lorsque les biens ne sont pas la propriété d'institutions de droit public, mais se trouvent exposés dans des endroits publics conformément à des dispositions de droit privé selon lesquelles des particuliers ou de tierces entités publiques proposent et les musées publics acceptent la mise d'oeuvres à disposition du public, (p. ex. les biens déposés par des personnes privées, les biens remis en prêt par des associations de soutien, les biens donnés ou légués avec charges notamment sous forme de fondation dite ficuciaire, les biens prêtés à titre d'expositions temporaires).

Le régime juridique de ces biens (qui seront d'autant plus nombreux que le Musée sera plus autonome et jouira de la personnalité juridique!) ne peut pas, par définition, en principe, être celui des biens de propriété publique. Il n'existe en outre, à notre connaissance, en Suisse, aucun régime de droit public pour les biens privés utilisés par des personnes ou entités de droit public.

Dès lors le régime applicable ne peut, en principe, être que celui de la propriété privée; ce régime sera identique dans tous les musées que ceux-ci soient publics ou privés.

La présence de tels biens soulève, cependant, la question de savoir si les musées publics peuvent accepter en dépôt, en legs, en donations, en prêt de tels biens et à quelles conditions.

Sur le principe même, il est remarquable que la pratique ne paraît faire aucune distinction entre les actes juridiques ne transférant au Musée que la jouissance des biens et ceux lui en accordant la propriété.

A titre d'exemple, le Musée cantonal des Beaux-Arts du canton de Vaud accepte le dépôt d'oeuvres même à titre définitif, sous réserve de l'approbation de l'autorité de surveillance; le fait que ces oeuvres sont en dépôt est mentionné sur elles; elles doivent être exposées publiquement; elles restent bien entendu la propriété des déposants. De même, dans le canton de Vaud, lorsqu'une succession est dévolue à l'Etat ou lorsqu'une donation est faite, les biens qu'elle comporte ne deviennent propriété publique que sous réserve d'acceptation par les autorités intéressées et par l'administration des finances; il faut en effet éviter que les charges liées à la succession ou à la donation soient exorbitantes.

Le Musée du Rietberg est réticent envers les dépôts en raison des frais que ceux-ci peuvent entraîner, sauf si l'objet est d'un intérêt exceptionnel ou si le déposant s'engage à transférer la propriété des objets le moment venu. Le Kunsthaus accepte des prêts par l'intermédiaire de la *Züricher Kunstgesellschaft* selon un contrat très bref obligeant le Musée à conserver et à assurer l'oeuvre.

Le Musée historique de Berne selon l'art. 434 de son règlement n'accepte des dons d'objets et des prêts que si les objets présentent un intérêt pour ses collections auxquelles il les intègre avec indication du nom du donateur ou du prêteur. Les donations ou prêts importants qui nécessitent des frais importants d'adaptation, des conditions ou des locaux d'exposition et ceux qui comportent des charges importantes, ne sont acceptés que selon une procédure particulière.

Il peut être intéressant de mentionner que la Confédération fait signer aux musées cantonaux des certificats de reconnaissance de dépôt lorsqu'elle dépose auprès d'eux des objets dont elle est la propriétaire. Il s'agit d'un dépôt de même nature que n'importe quel dépôt effectué par une personne privée, sous la réserve que l'objet déposé fait partie du patrimoine administratif de la Confédération.

c. Les conséquences d'une aliénation illicite

Il est bien entendu que les aliénations illicites de biens privés déposés dans des musées ou prêtés aux musées comme celles de biens publics entraînent des conséquences civiles, pénales et administratives.

Sur le plan civil, la propriété des biens n'est acquise valablement que par les tiers de bonne foi (art. 714 du Code civil). En outre, le responsable de l'aliénation illicite devra réparation au propriétaire public ou privé du fait du dommage que l'aliénation illicite lui cause.

Sur le plan pénal, l'aliénateur non-autorisé commet le délit d'abus de confiance (art. 140 du Code pénal), celui de gestion déloyale (art. 159) ainsi que le cas échéant, celui de gestion déloyale des intérêts publics (art. 314).

Sur le plan administratif, l'agent viole ses devoirs de fonctions et s'expose à des sanctions à ce titre. En outre, il se peut que l'auteur de l'aliénation illicite viole les rares règles de droit administratif relatives à l'interdiction d'exportation des objets d'art figurant dans le droit cantonal; il s'expose alors aux mêmes sanctions administratives et pénales, que les conservateurs de musées privés ou les amateurs d'art, toute personne, notamment violant ces interdictions.

En effet, certains cantons ont prévu une obligation d'annoncer les déplacements des objets protégés (*v.* 2.c.i. *infra*) et leur aliénation (*v.* 2.c.ii *infra*). D'autres cantons (*v.* 2.c.iii *infra*) ont même interdit l'exportation des objets protégés hors du territoire cantonal. Cette interdiction ne peut cependant être valable qu'envers les exportations à l'étranger dès lors que les cantons ont seuls la compétence de la prévoir; en revanche, à notre sens, elle ne saurait être valable à l'intérieur de la Confédération dès lors que celle-ci représente un marché unifié et unique et ne peut connaître d'interdictions d'exportation internes à la Suisse en l'absence de dérogations expressément prévues dans la Constitution. Si les cantons souhaitent empêcher l'exportation hors du canton mais en Suisse, ils ne peuvent y parvenir que par la voie d'un droit de préemption. Encore ce droit ne peut-il s'exercer qu'à l'occasion d'exportations à titre onéreux! A défaut, il faudrait recourir à l'expropriation pour autant que la loi en prévoie la possibilité.

2. *Les musées privés*

Les musées privés suivants ont bien voulu répondre à nos interrogations: Fondation Alfred et Eugénie Baur-Duret (collections) à Genève; Fondation in memoriam comtesse Tatiana Zoubov à Genève; Fondation Pierre Gianadda à Martigny; Fondation Oscar Reinhart à Winterthour; Fondation E.G. Bührle à Zurich (de façon extrêmement sommaire), Kunstmuseum Winterthour, Am-Rhyn-Haus, Donation Rosengart, Lucerne.

a. Les structures juridiques

Il est frappant de constater que les musées privés ici envisagés ont tous la forme de fondations de droit privé, à l'exception du Kunstmuseum de Winterthour qui est une association de droit civil sans but lucratif et du Musée Am-Rhyn-Haus qui gère la Donation Rosengart composée exclusivement d'oeuvres de Picasso, pour le compte de la Ville de Lucerne.

La fondation, en droit suisse se caractérise par le fait qu'une personne physique ou morale met, de manière irrévocable, à la disposition d'une personne morale qu'elle institue un ensemble de biens qui peuvent être des objets individualisés ou des sommes d'argent. La création de la fondation a lieu du vivant du fondateur ou, par testament, à la mort de celui-ci; elle est soumise à des conditions de forme, notamment, elle doit faire l'objet d'un acte notarié.

De manière générale, une fondation est dirigée par un Conseil, sous la surveillance de l'autorité publique fédérale ou cantonale dont relèvent les activités de la fondation. La surveillance tend à faire en sorte que les voeux du fondateur soient respectés, les biens de la fondation soient utilisés aux fins voulues par le fondateur et aucune mesure ne soit prise qui puisse mettre en cause les buts et les activités de la fondation.

Les associations sont des groupements de personnes constitués en personnes morales ayant la volonté de créer une collectivité indépendante poursuivant un but défini par les statuts de l'association. Aucune autorité étatique n'exerce une surveillance sur les activités de l'association dès lors que le législateur a considéré que les membres de l'association étaient en mesure de contester devant les tribunaux les actes des organes de l'association qu'ils considéreraient comme contraires aux buts et aux intérêts de l'association.

Une donation transfère la propriété de biens d'une personne à une autre; elle peut être accompagnée de charges qui limitent le droit du donataire de disposer des biens reçus.

b. Le régime des biens

Comme on l'a constaté, lorsque le musée a la forme de la fondation de droit privé ou de la donation, la volonté du fondateur est essentielle.

Il convient dès lors de distinguer les modalités selon lesquelles les biens ont été remis à la fondation ou donnés. Ainsi, le fondateur ou le donateur peut avoir donné une somme d'argent destinée à l'achat d'oeuvres. En principe, alors, le Conseil ou le donataire est libre de disposer des sommes reçues. Cependant, la liberté laissée au Conseil ou au donataire sera le plus souvent soumise à des charges. Ainsi la fondation ou le donataire ne pourra acheter que certains objets définis par le fondateur ou le donateur. Dans ces deux cas, à notre sens, le Conseil ou le donataire pourra revendre des objets acquis pour s'en procurer d'autres de même nature.

Parfois aussi, la fondation ou la donation aura seulement pour but d'acquérir avec les moyens mis à sa disposition par le fondateur ou le donateur un bâtiment déterminé pour exposer des oeuvres d'art déterminées ou non, léguées ou non par le fondateur.

Dans les hypothèses envisagées jusqu'ici, la fondation ou le donataire pourra à notre sens accepter en dépôt dans ses locaux ou prêter à des tiers à titre temporaire en principe, notamment en vue d'échanges ou d'expositions temporaires des oeuvres relevant de la collection faisant l'objet de la fondation ou de la donation. Eventuellement, il pourra même accepter des dons parts ou legs de tierces personnes, tant que les oeuvres reçues entrent dans le cadre de la collection.

Cependant, le plus souvent, le Conseil ou le donataire est étroitement lié par la volonté du fondateur ou le donateur de pérenniser la collection qu'il avait entreprise. Ainsi souvent, le fondateur ou le donateur interdit toute modification de la collection et prohibe toute aliénation, toute acquisition voire tout prêt ou dépôt.

Il peut exiger que les objets restent exposés dans les lieux où ils se trouvaient lors de l'établissement de la fondation (ou lors de la donation) ou même demeurent à l'endroit précis où ils étaient.

Le fondateur peut enfin (mais aussi parfois sous forme de donations entre vifs), normalement par un acte testamentaire, remettre sa collection à un musée public ou privé existant en imposant de multiples charges. Une telle remise de biens sous forme de fondation sans personnalité est dite fondation fiduciaire, le musée bénéficiaire étant propriétaire fiduciaire des biens et n'ayant dès lors pas le droit d'en disposer. C'est pourquoi de telles remises de biens sont sujettes à l'acceptation de leur bénéficiaire. Après acceptation, ce dernier est, en effet, tenu de respecter les conditions posées par le donateur/fondateur.

Si nous examinons les règles applicables dans les musées privés que nous avons cités, nous constatons que les situations les plus diverses se rencontrent.

Ainsi, selon les statuts de la Fondation Baur-Duret (collections), le but de la fondation est de devenir propriétaire de la collection d'art chinois et japonais de M. et Mme Alfred Baur-Duret, d'administrer cette collection et de la montrer au public et de 'devenir propriétaire de biens mobiliers et immobiliers pour permettre la pleine réalisation du but de la fondation'. Les fondateurs ont doté la fondation d'un capital de Sfr. 10,000. Il est interdit de transporter la collection hors du canton de Genève; celle-ci pourra être placée dans un musée propre ou, sous une forme individualisée, dans un musée existant. Surtout.

> 'cette collection ... doit former un tout; aucun objet ne doit être cédé, vendu ou échangé, elle ne pourra être groupée avec d'autres objets ou collections, les fondateurs désirant expressément que celle-ci, constituée avec le plus grand soin, soit conservée intégralement dans son état actuel. Par contre, si M. ...
> (aujourd'hui décédé) avec la collaboration duquel cette collection a été en grande partie exécutée et qui jouit de l'entière confiance des fondateurs, soumettait et recommandait au Conseil de Fondation d'autres acquisitions d'objets de collection, les fondateurs désirent que ses offres soient toujours, autant que possible, prises en considération. En dehors de cela, il ne devra pas être fait d'acquisitions.'

Les statuts de la fondation comtesse Tatiana Zoubov ne contiennent aucune règle sur la politique de vente, le dépôt d'oeuvres dans le Musée ou la donation d'oeuvres par de tierces personnes.

La Fondation P. Gianadda a des buts qui dépassent la conservation d'objets d'art. Elle a pour fins la conservation et la mise en valeur des vestiges d'un temple gallo-romain; d'offrir les espaces nécessaires à la présentation des objets archéologiques découverts à Martigny, d'utiliser à des fins culturelles les biens de la Fondation et de contribuer à l'essor culturel de Martigny. La Fondation collabore avec la Ville de Martigny et avec l'Etat du Valais. Il va de soi que la Fondation bénéficie d'un très large pouvoir de disposer des biens. En particulier, les statuts prévoient que parmi les ressources de la Fondation figure 'le produit des ventes'.

La Fondation O. Reinhart doit être conservée en l'état. Ni achat ni vente ne sont autorisées. Aucune donation ne peut être acceptée. Des expositions temporaires des collections graphiques non-exposées en permanence sont organisées dans des locaux réservés à ces fins. Des prêts à l'extérieur ne sont admissibles que 'dans des situations inévitables sur le plan scientifique'.

La Donation Rosengart ou Musée Am-Rhyn-Haus ne comprend que des oeuvres de Picasso. L'acte de donation précise que les oeuvres ne peuvent être ni vendues ni échangées et que les seules acquisitions permises doivent toutes non seulement être approuvées mais émaner de la famille Rosengart dont seule une personne subsiste à l'heure actuelle.

Un musée privé sous forme d'association a par définition une plus grande liberté d'action. Il se trouve, en effet, sous réserve de restrictions figurant dans les statuts, dans la même situation qu'un collectionneur privé.

A titre d'exemple de restriction statutaire, on pensera à celle figurant dans les statuts du *Kunstverein* de Winterthour dont le but est notamment de rassembler une collection d'art, une bibliothèque et des archives, de les exposer dans le Musée, de façon aussi permanente que possible et d'organiser des expositions temporaires d'artistes contemporains. Ce but laisserait suppposer une grande liberté de manoeuvre. Cependant, l'art. 15 des statuts qui ne peut, selon l'art. 10 *let.* a) être révisé qu'à l'unanimité' des membres, interdit l'aliénation totale ou partielle de la collection. Le Musée de Winterthour admet dans la pratique le dépôt d'oeuvres dans le Musée, sous réserve de l'acceptation du prêt par le Comité de l'Association.

c. Les conséquences d'une aliénation illicite

Les conséquences civiles et pénales de la violation des règles statutaires des fondations et associations ou des charges des donateurs constituant des musées privés sont identiques à celles de la violation des règles des musées publics.

Sur le plan administratif, les membres des conseils de fondation indélicats seront l'objet de sanctions de la part de l'autorité de surveillance pouvant aller jusqu'à la révocation.

En outre, la violation des règles de droit public sur l'interdiction de déplacer ou d'exporter les objets d'art entraîne les sanctions prévues dans ces dispositions que nous avons déjà mentionnées.

i. Par exemple, art. 5 loi sur la conservation des objets d'art et des monuments historiques du 16 mars 1902 de Berne qui soumet aussi à autorisation la mise en gage; art. 7 avec la même extension, de l'ordonnance sur la protection de la nature et des traditions et la conservation des antiquités et monuments historiques du 29 novembre 1927 de Schwyz; art. 4 avec la même extension, ordonnance concernant la sauvegarde des antiquités du 10 octobre 1921 de Bâle-campagne; art. 14 loi sur la protection des monuments historiques et artistiques du 15 avril 1946 du Tessin, en outre, l'art. 43 autorise l'autorité à ordonner le dépôt des biens en un lieu déterminé si leur transfert risque de les mettre en danger pour une période d'une semaine pour lui permettre de prendre des mesures telles que la préemption, art. 66 loi sur la protection de la nature, des monuments et les sites du 10 décembre 1969 de Vaud (même remarque que pour Berne); art. 5 loi sur la conservation des objets d'art et des monuments historiques du 9 novembre 1978 du Jura (même remarque que pour Berne).

ii. Par exemple, art. 11 loi sur la protection des monuments historiques du 8 mars 1960 de Lucerne conférant un droit de préemption; art. 52 loi sur la protection des traditions du 24 avril 1988 de Nidwald pour le même motif et sauf si l'aliénation a lieu en faveur du conjoint ou d'un membre de la famille domicilié à Nidwald; art. 9 ordonnance sur la protection des monuments historiques du 18 avril 1962 de Soleure; art. 10 ordonnance sur la protection de la nature et du patrimoine culturel du 27 novembre 1946 des Grisons; art. 5 loi sur le Valais du 28 novembre 1906 concernant la protection des objets d'art et des monuments historiques aux fins du droit de préemption; art. 36 loi sur la protection des monuments historiques du 26 octobre 1964 de Neuchâtel; art. 26 loi sur la protection des monuments, de la nature et des sites du 4 juin 1976 de Genève.

iii. Par exemple, art. 5 loi sur la conservation des objets d'art et les monuments historiques du 16 mars 1902 de Berne à l'exception du cas où le propriétaire transfère son domicile hors du canton; art. 7 ordonnance sur la protection de la nature et des traditions et la conservation des antiquités et monuments historiques du 29 novembre 1927 de Schwyz; art. 4 ordonnance concernant la sauvegarde des antiquités du 10 octobre 1921 de Bâle-campagne; art. 15 ordonnance concernant la protection des traditions du 27 novembre 1944 d'Alpenzell-Rhodes Intérieures; art. 1 ordonnance sur la protection de la nature et du patrimoine culturel du 27 novembre 1946 des Grisons; art. 15 loi sur la protection des monuments historiques et artistiques du 15 avril 1946 du Tessin qui réserve les exportations temporaires, les échanges n'appauvrissant pas le canton et les exportations aux fins de restauration; art. 5 loi sur la conservation des objets d'art et des monuments historiques du 9 novembre 1978 du Jura (avec la même précision que pour Berne).

Art. 12 loi sur la protection des monuments historiques du 8 mars 1960 de Lucerne, et art. 53 loi sur la protection des traditions du 24 avril 1988 de Nidwald, ont prévu un devoir d'annoncer ouvrant un droit de préemption.

United Kingdom

NATIONAL REPORT ON TOPIC 1. FREEDOM OF MUSEUMS TO SELL, TRADE OR OTHERWISE DISPOSE OF OBJECTS OF ART IN THEIR COLLECTION*

Adrian Barr-Smith**

1. The disposition of works of art in the United Kingdom is governed by:
   i. statutes controlling individual collections;
   ii. the Museums Association code of conduct;
   iii. United Kingdom export legislation.

a. Powers

The question whether a museum may sell, trade or otherwise dispose of an object or objects in its collection appears to depend on the specific powers granted to the museum. Many major museums are established by statute. The relevant enabling Act may provide either that the museum cannot dispose of the works held in its collections at all, or that it may make some limited dispositions.

b. National Gallery/Tate Gallery

Neither the National Gallery Act 1856 nor the National Gallery and Tate Gallery Act 1954 gives the relevant museum trustees any power of disposition at all.

c. British Museum

The British Museum Act 1963 provides that an object may be disposed of if:
   i. the object is a duplicate of another object; or
   ii. it appears to the trustees that the object was not made earlier than the

* The author acknowledges the invaluable assistance of Angela Jackson and Joshua Drapkin in the production of this material.

** Denton Hall Burgin & Warrens, Sollicitors, London. Consistent with our policy when giving comment and advice on a non-specific basis, Denton Hall Burgin & Warrens cannot assume legal responsibility for the accuracy of any particular statement. In the case of specific problems, it is recommended that professional advice be sought.

year 1850 and substantially consists of printed matter and the trustees hold a copy of the object made by photography or a process akin to photography; or

iii. in the opinion of the trustees, the object is unfit to be retained in the collection of the museum concerned and can be disposed of without detriment to the interests of students.

d. Victoria and Albert Museum

The National Heritage Act 1983 provides that the Victoria and Albert Museum trustees may only dispose of an object if:

i. they possess a duplicate; or
ii. the object is in their opinion unsuitable for retention in their collections and can be disposed of without detriment to the interests of students or other members of the public; or
iii. the object is sold to, given to or exchanged with one of a specified number of institutions; or
iv. the Board of Trustees is satisfied that the object has become useless for the purposes of their collections by reason of damage, physical deterioration or infestation, etc.

e. Local museums

The Museums Association lays down a code of practice for museum authorities. The most recent revision of this code was accepted at the 1987 Annual General Meeting of the Association.

f. Code of practice

The code emphasizes the general presumption in the United Kingdom that exists against any disposition by a public collection. The code acknowledges that local museums are less likely to be controlled by the statutory restrictions which apply to major institutions, and takes as its starting point the report of the Committee of Inquiry into the Sale of Works by Public Bodies (1964). This code provides that in most cases works should not be sold unless the sale is duly authorized by the relevant body, such as the Courts, the Charity Commissioners (most public collections in the United Kingdom having charitable status), the Ministry of Education, or a Local Act of Parliament.

g. Donor's restrictions

Certain collections like the Wallace Collection in London or the Burrell Collection in Glasgow, originally private bequests, have extremely strict rules on the lending or disposition of the objects contained within them, which effectively prevent any sale, trade or disposition.

h. Reform

Although museums' powers of disposition are limited, the Arts Minister last year suggested widening the powers of the National Gallery and the Tate Gallery to allow freedom to dispose of and/or to replace items in their collections. Various museum trustees rejected his proposals, fearing that to put dispositions on a statutory basis might lead to their later being denied direct government funding.

2. If a museum is empowered to sell works, the Museums Association's code of practice provides that they may be sold:

i. only after due consideration; and
ii.a. within the museum community to which the work should first be offered; or
b. to a party *not* a museum, only if the museum community has been allowed an opportunity (via notice in the Museums Bulletin) to express an interest in acquiring the work, and two months from the date of the notice have elapsed.

It should be noted especially that the decision to dispose of works of art should be the decision of the governing body and not of an individual curator. The museum should apply the proceeds of sales towards acquisition of other works.

3. Any museum which is empowered to do so may sell objects of art, subject to the considerations above, or not specifically prohibited by its articles of establishment.

4. The question whether a museum is authorized to sell an object of art which was part of a gift from a private person and whether there is a period prior to which such a sale cannot be made depends on the terms of the gift. There is no relevant statutory restriction placed on the freedom of an individual to deal with property owned by him outright.

5. If their articles of establishment permit, museums may transfer or lend objects between themselves. Indeed, public collections often make transfers between themselves, such as the swap two years ago between the Tate Gallery and the Victoria and Albert Museum of their respective examples of post-baroque sculpture with the result that the former held all the sculpture pre-dating Rodin, and the latter held all the examples post-dating him.

The museums may also make joint purchases such as the recent purchase by the National Gallery and the National Gallery of Wales at Cardiff of a work by Poussin (*The Finding of Moses*) under a scheme whereby the picture spends six months in each gallery. No United Kingdom galleries currently share works with foreign collections.

Works are often loaned or transferred to foreign galleries for the purposes of *temporary* exhibitions on terms agreed between the two institutions.

For a work to be exported permanently, rather than transferred temporarily, it must first be sold. For the purpose of sale, an export licence may be required. On this point, *see* under 7. *infra*.

6. I am not aware of any cases in which an object of art held by a museum or belonging to the United Kingdom's 'cultural patrimony' was exported, sold or otherwise disposed of. Museums and galleries of any size are usually in public ownership, and the overriding presumption against sale will apply.

7.a. A museum has sold an object of art belonging to a nation's cultural patrimony.

i. 'Cultural patrimony'
There is no formal register of National Cultural Goods in the United Kingdom but a concept of the Nation's 'cultural patrimony' does exist in the guise of the 'Waverley Criteria'. These are applied by the Export Reviewing Committee in assessing the importance of a work of art for which an export licence is required.

ii. General export licence
If they fall within certain limits, works may be exported under an Open General Export Licence under the supervision of the Department of Trade and Industry and of Her Majesty's Customs and Excise.

iii. Full licence
A full licence is required for any object which is *over fifty years of age and* which has a *value in excess of* £20,000 apart from pictures where the figure is £40,000 and portraits, arms and armour and certain textiles where the figure is £5,000. A licence is required for all manuscripts and archaeological material.

iv. Application of 'Waverly Criteria'
If an item has been imported within the last fifty years an export licence is normally granted. Otherwise the application is referred to an Expert Adviser. If the Expert Adviser decides that the work meets one or more of the 'Waverley Criteria', the work is referred to the Reviewing Committee.

The 'Waverley Criteria' apply if the object is:

a. *'so closely connected with our history or national life that its departure would be a misfortune';*
This was originally intended to catch such objects as the Alfred Jewel or the manuscript of 'Grey's Elegy', but it is interpreted in a somewhat wider context to include items which are of major importance for local history, or which are part of collections which are of the greatest historical significance, or which are associated with significant historical events.

b. or 'of outstanding aesthetic importance';
This criterion is not restricted to great works of painting or sculpture, but may be applied as well to an exquisite snuff box as to a painting by Poussin. Even in the case of a work by a great painter, account will be taken of the condition as well as the quality of the work in question and the extent of any damage or restoration to which it may have been subjected.

c. or *'of outstanding significance for the study of some particular branch of art, learning or history'*.
The criterion is applied with rigour to objects which are important *for* the study of some significant branch of art, learning or history rather than merely interesting *to* study.

v. Delay mechanism
If the work is sufficiently important, a delay mechanism comes into operation to give public collections in the United Kingdom an opportunity to buy the work at current market price.

vi. Remedies
If an attempt is made to sell the work abroad and the conditions of the Open General Export Licence are breached or an individual export licence is not obtained, the goods may be seized and are liable to forfeiture to the Crown. The person attempting to export them is in addition liable to a penalty. (Customs and Excise Management Act 1979).

7.b. A museum has sold an object of art not classified or not registered as a 'national cultural good' to a private person or to another museum.

If a work is sold by a museum in contravention of powers granted to the museum's trustees by the museum's articles of establishment, then the sale will be in breach of trust. An action may be brought by the Attorney General to enforce that trust in the Chancery Division of the High Court.

The equitable doctrine of 'following' governs the recovery of such a work, so far and so long as it is capable of being identified. However, if it has come into the hands of a bona fide purchaser for value without notice of the trust, then it cannot be so recovered and title in it will pass to the purchaser.

If a work is sold in breach of the museum's enabling Act, the museum trustees may additionally be liable for breach of statutory duty.

7.c. A museum has exchanged an object of art classified or registered as a 'national cultural good' or, alternatively, not classified or registered as a 'national cultural good' with another museum in the United Kingdom or abroad.

The answers to these questions will depend on the individual case, and on the rules governing a museum's power to deal with objects in its collection indicated above.

7.d. A museum has sold an object of art to a private person or another museum because its aesthetic value was lower at the time of the sale than at the time of its acquisition because of an error in the appraisal of its authenticity.

A higher price cannot be demanded. Public policy as regards museums and public collections, and the code of practice laid down by the Museums Association, is generally set against permitting museums extensive powers of disposal, exactly to avoid situations like this.

TOPIC 2. FREEDOM OF COLLECTORS TO SELL OR GIVE AWAY ALL OR PART OF THEIR COLLECTIONS

LIBERTE DU COLLECTIONNEUR DE DISPOSER DE TOUT OU PARTIE DE SA COLLECTION

General Report

General Report

TOPIC 2. FREEDOM OF COLLECTORS TO SELL OR GIVE AWAY ALL OR PART OF THEIR COLLECTIONS

Hans Koenig*

I. THE COLLECTOR'S POSITION

The issues regarding the right of a collector to dispose of part or all of his collection and the limits imposed on his rights by the legislation in various countries are certainly not so controversial or topical as de-accessioning effected by museums. However, he is often faced with legal problems in his activities as a collector.

What does a collector want to do and what are his objectives?

- (start or) pursue collecting objects of art;
- improve his or her collection (weed out, exchange, sell, purchase again, change direction of collecting, etc.);
- dispose of his or her collection;
  - i. sell part or all of it during his lifetime in his country or abroad;
  - ii. donate part or all of it to an individual or to an institution, in particular to a museum; possibly found a museum or participate in its establishment;
  - iii. make permanent or temporary loans to public or private collections;
  - iv. take his or her collection with him when he moves his residence to another country; move part of it to a secondary residence in another country;
  - v. leave it as part of his estate (succession) to his family or to other heirs including museums and other public institutions in his country or abroad.

It may be added that a serious collector will safeguard the appropriate conservation of art objects in his possession, repair and restore them, gather information, effect studies and research, encourage and support living artists. Needless to say that most public collections owe their enrichment and, in quite a number of cases, their existence to collectors; there often is a close symbiotic relationship between collectors, dealers or auction houses, museum staff and scholars.

---

* Former Secretary-General, International Chamber of Commerce.

There are persons who own and/or buy art objects without being collectors in the sense of the term as defined above. Particularly in recent times, works of art have been bought purely as an investment or as part of a speculative venture. This is of course a perfectly legitimate activity, but it is outside the field of true collecting although sometimes the borderline may be blurred. Furthermore there are owners of works of art who inherited them; in many cases, such works of art have been in the family for generations. And, of course, there are persons who, without being true collectors, like to surround themselves with beautiful objects some of which are genuine works or objects of art! For the purpose of this paper they are assimilated to the collector since the legal implications are practically the same for all groups.

It should be underlined, that there are only very few legal or regulatory provisions relating specifically to collectors. Also, many of the collector's problems and interests will coincide with those of the art and antique dealers, auction houses and museum professionals.

There are few examples where the legal treatment applied to an entire collection differs from that of individual items from a collection (except for rare cases where the authorities felt that a collection should be preserved in its entirety).

The laws and regulations referred to below generally do not or only very partially apply to works of art executed by contemporary artists.

II. LAWS AND REGULATIONS AFFECTING THE COLLECTOR IN HIS FREEDOM OF DISPOSAL

1. Restrictions of the Right of Ownership

In order to dispose of a work of art one would normally have to own it. There are a number of legal restrictions to ownership in most countries, more stringent in some than in others.

In Greece, e.g., the State is the permanent and absolute owner of all antiquities of Greek (or Roman) origin prior to 1830 (Law 5311/1932).[1] It is now recognized that this law also extends to movable objects dating from the period between 1453 (conquest of Constantinople) and 1830.[2] The government may also grant special protection by the State to works of art executed after 1830.[3] Such protection was given to icons up to 1900.

There are therefore no owners but holders or possessors of such works of art who can be either collectors or persons who inherited Greek works of art. This has not prevented important private collections from being established, e.g., the Goulandris Collection of Cycladic art which a few years ago

1. *See* the 'National Reports' following this 'General Report'.
2. Decision of the Supreme Court 407/1972.
3. Law 1469/1950.

was transformed into a private museum. It should be noted that this particular protective system and its restrictions do not apply to works of art of other origins.

Other States have adopted very similar concepts of protection and ownership such as Guatemala and other Latin American countries in which the ownership of the State of all works of art of national origin, including those not yet discovered, has been established.

In all countries where works of art and historical objects are protected by classifying, listing or registering, the owner of such works and objects generally has the duty to guarantee their good state of conservation, to keep them *in situ* and to notify authorities of an intended change of their location which usually will be subject to the approval of responsible authorities. In a number of cases subsidies and/or fiscal relief may compensate such obligations.

2. *Disposal of Works and Objects of Art Within the Collector's Country*

In all countries where protected works and objects are classified, listed or registered the disposal by a collector is regulated. The procedure in the case of a sale may include in particular notification to and approval by the responsible authorities and the right of pre-emption by the State. While notification and approval are the general rule in all these countries, the right of pre-emption exists in many but not all countries, e.g., Spain, France, Italy and Greece.

In Greece there exists a curious discrimination against the collector when the State exercises its right of pre-emption. While a normal holder of an antiquity will be compensated to the amount of the price agreed between the parties, a collector will only receive fifty percent of that amount.

The same rules as for sales will generally apply to gifts and donations. Often the government will consider donations to museums and public institutions more favourably than gifts to private persons. Also a donation to a museum will be more interesting both for the collector and the museum from the point of view of taxation.

A private collection which is part of an estate usually receives the same treatment as any other part of the estate, unless it is bequeathed to a museum. The possibility of an offer of surrender of part of a collection in an estate in lieu of payment of estate taxes (*dation*) was first enacted in the United Kingdom[4] and has been since adopted by several other countries either through appropriate legislation[5] or pragmatic action by government.[6]

4. Law of 1956.
5. France, Italy, Spain, Belgium, State of Maine (USA).
6. E.g., the United States. Cf. R. OBERSON, 'Rapport général - Fiscalité' and J.-L. BISMUTH, 'Rapport général, Dation en paiement d'oeuvres d'art' in ICC Institute, ed., *International Sales of Works of Art/La Vente Internationale d'Oeuvres d'Art* (ICC Publishing/ Kluwer, Paris/Deventer 1990) pp. 315–333 and pp. 481–560.

Collectors may want to dispose of part or all of their collection as temporary or permanent loans to museums and exhibitions. In the United States of America there was a notable tax incentive for such loans. This system, which has largely contributed to the enrichment of American museums, has been drastically modified by the new United States Tax Reform Act from 1986. However there still are some tax advantages in various countries as well as immaterial benefits in loaning privately owned works of art to museums.

It would follow, that if classified or listed works of art are subject to a restrictive regulation, the collector may dispose of unclassified or unlisted works of art freely. This, however, is not always the case.

Leaving aside the cases of Greece, Guatemala and others, where the notion of State ownership replaces that of classification or listing, there is in some countries, e.g., France, Spain and Italy, an uncertainty whether a work or object of art can be freely disposed of, even if so far it has not been classified. The responsible authorities, according to relevant legislation, have a more or less discretionary power to classify a work of art when it appears on the market, irrespective of the nature of the transaction – sale between two collectors, through an art dealer or by public auction. Obviously the inventory of classified objects cannot be complete in any country, but the lack of criteria or their vague wording create a climate of ambiguity which is highly unsatisfactory.

An example may serve to illustrate this point. In a European country with strict legislation regarding the protection of cultural goods, a painting by Van Gogh was acquired over ten years ago by a foreigner. The painting was to remain in the country, held by a foreign resident. It was further stipulated that after the departure of the foreign holder, the *Van Gogh* was to become the property of an internationally renowned private museum of modern art, again in the same country. At the time of the transaction, the parties, including the responsible authorities, felt that all had been done in accordance with the relevant laws and regulations. When the foreign holder left his host country a few months ago, the transfer to the private museum was to be implemented. At this moment, the authorities seized the painting, arguing that the original transaction had not followed the required procedure in all points, and transferred it into a public museum. A compensation corresponding to the value the painting had had more than ten years previously was offered to the owner who, understandably, did not see it the same way. At present, the issue is still pending.

3. *Moving Items of a Collection to Other Countries*

Obviously laws and regulations regarding the disposal of a work of art outside the boundaries of a country are much more stringent.

Even countries where disposal inside the country is not subject to any regulation, e.g., Sweden, have introduced provisions regulating and restricting the export of certain categories of objects.[7] It should also be noted, that not only sales, but also gifts and donations, bequests, exchanges, loans or personal removals are generally subject to the rules regulating export. The export for sale of classified objects is in many cases virtually prohibited (Italy, Spain, Greece, France, Portugal, Austria). In other countries, e.g., Japan, export will be excluded for objects of the most highly protected categories of national treasures and important cultural properties.

In other countries with a less comprehensive system of protection, it is at least theoretically possible to export a classified object, e.g., in the Federal Republic of Germany.[8] However, since the relevant German laws entered into force in 1955, only two applications for the granting of an export licence were made. Also because the number of objects classified in Germany, as is also the case in the Netherlands,[9] is relatively low,[10] an impact on the art market has not been felt.

The system in the United Kingdom recently was subject to much attention in the British and international media, when Canova's *Three Graces* belonging to the Duke of Bedford were to be sold to the Getty Museum. Any work or object of art to be sold to a buyer outside the United Kingdom requires a special export licence, if the value of the transaction is higher than an amount which varies according to the type of object. If an officially appointed expert feels, that the object should not leave the country, a reviewing committee of the Board of Trade will consider the case and may block the export for three months. If a British museum is willing and capable of acquiring it at the agreed price, the work of art goes to the museum provided the owner agrees. Should he not agree, the object remains in his possession, but he cannot apply for an export licence again before a period of ten years. If the funds required for the payment of the agreed price cannot be mobilized by the museum, the object may be exported.

Suggestions were recently made to modify the system by appropriate new legislation. However, so far, it has worked well and has the advantage of being both fair and flexible, apart from the fact, that during the last years British museums have been exceedingly short of funds and have not always been able to acquire desirable objects. At the time this text was drafted, it was not yet clear which way would be chosen to keep the *Three Graces* in the United Kingdom, especially in view of the question as to whether this

7. Law SOU 1988:950.
8. Law of 5 August 1955, Art. 5.
9. Conservation of Cultural Heritage Act of 1 February 1984, Decree of 13 March 1985.
10. The register of protected cultural property published in October 1988 by the Federal Ministry of the Interior on the basis of the lists established by the *Länder* includes around 300 works of art; incidentally in these lists, there appears an amazing disparity as to numbers which cannot be explained by the relative richness of the regions constituting the Federal Republic of Germany.

sculpture was part of a protected building, in which case other legal provisions might prevail.

The declaration of an export ban for an object so far not classified can of course have practical consequences for a collector wanting to sell an item of his collection. In an interesting decision from 1982 the French *Conseil d'Etat* decided that the State was not responsible for financial disadvantages arising from the export stop pronounced by the French administration, for a 14th century Chinese porcelain jar the price of which realized at public auction was considerably lower than the international market price.[11] However, in a more recent case the French administration showed its flexibility by granting an export licence for a major work of art: *Les noces de Pierrette* by Picasso, after the owner had offered another master painting by the same artist to the Musée Picasso.

Gifts and inheritances, where the beneficiaries live abroad, are systematically treated as export. However, one could hold the view that donations and bequests in favour of a foreign museum should be considered to be of a different nature. So far, this is not generally recognized, although in a few instances donations by collectors to foreign museums could be made. However, these donations did not have a very high material value. In another instance, a foreigner, having spent most of his life in Turkey, was allowed to leave part of his collection to beneficiaries outside the country, among them a museum, provided the bulk of the collection went to a Turkish museum.

Exchanges between collections would be desirable, but are rare, in particular when one of the States in which a collection is located, has very strict export regulations. One positive example concerning Greece can be mentioned: an important item of a Greek private collection could be exchanged against a more desirable sculpture in a museum in the United States.

Loans from private collections to temporary exhibitions abroad require export licences and the authorization of the relevant authorities. The permission will be facilitated if the exhibition is also shown in the country of origin of the loaned objects. Permanent loans to foreign museums are much rarer and generally frowned upon by the country of origin.

The removal of a collection or part of it, if a collector either wants to bring it to a secondary residence in another country or permanently wants to leave the country, raises delicate issues, if the items of the collection are classified or can be classified when the collector reveals his intention. Then the export restrictions mentioned above will usually apply. Sometimes a temporary export licence for a limited period of time can be granted in the first case, it being understood that the collection or part of it will return to the country where the collector originally had his residence.[12]

A foreign resident in a European country, to cite another instance,

11. Decision of the *Conseil d'Etat*, 7 October 1987.
12. This possibility was mentioned by the Report on the Austrian situation (*see infra* p. 169) but would also apply in a number of other countries.

acquired a painting by Van Gogh ten years ago. When recently he wanted to return to his own country, he was forbidden to take the painting with him; the government authorities offered to buy it, but at the price he had paid ten years before. Needless to say, he did not agree to that offer and the matter is still pending.

On the whole a collector does not have any special legal status except for provisions which render his position less favourable than that of other citizens.

III. EVALUATION OF LAWS RESTRICTING THE COLLECTOR'S FREEDOM OF DISPOSAL

World-wide there is an increasing trend towards the protection of works and objects of art within a country. This world-wide trend is basically a positive and necessary one and must be welcomed. In many countries protective measures were triggered off by a continuous exodus of works of art; in a number of countries, such as China, Turkey, Greece or Italy, archeological works of art, taken out of the country, resulted from wild and unscientific digs. Some of this still goes on and collectors bear a responsibility not to encourage – sometimes unknowingly – such illegal acts. One of the major aims of the Unesco Convention from 1970 is to put a stop to this pilfering of national cultural heritage. The Council of Europe's Convention on Archeological Treasures from 1969 goes into the same direction.

It should be noted that in several countries such as Italy, France, Greece and others, government protection of national patrimony and restrictions of the disposal of works of art go back to the early years of this century. Already during the second half of the nineteenth century, governments prevented the export of art works through individual measures.

The objectives of specific legislation seem to be very similar, although the scope and the extent of protection granted and intervention permitted to government authorities vary greatly from country to country.

As to the terminology used to describe what is to be protected, just to give a few examples, one notes an amazing variety:

- national patrimony (France)
- cultural goods (Italy and Austria)
- historical patrimony and goods of cultural interest (Spain)
- cultural property (F.R. Germany and Japan)
- movable cultural patrimony (Belgium)
- cultural heritage (Netherlands).

Neither the terminology used nor the wording of the preambles of national laws give a clear indication as to what is to be protected and how it is to be protected; even the substantive contents of the various laws do not always permit to draw clear conclusions to that effect.

As to the scope of protective legislation two groups can be distinguished.

One group includes the States where protection exclusively or mainly focuses on works of national origin. This applies, for example to Greece, Turkey, China, Thailand, most Latin American countries and New Zealand; even the only relevant American act aims at protecting the trade and export of artifacts made by the North American Indians. But also in countries such as the Netherlands, Sweden and Japan, the national legislation and its enforcement show a bias in favour of objects of national origin or having direct links with the country's political or cultural history. A similar concept underlies action by the Swiss cantons, although such action so far has had little or no influence on the movement of works of art.

The other group includes countries where a universal protection of a country's art treasures irrespective of their origin prevails. In these countries public and private collections are supposed to reflect the whole breadth of cultural and artistic creations throughout the world. Examples of this group are France, Italy, Spain and the F.R. Germany. Also in the United Kingdom, where the notion of national cultural patrimony has no official existence, the regulation of the export of works of art is inspired by the same concept.

Another distinction between two groups of countries based on different criteria, i.e., the nature and the extent of a government's intervention, can be proposed. On the one hand, there are countries where the State, irrespective of whether the works of art are of national or universal origin, claims an almost all embracing right of control and intervention. Examples of such countries are Italy, Spain, France and Greece. The other group would include countries where only a fairly limited number of objects frequently, but not always, incorporated in a list, are subject to government restrictions. Examples for this type would be the Netherlands, the F.R. Germany and Sweden.

For want of a better word one might call the first group the 'total claim countries' and the second group the 'selective claim countries'.

Finally, there are countries where for practical purposes no restrictions apply, such as the United States and Switzerland.

Between the legislator's intention and the letter of the law on the one hand and the actual implementation of such laws on the other hand is often a wide difference.

In several countries, laws were adopted some time ago, but the regulations allowing their implementation have not yet been approved. This applies, e.g., to the Belgian law from 1960, although the gap has been partially filled by the Communities (the Flemish, French and German Communities in Belgium) which since 1960 have been given a share of the State's responsibility in cultural matters.

Another problem is raised by laws providing mechanisms that are partly unsuited for fulfilling their purpose. For instance, in Greece the perpetual and absolute ownership of Greek works of art prior to 1830, in particular archeological objects, coupled with other provisions of the law from 1931 – e.g., provisions for compensation – have not helped to encourage finders or holders to do what they are supposed to do. Suggestions for remedying this situation have been sporadically put forward in Greece during the recent years, aiming *inter alia*, at reorganizing the Greek arts and antique trade or establishing a national antiques exchange.

In some countries national law is so far-reaching and so ambitious that there is an inbuilt obstacle to its enforcement and implementation, if only on account of the enormous amount of bureaucratic effort involved.

Often neither the funds nor the space or equipment nor the staff, which would be required to make the laws work, are available. While private sponsorship and funding may help and provide some relief, this certainly is not the adequate answer to the problem.

As mentioned under I., *supra* the criteria for imposing restrictions on the disposal of works and objects of art are very general; sometimes they are vague to the point of being almost meaningless and offer no clue to the collector or owner of the work of art. The indication of thresholds, expressed in monetary terms, for restrictions to intervene, have the disadvantage of being soon outdated as a consequence of currency depreciation, inflation and the development of the art market.

On the whole, there is in many places a deplorable lack of transparency in this area. A collector can often not be certain what he may own or possess, what he may dispose of and how he is allowed to do it. Consequently a collector, assuming that he is a law abiding person, will have unduly to weigh the possibilities and the risks of what he intends to do. To quote an example: A collector who, while being the citizen of a country A with a strongly restrictive, but not too efficiently implemented legislation, has effected all his collecting activities over the last thirty years in countries B, C, D, etc. Parts of the collection are on loan in other countries' museums and it is unlikely that the collection which he established abroad will ever be brought into his own country. There are quite a few other examples of that type. In many cases a collector, without openly violating the law, will try to bypass existing restrictions.

Clearly, while the aims of the legislation for the protection of national cultural heritage must be supported, the present situation as seen from an international standpoint – and collecting usually is an international activity – is neither logical nor satisfactory.

At the national level it is up to government, parliament and the voting citizen to ensure that wherever a national law and its application need to be improved such improvement be initiated. The same parties should try to obtain that the means deployed by authorities are commensurate to the desired effect.

To what extent is it possible to reach more international understanding, possibly a rapprochement or even a certain harmonization of legislation?

The Unesco Convention from 1970 may make a contribution if it leads to closer co-operation between administrations.[13] The same can be hoped from

13. It is interesting to note that among the industrialized nations only the USA, Greece, Italy, Spain and Portugal have ratified the convention. Editor's note: the text of the Convention and a list of the countries that have ratified it is reproduced in *International Sales of Works of Art/La Vente Internationale d'Oeuvres d'Art*, ICC Institute, ed., (ICC Publishing/Kluwer, Paris/Deventer 1990) in French pp. 171–185, and in English, pp. 187–200.

the European Convention on the protection of archeological heritage from 1969, drafted by the Council of Europe, though it covers an even smaller part of the issues we are dealing with.

Recently the Commission of the European Communities has released a communication to the Council of the Communities on the needs arising from the abolition of frontiers in 1992 with regard to the protection of national treasures.[14] Art. 36 of the Rome Treaty allows Member States to maintain prohibitions and restrictions on imports and exports on grounds of the protection of national treasures. In principle this article will continue to apply, but checks on goods and persons currently carried out at the communities' internal frontiers should be abolished. Also checks and formalities currently applied in intra-community trade for tax reasons (VAT) should disappear.

The communication mentions that proposals for a central monitoring of protective procedures might be made by the Commission. It continues however that 'an extremely strict system requiring a large number of authorizations and frequent involvement of the authorities, etc. can be applied only in respect of a limited number of objects; otherwise it would either fail to operate effectively in practice or unduly restrict lawful trading',[15] a statement which can certainly be endorsed (*see* this section, *supra*). The Commission recognizes that at present a harmonization of national legislation would be extremely difficult, even unfeasible, but makes a number of interesting suggestions, e.g., introducing registers listing specific objects rather than referring to categories and groups comprising an unknown and indefinite number of objects for the purpose of monitoring and procedures of control.

The practical approach includes the desired mutual recognition of Member States' law and the determination of possibilities for the return of national treasures unlawfully dispatched (in the Commission's language no exporting is possible in the movement of goods between Member States after 1992) to the country of origin.

Since it was drafted for the purposes of the single Common Market many other aspects of interest to the Symposium are not touched upon by the Communication, but the Commission's initiative may trigger off efforts to ensure better compatibility between the national legislations of Member States.

In conclusion, one can only repeat what Professor Raoul Oberson said in his report on fiscal issues to the 1988 Symposium,[16] namely that those involved in the world of art and antiques have so far not been able to sensitize governments and administrative practice to the actual needs.

---

14. Commission of the European Communities, Communication from the Commission to the Council on the Protection of National Treasures Possessing Artistic, Historic or Archaeological Value: Needs Arising from the Abolition of Frontiers in 1992, COM (89), 594 from 22 November 1989.
15. Communication, paras. 19 and 20.
16. *See* n.6.

National Reports

Austria

NATIONAL REPORT ON TOPIC 2. FREEDOM OF COLLECTORS TO SELL OR GIVE AWAY ALL OR PART OF THEIR COLLECTIONS*

Ignaz Seidl-Hohenveldern**

1. A private collector can sell or give as a gift all or part of a collection belonging to him but classified as a 'national cultural good' to anybody in Austria after having informed the Federal Monuments Office. If the collection, as a unit, is a monument, the collection can only be auctioned as a unit. Gifts to persons abroad require permission.

2. The price will be determined by the law of supply and demand. Where permission for delivery or export hinge on the value of the object, the value prior to the sale will be determined by a neutral expert.

3. In regard to the question whether a collector can sell or give as gift an object of art belonging to him which is not classsified as a national cultural good, if the object is a monument (cf. the general presumption to this effect in Art. 2(1) of the Federal Law on the Protection of Monuments), such act must be notified to the Federal Monuments Office if the object is to remain in Austria. If the object is to be exported, permission for export must be obtained.

4. A private collector may choose freely the country in which the objects of art belonging to him will be situated only after having obtained permission for export. The Federal Law Prohibiting the Export of Cultural Property provides no exception for such a case. However, such a dual resident may obtain a temporary export permit for three years, which may be extended up to nine years pursuant to Art. 7(1) of this Law.[1] The owner may be requested to give a surety for the final return of the objects to Austria up to twice the amount of the object's sales value abroad or in Austria. The transfer of the Liechtenstein Collection from Vienna to Liechtenstein in 1944 does not constitute a contrary precedent. The Prince could rely on the extraterritoriality of his collection. If, under international law, an ambassador returning to the sending State may freely export his household goods,

---

* Editor's note: *see also* 'Austria: Introduction' in Part One.

** Professor, Institut für Völkerrecht und Internationale Beziehungen, Vienna.

1. N. HELFGOTT, *Ausfuhrverbotsgesetz für Kulturgut* (Vienna, Manz 1987) p. 31.

such right – *de minore ad maius* – cannot be denied to the Prince entitled to send ambassadors.[2]

2. Cf. I. SEIDL-HOHENVELDERN, 'Ausfuhr und Rückführung von Kunstwerken', in KÖLZ/THÜRER, eds., *Festschrift für Dietrich Schindler* (Basle 1989) pp. 141–142.

Belgique

RAPPORT NATIONAL SUR LE SUJET 2. LIBERTE DU COLLECTIONNEUR DE DISPOSER DE TOUT OU PARTIE DE SA COLLECTION*

Francis Haumont**

1. La réponse à la question de savoir si un collectionneur privé peut vendre ou faire donation d'un objet d'art d'une collection d'objets d'art lui appartenant, bien que classé comme élément du patrimoine culturel national nécessite l'examen de plusieurs hypothèses selon les Communautés et selon le type de classement.

Si le bien est classé, la vente ne pourra se faire que moyennant l'autorisation de l'Exécutif en Communauté française et en Communauté germanophone. En revanche, en Communauté flamande, la vente ne sera pas soumise à autorisation préalable de l'Exécutif. Nonobstant cette vente, le bien restera classé.

Il convient de mentionner également une disposition du décret flamand du 17 novembre 1982 qui impose que, sauf autorisation de l'Exécutif, les objets classés soient gardés *in situ*.[1] Cela implique donc que la vente ne serait pas soumise à autorisation de l'Exécutif, mais que le déplacement de l'oeuvre vendue le serait.

Bien que l'hypothèse soit plus rare, si l'objet d'art appartenant au collectionneur privé est soumis au régime de la domanialité publique, il sera inaliénable. La vente ne pourrait se faire que moyennant une désaffectation préalable de l'objet.

Enfin, en ce qui concerne l'exportation par un collectionneur privé d'une oeuvre d'art non classée et non affectée au domaine public, mais faisant partie de la liste des biens du patrimoine culturel de la Nation en vertu de la loi du 16 mai 1960, elle ne pourra, dans l'état actuel de la réglementation, être interdite.

En ce qui concerne les donations d'oeuvres non classées ou non affectées au domaine public, il convient de noter qu'elles ne peuvent se faire aux musées dépendant des autorités administratives ou aux musées privés constitués en association sans but lucratif ou en fondation que moyennant l'approbation d'une autorité de tutelle ou du Ministère de la Justice.[2]

---

* Note d'Editeur: *v.* pour 'l'Introduction au Rapport', *supra* p. 31.

** Chargé de cours à l'Université Catholique de Louvain, Avocat au Barreau de Bruxelles.

1. Art. 8, §1er.
2. Arts. 910 et 937 Code civil.

2. Dans toutes les hypothèses où la vente peut avoir lieu, le prix est fixé librement par les protagonistes de la vente ou par le marché.

3. Dès lors que le collectionneur a la libre disposition de l'objet d'art (non-classé) lui appartenant, il peut le vendre ou en faire don à qui il veut en ce compris, comme nous l'avons vu, à l'étranger. Mentionnons, sans que ce mécanisme puisse être assimilé à celui de la donation, la dation d'un objet d'art en paiement des droits de succession. Cette dation ne dépend pas uniquement du bon vouloir du collectionneur. Elle doit répondre à plusieurs conditions et notamment à l'acceptation du Ministre des Finances qui, pour ce faire, recueille l'avis de la commission chargée de l'évaluation des oeuvres d'art.

4. Pour rappel, si le bien est classé, il doit rester, *in situ*, sauf autorisation préalable.[3]

Pour les autres biens, le collectionneur est libre de placer les objets où il veut pour autant, bien entendu, qu'il respecte les réglementations douanières fiscales des pays concernés.

3. Loi du 7 août 1931, art. 19, al. 2; Décret flamand du 17 novembre 1982, art. 8, §1er.

F. R. Germany

NATIONAL REPORT ON TOPIC 2. FREEDOM OF COLLECTORS TO SELL OR GIVE AWAY ALL OR PART OF THEIR COLLECTIONS*

Ludger Bischop**

Generally, German legislation is liberal for the collectors except where the exportation of 'cultural goods' is concerned.

In accordance with the Law of 5 August 1955, it is necessary to obtain an authorization to export a work of art belonging to the national 'German cultural patrimony' and listed as such in the national cultural register. The German system for controlling the export of cultural goods is situated between the liberalism of the United States and Swiss situations and the interdictory approach established by the French, Spanish and Italian laws.

To register a work of art as a cultural good, it is necessary that either the owner of the work of art in question, or a third party, applies for registration as a cultural good for a work of art from the regional public authority (*Land*). An expertise is the prequisite condition for a definitive registration of the work of art as a cultural good. A cultural good is specified by the German Law of 1955 as follows: a cultural good which is either of German or foreign origin, belongs to the German cultural patrimony if it has to be seen as a part of the German cultural patrimony because of its own artistic or cultural value or because of its importance for the cultural development in Germany.

The most important result of such a registration is the need to request an authorization in order to export the work of art concerned. An expert from the Federal Ministry of Internal Affairs has to give an opinion before an authorization is accepted. The authorization is given if the export of the work of art does not constitute a loss for the German cultural patrimony. Therefore, the property rights of the owner of a work of art registered in the cultural register are restricted. Compensation can be granted to the owner of the registered work of art when he is not authorized to export this work of art: he can be exempted from the capital tax or inheritance tax; he can also receive financial compensation in the case where he loses an opportunity to sell the work of art abroad, but this compensation is meaningless due to

* Editor's note: This Report is an English language summary of the German language National Report on Topic 2.

** Research Assistant, Institute for International Business Law, Westfälischen Wilhelms-Universität, Münster.

the recent record-prices reached by the sale of paintings. The owner of the registered work of art must keep the authorities informed when the work of art is moved from one location to another.

The exportation of a registered work of art without an authorization is punished by criminal sanctions (prison or payment of an amount of up to DM 300,000). When the work of art has been sold abroad, it is questionable whether or not the German authorities have the possibility of taking the registered work of art from the possession of the third party.

In practice, the Law of 1955 on the protection of the German cultural patrimony has not been applied in many cases. One of the reasons for this situation is due to the fact that the number of registered works of art is limited (501 of which 277 are for cultural goods and 224 for archives). There has not been a case where a registered work of art has been exported without authorization and there have only been two requests for authorization for exportation.

In conclusion, the liberal and very unrestricted policy adopted in the application of the Law of 1955 by the German authorities leads to the idea that the policy in Germany is not to restrict the trade in works of art.

Grèce

RAPPORT NATIONAL SUR LE SUJET 2. LIBERTE DU COLLECTIONNEUR DE DISPOSER DE TOUT OU PARTIE DE SA COLLECTION

Antonias Dimolitsa*

La même distinction que ci-dessus[1] doit être faite: c'est à dire, il faut encore distinguer les antiquités (I.) des oeuvres récentes, pas spécialement protégées (II.).

I. ANTIQUITES

Bien que les collectionneurs d'objets archéologiques (art. 23–24 loi 5351/1932) jouissent de certains privilèges d'ordre patrimonial ou scientifique ressemblant aux attributs d'un droit de propriété, le contrôle de l'Etat est toujours présent derrière l'exercice de ces privilèges, ce qui se justifie par l'intérêt public que représentent en même temps ces collections.

Pour toute vente d'un objet archéologique appartenant à une collection privée, une autorisation spéciale du Ministère de la Culture est nécessaire. L'Etat peut d'ailleurs acheter tout objet archéologique à vendre par un collectionneur, à la moitié du prix offert à celui-ci (art. 31 loi 5351/1932).

Cette disposition revient à créer en matière de vente un traitement plus sévère pour les collectionneurs que pour les simples détenteurs d'objets archéologiques. Si la vente d'objets archéologiques par ces derniers est possible sur simple déclaration de l'acte au Ministère, l'autorisation spéciale prévue pour les collectionneurs présuppose un examen précis de tous les éléments de la vente par le comité compétent du Ministère de la Culture.

Un refus de l'autorisation doit pourtant, à notre avis, être motivé: les collectionneurs jouissant quand même d'un droit privé sur leurs collections, le refus de l'autorisation doit se fonder sur une raison plausible dérivant de l'esprit de la loi, ce qui pourrait par exemple constituer le danger d'une exportation illicite ou le manque de garanties pour la sauvegarde des oeuvres chez l'acquéreur. Un refus injustifié équivaudrait, à la limite, à une atteinte d'un droit privé par l'Etat et créerait une obligation d'indemnisation à sa charge.

---

* Avocat, Athènes.

1. Note d'Editeur: *v.* pour 'l'Introduction au Rapport' *supra* p. 39.

Si la vente d'objets archéologiques de collections est spécialement prévue par la loi, ceci n'est pas le cas pour la donation de ces objets. Il ne fait pourtant pas de doute que la même disposition ci-dessus doit s'appliquer en la matière. Par conséquent, l'autorisation du Ministère de la Culture est nécessaire et sera accordée si le bénéficiaire acquiert son agrément. Ce serait plutôt le cas quand le bénéficiaire est un musée ou une fondation situés en Grèce et moins facilement le cas quand il est un particulier. Il serait d'ailleurs plutôt à exclure que l'autorisation puisse être accordée quand le bénéficiaire est une personne physique ou morale étrangère.

En ce qui concerne l'exportation d'objets archéologiques appartenant à une collection, sont applicables les mêmes dispositions que pour les simples détenteurs de pareils objets. Peuvent par conséquent être librement exportés les objets importés et déclarés à leur importation (art. 18 loi 5351/1932). Pour toute autre exportation, une licence spéciale émise par le Ministère de la Culture suivant une décision du Conseil Archéologique est nécessaire (art. 19 loi 5351/1932). En revanche, l'échange d'objets archéologiques 'multiples' – dans le sens de l'existence de plusieurs exemplaires du même objet dans la collection – par les collectionneurs privés contre des objets archéologiques de valeur analogue appartenant à des collections de musées étrangers est permis par la loi (art. 29 loi 5351/1932). La valeur de ces objets est estimée d'une manière définitive par un Comité composé de trois membres, un représentant du collectionneur privé, un éphore d'antiquités et une personne nommée par le Président de la Cour de Cassation (art. 11 loi 5351/1932).

Les collectionneurs d'oeuvres d'art récentes, non spécialement protégées, sont libres de vendre, donner, importer, exporter ou envoyer d'une résidence à l'autre pareilles oeuvres sans aucune restriction. Il suffit seulement, en vue d'une exportation, de remplir une simple formalité consistant à faire passer l'oeuvre au contrôle d'un bureau spécial de la Pinacothèque Nationale qui y mettra un sceau spécial attestant qu'il s'agit d'une oeuvre d'art contemporain (i.e., qui ne tombe pas sous le régime des oeuvres protégées). Des droits de douane ne sont d'ailleurs pas perçus à l'entrée ou la sortie de ces oeuvres d'art.

Italie

RAPPORT NATIONAL SUR LE SUJET 2. LIBERTE DU COLLECTIONNEUR DE DISPOSER DE TOUT OU PARTIE DE SA COLLECTION*

Tommaso Alibrandi**

1. Si le bien ou la collection (pour la collection, il faut que le démembrement ait été autorisé par le Ministre aux termes de l'art. 5 de la loi 1089/39) fait l'objet d'une contrainte, la personne privée ne peut le vendre sans notification préalable à l'Etat, afin que ce dernier soit en mesure d'exercer le droit de préemption (toujours dans le cadre territorial). S'ils ne font pas l'objet d'une contrainte, elle peut les vendre librement. S'ils font l'objet d'une contrainte, elle peut les vendre à une Fondation, à condition d'avoir l'autorisation de l'Etat.

2. Si la vente se fait dans le cadre de la CE, c'est le Ministre qui l'établit; sinon le prix est fixé dans le bordereau d'exportation ou par la Commission paritaire.

3. Un collectionneur privé peut vendre ou faire donation d'un objet d'art lui appartenant et qui n'est pas 'classé' à condition que cela soit notifié à l'Etat afin qu'il puisse être en mesure d'exercer le droit de préemption au cas où le bien ferait l'objet d'une contrainte. Et, de toute façon, l'intervention du Ministre est obligatoire pour les oeuvres déclarées au moment de l'exportation.

Il peut vendre ou faire une donation à une personne de son choix, un musée de son choix, par une vente publique aux enchères, ou à l'étranger à condition de passer par le Bureau des exportations (*Ufficio Esportazione*) qui peut adopter l'une des trois alternatives suivantes: veto, proposition de contrainte ou proposition d'acquisition au Ministère du Bureau central pour les biens AAAAS (*Ufficio Centrale per i Beni AAAAS*) aux fins de l'exercice du droit d'achat.

4. Un collectionneur privé peut choisir le pays où il va placer les objets d'art qui lui appartiennent. Si les objets ne font pas l'objet d'une importation temporaire, il doit les présenter au Bureau des exportations. S'ils font au

---

* Note d'Editeur: *v.* pour 'l'Introduction au Rapport' *supra* p. 41.

** Professeur, Libera Università Internazionale degli Studi Sociali, Facoltà di Scienza Politiche, Rome.

contraire l'objet d'une importation temporaire, il peut choisir librement le pays.

Lorsqu'il présente les objets d'art au Bureau des exportations et demande l'autorisation d'exporter, le Bureau peut répondre de la façon suivante:

a. si les objets ne sont pas sujets à contrainte, il peut proposer la contrainte au Ministère (Div. V);
b. il peut autoriser l'exportation au cas où les biens ne feraient pas l'objet d'une contrainte;
c. il peut mettre un veto à l'exportation.

L'exportateur peut choisir le pays à condition de donner, sur le formulaire du Bureau des exportations, l'adresse de son domicile à l'étranger.

The Netherlands

NATIONAL REPORT ON TOPIC 2. FREEDOM OF COLLECTORS TO SELL OR GIVE AWAY ALL OR PART OF THEIR COLLECTIONS*

Anton A. Quaedvlieg**

1. Objects of art belonging to a private collector (or private museum) may be placed on the List of Protected Objects by virtue of the Conservation of Cultural Heritage Act (*see* Introduction, II.*2*).

If the object in question has been placed on the List, the owner must *report* and obtain *permission* for the intended sale or transfer (for further details *see* the Introduction, II.*2*.f). Furthermore, under Art. 6 of the Act the owner is required to inform the purchaser (or transferee or assignee) beforehand of the fact that the object is listed.

A breach of these obligations may vitiate the contract of sale by reason of mistake, misrepresentation or breach of duty, not to mention the consequences under criminal law that are attached to violation of the Conservation of Cultural Heritage Act.

2. In principle the price would be determined in free negotiations. If the Minister objects to the sale or transfer, such objection will at the same time constitute an offer to purchase on the terms and conditions as indicated in the Introduction, II.*2*.f. If the price has already been determined, the State will have to pay the same price. In the case of an auction, the Minister may himself enter a bid.[1]

In other cases, the Minister will, immediately after having given notice of his objection, commence negotiations with the owner on the purchase price and other conditions of sale. If the negotiations do not result in an agreement, the price will be determined by the District Court at The Hague, which is required to obtain the advice of experts. Up to one month after the purchase price has been determined, both the Minister and the owner may decide not to go through with the transaction (Art. 13 of the Conservation of Cultural Heritage Act).

* Editor's note: *see also* 'The Netherlands: Introduction' in Part One.

** Professor, Catholic University of Nijmegen. The author gratefully acknowledges the assistance of the law firm Trenité Van Doorne, Amsterdam with which he was associated during the writing of this Report. Report translated by F. C. Compton.

1. P.J.J. VAN BUUREN and S.C.H. KONING, 'Wet tot Behoud van Cultuurbezit', *Ars Aequi* (1985) p. 86.

Naturally there is the possibility that the private collector has acquired the object on the condition that he would not sell or otherwise dispose of it. In Topic 1 at paragraph 4, we have already mentioned the private law consequences of such a condition.[2]

3. In principle there are no restrictions to the sale or donation of objects of art not classified as a national cultural good. However, the owner must remember that, in some cases, when there is a proven intention to sell, transfer or give away the objects, they may be placed on the List of Protected Objects by means of a summary procedure.

4. As to the question of whether the private collector has the free choice of the country in which the objects of art belonging to him may be situated, if objects of art are listed as protected objects pursuant to the Conservation of Cultural Heritage Act, the owner is not allowed to change the location where the object is situated unless and until his intention to do so has been reported (Art. 7.1 Conservation of Cultural Heritage Act) and the Minister has given permission, or at any rate has made no objection.

2. *See supra* p. 124.

Spain

NATIONAL REPORT ON TOPIC 2. FREEDOM OF COLLECTORS TO SELL OR GIVE AWAY ALL OR PART OF THEIR COLLECTIONS*

Miguel Virgós Soriano**

1. There are no specific rules for collections of works of art. Each of the objects forming part of the collection may be disposed of separately.

Freedom to dispose and autonomy to choose the buyer are the basic policies. The State reserves for itself a right of pre-emption to acquire classified objects under the same conditions agreed with the private buyer (Arts. 40–43 Royal Decree 111/1986).

Freedom to export is severely limited.

Foreigners can acquire as many items of cultural property as they wish. However, some objects cannot leave the country. The law orientates its policy toward the preservation *within* Spain of cultural property. Items of cultural property officially classified as 'of cultural interest' cannot be exported. Objects recorded in the General Inventory of movables of special importance and items of cultural property more than one hundred years old may be exported, whether by its owner for personal purposes or to trade with it, but require a special permit. Obviously, such a permit will be more difficult to obtain in the case of cultural property recorded in the Inventory.[1]

2. In regard to private transactions, the price would be determined by agreement. Foundations are subjected to certain requirements such as authorization, justified appraisal, etc. (*see* Arts. 27, 31 and 33 of the Decree on Private Cultural Foundations 2930/1972).

In regard to sales or gifts to public museums, the object has to be subjected to appraisal by an official expert, normally the Board for the Classification, Appraisal and Export (*see* Art. 8(e) and (f) Royal Decree 111/1986).

3. In regard to selling or giving as a gift an object of art not classified as a

---

* Editor's note: *see also* 'Spain: Introduction' by B. CREMADES in Part One.

** Associate Professor, Facultad de Derecho, Universidad Autónoma de Madrid.

1. *See* J.D. GONZALES CAMPOS and M. VIRGOS SORIANO, 'Law and Practice of International Art Trade in Spain' in ICC Institute, ed., *International Sales of Works of Art/La Vente Internationale d'Oeuvres d'Art* (ICC Publishing/Kluwer, Paris/Deventer 1990) pp. 103–126 at pp. 118–120. *See also* Art. 5 1985 *Ley del Patrimonio Histórico Español.*

'national cultural good', freedom to dispose is the general rule. Freedom to export is partially limited.

Objects of art less than one hundred years old and not recorded in the Inventory, for example, works of living artists, and objects of art legally imported (identified by means of a special import custom form and during ten years from import) are subject to 'free international trade'. Only some formal requirements must be complied with for their export.

Objects more than one hundred years old require a special permit to leave the country (*see* under 1. *supra*).

4. In regard to the question under which conditions a private collector may choose freely the country in which the objects of art will be situated, preservation within Spain of relevant items of cultural property is the basic policy of the Spanish 1985 Law. If the objects of art are less than one hundred years old, or were imported into Spain (within a ten-year limit) the collector has complete freedom.

For any other kind of items of cultural property, the collector will require a special permit. Objects of art classified as property 'of cultural interest', i.e., the most important objects of the Spanish Historical Patrimony, cannot be exported.[2]

2. *Ibid.*

Suisse

RAPPORT NATIONAL SUR LE SUJET 2. LIBERTE DU COLLECTIONNEUR DE DISPOSER DE TOUT OU PARTIE DE SA COLLECTION

Blaise Knapp*

En droit suisse, le droit de commercer et, plus généralement, le droit de vendre des biens, sont régis par trois principes fondamentaux:

a. la liberté du commerce et de l'industrie garantie par l'art. 31 de la Constitution fédérale;
b. la liberté contractuelle qui en découle et qui est le fondement du droit des contrats et des obligations en général;
c. la garantie de la propriété privée qui est affirmée à l'art. 22*ter* de la Constitution.

Bien entendu, ces principes s'appliquent aussi au commerce et à l'aliénation des objets d'art.

Dès lors, en règle générale, les collectionneurs peuvent disposer librement de leurs objets en général et de leurs objets d'art en particulier.

Cependant, la liberté contractuelle peut être limitée soit par des engagements de droit privé auxquels le collectionneur a souscrit, soit par des règles de droit public adoptées pour restreindre la liberté du commerce et de l'industrie et la garantie de la propriété.

La liberté contractuelle du collectionneur propriétaire d'objets d'art peut être limitée par des obligations encourues spontanément par lui. On songera ici p. ex. au propriétaire qui n'est qu'un fiduciaire ou au propriétaire qui a reçu et accepté des biens dans le cadre d'une donation entre vifs ou à cause de mort, complétée par des charges ou qui a bénéficié d'un legs assorti de charges limitant son droit de diposer.

La liberté contractuelle du collectionneur non-propriétaire est bien entendu limitée dans la mesure où ses obligations contractuelles vis-à-vis du propriétaire limitent son pouvoir de disposer. On songera ici notamment à l'usufruitier, au locataire ou à l'acheteur d'oeuvres d'art en leasing.

La liberté contractuelle du collectionneur peut, en outre, être limitée dans le cadre des restrictions à la liberté du commerce et de l'industrie ou à la garantie de la propriété imposées par l'Etat, de sorte que les contrats conclus par les collectionneurs, contraires à ces règles de droit public, sont nuls en vertu de l'art. 20 du Code des obligations.

---

* Professeur, Université de Genève, Faculté de Droit, Genève.

Ces restrictions peuvent porter sur l'utilisation des objets elle-même ou sur certains actes de disposition dans le cadre d'opérations commerciales ou non. On connaît ainsi, d'une part, le classement des objets à protéger et, d'autre part, les limites imposées au commerce des objets ou, plus généralement au droit de disposer en qualité de propriétaire des objets.

En effet, selon la pratique en Suisse, les restrictions concernant le commerce des objets d'art ne peuvent s'appliquer qu'aux personnes faisant profession de commerçants en objets d'art. En revanche, les propriétaires d'objets ne peuvent se voir opposer des limites qu'en dérogation au droit de libre disposition compris dans la garantie de la propriété.

De telles restrictions ne sont cependant opposables au collectionneur que si elles sont valables.

Ceci signifie que les restrictions doivent émaner d'une autorité compétente, avoir été adoptées selon la procédure législative en vigueur, avoir été publiées (validité formelle), trouver un fondement dans la loi, être d'intérêt public et respecter les principes de la proportionnalité, de l'égalité de traitement et du respect de la bonne foi (validité matérielle).

A l'heure actuelle, la question de la protection des biens culturels mobiliers relève de la législation cantonale. Seuls quelques cantons ont adopté des règles concernant la liberté contractuelle des collectionneurs.

Ces limites prévoient une procédure de classement de certains biens dignes de protection. Pour le surplus, les interdictions s'adressent plutôt aux propriétaires qu'aux commerçants d'objets d'art (*voir* à ce sujet notre rapport sur la liberté des musées de procéder à des transactions d'objets d'art *supra* pp.135 *et seq.*). Aussi elles restreignent la liberté de déplacer les objets, confèrent aux collectivités cantonales ou communales la faculté d'exercer un droit de préemption en cas d'aliénation, interdisent l'exportation des objets protégés hors du canton.

Il résulte de cette situation juridique qu'en principe, les collectionneurs peuvent librement vendre ou donner en Suisse ou à l'étranger les objets classés et non-classés mais qu'en revanche, dans certains cantons, certaines ventes et donations d'objets classés ne peuvent avoir lieu valablement que sous réserve d'obtenir une autorisation préalable de l'autorité ou de démontrer que l'autorité a refusé d'exercer son droit de préemption; parfois même l'acte de disposition ne doit pas entraîner l'exportation des biens culturels protégés.

United Kingdom

NATIONAL REPORT ON TOPIC 2. FREEDOM OF COLLECTORS TO SELL OR GIVE AWAY ALL OR PART OF THEIR COLLECTIONS*

Adrian Barr-Smith**

1. In regard to the question whether a private collector may sell or give as a gift all or part of the collection belonging to him but classified as a 'national cultural good', as noted in 'United Kingdom: National Report on Topic 1', *supra*, there is no register of 'national cultural goods'. Customs and Excise restrictions on the movement of goods, and the 'Waverley Criteria' apply to the *export* of goods. Therefore, a collector will face no special difficulty in regard to the sale or gift to (i) a private person of his choice; (ii) an auction house; (iii) a museum of his choice; (iv) a private foundation (charity); or (v) any foreign person, auction house, museum or foundation in any country.

2. In situations (i) to (iv) above, it is likely that the price would be agreed with the assistance of a mutually agreed expert.

In situation (v) above, the sale price would be determined in the same way. However, in the context of valuation for export purposes, the price would be mutually agreed between the vendor on the one hand and the Export Reviewing Committee's expert adviser on the other.

If an object of art is sold to a public collection, then the price is likely to be determined in the same way as between any other vendor and purchaser. This will be the case even if the vendor wishes to take advantage of the tax concessions comprised in the 'acceptance-in-lieu' scheme, whereby an offer of a pre-eminent object can be made by an estate, and the 'special price' can be off-set against inheritance tax. The Export Reviewing Committee is presently recommending modifications to this scheme to make it more attractive.

3. In regard to the question whether a private collector can sell or give as a

* The author acknowledges the invaluable assistance of Angela Jackson and Joshua Drapkin in the production of this material.

** Denton Hall Burgin & Warrens, Solicitors, London. Consistent with our policy when giving comment and advice on a non-specific basis, Denton Hall Burgin & Warrens cannot assume legal responsibility for the accuracy of any particular statement. In the case of specific problems, it is recommended that professional advice be sought.

gift an object of art belonging to him which is not classified as a 'national cultural good' to either a private person of his choice or to an auction house, there are no relevant restrictions on an individual's freedom to deal with property which he owns outright.

If he intends to transfer the property *abroad* either for sale or as a gift then, depending on the value of the object, a full export licence may or may not be required. If a licence is required, then the property will be considered by the expert adviser, who may or may not recommend the object to the Export Reviewing Committee for consideration in the light of the 'Waverley Criteria'.

4. A collector's freedom to move works of art in his possession from one residence to another is subject to the guidelines regarding export outlined above. The Export Reviewing Committee is unwilling to curtail the freedom of a collector to have his property with him wherever he may be and the Committee is presently considering ways of reconciling this freedom with the restrictions placed on the export of works of art.

TOPIC 3. RIGHTS OF ARTISTS AND THEIR HEIRS

DROITS DES CREATEURS ET DE LEURS HERITIERS

Introduction

TOPIC 3: RIGHTS OF ARTISTS AND THEIR HEIRS

This session, which was chaired by *Prof. Pierre Lalive*, introduced for the first time within the framework of this series of Symposia on International Trade in Art, the question of artists' rights.

The session covered the relationships between the artist and the various participants in the art market and examined the impact that the developments in this market during recent years, such as record prices and rapid turnover, have had on the position of artists.

The replies to the Questionnaire depicted the great variety in national laws defining the nature and scope of the rules concerning the protection of artists and led to the conclusion that there is no uniform legal regime for the protection of artists. This was particularly evident from the diverse legal regimes governing rights of authors or copyrights and *droit de suite* described in the National Reports, and was supported by the description of practices existing today in various countries in the field of artists' rights management.

Ms. Jacqueline de Jong, an established internationally known artist and *Mr. Blek*, a young artist starting his international career opened the session with accounts of their experiences in coping with problems of artists' rights, particularly those created by the evolution of national and international art markets.

Two other participants in the art market then presented their experiences: *Mr. Jean-Marc Gutton*, the administrator of an artists' rights collecting society (*see infra*, pp. 329–339) and *Mr. Richard Crewdson*, as a representative of the point of view of art galleries (*see infra*, pp. 341–346). Both emphasized the lack of institutions providing advice to artists and their heirs concerning the management of their relationships with museums and galleries. This problem is even more complex when examined at the international level because of the lack of conformity in national laws concerning *droit d'auteur* or copyrights. *Prof. Jean-Louis Bismuth* described a number of the legal aspects of these rights (see *infra*, pp. 193–220). Despite the fact that some laws converge on certain points, complex legal situations arise, for example, when an international inheritance must be organized. He also described the distortions existing regarding the free circulation of works of art within the European Community, due to the differences in national rules, in particular, in regard to the (non-) existence of the *droit de suite* (right to proceeds from sub-sequent transactions) and variations in moral rights.

There was general concern about, and criticism of the current situation, as well as general agreement among the panelists on the desirability of harmonizing the various legal regimes. Nevertheless, there was no agreement concerning the substantive rules to be adopted to achieve such a harmonization, in particular in regard to the *droit de suite*. Some panelists suggested that it be eliminated; others were in favour of it being maintained, sometimes on the condition that it be modified.

The general discussion showed that due to the complex international legal issues arising from the protection of artists and their heirs, such persons need legal advisors, but generally lack the financial resources to pay them.

List of Participants in Discussion

First Discussion
Philippe Kahn (France)
Javier Gutierrez Vicen (Spain)
Jean Chatelain (France)
Th. Weyland (Netherlands)
Elwood A. Rickless (United Kingdom)
Henri Carpentier (Canada)

Second Discussion
Jane Gregory Rubin (United States)
John Henry Merryman (United States)
Mariette Prinze (Belgium)
Ignaz Seidl-Hohenveldern (Austria)
Joe Och (United Kingdom)
Christian Wegenius (Sweden)
Philippe Simmonot (France)

General Report

Rapport Général

SUJECT 3. DROITS DES CREATEURS ET DE LEURS HERITIERS

Jean-Louis Bismuth*

L'examen des différents rapports complété par l'analyse des réglementations nationales de propriété littéraire et artistique aide à dresser un tableau des convergences et des divergences entre lois étatiques, en ce qui concerne tant les droits des artistes (I.) que ceux de leurs héritiers (II.).

I. LES DROITS DES ARTISTES

Une rapide synthèse de droit comparé commande d'opérer une distinction entre les droits pécuniaires (1.) et le droit moral (2.) des artistes.

1. LES DROITS PÉCUNIAIRES DES ARTISTES

Un examen comparé des législations nationales relatives au droit d'auteur aide à dresser l'état des convergences et des divergences existant entre ces législations.

Le constat de convergence a trait aux rapports entre les droits pécuniaires des artistes et le droit de propriété sur les oeuvres d'art (*A.*); le constat de divergence intéresse, quant à lui, le contenu des droits pécuniaires des artistes (*B.*).

A. Constat de convergence: Les rapports entre droits pécuniaires des artistes et droit de propriété sur les oeuvres d'art

Il importe d'apprécier la portée de ce phénomène (i.) puis d'en souligner la limite (ii.).

i. Portée de la convergence

Elle se trouve illustrée par deux solutions concernant l'une, l'indépendance des droits pécuniaires par rapport à la propriété de l'oeuvre d'art (*a.*),

* Professeur Agrégé, Faculté de droit, Université de Paris XI; Avocat à la Cour de Paris; Associé Jeantet et Associés Paris.

l'autre, le droit de représentation de l'artiste après aliénation de son oeuvre (*b.*).

a. Indépendance des droits pécuniaires de l'artiste par rapport à la propriété de l'oeuvre d'art

La plupart, sinon la totalité, des lois nationales sur le droit d'auteur affirme l'indépendance des droits pécuniaires des artistes par rapport à la propriété de l'objet matériel incorporant l'oeuvre d'art. Ainsi, l'art. 29 al. 1 de la loi française du 11 mars 1957 affirme-t-il: 'la propriété incorporelle est indépendante de la propriété de l'objet matériel'.[1]

Cette règle dite d'indépendance est également affirmée, entre autres:

- en droit belge, comme l'illustre l'art. 19 de la loi belge du 22 mars 1886 cité dans leur rapport par Messieurs Coppens et Strowell,[2]
- en droit suisse, ainsi qu'en témoigne l'art. 9 al. 3 de la loi fédérale du 7 décembre 1922 signalé par Monsieur Perret dans sa contribution,[3]
- par l'art. 3 de la loi espagnole du 11 novembre 1987 et l'art. 10 de la loi portugaise de 1985.[4]

Elle se trouve également posée à l'art. 202 du Copyright Act des Etats-Unis, ainsi que l'indique le rapport de Monsieur Karlen.[5]

La conséquence que les lois nationales tirent de la règle dite d'indépendance est la suivante: le transfert de la propriété de l'oeuvre d'art, par l'effet d'un acte de disposition à titre gratuit (donation) ou à titre onéreux (vente), n'entraîne pas, *ipso facto*, au profit du nouveau propriétaire de l'oeuvre d'art, transfert des droits pécuniaires.

Cette solution, ainsi exprimée à l'art. 29 de la loi française et l'art. 9 de la loi helvétique[6] – qui fait l'objet dans certaines législations nationales d'une

1. Sur cette disposition, cf. not. H. DESBOIS, *le Droit d' Auteur en France* (Dalloz, 3ème éd. 1978) n° 310 *et seq.*, p. 402 *et seq.*; P. SIRINELLI, *Le Droit moral de l'auteur et le Droit commun des contrats* (Thèse Paris II) p. 438 *et seq.*
2. Rapport de Ph. COPPENS et A. STROWELL, II.2.b.i.
3. Rapport suisse de F. PERRET, I.*3*.
4. Art. 3–1° de la loi espagnole sur la propriété intellectuelle, n° 22 du 11 novembre 1987, *Revue Internationale du Droit d'Auteur* (RIDA) Tome 1988, n° 138, pp. 332 *et seq.*; sur cette loi, A. DELGADO, 'La nueva ley espanola sobre propriedad intelectual', RIDA octobre 1988, n° 138, p. 199 *et seq.*; art. 10–1 du code portugais du droit d'auteur et des droits voisins (tel que modifié par le Décret-loi n° 63/85 du 14 mars 1985 et par la loi modificative n° 45/85 du 17 septembre 1985, RIDA, juillet 1986, n° 129, p. 194 *et seq.* (ci-après dénommée la loi portugaise); sur cette nouvelle législation, L. F. REBELLO, 'La nouvelle législation portugaise sur le droit d'auteur', RIDA, juillet 1986, n° 129, p. 3 *et seq.*
5. Rapport P. H. KARLEN, II.
6. Ainsi, l'art. 29 al. 2 de la loi française du 11 mars 1957 énonce-t-il que l'acquéreur de l'objet matériel 'n'est investi, du fait de cette acquisition, d'aucun des droits prévus par la présente loi...'; pour sa part, l'art. 9 al. 3 de la loi helvétique – reproduit par F. PERRET dans son rapport (I.3) – dispose que 'sauf convention contraire, le transfert de la propriété d'un exemplaire d'une oeuvre n'entraîne pas celui du droit d'auteur, même s'il s'agit de l'exemplaire original'.

exception expresse, lorsque l'oeuvre d'art est un portrait[7] – soulève une question: quels sont les attributs pécuniaires du droit d'auteur dont le transfert de l'oeuvre d'art n'emporte pas cession automatique en faveur du nouveau propriétaire de ladite oeuvre?

Si on laisse de côté le droit de suite, attribut pécuniaire – évoqué plus loin – qui est au coeur d'une divergence majeure entre lois nationales,[8] les prérogatives patrimoniales des artistes se regroupent, dans la plupart des réglementations étatiques, autour de deux droits pécuniaires: le droit de représentation, le droit de reproduction *lato sensu* (dans la mesure où la notion de droit de reproduction n'a pas, ainsi qu'il sera souligné ci-dessous,[9] le même contenu, selon les Etats en cause).

Précisément la règle dite d'indépendance ne joue pas, dans nombre de législations nationales, lorsqu'est en cause le droit de représentation.

b. Le droit de représentation de l'artiste après aliénation de son oeuvre

Les droits étatiques examinés dans le cadre du présent colloque, se signalent ici par une même position: sous réserve d'une convention spécifique entre l'artiste et l'acquéreur de l'oeuvre d'art, l'artiste se trouve dépouillé du droit de représentation, à partir du moment où il a aliéné la propriété de son oeuvre.

Monsieur Karlen est, à cet égard, très clair, s'agissant du droit américain.[10] La même solution prévaut aux Pays-Bas, en Belgique et en Suisse;[11] bien que la question n'ait pas été clairement débattue, le droit français adopte, semble-t-il, une position identique.[12]

Il reste que certains ont réclamé la reconnaissance au profit de l'artiste d'un droit de représentation (parfois dénommé 'droit de monstration') à l'égard des oeuvres d'art s'incorporant dans les collections publiques et ce,

7. Sur cette question, *v.* ainsi, rapport belge de Ph. COPPENS et A. STROWEL (II.2.b.i et n.53) citant en ce sens l'art. 20 al. 2 de la loi belge du 22 mars 1886; arts. 19 et 20 de la loi néerlandaise sur le droit d'auteur du 23 septembre 1912, sur lesquels, rapport A. A. QUAEDVLIEG, I.*13*; art. 60 de la loi allemande du 9 septembre 1965; art. 55 de la loi autrichienne du 9 avril 1936.
8. *V. infra* pp. 202 *et seq.*
9. *V. infra* pp. 199–200.
10. Rapport P. H. KARLEN, II: 'Without a contractual promise, once the artist sells the work, she cannot demand its return for exhibition purposes.'
11. Rapport néerlandais de A. A. QUAEDVLIEG, II.*4*, rapport belge Ph. COPPENS et A. STROWEL, II.2.c et n. 101, rapport suisse de F. PERRET, I.*3*.a; F. PERRET signale toutefois (I.*3*.a) que sous l'empire de la loi fédérale actuelle, la question de savoir si l'aliénation de l'exemplaire original de l'oeuvre constitue un acte de publicité suffisant, entraînant la perte pour l'auteur de son droit exclusif d'exposer l'oeuvre, paraît être l'objet d'une controverse doctrinale; le rapporteur suisse précise toutefois (II.*3*.b) que le projet de révision de la loi fédérale actuelle établi par la 3ème Commission d'experts en date du 18 décembre 1987 avait prévu à l'art. 15 al. 3 de son projet que sauf convention contraire, le propriétaire d'un exemplaire d'une oeuvre d'art est en droit de l'exposer publiquement, même lorsque ladite oeuvre n'a pas encore été rendue publique; mais F. PERRET d'indiquer que le projet de révision du Conseil Fédéral du 19 juin 1989 n'a pas retenu la solution préconisée par la 3ème Commission d'experts.
12. *V.* à cet égard, H. DESBOIS, *op cit.*, n° 259, p. 329.

pour compenser la privation du droit de suite infligée, en pareil cas, aux artistes; de fait, une oeuvre se trouve soustraite au commerce juridique, dès l'instant où elle entre dans les collections publiques,[13] ce qui prive alors le droit de suite des artistes de toute portée pratique.

Un pays – dont la législation ne fait pas partie de la législation étatique étudiée à l'occasion du présent colloque – se démarque par sa position spécifique: le Canada.

En effet, la loi canadienne du 8 juin 1988 institue au profit des artistes un droit de présentation au public de leurs oeuvres à l'occasion d'expositions publiques;[14] la portée pratique de cette réforme est, néanmoins, restreinte par une règle transitoire, en vertu de laquelle le droit de présentation mis en place ne joue que pour les oeuvres créées à partir de l'entrée en vigueur de la législation du 8 juin 1988.[15]

La solution selon laquelle l'aliénation de l'oeuvre d'art a pour effet de dépouiller l'artiste du droit de représentation sur l'oeuvre revêt une double signification.

D'un côté, l'artiste ne peut pas exiger de la personne devenue propriétaire de l'oeuvre d'art accès à ladite oeuvre, en vue d'une exposition publique de celle-ci; c'est ce qu'illustre notamment une décision néerlandaise signalée par Monsieur Quaedvlieg dans son rapport.[16]

L'on mesure par là-même, l'ingérence – à laquelle la plupart des législations nationales n'a pas consenti – dans le droit de propriété des oeuvres d'art qu'impliquerait l'existence d'un droit de 'monstration'.

Dans sa contribution relative au droit suisse, Monsieur Perret signale que le projet de réforme émanant de la 3ème Commission d'Experts a toutefois reconnu à l'artiste le droit d'accès à l'oeuvre pour une exposition publique; mais Monsieur Perret de préciser qu'une telle suggestion n'a pas été reprise dans le projet de réforme par le Conseil Fédéral.[17]

De l'autre, l'exposition publique de l'oeuvre d'art par le propriétaire de celle-ci ne se trouve par subordonnée au consentement de l'artiste ou au versement d'une rémunération au profit de ce dernier.

C'est ce qui ressort ainsi des dispositions de l'art. 23 de la loi néerlandaise du 23 septembre 1912.[18]

---

13. Sur ce point, *v.* not. J. CHATELAIN, *Administration et Gestion des musées, Manuel de l'Ecole du Louvre* (1987, La Documentation Française) p. 279 *et seq*.
14. *V.* paragraphe 3.1.g du Copyright Act tel que modifié par la loi du 8 juin 1988, RIDA, octobre 1989, n° 142, p. 406 et spéc. p. 407.
15. Cette règle transitoire a été critiquée par V. NABHAN, 'Coup d'oeil sur les modifications à la loi sur le droit d'auteur au Canada', RIDA, octobre 1989, n° 142, p. 175 et spéc. pp. 183–185.
16. Rapport néerlandais A. A. QUAEDVLIEG (II.*4*) citant une décision rendue par le Président de la Cour de District de Leeuwarden du 15 décembre 1971 confirmée par un arrêt de la Cour d'Appel de Leeuwarden du 14 juin 1972.
17. Rapport suisse F. PERRET (II.*3*.b).
18. L'art. 23 de la loi néerlandaise su le droit d'auteur du 23 septembre 1912 dispose en effet que 'sauf convention contraire, le propriétaire d'une oeuvre de dessin, de peinture, d'architecture, de sculpture, ou des arts appliqués est autorisé à l'exposer publiquement ou à la reproduire dans un catalogue, sans le consentement du titulaire du droit d'auteur et ce, en vue de la vente'.

Messieurs Coppens et Strowel signalent pourtant, dans leur rapport de droit belge, une exception à la solution selon laquelle l'aliénation de l'oeuvre d'art dépouille l'artiste de son droit de représentation: il s'agit de celle que dictent, en cas de représentation télévisuelle de l'oeuvre d'art, les dispositions de l'art. 11 bis al. 1 de la Convention de Berne; et les auteurs d'illustrer ladite exception en évoquant l'exemple de la diffusion à la télévision flamande, au cours de l'année 1972, d'un concert dans la grande salle du Casino de Knokke le Zout dont les murs avaient été peints par l'artiste belge Magritte.[19]

Le constat de convergence entre réglementations nationales que l'étude des relations entre droits pécuniaires des artistes et droit de propriété sur l'oeuvre d'art permet de vérifier, se heurte à une limite qu'il convient présentement d'exposer.

ii. Limite de la convergence

Cette limite intèresse le droit de reproduction de l'artiste après aliénation de son oeuvre; le point est ici plus exactement de savoir si l'artiste jouit d'un droit d'accès à son oeuvre, une fois celle-ci aliénée, en vue de l'exercice de son droit de reproduction.

La reconnaissance au profit de l'artiste d'un tel droit d'accès est posée à l'art. 25 de la loi allemande du 9 septembre 1965.[20] Monsieur Lohaus, dans son rapport, fait, à cet égard, état d'une décision allemande du 8 décembre 1983, mettant en oeuvre le droit d'accès de l'artiste en vue de l'exercice du droit de reproduction, dans une espèce concernant les masques mortuaires de Max Liebermann.[21]

L'art. 14 – 7° de la loi espagnole de 1987 reconnaît de même à l'artiste un même droit d'accès.[22]

Le droit français se signale par une solution identique, encore que l'art. 29 al. 3 de la loi du 11 mars 1957 – texte qui ne paraît avoir suscité aucune jurisprudence – ne prévoie le droit d'accès de l'artiste, que dans l'hypothèse d'un abus notoire du propriétaire de l'oeuvre d'art,[23] ce qui semble bien témoigner du souci de cantonner la restriction au droit de propriété sur

19. Rapport belge Ph. COPPENS et A. STROWEL, (II.*2*.c et n.103.)
20. De fait, l'art. 25 de la loi allemande du 9 septembre 1965 précise que 'l'auteur peut exiger que le possesseur de l'original ou d'une reproduction de son oeuvre lui donne accès auprès de cet original ou de cette reproduction, dans la mesure où cela est nécessaire pour la réalisation de reproductions ou pour des arrangements de l'oeuvre et pour autant que cela ne lèse pas les intérêts légitimes du possesseur'.
21. La décision du 8 décembre 1983 subordonne toutefois l'exercice du droit d'accès de l'artiste à son oeuvre à la souscription par celui-ci d'une police d'assurance en vue de couvrir le risque de détérioration de l'oeuvre.
22. L'art. 14-7° de la loi espagnole du 11 novembre 1987 précise toutefois en son al. 2 que le droit d'accès ainsi reconnu à l'auteur 'ne permet pas d'exiger le déplacement de l'oeuvre' et cette même disposition de poursuivre: 'l'accès à (l'oeuvre) s'effectuera au lieu et sous la forme qui occasionnent le moins d'inconvénients au détenteur, lequel sera indemnisé, le cas échéant pour tout dommage ou préjudice qui lui est causé'; cprer., sur ce dernier point, la décision allemande du 8 décembre 1983 citée *supra* n. 21.
23. *V.* ainsi, Cl. COLOMBET, *Propriété littéraire et artistique et droits voisins* Dalloz, 4ème Edition 1988) n° 157, p. 171.

l'oeuvre d'art que postule, par nature, le droit d'accès de l'artiste à son oeuvre.

Ce droit d'accès, bien qu'il ne soit pas expressément visé par la loi fédérale de 1912, est, note Monsieur Perret, reconnu par la doctrine suisse comme un complément nécessaire du droit de reproduction.[24]

La prérogative de l'artiste ici examinée n'est pas, en revanche, consacrée par le droit belge; Messieurs Coppens et Strowel signalent toutefois, dans leur contribution, que la proposition de loi belge dite proposition Lallemand suggère d'instituer de manière explicite un tel droit d'accès.[25]

La position du droit néerlandais concernant ce droit est, par contre, plus nuancée, ainsi que le mentionne Monsieur Quaedvlieg dans son rapport de droit néerlandais; celui-ci indique, en effet, qu'il n'existe pas, dans ce droit, une règle prescrivant d'imposer au propriétaire de l'oeuvre d'art le droit d'accès dont il est présentement question.[26]

Pour sa part, la position du droit américain apparaît plus tranchée; Monsieur Karlen souligne ainsi que l'artiste, même s'il conserve, par l'effet de la règle dite d'indépendance, analysée plus haut,[27] le droit de reproduction sur son oeuvre, n'est plus en mesure de l'exercer, dès lors que le propriétaire de l'oeuvre d'art lui refuse l'accès à ladite oeuvre.[28]

Perceptible lorsque sont en cause les relations entre les droits pécuniaires des artistes et le droit de propriété sur l'oeuvre d'art, la divergence entre les lois nationales de droit d'auteur s'accentue, dès l'instant où l'on s'attache à une étude de droit comparé prenant pour cible le contenu des droits pécuniaires.

B. Constat de divergence entre lois nationales: le contenu des droits pécuniaires des artistes

Ce constat de divergence, déjà sensible, s'agissant du droit de reproduction (i.), prend un relief plus marqué, lorsque l'on s'attache à l'étude du droit de suite (ii.).

i. Le droit de reproduction

Cette prérogative pécuniaire, traditionnellement présentée comme un attribut mineur, revêt présentement une plus grande importance du fait de la prolifération de différents supports matériels, qu'il s'agisse ainsi des cata-

---

24. Rapport suisse F. PERRET, II et les références doctrinales citées.
25. Rapport belge Ph. COPPENS et A. STROWEL, II.*2*.d; sur cette proposition de loi Lallemand, cf. C. DOUTRELEPONT, 'Une proposition de révision de la loi belge du 22 mars 1986', RIDA, octobre 1987, n° 134, p. 71 *et seq*.
26. Rapport néerlandais A. A. QUAEDVLIEG, II.*1*.a.
27. Cf. *supra* pp. 194–195.
28. Ph. KARLEN explique dans son rapport (II) que cette solution est dictée par les dispositions de l'art. 109 du Copyright Act du 19 octobre 1976; sur cet art. 109, cf. not F. POLLAUD-DULIAN, *Le droit de destination, Le sort des exemplaires en droit d'auteur* (Bibl. Dr. priv., T. 205, LGDJ 1989) n° 368 *et seq*., p. 308 *et seq*.

logues diffusés en vue de la vente d'oeuvres d'art, de l'édition d'ouvrages de vulgarisation à l'usage de touristes, de livres d'érudition (ayant trait notamment à l'histoire de l'art), de biographies d'artistes, de collections proposées à des consommateurs sous forme de fiches et de cartes reproduisant des oeuvres d'art.

L'essor que connaît ainsi le droit de reproduction ne peut que venir renforcer l'intérêt pratique des divergences opposant les législations de droit d'auteur; ces divergences concernent, entre autres, la notion de droit de reproduction (*a.*), les exceptions au droit de reproduction (*b.*).

a. La notion de droit de reproduction

Les réglementations nationales se scindent ici en deux groupes: relèvent en particulier du premier groupe la loi française et la loi belge; ces deux législations optent, en effet, pour une conception large et synthétique du droit de reproduction; conception en vertu de laquelle, en effet, le droit de reproduction, ce dernier ne recouvrant uniquement que la fixation matérielle mise en circulation et les modes de distribution desdits supports.[29]

La conséquence attachée à une telle acception du droit de reproduction est que la prérogative de l'artiste ou de son ayant-droit ayant pour objet la mise en circulation des exemplaires de l'oeuvre ne peut pas s'épuiser, dans la mesure où elle se rattache à un droit – le droit de reproduction – lequel ne s'épuise pas aussi longtemps qu'il n'est pas tombé dans le domaine public.[30]

Le nombre des législations nationales relevant du second groupe est bien plus important. Ressortissent, en effet, au second groupe, une multitude de pays, tels que l'Allemagne Fédérale, les Pays-Bas, le Royaume Uni, le Danemark, l'Espagne, la Suisse, l'Autriche, la Suède, la Norvège, la Finlande, l'Islande, les Etats Unis.[31]

Ces Etats se caractérisent, de fait, par une conception étroite du droit de reproduction, ce dernier ne recouvrant uniquement que la fixation matérielle de l'oeuvre, c'est-à-dire la fabrication des exemplaires de celle-ci.

Il s'ensuit que c'est en vertu d'un droit pécuniaire – le plus souvent dénommé droit de distribution – distinct du droit de reproduction *stricto sensu* que l'artiste ou son ayant-droit sera habilité à mettre les exemplaires de l'oeuvre à la disposition du public.

Il n'y aurait sans doute pas de différence significative entre les deux groupes de législations, si celles qui consacrent l'existence d'un droit de distribution autonome par rapport au droit de reproduction n'affectaient pas ce droit d'un terme extinctif fixé généralement au moment de la première vente de l'exemplaire.

De fait, dès qu'un exemplaire est mis pour la première fois en circulation

29. *V.* en ces sens not. F. POLLAUD-DULIAN, *op. cit.*, n° 103 *et seq.*, p. III *et seq.*, n° 158 *et seq.*, p. 156, *et seq.*
30. *V.* en ce sens not. F. POLLAUD-DULIAN, *op. cit.*, n° 158, p. 156; n° 329, p. 284.
31. Sur une analyse de ces différentes législations, cf. not. F. POLLAUD-DULIAN, *op. cit.*, n° 335 *et seq.*, p. 290 *et seq.*, n° 439 *et seq.*, p. 347 *et seq.*

(dans la plupart des cas sous forme d'une vente), le droit de distribution s'épuise en tant qu'il prend pour cible ledit exemplaire.[32]

Mieux encore, l'épuisement du droit de distribution jouera dans certains pays, même si la première mise en circulation de l'exemplaire de l'oeuvre d'art se localise en dehors des frontières de l'Etat en cause; autrement dit, le droit de distribution fera, en pareil cas, l'objet d'un épuisement international.

C'est le cas des législations en vigueur dans les pays scandinaves;[33] une même solution prévaut en Suisse, ainsi que le souligne Monsieur Perret dans son rapport.[34]

La portée juridique de la règle de l'épuisement international du droit de distribution peut être mesurée à la lumière de l'exemple suivant: un ouvrage ayant pour thème la biographie d'une artiste est édité en France; cette biographie renferme des reproductions de toiles autorisées en France par ceux qui sont titulaires du droit de reproduction *lato sensu*, à savoir des héritiers de l'artiste et/ou éventuellement une société française de gestion des droits d'auteur; l'ouvrage en question est ultérieurement importé en Suisse; en application de la règle sus-évoquée, en vigueur en Suisse, d'épuisement international, le droit de distribution, tel que défini et régi par le droit suisse, a été épuisé à l'égard des exemplaires de l'ouvrage mis en circulation pour la première fois en France, il s'ensuit que les héritiers de l'artiste et/ou le cas échéant, une société suisse de gestion des droits d'auteur n'ont pas à consentir à la vente en Suisse desdits exemplaires.

b. Les exceptions au droit de reproduction

Deux séries de situations, en autres, sont le siège d'une divergence entre les lois nationales: l'hypothèse des oeuvres d'art situées dans des lieux publics (§1.); celle des catalogues d'exposition ou de vente aux enchères publiques (§2.).

§1. Les oeuvres d'art situées dans des lieux publics

Le point de savoir si de telles oeuvres d'art donnent prise au droit de reproduction est à l'origine d'une divergence perceptible.

Sous l'empire de certaines législations, le simple fait que l'oeuvre d'art soit située dans un lieu public rend pleinement licite sa reproduction sans le consentement de l'auteur ou de ses ayant droits; il en est ainsi en droit

32. Sur l'examen de la théorie et de la pratique de l'épuisement du droit de distribution en Allemagne, cf. F. POLLAUD-DULIAN, *op. cit.*, n° 439 *et seq.*, p. 347 *et seq.*; sur la règle de l'épuisement du droit intellectuel, cf. B. CASTELL, *L'épuisement du droit intellectuel en droits allemand, français et communautaire* (PUF 1989).

33. Sur ces législations, cf. not. F. POLLAUD-DULIAN, *op. cit.*, n° 349 *et seq.*, p. 296 *et seq.* spéc. n° 356 *et seq.*, p. 299 *et seq.*

34. Rapport suisse F. PERRET, II.4a; adde, F. POLLAUD-DULIAN, *op. cit.*, n° 336 *et seq.*, p. 290 *et seq.*

espagnol et en droit allemand;[35] selon d'autres législations, la reproduction sans le consentement de l'auteur n'est licite que si l'oeuvre d'art n'est pas l'élément essentiel de la reproduction, solution qui est celle du droit néerlandais, du droit belge, du droit français.[36]

§2. Les catalogues d'exposition ou de vente aux enchères publiques

Ils constituent un autre foyer de divergence.

Dans certains pays, en effet, la règle est la libre reproduction sans le consentement de l'auteur ou de ses ayant droits des oeuvres d'art reproduites dans lesdits catalogues. Telle est la solution qui prévaut aux Pays Bas, en Allemagne, Suisse et avec quelques nuances en Autriche.[37] La règle de la libre reproduction n'était pas en revanche clairement admise en France jusqu'au 22 janvier 1991.[38]

---

35. L'art. 35 de la loi espagnole du 11 novembre 1987 dispose que 'les oeuvres situées de façon permanente dans des parcs, des rues, des places ou d'autres voies publiques peuvent être reproduites, distribuées et communiquées librement au moyen de peintures, de dessins, de photograhies, et de procédés audiovisuels'; dans le même sens, l'art. 59 de la loi allemande du 9 septembre 1965 considère 'comme licite la reproduction, par le moyen de la peinture ou du dessin, par la photographie ou par la cinématographie, des oeuvres qui se trouvent de façon permanente sur des voies, des rues ou des places publiques...'.
36. Cf. rapport néerlandais A. A. QUAEDVLIEG, I.*12* et la jurisprudence citée; rapport belge Ph. COPPENS et A. STROWEL, II.*2*.b.i et les références citées ns. 56 à 59; adde s'agissant du droit français, H. DESBOIS, *op cit.*, n° 255, p. 323–325, commentant en particulier un jugement rendu par le Tribunal Civil de Mirecourt du 10 juillet 1924 (publié in D. H. 1924.680); cf. également le très récent arrêt rendu par la lère Chambre de la Cour de Paris le 23 octobre 1990 (dont un extrait a été notamment publié, in J.C.P. 1990, éd. E. I. 20567) considérant comme justifiée la condamnation pour contrefaçon de sociétés ayant commercialisé des cartes postales représentant 'La Géode' sans autorisation de la Cité des Sciences et de l'Industrie, chargée de sa gestion et cessionnaire des droits d'auteur de l'architecte; l'arrêt, pour ce faire, souligne, entre autres, que la loi française du 11 mars 1957 relative aux droits d'auteur 'n'ayant prévu aucune disposition venant restreindre la protection des droits relatifs aux oeuvres d'art situées dans un lieu accessible au public, il appartient en conséquence aux seuls titulaires de ces droits de consentir à leur reproduction'; dans cette espèce, contrairement à celle à l'origine du jugement rendu le 10 juillet 1924 par le Tribunal Civil de Mirecourt, le monument constituait bien l'élément central de la reproduction.
37. Art. 23 de la loi néerlandaise du 23 septembre 1912 (cité par A. A. QUAEDVLIEG I.*14*); art. 58 de la loi allemande du 9 septembre 1965; art. 54–2 de la loi autrichienne du 9 avril 1936 qui admet la licéité de la reproduction des oeuvres d'art dans des catalogues, à la condition que ces derniers soient 'diffusés gratuitement ou à un prix n'excédant pas (leur) prix de revient'.
38. L'arrêt rendu par la lère Chambre civile de la Cour de Cassation le 13 avril 1988 (sur lequel cf. M. VIVANT, 'Pour une compréhension nouvelle de la notion de courte citation en droit d'auteur'; J. C. P. 1989, éd. G. I 3372; adde B. EDELMAN, 'Chronique de propriété littéraire et artistique', J. C. P. 1989, éd. G, I 3376 n° 12) paraît bien militer en faveur de la solution selon laquelle la reproduction d'oeuvres d'art dans les catalogues donne prise aux droits de reproduction; cet arrêt casse, en effet, un arrêt rendu par la Cour de Paris le 13 mai 1986 (in B. EDELMAN, 'Chronique de propriété littéraire et artistique', J. C. P. 1987, éd. G, I 3312 n° 17–20 et Annexe 4) pour avoir estimé qu'un ouvrage pouvait licitement reproduire 16 poinçons dessinés à la plume (au motif notamment que le nombre des reproductions incriminées, étant infime par rapport à celles que renfermait l'ouvrage contrefait, était assimilable à une courte citation), dès lors que chacun des dessins reproduits, 'qui constituaient en eux-mêmes des oeuvres protégées par la loi du 11 mars 1957, faisait l'objet d'une reproduction intégrale qui ne pouvait s'analyser comme une courte citation'. Cass. Civ. I 22 janvier 1991, D. 1991 I.R. 47.

De fait, la question de savoir si les catalogues d'exposition de vente aux enchères publiques peuvent licitement renfermer, sans le consentement de l'auteur ou de ses ayant droit, des reproductions d'oeuvre d'art est à l'origine d'une divergence récente de position que la Cour de Cassation vient de trancher le 22 janvier 1991, en condamnant explicitement la règle de libre reproduction (*v.* note 38), entre la première Chambre et la quatrième Chambre de la Cour de Paris, ainsi que l'illustrent les arrêts respectivement rendus, dans deux espèces qui concernaient des catalogues renfermant des reproductions de toiles d'Utrillo, les 20 mars 1989 et 3 juillet 1989.[39]

Déjà perceptibles au stade du droit de reproduction, les divergences entre lois nationales relatives au droit d'auteur s'aggravent, lorsque l'on s'attache à l'examen de cet autre attribut pécunaire du droit de l'artiste que constitue le droit de suite.

ii. Le droit de suite

Le droit de suite qui est au coeur des préoccupations essentielles du commerce international des oeuvres d'art peut être défini comme le droit de l'auteur d'une oeuvre graphique ou plastique et des héritiers de celui-ci de participer au produit de toutes ventes de l'oeuvre d'art en cause.[40]

L'on sait que la raison traditionnellement avancée pour justifier le droit de suite réside:

- dans le faible intérêt pécuniaire que le droit de reproduction représenterait pour l'artiste, spécialement lorsqu'il n'a pas atteint un certain degré de notoriété,
- et dans la nécessité corrélative d'associer l'artiste et ses héritiers aux plus-values importantes que les oeuvres de l'artiste peuvent être appelées à accuser, bien après le moment où l'artiste les aura aliénées.

L'explication qui précède[41] – dont l'on peut d'ailleurs se demander si le développement, évoqué plus haut, du droit de reproduction[42] n'en atténue pas la force – n'a pas pour autant conduit, loin s'en faut, à une large reconnaissance par les législations nationales relatives au droit d'auteur.

De fait, ce qui constitue une première divergence, le droit de suite n'existe pas dans nombre d'Etats, tels que les Pays-Bas, la Suisse, le Royaume Uni, les Etats-Unis (à l'exception de la Californie), la Suède,

39. Sur ces deux arrêts, cf. not B. EDELMAN, 'Chronique de propriété littéraire et artistique', J. C. P. 1990, éd. G, I 3433 n° 10–13.
40. Sur le droit de suite dans la loi française, cf. not. H. DESBOIS, *op. cit.*, n° 289 *et seq.*, p. 374 *et seq.*; Cl. COLOMBET, *op. cit.*, n° 206 *et seq.*, p. 210 *et seq.*
41. Cf. *supra* p. 202 (ii).
42. Cf. *supra* pp. 198–199.

l'Autriche, la Grèce,[43] alors qu'il a été introduit dans d'autres Etats, comme la France, la Belgique, l'Italie, l'Allemagne, l'Espagne, le Portugal et, outre atlantique, l'Etat de Californie.[44]

Il ne faut pas pour autant croire que le droit de suite obéit, dans l'ensemble des législations qui le consacrent, aux mêmes règles; des divergences existent qui gravitent, entres autres, autour du domaine (*a.*) et du régime (*b.*) du droit de suite.

a. Domaine du droit de suite

La délimitation du champ d'application du droit de suite peut être entreprise à un double point de vue: quant aux oeuvres d'art couvertes par le droit de suite (§1.); quant aux opérations donnant prise au droit de suite (§2.)

§1. Oeuvres d'art couvertes par le droit de suite

Si l'on excepte la question spécifique des manuscrits d'oeuvres littéraires et artistiques,[45] la délimitation du domaine matériel du droit de suite impose de définir la notion d'oeuvre originale, dans la mesure où ce n'est qu'à l'égard d'une telle oeuvre que le droit de suite se conçoit et a vocation à jouer; c'est ce que, d'ailleurs, rappellent expressément les lois française, allemande, italienne, portugaise de même que le Code civil californien.[46]

Mais la notion d'oeuvre originale soulève précisément une difficulté pratique, s'agissant des gravures, tapisseries et sculptures.

Pour les gravures, c'est la planche que l'artiste a burinée qui porte l'empreinte de sa personnalité; pour les tapisseries et les sculptures, ce sont

---

43. Rapport néerlandais A. A. QUAEDVLIEG. II.*3* et les références citées n. 31 (rapporteur indiquant que la question du droit de suite a fait l'objet aux Pays Bas d'un débat qui n'a toutefois pas abouti à l'introduction d'un tel droit dans la législation néerlandaise); rapport suisse F. PERRET, II.*9* (M. PERRET soulignant à cet égard que la 3ème Commission d'experts, chargée d'établir un projet de révision de la loi fédérale sur les droits d'auteur du 7 décembre 1922 n'a pas donné suite à la requête formulée par la Société des peintres, sculpteurs et architectes suisses invitant ladite Commission à introduire le droit de suite dans son projet); rapport anglais A. BARR-SMITH, paragraphe 1; rapport américain P.H. KARLEN, II; rapport suédois C.H. WEGENIUS; rapport autrichien I. SEIDL-HOHENVELDERN; rapport grec. A. DIMOLITSA, 3.

44. Art. 42 de la loi française du 11 mars 1957; loi belge du 21 juin 1921 complétée par l'arrêté royal du 23 septembre 1921; sur ces deux textes, cf. rapport belge Ph. COPPENS et A. STROWEL II.2.*b*.; art. s.144 à 155 de la loi italienne du 22 avril 1941; art. 26 de la loi allemande du 9 septembre 1965; art. 24 de la loi espagnole du 11 novembre 1987; art. 54 de la loi portugaise.

45. L'inclusion des manuscrits d'oeuvres littéraires et artistiques dans le domaine matériel du droit de suite n'est pas ainsi expressément prévue par l'art. 42 al. ler de la loi française du 11 mars 1957; contre cette inclusion, cf. H. DESBOIS, *op. cit.*, n° 303, p. 394; certaines législations visent expressément, en revanche, les manuscrits; cf. p. ex. art. 144 de la loi italienne du 22 avril 1941; art. 54–1 de la loi portugaise, cf. dans le même sens, art. 14*ter*-1 de la Convention de Berne.

46. Art. 42 al. ler de la loi française du 11 mars 1957; art 26–1 de la loi allemande du 9 septembre 1965; art. 145 de la loi italienne du 22 avril 1941; art. 54–1 de la loi portugaise; Sect. 986–c–2 du California Civil Code ('Fine art means original painting, sculpture, or drawing, or an original work of art in glass').

respectivement le carton et le modèle en platre ou en terre cuite. Limiter toutefois le droit de suite à la planche, au carton, au modèle en plâtre ou en terre cuite conduirait à exclure du domaine du droit de suite les gravures, tapisseries, sculptures destinées à circuler en une pluralité d'exemplaires.

Exclusion injustifiée, s'agissant, en particulier, des supports matériels fabriqués en nombre limité sous le contrôle étroit de l'artiste à partir de la matrice et portant, dès lors, la marque de son génie créateur.

C'est pour cette raison qu'en France la Chambre Nationale des Commissaires Priseurs, d'une part, les sociétés françaises d'auteurs ADAGP et SPADEM, d'autre part, ont conclu des 'accords d'usage' définissant l'interprétation conventionnelle de l'oeuvre originale au sens des dispositions de la loi française relatives au droit de suite et faisant, à cet égard, jouer le droit de suite sur un nombre limité d'exemplaires pouvant être considérés comme l'émanation de l'artiste lui-même.[47]

Dans un arrêt qu'elle a rendu le 18 mars 1986, la première Chambre Civile de la Cour de Cassation se référant à ces 'accords d'usage', a donné une interprétation large du concept d'oeuvre originale, à l'occasion d'un litige survenu en relation avec une vente aux enchères de trois bronzes de Rodin portant le cachet du musée Rodin et réalisés par un fondeur réputé après le décès du sculpteur.[48]

§2. Les opérations donnant prise au droit de suite

Certaines législations cantonnent le champ d'application du droit de suite aux ventes faites aux enchères publiques; il en est ainsi de la loi belge;[49] cette même solution prévaut actuellement en France, le texte d'application devant préciser les modalités de mise en oeuvre du droit de suite, en présence d'une vente par l'intermédiaire d'un négociant, n'ayant pas encore été édicté.[50]

D'autres législations, en revanche, visent aussi bien les ventes publiques que celles conclues par l'intermédiaire d'un commerçant; pareille solution est ainsi retenue par les législations allemande, espagnole, portugaise;[51] tout en retenant la même règle, la législation californienne comporte néanmoins une restriction, signalée par Monsieur Karlen dans sa communication, ayant trait aux ventes entre négociants pendant une période de dix années après la vente initiale de son oeuvre par l'artiste.[52]

---

47. Nous remercions M. AUBOIN, Directeur des Services Juridiques de la SPADEM de nous avoir communiqué un exemplaire de ces 'accords d'usage'.
48. Cass. Civ. I 18 mars 1986, J.C.P. 1987, éd. G. II 20723 concl. GULPHE, Rev. trim, dr. com. 1987.56 observ. A. FRANÇON; RIDA, juillet 1986, n° 129, p. 138, concl. GULPHE.
49. Rapport belge Ph. COPPENS et A. STROWEL, II.*2*.b (les rapporteurs belges signalent (II.*2*.b *in fine*) qu'une doctrine a proposé d'étendre l'application du droit de suite aux ventes privées); cprer., art. 144 et 149 de la loi italienne du 22 avril 1941 (le droit de suite est limité aux ventes publiques (art. 144) mais celles-ci ne sont pas uniquement circonscrites (cf. art. 149) aux ventes faites aux enchères publiques).
50. Cf. ainsi, H. DESBOIS, *op. cit.*, n° 308, p. 399.
51. Art. 26-1 de la loi allemande du 9 septembre 1965; art. 24-1 de la loi espagnole du 11 novembre 1987; art. 54-1 de la loi portugaise (sol. impl.).
52. Cf. Sect. 986-a-1 et Sect. 986-b-6 du California Civil Code.

b. Le régime du droit de suite

Deux questions appellent ici un bref commentaire concernant, l'une, l'inaliénabilité (§1.) l'autre, le montant (§2.) du droit de suite.

§1. Inaliénabilité du droit de suite

Contrairement aux autres droits pécuniaires de l'artiste, le droit de suite, dans la plupart des législations qui le consacrent, est inaliénable à titre tant gratuit qu'onéreux, ce, dans le but de protéger l'artiste contre lui-même; cette inaliénabilité – dont le corollaire est l'insaisissabilité du droit de suite – est affirmée ainsi par les droits belge, français, espagnol, portugais;[53] elle est, au demeurant, dictée par l'art. 14*ter* de la Convention de Berne.[54]

§2. Montant du droit de suite

S'agissant de la liquidation du montant du droit de suite, les législations qui consacrent le droit de suite, retiennent, selon le cas, l'une ou l'autre des deux formules suivantes:

- aux termes de la première, le montant du droit de suite représente un pourcentage du prix de la vente; c'est la solution la plus communément retenue; ainsi le montant du droit de suite est fixé à 2% du prix de la vente en Espagne, 3% en France, 5% en Allemagne, 6% au Portugal, 6% en Belgique si le prix de la vente est égal ou supérieur à 50.000,00 Francs Belges;[55]
- suivant la seconde formule qui a été adoptée par la législation italienne, le montant du droit de suite est un pourcentage de la plus value acquise par l'oeuvre d'art; l'examen de cette législation démontre la complexité que soulève l'application d'une telle méthode de calcul.[56]

---

53. Art. 1 de la loi belge du 21 juin 1921 cité par le rapport belge Ph. COPPENS et A. STROWEL, II.2.b; art. 42 al. ler de la loi française du 11 mars 1957; art. 24–3 de la loi espagnole du 11 novembre 1987; art. 54–3 de la loi portugaise.
54. Art. 14*ter*-1 de la Convention de Berne visant expressément le 'droit inaliénable' de l'auteur à être intéressé aux opérations de vente dont l'oeuvre est l'objet après la première cession opérée par l'auteur'.
55. Art. 24–1 de la loi espagnole du 11 novembre 1987; art. 42 al. 3 de la loi française du 11 mars 1957; art. 26–1 de la loi allemande du 9 septembre 1965; art. 54–1 de la loi portugaise; art. 2 de la loi belge du 21 juin 1921, sur lequel, rapport Ph. COPPENS et A. STROWEL, II.2.b (les rapporteurs belges reproduisent le barême des différents pourcentages calculés en fonction du prix de vente de l'oeuvre, le tarif ne pouvant excéder 6%, ainsi qu'indiqué au texte (*supra* n. 50); les rapporteurs belges précisent que par un arrêt du 28 septembre 1984, la Cour de Cassation belge a considéré que les différents tarifs du droit de suite n'étaient pas, contrairement aux taux proportionnels prévus dans le Code de l'impôt sur les revenus, applicables par tranches, en sorte que le prix de vente global de l'oeuvre détermine la mise en jeu d'un tarif unique du droit de suite; Ph COPPENS et A. STROWEL précisent, par ailleurs, que le barême actuel n'a pas été modifié depuis 1921 et pour cette raison devrait être révisé, compte tenu de l'érosion monétaire).
56. Arts. 145 et 152 de la loi italienne du 22 avril 1941; la réglementation californienne semble, dans une certaine mesure, s'inspirer de la même méthode de calcul que celle retenue par la loi italienne; de fait, si en vertu de la Sect. 986–a–1 du California Civil Code, le droit de suite est égal à 5% du montant de la vente, en application de la Sect. 986–b–4, la Sect. 986–a–2 n'est pas applicable 'to the resale of the work of fine art for a gross sales price less than the purchase price paid by the seller'.

D'un autre côté, les législations ayant introduit le droit de suite explicitent souvent les modalités de recouvrement du montant de ce droit; en témoignent les lois allemande, française, californienne.[57]

La césure – que l'étude du droit de suite révèle – entre deux groupes d'Etats (ceux qui ignorent le droit de suite et ceux qui le reconnaissent) se retrouve-t-elle, lorsque l'on s'attache à l'examen du droit moral des artistes?

2. LE DROIT MORAL DES ARTISTES

Un constat de convergence mérite d'être formulé, surtout depuis 1988, année au cours de laquelle les Etats-Unis ont adhéré à la Convention de Berne et qui constitue le millésime de la nouvelle loi du Royaume Uni sur le droit d'auteur.[58]

Convergence qui intéresse les deux prérogatives du droit moral que sont le droit au respect et à la paternité de l'oeuvre d'art (*A.*) mais qui cède la place à une divergence entre lois nationales, dès l'instant où sont en cause les autres prérogatives du droit moral (*B.*).

A. Constat de convergence entre lois nationales: le droit au respect et à la paternité de l'oeuvre d'art

L'ensemble des lois des Etats européens examinées dans le cadre du présent colloque reconnaissent à l'artiste tant le droit de revendiquer la paternité de son oeuvre que le droit au respect de celle-ci, droit au respect impliquant que l'artiste ou éventuellement ses héritiers soient fondés à s'opposer à toute déformation ou mutilation de l'oeuvre d'art.

La reconnaissance formelle des deux prérogatives sus-énoncées peut être ainsi illustrée par les lois française, autrichienne, allemande, italienne, néerlandaise, espagnole, portugaise, anglaise.[59]

Une même solution prévaut en droit suisse et en droit grec, le droit moral étant toutefois fondé non pas sur les règles gouvernant le droit d'auteur mais sur celles du Code Civil régissant les droits de la personnalité.[60]

---

57. Paragraphes 3 à 6 de l'art. 26 de la loi allemande du 9 septembre 1962; décret français du 17 septembre 1920, sur lequel, cf. not. H. DESBOIS, *op. cit.*, n° 308, pp. 399–401 paragraphes 3,4,5 et 6 de la Sect. 986–a du California Civil Code.
58. Sur la nouvelle loi du Royaume Uni relative aux droits d'auteur, cf. not. D. de FREITAS, 'The United Kingdom new copyright law', RIDA, janvier 1990, n° 143, p. 25 *et seq*.
59. Art. 6 al. ler de la loi française du 11 mars 1957, sur lequel, cf. not. Cl. COLOMBET, *op. cit.*, n° 138 *et seq*. p. 156 *et seq*.; art. 19–1 de la loi autrichienne du 9 avril 1936; arts. 13 et 14 de la loi allemande du 9 septembre 1965; art. 20 de la loi italienne du 22 avril 1941; art. 25 de la loi néerlandaise du 23 septembre 1912; art. 14–3 et art. 14–4 de la loi espagnole du 11 novembre 1987; art. 56–1 de la loi portugaise; arts. 77 et 80 de la loi anglaise de 1988, sur lequels, D. de FREITAS, étude précitée, RIDA, janvier 1990, n° 143, p. 25 *et seq*.; spéc. p. 54 *et seq*.
60. Arts. 28 et 29 du Code Civil suisse, sur lesquels, rapport F. PERRET, II.*5*. et *6*; arts. 57 et 59 du Code Civil grec, sur lesquels, rapport A. DIMOLISTA, 2 et 3.

La consécration du droit à la paternité de l'oeuvre et du droit au respect de celle-ci figure, outre-atlantique, dans les réglementations californienne et de l'Etat de New York, c'est-à-dire, explique Monsieur Karlen dans son rapport, dans le droit des deux Etats fédérés qui sont aux Etats-Unis les principaux marchés de l'art.[61]

On observera que le droit au respect a suscité en France une intéressante jurisprudence apportant des éléments de réponse aux délicats problèmes que pose la rencontre de cette prérogative du droit moral et du droit de propriété sur l'oeuvre d'art; rencontre conflictuelle au terme de laquelle le droit au respect de l'oeuvre affirme sa primauté au détriment du droit de propriété mais se trouve néanmoins sacrifié, dès l'instant où la sécurité du public exige qu'il en soit ainsi.[62]

Le conflit entre le droit au respect de l'oeuvre et le droit de propriété se trouve également illustré en Allemagne, par une décision – évoquée par Monsieur Lohaus – rendue par une juridiction berlinoise le 8 juin 1912 concernant l'espèce dans laquelle le propriétaire d'un immeuble où se trouvait une fresque représentant des femmes nues, avait repeint la fresque pour dissimuler la nudité des personnages; espèce qui n'est pas sans faire écho au litige porté devant les juges français dans l'affaire des Fresques de Juvisy.[63]

Cette convergence entre lois nationales prend, il est vrai, toute sa dimension, *prima facie*, à la lumière de l'art. 6*bis* de la Convention de Berne, article qui consacre expressément le droit de l'auteur à la paternité et au respect de son oeuvre.[64]

La portée de cet art. 6*bis* ne doit toutefois pas être exagérée, et ce, pour deux raisons:

- d'une part, le fondement assigné aux deux prérogatives du droit moral entrant dans les prévisions de l'art. 6*bis* paraît bien exclure tout rattachement du droit moral aux droits de la personnalité, alors qu'un tel rattachement est prescrit par différentes lois nationales (les lois française, suisse, grecque), puisque le droit n'est protégé par l'art. 6*bis* précité que pour autant qu'il y ait atteinte à la réputation et à l'honorabilité de l'artiste;[65]
- d'autre part, les deux prérogatives du droit moral visées à l'art. 6*bis* semblent pouvoir être susceptibles de renonciation.[66]

---

61. Sect. 987-c du California Art Preservation Act; Sect. 14.03 du New York Arts and Cultural Affairs Law; sur ces deux textes, cf. rapport KARLEN et les réf. cit. ns. de 13 et 14.
62. Sur cette jurisprudence, cf. not. Ph. COPPENS et N. VERHEYDEN-JEANMART, 'La Propriété d'une oeuvre d'art et les droits moraux de l'artiste', Annales de droit de Louvain, numéro spécial 3/4 1988, *Le droit et l'objet d'art*, p. 285 *et seq.*, spéc. p. 332 *et seq.*
63. Trib. Civ. Versailles du 3 juin 1932. D.H. 1932.487; C. Paris 1934, D.H. 1934.385.
64. Sur cet art. 6*bis*, cf. not. H. DESBOIS, A. FRANÇON, A. KEREVER, 'Les Conventions internationales du droit d'auteur et des droits voisins', Dalloz 1976, n° 176, p. 209–211.
65. Sur la critique de cette solution, cf. not. H. DESBOIS, A. FRANÇON, A. KEREVER, *op. cit.*, n° 175, p. 211.
66. Cf. ainsi J.C. GINSBURG et J.M. KERNOCHAN, 'One Hundred and Two years later: the US joins the Berne Convention', RIDA, juillet 1989, n° 141, p. 57 *et seq.*, spéc. p. 137 et les réf. citées n. 112, p. 187.

Or, dans différentes législations, le droit à la paternité et au respect de l'oeuvre est expressément présenté comme inaliénable et donc insusceptible de renonciation; c'est le cas en France, en Espagne, au Portugal;[67] la question de savoir si une telle renonciation est concevable est, en revanche discutée en Belgique, ainsi que nous l'indiquent Messieurs Coppens et Strowel dans leur rapport national.[68]

Par ailleurs, l'on pourrait de prime abord penser que l'adhésion des Etats-Unis le 31 octobre 1988 à la Convention de Berne a accentué, en l'étendant aux Etats-Unis, le phénomène de convergence entre lois nationales relativement au droit à la paternité et au droit au respect de l'oeuvre, dans la mesure où le Copyright Act américain ne consacre pas traditionnellement l'existence d'un droit moral au profit de l'auteur.

Or, en fait, l'adhésion des Etats-Unis à la Convention de Berne n'a pas conduit les Etats-Unis à introduire dans l''Implementation Act' de ce traité une réglementation matérielle spécifique sur le droit moral.[69]

L'explication avancée – que Monsieur Karlen relate dans son rapport – est la suivante: les règles du droit existant sont en mesure d'assurer la protection des prérogatives du droit moral donnant prise à l'art. 6*bis* de la Convention de Berne.[70]

A titre d'exemple, est-il indiqué, le droit au respect de l'oeuvre peut être sauvegardé par la législation fédérale sur la concurrence déloyale – ainsi qu'en témoigne l'affaire *Gillian c. American Broadcasting Co.* plus connue sous le nom de l'affaire Monty Python[71] – de même que par le Sect. 106 du Copyright Act.[72]

Le constat d'une convergence relative que permet d'établir l'étude comparée des législations nationales concernant le droit à la paternité et au respect de l'oeuvre cède le pas au constat d'une certaine divergence, s'agissant des autres prérogatives du droit moral.

B. Constat de divergence entre lois nationales: les autres prérogatives du droit moral

Cette divergence prend pour cible le droit de divulgation (i.) et de manière encore plus nette le droit de retrait ou de repentir (ii.).

---

67. Art. 6 al. 3 de la loi française du 11 mars 1957, sur lequel cf. not Cl. COLOMBET, *op. cit.*, n° 130, pp. 150–151; art. 14 al. ler de la loi espagnole du 11 novembre 1987; art. 56–2 de la loi portugaise.
68. Rapport belge Ph. COPPENS et A. STROWEL, II.*1*.b.
69. *V.* ainsi, A. DIETZ, 'Les Etats-Unis et le droit moral: Idiosyncrasie ou rapprochement', RIDA, octobre 1989, n° 142 p. 223 *et seq.*, spéc. 233 *et seq.*
70. *V.* ainsi, J. C. GINSBURG et J. M. KERNOCHAN, étude précitée, RIDA, juillet 1989, n° 141, p. 57 *et seq.*, spéc. p. 123 *et seq.*; adde, B. EDELMAN, 'Entre copyright et droit d'auteur: l'intégrité de l'oeuvre de l'esprit', D. 1990 Chron., p. 295 *et seq.* spéc. n° 3–11.
71. Sur cette affaire, cf. not. J.C. GINSBURG et J.M. KERNOCHAN, étude précitée, RIDA, juillet 1989, n° 141 spéc. 143–145.
72. *V.* ainsi, A. DIETZ, étude précitée, RIDA, octobre 1989, n° 142, spéc. p. 241.

i. Le droit de divulgation

Ce droit défini comme celui conféré à l'artiste de décider du moment et du mode de communication de son oeuvre au public est le siège d'une divergence sensible entre les lois nationales des pays européens et la réglementation des Etats-Unis.

La reconnaissance au profit de l'artiste du droit de divulgation est, de fait, consacrée par une pluralité d'Etats européens: la France, la Belgique, l'Allemagne, l'Italie, la Suisse, la Suède, l'Espagne.[73]

Par l'exercice du droit de divulgation, dans les pays qui consacrent cette prérogative, l'oeuvre cesse de faire corps avec la personne de l'artiste pour entrer dans le commerce juridique, ce qui emporte notamment deux conséquences:

- aussi longtemps que le droit de divulgation n'est pas exercé, l'oeuvre d'art n'est pas saisissable; c'est ce que souligne expressément la loi belge, comme le rappellent Messieurs Coppens et Strowel dans leur rapport;[74]
- en droit international privé, c'est du moins la règle de conflit de lois formulée par la jurisprudence française, la loi applicable à l'existence des droits pécuniaires est la loi de première publication de l'oeuvre, puisque c'est précisément à la date à laquelle l'oeuvre est divulguée que naissent les attributs patrimoniaux du droit d'auteur.[75]

On observera, d'un autre côté, que le droit de divulgation soulève, au plan de sa mise en oeuvre, une difficulté: celle de déterminer l'initiative de l'artiste impliquant de manière non équivoque l'exercice d'un tel droit. Question qui a suscité en France une jurisprudence illustrée par deux espèces célèbres, celles du peintre Whistler et du peintre Rouault.[76]

Contrairement aux législations nationales sus-mentionnées, le droit américain ne reconnait pas explicitement le droit de divulgation, ainsi que le fait observer Monsieur Karlen dans sa communication.[77] Toutefois, note

---

73. Art. 19 de la loi française du 11 mars 1957 sur lequel, spéc. O. LALIGANT, *La divulgation des oeuvres artistiques, littéraires et musicales en droit positif français*, Bibl. dr. piv. T. 176, LGDJ 1983; rapport belge Ph. COPPENS et A. STROWEL, II.*1*.a; adde, Ph. COPPENS et N. VERHEYDEN-JEANMART, étude précitée, *Annales de droit de Louvain*, p. 285 *et seq.*, spéc. p. 290 *et seq.*; art. 12 de la loi allemande du 9 septembre 1965; rapport suisse F. PERRET citant l'art. 12-1-3° de la loi fédérale suisse du 7 décembre 1922; rapport suédois de C. WEGENIUS; art. 14-1° de la loi espagnole du 11 novembre 1987.
74. Art. 9 de la loi belge du 22 mars 1886 cité par le rapport Ph. COPPENS et A. STROWEL, II.; adde Ph. COPPENS et N. VERHEYDEN-JEANMART, étude précitée, *Annales de droit de Louvain*, spéc. p. 315.
75. *V.* ainsi, Cass. Civ. I 22 décembre 1959, *Soc. Fox – Europa c. Soc. Le Chant du Monde*, D. 1960.93 note G. HOLLEAUX, Rev. Trim. du Dr. com. 1960.351 n° 2 observ. H. DESBOIS, Rev. Crit. dr. intern. Priv. 1960.361 note F. TERRÉ; C. Paris 24 avril 1974, *Soc. Galba Films. c. Friedman*. Rev. Crit. dr. intern. Priv. 1975.440 note G. BONET et, sur pourvoi Cass. Civ. I 15 décembre 1975, Rev. Crit. dr. intern. Priv. 1976.515 note G. B.; cf. toutefois, Cass. Crim. 5 janvier 1988, *Moubarak c. Sacem*, RIDA, 1988,204; *V.* ég., bien que moins net, Cass. Crim. 31 mars 1987, *Saumagnac c. Sacem*, RIDA, 1988.198.
76. Sur ces deux espèces, cf. not. Ph. COPPENS et N. VERHEYDEN-JEANMART, étude précitée, *Annales de droit de Louvain*, spéc. p. 293 *et seq.*
77. Rapport américain P. H. KARLEN, II.

Monsieur Karlen, l'artiste est titulaire d'un droit de distribution au public des exemplaires, ce, en vertu de la Sect. 106 – 3 du Copyright Act, qui, selon le rapporteur, est l'équivalent du droit de divulgation;[78] mais, précise Monsieur Karlen, pour être investi d'un tel droit de distribution, encore faut-il que l'auteur n'ait pas créé l'oeuvre pour son employeur ou un donneur d'ordre (hypothèse du *work made for hire*)[79] ou qu'il n'ait pas cédé son copyright.

Autrement dit, lorsque l'artiste conclut avec un client déterminé (un particulier, une galerie ou toute autre entreprise, un musée) un contrat de commande ou de mécénat, il entre alors dans le champ d'application de la catégorie des *works made for hire*; en pareil cas, il n'est pas corrélativement titulaire du droit de distribution que l'on peut, de fait, présenter légitimement comme un équivalent du droit de divulgation, ce, à la lumière de deux décisions qui ont conféré au droit de distribution une connotation morale indéniable, à savoir l'arrêt rendu par la Cour Suprême des Etats-Unis dans l'affaire Harper and Row Publishers et celui de la Cour d'Appel du deuxième Circuit dans l'affaire *Pierre Salinger c. Random House*.[80]

ii. Le droit de retrait ou de repentir

Cet attribut moral – dont l'examen fait apparaître une divergence encore plus nette entre les lois nationales ici étudiées – vise, comme on le sait, à satisfaire le scrupule de conscience de l'auteur regrettant d'avoir divulgué son oeuvre et souhaitant se délier des conventions par l'effet desquelles il a cédé tout ou partie de ses droits pécuniaires sur l'oeuvre.[81]

Le droit de retrait ou de repentir – qui a ainsi pour objet spécifique, non pas les contrats de commande d'oeuvre d'art ou de mécénat, mais les conventions de cession des droits patrimoniaux – est reconnu par diverses législations de pays membres de la C.E. tels que la France, l'Italie, l'Allemagne, l'Espagne, le Portugal;[82] une récente proposition de loi belge vise à introduire cet attribut extra-patrimonial du droit d'auteur, comme le signalent Messieurs Coppens et Strowel dans leur rapport.[83]

---

78. Rapport américain P. H. KARLEN, II et la référence citée n. 25.
79. Cf. Sect. 201–b du Copyright Act; adde, rapport américain P. H. KARLEN, II et sa n. 23.
80. Sur ces deux affaires, cf. not. J. C. GINSBURG, 'L'évolution récente du droit d'auteur aux Etats Unis', RIDA, juillet 1987 n° 133, p. 111 *et seq.*, spéc. p. 157 *et seq.*
81. *V.* ainsi, H. DESBOIS, *op. cit.*, n° 392, p. 483.
82. Art. 32 de la loi française du 11 mars 1957, sur lequel, cf. not. H. DESBOIS, *op. cit.*, n° 392 *et seq.*, p. 483 *et seq.*; Cl. COLOMBET, *op. cit.* n° 163 *et seq.*, p. 176 *et seq.*; arts. 142 et 143 de la loi italienne du 22 avril 1941; art. 42 de la loi allemande du 9 septembre 1965; art. 14–6° de la loi espagnole du 11 novembre 1987; art. 62 de la loi portugaise.
83. Art. 11 de la proposition de révision de la loi belge du 22 mars 1886, citée par le rapport Ph. COPPENS et A. STROWEL, II.*1*.c (les rapporteurs belges commentent toutefois un arrêt rendu par la Cour de Cassation belge en date du 12 septembre 1975 (II.*1*.c de leur rapport), lequel semble avoir reconnu le droit de retrait ou de repentir; sur cet arrêt cf. également Ph. COPPENS et N. VERHEYDEN-JEANMART, étude précitée, *Annales de droit de Louvain*, spéc. p. 329 *et seq.*

Le droit de retrait ou de repentir, en revanche, n'existe pas dans la législation néerlandaise; de même, il ne semble pas être reconnu au Royaume-Uni; pareillement, en tant qu'attribut du droit moral, ce même droit n'est pas consacré aux Etats-Unis, précise le rapport de Monsieur Karlen;[84] néanmoins, explique le rapporteur américain, il existe aux Etats-Unis des mécanismes juridiques susceptibles de satisfaire le même but que celui que s'assigne le droit de retrait ou de repentir, tel que, par exemple, les règles sur la concurrence déloyale; et Monsieur Karlen de signaler en ce sens une affaire *CBS-Inc. c. Gusto Records Inc.*[85]

Dans les législations où il est consacré, le droit de retrait ou de repentir soulève une question au stade de son application: peut-il être mis en oeuvre, lorsqu'il s'agit, non pas des attributs pécuniaires du droit d'auteur, mais du support matériel de l'oeuvre?

Dans quelle mesure, à cet égard, le droit de retrait ou de repentir peut-il paralyser la circulation des oeuvres d'art et compromettre le droit de propriété sur celles-ci?

Dans leur rapport de droit belge, Messieurs Coppens et Strowel expliquent de manière pertinente que le droit de retrait ou de repentir doit être enfermé dans une double limite: d'un côté, il n'est susceptible de jouer qu'à compter du moment où l'oeuvre d'art est divulguée; de l'autre, il ne peut plus être mis en oeuvre dès l'instant où l'oeuvre d'art a été aliénée.[86]

La première limite n'apparaît pas clairement à l'examen du droit positif français, l'hypothèse dans laquelle l'artiste refuse de livrer une oeuvre commandée relevant plutôt du droit de divulgation; la seconde se trouve, par contre, illustrée par l'arrêt de la Cour de Paris du 19 avril 1961 concernant la toile de Vlaminck 'Champ de blé'; pour les juges d'appel, en effet, si l'artiste 'est entièrement libre de dire quand l'oeuvre lui paraît indigne de lui, il perd son droit au repentir au moment où il livre cette oeuvre', solution qui évite une véritable expropriation du propriétaire de l'oeuvre d'art au profit de l'artiste.[87]

Assurément, appliqué au support matériel de l'oeuvre d'art, le droit de retrait ou de repentir, enfermé dans la double limite esquissée plus haut[88] (la première étant dictée par le souci compréhensible de distinguer cet attribut moral du droit de divulgation, la seconde étant animée par la préoccupation de préserver le droit de propriété sur le support matériel de l'oeuvre), se voit corrélativement impartir un champ d'intervention particulièrement étroit.

Constat de convergence dont il ne faut pas exagérer la portée, constat de divergence, c'est autour de ces deux axes que semble devoir s'articuler

84. Rapport américain P. H. KARLEN, II.
85. Cf. rapport américain P. H. KARLEN, n. 39.
86. Rapport belge Ph. COPPENS et A. STROWEL, II.*1*.c; adde Ph. COPPENS et N. VERHEYDEN-JEANMART, étude précitée, *Annales de droit de Louvain*, spéc. p. 321 *et seq*.
87. Paris 19 avril 1961, RIDA, janvier 1962, p. 119.
88. Cf. *supra*, référence au rapport du droit belge.

l'étude, en droit comparé, des droits pécuniaires et du droit moral de l'artiste. Cette même approche doit-elle également guider la condition juridique des héritiers de l'artiste?

II. LA DEVOLUTION SUCCESSORALE DES DROITS DES ARTISTES

A cet égard, si l'examen des règles qui gouvernent dans les différents systèmes juridiques concernés la dévolution successorale des droits pécuniaires amène à relever l'existence d'un certain constat de convergence (1.), c'est, en revanche, sur un constat de divergence que débouche une étude de droit comparé consacrée à la dévolution successorale du droit moral (2.).

1. CONSTAT DE CONVERGENCE ENTRE LOI NATIONALE: LA DEVOLUTION SUCCESSORALE DES DROITS PECUNIAIRES

Cette convergence doit être mesurée à deux stades: au plan des règles de dévolution successorale (*A.*), au plan à celui de la durée des droits pécuniaires dévolus (*B.*)

A. Règles de dévolution successorale des droits pécuniaires

Il importe d'apprécier la portée du phénomène de convergence (i.) avant de tenter d'en esquisser les limites (ii.).

i. Portée du constat de convergence

Dans la plupart des législations nationales, les droits pécuniaires des artistes sont transmissibles à cause de mort aux héritiers des artistes, selon les règles ordinaires de la dévolution successorale. Cette solution est ainsi affirmée par les lois allemande, italienne, suisse, autrichienne, espagnole, suédoise, néerlandaise, anglaise.[89]

Poser le principe que les règles ordinaires de la dévolution successorale sont applicables aux droits pécuniaires des artistes n'est pas sans implications en droit international privé. En effet, dans les droits nationaux, tels que le droit français, où la loi applicable à la dévolution de la succession mobilière est la loi du dernier domicile du défunt,[90] le fait pour un artiste de transférer

89. Art. 28-1 de la loi allemande du 9 septembre 1965; art. 115 de la loi italienne du 22 avril 1941 (sol. impl.); rapport suisse F. PERRET, III; art. 3.1 de la loi autrichienne du 9 avril 1936; rapport suédois Ch. WEGENIUS; rapport néerlandais A.A. QUAEDVLIEG III; art. 90-1 de la loi anglaise du 15 novembre 1988.

90. Sur la règle française de conflit de lois soumettant les successions mobilières à la loi du dernier domicile du défunt, cf. not. Y. LOUSSOUARN et P. BOUREL, *Droit international privé* (Dalloz, 3ème éd. 1988) n° 430, p. 664 *et seq*.

dans un autre Etat son domicile est de nature à affecter l'existence et/ou la consistance des droits pécuniaires dévolus à ces héritiers.

Prenons ainsi l'exemple d'un artiste italien qui vit en France où existe le droit de suite et qui se retire en Suisse quelques années avant sa mort.

Au regard du droit international privé français, la loi gouvernant la dévolution successorale de l'artiste est la loi suisse, laquelle, contrairement au droit français, ignore le droit de suite;[91] dans l'exemple qui précède, la dévolution du droit de suite aux héritiers de l'artiste paraît corrélativement compromise.

ii. Limites du constat de convergence

Deux séries de limites, entre autres, semblent devoir être évoquées concernant, l'une, la dévolution successorale du droit de suite (*a.*), l'autre, les prérogatives des héritiers (*b.*).

a. La dévolution successorale du droit de suite

L'accent mérite ici d'être porté sur les dispositions de l'art. 42 al.2 de la loi française du 11 mars 1957, ces dispositions organisant en effet une dévolution successorale spécifique du droit de suite.

D'un côté, l'art. 42 al. 2 exclut clairement les légataires de la dévolution successorale du droit de suite; en d'autres termes, le droit de suite ne peut être légué, solution qui semble être la conséquence de l'inaliénabilité du droit de suite, l'artiste ne pouvant disposer, même à titre gratuit et à cause de mort, du droit de suite dont il est investi par la loi française du 11 mars 1957.

De l'autre, par son arrêt Utrillo du 19 octobre 1977, la Cour de Cassation française est venue prendre parti en faveur de la thèse selon laquelle par 'héritiers' au sens de l'art.42 al. 2, il convient d'entendre 'héritiers de sang et non pas héritiers déterminés par les règles ordinaires du droit successoral'.[92]

Cet arrêt – qui opérait un revirement par rapport à deux arrêts antérieurs rendus par la même Cour Suprême dans les affaires Dufy et Monnet[93] – restreignait ainsi le champ d'application du droit de suite, une fois l'auteur décédé et renforçait corrélativement le particularisme des règles françaises en cette matière.

L'arrêt récent du 11 janvier 1989 rendu par la Cour de Cassation dans l'affaire du peintre Braque[94] marque toutefois un abandon de la jurisprudence Utrillo, ce qui, dès lors, atténue la première limite, ici évoquée,

---

91. Cf. *supra* p. 202–203 et n. 43.
92. Cass. Civ. I 19 octobre 1977 D. 1978.109 note H. DESBOIS, J.C.P. 1978, éd. 2 18815 note R. LINDON.
93. Cass. Civ. I 10 juin 1968, *Dufy*, D. 1968.633, concl. R. LINDON, Rev. Trim. Dr. Com. 1969.781 observ. H. DESBOIS; Cass. Civ. I 9 février 1972, *Monnet*, D. 1972.289, concl. R. LINDON, Gaz. Pal. 1972. 2. 539 note R. SARRAUTE.
94. Cass. Civ. 11 janvier 1989, D. 1989.308, 2ème espèce, note B. EDELMAN, J.C.P. 1989, éd. G II 21378 note A. LUCAS, D.1990, Sommaires Commentés p. 51 observ. Cl. COLOMBET.

au constat de convergence et, par là même, renforce la portée d'un tel constat.

b. Les prérogatives des héritiers

Ici encore, l'expérience juridique française appelle l'attention.

Aux termes d'une disposition originale figurant à l'art. 20 de la loi française du 11 mars 1957, le tribunal de grande instance est autorisé à prendre toutes mesures appropriées en cas d'abus notoire de la part des héritiers dans l'usage ou le non usage du droit de divulgation comme (cette seconde solution ayant été introduite par la loi du 3 juillet 1985) dans l'usage ou le non usage des droits pécuniaires.[95]

Dans la célèbre affaire du peintre Foujita, les juridictions françaises ont eu à apprécier si la veuve de ce peintre commettait un abus notoire dans le non usage des droits de reproduction dont elle était dévolutaire sur les oeuvres de son mari, en refusant aux auteurs d'un ouvrage consacré à la vie de Foujita et à l'éditeur de cet ouvrage l'autorisation de publier dans le livre en préparation 1.200 reproductions d'oeuvres du peintre.

Le mérite des décisions rendues dans cette espèce[96] est, entre autres, de soulever la question de savoir si l'intérêt du public, plus exactement, l'accès à la culture du public français, peut servir d'élément de référence pour apprécier l'abus notoire dans le non usage par un héritier des droits pécuniaires qui lui sont dévolus au décès de l'artiste.

Autrement dit, l'enjeu était finalement de savoir, dans cette espèce, si le droit d'auteur en France n'a pas vocation à se rapprocher du système du copyright, dès l'instant où, par suite du décès de l'artiste, ne sont en cause que les droits pécuniaires des héritiers de celui-ci.[97]

B. La durée des droits pécuniaires dévolus aux héritiers

Essayons, ici encore, d'apprécier succinctement la portée du phénomène de convergence (i.) avant de tenter d'en appréhender les limites (ii.)

i. Portée du constat de convergence

Dans la plupart des lois nationales, la durée des droits pécuniaires dévolue aux héritiers est, comme le prescrit d'ailleurs l'art. 7 de la Convention de Berne, de 50 ans après le décès de l'artiste, s'agissant des oeuvres divulguées du vivant de celui-ci.

95. Sur l'adjonction résultant plus précisément de l'art. 7 de la loi du 3 juillet 1985, cf. not. Cl. COLOMBET, *op. cit.*, n° 266, p. 273 n. 1 et les références citées.
96. Trib. Gr. Inst. Nanterre 15 septembre 1986, RIDA, janvier 1987, n° 131, p. 268, Rev. Trim. Dr. Com. 1987.60 observ. A. FRANÇON; C. VERSAILLES, RIDA, avril 1988, n° 136, p. 161, D. 1987.382 note B. EDELMAN; Cass. Civ. 28 février 1989, D. 1989.557 note S. DURRANDE, D. 1990, Sommaires Commentés 1990 p. 51 observ. Cl. COLOMBET.
97. Cf. ainsi, note S. DURRANDE citée *supra* n. 96.

Cette solution est retenue, par exemple, par les lois française, néerlandaise, italienne, suisse, suédoise, portugaise.[98]

ii. Limites du constat de convergence

La première limite tient au fait que dans certaines législations, la durée des droits pécuniaires des héritiers, pour les oeuvres divulguées, est selon le cas inférieure à 50 ans – il en est ainsi en Californie, s'agissant du droit de suite[99] – ou supérieure à 50 ans.

Ainsi la durée des droits patrimoniaux dévolus aux héritiers est-elle de 60 ans en Espagne et de 70 ans en Autriche et en Allemagne.[100]

Les divergences qui ainsi peuvent exister entre lois nationales, quant à la durée des droits patrimoniaux dévolus aux artistes, ne sont pas sans implications juridiques, en particulier dans l'espace communautaire, lorsque des exemplaires d'une oeuvre d'art mis licitement en circulation dans un Etat membre de la C.E. où la durée est de 50 ans avec le consentement de l'auteur ou de son ayant droit sont importés dans un autre Etat membre de la C.E. qui prévoit une durée de protection plus longue.[101]

La seconde limite au phénomène de convergence envisagé plus haut intéresse la durée des droits patrimoniaux des héritiers, en présence d'oeuvres non divulguées.

Il existe, en effet, une divergence entre les lois nationales quant au mode de calcul de la durée de protection.

Une simple approche de droit comparé, circonscrite à la France, l'Italie, l'Allemagne, le Portugal, l'Espagne, permet de relever la grande diversité des solutions respectivement retenues.[102]

2. CONSTAT DE DIVERGENCE ENTRE LOIS NATIONALES: LA DEVOLUTION SUCCESSORALE DU DROIT MORAL

Un tel constat s'impose, dans la mesure où, selon certaines législations

---

98. Art. 21 al. 2 de la loi française du 11 mars 1957 (cette disposition étant toutefois la durée de protection à 70 années pour les compositions musicales avec ou sans paroles); rapport néerlandais A. A. QUAEDVLIEG, III; art. 25 de loi italienne du 22 avril 1941; art. 36 de la loi fédérale suisse du 7 décembre 1922 cité par le rapport F. PERRET III; rapport suédois Ch. WEGENIUS; art. 30 de la loi portugaise.
99. Sect. 986-a-7 du California Civil Code.
100. Art. 26 de la loi espagnole du 11 novembre 1987; art. 60 de la loi autrichienne du 9 avril 1936; art. 64 de la loi allemande du 9 septembre 1965.
101. Cf. sur ce point, à propos de phonogrammes, Cour de Justice des Communautés Européennes 24 janvier 1989, EMI, RIDA, juillet 1989, n° 141, p. 235 note A. KEREVER, J.C.P. 1989, éd. G. II 21241 concl. M. DARMON, Rev. Trim. Dr. Com. 1989.464 observ. A. FRANÇON.
102. Cprer. art. 23 al. ler de la loi française du 11 mars 1957 (sur lequel cf. not. Cl. COLOMBET, *op. cit.*, n° 284, p. 290); art. 31 de la loi italienne du 22 avril 1941; art. 64 de la loi allemande du 9 septembre 1965; art. 31 de la loi portugaise; art. 27-1 de la loi espagnole du 11 novembre 1987.

nationales, le droit moral n'est pas transmissible aux héritiers (*A.*), alors que d'autres législations prévoient cette transmissibilité (*B.*).

A. Législations nationales en vertu desquelles le droit moral n'est pas transmissible aux héritiers

En Suisse, ainsi qu'il a été mentionné plus haut, le droit moral est rattaché aux droits de la personnalité, en sorte, comme le signale le rapporteur suisse Monsieur Perret, le droit moral s'éteint à la mort de l'artiste.[103]

Par voie de conséquence, les héritiers de l'artiste ne peuvent faire valoir que leur propre droit à la personnalité, pour s'opposer, après la mort de l'artiste, à des mutilations ou à des altérations de ses oeuvres.[103]

Monsieur Perret fait toutefois part du souhait exprimé par la doctrine helvétique de voir introduire la règle d'une dévolution successorale du droit moral, pour une durée égale à celle des droits pécuniaires, au profit des héritiers les plus proches du défunt (conjoint et enfants).[103]

Un tel souhait rejoint, au demeurant, nous précise Monsieur Perret, la règle que propose d'instituer le Projet de réforme du droit d'auteur élaboré par le Conseil Fédéral et la troisiéme Commission d'experts.[103]

Parce qu'elle rattache le droit moral aux droits de la personnalité, à l'égal de la Suisse, la Grèce, tout comme la Suisse, ignore la dévolution du droit moral, solution que critique le rapporteur de ce pays.[104]

B. Législations nationales en vertu desquelles le droit moral est transmissible aux héritiers

Si la plupart des droits nationaux prévoit une telle dévolution, des divergences apparaissent, lorsque l'examen de droit comparé prend pour cible les dévolutaires du droit moral (i.) et la durée du droit moral dévolu aux héritiers (ii.)

i. Les dévolutaires du droit moral

Deux solutions sont concevables, selon que le droit est dévolu conformément au droit commun successoral (*a.*) ou selon qu'il fait l'objet d'une dévolution spécifique (*b.*).

a. Dévolution du droit moral conforme au droit commun successoral
Cette solution est celle retenue par la loi anglaise sur le droit d'auteur de 1988, par les droits allemand, autrichien, italien, espagnol, portugais.[105]

---

103. Rapport suisse F. PERRET, III. 2.
104. Rapport grec A. DIMOLITSA, 4.
105. Art. 95 de la loi anglaise du 15 novembre 1988; art. 28 1° de la loi allemande du 9 septembre 1965; art. 23 1° de la loi autrichienne du 9 avril 1936; art. 23 et 24 de la loi italienne du 22 avril 1941; art. 15–1 de la loi espagnole du 11 novembre 1987; art. 57–1 de la loi portugaise.

b. Dévolution spécifique du droit moral par rapport au droit commun successoral

L'on doit ici mettre l'accent sur la solution originale qu'édicte l'art. 19 de la loi française du 11 mars 1957; cette disposition organise en effet un ordre spécifique des dévolutaires du droit de divulgation, à savoir: les descendants, le conjoint survivant, les héritiers autres que descendants et légataires universels ou donataires de l'universalité des biens à venir. La règle de dévolution successorale posée à l'art. 19 n'est pas, en revanche, expressément applicable aux autres attributs successoralement transmissibles du droit moral, c'est à dire le droit à la paternité et le droit au respect de l'oeuvre (le droit de retrait ou de repentir n'étant pas, en ce qui les concerne, transmissible aux héritiers). De fait, l'art. 6 de la loi française du 11 mars 1957 se borne à affirmer que le droit moral est 'transmissible à cause de mort aux héritiers de l'auteur'.

Or, une doctrine importante suivant en cela la position exprimée par le Professeur Desbois, avait opté pour l'analyse suivante: la règle de dévolution successorale édictée à l'art. 19 est applicable également au droit à la paternité et au droit au respect de l'oeuvre.[106]

Cette thèse a été retenue par la Cour de Paris, dans un arrêt du 17 décembre 1986 concernant Monsieur Fabris.[107] Monsieur Fabris, légataire universel de la veuve d'Utrillo, elle-même donataire de l'universalité des biens d'Utrillo, avait fait procéder en 1982 à la saisie-contrefaçon d'une toile attribuée à Utrillo dont il contestait l'authenticité; pour ce faire, il se fondait sur sa qualité de dévolutaire du droit moral sur les oeuvres du peintre; sa prétention fut repoussée par la Cour de Paris, Monsieur Fabris n'entrant pas dans la catégorie des héritiers figurant à l'art. 19 de la loi 11 mars 1957.

L'arrêt de la Cour d'Appel du 17 décembre 1986 a néanmoins été annulé par la première Chambre Civile de la Cour de Cassation le 11 janvier 1989;[108] dans son arrêt de censure, la Cour Suprême énonce clairement que 'le droit de l'auteur au respect de son nom, de sa qualité, de son oeuvre est transmissible à cause de mort à ses héritiers selon les règles ordinaires de la dévolution successorale'.

L'arrêt du 11 janvier 1989 a une double signification:

- en limitant les termes de l'art. 19 de la loi du 11 mars 1957 au seul droit de divulgation, la Cour de Cassation atténue largement, dans une perspective de droit comparé, la divergence par rapport aux autres législations nationales que matérialise la règle de dévolution spécifique posée à l'art. 19 précité;
- c'est la loi gouvernant la dévolution de la succession mobilière de l'artiste et non pas la loi nationale de celui-ci qu'il convient de consulter pour déterminer les héritiers de l'artiste et savoir si lesdits héritiers sont dévolutaires du droit à la paternité et du droit au respect de l'oeuvre.

---

106. Sur une présentation de cette doctrine, cf. B. EDELMAN, note in D. 1989.309-310 n° 3-5.
107. C. Paris 17 décembre 1986 J.C.P. 1987, éd. G. II 20899 note B. EDELMAN.
108. Cass. Civ. 11 janvier 1989 D. 1989.308, lère espèce note B. EDELMAN.

Concernant ce second point, prenons l'exemple d'un peintre français qui, pendant toute sa carrière, a vécu en France mais qui se retire à Genève où il décède quelques années plus tard, laissant pour lui succéder deux enfants légitimes, tous deux de nationalité française.

En droit international privé français, la loi applicable à la dévolution de la succession mobilière de l'artiste est la loi suisse, loi du dernier domicile du défunt;[109] or en droit suisse, comme on l'a vu, le droit moral n'est pas transmissible aux héritiers; il s'ensuit que les enfants du peintre ne seraient pas recevables à faire procéder à la saisie-contrefaçon en France d'une toile de leur auteur, en se prévalant de la qualité – que leur dénie la loi suisse, laquelle est pour le droit français, la loi applicable – de dévolutaires du droit moral de l'artiste; à moins que le juge français considère que la loi suisse est contraire à l'ordre public au sens du droit international privé français, en ce qu'elle frappe d'intransmissibilité successorale le droit moral de l'artiste.

ii. La durée du droit moral dévolu aux héritiers

Selon le cas, la durée du droit moral est égale à celle des droits pécuniaires ou se caractérise par sa perpétuité.

La durée du droit moral est égale à celle des droits pécuniares en droit allemand, autrichien, néerlandais, suédois, anglais.[110]

Le droit français et, dans une moindre mesure, les droits espagnol et portugais se démarquent de cette position.

La perpétuité de principe du droit moral est posée en droit français à l'art. 6 de la loi du 11 mars 1957 et réaffirmée, à propos du droit de divulgation, à l'art. 19 dernier alinéa de la même loi. L'on observera néanmoins que l'analyse doctrinale consacrée par l'arrêt Utrillo rendu par la Cour de Paris le 17 décembre 1986[111] impliquait la disparition à la première génération de la dévolution successorale de l'ensemble des attributs du droit moral, en l'absence d'héritiers par le sang.

De fait, dans son arrêt du 17 décembre 1986, la Cour de Paris, après avoir souligné que la dévolution successorale spécifique du droit de divulgation doit être étendue aux autres attributs du droit moral, a jugé que 'la présomption de fidélité aux intentions de l'auteur sur laquelle repose l'art. 19 ne saurait être étendue à des personnes qui n'ont aucun lien de rattachement avec l'auteur lui-même'.

En censurant par son arrêt du 11 janvier 1989, la décision du 17 décembre 1986, la Cour Suprême[112] a restitué à la perpétuité du droit moral toute sa rigueur.

109. Cf. *supra* p. 212 et n. 90.

110. Art. 64 de la loi allemande du 9 septembre 1965; rapport néerlandais A. A. QUAEDVLIEG, III; rapport suédois Ch. WEGENIUS; art. 86-1 de la loi anglaise du 15 novembre 1988, sur lequel de FREITAS, étude précitée, RIDA, janvier 1990, n° 143, p. 63.

111. Cf. *supra* p. 217 et n. 107.

112. Cf. *supra* p. 217 et n. 108.

Ce qui accentue le contraste existant entre le droit français d'une part, les droits espagnol et portugais d'autre part.

De fait, selon la législation espagnole, la perpétuité n'est attachée qu'au droit à la paternité et au respect de l'oeuvre; par contre, le droit de divulgation dévolu aux héritiers ne dure que 60 années après le décès de l'auteur,[113] durée qui est, comme on l'a relevé celle dans laquelle la loi espagnole enferme les droits pécuniaires dévolus aux héritiers.[114]

Pour sa part, le Portugal habilite les héritiers de l'artiste à exercer les prérogatives du droit moral, aussi longtemps que l'oeuvre n'est pas tombée dans le domaine public et confère au seul Ministère de la Culture, une fois que la durée de protection des droits pécuniaires (50 ans après le décès de l'artiste) est expirée, la défense de l'authenticité et de l'intégrite de l'oeuvre.[115]

Par les prérogatives ainsi conférées au Ministère de la Culture, le Portugal semble pouvoir être rangé dans la catégorie des Etats qui adoptent la règle de la perpétuité du droit moral; à la différence toutefois du droit français, les héritiers sont dépossédés des prérogatives liées au droit moral, une fois l'oeuvre d'art est tombée dans le domaine public.

III. CONCLUSION

En dernière analyse, l'examen des règles nationales gouvernant les droits des artistes et de leurs héritiers fait apparaître des points communs entre les lois nationales mais également des divergences souvent sensibles en ce qui concerne, plus particulièrement, le droit de suite et, dans une moindre mesure, le droit moral.

Divergences dont les conséquences, du point de vue de la libre circulation internationale des oeuvres d'art, peuvent être sensibles car l'inclinaison naturelle et compréhensible des opérateurs intervenant sur le marché international de l'art est de localiser les transactions sur les oeuvres d'art dans les zones de moindre protection des artistes et de leurs héritiers.

Assurément, pour remédier aux distorsions de concurrence entre les différents marchés de l'art résultant des divergences entre législations relatives au niveau de protection des artistes et de leurs héritiers, une harmonisation des règles nationales sur le droit d'auteur apparaît souhaitable; mais qui dit harmonisation dit nivellement; va-t-il alors s'agir d'un nivellement vers le haut ou vers le bas?

Un nivellement vers le haut risque fort de se heurter à l'opposition des Etats où la protection des artistes et de leurs héritiers est plus faible, en particulier s'agissant des pays ignorant le droit de suite.

Mais un nivellement vers le bas ne risquerait-il pas, quant à lui, de

113. Arts. 15–1 (concernant le droit à la paternité et le droit au respect de l'oeuvre) et 15–2 (concernant le droit de divulgation) de la loi espagnole du 11 novembre 1987.
114. Cf. *supra* p. 215.
115. Cf. arts. 57–1 et 57–2 de la loi portugaise.

décourager et, par là même, de tarir la création artistique, ce qui pourrait, par contrecoup, conduire à terme à un assèchement du marché international des oeuvres d'art.

Un juriste français, Charles Lyon Caen écrivait en 1881 que 'le développement intellectuel littéraire et artistique d'un pays est en raison directe de la protection accordée aux auteurs nationaux et étrangers'.[116]

Ce point de vue, exprimé il y a plus de 100 ans, demeure on ne peut plus actuel.

116. Phrase reproduite par C. DOUTRELEPONT, 'Une proposition de révision de la loi belge du 22 mars 1886', RIDA, octobre 1987, n° 134, p. 71, n° 1.

National Reports

Austria

NATIONAL REPORT ON TOPIC 3. RIGHTS OF ARTISTS AND THEIR HEIRS*

Ignaz Seidl-Hohenveldern**

1. The Austrian Copyright Act (*Urheberrechtsgesetz* (UrhG) BGBl 1936/III in the version of BGBl 1973/142)[1] gives the author a number of different rights. These rights protect the author's economic and intellectual interests:

- The author has the right to release the first public information as to the contents of his work of literature or of his film-work (Art. 14(3) UrhG).
- He has the exclusive right to adapt and translate the work. The author of a translation or adaptation of the work may use that only as far as the author of the original work agrees (Art. 14(7) UrhG).
- The author has the exclusive right to copy the work by any means and to any extent. This right includes the right to realize designs and plans (Art. 15(1) UrhG).
- The author has the exclusive right to distribute the work in a way that makes it public (Art. 16(1) UrhG).
- As long as the work is not opened to the public with the author's consent, this right of distribution also includes the exclusive right of the author to make the work available for the public especially by an exhibition or a similar use of the work.
- The author has the exclusive right to broadcast his work (Art. 17 UrhG).
- The author has the exclusive right to perform, recite or lecture on his work before the public (Art. 18 UrhG).
- The right to decide whether or not the work may be published is not explicitly mentioned in the UrhG. It is part of the rights mentioned above. If the author, e.g., gives his permission for broadcasting, this permission includes the right to make the work available to the public by broadcasting.
- The author has the right to be acknowledged as author (Art. 19 UrhG).
- It is the author's right to decide whether and how he may be named on the work as the author (Art. 20 UrhG).

* Editor's note: *see also* 'Austria: Introduction' in Part One.

** Professor, Institut für Völkerrecht und Internationale Beziehungen, Vienna. This Report was prepared with the assistance of *Dr. Guido Kucsko*, Vienna.

1. Cf. DITTRICH, *Urheberrechtsgesetz*.

- The person who has the consent of the author to use the work in a public way is not allowed to change the work, its title or the author's sign, unless agreed by the author or permitted by law (Art. 21 UrhG). For the original of a work of fine art, this is true even if the work is not used in a way that makes it public (Art. 21(2) UrhG).
- The owner of a work has to make it available to the author as far as it is necessary for the author to copy his work (Art. 22 UrhG). Nevertheless, the owner of the work is not obliged to give the work to the author or to keep it in good condition.

The artist can prohibit any use of the work contrary to the above-mentioned rights.

Any use of the work in the above-mentioned way requires the consent of the artist.

Artists can exploit their work commercially not only by selling the original work. They can exploit it also by giving the exclusive or non-exclusive licence to a third party for using this work in a way mentioned above.

2. Regarding the exercise of rights:

- As mentioned above, the author has the sole right to disclose the work to the public (right of exhibition) as long as the work has not been disclosed with the consent of the author.
- As mentioned above, the author has the exclusive right to reproduce his work.
- The same is true for the right to perform a work.
- As described above, the right to use a work is limited by the exclusive rights of the author.
- The Austrian Copyright Act does not provide for such a *droit de suite* as the right to receive royalties and resale proceeds from a work.
- The artist does not have the right to exhibit a work even if it is owned by a private person and whether or not it is held in a private or public place. This results *a contrario* from Art. 22 UrhG mentioned *supra*.
- There are no specific regulations for the right to withdraw an authorization given by the artist to reproduce, disclose or perform a work.
- There is no special right prohibiting the work being destroyed.
- The right to oppose the exhibition of a work whether or not it has been exhibited previously is only given if the work has not been opened previously to the public with the author's consent.
- As mentioned above, the artist has the right to object to any substantial alteration or relocation of a work which threatens its integrity (Art. 21 UrhG).
- As mentioned above, the artist has the right to be recognized as the creator of the work (Arts. 19 and 20 UrhG).

Generally speaking, there is no difference between the use by a gallery or a museum. There are no special requirements for the exercise of these rights. The copyright exists from the day of the creation of the work. There is no need for registration or other formalities. The copyright is inheritable. Therefore, the rights of the artist may be used by his heirs after the artist's death.

In respect to some details, there might be some exemptions. For instance, it is allowed to copy and distribute a work of fine art from the original that is part of a public collection, if it is copied for a catalogue for the visitors of the collection. A similar exemption is made for catalogues made for (auction) sales (Art. 54 Z (1) and (2) UrhG).[2]

3. The copyright as such is not transferable by contract but it is inheritable (Art. 23 UrhG). It may pass to the heirs by law or by last will.

2. Cf. G. KUCSKO, 'Die Katalogfreiheit' in R. DITTRICH, ed., *Festschrift 50 Jahre Urheberrechtsgesetz* (Vienna, Manz 1986) pp. 191–197.

Belgique

RAPPORT NATIONAL SUR LE SUJET 3. DROITS DE CREATEURS ET DE LEURS HERITIERS*

Philippe Coppens** et Alain Strowel***

I. INTRODUCTION

L'idée de reconnaître des droits aux créateurs est relativement récente. La protection de ceux-ci est assurée, en Belgique, par la loi du 22 mars 1886[1] et par les Conventions internationales de Berne du 9 septembre 1886[2] et de Genève du 6 septembre 1952.[3] La Convention de Berne, dite Convention d'Union, revêt en droit interne une singulière importance: d'une part, la loi du 27 juillet 1953 permet au créateur d'invoquer en Belgique les dispositions de la Convention qui lui sont plus favorables que la loi du 22 mars 1886; d'autre part, conformément à la jurisprudence de la Cour de cassation,[4] les dispositions directement applicables de cette Convention doivent prévaloir sur les normes de droit interne qui sont incompatibles avec elle.

La loi belge et la Convention d'Union accordent leur protection aux créateurs d'oeuvres littéraires et artistiques. La protection est soumise à

* Note d'Editeur: *v*. 'Belgique: Introduction', Francis HAUMONT, *supra* pp. 31–38.

** Assistant en droit à l'Université catholique de Louvain, Centre de philosophie de droit.

*** Assistant en droit aux Facultés universitaires Saint-Louis, Avocat au Barreau de Bruxelles, Stipendiat au Max-Planck-Institut, Munich.

1. La loi du 22 mars 1886 a été modifiée à plusieurs reprises: un principe de réciprocité à l'égard des étrangers a été introduit par la loi du 5 mars 1921 (art. 38); deux lois portant la date du 25 juin 1921 ont introduit des dispositions relatives au droit de suite et à la prolongation de la durée du droit pour cause de guerre; par ailleurs, le droit de citation de l'article 13, dont le champ d'application se réduisait aux oeuvres littéraires, a été étendu aux autres oeuvres d'art par la loi du 11 mars 1958 (art. 21*bis*).
2. La Convention de Berne est approuvée par la loi belge du 30 septembre 1887; elle a été modifiée à diverses reprises, notamment à Bruxelles le 26 juin 1948. Cette modification fut introduite dans l'ordre interne par la loi du 26 juin 1951. C'est cet état du texte que nous retiendrons ici bien que la Convention ait encore été révisée à Stockholm le 14 juillet 1967 et à Paris le 24 juillet 1971. La loi belge du 26 septembre 1974 a rendu applicable les seules dispositions administratives de l'Acte de Stockholm, tandis que l'Acte de Paris est resté lettre morte en droit belge. (*v*. pour plus de détails, A. BERENBOOM, *Le droit d'auteur* (Bruxelles, Larcier 1984) p. 180 et suivantes; P. EECKMAN, 'Kunst en auteursrecht', *Kunst en Recht*, K. RIMANQUE, éd. (Antwerpen, Kluwer 1985, pp. 50–53).
3. La Convention de Genève est approuvée par la loi belge du 20 avril 1960.
4. Cass., 27 mai 1971, Pas, 1971, 1, 886 et les conclusions de W. GANSHOF VAN DER MEERSCH.

deux conditions: l'oeuvre doit être une création originale et revêtir une certaine forme, au demeurant tout à fait variable. D'autres critères, singulièrement ceux du beau ou du mérite ne peuvent être retenus. En principe, la protection juridique d'un créateur n'est pas préalablement soumise à un jugement esthétique.[5] Reste qu'en pratique, les juges sont souvent amenés – le cas typique est celui des photographies[6] – à émettre un jugement esthétique et à en faire dépendre la protection.

Ce rapport ne concerne que les arts qualifiés de 'plastiques' et, tout spécialement, la peinture et la sculpture. On distingue classiquement, parmi les droits de l'auteur, deux sortes de prérogatives: les droits moraux du créateur de l'oeuvre et ses droits patrimoniaux. Les premiers, dérivés du droit de la personnalité ne trouvent, que pour partie, un ancrage légal.[7] Leur étude fera l'objet du point 1. de la deuxième section. Les droits patrimoniaux trouvent, par contre, un appui stable dans les textes légaux.[8] Ils feront l'objet du point 2. de cette seconde section. La troisième section sera consacrée à la question de savoir si et dans quelle mesure ces droits peuvent être attribués aux héritiers.

La jurisprudence belge – à tout le moins, celle qui est relative aux droits moraux de l'artiste – est peu abondante. Mais, de même qu'en d'autres matières, la doctrine et la jurisprudence belges interprètent et assimilent largement dans l'ordre juridique interne certaines solutions dégagées par la doctrine et la jurisprudence françaises. Cette influence s'exerce d'autant plus facilement que, comme il a été relevé ci-dessus, les droits moraux de l'artiste ne trouvent en Belgique qu'une assise légale partielle. Cette lacune pourrait toutefois être largement comblée si une récente proposition de loi relative aux droits d'auteur, aux droits voisins et à la copie privée d'oeuvres sonores et audiovisuelles était adoptée[9]. Aussi, nous mentionnerons, pour chaque prérogative étudiée, les solutions indiquées dans cette proposition, qui devrait être adoptée prochainement. Enfin, sauf lorsque nous le préciserons dans le texte qui suit, il n'y a pas lieu de réserver un sort particulier

---

5. *V.* p. ex., Bruxelles, 29 septembre 1965, J.C.P., 1966, 14820 et note A. FRANCON: 'Attendu que, dans les litiges qui, comme celui-ci, mettent en cause le droit de l'auteur au respect de sa personnalité à travers son oeuvre esthétique, les juges n'ont point à porter un jugement de valeur esthétique.'
6. *V.* p. ex., civ. Liège, 27 janvier 1984, Jur. de Liège, 1984, p. 129: 'Les photographies banales qui ne révèlent pas une conception intellectuelle créant chez celui qui les voit et les regarde un sentiment d'art ne sont pas protégées par la loi du 22 mars 1886'.
7. Comme nous l'avons souligné plus haut, les droits moraux sont centrés sur la personnalité de l'artiste. Les droits moraux de divulgation, de paternité et de respect de l'oeuvre sont visés par les art 8 et 9 de la loi du 22 mars 1886 et l'art. 6*bis* de la Convention de Berne. Le droit moral de repentir et de retrait fait l'objet d'une construction doctrinale et, dans une mesure qu'il nous appartiendra de préciser, jurisprudentielle.
8. Cf. entre autres, les arts. 1, 15, 16, 19 de la loi du 22 mars 1886, la loi du 25 juin 1921 sur le droit de suite ainsi que les arts. 9 à 12 de la Convention de Berne.
9. Cf. Sénat de Belgique, session extraordinaire de 1988, n° 329–1; sur cette proposition, *v.* C. DOUTRELEPONT, 'Une proposition de révision de la loi belge du 22 mars 1886: un pas de plus vers l'uniformisation du droit d'auteur dans le Marché commun?', *Revue Internationale du Droit d'Auteur* (R.I.D.A.) 1987, n° 134, p. 70 *et seq.*

aux droits, tant moraux que pécuniaires, selon qu'ils sont exercés à l'égard d'une galerie d'art ou d'un musée.

II. LES DROITS DES CREATEURS SUR LEURS OEUVRES

1. Les droits moraux de l'artiste

a. Le droit de divulgation

L'art. 1 de la loi belge du 22 mars 1886 stipule que 'l'auteur d'une oeuvre littéraire ou artistique a seul le droit de la reproduire ou d'en autoriser la reproduction, de quelque manière et sous quelque forme que ce soit'. L'art. 9 de cette même loi énonce, par ailleurs, que 'sont toujours insaisissables les oeuvres littéraires ou musicales, tant qu'elles sont inédites, et, du vivant de l'auteur, les autres oeuvres d'art, tant qu'elles ne sont pas prêtes pour la vente ou la publication'.

Ces dispositions reconnaissent, de manière indirecte, au créateur le droit exclusif et le pouvoir discrétionnaire de divulguer son oeuvre. Le principe ne pose pas de difficultés. Il est bien établi en droit belge. Il n'en va pas de même de sa définition et de son application. Car, en effet, qu'appelle-t-on la divulgation? Et quand est-elle réalisée? L'étude de la doctrine française révèle un nombre impressionnant de conceptions différentes qu'il ne nous est pas possible ici de recenser.[10] On admettra ici que la divulgation est l'acte par lequel le créateur ou, à sa mort, la personne habilitée à cette fin, manifeste sans équivoque sa volonté de communiquer son oeuvre au public.

Mais quelle est précisément cette manifestation non équivoque qui réalise la divulgation? Différents critères peuvent être avancés, qui ne sont pas tous d'égale valeur:[11]

- l'aliénation de l'oeuvre, à titre onéreux ou à titre gratuit, indique avec certitude la volonté de l'auteur de la divulguer, même si elle n'est qu'une ébauche ou une esquisse;
- la déclaration, par le créateur, de l'achèvement de son oeuvre a été retenue comme critère de divulgation par la Cour d'appel de Bruxelles.[12] Cette juridiction a en effet décidé qu'une telle déclaration signifiait que l'artiste considérait son oeuvre 'comme prête pour la vente et aussi pour la publication, puisqu'il la savait destinée à figurer au musée de l'Etat de Bruxelles; que, partant, elle cessait dès ce moment d'être insaisissable, aux termes de l'art. 9 de la loi du 22 mars 1886'. Le critère de l'achève-

10. Cf. sur ce point, O. LALIGANT, *La divulgation des oeuvres artistiques, littéraires et musicales en droit positif français* (Paris, L.G.D.J. 1983).
11. *V.* pour plus de développements, Ph. COPPENS et N. VERHEYDEN-JEANMART, 'La propriété d'une oeuvre d'art et les droits moraux de l'artiste', *Annales de droit de Louvain*, 1988, n° 3-4, pp. 293 à 298.
12. Bruxelles, 31 mars 1888, Pas., 1888, II, p. 196.

ment pose cependent plusieurs difficultés. Il va de soi que seul l'artiste peut réputer son oeuvre achevée. Mais, même dans ce cas, y-a-t-il divulgation?

Dans la célèbre affaire Whistler,[13] la Cour d'appel de Paris, puis la Cour de Cassation, ont refusé d'admettre que l'exposition au Salon du Champ de Mars du tableau commandé et la déclaration du peintre selon laquelle ce tableau était 'un petit chef d'oeuvre' entraînent *ipso facto* la divulgation. L'achèvement ne peut, nous semble-t-il, être retenu comme critère nécessaire et suffisant: l'inachèvement de l'oeuvre ne fait pas obstacle à sa divulgation;

- l'exposition publique de l'oeuvre n'emporte pas nécessairement divulgation de celle-ci. Elle doit être corroborée par d'autres éléments, par exemple la volonté de vendre;
- la livraison de l'oeuvre, en exécution d'un contrat, implique normalement la volonté de divulguer. Cette hypothèse doit cependant être distinguée du cas de la possession de l'oeuvre par un tiers. En effet, la seule possession n'entraîne pas nécessairement divulgation, surtout si elle résulte d'une livraison assortie de réserves. Le tiers devra alors être considéré comme dépositaire. Il s'agira donc d'une détention et non pas d'une possession. L'affaire Rouault[14] en fournit, pour la France, un exemple illustre;
- la signature de l'oeuvre n'est ni un critère nécessaire ni un critère suffisant pour entraîner la divulgation. La doctrine et la jurisprudence belges et françaises sont, sur ce point, unanimes. La Cour d'appel de Bruxelles, dans l'arrêt précité, a ainsi décidé 'qu'il n'est pas indispensable, pour qu'un tableau soit prêt pour la vente ou la publication, que l'auteur y ait apposé sa signature'.

Il ressort de ce qui précède que la plupart des critères, pris isolément, ne sont pas suffisants. Bien plutôt, ils agissent comme présomption et doivent se renforcer mutuellement pour qu'on puisse y trouver un ensemble d'éléments décisifs qui manifestent une volonté de divulguer l'oeuvre créee.

Deux autres questions, du reste fort liées, méritent encore de retenir l'attention. La première est relative au point de savoir si l'artiste peut renoncer contractuellement à son droit moral de divulgation. Une certaine doctrine belge s'est prononcée affirmativement en se fondant sur l'arrêt de

---

13. Trib. civ. Seine, 20 mars 1895 et Paris 2 décembre 1897, D. P., 1898, note. M. PLANIOL; S., 1900, II, 201, note A. WAHL; Cass. civ. 14 mars 1900, D. P., 1990, 447, rapport RAU et conclusions DESJARDIN.
14. Trib. civ. Seine, 10 juillet 1946, Gaz. Pal., 1946, II, 108 et conclusions GEGOUT; J. C. P., 1947, II, 3405, et note PLAISANT; D. S., 1947, 98 et note DESBOIS; Appel Paris, 19 mars 1947, Gaz. Pal., 1947, I. 84, et conclusions FRECHTE; D. S., 1949, 20, et note DESBOIS. La Cour de Paris décida en l'espèce 'qu'il n'y a pas transfert à un marchand de tableaux de la propriété de toiles non achevées, ni signées qu'un peintre lui a remises, avec faculté de les reprendre pour les retoucher, la livraison effective ne devant s'opérer qu'au fur et à mesure de l'accomplissement du travail, dans un atelier-d'ailleurs mis à la disposition de l'artiste par le marchand.'

la Cour d'appel de Bruxelles déjà cité.[15] Il s'agit là d'une mauvaise interprétation. Car l'élément essentiel de cet arrêt est, sans nul doute, que l'artiste avait déclaré expressément que son tableau était achevé. Le fait, pour un créateur, de s'engager à livrer un tableau, le cas échéant inachevé, pour une date déterminée ne peut signifier une renonciation à son droit de divulgation. Par ailleurs, la solution contraire conduit logiquement à une impasse dès lors que personne ne conteste que l'artiste ne peut jamais être contraint d'exécuter l'oeuvre promise. La solution ici critiquée, est, enfin, incompatible avec l'essence des droits moraux qui, indissolublement liés à la personnalité de l'artiste, sont par nature rebelles à toute forme de renonciation. Le droit de divulgation doit, nous semble-t-il, rester inaliénable. Ce principe est parallèle à celui qui interdit l'exécution forcée de l'oeuvre promise. Il faut donc admettre qu'en droit belge, la renonciation contractuelle au droit de divulgation est impossible.

La jurisprudence française s'est par ailleurs souvent prononcée en ce sens. Dans l'affaire Rouault précitée, la Cour d'appel de Paris a décidé sans ambiguïté que ce droit s'exerce 'nonobstant toutes conventions contraires'. La combinaison des arts. 6 et 19 de la loi française du 11 mars 1957 confirme textuellement cette impossibilité.[16] Pour les autres droits moraux, cette règle doit être nuancée en fonction des espèces litigieuses. Aucune réponse décisive ne peut être apportée. Les solutions défendues varieront selon les critères retenus. Les juges ont, en cette matière, un large pouvoir d'appréciation. Toutefois, et nous abordons ici la seconde question, l'impossibilité de renoncer au droit de divulgation ne signifie pas que l'artiste ne sera jamais contraint de réparer les conséquences dommageables résultant, pour le tiers, de l'exercice de cette faculté incessible. Le caractère discrétionnaire du droit de divulgation est en effet limité par la théorie de l'abus de droit. Il ne s'agit pas cependant d'une limite au principe du droit moral de divulgation, car le théorie de l'abus de droit ne sanctionne que l'exercice fautif de celui-ci. La différence est importante.

En Belgique, singulièrement depuis l'arrêt de la Cour de Cassation du 19 septembre 1983, le fondement juridique de la théorie peut se trouver dans l'art. 1134 al. 3 du Code civil.[17] Le principe de l'exécution de bonne foi des conventions impose aux parties contractantes de ne pas faire un usage abusif

15. A. BERENBOOM, *op cit.*, p. 124.
16. *V.* p. ex., H. DESBOIS, *Le droit d'auteur en France* (Paris, Dalloz, 3 éd., 1978) n° 406, p. 498: 'au moment où il accepte de brosser une toile pour le compte du client, le peintre n'exerce pas encore le droit de divulgation que lui réserve en propre l'article 19 §1er et dont l'article 6 lui interdit de se priver'; dans le même sens, S. STRÖMHOLM, 'Le refus par l'auteur de livrer une oeuvre de l'esprit cédée avant son achèvement', in *Hommage à H. Desbois* (Paris, 1974) n° 5, p. 76.
17. Cass. 19 septembre 1983, R. C. J. B., 1986, p. 283 et la note J. L. FAGNART, 'L'exécution de bonne foi des conventions'. Comme le relève cet auteur, l'arrêt ne dit pas que le fondement de la théorie en matière contractuelle ne peut plus se trouver dans l'art. 1382 du Code civil; par ailleurs, sur cette théorie, on lira avec profit la note classique de P. VAN OMMESLAGHE, 'Abus de droit, fraude aux droits des tiers et fraude à la loi', note sous Cass. 10 septembre 1971, R. C. J. B., 1976, pp. 303 à 350.

des prérogatives qu'elle tirent du contrat. Ce principe pourra être utilement invoqué dans le cadre des contrats de commande d'une oeuvre d'art. On ne peut, ici, développer les critères classiques qui définissent l'abus de droit. Il est cependant opportun de rappeler que la jurisprudence belge a profondément évolué. Car, si, initialement, un sujet de droit abusait de ses droits lorsqu'il les exerçait dans l'intention de nuire, les Cours et tribunaux ont rapidement retenu d'autres critères moins stricts: l'absence d'intérêt, le choix sans utilité du mode d'exercice du droit le plus dommageable pour le tiers, la disproportion entre l'intérêt servi et l'intérêt lésé, le détournement du droit de sa fonction sociale et le comportement anormal.[18]

Dans une décision du 19 décembre 1966, le Tribunal civil d'Anvers a fait, incidemment, référence à la théorie de l'abus de droit.[19] En l'espèce, Sartre s'opposait à la représentation de sa pièce 'Les Mains sales' en raison 'de la fausse interprétation qui pourrait être donnée à la pièce dans le contexte politique actuel'. Le tribunal lui donna raison mais les attendus témoignent de sa réticence à adopter une telle solution: il laisse penser que s'il n'avait pas siégé en référé, il eut fait prévaloir la théorie de l'abus de droit. Celle-ci trouve d'ailleurs à s'appliquer à l'égard de tous les droits subjectifs de l'auteur.

La nouvelle proposition de loi belge relative au droit d'auteur reconnaît expressément le droit moral de divulgation (art. 4). Elle tend par là à exprimer textuellement ce droit qui n'est pas entièrement assuré par les arts. 1 et 9 de la loi du 22 mars 1886.

L'art. 4 de cette proposition stipule que 'le droit d'auteur est mobilier, cessible et transmissible, en tout ou en partie, conformément aux règles du Code civil'. Cet article figure dans le chapitre II, intitulé 'Du droit d'auteur', qui traite, notamment, des droits moraux. Si l'état actuel du texte de la proposition était adopté par le législateur, il faudrait, semble-t-il admettre que le créateur pourrait renoncer contractuellement à ses droits moraux. Nous avons déjà noté qu'une telle solution, appliquée au droit de divulgation, ne nous paraît pas souhaitable.

b. Le droit de paternité

Le droit à la paternité n'est pas consacré dans la loi belge actuellement en vigueur. Cela n'a pourtant guère d'effets pratiques, dès lors qu'il est reconnu par l'art. 6*bis* de la Convention de Berne qui, rappelons-le, a été approuvée par la loi belge du 26 juin 1951. L'art. 6*bis* s'applique donc dans l'ordre juridique interne. La reconnaissance du droit de paternité a pour conséquence que tout auteur a droit à ce que son oeuvre soit publiée avec sa signature.[20] La loi belge se montre soucieuse d'assurer une protection étendue à l'artiste en sanctionnant de lourdes peines 'l'application méchante

---

18. Sur ceci, cf. J. L. FAGNART, *op. cit.*, spéc. n° 32, p. 313 et les références citées.
19. Civ. Anvers (réf.), 19 décembre 1966, J. T., 1967, p. 224 et la note L. V. B.
20. Cf. civ. Bruxelles, 25 février 1954, J. T., 1954, p. 279.

ou frauduleuse sur un objet d'art, un ouvrage de littérature ou de musique, du nom d'un auteur, ou de tout signe distinctif adopté par lui pour désigner son oeuvre' (art. 25).[21] Des corollaires importants au droit de paternité sont, bien entendu, le droit à l'anonymat et au pseudonyme. Personne ne peut être contraint de reconnaître la paternité de son oeuvre.

La question de savoir si on peut renoncer à son droit de paternité est discutée dans la doctrine belge. Il faut, nous semble-t-il, affirmer minimalement que l'artiste ne peut renoncer à la paternité d'une oeuvre entièrement réalisée. Cette solution assure une protection élémentaire contre diverses pressions économiques qui pourraient s'exercer à l'encontre du créateur. Notons que l'art. 6 de la loi française de 1957 rejette la possibilité d'une telle renonciation.

La nouvelle proposition de loi belge dispose, à son art. 10, que 'même après la cession du droit d'auteur, l'auteur a le droit de s'opposer à l'exécution, la représentation, la publication ou l'exposition de l'oeuvre, sans son nom ou sous un autre nom que le sien ainsi qu'à toute déformation, altération ou autre atteinte à son oeuvre. L'auteur jouit du droit au respect de son nom, de sa qualité et de son oeuvre'. Le droit à la paternité y est donc expressément affirmé. Toutefois, par identité de motifs avec ce que nous avons vu à propos du droit de divulgation, la proposition reste ambiguë sur le point de savoir si, et dans quelle mesure, elle entend réserver la possibilité d'y renoncer.

c. Le droit de repentir et de retrait

L'oeuvre attire celui qui s'y consacre vers le point ou elle est à l'épreuve de son impossibilité' écrit M. Blanchot.[22] Le visible, dans l'oeuvre, n'est en effet jamais que le voile partiellement déchiré de la présence d'un monde. Et un nouveau dévoilement d'une nouvelle présence ne fera pas un pas pour retrouver l'unité perdue. Ce n'est pas à dire qu'avant l'oeuvre, rien n'ait été fait mais bien qu'après l'oeuvre, tout reste à faire. L'invisible dévoilé est le signe d'une présence absente. Aucune oeuvre ne totalise donc l'urgence du monde à exprimer mais la première, comme chaque oeuvre ultérieure 'va jusqu'au fond de l'avenir'.[23] Et pourtant, malgré l'inéluctable inachèvement de leur travail, le peintre ou le sculpteur, en prononçant le vouloir être dans la violence du commencement, font comme si l'oeuvre se dirigeait vers la voie de son achèvement pour que s'élève enfin 'une page à la puissance du ciel étoilé'.[24]

Il ne fait guère de doute qu'en créant, l'artiste se repent sans cesse. Chacun sait que l'oeuvre se fait en se défaisant. Mais la singularité du droit de repentir consiste précisément à en fixer une limite temporelle, eu égard

---

21. *V.* pour un cas d'espèce, civ. Bruxelles, 14 juillet 1931, Pas., 1931, p. 161.
22. M. BLANCHOT, *L'espace littéraire* (Paris, Gallimard 1955) p. 101.
23. M. MERLEAU-PONTY, *L'oeil et l'esprit* (Paris, Gallimard 1969) p. 92.
24. P. VALÉRY, *Variétés I et II* (Paris, Gallimard 1930) p. 268.

aux actes juridiques accomplis par l'artiste, et au-delà de laquelle le constat d'inachèvement ne lui permet plus de refaire l'oeuvre, fut-ce une dernière fois. Le droit de retrait et de repentir ne pose donc de problèmes que lorsqu'il s'oppose à la force obligatoire des contrats.

La doctrine a largement étudié le droit de repentir et de retrait mais demeure hésitante sur son contenu et, partant, sur ses limites. De même, la terminologie est mal assurée. L'art. 32 al. 1 de la loi française parle du repentir *ou* du retrait. La loi belge et la Convention de Berne n'en parlent pas. Mais, malgré l'absence de dispositions légales, la doctrine belge reste curieusement divisée sur sa qualification: certains parlent de droit de repentir; d'autres, de droit au retrait.

Les moments du repentir varient en fonction des actes juridiques dont a fait l'objet l'oeuvre sur laquelle le créateur désire opérer le retrait. Le repentir peut ainsi intervenir avant ou après la divulgation de l'oeuvre, que celle-ci ait fait l'objet d'un contrat de commande ou que les droits patrimoniaux y afférents aient été cédés. Le repentir peut également saisir l'artiste lorsqu'il a aliéné la propriété matérielle de son oeuvre. Mais cette dernière hypothèse montre à suffisance que l'exercice du droit de repentir ne peut intervenir à chacun de ces moments.

Le droit de repentir doit être radicalement distingué du droit de divulgation. Sans cette autonomie, il perd tout intérêt. Aussi, s'il est admis, son exercice ne peut débuter qu'à partir du moment où la divulgation est dèfinitivement réalisée. La question de l'exercice initial du droit de repentir est donc totalement liée à celle de la définition de la divulgation. Ainsi, si l'artiste refuse de livrer une oeuvre commandée, il exerçera en réalité son droit de divulgation et non son droit de repentir. Ces points ont été analysés plus haut. Par ailleurs – seconde limite – le droit de repentir ne peut plus s'exercer lorsque l'oeuvre a fait l'objet d'un transfert de propriété. La doctrine est unanime sur ce point: repousser cette limite reviendrait en effet à offrir au créateur un véritable droit d'expropriation.[25] La jurisprudence, elle non plus, n'a jamais admis la possibilité pour l'artiste de modifier une oeuvre transférée.[26]

S'il est établi que le droit de repentir ne peut s'exercer avant la divulgation et après l'aliénation de l'oeuvre, il demeure, entre ces deux moments, l'espace d'un temps: l'oeuvre est divulguée mais n'est pas pour autant

25. *V.* en Belgique, J.G. RENAULD, *Droit d'auteur et contrat d'adaptation* (Bruxelles, Larcier 1955) p. 133; F. VAN ISACKER, *De morele rechten van de auteur* (Bruxelles, Larcier 1961) n° 103, p. 116; G. LEROY, 'Le droit de repentir', J.T., 1979, p. 211.

26. *V.*, pour un bel exemple, Paris, 19 avril 1961, R.I.D.A., janvier 1962, p. 119: un amateur avait acquis une toile intitulée 'Champ de blé', puis l'avait confiée au marchand attitré du peintre Vlaminck, en lui précisant qu'un acheteur potentiel s'était présenté mais exigeait un certificat d'authenticité. Peu après, la toile lui fut restituée mais le peintre y avait effacé sa signature et l'avait déclarée fausse. La Cour condamne les agissements du peintre par ces deux considérants très significatifs: 'Considérant en effet que dans l'hypothèse où il serait l'auteur de l'oeuvre, s'il est entièrement libre de dire quand celle-ci lui paraît indigne de lui, il perd son droit au repentir au moment où il livre cette oeuvre qui, dans l'espèce, est de plus revêtue de la signature, marque de son achèvement'; 'Considérant d'autre part, qu'au cas où la toile n'aurait pas été peinte par l'artiste, rien n'autorisait ce dernier à mutiler luimême un tableau dont il n'était pas propriétaire.'

aliénée purement et simplement. Les conflits surgissent dans cet intervalle, lorsque des contrats de cession des droits patrimoniaux sont conclus.

Depuis plusieurs années, certains auteurs belges ont reconnu l'existence d'un droit de repentir. Le fondement qu'ils donnent à cette prérogative varie toutefois fortement.

Pour F. van Isacker, le droit de repentir trouverait une base textuelle dans l'art. 1794 du Code civil et, le cas échéant, dans l'art. 14 de la Constitution.[27] Le premier texte, qui reconnaît le droit du maître de l'ouvrage de rompre unilatéralement, moyennant des dommages-intérêts, le contrat d'entreprise, est cependant fort éloigné de l'idée de droit moral et ne s'applique pas à tous les cas d'espèce; le second garantit la liberté des idées – notamment artistiques – mais ne confère pas la faculté de retirer du circuit économique la forme dans laquelle ces idées sont exprimées.[28]

Pour J. G. Renauld, il convient de tenir compte de la nature particulière des contrats de cession de droits patrimoniaux relatifs à une oeuvre d'art. Cet éminent auteur écrivait ceci:

> 'L'exploitant ne devient point maître absolu des droits transférés et la cession du droit d'édition ou de représentation ne coupe pas tout lien entre l'artiste et son oeuvre. En l'exploitant, l'éditeur met en jeu la personnalité de son auteur. Il est normal que ce dernier puisse mettre fin à la diffusion de l'oeuvre, lorsqu'elle est de nature à léser ses intérêts moraux essentiels. Nous croyons donc que rien n'empêche également en droit belge, le principe même du droit de repentir.'[29]

La reconnaisance du droit de repentir de l'auteur paraît ici doublement fondée: d'une part sur le constat que l'oeuvre n'est pas un acte détachable de son auteur; d'autre part, sur la prééminence du droit moral par rapport aux droits, sinon réels, du moins personnels d'une tierce personne; où on retrouve la conception à la base du droit d'auteur, selon laquelle l'oeuvre est définitivement liée à son créateur, et, par là, une philosophie de l'art qui doit être qualifiée d'Esthétique subjectiviste. Par ailleurs, la prééminence du droit d'auteur comme 'écho sublime' des droits de la personnalité se manifeste de jour en jour. La désacralisation de l'oeuvre est le mouvement inverse de la sacralisation de l'artiste.

Ce double fondement paraît suffisant pour recevoir le droit de repentir en droit belge. La Cour de cassation a, nous semble-t-il, reconnu ce droit dans son arrêt du 12 septembre 1975.[30] Les faits de la cause étaient les suivants:

27. F. VAN ISACKER, *op. cit.*, pp. 120–122.
28. Sur ce point, cf. F. GOTZNEN, observations sous Cass. (1ère ch.), 12 septembre 1975, J. T., 1976, p. 727; G. LEROY, *op. cit.*, p. 213.
29. J. G. RENAULD, *op. cit.*, p. 135.
30. Cass., 12 septembre 1975, J. T., 1976, p. 723 et note F. GOTZEN. Le professeur L. VAN BUNNEN rejoint notre position. Mais, après avoir admis que 'la Cour suprême, en consacrant prétoriennement cette faculté de se raviser, en indique aussitôt les étroites limites', il ajoute: 'ainsi restreint, le retrait est assimilable au refus de divulgation, ce qui permettrait de lui donner la même base textuelle que ce dernier, c'est-à-dire l'art. 9 de la loi du 22 mars 1886', in 'Examen de jurisprudence – Droit d'auteur, dessins et modèles – (1973–1977)', R. C. J. B., 1978, n° 22, p. 553. Nous avons montré plus haut que le droit de repentir ne peut être ainsi assimilé au droit de divulgation.

le sénateur Van den Daele, président du conseil d'administration du 'Secteur public d'Electricité' avait accordé une interview destinée à prendre place dans une émission de la télévision belge de langue néerlandaise (BRT) et relative à la structure du secteur électricité en Belgique. Par la suite, sans doute inquiet du destin de son interview, il exigea que la BRT lui laisse la possibilité de vérifier l'ensemble de l'émission. Devant le refus de la BRT, il prétendit alors opérer le retrait de sa contribution et assigna l'organisme de télévision au nom de son droit moral. Les attendus dans lesquels la Cour fait référence au droit de retrait méritent d'être reproduits:

> 'Attendu qu'il ressort, en effet, des constatations souveraines de l'arrêt que le demandeur avait exigé le retrait de sa contribution au reportage, non parce qu'il désirait y apporter des modifications ou parce qu'il ne l'approuvait plus, mais uniquement parce qu'il invoquait des droits qu'il n'avait pas sur l'ensemble du reportage.
> 'Qu'une telle prétention est étrangère au droit de retrait qu'un auteur est en droit de faire valoir
> 'Attendu que, après avoir ainsi légalement admis qu'en l'espèce, le demandeur avait invoqué à tort le droit de "retrait" (ou de repentir) et le droit de "divulgation" liés au droit d'auteur...'.

Dans les attendus qui précèdent, la Cour de cassation nous paraît avoir reconnu l'existence d'un droit de retrait ou de repentir en droit positif belge et l'avoir défini comme le droit, pour un créateur, d'opérer le retrait d'une oeuvre, tantôt provisoirement pour la modifier, tantôt définitivement en la désavouant.[31] Le sommaire de l'arrêt est, à cet égard, beaucoup plus explicite puisqu'il affirme que 'l'auteur ne peut faire valoir le droit de retrait si son but est autre que la modification ou le désaveu de l'oeuvre'.

Si la Cour a, il est vrai, abordé le problème du droit de repentir de manière indirecte, puisque cette question n'était pas au coeur des débats, il n'en demeure pas moins qu'elle a décidé que le demandeur invoquait, en l'espèce, une prétention étrangère au droit de retrait qu'un auteur est en

31. Contra: A. BERENBOOM, *op. cit.*, n° 114, p. 312; de manière prudente, G. LEROY écrit: 'il serait difficile de ne pas inférer de ces attendus que la Cour reconnaît indirectement le droit de retrait et de repentir', *op. cit.*, p. 212; de même, F. GOTZEN note: 'd'aucuns diront peut-être que l'arrêt du 12 septembre 1975 ne doit pas nécessairement être interprété dans le sens d'une reconnaissance du droit de repentir et que par conséquent rien ne presse', *op. cit.*, p. 728. Ces deux auteurs semblent admettre 'sur la pointe des pieds' l'idée que la Cour a reçu le droit de repentir. J. PERLBERGER s'interroge: 'une personne interviewée bénéficie-t-elle à *l'instar d'un auteur* (nous soulignons) du droit de retrait sur ce qu'elle a déclaré?', 'Chronique de jurisprudence: le droit d'auteur (1976–1985)', in J.T., 1986, n° 59, p. 635 et J. CORBET écrit: 'De auteur kan zijn berouwrecht niet laten gelden indien hij een ander doel nastreeft dan de wijziging of de intrekking van zijn werk' [L'auteur ne peut utiliser son droit de repentir que pour modifier son oeuvre ou pour la rendre non accessible.], 'Vijf jaar auteursrecht (1975–1979)', in R.W., 1983–1984, col. 1129.

droit de faire valoir'. Comment comprendre ce passage, si ce n'est en constatant que la Cour de cassation, en disqualifiant une prétention comme droit de retrait en a, par là-même, reconnu l'existence?

Cette solution va, du reste, dans le sens de plusieurs législations européennes.[32] Les modalités d'exercice du droit de repentir restent toutefois délicates et rendent plus impérieuses encore la nécessité d'une réforme législative en Belgique.[33] A cet égard, trois points doivent encore être signalés:

(1) L'exercice du droit de repentir implique une indemnisation du cessionnaire des droits d'exploitation. On admet généralement que l'indemnité doit couvrir le *damnum emergens* (perte réellement subie) et le *lucrum cessans* (manque à gagner). On insiste également sur le fait que l'indemnisation doit être préalable à l'exercice du droit de repentir. Ces modalités peuvent toutefois laisser penser que l'on retire d'une main (sévérité de l'indemnisation), ce que l'on donne de l'autre (droit de repentir comme faculté exorbitante de la force obligatoire des contrats).

(2) Le droit de repentir n'est pas un droit discrétionnaire dès lors qu'il peut faire l'objet d'un abus et, partant, il entre dans le champ d'application de la théorie extensive de l'abus de droit.

(3) Le sort de l'oeuvre, après l'exercice de droit de repentir, a, parfois, agité la doctrine. On a cru que M. Planiol, dans un texte isolé, préconisait la destruction de l'oeuvre.[34] Mais cette opinion excessive était exprimée à propos de l'affaire Whistler dans laquelle la nécessité de rendre le portrait méconnaissable résultait du principe des droits de la personnalité du modèle, Lady Eden. Rien ne justifie en principe une quel-conque destruction de l'oeuvre. Le principe d'une indemnisation et l'instauration d'un droit de priorité au profit du cessionnaire, pour le cas où le créateur, regrettant son repentir, réintroduisait l'oeuvre dans le circuit économique, doivent suffire.

La nouvelle proposition de loi belge reconnaît, dans son art. 11, le droit de repentir. Cette disposition, au demeurant pratiquement identique à l'art. 32 de la loi française, assortit l'exercice de ce droit de conditions très strictes. Il ne pourra s'exercer à l'encontre du propriétaire de l'oeuvre, qui l'a acquise sans réserve. Ainsi, conformément à l'exposé des motifs de cette proposition, un peintre ne pourra pas retirer un tableau d'une collection privée ou d'un musée qui l'a acquis régulièrement ou exiger d'y faire des retouches. Et, si le créateur entend se repentir d'une autorisation d'exploitation, ce sera à charge pour lui d'indemniser préalablement le cessionnaire du

32. Cf. les arts. 32 de la loi française du 11 mars 1957, 142 de la loi italienne du 22 avril 1941 et le paragraphe 42 de la loi allemande du 9 septembre 1965.
33. Cf. *infra*.
34. M. PLANIOL, note sous Trib. civ. Seine, 20 mars 1895, D., 1898, p. 465.

préjudice que ce repentir pourra lui causer. Par ailleurs, si, postérieurement à l'exercice du droit de repentir, l'auteur décide de publier à nouveau son oeuvre, il sera tenu d'offrir par priorité son droit d'auteur au cessionnaire originaire à des conditions équitables.

d. Le droit au respect de l'oeuvre

Si, dans l'état actuel des textes, le droit de repentir peut apparaître comme une construction prétorienne, le droit au respect de l'oeuvre d'art est expressément visé par les arts. 8 de la loi du 22 mars 1886 et par l'art. 6*bis* de la Convention de Berne.[35]

Contrairement aux juridictions belges, les Cours et tribunaux français ont, à plusieurs reprises, été amenés à se prononcer sur des conflits relatifs au non-respect d'une oeuvre par un tiers détenteur ou propriétaire de celle-ci. Dans le cadre du présent rapport, il ne nous appartient pas d'analyser ces différentes affaires.[36] Nous tenterons seulement de systématiser certains critères qui ressortent de la jurisprudence française et qui pourraient être adoptés par les juridictions belges. Il serait toutefois fort présomptueux d'y voir des règles générales. Il convient plutôt de proposer certains paramètres qui, selon les circonstances, permettraient au juge de donner une solution à ce type de conflit très particulier.

L'analyse de la motivation qui pousse le propriétaire de l'oeuvre à la modifier, à la laisser dépérir, ou même à la détruire est récurrent dans toutes les décisions. S'il a agi dans l'intention de nuire, le propriétaire a certainement abusé de son droit. D'une façon tout à fait générale, on peut affirmer que le droit moral au respect de l'oeuvre est, à tout le moins, protégé par la théorie de l'abus du droit de propriété. Cependant, plus radicalement, certaines décisions exigent du propriétaire qu'il rapporte la

35. L'art. 8 de la loi du 22 mars 1886 dispose que 'le cessionnaire du droit d'auteur, ou de l'objet qui matérialise une oeuvre de littérature, de musique ou des arts du dessin, ne peut modifier l'oeuvre, pour la vendre ou l'exploiter, ni exposer publiquement l'oeuvre modifiée, sans le consentement de l'auteur ou de ses ayant cause'; l'art. 6*bis* de la Convention de Berne stipule que: 'Indépendamment des droits patrimoniaux d'auteur, et même après la cession desdits droits, l'auteur conserve pendant toute sa vie, de droit de revendiquer la paternité de l'oeuvre et de s'opposer à toute déformation, mutilation ou autre modification de cette oeuvre ou à toute autre atteinte à la même oeuvre, préjudiciable à son honneur et à sa réputation'. Ces derniers termes restreignent le champ d'application de cette règle par rapport à l'art. 8 de la loi du 22 mars 1886; on peut y lire le passage d'un critère individuel et subjectif (dans la loi belge de 1886) à un critère social et objectif (dans la Convention); cfr., à ce propos, M. FABIANI, 'Le droit de l'auteur à l'intégrité de son oeuvre', R.I.D.A., 1964 p.87.

36. *V.* sur ce point, Ph. COPPENS et N. VERHEYDEN-JEANMART, *op. cit.*, spéc. pp. 333 à 340; pour un litige récent en Belgique et une analyse du droit au respect de l'oeuvre, *v.* A. STROWEL, 'L'affaire Somville: une question de droits ou une pesée des intérêts?' *Journal des Procès* 1989, n° 148, pp. 8 à 10.

preuve d'un motif légitime, voire de la force majeure, pour s'exonérer de tout reproche.[37]

Un second critère souvent avancé consiste à distinguer selon que l'oeuvre figure dans un espace public ou dans un lieu privé. Cette distinction met en évidence l'idée selon laquelle la réputation de l'artiste est davantage atteinte par le regard public porté sur l'oeuvre. Les juridictions semblent ainsi se montrer plus sévères à l'égard des autorités publiques qui n'ont pas assumé pleinement les charges qui leur incombent en tant que gardiennes de l'oeuvre.[38] Il doit pourtant moins s'agir d'un contraste absolu que d'une différence de degré.[39]

Deux autres critères, assez complémentaires, sont relatifs au caractère utilitaire ou non utilitaire de l'oeuvre et au respect d'un minimum de durée d'existence de celle-ci. Mais ces critères, d'un maniement très délicat, semblent faire ressurgir l'idée du mérite de l'oeuvre d'art. Ne s'agit-il pas, en effet, d'opérer une distinction fragile sinon impossible entre l'oeuvre utilitaire et l'oeuvre 'pure', cette dernière devant bénéficier, en définitive, d'un respect accru et d'une durée de protection plus grande?

Plus généralement, il convient de se demander s'il n'est pas opportun d'exiger du propriétaire qu'il prévienne l'artiste des actes qu'il entend poser sur l'oeuvre acquise. Certaines décisions reprochent du reste au propriétaire d'avoir agi à l'insu de l'artiste.[40] Dans cette optique, il serait sans doute souhaitable d'aménager les modalités d'une préalable reprise de l'oeuvre par l'artiste avant une modification ou une destruction éventuelle.[41]

Ainsi défini, et donc limité, le droit moral au respect de l'oeuvre, à son intégrité, doit être affirmé, fut-ce à l'encontre du propriétaire de l'objet d'art. La doctrine belge semble généralement réticente à admettre cette évolution.[42] D'autres paraissent l'accepter en soumettant, à très juste titre,

---

37. *V.* p.ex., aff. Scrive, Trib. civ. Paris, 14 mai 1974, R. I. D. A., 1975, LXXXIV, p. 219; Paris, 10 juillet 1975, R. I. D. A., 1977, LXXXXI, p. 114 et la note A. FRANCON; D., 1977, p. 342 et la note C. COLOMBET; aff. *Dubuffet*, Trib. gde Inst. Paris, 23 mars 1977, R. I. D. A., 1977, LXXXXIII, p. 191 et la note H. DESBOIS; Paris, 2 juin 1978, D., 1979, p. 14 et la note C. COLOMBET; Cass., 8 janvier 1980, J. C. P., 1980, 1936 et la note R. LINDON; R. I. D. A., 1980, n° 104, p. 152; D., 1980, p. 83 et la note B. EDELMAN.
38. Cf. aff. *Sudre et fontaine du Roussillon*, C. E., 3 avril 1936, D., 1936, III, p. 57 et les conclusions du commissaire JOSSE, note M. WALINE; Conseil préf. Montpellier, 9 décembre 1936, Gaz. Pal., 1937, I, p. 34.
39. *V.* H. DESBOIS, note sous Paris, 30 mai 1962, D., 1962, p. 574.
40. Cf. aff. Scrive, précitée.
41. H. DESBOIS, *op. cit.*, n° 460, p. 505, propose une faculté de rachat; dans le même sens, C. COLOMBET, *Propriété littéraire et artistique*. (Paris, Dalloz 1976) n° 158, p. 179. On aperçoit mal toutefois la justification d'un rachat lorsque le propriétaire de l'oeuvre la destinait à la destruction; en ce sens, A. FRANCON, note sous Paris, 10 juillet 1975, *op. cit.*, p. 122. Il reste possible, bien entendu, de prévoir dans le contrat de vente une clause de non-destruction. Mais la relativité des conventions ne permet pas de la rendre opposable au tiers acquéreur de l'oeuvre.
42. *V.* P. EECKMAN, 'Kunst en auteursrecht', *op. cit.*, p. 79.

son exercise au contrôle de l'abus de droit.[43]

L'art. 10 de la nouvelle proposition de loi définit le droit au respect de l'oeuvre de manière plus large que les arts. 8 de la loi actuelle et 6*bis* de la Convention de Berne. Même après la cession du droit d'auteur, il est prévu que l'artiste aura le droit de s'opposer à 'toute déformation, altération ou autre atteinte à l'oeuvre'. Aussi, les anciennes limites, qui subordonnaient l'exercice de ce droit au fait que l'atteinte soit préjudiciable à l'honneur ou à la réputation de l'auteur (art. 6*bis* de la Convention) ou à la circonstance que le propriétaire de l'objet d'art modifiait celui-ci en vue de vendre, exploiter ou exposer publiquement l'oeuvre (art. 8 de la loi du 22 mars 1886), sont abandonnées.

2. *Les droits pécuniaires*

La loi belge sur le droit d'auteur n'établit, à l'inverse de la loi française ou allemande, aucune classification systématique des divers droits pécuniaires. La doctrine considère de façon unanime que ces droits, qui visent à assurer à l'auteur une rémunération pour tout acte d'exploitation de son oeuvre, se composent de deux droits principaux: le droit de reproduction, c'est-à-dire le droit de fixer l'oeuvre sous une forme matérielle qui en permet la duplication, et le droit de représentation, c'est-à-dire le droit exclusif d'autoriser toute exécution publique de l'oeuvre.

Compte tenu de notre perspective, il ne sera pas ici question du droit de représentation (ou d'exécution) qui s'applique aux oeuvres littéraires et musicales mais ne concerne pas les auteurs d'oeuvres plastiques. En tout cas, pas au premier chef. En effet, on ne doit pas oublier qu'avec la disparition des limites entre les divers domaines artistiques, certains 'objets' d'art contemporain peuvent prendre des formes qui sont sujettes à représentation plutôt qu'à reproduction – songeons aux oeuvres mises en scène par des artistes conceptuels contemporains comme Yves Klein,[44] Fred Forest,

43. A. BERENBOOM, *op. cit.*, n° 112, p. 129; mais l'interprétation du texte de cet auteur est délicate, car il n'opère pas la distinction, pourtant essentielle, entre le conflit de l'artiste et du propriétaire, d'une part, et celui, moins complexe, de l'artiste et du cessionnaire des droits d'exploitation, d'autre part; A. PUTTEMANS, 'Les auteurs sont-ils responsables de leurs actes?', *Les journées du droit d'auteur* (Bruxelles, Bruylant 1989) n° 16, p. 313.

44. Donnons l'exemple de l'action d'Yves Klein consistant à céder des 'Zones de sensibilité picturale immatérielle'. En 1958, Klein expose le Vide: le spectateur entre dans une galerie complètement vidée de tous ses objets, et donc imprégnée de ce que Klein appelait une sensibilité picturale immatérielle. Ce Vide, Klein le vendait à travers un rituel assez compliqué qui venait compenser l'immatérialité de l'oeuvre. L'amateur intéressé par l'achat d'une Zone devait la payer en poids d'or. Contre cet or, le collectionneur recevait un certificat. Au moment où Klein dispersait cet or dans l'eau de la Seine, le collectionneur devait brûler son reçu, ce qui fait que, si, pour toute cession du Vide, il y avait échange de biens matériels, en fin de compte, il ne restait rien de cette matière. Dans ce cas, l'oeuvre d'art se réduit bien évidemment à ce rituel, à cette représentation. Pour d'autres exemples, *voir* le numéro spécial d'*art press* (sept. 1989, n° 139, le précédent exemple est cité à la p. 47 de ce numéro) consacré à l'art conceptuel.

Ian Wilson ou Philippe Thomas.[45]

On a par ailleurs pu qualifier le droit qu'a l'auteur de consentir ou non à la présentation de son oeuvre plastique par la télévision comme une 'sorte de droit d'exécution publique *sui generis*';[46] nous considérons plutôt ce droit comme un droit d'exposition publique et nous en traiterons dans une section à part 2.*c*.

De plus, le droit de reproduction n'est lui-même pas particulièrement adapté à l'exploitation des oeuvres d'art plastique:[47] en effet, en règle générale, l'artiste plasticien trouve l'essentiel de ses revenus dans la vente de l'oeuvre originelle, qu'il s'agisse d'un exemplaire unique – pensons à la peinture – ou d'un nombre limité d'exemplaires originaux, comme dans le domaine de la sculpture.[48] Seules certaines oeuvres graphiques sont destinées à être commercialisées sous forme de reproductions, par exemple en vue d'illustrer des livres. On a donc pu soutenir à juste titre que le mécanisme de protection par les deux prérogatives classiques, consacrées par la loi sur le droit d'auteur du 22 mars 1886, 'joue un rôle relativement modeste dans l'exploitation économique des oeuvres d'art plastique'.[49]

C'est en vue de mettre sur le même pied les artistes plasticiens avec les auteurs d'oeuvres littéraires ou musicales, qui, eux, profitent amplement de leurs droits de reproduction et de représentation, que les premiers se sont vus reconnaître, en Belgique depuis la loi du 21 juin 1921, un droit supplémentaire: le droit de suite (voir point 2. *b*). Ce droit leur permet de profiter de la plus-value que prend leur oeuvre après sa première aliénation. Si on a parfois argué de ce que ce droit était reconnu par une loi spéciale, en marge de la loi de 1886, pour contester sa nature de droit d'auteur, la doctrine est néanmoins d'accord pour ranger le droit de suite parmi les droits d'auteur.

Il sera enfin question de deux droits, certes accessoires, mais qui concernent spécifiquement les oeuvres d'art plastique; le droit, déjà cité, d'exposer publiquement via la télévision une oeuvre d'art plastique (2. *c*), droit consacré par la Convention de Berne et le droit d'accès (2. *d*) à l'oeuvre d'art à des fins de reproduction, droit que la proposition de loi allemande envisage d'introduire dans notre législation.

a. Le droit de reproduction

i. Généralités

Selon l'art. 1er de la loi de 1886, 'l'auteur d'une oeuvre littéraire ou

45. Au sujet des questions que pose, au droit d'auteur, l'art contemporain, notamment l'art conceptuel, le land art et l'anti-art, v. A. STROWEL, 'Droit et objet d'art. Réflexions en marge d'un colloque', Ann. dr. 1990.
46. F. VAN ISACKER, *Kritische synthese van het Belgische auteursrecht* (Antwerpen, Kluwer 1985) p. 51.
47. Ces prérogatives ne sont d'ailleurs pas énoncées aux articles 19 à 21, composant la section 4 de la loi sur le droit d'auteur, consacrée spécifiquement aux oeuvres plastiques.
48. P. EECKMAN, 'Kunst en auteursrecht', *op. cit.*, p. 69.
49. *Ibid*, p. 69.

artistique a seul le droit de la reproduire ou d'en autoriser la reproduction, de quelque manière et sous quelque forme que ce soit', c'est-à-dire quel qu'en soit le mode de reproduction, l'étendue, la matière dans laquelle elle se réalise, ou encore le caractère lucratif ou non de son utilisation.[50]

Le législateur de 1886 a ainsi attribué à l'auteur un très large droit d'exclusivité. L'art. 19, relatif aux oeuvres plastiques, vient confirmer ce monopole légal en précisant que 'la cession d'un objet d'art n'entraîne pas cession du droit de reproduction au profit de l'acquéreur'. Ce faisant, le législateur a clairement réaffirmé le principe à la base du droit intellectuel, selon lequel la propriété matérielle d'une oeuvre est à dissocier de la propriété intellectuelle.

L'auteur conserve donc, à défaut de convention contraire,[51] le droit de reproduction sur l'oeuvre qu'il a vendue.[52] Il n'y qu'un cas où l'acheteur d'une peinture, d'un dessin, d'une sculpture acquiert une portion du droit de reproduction: lorsque l'oeuvre constitue un portrait.[53] En effet, comme le prévoit l'art. 20 al. 2 de la loi de 1886, le propriétaire de l'oeuvre d'art a, moyennant l'assentiment de la personne représentée, le droit de faire reproduire le portrait, 'sans toutefois que la copie puisse porter l'indication du nom de l'auteur'.

Le principe du consentement préalable de l'auteur pour toute reproduction est encore tempéré dans un certain nombre de cas.

- Ainsi, on considère généralement que la reproduction peut être librement effectuée lorsqu'elle a un caractère privé.[54] Les termes généraux de l'art. 1er précité et l'absence de disposition permettant expressément la reproduction privée ont cependant conduit certains à considérer que toute forme de reproduction est interdite, quand bien même elle est effectuée à titre privé.[55]
- Mentionnons encore une deuxième exception, importante compte tenu de notre sujet: selon la jurisprudence, est admise la reproduction de certaines oeuvres exposées sur la voie publique 'lorsque l'oeuvre d'art n'est qu'un élément inséparable d'un objet plus vaste qui ne bénéficie pas de la

---

50. A. BERENBOOM, *op. cit.*, p. 80.
51. Notons au passage que les conventions, qui peuvent être tacites pourvu que la volonté de céder soit certaine (A. BERENBOOM, *op. cit.*, p. 97), s'interprètent restrictivement et en faveur de l'auteur; de plus, la portée de l'accord entre les parties est limitée aux modes d'exploitation connus au moment de l'accord.
52. P. WAUVERMANS, *Le droit des auteurs en Belgique* (Bruxelles, Société belge de Librairie 1894) p. 296, n° 333.
53. F. VAN ISACKER, *Kritische synthese, op. cit.*, p. 78.
54. Dans ce sens: P. POIRIER, 'Le droit d'auteur', *Les Novelles, Droits intellectuels*, (Bruxelles, Larcier 1936) p. 892, n° 312; P. RECHT, *Le droit d'auteur en Belgique* (Bruxelles, Larcier 1955) p. 167; A. BERENBOOM, *op. cit.*, pp. 81 et 105 *et seq.*
55. Dans ce sens: F. VAN ISACKER, *De exploitatierechten van de auteur* (Bruxelles, Larcier 1963) p. 180, n° 204; du méme, 'Het reproduktierecht zoals het heden ten dage waait en draait in het Belgisch auteursrecht', F. GOTZEN (éd.), *Reprographie* (Antwerpen, Kluwer 1978) p. 3 *et seq.* et surtout pp. 9–11. Pour une position intermédiaire, *v.* P. WAUVERMANS, *op. cit.*, p. 222, n° 223. Selon ce dernier auteur, la copie qui a été exécutée pour l'usage personnel du copiste ouvre la possibilité d'une action non sur la base de la loi de 1886 mais sur celle de la responsabilité civile (art. 1382 du Code civil).

protection de la loi'.[56] C'est ainsi que l'on pourra, par exemple, publier la photographie d'une rue sans devoir demander l'autorisation des architectes de chacune des maisons. En-dehors de ces cas, les sculptures érigées dans un lieu public (square, parc, station de métro), les peintures murales, les immeubles et autres oeuvres d'architecture ne peuvent 'être reproduits dans un journal ou un dépliant publicitaire ou encore, sous forme de carte postale,[57] de photos de presse, d'objets,[58] de gadgets ou de publicité'.[59]

- L'art. 21*bis* de la loi de 1886 vient apporter une troisième limitation au droit de reproduction. Selon cette disposition en effet:

> 'l'autorisation de l'auteur n'est pas requise pour la reproduction, l'enregistrement et la communication publique de courts fragments d'oeuvres littéraires ou artistiques, à l'occasion de comptes rendus des événements d'actualité par la photographie, la cinématographie, la radiophonie ou la télévision. Il en est de même pour la reproduction et la communication publique d'oeuvres plastiques dans leur totalité, mais seulement dans les limites des nécessités de l'information d'actualité.'

Cet article, introduit dans la loi en 1958, apporte une restriction au droit de reproduction, lorsque l'oeuvre est citée à des fins d'information (alors que c'est depuis 1886 que la loi sur le droit d'auteur dispose à son art. 13 que la citation littéraire ne comporte aucune atteinte au droit de reproduction de l'auteur).[60] L'art. 21*bis* (contrairement à l'art. 13) vise toutes les oeuvres; sa portée est néanmoins étroite en ce que les citations informatives sont libres seulement dans le cas de la photographie, de la cinématographie, de la radiophonie et de la télévision.[61] Les travaux préparatoires font ressortir que le législateur n'a voulu prévoir d'exception qu'en faveur des moyens modernes d'information; dans ce cas seulement manque en effet le temps pour obtenir les autorisations nécessaires des auteurs.[62] De la différence de formulation entre les alinéa 1

---

56. Conclusions du Procureur général Hayoit de Termicourt avant Cass., 14 avril 1955, Pas., 1955, I, p. 884 (cité par A. BERENBOOM, *op. cit.*, p. 83, n° 66).
57. A propos de la reproduction sur carte postale du mémorial du Mardasson de Bastogne: Cass. 14 avril 1955, Pas., 1955, I, p. 884.
58. A propos de la reproduction de l'Atomium sous forme de maquettes presse-papier, de décalcomanies, de fanions et d'impression en relief sur articles de maroquinerie: Bruxelles, 22 avril 1959, J.T. 1959, pp. 562–564 et Corr. Bruxelles, 12 novembre 1958, J.T. 1959, pp. 566–569.
59. A. BERENBOOM, *op. cit.*, p. 83.
60. Par conséquent, avant 1958, il est toujours interdit de 'citer' une oeuvre plastique. C'est ainsi que le peintre Strebelle assigna le *Journal de Charleroi*, pour avoir publié une photo prise à l'occasion du vernissage du 'Salon des Artistes Wallons' en 1946, photo qui représentait une de ses oeuvres; le *Journal* fut à l'époque condamné par la juridiction suprême (*v.* Cass., 4 décembre 1952, Pas., I. p. 215).
61. F. VAN ISACKER, *Kritische synthese, op. cit.*, pp. 87 et 89.
62. J. CORBET, *Cinq ans de jurisprudence en matière de droit d'auteur* (t. II 1965–1969) (Bruxelles, SABAM 1972) p. 4. Ce qui, ainsi que le remarque F. VAN ISACKER (*Kritische synthese, op. cit.*, p. 89) peut avoir cette conséquence absurde qu'un musicologue ne pourra illustrer une conférence en reprenant un thème musical au piano, sans avoir obtenu l'autorisation de l'auteur.

et 2 de l'art. 21*bis*, on a pu déduire que la mesure d'exception est plus large pour les oeuvres plastiques que pour les oeuvres littéraires et musicales; dans le cas des premières, la citation pourrait se faire sans qu'il soit nécessaire qu'elle figure dans un 'compte rendu'. C'est ainsi que des exploitants de galeries d'art, qui avaient édité des catalogues des oeuvres mises en vente, voulaient les assimiler à de 'l'information d'actualité', quoi qu'il ne soit pas donné de 'compte rendu'. Un jugement de 1965[63] a condamné cette thèse et réaffirmé que l'exception devait être interprétée au sens le plus strict.[64]

- Par ailleurs, la parodie, conformément à l'avis de la doctrine et de la jurisprudence,[65] échappe à l'autorisation de l'auteur, quoi qu'aucun texte ne cite cette quatrième exception au droit de reproduction. Cette limite au droit d'auteur mérite d'autant plus d'être mentionnée que l'art visuel contemporain est devenu de plus en plus parodique – pensons simplement à A. Warhol. On a même pu écrire que l'appropriation des oeuvres passées, notamment sur le mode parodique, était désormais au coeur de l'art d'avant-garde, qui, sans cesse, défie les valeurs traditionnelles, telles que celles d'auteur et d'originalité.[66]

ii Droit de destination et droit de prêt/location

Le droit de reproduction s'est vu reconnaître, selon certains,[67] une très large portée dans la jurisprudence, à la suite d'un important arrêt de la Cour de Cassation.[68] Selon la thèse de F. Gotzen, la Cour aurait dans cet arrêt consacré le droit pour les auteurs de contrôler l'usage qui est fait de leurs oeuvres après leur première aliénation et ce droit, qui est appelé 'droit de destination',[69] serait opposable à tous. Il semblerait en effet logique d'admettre que l'auteur, qui reçoit, conformément à l'art. 1er de la loi de 1886, le droit exclusif d'interdire toute reproduction ainsi que celui d'interdire toute reproduction ainsi que celui d'autoriser la reproduction 'de quelque manière et sous quelque forme que ce soit', ne sort pas de son droit 'quand il se contente de réserver à une certaine destination les exemplaires

63. Trib. 1ère instance d'Anvers, 29 juin 1965, R. W., 1965–66, col. 1314; R. I. D. A., Li, p. 3.
64. J. CORBET, *op. cit.*, p. 4. Dans ce sens aussi: A. BERENBOOM, *op. cit.*, p. 113.
65. A BERENDBOOM, 'La parodie', Ing.-Cons., 1984, pp. 73–84.
66. J. CARLIN, 'Culture Vultures: Artistic Appropriation and Intellectual Property Law', *Columbia – VLA Journal of Law & the Arts*, 1988, vol. 13. pp. 103–143.
67. *V.* F. GOTZEN, *Het bestemmingsrecht van de auteur* (Bruxelles, Larcier 1975); P. EECKMAN, *op. cit.*, p. 68; J. CORBET, 'La Convention de Berne et la loi belge sur le droit d'auteur', *Le droit d'auteur*, 1986, p. 228.
68. Cass., 19 janvier 1956, Pas., 1956, I, p. 484.
69. A propos de ce droit de destination, *v.* encore les Actes de colloque de l'ALAI qui s'est tenu à Munich du 5 au 8 décembre 1988 et était consacré, entre autres, aux problèmes posés par la distribution des exemplaires d'oeuvres protégées. *V.* encore le compte rendu par A. STROWEL, 'Actualité du droit d'auteur', Ing.-Cons., 1989, pp. 2–8.

reproduits avec son autorisation conditionnelle'[70] (selon l'adage: 'Qui peut le plus, peut le moins'). C'est ainsi que l'auteur pourrait règler le nombre des exemplaires, leur circulation, leur mode d'utilisation et imposer ces restrictions aux tiers acquéreurs des reproductions; l'artiste peintre pourrait, par exemple, exiger que les acheteurs des reproductions de son oeuvre n'en fassent qu'un usage privé. Notons cependant que la thèse du droit de destination a été profondément mise en question par la doctrine.[71]

C'est encore en invoquant l'existence d'un tel droit de destination que des commentateurs ont reconnu aux auteurs le droit de s'opposer à la location et au prêt de leurs oeuvres, malgré le fait que la loi de 1886 n'a pas explicitement consacré de droit de prêt ou de location. Dans les faits, le recours au prêt et à la location des exemplaires d'oeuvres s'est généralisé, sans qu'aucune rémunération ne soit en contrepartie versée au profit des ayant droit, ce qui permet de douter de l'incidence pratique de l'arrêt de Cassation du 19 janvier 1956 et de la construction doctrinale du droit de destination.[72]

A première vue, la récente proposition de loi Lallemand ne reconnaît pas plus le droit de location/prêt que la loi de 1886. On a cependant pu soutenir[73] que la proposition accordait à l'auteur un véritable droit exclusif d'autoriser ou d'interdire le prêt ou la location de ses oeuvres, dans la mesure où l'auteur a le droit d'autoriser la publication de son oeuvre et où l'art. 1er, 6° précise qu'il faut entendre par 'publication: divulgation au public d'un ou de plusieurs exemplaires d'une oeuvre, notamment par la vente, le prêt ou la location'. Il nous paraît tout à fait prématuré de se prononcer sur la probabilité qu'une telle prérogative soit introduite dans notre future législation, à un moment où le texte proposé n'a pas encore fait l'objet d'une discussion au Parlement. Ajoutons que, tant le procédé consistant à donner un catalogue de définitions dans un chapitre préliminaire de la loi, que les définitions elles-mêmes, dont celle de la 'publication', ont fait l'objet de critiques sévères.[74]

iii. Droit d'adaptation

Par droit d'adaptation, il faut entendre le droit exclusif de l'auteur d'adapter ou de laisser adapter son oeuvre, ainsi que le droit de l'auteur originaire et de l'adaptateur d'exploiter ensemble l'oeuvre dérivée. Certains ont distingué ce droit du droit de reproduction et l'ont traité à part.[75]

Vu que la loi de 1886 ne consacre pas clairement ce droit – il n'en est

70. F. GOTZEN, *op. cit.*, p. 379.
71. A. BERENBOOM (*op. cit.*, p. 99) estime par exemple qu'elle 'ne repose pas sur des bases légales bien solides'.
72. Dans ce sens, F. VAN ISACKER, *Kritische synthese, op. cit.*, p. 73.
73. *V.* C. DOUTRELEPONT, 'Initiatives législatives en droit d'auteur', *Journal des Procès*, 18 novembre 1988, n° 138, p. 19.
74. A. BERENBOOM, Une nouvelle loi sur le droit d'auteur J.T., 1989, pp. 117–118.
75. Dans ce sens, F. VAN ISACKER, *Kritische synthese, op. cit.*, p. 53 *et seq*; P. EECKMAN, *op. cit.*, p. 69.

qu'accessoirement question à l'art. 17,[76] à propos des oeuvres musicales – le droit d'adaptation est surtout un droit d'origine prétorienne,[77] qui découle de la reconnaissance du droit exclusif de reproduction à l'art. 1 de la loi. Suivant en cela une doctrine majoritaire, nous rangeons donc ce droit sous le droit de reproduction.[78]

Si les problèmes d'adaptation concernent avant tout les oeuvres littéraires et leur transposition au cinéma, théâtre – il n'est néanmoins pas rare que des oeuvres plastiques soient transposées d'un genre à un autre: ainsi, à partir d'une peinture ou d'un dessin, on composera une gravure, un vitrail ou une tapisserie. De même, la photographie d'une statue pourra, le cas échéant, si sa composition présente un caractère d'originalité, constituer une oeuvre dérivée.[79]

Le créateur originaire conserve dans ces hypothèses le droit exclusif d'adapter ou de laisser adapter son oeuvre, ce qui veut dire qu'il précisera de façon souveraine les conditions, pécuniaires ou autres, de l'adaptation; de plus, le droit de l'adaptateur se voit encore limiter par le droit moral à l'intégrité de l'auteur originaire. Une fois que l'oeuvre dérivée a vu le jour, coexistent sur cette dernière deux parcelles de souveraineté, l'une appartenant à l'auteur originaire, l'autre à l'adaptateur. C'est au juge qu'il revient, en cas de litige, de trouver un équilibre délicat entre les prérogatives de ces deux titulaires.

b. Le droit de suite[80]

La loi du 21 juin 1921 (Moniteur, 20 août) accorde aux auteurs d'oeuvres plastiques un droit en cas de vente publique de l'original de leur oeuvre. L'arrêté royal du 23 septembre 1921 organise le mode de perception de ce droit.

Ce sont des considérations d'équité qui ont motivé l'adoption de cette loi: le peintre et le sculpteur devaient pouvoir participer à la fortune de leurs

---

76. Selon cet article, 'le droit d'auteur sur les compositions musicales comprend le droit exclusif de faire des arrangements sur des motifs de l'oeuvre originale'.
77. F. VAN ISACKER, *Kritische synthese, op. cit.*, p. 54.
78. Dans ce sens, A. BERENBOOM, *op. cit.*, pp. 80 et 84 *et seq.*; J.G. RENAULD, *Droit d'auteur et contrat d'adaptation* (Bruxelles, Larcier 1955) p. 100, qui écrit: 'Ainsi, est-ce à bon droit, pensons-nous, que la doctrine belge s'accorde à dire que le droit de reproduction comporte comme l'un de ses attributs, le droit de reproduire l'oeuvre sous une forme modifiée ou adaptée.'
79. *Ibid.*, p. 60 et J.G. RENAULD, *op. cit.*, p. 172 *et seq.*
80. Comme on l'a écrit (R. PLAISANT, 'Le droit de suite', *Le droit d'auteur*, 1969, p. 161), les fondements théoriques du droit de suite sont discutables. Généralement considéré en France comme un droit économique – au motif qu'il est défini à l'art. 42 de la loi du 11 mars 1957 qui se trouve sous le titre II 'de l'exploitation des droits patrimoniaux de l'auteur' – le droit de suite revêt cependant un caractère inaliénable, dont certains ont déduit qu'il s'apparentait plus au droit moral qu'au droit patrimonial (*v.* sur cette discussion: A. DE MARESCHAL DECAMME, *Le droit de suite en France* (thèse Paris 2, 1983) chapitre premier). Nous le considérons ici, conformément à l'opinion largement dominante de la doctrine belge, comme un droit économique.

oeuvres, il fallait donc leur permettre de recueillir une part du prix de vente de l'oeuvre.[81]

On a aussi estimé que ce régime se justifiait, dans un souci de symétrie avec les autres auteurs, puisque les auteurs d'oeuvres plastiques ne perçoivent plus aucun profit de leur oeuvre une fois celle-ci vendue, alors que l'écrivain et le compositeur continuent à tirer des revenus de la reproduction et de la représentation de leurs oeuvres.[82].

Le régime instauré en Belgique s'écarte pour partie des dispositions introduites à l'art. 14*bis*[83] de la Convention de Berne à l'occasion de la révision de Bruxelles (1948):[84]

- la loi belge ne vise que les oeuvres plastiques, alors que la Convention s'applique également aux manuscrits originaux des écrivains et compositeurs;
- elle ne concerne que les ventes publiques, tandis que la Convention porte sur toute espèce de vente, y compris les cessions privées;
- elle ne vise que les héritiers et ayant cause de l'auteur; la Convention s'étend de plus aux institutions publiques au profit desquelles une législation nationale peut établir le droit de suite.

Par contre, loi belge et Convention de Berne se rejoignent en ce qu'elles visent toutes deux les seuls originaux, c'est-à-dire les exemplaires réalisés par l'artiste lui-même.[85] Le droit de suite s'applique essentiellement aux oeuvres relevant de la peinture, du dessin, de la sculpture, de la gravure, de la lithographie; sont exclues du bénéfice de ce droit les oeuvres d'architecture et celles des arts appliqués.

Tout comme l'art. 14*bis* al. 1) de l'Acte de Bruxelles, l'art. 1er de la loi belge précise que le droit de suite est un droit inaliénable. On évite ainsi que, sous la pression des circonstances, l'artiste ne le cède de son vivant; par contre, ce droit n'est pas personnel[86] et, depuis un jugement du tribunal civil de Gand de 1967,[87] il semble confirmé que l'auteur puisse en disposer par voie testamentaire.[88] Le régime belge s'écarte sur ce point du régime

81. *V. Guide de la Convention de Berne pour la protection des oeuvres littéraires et artistiques* (*Actes de Paris*, 1971) (Genève, OMPI 1978) p. 105.
82. A. BERENBOOM, *op. cit.*, p. 122.
83. Dans la version révisée en 1971 à Paris, il s'agit de l'art. 14*ter* de la Convention.
84. Nous reprenons ici l'énumération des différences entre les deux régimes faite par P. RECHT, *op cit.*, pp. 206-207 et reprise par J. CORBET, *La Convention de Berne, op. cit.*, p. 226.
85. *Guide de la Convention de Berne, op. cit.*, p. 106.
86. *Ibid.*
87. *V.* Tribunal civil de Gand, 26 juin 1967, R.W., 1967-68, col. 490 qui soutient que, si 'le droit de suite est en principe inaliénable, cela ne vaut cependant pas pour le transfert juridique à cause de mort'. *V.* également la note de J. CORBET sous cette décision (R.W., col. 493-494).
88. Dans ce sens, P. RECHT (*op. cit.*, p. 208) soutenait déjà que 'les héritiers comprennent les successeurs irréguliers aussi bien que les successeurs légitimes, les légataires universels ou à titre universel.'

français, tel qu'il résulte de la loi française du 11 mars 1957 (art. 42).[89]

En ce qui concerne les taux de perception de ce droit, l'art. 2 de la loi belge les fixe comme suit:

2% de 1000 FB à 10.000 FB
3% de 10.000 FB à 20.000 FB
4% de 20.000 FB à 50.000 FB
6% au-dessus de 50.000 FB

Depuis l'arrêt de la Cour de Cassation du 28 septembre 1984,[90] il est établi que ces taux, contrairement aux taux proportionnels prévus dans le Code de l'impôt sur les revenus, ne s'appliquent pas par tranche; autrement dit, c'est le prix de vente global qui détermine le taux unique du droit de suite. On a par ailleurs souligné que le barême, actuellement appliqué, est resté inchangé depuis 1921 et qu'il devrait donc être revu, compte tenu de l'érosion monétaire.[91]

Quant aux modalités de la perception, l'art. 3 de la loi dispose que 'le vendeur, l'acheteur et l'officier ministériel qui procèdent à la vente sont tenus solidairement, envers l'artiste ou ses ayant cause, des droits prévus'. L'arrêt de Cassation précité est venu préciser ce qu'il fallait entendre par 'vendeur': 'non seulement celui qui, selon le droit civil, aliène son droit de propriété contre paiement, mais aussi celui qui, selon le droit commercial, vend pour le compte du propriétaire, en agissant en son nom propre et en tant que vendeur à l'égard de l'acheteur et des tiers'.[92]

Dans la pratique, le droit de suite est payé par l'acheteur et versé par la salle de vente auprès du receveur du droit de suite. Ce dernier ne vérifie pas l'exactitude des comptes, ce qui apparaît à certains comme une lacune.[93] L'auteur peut donner mandat à une association ou à une société d'auteurs de percevoir les sommes à sa place.[94] L'arrêté royal du 23 septembre 1921, en application de la loi sur le droit de suite, précise en outre à son art. 6 que 'deux fois par an, en janvier et en juillet, le Moniteur publiera la liste des artistes qui ont donné procuration à une association pour percevoir en leur nom le droit de suite.'

Un auteur[95] a proposé d'étendre l'application de la loi aux ventes privées, à l'instar de la loi francaise. L'expérience d'autres pays, de la France en particulier, montre l'ineffectivé d'une telle disposition, vu notamment la difficulté de contrôler ces ventes.

Par contre, la proposition du même auteur d'uniformiser le tarif au taux le

89. A ce sujet, *v*. R. PLAISANT, *op. cit.*, pp. 158–159.
90. Cass., 28 septembre 1984, R. W., 1984–85, col. 2702–2704.
91. *V*. le numéro spécial de *Arts Antiques Auctions*, octobre 1989, p. XLVI et la proposition de mise à jour du barême. Par ailleurs, l'article critique le principe de la progression des taux qui joue au détriment de l'artiste moins connu et moins coté.
92. Cass., *op. cit.*, col. 2704.
93. Dans ce sens, J. CORBET, *op. cit.*, p. 226.
94. *Arts Antiques Auctions, op. cit.*, p. XLVI.
95. F. VAN ISACKER, *op. cit.*, pp. 362–363.

plus élevé (6%) a été récemment approuvée par certains.[96] D'autres ont considéré que la Commission des Communautés Européennes se devait, dans la perspective du marché unique, de proposer une directive prévoyant la perception d'une taxe de 1% sur toutes les oeuvres d'art vendues par n'importe quel canal.[97] Cette formule offrirait l'avantage de mettre les différents marchés nationaux sur le même pied d'égalité. Rappelons à ce sujet que le Commission des Communautés Européennes a dénoncé depuis longtemps la distorsion de la concurrence qui résulte de la divergence entre les législations des pays membres: certains ne connaissent pas le droit de suite (en 1980, seuls six pays de la CE disposaient d'une législation à ce propos) et, parmi ceux qui le connaissent, d'importantes différences de taux persistent.[98] L'imposition d'une taxe de 1% aurait encore l'avantage de ne guère jouer en faveur des pays hors CE, qui ne connaissent pas ce droit.

On a encore suggéré de relever le montant plancher, à partir duquel le droit de suite est dû, de 1000 à 10.000 FB.[99]

La proposition de loi Lallemand,[100] qui intègre le droit de suite à la loi sur le droit d'auteur, reprend à ses arts. 37 à 40 l'essentiel des dispositions de la loi du 25 juin 1921, actuellement toujours en vigueur. Elle s'en écarte cependant sur la question du tarif et du plancher: suivant en cela les récentes suggestions de la doctrine, elle fixe un taux uniforme de 6% et remonte le prix de vente plancher à 10.000 FB.

c. Le droit d'exposer publiquement une oeuvre d'art plastique via la télévision

La Convention de Berne, depuis l'Acte révisé de Bruxelles, reconnaît à son art. 11*bis* al. 1 que les auteurs d'oeuvres littéraires ou artistiques jouissent du droit exclusif d'autoriser la radiodiffusion de leurs oeuvres. Ce droit, qui n'est pas reconnu dans la loi de 1886, peut néanmoins être invoqué par tout belge, dans la mesure où il lui est plus favorable que les dispositions de la loi interne.

Ce droit constitue en fait une exception au droit d'exposition publique en général qui veut que l'auteur ou l'acquéreur du *corpus mechanicum* d'une oeuvre dispose du droit de l'exposer au public. Ce droit ne constitue en fait pas un droit d'auteur mais un droit commun découlant du droit de propriété de l'art. 544 du Code Civil. Si donc l'auteur a le droit d'exposer publiquement son oeuvre, c'est parce qu'il est le propriétaire du *corpus mechanicum*; dès

96. Dans ce sens: W. JUWET, 'Het volgrecht', in *Honderd jaar Auteurswet* (sous la direction de J. CORBET) (Deurne 1986) p. 91; J. CORBET, *op cit.*, p. 227.
97. *Arts Antiques Auctions, op. cit.*, p. XLIX.
98. *L'action de la Communauté européenne dans le secteur culturel (Documentation européenne*, 1980/3) p. 22. *V.* encore à ce sujet: A. DIETZ, 'The Harmonization of Copyright in the European Community', in IIC, 1985/4, pp. 404–405.
99. W. JUWET, *op. cit.*, pp. 90–91.
100. *V. supra.*

que la propriété sur le support matériel de l'oeuvre est transférée, le droit d'exposition appartient au nouvel acquéreur.[101]

Si le droit d'exposer publiquement à la télévision une oeuvre plastique a été lui expressément reconnu comme droit d'auteur, c'est dû au fait que la présentation au public via la télévision est moins étroitement liée à l'exercice normal du droit de propriété.[101]

Ce droit de l'artiste plasticien trouva à s'appliquer en 1972, à l'occasion de la diffusion à la télévision flamande du concert de la chanteuse Liesbeth List donné au casino de Knokke. En effet, les murs de la grande salle de ce casino ont la particularité d'avoir été peints par R. Magritte. Les producteurs de l'émission de variété avaient fait abondamment usage de ce décor surréaliste et la société de télévision acquitta la facture spéciale que lui avait présentée la société d'auteurs pour rémunérer cet usage de l'oeuvre de Magritte.[103]

d. Le droit d'accès à l'oeuvre plastique

Ce droit n'est pas consacré dans la loi de 1886. La proposition de loi Lallemand envisage de l'introduire; l'art. 35 al. 2 de cette proposition dispose en effet que 'l'auteur aura accès à son oeuvre pour l'exercice du droit de reproduction, sauf convention contraire'.

Plutôt que de spécifier que l'auteur peut renoncer à ce droit par convention, nous estimons qu'il vaudrait mieux préciser, tout comme l'a fait la loi allemande à son §25,[104] que ce droit peut être exercé 'aussi longtemps qu'il ne s'oppose pas aux intérêts légitimes du propriétaire' de l'oeuvre d'art. L'éventuel conflit devrait ainsi être résolu à travers une balance des intérêts en présence.

III. L'ATTRIBUTION DES DROITS D'AUTEUR AUX HERITIERS

L'art. 3 de la loi du 22 mars 1886 dispose que 'le droit d'auteur est mobilier, cessible et transmissible, en tout ou en partie, conformément aux règles du Code civil'. En d'autres termes, l'ordre de dévolution successorale des droits d'auteur est réglé par le droit commun des successions (art. 718 *et seq.* du Code civil).

Par ailleurs, l'art. 2 prévoit que le droit de reproduire l'oeuvre littéraire ou artistique ou d'en autoriser la reproduction 'se prolonge pendant cinquante ans après le décès de l'auteur au profit de ses héritiers ou ayant

---

101. F. VAN ISACKER, *Kritische synthese, op. cit.*, p. 80; du même, *De exploitatierechten, op. cit.*, pp. 161–162.
102. *Ibid.*, p. 81.
103. L'exemple est emprunté à F. VAN ISACKER, *Kritische synthese, op. cit.*, pp. 51–52.
104. Sur cette disposition, *v.* W. NORDEMANN, K. VINCK, P. W. HERTIN, *Urheberrecht Kommentar* (Stuttgart, Berlin, Köln, Mainz 1988) 7ème éd., pp. 158–160.

droits'. Mais ce texte ne vise formellement que le droit de reproduction de l'oeuvre qui constitue une des prérogatives patrimoniales de l'auteur.

Enfin, l'art. 6*bis* de la Convention de Berne, applicable en droit belge, prévoit qu'à la mort de l'auteur (et sauf s'il a confié à un tiers la sauvegarde de ses droits moraux), les personnes habilitées à cette fin par leur législation nationale conservent:

> 'au moins jusqu'à l'extinction des droits patrimoniaux' (al. 2), 'le droit de revendiquer la paternité de l'oeuvre et de s'opposer à toute déformation, mutilation ou autre modification de cette oeuvre ou à toute autre atteinte à la même oeuvre, préjudiciables à son honneur ou à sa réputation' (al. 1).

Nous retrouvons donc l'opposition récurrente entre les droits patrimoniaux de l'artiste et ses droits moraux.

1. Le statut des droits patrimoniaux de l'artiste décédé

Ceux-ci sont protégés par l'art. 2 de la loi du 22 mars 1886 et par l'art. 7 de la Convention de Berne: la durée de protection s'étend à la vie de l'auteur et se prolonge, après sa mort, pendant 50 ans.

Conformément au droit commun, les droits patrimoniaux peuvent faire l'objet de dispositions testamentaires ou de legs. L'auteur peut ainsi en disposer mais aussi restreindre les modalités et l'étendue d'exercice de ces droits par les bénéficiaires futurs. Les héritiers et légataires pourront, par ailleurs, les céder.

En cas d'indivision, les droits patrimoniaux sont, en principe, régis par les conventions conclues entre les parties indivisaires. A défaut de conventions, l'art. 6 de la loi belge prévoit qu'aucun des copropriétaires ne pourra les exercer isolément. Or, ces droits sont, dans la plupart des cas, indivisibles. Aussi, l'art. 815 du Code civil, selon lequel 'nul ne peut être contraint de demeurer dans l'indivision et le partage peut toujours être provoqué, nonobstant prohibitions et conventions contraires', est tempéré par l'alinéa 1, in fine, de l'art. 6 précité: le juge a un pouvoir élargi en cas de désaccord des indivisaires. Après avoir réputé indivisibles les droits patrimoniaux litigieux, il pourra, par exemple, nommer un curateur pour les exercer.

Les droits d'exploitation exercés par les héritiers peuvent-ils faire l'objet d'abus? La Cour d'appel de Versailles a répondu positivement.[105] Les enseignements de cet arrêt ne sont pas, en tant que tels, transposables en droit belge car nous ne connaissons pas un équivalent de l'art 20 de la loi française qui permet au Tribunal de prendre toute mesure appropriée en cas d'abus notoire, de la part des représentants de l'auteur décédé, dans l'usage ou le non-usage du droit de divulgation ou des droits d'exploitation. Mais les

105. Aff. *Foujita*, appel Versailles (1ère ch.), 3 mars 1987, D.S., 1987, p. 382 et note B. EDELMAN.

critères retenus par cette juridiction pour affirmer que la veuve du peintre Foujita abusait de son droit d'exploitation en refusant de donner son autorisation à la publication d'un livre sur son mari sont significatifs. La Cour de Versailles fait valoir deux critères majeurs: lorsque l'oeuvre est divulguée, il faut présumer, eu égard bien entendu à d'autres éléments de fait, que son auteur a entendu lui donner le plus grand rayonnement possible, sauf s'il a exercé son droit au retrait; et il convient également, dit la Cour, d'éviter qu'une atteinte soit portée 'à la perpétuation de la renommée d'un artiste français de grand talent'. N'est-il pas assez étonnant que l'abus, retenu ici par la Cour, a pour résultat de faire prévaloir la volonté incertaine d'un mort et l'intérêt général d'une culture sur la volonté expresse de la titulaire du droit subjectif d'exploitation?

2. Le statut des droits moraux de l'artiste décédé

Les droits moraux se transmettent-ils, après la mort de l'artiste de la même manière et pour la même durée que les droits d'exploitation? Deux principes doivent guider les solutions qu'on apporte à cette question. S'agissant de protéger la création de l'auteur décédé, dans le système subjectiviste des droits d'auteur, le premier principe exige qu'on reste fidèle à la volonté qu'il a, éventuellement, exprimée. Le second principe exige qu'en l'absence d'une telle volonté, on se tourne davantage vers l'oeuvre. La jurisprudence française, notamment dans l'arrêt Foujita, montre, sans doute de manière prudente, que la notion d'intérêt général peut jouer un rôle important.

Dans un intéressant arrêt, la Cour d'appel de Bruxelles s'est prononcée sur le point de savoir si et dans quelle mesure des héritiers pouvaient faire valoir le droit au respect d'une oeuvre écrite par des auteurs décédés.[106] Les faits de l'espèce étaient les suivants. En 1963, Béjart réalisa l'opérette 'La veuve joyeuse' pour le Théatre royal de la Monnaie à Bruxelles. Or, le célèbre chorégraphe, tout en utilisant scrupuleusement le texte des auteurs, l'interpréta, par la magie de la chorégraphie, comme une oeuvre engagée. Les auteurs la voulaient dénuée de toute intention sociale, politique ou moralisatrice. La chorégraphie de Béjart lui donna, par contre, le ton d'une critique d'une société jouisseuse et insouciante des difficultés d'existence de certaines classes défavorisées. Les héritiers des auteurs assignèrent alors Béjart en soutenant que sa mise en scène constituait une atteinte au droit au respect de l'oeuvre dont ils étaient dépositaires. Les attendus suivant méritent d'être reproduits:

> 'Attendu d'abord que le caractère essentiellement personnel du droit au respect de l'oeuvre, comme de toutes les prérogatives inhérentes au droit moral, empêche que soit donné au cessionnaire du droit de représentation une autorisation générale d'apporter à l'oeuvre toute modification qu'il estimerait désirable

106. Bruxelles, 29 septembre 1965, J. C. P., 1966, 14820, note A. FRANCON.

> au risque de la déformer en portant préjudice à la réputation de l'auteur; que c'est seulement en parfaite connaissance de cause et par un acquiescement formel, exempt de toute ambiguïté, que l'auteur ou ses ayant droit peuvent approuver de telles initiatives de leur cocontractant.'

Deux remarques peuvent être formulées à propos de cet arrêt:
a. Singulièrement pour ce qui concerne les oeuvres littéraires, le droit au respect n'est pas uniquement le droit de voir respectée l'intégrité matérielle de l'oeuvre. On peut en effet respecter le texte tout en trahissant son esprit. Ce type d'atteinte entre dans le champ d'application de l'art. *6bis* de la Convention de Berne qui protège 'toute autre atteinte à la même oeuvre'.
b. Par ailleurs, nous avons vu plus haut que la question de la renonciation aux droits moraux est loin de recevoir une réponse univoque. Trois positions peuvent être rencontrées: soit on affirme que les droits moraux sont tellement liés à la personnalité de l'auteur qu'il ne peut y renoncer; soit on prétend, fut-ce avec des nuances, que rien ne s'oppose à une telle aliénation; soit, et c'est le moyen terme retenu par la Cour de Bruxelles, la renonciation aux droits moraux est possible, mais uniquement dans un cadre formel très strict: la volonté de l'auteur ne peut être présumée; elle doit être expressément formulée.

Les conflits qui peuvent surgir à propos des droits d'auteur ne peuvent que très rarement recevoir, a priori, une solution décisive.

Les droits d'exploitation sont, en principe, transmis sans réserve aux héritiers. L'affaire Foujita montre cependant qu'une telle solution, qu'on eut pu croire certaine, a été abandonnée au profit d'une construction assez étrange au terme de laquelle le droit subjectif patrimonial d'exploitation transféré aux héritiers s'est vu repoussé par la notion d'intérêt général et par 'l'interprétation divinatoire d'une volonté d'outre tombe'.[107]

La transmission des droits moraux aux héritiers de l'auteur est beaucoup plus controversée. En Belgique, certains l'admettent à titre perpétuel, au-delà donc de la durée de survie des droits patrimoniaux fixée à 50 ans, aussi bien par la loi belge que par la Convention de Berne.[108] Cette solution pose alors la question de l'exercice des droits moraux sur une oeuvre tombée dans le domaine public. D'autres limitent le droit des héritiers à certains attributs du droit moral et pour une période limitée à la durée des droits d'exploitation.[109] Les héritiers agissent *in nomine auctoris* et, partant, ils doivent avant tout se conformer à la volonté exprimée par le *de cujus*. Il ne leur appartient donc pas de divulguer une oeuvre que l'auteur défunt

107. F. RIGAUX, 'Le droit, à la découverte de l'art' in *Annales de droit de Louvain*, 1988, n° 3–4, p. 483.
108. P. RECHT, *Le droit d'auteur en Belgique, op. cit.*, n° 15, p. 77.
109. F. VAN ISACKER, *De morele rechten, op. cit.*, n° 125 à 129, pp. 135 à 139.

entendait garder secrète. D'autres, enfin, s'opposent sans nuance à une telle transmission.[110]

Cette dernière position est sans nul doute excessive. La transmission aux héritiers des droits moraux de paternité et de respect de l'oeuvre est reconnue par l'art. 6*bis* al. 2 de la Convention de Berne. Ce texte est applicable[111] et a été appliqué en Belgique.[112] Ces droits moraux sont, après la mort de l'auteur et, sauf manifestation contraire expresse de celui-ci, maintenus au profit des héritiers 'au moins jusqu'à l'extinction des droits patrimoniaux'. Les termes 'au moins' permettent aux législateurs nationaux d'étendre la durée d'exercice de ces droits. A ce jour, le législateur belge n'a toutefois pas mis en oeuvre cette possibilité.

Minimalement, il faut reconnaître que les droits moraux de paternité et de respect de l'oeuvre peuvent être exercés pendant 50 ans par les héritiers ou légataires de l'auteur défunt. Par ailleurs, la question de l'extension de cet exercice aux droits de divulgation et de repentir ne peut recevoir de réponse décisive. En l'absence d'une volonté manifeste du *de cujus*, les litiges seront sans doute tranchés dans le sens d'une extension ou d'un affaiblissement[113] des droits moraux selon les critères que les juridictions retiendront et, singulièrement, en fonction de l'idée qu'elles se feront de l'intérêt général de voir une oeuvre entrer dans le patrimoine culturel de leur communauté.

---

110. A. BERENBOOM, *op. cit.*, n° 161, p. 177 prétend que la transmission à cause de mort du droit moral est injustifiable car 'personne ne peut se substituer à l'artiste pour exprimer ce qui est si intimement lié à sa personnalité' (n° 161). Mais, dans le même temps, il défend la thèse qu'on peut contractuellement renoncer au droit de divulgation (n° 105). Si on comprend bien, les droits moraux ne sont transmissibles et cessibles que du vivant de l'auteur; et, partant, la force de liaison du droit moral à son auteur est renforcée par la mort de son titulaire. Ses droits moraux meurent avec lui.
111. Contra, mais à tort, A. BERENBOOM, *op. cit.*, n° 161; dans notre sens, *Guide de la Convention de Berne, op. cit.*, p. 46.
112. Cf. aff. *Veuve joyeuse, supra.*
113. *V.* O. LALIGANT, *op. cit.*, p. 428.

République Fédérale d'Allemagne

RAPPORT NATIONAL SUR LE SUJET 3. DROITS DES CRÉATEURS ET DE LEURS HERITIERS*

Ulrich Lohaus**

I. INTRODUCTION

Les droits des créateurs sont définis par la loi sur le droit d'auteur et les droits voisins (*Urheberrechtsgesetz*) du 9 Septembre 1965. Les oeuvres d'art entrent dans le champ d'application de cette loi (cf. para. 2 I n° 4).

II. DROIT D'AUTEUR ET DOMAINE PUBLIC

Les oeuvres d'art ont une double nature:
matérielle/corporelle et spirituelle/incorporelle.
De plus, tout le monde participe à la vie culturelle; c'est pourquoi, il est nécessaire de distinguer ce qui est la propriété spirituelle d'un individu (et donc protégeable par le droit d'auteur) et ce qui appartient au domaine public. Le critère de distinction est le fait que l'artiste a créé une oeuvre qui porte la marque de sa personnalité, individualité et est de ce fait unique. En conséquence, le champ du droit d'auteur n'inclut pas les oeuvres d'art qui ne sont pas l'expression de l'individualité de l'artiste; ces oeuvres appartiennent au domaine public.

III. LE DROIT D'AUTEUR DANS LES ARTS PLASTIQUES

1. Caractéristiques du droit d'auteur

Le droit d'auteur comprend 3 aspects:

- il est un droit subjectif attaché à la personne de l'artiste qui peut l'opposer *erga omnes*;

---

* Note d'Editeur: résumé en français du rapport en allemand.

** Assistant de recherche à l'Institut du Droit des Affaires Internationales, Westfälischen Wilhelms-Universität, Münster.

- il protège les intérêts de l'artiste sur son oeuvre et le contenu de cette dernière;
- il est un droit absolu.

2. Le contenu du droit d'auteur

A. Observations générales

Le paragraphe 11 de la loi étend la protection du droit d'auteur à la relation spirituelle et personnelle qui existe entre l'artiste et son oeuvre, de même qu'à l'utilisation de cette oeuvre par l'artiste.

Deux observations permettent de mieux comprendre le système de protection du droit d'auteur:
le droit d'auteur protège la personne même de l'artiste et seulement en second lieu ses oeuvres;
le droit d'auteur est dichotomique: il s'attache aussi bien à l'aspect corporel de l'oeuvre (droits patrimoniaux, cf. paras. 15 à 24 de la loi) qu'à son aspect immatériel: la personnalité de l'artiste et la projection de cette dernière dans l'oeuvre (droit moral, cf. paras. 12 à 14 de la loi).

B. Les droits patrimoniaux

Ils sont définis par les paragraphes 15 à 24 de la loi.

i. Caractères communs des droits patrimoniaux
Ils sont exclusifs et absolus (cf. para. 15 de la loi). Ils poursuivent deux objectifs:

- permettre à l'artiste d'exploiter économiquement son oeuvre;
- lui reconnaître le droit de choisir les formes de cette exploitation et la personne qui en sera chargée (principe du consentement de l'auteur).

Ainsi l'imprimeur qui tire sans l'autorisation de l'artiste des exemplaires supplémentaires de son oeuvre, et qui les garde et les publie sans le consentement exprès de l'artiste, viole le paragraphe 16 de la loi sur le droit d'auteur. L'artiste a les droits de jouissance sur son oeuvre et à une rémunération appropriée qui sont crées dès le moment de la création de l'oeuvre. Il a le droit à cette rémunération même si son oeuvre est adaptée ou façonnée par d'autres (para. 23 de la loi).

ii. Les droits patrimoniaux au sens strict du terme
Ces droits portent sur l'exploitation de l'oeuvre dans sa forme corporelle et sont: le droit de reproduction, de divulguer et de représentation. (cf. para. 15 de la loi).

a. Le droit de reproduction
C'est le droit de fabriquer des reproductions de l'oeuvre, de fixer la forme

matérielle de l'oeuvre qui est ainsi rendue directement ou indirectement perceptible à tout être humain (cf. para. 16 de la loi).

Il peut s'agir d'une reproduction directe ou indirecte; la reproduction directe est la reproduction d'oeuvre originale; la reproduction indirecte est la reproduction d'une autre reproduction. La question se pose de savoir si la fabrication d'un moyen de reproduire une oeuvre (négatifs, clichés) constitue une reproduction ou pas. Si l'on admet qu'une oeuvre peut être indirectement perceptible, la fabrication de négatifs ou de clichés devrait être considérée comme une reproduction. De ce fait le consentement de l'artiste est nécessaire pour une telle fabrication.

Doit être considéré comme une reproduction le fait de recréer une oeuvre originale endommagée. Est également une reproduction le fait de photographier une oeuvre d'art. La reproduction de photographies est par contre une éxécution (para. 19 IV de la loi).

b. Le droit de publication

Ce droit est visé par les paragraphes 15 I n° 2 et 17 de la loi. C'est le droit d'offrir au public et de commercialiser l'oeuvre ou sa reproduction sous sa forme corporelle.

Une oeuvre d'art est divulguée lorsqu'elle est offerte à la vente, à un prêt ou à une location, ou bien publiée (c'est à dire mise à la disposition du public).

Une oeuvre seulement exposée dans un musée sans pouvoir être achetée n'est pas divulguée au sens du paragraphe 17 I de la loi. Lors d'une exposition d'une oeuvre dans une galerie, celle-ci n'est pas vendue au directeur de la galerie par l'artiste, mais ce dernier a cédé non seulement le droit d'exposer mais également le droit de publication et ce, tacitement lors de l'accord de commission. Celui qui détient le droit de reproduction peut ne pas détenir le droit de publication, ce qui peut poser problème, car la divulgation d'une oeuvre implique souvent sa reproduction.

En tout cas l'auteur et l'artiste épuisent leur droit de publication par la première vente de leur oeuvre; cette règle de l'épuisement (*Erschöpfungsgrundsatz*) ne s'applique que s'ils ont cédé la jouissance de l'oeuvre de façon définitive. Ainsi lorsqu'un artiste cède ses droits de divulguer à une imprimerie d'art, son droit de publication s'épuise s'il a renoncé à signer ou coloriser l'oeuvre à reproduire. Lors d'une vente d'un objet d'art avec une clause de réserve de propriété, se pose la question de savoir si cette règle de l'épuisement s'applique immédiatement. La question reste sans une réponse unanime de la Doctrine. Une autre possibilité pour que la règle de l'épuisement s'applique est que le détenteur légitime des droits ait donné son accord à la publication. Cependant cette règle de l'épuisement trouve une limite dans l'existence du droit de suite qui appartient à l'artiste.

c. Le droit de représentation

Le droit de représentation est défini au paragraphe 18 de la loi. C'est le droit de représenter une oeuvre (ou sa reproduction) non publiée. Il permet de protéger les oeuvres d'art non publiées. Le commerce de l'art serait difficile si le consentement de l'artiste était nécessaire pour exposer des oeuvres publiées. Par le contrat qui lie l'artiste et une galerie d'art, le droit de représentation est cédé pour une certaine période et pour certains lieux; la galerie a l'obligation d'exposer l'oeuvre; l'artiste s'oblige a interdire l'exposition de ses oeuvres dans les mêmes lieux aux mêmes périodes.

iii. Les droits patrimoniaux au sens large du terme
Ces droits concernent le transfert de l'oeuvre sous ses aspects immatériels.

a. Le droit d'exécution
Le para. 19 IV 1 de la loi définit le droit d'exécution comme le droit de rendre perceptible une oeuvre d'art par des moyens techniques. C'est le cas par exemple de projections publiques de photographies.

b. Le droit de diffusion
Le droit de diffusion est le droit de rendre accessible l'oeuvre par l'intermédiaire de sa diffusion sur les ondes (para. 20 de la loi). Ce droit n'est applicable aux oeuvres d'art que si ces dernières servent d'illustration à une émission télévisée ou si un programme porte sur l'oeuvre d'un artiste ou d'un sculpteur.

iv. Le droit patrimonial au sens large
La liste des droits patrimoniaux décrits dans la loi n'est pas exhaustive; ainsi les artistes peuvent se prévaloir d'autres droits patrimoniaux portant sur des exploitations de leurs oeuvres sur d'autres médias et se réserver de nouveaux droits pour de futurs types d'exploitation.

v. Les restrictions aux droits patrimoniaux
Les droits patrimoniaux ne peuvent pas préserver les droits d'un seul individu; le bien commun, les intérêts de l'art et des sciences doivent également être pris en considération, de ce fait l'exercice de ces droits peut être limité conformément aux paragraphes suivants de la loi:

a. Para. 46
La publication et la reproduction d'oeuvres qui font partie d'une collection sont permises si elles sont faites à des fins éducatives, pour l'église ou les écoles. L'artiste doit en être informé; 2 semaines après l'envoi de cette information, la reproduction peut commencer. L'artiste doit être rémunéré.

b. Para. 47
Les écoles et autres institutions éducatives ont le droit de fabriquer des copies vidéo seulement pour des fins éducatives. L'artiste ne recevra pas de rémunération si les copies vidéo sont effacées après une certaine période.

c. Para. 50
La reproduction d'oeuvres, leur publication ou reproduction publique à des fins d'information et d'actualités utilisées par la presse est libre de tout contrôle de l'artiste.

d. Para. 51
Le droit de citation permet de reproduire et de publier une oeuvre sans le consentement de l'auteur et sans rémunérer ce dernier.

e. Paras. 53, 54
Le droit à la copie privée autorise la reproduction par photocopie ou autre moyen d'une oeuvre si la copie est utilisée à des fins priviés par une personne physique ou morale. Si une oeuvre est susceptible d'être reproduite à des fins privées, les fabricants du matériel servant à la reproduction sont tenus de rémunérer l'artiste et l'informer du nombre d'appareils utilisés à cette fin.

f. Para. 59
Les oeuvres qui se trouvent dans des lieux publics peuvent sans l'autorisation du détenteur de droits être reproduites (au moyen de techniques picturales, graphiques, photographiques ou cinématographiques), publiées et rendues publiques.

g. Para. 60
Ce paragraphe concerne le cas d'un portrait d'une personne physique qui en réclame la propriété; le droit d'auteur par contre demeure au peintre. Mais celui qui a commandé le portrait (ainsi que ses héritiers) a le droit de le faire reproduire.

C. Le droit moral

Le contenu du droit moral est défini aux paragraphes 12, 13 et 14 de la loi. Ce sont les droits de divulgation, de paternité et d'opposition. Mais il peut être plus vaste.

i. Le droit moral au sens strict du terme

a. Le droit de divulgation
Le droit de divulgation est défini au paragraphe 12 de la loi. C'est le droit de l'auteur de décider si son oeuvre sera rendue publique, quand elle le sera et comment.

Une oeuvre d'art est divulguée normalement par le fait de la vendre ou de la prêter à un musée. Le choix des circonstances de la divulgation de son oeuvre relève de la seule décision de l'artiste.

b. Le droit de paternité
C'est le paragraphe 13 de la loi qui définit le droit de paternité. Il sert de base à toute action contre un plagiat et pour être cité. Ce paragraphe permet également à l'artiste de décider comment il signera son oeuvre (pseudonyme, signe ou autres manières). Il lui permet également de s'opposer à ce que sou nom soit lié à son oeuvre.

c. Le droit d'opposition
L'artiste a le droit d'interdire toute altération ou autre dommage faits à son oeuvre, à la condition que ceux-ci portent atteinte aux intérêts spirituels de l'artiste pour son oeuvre ou à la réputation de l'artiste (cf. para. 14 de la loi). Une hypersensibilité de l'artiste n'empêche pas l'exercice de ce droit.

Ce droit peut être exercé même si l'oeuvre est la propriété d'un tiers. Mais l'artiste ne peut pas s'opposer à des modifications peu importantes, de même il ne peut pas se prévaloir de ce droit lorsque des modifications ont été apportées à une de ses oeuvres qui se trouve dans un lieu privé et qui, de ce fait, est vue par un nombre limité de personnes.

ii. Le droit moral au sens large du terme
Les droits liés à la personne de l'artiste sont basés sur la nécessité de protéger les intérêts spirituels, personnels et l'idéal de l'artiste et sur l'idée que l'oeuvre créée par ce dernier porte son empreinte. Ces principes fondamentaux du droit d'auteur sont la base d'une conception plus large du droit moral. Ainsi, c'est sur cette base que l'auteur bénéficie d'autres droits comme ceux d'accès à ses oeuvres (para. 25), celui d'interdire des modifications en cas de cession des droits d'utilisation (para. 39) et celui de retrait (paras. 41 et 42).

D. Les autres droits détenus par l'auteur

D'autres droits sont reconnus à l'auteur qui peuvent être patrimoniaux (droit de suite, droits à rémunération pour des emprunts (seulement utilisés dans la littérature)) ou liés au droit moral (droit d'accès). Les paragraphes 25 à 27 définissent ces droits.

i. Le droit de suite
Le droit de suite est le droit pour l'artiste de recevoir un pourcentage (5%) du produit de la vente (quelle que soit sa forme) d'une de ses oeuvres bien que cette dernière ne lui appartienne plus puisqu'il l'a lui-même vendue depuis longtemps (para. 26).

a. Le principe à la base de la règle
Le fondement du droit de suite est l'idée que l'artiste a droit à une part du bénéfice crée par la vente d'une de ses oeuvres. L'artiste et ses ayant droit doivent pouvoir recevoir une partie des bénéfices, surtout si le prix de vente de l'oeuvre a augmenté depuis sa première vente par l'artiste.

b. Les conditions d'exercice du droit
Le droit de suite ne s'applique qu'aux arts plastiques et qu'en cas de vente d'une oeuvre d'art originale. Le fait que l'oeuvre doit être originale, pose un problème lorsqu'il s'agit d'oeuvres nécessitant des moulages ou des mises en forme. En général, sont dans ce cas considérées comme 'originales' les

oeuvres coulées dans des moulages produits par l'artiste lui-même et avec son accord. La vente qui occasionne le paiement d'un droit de suite doit obligatoirement être faite par un marchand d'oeuvres d'art ou une maison aux enchères. Il doit s'agir naturellement d'une deuxième vente de la même oeuvre d'art; la première vente n'ouvre pas de droit de suite au bénéfice de l'artiste.

c. Les conséquences de l'application du droit de suite
L'artiste a droit à un paiement de 5% du montant du prix de la vente à moins que ce dernier soit inférieur à 100 DM. L'artiste ne peut y renoncer. La personne qui doit payer ce montant est le vendeur. Une procédure d'exécution forcée ne peut pas s'exercer à l'encontre de ce droit.

d. Les droits accessoires de l'artiste
L'artiste a le droit de demander aux maisons aux enchères et aux galeries d'art quelles oeuvres originales créées par lui ont été vendues. Il a le droit de connaître les noms et adresses des vendeurs de ses oeuvres et le montant du prix d'aliénation. Les maisons de vente aux enchères et les galeries peuvent lui refuser de lui donner ces informations s'ils lui paient le montant qui lui est dû. Ce droit d'obtenir des renseignements ne peut être qu'exercé que par une société d'auteurs. Cette dernière peut ainsi vérifier la véracité des informations mentionnées qui ont été données à l'artiste. Tous ces droits sont prescrits en 10 ans.

En Allemagne, le droit de suite, y compris les droits d'information et de contrôle, est géré par la société d'exploitation *Bild-Kunst* (*Verwertungsgesellschaft (VG) Bild-Kunst*). Cette dernière a passé un accord-cadre en 1980 avec l'association des commerçants de l'art. L'accord établit une société de compensation (*Ausgleichsvereinigung Kunst*). Cette société encaisse les paiements forfaitaires du commerce d'oeuvres d'art pour le droit de suite. Le pourcentage que les commerçants d'art et les commissaires-priseurs doivent lui payer s'élève à 1,3% des recettes atteintes par la vente des oeuvres d'art. Ce pourcentage est utilisé pour financer le système de sécurité sociale des artistes. La société d'exploitation *Bild-Kunst* partage ces montants entre les artistes.

ii. Le droit d'accès à l'oeuvre
Conformément au paragraphe 25 I de la loi, l'artiste a le droit de demander au détenteur de l'original ou d'une reproduction d'une de ses oeuvres d'y avoir accès, si cela lui est nécessaire afin d'en faire des reproductions ou d'y retravailler et si cela ne porte pas atteinte à des intérêts justifiés de son détenteur (en cas d'un portrait de famille du détenteur par exemple). Au cas où l'artiste ne possède plus d'exemplaire de son oeuvre, il est clair que le détenteur de l'original sera obligé de lui en laisser l'accès. Mais c'est au détenteur qu'il appartient de fixer les modalités d'accès à l'oeuvre et de réclamer le cas échéant le paiement des coûts y afférent.

3. *Les conditions d'exploitation des droits d'auteur*

A. Observations générales

Un artiste ne peut pas transmettre une partie ou la totalité du droit d'auteur à un tiers. Il peut céder (para. 31 I 1) à un tiers le droit d'utiliser son oeuvre pour l'exploiter sous une forme ou une autre. De tels droits d'utilisation sont indépendants des droits patrimoniaux, bien que leur contenu soit le même.

L'exploitation des oeuvres par cession des droits d'utilisation peuvent suivre deux voies: l'artiste peut céder les droits à la *VG Bild-Kunst* qui cède certains de ses droits à des tiers; il peut aussi céder directement certains droits pour certaines formes d'exploitation par contrat (avec par exemple un éditeur d'art).

B. La cession des droits d'utilisation

La cession de droits d'utilisation suit les règles de cession d'autres droits (cf. paras. 398 *et seq*. du Code civil allemand). Le contrat de cession des droits d'utilisation d'une oeuvre future doit être en forme écrite (cf. para. 40 de la loi). Les contrats qui lient les artistes et les galeries sont conclus pour 5 ans avec un préavis de 6 mois.

C. Les formes d'utilisation

i. La simple utilisation
C'est le droit cédé à l'acquéreur d'utiliser l'oeuvre sous la forme autorisée par le contrat de cession en même temps que l'auteur ou un détenteur légitime du droit d'auteur (para. 31 II).

ii. L'utilisation exclusive
Elle existe lorsque son détenteur est fondé à utiliser l'oeuvre de façon exclusive (même par rapport à l'auteur) sous la forme autorisée par le contrat et à en céder l'utilisation simple (cf. para. 31 III de la loi).

D. Les limitations aux droits d'utilisation

Chaque artiste a sa propre manière d'exploiter son oeuvre. Le paragraphe 32 de la loi prescrit des limitations dans le temps et l'espace du droit d'utilisation ainsi que des limites relatives au contenu.

i. Les limites liées au contenu
Il est possible de céder chacun des droits de reproduction, de divulguer etc. à des personnes différentes.

ii. Les limites dans le temps et l'espace
Ces limites sont très fréquentes, en cas de cession de droit de diffusion.

iii. La théorie de la destination (*Zweckübertragungstheorie*)
Le paragraphe 32 prend en compte le but poursuivi par l'artiste. C'est par l'interprétation du contrat que l'on connaît la portée de cette destination. La jurisprudence a développé la 'théorie de la destination' selon laquelle le but de la cession est déterminant pour établir sa portée. Cette théorie a été adoptée par le législateur (cf. para. 31 V). L'artiste conserve le droit de décider de la divulgation et de l'exploitation d'une adaptation de son oeuvre bien que les droits d'utilisation aient été cédés (cf., para. 37 I de la loi).

E. Les honoraires de l'artiste

En pratique souvent les artistes doivent se contenter d'honoraires convenus. Le paragraphe 36 I (appellé souvent le paragraphe du *bestseller*) reconnaît à l'artiste le droit de demander une augmentation de la contre-partie convenue dans le contrat de cession des droits d'utilisation, lorsqu'il existe une grande différence entre le fruit de l'exploitation et cette contre-partie. L'artiste ne peut renoncer à ce droit qui se prescrit en 2 ans.

F. Le droit de retrait

i. Le retrait pour non exercice
Si l'artiste a conclu une cession exclusive de droits d'utilisation, il ne peut plus lui-même exploiter son oeuvre ou céder des droits à des tiers. De ce fait l'artiste est fondé à retirer les droits cédés à la personne qui n'exerce pas ses droits ou bien qui par exemple ne publie pas un livre contenant des reproductions de son oeuvre (cf. para. 41 de la loi). Ce non-exercice doit être du à des circonstances indépendantes de l'artiste. L'artiste doit observer un délai avant de retirer le droit d'utiliser son oeuvre. Le cas échéant, l'artiste doit dédommager le détenteur du droit.

ii. Le retrait pour cause de changement d'opinion
L'artiste peut retirer le droit d'utiliser son oeuvre si cette dernière ne correspond plus à son goût esthétique, à ses opinions, à sa vision de la vie (cf. para. 42 de la loi). Cette faculté reconnue à l'artiste entraîne une insécurité juridique pour les collectionneurs, les acquéreurs et les musées.

Ce droit peut être exercé par les héritiers de l'artiste. L'artiste doit dédommager le détenteur du droit.

IV. DROITS D'AUTEURS ET SUCCESSIONS

Les héritiers de l'artiste reçoivent l'ensemble de ces droits d'auteur (droits moraux et droits patrimoniaux; cf., paras. 28 et 30 de la loi et para. 1922 du Code civil allemand). L'artiste peut désigner par testament la personne fondée à exploiter ces droits et à en être le détenteur. Ces droits ont une durée de 70 ans après la mort de l'artiste (cf. para. 64 de la loi). Les oeuvres tombent dans le domaine public après cette période.

Grèce

RAPPORT NATIONAL SUR LE SUJET 3. DROITS DES CREATEURS ET DE LEURS HERITIERS*

Antonias Dimolitsa**

1. On devrait peut-être commencer par mentionner les lois grecques d'application générale en matière de propriété littéraire et artistique. Il s'agit de la loi 2387/1920 sur la 'propriété intellectuelle' avec les amendements qui y ont été portés depuis, le décret-loi 4254/1962 ratifiant la Convention Mondiale de Genève du 6 septembre 1952 et la loi 100/1975 ratifiant d'une part la révision de la Convention de Berne (Paris 1971) et, d'autre part, la Convention de Stockholm du 14 juillet 1967. Il faudrait encore mentionner le décret-loi 4264/1962 selon lequel les ressortissants grecs ont le droit de se prévaloir des dispositions de la Convention de Berne, si celles-ci s'avèrent plus favorables pour eux que les dispositions du droit grec.

Ces quelques indications permettent de cerner le régime général de protection de la propriété littéraire et artistique; celui-ci ne règle pas quand même directement le droit moral de l'auteur qui est plutôt considéré en Grèce comme un droit de la personnalité protégé par les arts. 57 et 59 du Code civil et non pas comme un droit de l'auteur dérivant des dispositions sur la propriété littéraire et artistique. Vu que ce chapitre concerne essentiellement le droit moral de l'auteur, il est nécessaire de citer le texte de ces deux articles du Code civil:

> '*Article 57. Droits sur sa propre personnalité*
> 'Celui qui, d'une manière illicite, est atteint dans sa personnalité, a le droit d'exiger la suppression de l'atteinte et, en outre, l'abstention de toute atteinte à l'avenir. Si l'atteinte concerne la personnalité d'une personne décédée, ce sont son conjoint, ses descendants, ascendants, frères et soeurs et les héritiers testamentaires qui possèdent ce droit.
> 'En outre, la prétention à des dommages-intérêts, suivant les dispositions relatives aux actes illicites, n'est pas exclue.'
> '*Article 59. Réparation du préjudice moral*
> 'Dans les cas prévus par les deux articles précédents, le tribunal peut, par son jugement rendu à la requête de celui qui a été atteint et compte tenu de la nature de l'atteinte, condamner en outre la personne en faute à réparer le

---

* Note d'Editeur: *v.* pour 'l'Introduction au Rapport', *supra* p. 39.

** Avocat, Athènes.

préjudice moral de celui qui a été atteint. Cette réparation consiste dans le paiement d'une somme d'argent, dans une mesure de publicité, et aussi dans tout ce qui est indiqué dans les circonstances.'

2. En tant que le droit de la personnalité, le droit moral de l'auteur est illimité dans le sens que la possibilité d'apparition de nouvelles manifestations de ce droit est toujours ouverte; les catégories dans lesquelles la doctrine a voulu classer ces manifestations, peuvent ainsi être élargies ou même dépassées. Ce caractère illimité signifie aussi que le droit moral n'est soumis qu'aux seules restrictions prévues par la loi ou impliquées par des contrats passés par l'artiste. Ces contrats ne doivent pas être quand même contraires aux bonnes moeurs, ce qui les rendrait nuls (arts. 178 et 179 C.c.); tel pourrait être le cas d'un contrat imposant à l'artiste de ne pas révéler sa paternité sur l'oeuvre, peut être aussi le cas d'un contrat – genre inconnu de la pratique en Grèce – passé par l'artiste et une galerie sur la base de laquelle l'artiste s'obligerait à transférer toutes ses oeuvres futures à la galerie, contre un salaire mensuel. Pour que les restrictions contractuelles soient licites et opposables à l'artiste, il faut encore que l'exécution du contrat ne crée pas une situation d'abus de droit (art. 281 C.c.).

Le droit moral est d'ailleurs protégé dès qu'il y a atteinte à l'oeuvre en tant qu'émanation de la personnalité de l'auteur, indépendamment des répercussions dommageables possibles à la personne de l'auteur ou à l'oeuvre. On devrait préciser cette remarque:

- par rapport au droit au respect de l'oeuvre, le droit grec (art. 15 loi 2387/1920) pourrait être considéré comme plus favorable à l'auteur que le droit conventionnel. Selon ce dernier (art. 6*bis* de la Convention de Berne), la protection est accordée à l'auteur en cas d'atteinte à l'oeuvre, sous condition que 'l'honneur ou la réputation' de celui-ci en aient été aussi touchées. Pareille condition n'existe pas en droit grec;
- toujours dans le cadre du droit au respect de l'oeuvre et pour le cas de déplacement, la protection existe en dehors de tout danger menaçant son intégrité en tant que telle. En 1954 le Conseil Municipal de Rhodes prit la décision d'enlever de la place centrale de la ville une sculpture de Christos Kapralos qui y était située depuis deux ans, après commande à l'artiste, pour la mettre en dépôt jusqu'à décision ultérieure du Conseil sur un autre endroit de placement. L'artiste ayant demandé l'annulation de l'acte administratif par devant le Conseil d'Etat, celui-ci émit sa décision 1465/9.11.1954 (Session Plénière, EEN 55, p. 78), décision considérée comme de principe en la matière. Elle déclara que l'artiste continue, même après la vente de son oeuvre, d'avoir un droit de se dresser contre toute altération ou déplacement de l'oeuvre; le lien moral et intellectuel qui existe entre l'artiste et son oeuvre persiste, malgré l'acquisition par des tiers de droits réels sur l'oeuvre – bien corporel; l'oeuvre d'art est toujours caractérisée par le nom de l'artiste et non par celui de son propriétaire; l'artiste a droit d'attaquer tout acte administratif qui reviendrait à être une atteinte à l'oeuvre.

3. Le droit moral de l'auteur est inaliénable mais son exercice peut être soumis à des restrictions contractuelles (sous les réserves ci-dessus). Il s'agirait surtout, pour les oeuvres d'art, d'un conflit du droit moral de l'auteur et du droit de propriété de l'acquéreur de l'objet matériel auquel est incorporée l'oeuvre. La résolution de ce conflit en droit grec (doctrine, jurisprudence mais aussi et surtout usages) serait comme il suit:

- le droit de l'artiste de s'opposer à toute atteinte á l'intégrité de son oeuvre, à toute reproduction ou exposition de celle-ci ou son droit de visiter ou retirer temporairement l'oeuvre pour l'exposer, prévaudrait sur le droit de propriété. Il est à noter, en l'occurrence, que les galeries n'ont pas le droit de réexposer les oeuvres qu'elles ont acquises sans le consentement de l'artiste;
- par contre, on ne voit pas comment le droit moral pourrait arrêter la destruction de l'oeuvre par le propriétaire du bien l'incorporant ou fonder une obligation subséquente de réparation du préjudice moral à sa charge. Les artistes n'ont pas d'ailleurs droit à un pourcentage sur le prix de revente de leurs oeuvres; le droit de suite n'étant pas prévu en droit grec, il y trouverait en outre difficilement un fondement.

4. Le droit moral de l'auteur s'éteint par sa mort. Le droit des personnes mentionnées dans l'art. 57 §1 al. 2 du C.c., cité ci-dessus, est propre à celles-ci; il ne leur est pas transmis suivant les règles du droit successoral. L'intransmissibilité du droit moral, mais aussi du droit propre des héritiers de l'art. 57, amène à l'impossibilité – *de lege lata* – de protection de la personnalité de l'auteur après la mort de ces personnes. Il s'agit là d'un inconvénient du système de protection du droit moral sous l'orbite des droits de la personnalité, auquel pourrait éventuellement remédier la création d'un 'droit moral public' fondé sur des considérations de protection du patrimoine culturel.

The Netherlands

NATIONAL REPORT ON TOPIC 3. RIGHTS OF ARTISTS AND THEIR HEIRS*

F. Willem Grosheide** and Lucas J. van Eeghen***

I. INTRODUCTION

Given the fact that international trade in art mainly has to do with sale and resale of works of art, with respect to the rights of artists and their heirs, generally speaking many different legal regimes are applicable. Those regimes all deal with works of art in terms of property, ownership and possession. For the purpose of this report only the following legal regimes shall be discussed:
- copyright law
- property law
- contract law
- tort law.

There is an inherent conflict between copyright on the one hand and property law and contract law on the other hand with tort law as an intermediary between them. The law of copyright determines copyright ownership, i.e., who has the power to exercise and protect the rights afforded by it in relation to the creation of a work of art. The law of property indicates who is the owner of a work of art, for instance, a piece of framed and painted canvas, and which entitlements stem therefrom. The law of contract regulates the relationship between the copyright holder and all those who are authorized by him to some sort of use of the work of art (e.g., by means of assignment or licensing of the copyright; sale or loaning of the work itself). Tort law plays its intermediary role in case of violation of copyright by making the infringer liable according to specific action on the basis of copyright law as well as to general action on the basis of the general law of torts.

From now on the accent in this report shall rest on copyright law (II.), the

* Editor's note: *see also* 'The Netherlands: Introduction' by Anton A. QUAEDVLIEG in Part One.

** Professor, University of Utrecht; Attorney at Law, Höcker, Spigt & Doeleman, Amsterdam.

*** Attorney at Law, Höcker, Spigt & Doeleman, Amsterdam.

other legal regimes mentioned being only dealt with in as far as they are connected with one or more questions posed in the Questionnaire (III.).

II. GENERAL OUTLINE COPYRIGHT LAW

From a systematical point of view, the copyright law of the Netherlands reflects the Roman legal tradition, be it that some aspects fit more into the Anglo-Saxon tradition (*see*, e.g., the rules for commissioned works and those made for hire).

Copyright law is codified in the *Auteurswet* 1912 (Copyright Act 1912; AW) and developed accordingly by judge-made law. It protects 'authors' as owners of copyright via the protection of their 'works' all in conformity with both the Berne Convention and the Universal Copyright Convention to which the Netherlands adhere. The WIPO translation into English of the Copyright Act, as amended by the Act of 27 October 1972 (*Staatsblad* (Stb.) 579), was published in 1970 *Copyright* 181–188 and in 'Netherlands' item 1, in *Copyright Laws and Treaties of the World*, Vol. 3 (Unesco, 1985). The last amendment was by the Act of 30 May 1985 (Stb. 307) in effect since 1 August 1985, by Royal Decree of 11 July 1985 (Stb. 412). *See* for the WIPO translation of this Amendment into English, 1986 *Copyright* 42–45.

'Authors' are in the first place persons who actually created the 'works'. However, not only natural persons can be original owners of copyright, the same can apply to a corporate body or a legal entity (Arts. 7, 8, 45a AW).

'Works' in the first place are intellectual creations in the fields of 'literature, science and arts', as the Copyright Act stipulates it (Art. 1 in conjunction with Art. 10 AW). In fact the domain is broader encompassing creation and communication of all cultural information including technological creations like computer software.

To be protected by copyright law, a work in the second place must meet the requirements for protection. The Copyright Act does not give the appropriate criteria; this has been done by the courts. According to the formula of the Supreme Court of The Netherlands (*Hoge Raad*; HR) copyright protects 'works which as a result of personal creation, have a personal character' (HR 27 January 1961, *Nederlandse Jurisprudentie* (NJ) 1962, 355). In other words: the general requirement for a work to be protected by copyright is that the work as a form of expression of the author's personal imagination, skill, knowledge and labour, is original. In practice the test to judge this is to investigate whether or not identical works might have been developed independently; if not, the work must be considered to be original (freedom of choice in expression test). This standard of originality is not very hard to meet.

Apart from this general requirement of originality with respect to only written material that is not original, Dutch copyright law accepts a second route to copyright protection. These so-called non-personal writings are, according to the Supreme Court of The Netherlands, protected, provided they have been published or are intended for publication. The scope of this additional protection however is somewhat limited: non-personal writtings are protected only against copying of the written document (HR 17 April 1953, NJ 1954, 211; HR 27 January 1961, NJ 1962, 355; HR 25 June 1965, NJ 1966, 116).

Dutch copyright law attributes to the copyright owner two categories of entitlement: moral rights and economic rights, considered to be unified in one, the so-called exclusive copyright (*auteursrecht;* cf. *droit d'auteur, Urheberrecht*; so it is not a synonym to the Anglo-Saxon term 'copyright'). As the Copyright Act stipulates it, this exclusive right is the authority of the owner of the copyright in a work to make copies thereof and to publish copies of the work, be it within the limitations set by the law (Arts. 1, 12, 13, 14 AW). Exclusivity in this respect means that the copyright owner can forbid any use of a work made or to be made, without his prior consent that can be labelled as copying or publishing. In other words: the copyright owner at the same time has non-pecuniary interests and economic interest in the reproduction, publication, presentation, communication or distribution of his work by whatever means (e.g., including two or three dimensional variants or broadcasting).

Although moral rights and economic rights are considered to be unified in one copyright they are of a different character. This can be shown best by a brief survey of both those categories of rights. Moral rights are inherent to a natural person who created the work; it is questioned whether or not moral rights can be attached to a legal person or entity. Moral rights are inalienable or non-transferable but they can be waived. In principle they can be exercised in spite of the transfer of the economic rights but only during the lifetime of the author, be it that the authority to do so goes to the successors when they are appointed for that purpose by will or codicil (Art. 25 AW).

According to the Copyright Act (Art. 25 AW) there are three types of moral rights:

- Right of paternity: the right to be identified as the author of a work and to claim publication under this name as well as the right to prevent publication of it under the name of another person. The same applies to the right to communicate a work under pseudonym or anonymously. Also involved is the right to prohibit the alteration of the name or use of it in connection with the work of another author (Art 25(1)(*a*) AW).
- Right of integrity: the right to prevent any distortion, mutilation or derogatory action in relation to a work (e.g., exposition in a defamatory context) that would be prejudicial to the author's honour, his name or his reputation. The same applies in case of any alteration of a work (in form or content) unless such a prohibition would be unreasonable (Art. 25(1)(*c*) and (*b*) AW).
- Right of control: the right to modify (e.g., corrections or improvements) a work after publication with the consent of the author in conformity with the rules of reason (Art. 25(4) AW).

Although it is not laid down in the Copyright Act, it is commonly agreed that a fourth moral right has to be added: *right of publication*. This right is in fact the most fundamental moral right giving to the author the right to decide on the publication of his work and the power to control the communication of a work to the public. As far as paintings and similar works of art are concerned, a specific provision has to be mentioned here (Art. 24 AW) giving the author the authority in spite of the transfer of the economic rights to make and produce in the future identical or similar paintings and the like.

Economic rights have to do with the exploitation of copyright. Consequently they are alienable or transferable and can be waived (Art. 2 AW). The economic rights are protected during the lifetime of the copyright owner who is a natural person and for fifty years *post mortem actoris* (Art. 37 AW). Special provisions apply in case of anonymous or pseudonymous publication of works as well as for works of legal entities (Art. 38 AW).

According to the Copyright Act (Arts. 1, 12, 13, 14 AW) there are two types of economic rights:

- Reproduction right: the right of the copyright owner to authorize the making of copies of his work, including the right to fixation of a work in a medium meant to expose the work to the public (e.g., print, film, videogram) (Arts. 1, 13, 14 AW).
- Communication right: the right to distribute a work by putting it at the disposition of the public by way of sale, rent, lease, exhibition, recitation, performance, broadcasting licence or any other act. In case of sale, according to court practice, the right is extinguished after the first sale. The same applies with respect to rent and lease but pending legislation aims at introducing a rental right for certain types of works under which works of art.

As already has been indicated, the copyright has to be exercised within certain limitations. The condition here is that the work has been communicated to the public by one way or another: so there are no limitations to copyright protection in unpublished works.

In principle, the copyright applies up to and including fifty years after the death of the author (cf. Berne Convention). In case of joint works, the longest surviving author is the starting-point. If it is not clear who the originator of the work is (it not being signed does not have to be decisive for this), the copyright expires fifty years after the first rightful publication. The same applies for posthumously published works, if published within fifty years after the death of the maker. Furthermore, in the Netherlands it is not possible to invoke the copyright in case the term of the corresponding right in the country of origination already has expired.

These limitations have to do with balancing out the interests of the copyright owner and those of the public at large. To be mentioned here are – apart from the extinguishing of the copyright already indicated – the following limitations: limitations with respect to justice and the functioning of public service (Arts. 11, 22 AW); limitations connected with the free flow of information (Arts. 15, 16a AW); limitations referring to educational purposes (Arts. 15, 15a, 16 AW); limitations involved with private or personal use (Arts. 16b, 17, 17a AW); limitations connected with works of art (e.g., monuments, buildings) permanently located in public places (Art. 18 AW); limitations referring to exposition and trade of works of art by the owner of the work (Art. 23 AW).

A word may be added with regard to infringement and remedies. Copyright is infringed through any restricted act done by a person who is not authorized to do so. In case of copyright infringement, the copyright owner may bring an action for an injunction, for damages and/or an account of profits as well as for an order to seize the infringing objects (Arts. 26–36b AW). The copyright is subject to the law of inheritance. As long as an inheritance, containing any copyright has not been divided, the consent of each of the successors will have to be acquired in order to exercise any right. Here it concerns specifically the exploitation rights. Moral rights can only be transferred by will or codicil. This does not alter the fact that in practice the owners of the exploitation right will often be able to resist undesired publications and/or reproductions. Also relatives who are not appointed by will or codicil are allowed to take action based on the tort law, if these relatives are being treated incorrectly. By relatives is meant in this connection: parents, spouse or children (Arts. 2(2), 25(4), 25a, 26, 27(2) AW).

III. QUESTIONNAIRE

1. Rights, Prohibitions, Consent, Exploitation

a. Rights held by artists on their work

moral rights
- right to publication
- right to paternity
- right to integrity
- right of control

economic rights
- reproduction right
- communication right

contractual rights
- assignment or licensing of the copyright
- sale or loaning of the work itself
- any other permission to use the copyright or the work itself.

b. Prohibitions to be made

As general rule any use of a protected work that can be labelled as a prerogative of the copyright owner by another than the copyright owner is legitimate only if proper authorization from the copyright owner is obtained prior to such use.

Any form of violation of one of the author's (cf. artist's) moral rights can be prohibited.

Any unauthorized act or violation of moral rights is a form of copyright infringement and liable to legal action for preventive or repressive measures (injunction, damages, fines, imprisonment).

c. Requirement of consent

Except in cases expressly prescribed by the law (e.g., limitations with respect to citation of a work) the prior consent of the copyright owner is required for any use of a protected work that can be labelled as a prerogative of the copyright owner.

d. Commercial exploitation

This can be done
- by the copyright owner himself (e.g., acting as his own agent)
- by way of assignment or license of the copyright to a third party or any other contractual bond.

2. *Conditions of Artists' Rights in Relation to Galleries and Museums*

a. Right to disclose, reproduce, perform, use a work

As far as the disclosure is concerned, after the first publication and communication of a work the right of the copyright owner (cf. artist) is extinguished in as far as he cannot block any further publication or communication of it, provided that no violation of the moral rights is at stake.

So once a painting has been publicly exposed for sale or put in an exhibition, any other exposure or exhibition of this particular work is allowed, provided that no moral right (e.g., right of integrity) is violated.

With respect to works of art which can be published and communicated by mechanical or electronical means such as videograms of performances, the distribution of the videogram does not extinguish the right of the copyright owner (cf. artist) to any further public performance, even using the particular videogram. So a museum needs prior consent for the exposition of a videoperformance.

On the basis of a special provision in the Copyright Act (Art. 23 AW) the right to publish and communicate can be extinguished without the copyright owner's (cf. artist's) prior consent or even against his wish in case a work of art has been bought from the copyright owner (cf. artist) before the first publication and communication has taken place. This will happen in all those cases that organizations, commercially exploiting works of art by means of a rental system, buy works of art and bring them to the rental market afterwards. The extinguishing of the publication and communication right being strictly related to a particular copy of a work of art, for all further exposition and exhibition of other copies of that work the prior consent of the copyright owner (cf. artist) again is required.

According to the Copyright Act (Art. 24 AW) the copyright owner (cf. artist) remains competent, provided that no agreement to the contrary has been made, to produce similar works of art (the statute reads 'paintings' but there is no good reason for this restriction). There is no consensus on the question to whom the copyright of such similar work belongs: the artist, the copyright owner, both of them?

As far as the reproduction right is concerned, the one to whom the copyright has been transferred or licensed is, be it within the possible limitations of the assignment or licence, authorized to make copies of the work. According again to Art. 23 AW the same right belongs to the owner of a protected work of art who wants to sell it and to expose it in an auction catalogue.

Under Art. 24 AW, the artist is not authorized to mechanically reproduce or copy works of art similar to that of which he transferred or assigned the copyright.

The author (cf. artist) has no statutory right to exhibit his work, be it owned by a private gallery or a museum or be it held in a private or public place. Contract or tort law will apply in such a case.

b. Right to re-sale royalties

Under Dutch copyright there is no such a right as a *droit de destination*. However, in due time a rental right will be introduced within the Copyright Act with respect to at least the lending of books and related materials by public libraries. It is under discussion whether or not such a rental right should also apply to works of art.

c. Right to destruction and/or alterations

The Copyright Act does not give provisions as to the destruction of a work of art neither with respect to the author (cf. artist) nor to the owner of the work. Contract and tort law will apply in such a case.

As far as the making of alterations is concerned this is one of the special moral rights which the Copyright Act (Art. 25 AW) gives to the author (cf. artist); the right has to be exercised in good faith. However, with respect to works of art this provision will seldom apply. The same article gives the author the right to object to the making of alterations; again this right has to be exercised in good faith.

The same applies to a relocation of a work of art, be it that most of the reported cases deal with relocation on the basis of contract law.

3. Assignment and Inheritance

Economic rights can be transferred and waived, moral rights can only be waived. Economic rights as well as moral rights can be inherited; as far as the latter are concerned, only in case special provision has been made by will or codicil. The general law of inheritance applies.

The Netherlands

NATIONAL REPORT ON TOPIC 3. RIGHTS OF ARTISTS AND THEIR HEIRS*

Anton A. Quaedvlieg**

I. RIGHTS HELD BY ARTISTS ON THEIR WORK

In this section the visual arts again take a key position. We will leave out some legal issues on the subject of photography, as far as they do not touch upon art trade as such (press and news photography, etc.).

Another subject we will leave out of discussion are the rights which the author may assert on manuscripts and/or writings that are kept in archives. There is no authoritative doctrine or guiding case law with regard to many aspects specifically connected with such rights. As even the Copyright Act itself takes no account of the special problems that may arise on the subject of archive-management, a dissertation on this point would be complicated and besides mainly hypothetical.

The rights which artists can invoke under Dutch law are chiefly derived from the *Auteurswet* ('Copyright Act') 1912. In 1975 a separate statute on the protection of industrial design was introduced, but this does not generally prevent one from invoking copyright protection, which in many ways would be preferable to the artist.

In cases where the Copyright Act does not provide a solution artists may, depending on the circumstances of the particular case, try and invoke the rule of 'good faith' to be observed between the parties to a contract, or Art. 1401 of the Civil Code (on tort).

An additional effect of Art. 1401 will, however, always be an exception.[1] A recent series of important rulings of the Supreme Court shows that

* Editor's note: *see also* 'The Netherlands: Introduction' in Part One.

** Professor, Catholic University, Nijmegen. The author gratefully acknowledges the assistance of the law firm Trenité Van Doorne, Amsterdam, with which he was associated during the writing of this Report. Report translated by F. C. Compton.

1. Supreme Court, 18 February 1949, *Nederlandse Jurisprudentie* (NJ) 1949, annotated by Ph. ANH, *Bijblad bij de Industriële Eigendom* (BIE) 1949, 42 annotated by VdM: 'Bonda non-solidifying salt' in the field of patent law; Supreme Court, 27 June 1986, NJ 1987, 191 annoted by vNH; *Intellectuele Eigendom en Reclamerecht* (IER) 1986, 78; BIE 1986, 280; *Computerrecht* 1986, 178 annoted by DOMMERING; *Ars Aequi* (AA) 1988, 257 with notes COHEN JEHORAM.

further protection in addition to the intellectual property rights is only very sparsely granted.

Assuming that the artist or his heirs are the lawful copyright owners, under Dutch law there is no difference between the rights they can assert against galleries or museums or anyone else, or between the conditions under which they may do so. To this extent the questions under I. and II. in the Questionnaire overlap. In an attempt to follow the sequence of the Questionnaire as closely as possible, I will under point I. give an overview of the artists' rights and the exceptions to those rights; as far as that subject returns in the first three items under point II. I refer to point I. Items 3. through 9. under point II. contain questions specifically directed at issues of moral rights, so I have concentrated the discussion of that aspect under point II.

1. Rights to Disclose, Reproduce and Perform a Work

Art. 1 of the Copyright Act gives the author of a work the exclusive right to publish, reproduce and perform that work. As far as the Act itself uses the word 'copyright' it means – save for exceptions – the exploitation rights, such as these are included in the concepts 'to publish' and 'to reproduce'.[2]

2. 'Fictitious Authors'

Generally speaking it is the maker himself who is regarded as the author and can therefore exercise the copyright (and moral rights). In some cases, however, this is not so and the copyright owner is a so-called 'fictitious author' as defined in the Copyright Act:

> 'Art. 6: If a work has been realized from the design of another person and under that person's direction and supervision, that person shall be regarded as the author.'

The Explanatory Memorandum on the 1912 Act gave an example which has frequently been cited since: the paintings which at Rubens' studio were realized from the master's design and under his direction and supervision.

In relation to Art. 6, G. Mom[3] mentions a ruling of the County Court (*Kantonrechter*) at Hilversum dated 8 June 1982. An advertising agency had commissioned a graphic designer to design containers for dairy products in accordance with that agency's instructions as to the desired size and colour.

2. S. GERBRANDY, *Kort commentaar op de Auteurswet 1912* (Arnhem 1988) p. 292.
3. G. MOM, (translated) 'On authors who are not "creators", and vice versa', *Beeldrecht-wijzer* ('s-Gravenhage 1987) p. 75 *et seq.*

The Court held that the advertising agency could not be regarded as fictitious author under Art. 6 of the Copyright Act.[4]

> 'Art. 7: The employer shall be regarded as the author of works which are realized within the framework of an employment relationship, unless the parties agree otherwise.
> 'Art. 8: If a public institution or association or corporation publishes a work as having originated from itself, and does so without naming the author, that institution, association or corporation shall be regarded as the author.'

3. *The Concept of 'Work'*

In a number of precedents mention is made of artists who relied on protection for achievements not covered by the concept of 'work' as defined by the Copyright Act.

The Copyright Act protects only original work that has been given a concrete shape or form.

Supreme Court, 28 June 1946, NJ 1946, 712, in *Van Gelder v. Van Rijn*: By the way in which he worked his material (wood) Van Gelder gave a particular artistic effect to the objects he created. However, the Supreme Court held that 'only design, which is the expression of that which has prompted the author to his labour, enjoys the protection of copyright'; the method of working as such is therefore not protected by copyright.

Just as an artist cannot claim exclusive rights to a *method of working* which gives a work a particular artistic individuality, so an artist cannot acquire exclusive rights to a particular *idea* or a particular *style*.

In the Explanatory Memorandum on the 1912 Act the legislator used an example taken from the visual arts: 'the potato-eating workman's family, the fisherman's children splashing about in the sea, the seamen's wives knitting on the beach, the cows in the milking enclosure, and other *subjects* so popular with our contemporary masters' have no copyright restrictions.[5]

a. No protection

President District Court Amsterdam, 1 November 1979, *Auteursrecht, tijdschrift voor auteurs- en mediarecht* (AMR) 1980, 13,; BIE 1980, 32, in *Henneman v. McCann-Erickson & others*: Artist Henneman's idea – drawings of floating papers that come alive – was borrowed in an advertizing campaign of a photocopier manufacturer. The Court held that the idea as such was not protected.

Appeal Court Arnhem, 6 March 1979, AMR 1980, 32; BIE 1981, 42, in

4. Cf. also VERKADE/SPOOR, *Auteursrecht* (Deventer 1985) p. 23.
5. Citation taken from: VAN LINGEN, *Auteursrecht in Hoofdlijnen* (Alphen a/d Rijn 1984) p. 66.

Bruna v. Rolf: The overall design of Bruna's works is marked by an individual and clearly recognizable style; merely a particular style does not deserve copyright protection; however, after very detailed reasoning, the Appeal Court held that the production and sale of the pictures was a civil wrong by virtue of Art. 1401 of the Civil Code.

District Court Utrecht, 4 December 1985, *Informatierecht AMI, tijdschrift voor auteurs-, media- en informatierecht* (AMI) 1987, 110; NJ 1987, 677; IER 1988, 45, in *Dick Bruna & others v. A. W. Bruna & Zoons Uitgevers Mij BV*; discussed by Prof. F.W. Grosheide in IER 1988, 43: The children's picture books designed by Dick Bruna are marked by an immediately recognizable style. The imitation of a style does not fall under the protection of the Copyright Act. However, the imitation combined with additional factors was held to be a civil wrong against Dick Bruna by virtue of Art. 1401 of the Civil Code.

b. Doubt

Appeal Court 's-Hertogenbosch, 11 February 1954, NJ 1954, 359, in *The Crown & others v. Beeldenatelier Jema* ('Hummel' figurines): The lower court held that the figurines were only an imitation of style, but the Appeal Court held that they were a virtually exact copy in modified form.

c. Protection granted

President District Court Haarlem, 28 June 1988, BIE 1989, 51: The Court held that a vase executed in a geometrical shape, obtained by joining together three sheets of glass in a particular way, was copyright protected, for – the Court reasoned – the claimant did not demand protection of *all* applications of three identically shaped sheets of flat glass glued together.

Supreme Court, 13 April 1984, NJ 1984, 524, annotated by LWH; AA 1984, 565, annotated by Cohen Jehoram: The Court held that comic strip characters 'Suske and Wiske' are copyright protected.

i. Work borrowed from existing, not copyright protected examples

President District Court Amsterdam, 8 June 1987, BIE 1987, 332, annotated by S. Boekman, in *Den Haan & Wagenmakers v. Herman Bauer*, trading under the name 'De Zilvervloot' (dress ornaments for dolls in traditional costumes): The Court held that there was no copyright protection for miniature replicas of dress ornaments worn with traditional costumes.

Appeal from President District Court Alkmaar, 15 July 1982, to Appeal Court Amsterdam, 14 June 1984, BIE 1986, 63 in *Borger v. Zoon* ('white cat in sitting position'): The District Court held that the plaintiff's statuette representing a white cat in a sitting position 'although no doubt a clever copy, is a copy of a cat sitting in a position such as one can observe in real live cats many times a day, so the statuette is not original' (!). The appeal was granted.

ii. No protection for work not sufficiently concretized
President District Court 's-Hertogenbosch, 31 March 1977, NJ 1977, 479, in *Arons v. Helmond City Council* ('Helmond civic centre'): The Court held that the written description of a plan to paint the main hall of a civic centre in a style to make it look like a circus tent was not specific enough to protect that idea as a work.

iii. Finally
Appeal Court Amsterdam, 7 April 1988, BIE 1989, 82, in *Cassina SpA v. Harvink Collection BV* ('Le Corbusier furniture'): The Court held that the fact that Le Corbusier's LC-2 armchair was intended for mass production is no bar to copyright.

4. The Exclusive Right to Disclose and Perform

If he is the copyright owner, the artist has the exclusive right to disclose and perform.

Supreme Court, 18 December 1953, NJ 1954, 258, in *Polak v. De Muinck* (art reproductions): The exclusive right to publication of a work (art reproductions in this case) does not embrace merely the publishing of one or more reproductions of that work, nor is it therefore exhausted by that action, but for *each* reproduction of that work the copyright owner's authorization is required. However, once a copy of the work has been legitimately put into the stream of commerce, copyright in respect of that particular copy has been exhausted or at any rate there is generally no restriction to the continued distribution of that copy.

Supreme Court, 25 January 1952, NJ 1952, 195, in *De Spaarnestad v. Favoriet* (the 'Leesportefeuille' case): Once magazines have been put into the stream of commerce the publisher can no longer oppose the rental of copies thereof to the public in so-called 'leesportefeuilles');[6] such rental does not constitute publication.

Supreme Court, 23 June 1961, NJ 1961, 423, in *Bolhoeve v. De Geillustreerde Pers*: Unsuccessful reliance on the doctrine of tort (Art. 1401, Civil Code) in an attempt at preventing in this way the rental of magazines in *leesportefeuilles*.

Supreme Court, 20 November 1987, AMI 1988, 15, annotated by HCJ; NJ 1988, 280, annotated by LWH, in *Stemra v. Free Record Shop*: Once a reproduction of a work (a gramophone record in this case) has been legitimately put into the stream of commerce this completes the publication

6. 'A *leesportefeuille* is a selection of periodicals, put in folders, supplied to subscribers and at intervals replaced. *Leesportefeuilles* are a feature of waiting rooms, lounges and hairdressing establishments in the Netherlands, if not elsewhere.' (Quote from: J. H. SPOOR, *Copies in Copyright* (Alphen a/d Rijn 1980) [published in English]; details on this and other precedents on p. 71 *et seq*.)

of that reproduction, and so any subsequent making available of that reproduction by rental – or offering it for rental – cannot be regarded as further publication within the meaning of the Copyright Act.

In 1986, however – unlike the similar case in 1952 – the Supreme Court did consider the offering for rental as such to be publication:

Supreme Court, 16 December 1986, NJ 1987, 613 (criminal action): The term 'publication of a work' also includes the offering for rental of video tapes to the public.

It seems difficult to reconcile these precedents with the so-called *Poortvliet* judgment:

Supreme Court, 19 January 1979, NJ 1979, 412, annotated by LWH; AMR 1979, 50, annotated by JHS; AA 1980, 311, annotated by HCJ. The Court held that by virtue of his copyright, author and illustrator Rien Poortvliet was justified in objecting to the sale of illustrations pasted on chipboard which had initially been introduced on the market as calendar illustrations.

5. *The Exclusive Right of Reproduction*

A significant number of learned writers in the Netherlands defend the argument that there must be a case of *appropriation* before a work may be regarded as an unauthorized reproduction; on the other hand, there are also legal experts who go against this argument and would give the author of a work a monopoly by virtue of which he can oppose any work that looks alike (accidentally or otherwise). The issue has not yet been decided by any judgment in the final instance.

Parody or satirizing work is often judged mildly when it comes to the question whether it should be regarded as an unauthorized adaption of the original. For the rest, case law speaks for itself:

County Court Maastricht, 23 January 1985/15 May 1985, AMI 1986, 21 ('D'r Kuëb va Heële'): Illustration, depicting the Church Square at Heerlen with sculpture and Roman church, published on picture postcards and loose-leaf reproductions which were regarded as reproductions of the sculpture. *See also* I.*13*. In the judgment, the sculpture is referred to as 'De Koempel van Hehle', which in itself (as an annoying corruption of the name of the work of art) is a nice example of infringement of the sculptor's moral rights.

County Court Leeuwarden, 23 September 1986, *Informatierecht* 1990, 16, in *Stichting Beeldrecht v. Stichting Hispel*: The artist is the author of a sculpture (coat of arms with a swan) which is affixed to the façade of the Fryske Akademy building. The case concerned the publication of a cartoon in which the swan's head had been replaced by the head of one Folkertsma (governor of the Fryske Akademy) and certain elements had been added to suggest fascism. The Court held that the drawing was of a satirical nature and could be regarded as a new original work; there was no evidence to prove that the integrity of the work of Chris Fokma, the artist, and Chris Fokma's personal integrity had been harmed.

District Court Rotterdam, 18 October 1966, NJ 1968, 415 (photographs of Delft Technical College): Photographic disclosure of the new assembly hall of the Technical College at Delft was held to be an infringement of copyright.

President District Court Assen, 26 January 1975, BIE 1977, 263, in *Naaldkunst-Lanarte BV & others v. H. Yntema* ('Sampler'): Plaintiff's drawing was used to design embroidery pattern; the Court decided this was a reproduction within the meaning of the Copyright Act.

County Court Amsterdam, 20 May 1983, AMI 1986, 126, in *Van Schaik v. Smelt*: Etchings, depicting cats, transferred to ceramic tiles. The judge took a serious view of the unlawful act *vis–à-vis* a fellow-artist and awarded 3,000 guilders in damages.

Appeal Court Amsterdam, 26 May 1983, BIE 1984, 266, in *Poortvliet & others v. Condor Gips*: The Court held that the three-dimensional imitation of drawings of gnomes constituted copyright infringement. Injunction granted against further publication and reproduction (no damages sought).

District Court Amsterdam, 3 July 1985, AMI 1986, 83, in *René Pierre Boin v. Jedezet Confectie-industrie*: This case concerned an advertising pamphlet with a photograph of a furniture showroom – cum art gallery – showing paintings by René Boin; 750,000 copies had been printed. The Court held that this constituted infringement of copyright as well as infringement of moral rights and awarded 10,000 guilders in damages.

A case similar to the one above is reported by C.G.M. Berendsen, 'Inbreuk en afbraak' (*Beeldrechtwijzer*, pp. 49/50). This concerned photographs of fashion models taken against a background showing work by Mari Boeijen, with captions in a typeface that corresponded with letters used by Boeijen in his work.

President District Court 's-Hertogenbosch, 26 September 1985, BIE 1986, 311, in *Cassina SpA v. Alphen International Agencies* ('Le Corbusier furniture'): The characteristic features of shape of the plaintiff's furniture, regarded as copyright-protected, reappeared recognizably in the defendant's furniture. The Court held that this was an unauthorized reproduction.

County Court The Hague, 1 October 1985, IER 1986, 9; AMI 1986, 83, in *Philip Mechanicus v. Stichting Bzztôh*: Drawn adaptation of photographic portrait on cover-page of literary magazine *Bzzletin*. The Court held that this was an unauthorized reproduction and awarded 850 guilders in damages.

County Court The Hague, 18 August 1987, IER 1987, 109, AMI 1988, 41, in *Stichting Beeldrecht v. Bedrijfsschap Schildersbedrijf and HCM Nederland BV*: Full-colour advertisement in which back and side of the red-and-blue Rietveld chair were visible. The Court held that this was an infringement of copyright of the Rietveld Estate and awarded 1,232 guilders in damages.

County Court Amsterdam, 29 July 1988, IER 1988, 107; *Informatierecht* 1990, 19, in *Stichting Beeldrecht v. Sigma Filmproductions BV*: The Court held that 'It would be an excessive encroachment on the right of ownership for an architect to be able to prohibit the filming of the interior of a home he has designed' (parts of the interior in view for ten minutes; furnishings and decoration not designed by architect; interior not the main aspect of the film.)

Appeal Court Arnhem, 24 January 1989, *Informatierecht* 1989, 126; *Kantongerecht* (KG) 1988, 144, in *Marris v. Millingen* ('replica in bronze'): Local Authority replaced defaced ceramic statue by a replica in bronze, without the artist's permission. The Court held that no harm had been done to the artist's honour and reputation, but nevertheless awarded damages (3,000 guilders).

6. *Copying or Quoting for the Purposes of Criticism, Review or Research*

Copying or quoting a work for the purposes of criticism, review or research (i.e., quoting from it in an article, column or scientific publication) does not infringe any copyright in the work (Art 15a of the Copyright Act), provided that various conditions under the Act are satisfied (such as the requirement of sufficient acknowledgement). For some categories especially – including works of visual art – there is the requirement that the copy must be clearly distinguishable from the original work by its size or the method of reproduction.

Copying or quoting for the purposes of criticism, review or research must be in accordance with what is generally accepted in society as reasonable and fair, and the number and volume of the parts or passages copied or quoted must be justified by the objective to be realized.

District Court The Hague, 29 December 1971, NJ 1972, 211, ('Portuguese fishermen'): The real purpose of using René Margotton's painting *Portuguese fishermen* for the cover-page of a catalogue was to decorate the catalogue and make it attractive. The Court held that this constituted copyright infringement, rejected the defence of fair dealing, and awarded 2,734 Belgian francs in damages for loss of royalties and 500 guilders in punitive damages.

District Court The Hague, 24 December 1986, *Informatierecht* 1987, 36, in *Stichting Beeldrecht v. Samsom Utigeverij*; An art magazine (*Kunstbeeld*) published by the defendant showed reproductions of certain paintings in an announcement and in an article, but the text of the announcement and the article did not mention the paintings.

The Court held that:

1. the connection between the reproductions and the announcement of an exhibition, necessary to rely on the defence of fair dealing, will also exist if the original works are present at the exhibition or are mentioned in the catalogue;
2. there is sufficient connection between the article and the reproductions to sustain a defence of fair dealing, since the works shown are clearly illustrative and characteristic of the subject of the article.

A striking aspect of the Court's reasoning is that for the purpose of judging of what is permitted as fair dealing a very important part is played by what is customary and considered acceptable in the circle of interested parties.

District Court 's-Hertogenbosch, 3 July 1987, AMI 1989, 24, in *Stichting*

Beeldrecht v. L.C.G. Malmberg BV ('Zienderogen kunst'): The defendant's book, using pictures and text combined, provides instruction in visual creation. The illustrations have no independent commercial function. The Court accepted the defence of fair dealing.

County Court Utrecht, 23 February 1989, *Informatierecht* 1989, 102, annotated by J.H. Spoor, in *Stichting Beeldrecht v. Utrechts Nieuwsblad*. In an article published at the opening of the new extension of the Centraal Museum, *Utrechts Nieuwsblad* used colour pictures of paintings by Charley Toorop and Karel Appel. The Court held that the article concerned the new extension of the museum and not the works shown, which are a random choice from the collection of the museum; the defence of fair dealing was rejected and the Court awarded 3,325 guilders in compensatory damages, but no additional damages.

7. *Work Disclosed by Public Authorities*

Art. 15*b* of the Copyright Act provides that it is not an infringement of copyright to disclose, perform or reproduce work previously disclosed by the public authorities, unless the public authorities have reserved copyright in the manner described in Art. 15*b*.

Supreme Court, 29 May 1987, NJ 1987, 1003; AMI 1987, 105, annotated by DWFV; *Rechtspraak van de Week* 1987, 128, in *Struycken and Unger v. Riet*. A postage stamp with the portrait of the Queen, designed by Struycken, was used in enlarged form as the illustration of a picture postcard. The public authorities (who published the stamp) had not reserved copyright. Struycken had *not* assigned the copyright to the public authorities. However, Art. 15*b* also applies if the copyright does not vest in the public authorities: Struycken could not invoke copyright (although he could invoke infringement of moral rights, since on the postcard Struycken's design was not shown in combination with the original typeface designed by Unger).

8. *Education*

Art. 16 of the Copyright Act allows the use of works for educational purposes, although this is subject to some conditions, including the requirements of sufficient acknowledgement and reasonable compensation. Furthermore, the quantity of material reproduced or copied must remain within the limits of what is generally accepted in society as reasonable and fair.

9. *Reporting Current Events*

Under Art. 16a of the Copyright Act, the artist cannot oppose quotation from or performance of a work for the purpose of reporting current events, to the extent that such quotation or performance is essential to the proper representation of the actual event that is the subject of the report.

10. Copying for Private Use

Under Art. 16b of the Copyright Act, no copyright is infringed by reproducing a work for the purpose of private study or use, provided that such reproduction is limited to a few copies and serves solely for the private study or use of the person who makes or orders the copy for his own benefit only. If the work is a work of visual art the copy must be clearly distinguishable from the original work by its size or the method of reproduction.

11. Authorized Copying by Organizations

Under Art. 17 of the Copyright Act, organizations, companies and institutions are permitted – on certain conditions – to make copies of *literary works* for internal use.

Appeal Court Amsterdam, 20 November 1980, *Auteursrecht* 1981, 69, annotated by H. M. van Niftrik: As the permission to copy is limited to *literary works* it does not extend to *photographs and drawings* included in the copied material. (In some cases this judgment may seriously restrict the practical effect of Art. 17).

12. Works Erected along Public Roads

Works of architecture and works of visual art which 'have been erected or are permanently displayed in or along public roads' may be reproduced/copied and published as long as the work is not the chief element of the representation and the reproduction/copy is clearly distinguishable from the original work by its size or the method of reproduction (Art. 18, Copyright Act).

County Court Rotterdam, 24 February 1983, NJ 1984, 677; AMR 1985, 14, in *Stichting Beeldrecht v. Rotterdam City Council* (Hans Wap's tramcar'): In this case, concerning Hans Wap's artistic decoration of a tramcar, the work was regarded as 'being permanently displayed in or along public roads'.[7] The Local Authority published a greeting card with a picture of the tramcar. The Court held that the tramcar was the chief element of the card and awarded damages of 2,000 guilders for copyright infringement and 1,000 guilders for failure to make acknowledgement of the artist.

7. A different opinion is held by K. J. BERKHOUT, 'Auteursrecht op visuele werken', *Beeldrechtwijzer*, p. 6.

13. Portraits

The Dutch Copyright Act makes a distinction between portraits that are commissioned (Arts. 19, 20) and portraits that are not ('non-commissioned portraits') (Art. 21).

The *commissioner* of a portrait, or, after his death, his relatives possess certain rights as to publication and reproduction of the commissioned portrait, while the *author* of the portrait is not authorized to disclose it without permission from the person portrayed or, up to ten years after that person's death, permission from his/her relatives, i.e., parents, husband/wife, children.

In the case of non-commissioned portraits, the person portrayed can oppose publication on the ground of a reasonable (moral or commercial) interest in non-disclosure. The same right vests in that person's relatives up to ten years after that person's death.

14. Owner's Rights

Art. 23 of the Copyright Act gives the owner of a drawing, painting, sculpture, work of architecture or work of applied art the right to exhibit the work or, with a view to selling it, to reproduce the work in a catalogue, without requiring permission from the copyright owner.

15. Author's Rights after Transfer

After the ownership of a painting work has been transferred, the author continues to have the right to make similar works, unless otherwise agreed by contract (Art. 24, Copyright Act).

16. Assignment and Licensing of Copyright

Copyright can be assigned (also partially) and licensed by the author. Pursuant to Art. 2(1) of the Copyright Act, assignments must be in writing. Licences are not required to be in writing; in some cases it is even assumed that an *implied* licence has been granted.

District Court Amsterdam, 27 August 1969, NJ 1969, 393, in *De Bezige v. Opera Mundi* ('Emmanuelle'): Once a partial assignment of copyright has been validly effected, any subsequent full or partial assignment of the rights so assigned does not require the author's permission, unless expressly agreed otherwise in the initial assignment.

District Court Assen, 25 May 1982, AMR 1983, 62, in *Georgette Magritte v. John Faber Posters BV* ('Magritte Posters'): John Faber Posters BV received permission from Arpo to produce 1,000 copies of René Magritte's work *La grande famille*. It turned out that Arpo had no authority to grant that sublicence.[8] The Court held that Faber, too, acted unlawfully *vis-à-vis* Magritte because he should have suspected that Arpo was not authorized to grant the licence and he could easily have checked this by making inquiries with Magritte. The Court awarded 1,500 guilders in damages.

County Court 's-Hertogenbosch, 29 March 1989, *Informatierecht* 1990, 18, in *Stichting Beeldrecht v. Uden City Council*: The owner requested permission to publish works in a catalogue. The artist replied by letter: 'inclusion of the works in a catalogue is not appreciated'. This reply was regarded as implied permission for publication, partly in view of the fact that the person who requested the permission was the owner of the works.

County Court Haarlem, 22 July 1988 and 14 October 1988, *Informatierecht* 1990, 18, in *Stichting Beeldrecht v. Kokke-Van der Willigen*. The artist gave permission for paintings depicting old golf shoes to be published in a golf magazine; nevertheless the Court held that the publication was an infringement of copyright because without the artist's knowledge or permission the photographs of the paintings had been inserted in a section used for advertising purposes.

County Court Amsterdam, 29 July 1988, IER 1988, 107; *Informatierecht* 1990, 19, in *Stichting Beeldrecht* v. *Sigma Filmproductions BV* (*see supra*, p. 283).

II. CONDITIONS REQUIRED FOR THE EXERCISE OF RIGHTS

1. Right to Publish, Reproduce and Perform

The rights to publish, reproduce and perform a work as well as the most important conditions required for their exercise have already been discussed under point I. In principle, there is no difference as to these conditions in relation to galleries or museums. I make the following two additional remarks on this subject.

a. The rights of the author and the owner (e.g., a museum) may come into conflict if, for example, the author wants to be able to (have others) make reproductions of works of his which hang in a museum. Would the museum be obligated to give the author the opportunity to do so?

Complications of this kind are not regulated by statute. A question such as the one posed above must be answered according to the circumstances of the case. Although in principle there is no rule which forces the owner to meet certain wishes of the author/copyright owner, in some cases a museum or gallery or other third party could possibly be sued for abuse of rights if they unreasonably refuse to meet the artist's wishes.

8. VERKADE/SPOOR, *op. cit.*, p. 290: The authority to grant a sublicence will depend on the content, nature and scope of the licence agreement concerned. WICHERS HOETH, in *Kort Begrip* (Zwolle 1984) p. 158, is very sure: 'After assignment the assignee can in principle assign the copyright to a third party; in the case of licences this is definitely not allowed.'

In connection with the right of reproduction I would also refer to Art. 24 of the Copyright Act (*see* I.*16*).

b. As many of the precedents quoted in this report show, litigation on behalf of artists is often conducted by Stichting Beeldrecht. Stichting Beeldrecht (1977)[9] – a copyright protection society organized under Dutch law – looks after the interests of visual artists in the protection and exploitation of their copyright. For those purposes the society obtains exclusive powers of attorney from the artists.

Verkade Spoor, p. 236, reports a judgment of the Appeal Court Amsterdam dated 9 May 1985 in *Stichting Beeldrecht v. Riet* (also briefly quoted in AMI 1986, 14) in which it was decided that moral rights cannot be exercised by any other person than the author and, consequently, cannot be exercised by Stichting Beeldrecht either, even if this is done in the artist's interest.

District Court Roermond, 17 September 1987, in *Uitgeverij Van Spijk BV v. Stichting Beeldrecht*: Publishers Van Spijk included reproductions of certain artists' work in an art book. The artists themselves had no authority to give permission for such publication because they had given Stichting Beeldrecht the exclusive power to protect their copyright interests. The Court held that the publishers knew or at any rate could have known that the artists were not authorized to give such permission.

2. *Right to Use a Work*

Under Dutch law it is difficult to envisage forms of use relevant to copyright law which would not be covered already by the exclusive powers of reproduction, publication and performance. The term 'use' does occur in Art. 29 of the Copyright Act, where it is provided that the copyright owner is not permitted to seize infringing goods that are in the possession, custody or control of a person who is not carrying on trade in similar goods and who has obtained the goods solely for his private *use*, unless that person himself has committed infringement of copyright.

3. *Right to Receive Royalties and Resale Proceeds from a Work*

As long as the author of a work is the copyright owner, he has the right to stipulate royalties to be paid by third parties on account of their exercise of rights which the Copyright Act reserves to the author of the work. If third parties exercise such rights without prior permission they will incur liability for compensation. There are few if any firm rules on determining the amount of compensation; in many cases the Court will award damages

9. For further details about Stichting Beeldrecht: K.J. BERKHOUT, 'Verbeelding', *Beeldrechtwijzer*, p. 107.

according to what it considers reasonable and fair. Such damages are usually a moderate amount. Besides, one must always bear in mind that in certain circumstances an *implied licence* to exercise certain rights may be deduced from the acts or conduct of the artist/copyright owner.

Dutch law does not grant the artist any rights of action in respect of resale proceeds. 'No wonder then that the major art auction houses are found in these countries' [the Netherlands and Britain].[10]

4. Right to Exhibit a Work

There are no rules under the Copyright Act pursuant to which the owners of works could be required by the author to make those works available for exhibition. If the artist wishes to reserve the right to exhibit works he has sold, he will have to negotiate a clause to that effect in the contract of sale, such clause preferably to be worded in such a way as to apply equally to any subsequent purchaser of the works. The standard contract of sale of art to the public authorities contains a provision by virtue of which works may be loaned to the artist for the purpose of an exhibition.[11]

Van Lingen[12] reports the case of a former mayor of the city of Leeuwarden who refused permission to display his portrait at an exhibition because he felt the painter had exaggerated the size of his ears. The artist failed in his attempt to obtain an injunction giving him leave to exhibit his work. The judgments in this case (President District Court Leeuwarden, 15 December 1971, upheld by Appeal Court Leeuwarden, 14 June 1972) have not been published.

5. Right to Withdraw an Authorization Given to Reproduce, Disclose or Perform a Work

Once an artist/copyright owner has given permission to reproduce, disclose or perform a work it will generally not be easy to withdraw such authorization. The Copyright Act contains no express recognition of the *droit de repentir*, although one does encounter some aspects of that right, such as the right to make alternations. However, even this right tends to be interpreted restrictively and applied only in respect of alterations in scientific works.

---

10. J. C. SMITHUIJSEN, 'Krijgertje in het auteursrecht', *Beeldrechtwijzer*, p. 72. In the early eighties, the introduction of a right of action was the subject of debate, also at government level, in the Netherlands, but the discussions did not result in the introduction of such right. Cf. DUBOIS, 'Het droit de suite – moet Nederland volgen?', AMR 1979, 36; DE BOER, 'Het volgrecht: een hersenschim', AMR 1980, 85; MOM, 'Volgrecht: een volgend recht?', AMR 1982, 132.
11. Standard contract public authorities, *see Beeldrechtwijzer*, p. 113 *et seq*.
12. *Auteursrecht in hoofdlijnen*, p. 126.

6. *Right to Destroy a Work*

The Copyright Act does not give the artist the right to destroy a work. In principle it must therefore be assumed that this right exists only if the artist is both the copyright owner and the owner of the work and if the work has not been placed on the list of protected objects (with the author's permission) by virtue of the Conservation of Cultural Heritage Act. If the artist has contracted obligations with respect to the work, he is liable for the consequences relating to such obligations arising out of the destruction of the work.

7. *Right to Oppose the Exhibition of a Work*

Art. 23 of the Copyright Act gives the owner of a drawing, painting, sculpture, work of architecture or work of applied art the right to display that work at a public exhibition without requiring permission from the person who owns the copyright in that work. In principle the artist can oppose the exhibition of a work if such exhibition is intended by a person who is not the owner (e.g., a lender) of the work.

In this connection it is irrelevant whether the work has ever been exhibited before. (*See*, however, II.*10*. b).

8. *Right to Object to Any Substantial Alteration or Relocation of a Work which Threatens its Integrity*

Under Art. 25(1)(*b*) of the Copyright Act, the artist has the moral right to object to *any* alteration of his work, unless such objection is unreasonable.

Supreme Court, 11 January 1983, 322 ('girl on suitcase') annotated by L. Wichers Hoeth: In this absurd criminal case one finds a wide selection of arguments with regard to the question as to what constitutes alteration of a work. A visual artist had supplied to the defendant – also a visual artist – photographs showing his daughter sitting on a suitcase, commissioning him to make silk-screen prints from the negatives of those pictures. The defendant had first prepared new negatives, in which he replaced the other man's daughter with his own daughter. The Supreme Court held that in an instance such as this there can only be a case of alteration if one reproduces the original mental creation in altered form. This, so the Court held, did not follow from the evidence of the case.

When it concerns a substantial alteration or relocation of a work which threatens its integrity, the artist has the right to object to such alteration or relocation by virtue of Art. 25(1)(*c*). Pursuant to Art. 25(3), he cannot waive this right.

Case law provides numerous examples of such incidents (including also incidents involving the destruction of a work).

Supreme Court, 21 March 1975, NJ 1975, 410: When the Local Authority of Amsterdam cleared the studio of Miletic, the sculptor (in connection with his eviction from the premises), works of this artist were damaged, some went missing and others were stored in unsuitable facilities. The Court held this to constitute a tort under Art. 1401, Civil Code (Art. 25, Copyright Act was not invoked).

Appeal Court Amsterdam, 16 June 1977, NJ 1978, 218; AMR 1978, 30; BIE 1978, 124, in *Koetsier v. Schiphol*: Wooden wall panels decorated with paintings by the plaintiff had been removed in connection with the intended alteration of a conference room. Removal for the purpose of alteration work was permitted. Immediately after their removal the panels warped through natural causes. The Court held that there was no case of alteration within the meaning of Art. 25, Copyright Act, nor a case of tort.

District Court Amsterdam, 15 November 1978, AMR 1979, 32, in *Toon de Haas v. Ulrich BV*: The artist's mural in an office building had been painted over with white paint, without his knowledge or consent. This constituted a violation of Art. 25(1)(*c*) of the Copyright Act and the Court awarded 2,000 guilders in damages.

District Court Amsterdam, 20 November 1985, *Informatierecht* 1985, 146, in *Hirs v. Amsterdam City Council*: The artist's charcoal drawing made on a wall hanging was removed during an exhibition and deposited in a dustbin. As a result the charcoal drawing was destroyed. The Court held that the Local Authority had acted in breach of its duty of care and awarded 1,500 guilders in damages.

President District Court Leeuwarden, 12 July 1988, IER 1988, 88, annotated by L. Wichers Hoeth; *Informatierecht* 1988, 17, in *Bonnema v. Tietjerkstradeel City Council*: Injunction granted under Art. 25, Copyright Act, restraining the Local Authority from fitting sunshades to the new town hall, on the ground that doing so would be regarded as mutilation of the architecture of the building.

President District Court Zwolle, 14 April 1989, *Informatierecht* 1989, 100; KG 1989, 90, in *Van Soest v. De Meerpaal BV*: A monumental painting (6 by 15 metres) had been made especially to be hung in 'De Meerpaal' building. Its relocation at a height of 2.20 metres (original height: 90 centimetres from the floor) was held to affect the integrity of the painting; the Court ordered the defendant to hang the painting at 90 centimetres from the floor.

President District Court Zwolle, 2 March 1988, BIE 1988, 177; AMI 1988, 128, in *F. van Klingeren v. Dronten City Council and community centre De Meerpaal BV*: The Court held that it was unreasonable for an architect, in reliance on his moral right, to oppose the alteration of a building which was essential to the preservation of that building as well as in accordance with its original designated purpose.

Supreme Court, 22 June 1973, NJ 1974, 61, annotated by BW, in *Erven Reijers v. Partrimonium* ('The Hands'): The governors of a school placed Reijer's sculpture in a different location, not the place originally agreed, where it could not be shown to its full advantage. The Court held that this constituted breach of contract.

Supreme Court, 29 May 1987, AMI 1987, 105, annotated by DWFV; NJ 1987, 1003, annotated by L. Wichers Hoeth:[13] A postage stamp with the portrait of the Queen had been reproduced in postcard-size enlargement; the Court held that the artist's moral rights had been infringed by the defendant's using a thicker and coarser typeface which harmed the artistic uniformity of picture and lettering of the original work as a whole. The Court awarded 2,000 guilders in damages to both the designer of the portrait and the designer of the typographical arrangements.

9. Right to be Recognized as the Creator of a Work

The right to acknowledgement of the author has been explicitly incorporated in Art. 25a of the Copyright Act since 1 October 1989; many learned writers assume, however, that this right also existed prior to that date, even though the Copyright Act did not say this in so many words. According to the letter of the law, the author of a work only had the right to oppose publication of his work under a different name, and the right to object to any alteration in the reference to the author, insofar as such reference was stated in or on the work or disclosed in connection therewith. According to the present wording of the Act the author has the right to oppose publication of his work without mention of his name or other reference to him as the author, unless such objection would be unreasonable.

District Court Haarlem, 8 January and 22 October 1985, NJ 1986, 619, in *Maes v. Koninklijke Vermande BV* ('Beeldend werken met jonge kinderen'). The Court held that the defendant was liable for damages on account of, *inter alia*, using the wrong name under photographs of the plaintiff inserted in a book published by the defendant.

President District Court Amsterdam, 27 August 1963, NJ 1963, 419; Appeal Court Amsterdam, 14 May 1964, NJ 1964, 453, in *Geesink v. Terra Nostra* ('Sprookjesparade'): It was not until 1963 that Terra Nostra first published drawings made by Geesink in 1944 under the title 'Sprookjesparade', all rights to which the author had assigned in 1944. As Geesink's style had completely changed since 1944 he considered it inappropriate for his name to be associated with the drawings any longer. The District Court granted an injunction restraining Terra Nostra from publishing the drawings under Geesink's name unless they would add the year 1944 to his name. The Appeal Court concurred. Both Courts based their decision on the rule of contractual good faith to be observed by Terra Nostra.

An issue still being debated is whether an artist is entitled to acknowledgement if pursuant to Arts. 7 or 8 of the Copyright Act another person or organization is considered to be the (fictitious) author (*see* III.*1*). Case law

13. Detailed paper on postage stamps: VERKADE, 'Postzegels en auteursrecht', *Filatelie Informatief* (July 1986) p. 2030.

and doctrine are divided on this issue, although case law shows a slight preference towards also granting the moral rights to the fictitious author.

Two examples:

President District Court Amsterdam, 20 August 1987, AMI 1988, 18, annotated by Cohen Jehoran, in *Zeinstra v. Thoth*: Pictures of various buildings designed by Zeinstra (as employee) were published in the guide *Amsterdam Architecture*. The Court held that Zeinstra was not entitled to acknowledgement.

Appeal Court Amsterdam, 10 February 1970, NJ 1971, 130, ('Savings book'): In this case the Court decided that the moral rights accrued to the *true* author.

Art. 9 of the Copyright Act provides that if the author of a work remains anonymous or uses a pseudonym, copyright in the work may be exercised by the person or organization named on or in the work as the publisher or, in the absence of a reference to the publisher, the person or organization named as the printer.

10. Other Rights Accruing to an Artist

Beside the rights described above, the Copyright Act grants the artist/copyright owner mainly the following rights:

a. As long as the copyright vests in the author it is not susceptible of any form of *beslag* (attachment)[14] (Art. 2(3)).

b. As long as the artist has not publicized a work he is entitled to demand a certain measure of discretion from persons who have a copy of it in their possession (Art. 12(2)); the exact tenor of the wording of this article, however, is not clear).

c. The author has the right to object to any alteration in the name or title of a work, insofar as such name or title is stated on or in the work or has been disclosed in connection therewith (Art. 25(1)(*a*)).

District Court Rotterdam, 2 October 1931, NJ 1932, 538, in *Corsari v. Johan Mulders Uitgeversmaatschappij* ('De Moord op no. 17 O.Z. Achterburgwal' or 'De Misdaad zonder Fouten'): The Court held that changing the title of a novel was an infringement of copyright (under Art. 25, Copyright Act).

County Court Amsterdam, 31 January 1983, AMI 1986, 105, in *Bergen v. De Geïllustreerde Pers BV* ('Margriet-cats'): The plaintiff was the author of painted portraits of cats which she had named *Bodo in der Tür* and *Frühlingstraum*. The magazine *Margriet* referred to these paintings as 'the

14. As a rule under Dutch law, *beslag* (attachment) of copyright as such is possible.

Margriet cats'. The Court held that this was an infringement of copyright (under Art. 25, Copyright Act) and awarded 3,000 guilders in damages (including additional damages).

d. Art. 25(1)(*c*) grants the author the moral right to object to any *alteration* of a work, unless such objection should be unreasonable. On this point, of course, often the question arises as to the difference between 'alteration' and 'multilation' of a work, as mentioned under II.8. The difference is that the author can waive his right to object to alteration but cannot waive his right to object to mutilation of his work.

e. Although strictly speaking this exceeds the scope of the Questionnaire it is interesting to add a few remarks about aspects of *maintaining* the rights of the artist/copyright owner in the Netherlands.

Art. 28 of the Copyright Act provides for a special and swift procedure of copyright *beslag* (attachment). However, it is not certain if such attachment is always possible, in connection with infringement of moral rights.

The Dutch *kort geding* (literally meaning 'brief action' and similar to the English 'interlocutory injunction' system) makes it possible for a plaintiff to obtain a court order within a short space of time (approx. three weeks, sometimes even sooner) which enables him to enforce a number of measures before the full trial of the action.

Awards of damages are generally rather modest and usually do not justify separate litigation. Although in principle it is not possible to seek damages in a *kort geding*, more and more cases occur – particularly cases of evident infringement – where the plaintiff asks for and the court will award a sum by way of advance on the damages ultimately expected to be awarded.

III. ASSIGNMENT OF RIGHTS TO HEIRS OF ARTIST

Copyright devolves by succession. One may also acquire copyright by bequest. If an individual whose identity is known is recognized as the author of a work the copyright in the work continues for fifty years from the 1st of January of the year following the year of the author's death.

After the author's death and until the expiry of the copyright the right to acknowledgement and the right to object to alteration and mutilation of the work will vest in the person appointed by the author by will or codicil (Art. 25(2), Copyright Act). The power to make such alterations in the work as are permitted in good faith according to the rules generally accepted in society will vest in the person appointed by the author by will or codicil, provided that it may reasonably be assumed that the author himself would have approved such alterations.

Berkhout[15] reports the following painful case. The maker of a glass

15. K. J. BERKHOUT, 'Auteursrecht op visuele werken', *Beeldrechtwijzer*, p. 5.

sculpture which had been affixed to an office building died while negotiations about the necessary restoration of the work were pending. He had omitted to appoint by will or codicil someone to exercise his moral rights. The insurance company which had its offices in the building immediately proceeded to have the work demolished (but did offer the widow the skip containing the pieces of glass . . .)

Verkade/Spoor[16] has pointed out the risk of a conflict – not regulated by the law – between the appointed custodian of the moral rights and the heirs who inherit the copyright exploitation rights, if the former, by virtue of the moral rights, considers further publication unwanted while the heirs wish to continue exploitation.

Under Art. 2(3) of the Copyright Act it is not possible after the author's death to attach the copyright in works not yet disclosed, which accrues to the person who has acquired it as the author's heir or legatee.

Works which are still the property of the author or his heirs cannot without their permission be placed on the list of protected objects under the Conservation of Cultural Heritage Act.

16. *Op. cit.*, p. 245.

Spain

NATIONAL REPORT ON TOPIC 3. RIGHTS OF ARTISTS AND THEIR HEIRS*

Miguel Virgós Soriano**

I. RIGHTS OF ARTISTS AND CONDITIONS FOR THEIR EXERCISE

'Intellectual property' is regulated by international treaties (Spain is party to the most important ones, the Berne Convention and the Universal Copyright Convention), and by the 22/1987 Act (*Ley de Propiedad Intelectual* 1987 LPI).

The subject of intellectual property is incorporeal. It has to be distinguished from the property of a physical object. From the point of view of intellectual property, the author enjoys both moral and economic rights in the work.

1. Moral Rights

Moral rights safeguard the non-commercial interest of the author and are enunciated in Art. 14 1987 LPI. These rights are inalienable and not to be renounced; the author may not transmit nor waive such rights. Moral rights are enforceable *erga omnes*. Some of them are protected on a temporary basis, i.e., life of the author; some are perpetual.

– Right of *paternity* (right to be recognized as author of the work). This right is perpetual (Art. 41 II 1987 LPI).

– Right to *divulge* (to make public) the work. It has a temporary character (*see* Arts. 15(2) and 40 1987 LPI). In cases of non-divulged works it lasts sixty years after the author's death. If the author has given (by contract) an authorization to divulge the work, which is a pre-condition for the grant of economic rights, he may withdraw it. But first, he must indemnify the due holder even for *lucrum cesans* (*see* Arts. 14(1) and 14(6) 1987 LPI).

The author has also the right to decide *how* the work is to be divulged.

The *owner* of the original of a work of plastic (pictorial, graphic, sculptural) or photographic art has a right to public exhibition of the said work,

* Editor's note: *see also* 'Spain: Introduction' by B. CREMADES in Part One.

** Associate Professor, Facultad de Derecho, Universidad Autónoma de Madrid.

with two exceptions: when the author has expressly excluded this right or when he objects to the exhibition because it is done under conditions which are prejudicial to his honour or professional reputation (Art. 56(2) 1987 LPI).

If the work has been classified as 'of cultural interest' according to the 1985 Act on the protection of the Spanish Patrimony, the owner has not only the right but even the obligation to allow the public contemplation of the work (see Arts. 13 and 9(4) 1985 Spanish Historical Patrimony Act (LPH)).

– Rights to *withdraw* the work from *commerce*, when the author's moral or intellectual convictions have changed. He must indemnify the holders of economic rights in the work for any loss they sustain. The author has *no* right to take the object back from its owner. Only rights of exploitation of the work, not property, are affected (Art. 14(6) 1987 LPI). It has a temporary character, i.e., the duration of the author's life.

– Right of *integrity* of his work. This right is perpetual (Art. 41 II 1987 LPI). It includes the right to object to any distortion, mutilation, modification of, or any derogatory action in relation to, the work, which would be prejudicial to his honour, reputation, or *legitimate interests*. The scope of the rule is therefore broader than Art. 6*bis* Berne Convention. The author may object to a relocation of a work that threatens its integrity.

Of course, the author may *agree* to a modification of the work.

– Right to *modify* or to *destroy* his work. There are two important limits to this right: vested rights of other persons (e.g., if the physical object has been sold, the author can only exercise this right with the consent of the actual owner) and protection of objects officially classified as 'of cultural interest' (the 1985 LPH follows a policy of preservation). It has a temporary character, i.e., the duration of the author's life.

– Right of *access* to the original (or rare copy) of his work. This right has an 'instrumental' character, insofar as it is necessary to enforce the right to divulge, or any other of his rights. It has the same limits as the principal right that the author wishes to enforce. The possessor of the object is entitled to adequate indemnity (Art. 14(7) 1987 LPI). Displacements of the work are only possible when permitted by its possessor.

2. *Economic Rights*

In regard to economic rights two categories must be distinguished:

– The right to *proceeds* (*droit de suite*), or right of authors of the plastic arts to participate in the proceeds of a further sale of the original. This right only embraces sales at public auction, commercial establishment, or by means of a merchant. The rate is two percent of the sales price (Art. 24 1987 LPI).

This right is *not* transmissible *inter vivos* nor *mortis causa*; it lasts only while the author is alive. It is not susceptible of renunciation; the author cannot waive the right to proceeds.

– The right of *exploitation*. This right encompasses, among others, the rights of reproduction, of distribution, of exhibition and also the right to communicate the work publicly. These rights have a temporary character. The term of protection extends sixty years after the death of the author or the publication of the work, in cases of anonymous or pseudonymous works and works divulged within sixty years after the death of the author (*see* Art. 26 1987 LPI). After this time the work falls into the 'public domain' (Art. 41 1987 LPI).

Exploitation rights are reserved to the author, subject to certain restrictions or exceptions in public interest. For example, museums may reproduce works without lucrative objectives for research purposes (Art. 37 1987 LPI). Works permanently located in public places may be reproduced, by means of paintings, drawings, photographs, etc. without consent (Art. 35 1987 LPI).

The *grant of rights to use and exploit* the work is possible. Economic rights are always conditioned by the moral rights of the author. *Inter vivos* grants of the right to use and exploit are made by *contract*, subject to a number of limitations:

Art. 43(1) 1987 LPI establishes the principle of 'purpose-restricted' interpretation of the assignment. Unless otherwise expressly stipulated, the grant lasts five years, is territorially limited, encompasses no more rights than strictly required by the objective pursued by the contract, and (Art. 48 1987 LPI) is considered as non-exclusive.

The sale of the original of a work does not thereby imply the grant of the exploitation rights. The buyer of an object of plastic arts, as such, has no right to exploit the work (Art. 56(1) 1987 LPI).

Global grants of exploitation rights of future works and agreements or promises not to create a work or works in the future, are void and null (Arts. 43(3) and 43(4) 1987 LPI).

The remuneration of the author may be a participation in the proceeds or a lump sum, which is subject to adjustment in cases of gross disproportion as a consequence of the success of the work (Art. 47 1987 LPI).

The contract must be in writing (Art. 45 1987 LPI).

II. ASSIGNMENT OF RIGHTS TO HEIRS

1. Moral Rights

– The rights of *paternity* and the right of *integrity* are perpetual (Arts. 15(1) and 41 II 1987 LPI). They pass to the person or institution appointed by the author in his last will. If the author did not designate any person, the rights pass to the heirs. If there are no heirs, the Public administrations are legitimized to exercise those rights in the interest of the author (Art. 16 1987 LPI). In this regard, therefore, it is possible for these moral rights to be assigned.

– *Other moral rights* die with the author. In the case of a non-divulged work, the heirs of the author or the person.expressly designated by him in his testament, may exercise the right to divulge the work during seventy years. In this regard, therefore, it is not possible to assign other moral rights.

2. Economic Rights

– The right to *proceeds* is not inheritable.
– *Exploitation* rights are inheritable. The general rules of inheritance are applicable, and exploitation rights pass to the heirs under a will, a testamentary agreement, or by virtue of the statutory rules of inheritance (Art. 42 1987 LPI). The existence of several systems of civil law within Spain (the so-called *Derechos forales*) with different inheritance principles must be taken into account.

Suisse

RAPPORT NATIONAL SUR LE SUJET 3. DROITS DES CREATEURS ET DE LEURS HERITIERS

François Perret*

I. REMARQUES GENERALES

Avant de répondre au questionnaire, ce qui revient à décrire sommairement les prérogatives qui, en droit suisse, compètent à l'auteur d'une oeuvre des beaux-arts, il convient de faire quelques remarques d'ordre général.

1. Tout d'abord, la loi fédérale concernant le droit d'auteur sur les oeuvres littéraires et artistiques du 7.12.1922 (LDA) est en voie de révision.

Dès lors et dans la mesure où les prérogatives conférées à l'auteur sont visées par cette révision, on indiquera également les solutions du projet du Conseil fédéral du 19 juin 1989 (FF 1989 III p. 465) lesquelles sont fondées sur le projet de la IIIe Commission d'experts du 18 décembre 1987, auquel il sera fait également référence.

2. Deuxième remarque: le droit d'auteur comprend des prérogatives patrimoniales et non patrimoniales.

Ces dernières formeraient, selon une certaine doctrine, l'objet du droit moral de l'auteur.

La loi actuelle sur le droit d'auteur prévoit essentiellement des droits de nature patrimoniale encore que certaines de ces dispositions, tel l'art. 12 ch. 4 (droit de divulguer l'oeuvre) paraissent viser des prérogatives non patrimoniales. Cela étant, dans plusieurs arrêts (ATF 169 II 155 = JT 1943 I 337; ATF 96 II 409, 420 = JT 1971 I 597, 599), le Tribunal fédéral a considéré que le droit moral de l'auteur faisait partie des droits de la personnalité protégés par les arts. 27 *et seq.* du Code civil suisse (CSS).

Comme l'a relevé la doctrine,[1] la distinction entre les prérogatives patrimoniales et non patrimoniales de l'auteur n'est pas heureuse; en effet, dans la plupart des cas, l'auteur qui souffre d'une atteinte à son droit moral est également lésé dans ses intérêts économiques.

Ainsi en est-il d'une divulgation de l'oeuvre sans l'accord de l'auteur,

---

* Professeur, Université de Genève; Avocat au Barreau de Genève.

1. TROLLER, *Immaterialgüterrecht*, vol. II, p. 682 *et seq.*

laquelle, si elle constitue indiscutablement une atteinte à sa personnalité, peut également lui causer un dommage de nature purement patrimoniale.[2]

La question de savoir s'il faut considérer les prérogatives de l'auteur selon la conception dualiste – distinction entre l'aspect patrimonial et non patrimonial du droit – ou moniste – le droit d'auteur est constitué par un faisceau de prérogatives patrimoniales et non patrimoniales liées entre elles – n'est pas purement académique. En effet, si l'on admet avec le Tribunal fédéral, que le droit moral de l'auteur est fondé sur les arts. 27 *et seq.* CCS, il est, comme tout autre droit de la personnalité, incessible et s'éteint avec la mort de son titulaire. Il en résulterait que les héritiers de l'auteur, même s'ils acquièrent par succession les droits de nature patrimoniale, ne pourraient en principe pas invoquer le droit moral pour s'opposer à une altération de l'oeuvre, à moins que la mutilation soit telle qu'elle porte atteinte à leurs propres intérêts personnels. On reviendra sur cette question dans la partie de ce rapport qui traite des droits des héritiers du créateur.

3. Troisième remarque: les oeuvres des beaux-arts ont ceci de particulier qu'elles s'identifient avec leur support matériel, à tel point qu'elles n'existent pas en dehors de l'exemplaire original.[3]

On ne saurait donc à propos des oeuvres des beaux-arts, assimiler le support matériel de la réalisation intellectuelle tel le tableau ou la sculpture à un simple exemplaire matériel de l'oeuvre, comme cela serait le cas du livre ou de la partition.[4] Cette identification de l'oeuvre avec son support matériel peut engendrer des conflits entre l'auteur et le propriétaire de l'exemplaire original, conflits qui sont spécifiques à cette catégorie d'oeuvres, en raison du caractère personnel que doit revêtir l'exécution matérielle de l'oeuvre; en ce qui concerne les oeuvres littéraires et musicales, ces mêmes conflits n'existent pas, l'oeuvre étant totalement séparable du corps matériel qui l'extériorise dans la réalité, de sorte qu'il ne peut y avoir de confusion entre le droit d'auteur qui porte sur l'oeuvre intellectuelle et le droit de propriété corporelle sur le support matériel de cette même oeuvre.

Certes, l'art. 9 al. 3 de la LDA en précisant que:

> 'Sauf convention contraire, le transfert de la propriété d'un exemplaire d'une oeuvre n'entraîne pas celui du droit d'auteur, même s'il s'agit de l'exemplaire original',

assure à l'auteur son droit exclusif sur l'oeuvre, nonobstant l'aliénation du support matériel.

En d'autres termes, de par cette disposition, la loi suisse souligne l'indépendance totale du droit d'auteur par rapport au droit de propriété

2. *V.* également CHERPILLOD, *Le droit d'auteur en Suisse* (Lausanne 1985) p. 37 *et seq.*
3. Cf. E. DEL BIANCO, *Le droit d'auteur et ses limites* (Lausanne 1951) p. 216.
4. Cf. M. PEDRAZZINI, 'Das Ausstellungsrecht an Werken der bildenden Künste' dans RSPIDA 1956, pp. 72, 80.

corporelle. Cela étant, comme on le verra plus loin, il existe des situations où le propriétaire du support matériel doit se voir attribuer certaines prérogatives de l'auteur, faute de quoi son droit de propriété serait illusoire; vice versa, ce même droit de propriété doit souffrir de restrictions pour permettre à l'auteur d'exercer en plein les prérogatives qui sont les siennes, en sa qualité de créateur de l'oeuvre.

II. LES PREROGATIVES DE L'AUTEUR

Ces prérogatives sont prévues à l'art. 12 de la LDA. L'énumération figurant dans la disposition précitée est exhaustive (ATF 64 II 162, 166 = JT 1938 I 522, 530); c'est également cette solution qu'a choisie le projet du Conseil fédéral (art. 10), alors que la IIIe Commission d'experts proposait une liste purement exemplative des prérogatives de l'auteur.

S'agissant des oeuvres des beaux-arts, les prérogatives du créateur sont les suivantes:

1. Droit exclusif de reproduire l'oeuvre par n'importe quel procédé (art. 12 al 1 ch. 1 LDA)

a. Cette prérogative se rapporte aussi bien à la reproduction pure et simple qu'à la reproduction modifiée. Le créateur peut transférer le droit de reproduction, avec ou sans modification, à un tiers. Si la cession porte également sur le droit de reproduction sous une forme modifiée de l'oeuvre, l'auteur n'en conserve pas moins son droit à l'intégrité de l'oeuvre. En conséquence, et nonobstant cette cession, il pourra interdire toute déformation, mutilation ou modification de l'oeuvre, ou toute autre atteinte qui serait préjudiciable à son honneur ou à sa réputation.

Selon le Tribunal fédéral, un tel droit résulte de l'art. 28 CCS (ATF 69 II 53 = JT 1943 I 337; ATF 96 II 409, 420 = JT 70 I 597, 599).

Le projet du Conseil fédéral (cf. art. 11 al. 2) et celui de la IIIe Commission d'experts (cf. art. 14 al. 2) ont expressément réservé le droit de l'auteur de s'opposer à toute déformation ou mutilation de l'oeuvre, nonobstant la cession du droit de reproduction à un tiers.

b. Si l'auteur, en aliénant le support matériel de l'oeuvre, n'a pas transféré le droit de reproduction à l'acquéreur dudit exemplaire, celui-ci ne peut en principe pas reproduire l'oeuvre, en particulier, en tirer des copies. Cette interdiction n'est toutefois pas absolue. Ainsi à teneur de l'art. 30 ch. 2 LDA, la reproduction, dans des catalogues édités par l'administration d'une collection publique, d'oeuvres d'art figuratif, d'après des exemplaires se trouvant à demeure dans cette collection, est licite.

Le chiffre 3 de cette même disposition précise qu'est également licite, la reproduction d'oeuvres des arts figuratifs d'après des exemplaires se trouvant à demeure sur les voies et places publiques.

2. Droit exclusif de réciter, représenter, exécuter ou exhiber l'oeuvre publiquement (cf. art. 12 al. 1 ch. 3 LDA)

Cette prérogative n'intéresse les oeuvres des beaux-arts qu'en ce qui concerne le droit de l'auteur d'exhiber l'oeuvre publiquement. Cette question est liée au droit du créateur d'exposer publiquement des exemplaires de l'oeuvre; elle sera traitée ci-après.

3. Droit exclusif d'exposer publiquement des exemplaires de l'oeuvre ou de livrer l'oeuvre à la publicité d'une autre manière tant que celle-ci n'est pas rendue publique (cf. art. 12 al. 1 ch. 4 LDA)

a. Cette prérogative est la conséquence du droit de première publication, sanctionnée non seulement par l'art. 12 al. 1 ch. 4 LDA, mais également par l'art. 11 de cette même loi. Selon cette prérogative, l'auteur a le droit exclusif de décider si, quand et de quelle manière son oeuvre sera divulguée. Comme le prévoit l'art. 12 al. ch. 4 LDA, ce droit s'éteint dès que l'auteur en a fait usage, soit lorsqu'il a consenti à ce que l'oeuvre soit rendue accessible à un nombre indéterminé de personnes.[5] Lorsque l'oeuvre a été ainsi rendue publique, l'auteur ne peut plus empêcher le propriétaire de son support matériel d'exposer à son tour ledit support.

Sous l'empire de la loi actuellement en vigueur, la question de savoir si l'aliénation de l'exemplaire original de l'oeuvre à un particulier est un acte de publicité suffisant, entraînant la perte pour l'auteur de son droit exclusif d'exposer l'oeuvre, paraît controversée. Pour le Prof. Pedrazzini,[6] la réponse à cette question doit être affirmative, dès lors qu'en aliénant le support matériel de l'oeuvre par une vente ou une donation, le créateur a considéré par là que son oeuvre était achevée et qu'ainsi elle avait acquis une existence autonome par rapport à sa personne.[7]

Le créateur pourrait certes par convention, obliger l'acquéreur à ne pas divulguer l'oeuvre et partant, à ne pas l'exposer publiquement, mais cette restriction serait, toujours selon cette doctrine, de nature purement obligationnelle, et ne s'imposerait pas à un acquéreur subséquent de l'exemplaire matériel. Ce serait dans ce sens qu'il conviendrait d'interpréter l'art. 33 LDA, qui prévoit que les exemplaires d'une oeuvre non rendue publique des arts figuratifs, exécutés et mis en circulation de manière licite, peuvent être exposés publiquement, même sans l'autorisation du titulaire du droit d'auteur, lorsque celui-ci ne peut être consulté.[8] Mais pour que l'auteur perde l'exclusivité du droit d'exposition, il faut que la propriété de l'exemplaire matériel ait été transférée, le simple transfert de la possession, par le truchement d'un contrat de prêt, n'étant pas suffisant.

---

5. Cf. TROLLER, *op cit.*, p. 688.
6. *Op cit.* dans RSPIDA 1956, p. 81.
7. Dans le même sens, TROLLER, *op cit.*, p. 688.
8. En sens contraire, DEL BIANCO, *op cit.*, p. 223.

b. Le projet du Conseil Fédéral (art. 10) n'a pas inclu au nombre des prérogatives de l'auteur, celles d'exposer publiquement des exemplaires de l'oeuvre, pas plus qu'il n'a repris le texte de l'art. 33 de l'actuelle LDA, de sorte que le problème que l'on a examiné sous *a.*, *supra* devrait être résolu en fonction de la seule interprétation de l'art. 9 al. 3 du projet, qui définit les conditions selon lesquelles une oeuvre est considérée comme divulguée – l'oeuvre doit avoir été rendue accessible à un grand nombre de personnes ne constituant pas un cercle de personnes étroitement liées au sens de l'art. 19 al. 1 litt. a) du projet.

Cette solution n'est pas satisfaisante et le projet du Conseil Fédéral aurait été bien inspiré de reprendre la version de la IIIe Commission d'experts, qui avait tranché le conflit existant entre le créateur et le propriétaire de l'exemplaire original de l'oeuvre en faveur de ce dernier; en effet, la Commission avait prévu à l'art. 15 al. 3 de son projet que sauf convention contraire, le propriétaire d'un exemplaire d'une oeuvre des arts figuratifs est en droit de l'exposer publiquement, même lorsque l'oeuvre n'a pas encore été rendue publique au sens de l'art. 12 de ce même projet, qui prévoit le droit à la première publication.

4. Droit exclusif de vendre, de mettre en vente et de mettre en circulation des exemplaires de l'oeuvre

a. Ce droit est épuisé par la première vente licite d'un exemplaire matériel de l'oeuvre. Il faut ici souligner qu'à teneur de l'art. 58 al. 1 LDA, cette première vente licite peut avoir lieu n'importe où dans le monde, nonobstant une éventuelle limitation territoriale fixée par le titulaire du droit d'auteur, dont la transgression n'entraînera que les sanctions prévues par le droit des contrats (art. 58 al. 2 LDA).

Cette dérogation au principe de la territorialité ne s'applique toutefois pas aux instruments mécaniques tels que disques, cassettes, sur lesquels sont enregistrées des oeuvres littéraires ou musicales et ce, en vertu de l'art. 3 de l'art. 58 LDA.[9]

La prérogative visée à l'art. 12 al. 1 ch. 2 LDA ne concerne, une fois l'exemplaire original aliéné, que des reproductions mécaniques de l'oeuvre d'art et ne présente donc pas pour l'artiste le même intérêt que s'il s'était agi d'une oeuvre littéraire ou musicale. En effet, en matière de créations littéraires et musicales, l'exécution matérielle par l'auteur est sans importance, de sorte que tous les exemplaires de l'oeuvre, sous réserve peut-être du manuscrit, ont une même valeur pour l'auteur et par voie de conséquence, pour les acquéreurs desdits exemplaires.

Tel n'est pas le cas avec la création artistique où le caractère personnel de l'oeuvre réside précisément dans son exécution matérielle, ce qui, comme on l'a relevé plus haut, fait qu'une oeuvre des beaux-arts n'existe pas en

9. Cf. art. 13 al. 3 de la Convention de Berne et RSPIDA 1988, p. 115 *et seq*.

dehors de l'exemplaire original. En conséquence, en aliénant l'exemplaire original de l'oeuvre, l'artiste transfert en quelque sorte par le truchement du corps matériel, ce qui constitue l'essentiel de sa création, même s'il conserve le droit de reproduction et de mise en circulation de copies de son oeuvre, réalisées par un procédé de fixation mécanique.

5. *Droit à la paternité de l'oeuvre*

Sous l'empire du système actuellement en vigueur, ce droit ne résulte pas de la LDA et découle des arts. 28 et 29 CCS.

Le projet du Conseil Fédéral (art. 9), de même que celui de la IIIe Commission d'experts (art. 11 al. 2) consacre en revanche, le droit du créateur de faire reconnaître sa qualité d'auteur de l'oeuvre et de décider sous quel nom l'oeuvre sera utilisée, les règles sur la protection de la personnalité demeurant réservées.

6. *Droit à l'intégrité de l'oeuvre*

Ce droit qui permet à l'auteur de s'opposer à toute déformation, mutilation ou autre modification de son oeuvre, ou à toute autre atteinte préjudiciable à son honneur ou à sa réputation, peut être exercé par l'auteur, nonobstant la cession du droit de reproduction de l'oeuvre, même sous une forme modifiée.

Il s'agit là d'une prérogative dite 'morale' de l'auteur qui résulte de l'art. 28 CSS (ATF 69 II 53 = JT 43 I 337; 96 II 409, 420 = JT 1971, 597, 599), et qui est expressément consacré par l'art. 6*bis* de la Convention de Berne.

Il faut noter que tant le projet du Conseil Fédéral (art. 11) que celui de la IIIe Commission d'experts (art. 14 al. 2) consacrent une disposition au droit de l'auteur à l'intégrité de son oeuvre.

A notre avis, l'exercice de ce droit devrait permettre à l'artiste d'interdire que l'exemplaire original de sa création soit placé par son propriétaire dans un environnement susceptible de nuire à sa réputation, par exemple, que la toile soit exposée avec d'autres oeuvres appartenant à une tendance que l'auteur réprouve.[10]

C'est également dans le cadre du droit à l'intégrité de son oeuvre que l'auteur devrait pouvoir s'opposer à la destruction de l'exemplaire matériel de l'oeuvre, lorsque celui-ci est unique. Cette prérogative n'est pas prévue par la LDA actuellement en vigueur et ne saurait, par ailleurs, être considérée comme relevant du droit moral de l'auteur, dès lors qu'elle est plutôt une condition nécessaire à l'exercice des droits patrimoniaux; en consé-

10. Dan ce sens, DEL BIANCO, *op cit.*, p. 220.

quence, et en l'état actuel de la législation, il y a donc une lacune que la doctrine souhaiterait voir combler.[11]

Cette lacune devrait subsister dans le nouveau droit en gestation, puisque le projet du Conseil Fédéral à la différence de celui de la IIIe Commission d'experts n'a prévu aucune disposition permettant à l'auteur de s'opposer, à certaines conditions, à la destruction de l'exemplaire matériel de l'oeuvre.

7. *Droit d'accès*

Cette prérogative devrait permettre à l'auteur d'exercer les prérogatives qui lui compètent – droit de reproduction – alors que l'exemplaire original de l'oeuvre a été cédé à un tiers et que le créateur n'a pas réalisé, avant cette aliénation, des copies de l'oeuvre par des procédés mécaniques. Le droit d'accès à l'oeuvre, qui ne figure pas au titre de prérogatives consacrées par l'art. 12 LDA ne relève, à notre avis, pas du droit moral de l'auteur, de sorte qu'il ne saurait trouver son assise dans les arts. 27 *et seq.* CSS qui protègent les droits de la personnalité.

Cela étant, le droit d'accès paraît être un complément nécessaire du droit de reproduction, de sorte que la majorité de la doctrine[12] l'admette précisément pour permettre à l'auteur d'exercer son droit exclusif de reproduction de l'oeuvre. Plus exactement, comme le relève cette doctrine, il serait abusif de la part du propriétaire d'opposer à l'auteur un refus à l'accès de l'oeuvre, lorsque le créateur souhaite exercer ses droits de reproduction et d'adaptation.[13]

Toutefois, cette même doctrine considère qu'en l'état actuel du droit, le créateur n'a pas le pouvoir d'imposer des obligations positives au propriétaire en vertu de son droit d'accès. Par exemple, l'auteur ne pourrait, selon cette doctrine, exiger du propriétaire qu'il lui remette l'exemplaire original de l'oeuvre aux fins de l'exposer publiquement.[14]

Il y a donc là encore une lacune qui ne sera pas comblée par le nouveau droit, puisque le projet du Conseil Fédéral, à la différence de celui de la IIIe Commission d'experts (art. 17 al. 2) n'a prévu aucune disposition permettant de trancher le conflit existant entre le créateur et le propriétaire de l'exemplaire original de l'oeuvre. Dans cette perspective, on relèvera que la IIIe Commission d'experts imposait au propriétaire le devoir de remettre l'exemplaire original de l'oeuvre à l'auteur afin que celui-ci puisse l'exposer en Suisse, pour autant que le créateur prouve un intérêt prépondérant. Pour garantir le propriétaire contre toute dégradation de l'exemplaire original, le propriétaire ou le possesseur pouvait subordonner la remise de l'oeuvre à la fourniture de sûretés.

---

11. Cf. TROLLER, *op cit.*, p. 694: DEL BIANCO, *op cit.*, p. 220 *et seq.*
12. Cf. TROLLER, *op cit.*, p. 695: DEL BIANCO, *op cit.*, p. 233 *et seq.*
13. Cf. DEL BIANCO, *op cit.*, p. 224.
14. *Ibid.* et TROLLER, *op cit.*, p. 695.

8. Droit de retrait

Telle qu'elle est posée dans le questionnaire, cette question vise deux situations qui doivent être soigneusement distinguées.

a. La première situation est celle où l'auteur a conclu un contrat emportant cession de certaines de ses prérogatives telles le droit de reproduction – contrat d'édition – lequel fait naître un rapport d'obligations durables. En droit suisse, tout contrat qui implique un élément de durée peut être résilié pour juste motif lorsque le rapport de confiance est rompu et que la continuation du contrat ne peut plus être raisonnablement exigée (p. ex., à propos du contrat de licence ATF 92 II 299 = JT 1967 I 247).

La résiliation pour juste motif ne confère pas au créateur un 'libre droit de résiliation' qu'il pourrait exercer à son gré. En fait, lorsque le juste motif n'a pas sa cause dans la personne de son co-contractant, l'auteur ne pourra mettre fin au contrat que si les circonstances sous l'empire desquelles la convention a été conclue ont été profondément modifiées, ce qui revient en quelque sorte à appliquer la 'clausula rebus sic stantibus'.[15]

b. La seconde situation vise celle d'un créateur qui, après avoir aliéné l'exemplaire original de son oeuvre, par hypothèse par une vente, entend le reprendre en vue de sa destruction. Le créateur peut estimer que l'oeuvre qu'il a réalisée n'est plus en harmonie avec sa production actuelle, et prétendre ainsi à retirer de la circulation une oeuvre, quand bien même l'exemplaire de celle-ci aurait été d'ores et déjà aliéné. Ce droit de retrait ou de repentir, dès lors qu'il ne touche pas un rapport obligationnel, lequel a déjà été dissous de par l'exécution des prestations des parties, ne devrait pas pouvoir être fondé sur le concept des justes motifs. Ce concept ne vise en effet que des liens obligationnels qui ne sont pas encore dénoués, ce qui n'est pas le cas d'une vente, qui est un contrat instantané. Dans ces conditions, le droit de repentir ne pourrait être fondé que sur le droit moral de l'auteur.

Mais en droit suisse, l'exercice des droits de la personnalité des arts. 27 *et seq.* CCS ne va pas jusqu'à permettre de porter atteinte au droit de propriété d'un tiers, en l'espèce au droit du propriétaire de l'exemplaire original de l'oeuvre. En l'absence d'une disposition légale, force est alors d'admettre que le droit de retrait ou de repentir, tel qu'envisagé dans la seconde situation que l'on vient de décrire n'existe pas en droit suisse.[16]

Au demeurant ni le projet du Conseil Fédéral, ni celui de la IIIe Commis-

15. Cf. M. PEDRAZZINI, 'Le contrat d'entreprise, le contrat d'édition, le contrat de licence' dans *Traité de droit privé suisse*, vol. VII, Tome I, 3, p. 92 *et seq.*; TROLLER, *op cit.*, p. 803.
16. Dans ce sens, DEL BIANCO, *op cit.*, p. 224 et TROLLER, *op cit.*, p. 696 qui réserve toutefois l'application éventuelle de la *clausula rebus sic stantibus*, à tort à notre avis, dès lors que le contrat entre le créateur et l'acquéreur a déjà été exécuté par la remise de l'exemplaire original de l'oeuvre contre paiement de son prix.

sion d'experts ne prévoit un droit de retrait ou de repentir susceptible d'affecter les droits de propriété de l'acquéreur de l'exemplaire original.

9. Droit de suite

Cette prérogative n'existe pas dans la loi actuelle sur le droit d'auteur.

Bien que la société des peintres, sculpteurs et architectes suisses (GSMBA) ait invité la IIIe Commission d'experts à introduire cette prérogative dans son projet, cette dernière n'a pas donné suite à cette requête et a motivé sa position de la manière suivante:

> 'La Commission a étudié le droit de suite pendant plusieurs séances et a chargé l'OFPI d'effectuer une enquête sur les conséquences de l'introduction d'un tel droit sur le marché de l'art. Il s'agissait de savoir si les grandes entreprises spécialisées dans les ventes aux enchères seraient touchées par le droit de suite, voire si elles envisageraient de déplacer le siège de leurs activités.
>
> 'Sur les sept entreprises contactées, quatre ont répondu. Il ressort de leur réponse que les oeuvres encore protégées ne représentent qu'une part relativement faible des transactions des entreprises internationales spécialisées dans les ventes aux enchères. L'introduction du droit de suite ne les amènerait pas à envisager le déplacement de leur siège; elles n'excluent cependant pas que les ventes d'oeuvres protégées soient confiées à leurs filiales à l'étranger, afin de les soustraire à la charge supplémentaire.
>
> 'La Commission s'est finalement ralliée à l'opinion qu'introduire le droit de suite n'entrait pas dans le mandat qu'elle avait reçu, à savoir réviser le projet. C'est pourquoi elle s'est abstenue d'intégrer une telle disposition dans le projet de loi. Elle estime cependant que le Parlement devrait débattre de l'opportunité d'introduire ce droit au profit des auteurs d'oeuvres des arts figuratifs.'[17]

Considérant ce qui précède, il n'est donc pas exclu que le droit de suite soit finalement intégré dans la nouvelle loi sur le droit d'auteur, bien que le projet du Conseil Fédéral, en ne prévoyant aucune disposition à cet effet, ait laissé la question ouverte.

III. LES DROITS DES HERITIERS DU CREATEUR

1. Comme déjà relevé dans la partie introductive du présent rapport, il convient de distinguer les droits patrimoniaux des droits non patrimoniaux. En ce qui concerne les premiers, leur durée est, d'après la loi actuelle, de cinquante ans après la mort de l'auteur (art. 36 LDA).

Les droit patrimoniaux du créateur étant par nature cessibles, ils seront transférés au décès de l'auteur à ses héritiers selon les règles de la dévolution prévues par le Code civil suisse (arts. 467 *et seq.*) pour autant naturellement

---

17. Cf. Rapport explicatif sur le projet de la IIIe Commission d'experts, pp. 9–10.

que cette loi soit applicable à la succession de l'auteur.

Une étude du droit successoral suisse déborderait le cadre du présent rapport. Cela étant, on rappellera qu'à teneur de l'art. 602 CCS, lorsqu'il y a plusieurs héritiers, tous les droits et obligations compris dans la succession restent indivis jusqu'au partage. C'est donc le régime de la propriété en main commune qui s'applique aux droits d'auteur dépendant de la succession indivise et ce jusqu'à ce que celle-ci soit partagée.

Si l'auteur a fait un legs de ses droits d'auteur à une personne qui peut ne pas être un héritier légal ou institué, les héritiers sont personnellement tenus d'exécuter ce legs et, partant, c'est contre eux que le légataire dirigera son action en délivrance du legs (cf. art. 485 CCS).

2. S'agissant maintenant des prérogatives morales de l'auteur, on a vu que selon la conception du Tribunal fédéral, celles-ci trouvaient leur fondement dans les règles sur la protection de la personnalité, plus particulièrement dans l'art. 28 CCS. Or, les droits personnels sont incessibles, intransmissibles et s'éteignent avec la mort de leur titulaire, de sorte que les héritiers ne pourraient invoquer que leurs propres droits à la personnalité, qui comprendraient la sauvegarde de la considération dont jouissait le créateur (cf. ATF 104 II 225 = JT 1979 I 546; ATF 101 II 191 = JT 1976 I 376), pour s'opposer à certaines mutilations ou altérations inadmissibles de l'oeuvre.

Cette solution n'est pas satisfaisante, car ce ne serait que dans des cas exceptionnels que les héritiers pourraient se prévaloir d'une atteinte à leur propre sentiment de piété envers le défunt.[18] Dans ces conditions, ne conviendrait-il pas d'admettre la théorie moniste et de considérer que les prérogatives patrimoniales et morales constituent un faisceau de droits indissociables, lequel est transmis aux héritiers à la mort du créateur?[19] Si l'on devait admettre cette conception, les héritiers acquerraient tous les droits du créateur, quelle que soit la nature des prérogatives transférées et ils pourraient exercer de tels droits jusqu'à l'expiration de la période de protection, soit cinquante ans selon le système actuellement en vigueur, qui a été repris par le projet du Conseil Fédéral, alors que la IIIe Commission d'experts avait proposé un délai de soixante-dix ans après la mort de l'auteur.

Une troisième solution consisterait à admettre que seuls les héritiers les plus proches du défunt (conjoint survivant, enfants) seraient habilités à exercer en leur propre nom, les prérogatives relevant du droit moral du créateur.[20]

On soulignera enfin que la conception moniste se reflète aussi bien dans le projet du Conseil Fédéral (cf. FF 1989 III p. 515) que dans celui de la IIIe Commission d'experts, de sorte que si les Chambres fédérales devaient adopter le projet de révision de la LDA, toute incertitude quant au sort des droits non patrimoniaux après la mort de l'auteur devrait être levée.

---

18. Cf. CHERPILLOD, *op cit.*, p. 69.
19. Dans ce sens, TROLLER, *op cit.*, p. 740.
20. Dan ce sens, CHERPILLOD, *op cit.*, p. 69.

United Kingdom

NATIONAL REPORT ON TOPIC 3. RIGHTS OF ARTISTS AND THEIR HEIRS*

Adrian Barr-Smith**

1. The rights of artist in their works fall into three categories: a. copyright; b. moral rights; and c. contractual rights.

a. Copyright

i. The Act
The new United Kingdom copyright legislation (Copyright, Designs & Patents Act 1988) applies to artistic works created after 1 August 1989. There are detailed transitional provisions dealing with the status of artistic works made before 1 August 1989.

ii. Works
Copyright subsists in an artistic work if it is sufficiently original (rather than of an artistic quality). For this purpose, artistic works include graphic works, photographs, sculptures, collages, works of architecture and works of artistic craftsmanship.

iii. Owner
The artist is usually the first owner of any copyright in the work. However, if the work was made in the course of the artist's employment, then copyright is owned by his employer. If the work was generated by a computer, then the copyright owner of the work is the person who made the arrangements necessary for the work to be generated.

iv. Term
Copyright in an artistic work expires at the end of the period of fifty years after the end of the calendar year in which the artist dies. If the identity of the artist is unknown, the copyright will expire fifty years after the end of

* The author acknowledges the invaluable assistance of Angela Jackson and Joshua Drapkin in the production of this material.
** Denton Hall Burgin & Warrens, Solicitors, London. Consistent with our policy when giving comment and advice on a non-specific basis, Denton Hall Burgin & Warrens cannot assume legal responsibility for the accuracy of any particular statement. In the case of specific problems, it is recommended that professional advice be sought.

the calendar year in which the work was first made available to the public (e.g., exhibited in public, or included in a film, broadcast or cable programme) with the requisite permission of the copyright owner. If the artistic work is computer-generated, the copyright expires at the end of the period of fifty years from the end of the calendar year in which the work was made.

v. Rights
The Act gives the owner of the copyright in a work the exclusive right in the United Kingdom to do the following restricted acts:
1. to copy the work including making a three dimensional work from a two dimensional work and vice versa;
2. to issue copies of the work to the public;
3. to broadcast the work or include it in a cable programme service.

vi. Infringement
Copyright in the artistic work is infringed by a person who without the licence of the copyright owner does, or authorizes someone else to do, any of these restricted acts. The Act also identifies acts of secondary infringement such as possessing or dealing with an infringing copy or providing the means for making an infringing copy.

vii. Exceptions
However, there are also certain exceptions whereby a copy, not amounting to a substantial part of the work, may be made in certain circumstances for the purposes of education; research or private study; criticism, review or news reporting; or incidental inclusion in another artistic work, or in a sound recording, film, broadcast or cable programme.

viii. Remedies
If copyright is infringed, the copyright owner may bring an action for remedies such as damages, and/or an account of profits (financial compensation) or an injunction (to prevent further infringement). Furthermore the owner of the copyright may apply to the court for an order that an infringing copy be delivered up to him. In certain cases, the copyright owner may have the right to seize the infringing copy himself.

b. Moral rights

The Act divides moral rights of artists into three categories: paternity, integrity and the right to prevent false attribution of work. The provisions relating to moral rights are new and, for the most part, will only apply to works created after 1 August 1989. There are also detailed transitional provisions.

i. Paternity
The author of an artistic work has the right to be identified as author (*if* he asserts that right) when the artistic work is exploited by others in certain

ways. This right of paternity continues so long as the work is in copyright. Such assertion may be contained in a copyright assignment, or given separately, (at any time) by written notice.

The right of paternity does not apply:

1. to a computer-generated work;
2. to anything done by or with the authority of the copyright owner where the copyright first vests in the employer;
3. publication in newspapers periodicals or collective works of reference;
4. certain other circumstances in which *copyright* is not infringed.

ii. Integrity

The artist has the right not to have his work subjected to derogatory treatment. '*Treatment*' means any addition to, deletion from or alteration to or adaptation of the work. Treatment is '*derogatory*' if it amounts to a distortion or mutilation of the work or is otherwise prejudicial to the honour or reputation of the author.

This right of integrity lasts so long as the work is in copyright.

The artist does not need to assert the right of integrity: the right is automatic unless waived by the artist. The right is subject to exceptions broadly similar to those for the right of paternity above.

iii. False attribution

An artist has the right not to have falsely attributed to him a work by a different artist.

The right in respect of false attribution continues for twenty years after the artist's death.

The right in respect of false attribution cannot be enforced by the artist, if previously waived by him.

c. Contractual rights

An artist may exploit commercially his work by means of:

1. sale of the work itself;
2. the licensing of copies which would otherwise be infringing copies;
3. the contractual assignment of his copyright in the work;
4. loaning a work for exhibition.

d. *Droit de suite*

There is no *droit de suite* in the United Kingdom. However, in theory, an artist could impose such a right by contract when selling the work. Such purchaser ('purchaser A') would be obliged to account for a percentage of the proceeds/profit when reselling the work to 'purchaser B'. The artist could also impose on purchaser A the obligation to sell the work only on like terms, and so on, down the purchase chain. However, the artist has a contract only with purchaser A. The artist would have no remedy against purchaser B for either failing to account for a percentage of proceeds or to sell on like terms.

2. The 1988 Act provides that copyright is transmissible on death by testamentary disposition. Depending on the terms of the bequest, an artist's heir may thus acquire copyright in a work for all or part of the copyright life, and in relation to all or some of the restricted acts.

The Act further provides that if a work as a piece of physical property, not previously published, is left under a will to an heir, then the copyright in that work (*if* owned by the deceased) will also pass to the heir, unless the will provides otherwise. (This is a new provision).

The moral rights of *paternity* and *integrity* (but not the right in respect of false attribution) may pass to the artist's estate on death. If the deceased did not leave such moral rights to a particular person, they generally follow the copyright.

United States

NATIONAL REPORT ON TOPIC 3. RIGHTS OF ARTISTS AND THEIR HEIRS

Peter H. Karlen*

I. RIGHTS HELD BY ARTISTS ON THEIR WORKS

American artists primarily rely on federal copyright laws[1] and moral rights statutes enacted only in nine states.[2] As indicated by the Congressional testimony supporting the Berne Convention Implementation Act of 1988,[3] the United States provides protection for artists equivalent to that required under Art. 6*bis* of the Berne Convention through state and federal unfair competition laws and state laws on defamation, invasion of privacy, and other common law doctrines.[4] Of course, while the artist owns the art object, he can protect it as would any other property owner and can object to its alteration, mutilation, or destruction without resorting to moral rights laws.

---

* Attorney at Law, La Jolla, California.

1. Title 17, United States Code (U.S.C.).
2. Cal. Civ. Code Sects. 987, 989; La.Rev.Stat.Ann. Sects. 51–2151 to 51–2156; Me.Stat.Ann. Tit. 27, Sect. 303; Mass.Gen.Laws Ann. ch. 231, Sect. 85S; N.J.Stat.Ann. Sects. 2A: 24A–1 to 2A: 24A–8; N.M.Stat.Ann. Sects. 13–4B–2 to 13–4B–3; N.Y. Arts & Cultural Affairs Law Sects. 11.01, 14.03; Pa.Stat.Ann. Tit. 73, Sects. 2101–10; R.I.Gen.Laws Sects. 5–62–2 to 5–62–6. *See also* ns. 15–16.
3. Public Law 100–568, 102 Stat. 2853 (1988).
4. *See* H.R. Rep. No. 100–609 at 38, 100th Cong. 2d Sess. (1988); S. Rep. No 100–352 at 9–10, 100th Cong. 2d Sess. (1988). Art. 6*bis* of the Berne Convention for the Protection of Literary and Artistic Works reads as follows:
'(1) Independently of the author's economic rights, and even after the transfer of said rights, the author shall have the right to claim authorship of the work and to object to any distortion, mutilation, or other modification of, or other derogatory action in relation to, the said work, which would be prejudicial to his honor or reputation.
'(2) The rights granted to the author in accordance with the preceding paragraph shall, after his death, be maintained, at least until the expiry of the economic rights, and shall be exercisable by the persons or institutions authorized by the legislation of the country where protection is claimed. However, those countries whose legislation, at the moment of their ratification of or accession to this Act, does not provide for the protection after the death of the author of all the rights set out in the preceding paragraph may provide that some of these rights may, after his death, cease to be maintained.
'(3) The means of redress for safeguarding the rights granted by this Article shall be governed by the legislation of the country where protection is claimed.'

The *droit de suite* (the artist's right to a share of resale proceeds) has not been recognized in the United States except in California.[5] The California statute follows French theory by allowing the artist a fixed percentage (five percent) of the resale price, but with many restrictions, as explained below (*see* pp. 319–320).

Design patents are a possibility for any artist who invents 'new, original, and ornamental' designs for 'articles of manufacture'.[6] However, most articles of manufacture are utilitarian items, so that artists considering design patent protection would be primarily commercial artists, and even they seldom apply for patents. After all, patent protection is expensive, hard to get, and short-lived.[7]

1. *What Can Artists Prohibit?*

a. Copyright law

Sect. 106 of the U.S. Copyright Act[8] provides affirmative exclusive rights. The artist owns exclusive rights to reproduce, prepare derivative works based on, publicly distribute copies of, publicly display, and publicly perform her work. The exclusive right to prepare derivative works is rather a broad right entitling the artist to prevent others from adapting the work in the same or other media of expression.[9] If the artist remains the copyright owner, anyone exercising any of these exclusive rights without her consent has infringed the copyright.[10] Thus, with some exceptions, the artist can stop other persons from reproducing, adapting, distributing copies of, performing, and displaying the work.

b. Moral rights

Moral rights legislation in the United States is limited to nine states,[11] although there is pending federal legislation, the Visual Artists' Rights Act of 1989.[12] Fortunately, moral rights statutes exist in the principal art markets,

---

5. California Civil Code Sect. 986.
6. 35 U.S.C. Sect. 171.
7. Fourteen years maximum is granted at 35 U.S.C. Sect. 173.
8. 17 U.S.C. Sect. 106.
9. According to Sect. 101 of the Copyright Act, 17 U.S.C. Sect. 101, a 'derivative work' is: 'a work based upon one or more pre-existing works, such as a translation, musical arrangement, dramatization, fictionalization, motion picture version, sound recording, art reproduction, abridgment, condensation, or any other form in which a work may be recast, transformed, or adapted. A work consisting of editorial revisions, annotations, elaborations, which, as a whole, represent an original work of authorship, is a "derivative work"....'
10. 17 U.S.C. Sect. 501.
11. *See supra* n. 2.
12. S. 1198, 101st Cong., 1st Sess. (1989).

New York[13] and California.[14] Those statutes modeled after the California law enable the artist to prevent the physical alteration, mutilation, defacement, and destruction of the artist's work; they also permit the artist to control crediting by allowing him to claim credit for his works of 'fine art' as well as to disclaim credit for 'just and valid reason'.[15] Those laws which follow the New York model also grant crediting rights but do not directly prohibit physical alteration, mutilation, or destruction; rather they prevent persons other than the artist from publicly displaying altered or mutilated works.[16]

Even in State jurisdictions without moral rights statutes, artists use unfair competition laws to control crediting. Traditional unfair competition law prevents 'passing off' goods as those of another merchant or manufacturer, particularly a better known merchant or manufacturer.[17] The artist wrongfully credited with a work of art can use unfair competition law to remove the credit.[18] Similarly, in a few cases, the courts have held that the wrongful removal or denial of a credit also amounts to unfair competition in the form of 'reverse passing off'.[19] Also, privacy laws can be used against false crediting when the artist's name is wrongfully associated with a work.[20] Attempts have been made to enforce moral rights using defamation laws, especially in relation to crediting.[21] An artist might argue that a credit for a mutilated work defames him, but this ploy has seldom been successful.

---

13. *See* New York statutes, *supra* n. 2. *See also*, DAMICH, 'The New York Artists' Authorship Rights Act: A Comparative Critique', 84 *Columbia Law Review* (1984) p. 1733.
14. *See* California statutes, *supra* n. 2. *See also*, KARLEN, 'Moral Rights in California', 19 *San Diego Law Review* (1982) p. 675.
15. *See* Massachusetts, California, Pennsylvania, and New Mexico statutes, *supra* n. 2.
16. *See* New York, Maine, Rhode Island, Louisiana, and New Jersey statutes, *supra* n. 2.
17. *See* 15 U.S.C. Sect. 1125(a), the principal federal unfair competition statute.
18. *See*, e.g., *Gilliam v. American Broadcasting Co.*, 538 F.2d 14 (2d Cir. 1976) discussed at n. 45 *infra*.
19. *See* e.g., *Smith v. Montoro*, 648 F.2d 602 (9th Cir. 1981).
20. *See* e.g., *Neyland v. Home Pattern Co.*, 65 F.2d 363 (2d Cir. 1933). *But see*, e.g., *Shostakovich v. 20th Century-Fox Film Corp.*, 80 N.Y.S.2d 575 (Sup.Ct. 1948), affd., 87 N.Y.S.2d 430 (1st Dept. 1949) (composer's privacy claim under Sect. 51 of the N.Y. Civil Rights Law denied); *Ellis v. Hurst*, 121 N.Y.S. 438 (Sup.Ct. 1910) (pseudonymity protected by privacy laws).
21. *See*, e.g., *Shostakovich v. 20th Century-Fox Film Corp.*, 80 N.Y.S.2d 575 (Supt.Ct. 1948), affd., 87 N.Y.S.2d 430 (1st Dept. 1949) (Soviet composer alleges that use of his music in anti-Communist film injures his reputation); *Geisel v. Poynter Products. Inc.*, 295 F. Supp. 331 (SDNY 1968) (the Dr. Seuss case wherein plaintiff claimed dolls reproduced from his illustrations were in poor taste and injured his reputation). *But see Ben-Oliel v. Press Publishing Co.*, 251 N.Y. 250, 167 N.E. 432 (1929) (false attribution of authorship of inaccurate literary work held defamatory).

II. CONDITIONS FOR EXERCISE OF RIGHTS

1. Right to Disclose a Work

The disclosure right, especially as developed in France, is not directly recognized under U.S. law. For instance, an American artist under circumstances similar to the *Rouault* case[22] might not prevail. The right to control how and when a work will be disclosed, not being separately recognized, must be protected using copyright laws, moral rights laws granting other rights, and unfair competition laws.

For example, an artist contending that a work he sold remains unfinished may try to invoke a moral rights statute (if enacted in his jurisdiction) to disclaim credit for 'just and valid reason'. That is, if the artist is contractually bound to distribute the work, she may be forced to deliver the art object while still entitled to disclaim credit for the work, thus making the work relatively valueless to the purchaser. If the artist remains the copyright owner, having not created the work 'for hire'[23] nor having transferred the copyright,[24] she can exercise her exclusive distribution right, which may be equivalent to a disclosure right.[25] However, this option is not available when the artist is not a copyright owner or has granted a copyright license to reproduce or distribute the work. Moreover, even if the artist is the copyright owner, Sect. 109 of the Copyright Act[26] provides exemptions for owners of the art object. For instance, whenever a dealer or museum purchases the art object without acquiring the copyright, as owner of the art object it may display and sell without violating the copyright, according to Sect. 109.

---

22. *Rouault c. Consorts Vollard*, [1947] S.Jur.II.3, [1947] *La Semaine Juridique* [J.C.P.] II, No. 3405 (Tribunal Civil de la Seine) (dealer's heirs sued artist who was under contract to give entire production to dealer; artist successfully claimed that canvases stored at dealer's premises were 'unfinished' and not be divulged).
23. A 'work made for hire', of which the employer is both 'author' and copyright owner is:
'(1) a work prepared by an employee within the scope of his or her employment; or
'(2) a work specially ordered – or commissioned for use as a contribution to a collective work, as part of a motion picture or other audio-visual work, as a translation, as a supplementary work, as a compilation, as an instructional text, as a test, as answer material for a test, or as an atlas, if the parties expressly agree in a written instrument signed by them that the work shall be considered a work made for hire....'
24. Sect. 204 of the Copyright Act, 17 U.S.C. Sect. 204, says that transfers of copyright ownership, other than by operation of law, are not valid unless there is a written instrument signed by the owner of the rights conveyed or the owner's duly authorized agent. Thus, an artist cannot lose a copyright unless the work is created for hire, conveyed in writing, or passed by operation of law after the artist's death. In particular, a copyright cannot be seized to satisfy a court judgment or otherwise involuntarily transferred. *See* 17 U.S.C. Sect. 201(e).
25. *See Chamberlain v. Feldman*, 300 N.Y. 135, 89 N.E.2d 863 (1949) (heirs of Mark Twain able to prevent publication of short story under older doctrine of common law copyright allowing perpetual control over disclosure).
26. 17 U.S.C. Sect. 109.

2. *Right to Reproduce a Work*

Reproduction rights are solely governed by federal copyright law. Sect. 106(1) of the Copyright Act[27] gives the artist the exclusive right to reproduce the work if he remains the copyright owner, not having created the work for hire or having transferred copyright.[28] Sect. 301 of the Copyright Act[29] pre-empts all state laws governing the same subject matter and same exclusive rights granted under the Copyright Act at Sect. 106; therefore, all state laws granting artists exclusive reproduction rights will be pre-empted and are of no force and effect.[30]

3. *Right to Perform a Work*

Again, federal copyright law under Sect. 106(4) grants the artist the exclusive right to perform a work,[31] and all state laws granting the same right are pre-empted.[32] Also, the performance right does not apply to 'pictorial, graphic, or sculptural works',[33] perhaps because such works are technically incapable of being performed. Rather, a pictorial, graphic or sculptural work is 'displayed'.

4. *Right to Receive Royalties and Resale Proceeds*

As mentioned above, the *droit de suite* does not exist in the United States except in California,[34] and the California statute has many exemptions. To claim the five percent royalty on resale proceeds, the artist must show that the gross proceeds are $ 1000 or more; such proceeds exceed the amount the seller originally paid for the work so that the seller has made a 'profit'; the artist must be either a U.S. citizen or a California resident for two years preceding the date of resale; and all sales for the first ten years after the

27. 17 U.S.C. Sect. 106(1). *See also* 17 U.S.C. Sect. 113 on reproduction rights in connection with useful articles.
28. *See supra* ns. 23–24.
29. 17 U.S.C. Sect. 301. One purpose behind the pre-emption statute was to create a uniform national law governing copyrights in both published and unpublished works.
30. Thus, common law copyright which had granted perpetual protection for unpublished works was mostly abolished. Nonetheless, vestiges of state law protection still survive. For example, state statutes may still provide protection for 'unfixed' (i.e., intangible) works of art. *See*, e.g., California Civil Code Sects. 980–82. This is because federal copyright law only covers works of art fixed in a tangible medium of expression (17 U.S.C. Sect. 102(a)).
31. The definition of 'perform' at 17 U.S.C. Sect. 101 is:
'To "perform" a work means to recite, render, play, dance, or act it, either directly or by means of any device or process, or, in the case of a motion picture or other audio-visual work, to show its images in any sequence or to make the sounds accompanying it audible.'
32. 17 U.S.C. Sect. 301.
33. 17 U.S.C. Sect. 106(4).
34. California Civil Code Sect. 986.

initial sale by the artist are exempt so long as *all* intervening sales are between dealers.[35] Other exemptions apply as well. The statute does have one broad application: it applies to all sellers who are California citizens no matter where the sale takes place and to all sales in California regardless of the seller's citizenship.[36]

The other kinds of royalties an artist gets are derived from her licensing or transferring copyrights. Generally, artists will either transfer or license a copyright for a fixed fee or for percentage royalties, or both. The more extensive the grant, the higher the payment. As mentioned below (*see* p. 324), U.S. copyrights are divisible, so the artist can either transfer the entire copyright or a part thereof or license some or all the constituent rights.

5. *Right to Exhibit a Work even if It Is Owned by a Private Person and whether or not It Is Held in a Private or Public Place*

Without a contractual promise, once the artist sells the work, she cannot demand its return for exhibition purposes. Moreover, as indicated above, once the artist sells the physical art object, even if she remains the copyright owner – which is usually the case – she cannot prevent the buyer from reselling or publicly displaying the work because of the exceptions at Sect. 109 of the Copyright Act.

Sect. 202 of the Copyright Act says that there is a distinction between the physical art object and the copyright in the work, which creates a 'standoff' between the artist as copyright owner and the purchaser as owner of the physical art object.[37] The artist-copyright owner has no right of access to the art object without a contract, so that, even though the artist has the exclusive reproduction rights, she may never be able to exercise them if the owner of the art object won't permit access. Similarly, the owner of the physical art object may not reproduce the work without the consent of the artist-copyright owner.

6. *Right to Withdraw an Authorization Given by the Artist to Reproduce, Disclose or Perform a Work*

It is possible to imagine a U.S. case yielding the same result as the *Anatole France* case,[38] but the artist licensing rights to a work usually cannot revoke

35. *Ibid.* at subdivisions (b), (c).
36. *Ibid.* at subdivision (a).
37. 17 U.S.C. Sect. 202. This means, for example, that sale or transfer of the physical art object does not cause a transfer or sale of the copyright, and vice versa.
38. *Anatole France c. Lemerre*, [1911] Pataille 1912.1.98. (famous author able to withdraw historical work after publisher delayed publication for approximately 25 years, by which time much of the book became outdated).

the grant if given under contract. As a 'moral right' the withdrawal right is not recognized under U.S. law. However, unfair competition law or crediting rights under moral rights statutes may be used to achieve withdrawal. For example, if circumstances changed so that use of the work would injure the artist's reputation, perhaps the artist can remove his credits from the work as per a moral rights statute. However, the artist would typically have to show a 'just and valid reason'. In an entertainment industry case a recording artist used unfair competition law to prevent use of older works packaged with more recent photographs of the artist which gave the false impression that these older works were his current creations.[39]

There is at least one other possibility. Under contract law a party may rescind (i.e., cancel) a contract because it was secured by fraud or duress or because of a lack or failure of consideration. For example, if a licensee fails to publish an artist's work within agreed-upon time limits, the artist might be able to rescind the agreement based on failure of consideration. Of course, the rescinding party must give prompt notice of rescission upon discovering the facts entitling him to rescind and must offer to restore to the other party all things of value received in exchange for similar restitution by the other party, thus putting the parties in the same position as before the contract. In essence, this achieves the same result as the withdrawal right which may be exercised only if the artist reimburses the other party.[40]

7. *Right to Destroy a Work*

As already indicated, under some but not all moral rights statutes, the artist can prevent others from destroying a work.[41] The artist himself has no right to destroy a work he created but sold to someone else. Perhaps he can prevent a public display if the work has been mutilated or altered, e.g., under the New York moral rights legislation and its progeny,[42] or he can disclaim credit for the work, as per the moral rights statutes following both the California and New York models.[43] Nonetheless, the physical art object no longer belongs to the artist, and he cannot destroy it.

8. *Right to Oppose the Exhibition of a Work whether or not It Has Been Exhibited Previously*

Again, there are no specific laws allowing the artist to oppose exhibition of a work, although the New York moral rights statute and its successors allow

39. *CBS, Inc. v. Gusto Records, Inc.*, 403 F.Supp. 447 (M.D. Tenn. 1974) (suit by vocalist Charlie Rich under Sect. 43(a) of the Lanham Trademark Act. 15 U.S.C. Sect. 1125(a)).
40. E.g., under the French law, Law No. 57–298 on Literary and Artistic Property Art. 32.
41. California, Pennsylvania, Massachusetts, and New Mexico statutes, *supra* n. 2.
42. The New York statute, as followed by the Rhode Island, Louisiana, New Jersey, and Maine statutes, *supra* n. 2.
43. *See* statutes, *supra* n. 2.

the artist to prevent the public exhibition of a mutilated or altered work.[44] If the artist remains both copyright owner and owner of the art object, then he can use his copyright to prevent public exhibition since public exhibition without his consent would be copyright infringement.[45] The artist can also insist upon not being credited with the exhibited work if he can show a 'just and valid reason', for example under moral rights statutes following the California and New York models.[46]

9. Right to Object to any Substantial Alteration or Relocation of a Work which Threatens its Integrity

Here, the artist must principally rely upon the moral rights laws modeled after the California statutes. These laws allow the artist to prevent alteration or mutilation of works.[47] However, there are no statutes which specifically govern *relocation* of a work. For instance, artist Richard Serra could not block relocation of his massive outdoor work *Tilted Arc*, originally installed in a New York City plaza. If the work is a landscape or environmental work whose relocation would actually destroy it because it is inextricably part of the landscape, then arguably moral rights statutes should apply. Relocation, in effect, may constitute a prohibited 'alteration' under the kind of statute enacted in California. Also, relocation may cause a public display of an altered work, to which the artist may object under the New York kind of moral rights law.

10. Right to Be Recognized as the Creator of a Work

Without contract rights the artist must either rely upon moral rights laws modeled after the California and New York statutes which give explicit rights to credit, or else unfair competition laws which recognize the tort of 'reverse passing off'. Earlier U.S. law, in the absence of moral rights legislation, never recognized the right to credit unless preserved by contract, or unless the court could find an 'implied' covenant to give credit.[48] For example, an implied covenant to give credit can be found within the context of publishing a book even though crediting might never be mentioned in the

---

44. *See* New York, Maine, Rhode Island, Louisiana, and New Jersey statutes, *supra* n. 2.
45. *See Gilliam v. American Broadcasting Co.*, 538 F.2d 14 (2d Cir. 1976) (the Monty Python case wherein broadcast of mutilated version of film was held outside of copyright licence and thus a copyright infringement).
46. *See* statutes, *supra* n. 2.
47. *See* California, Pennsylvania, Massachusetts and New Mexico statutes, *supra* n. 2.
48. *See Vargas v. Esquire*, 164 F.2d 522 (7th Cir. 1947), cert. denied, 335 U.S. 813 (1948); *Lake v. Universal Pictures Co.*, 95 F.Supp. 768 (S.D. Cal. 1950); *Clemens [Mark Twain] v. Press Publishing Co.*, 122 N.Y.S. 206 (Sup.Ct. 1910); *Ellis v. Hurst*, 121 N.Y.S. 438 (Sup.Ct. 1910).

publishing agreement.[49] After all, every writer expects to have her name on the book cover even though credits may not be mentioned in the publishing agreement. The covenant is 'implied' because it arises from the circumstances of the transaction rather than from an explicit reference.

11. Other Rights Accruing to an Artist

Other rights which accrue to artists are derived from miscellaneous state laws. For example, California and a few other states have laws which regulate consignment sales of goods, including works of art, which require the consignee (i.e., the art dealer) to inform the consignor (i.e., the artist) about the name and address of the buyer and sales price for each work sold by the consignee.[50] This kind of law enables the artist to trace where his works have gone for purposes of enforcing copyrights, resale royalty rights, and other miscellaneous rights.

Many states have enacted artist-dealer relations laws governing consignment sales by dealers.[51] Included within these states are the principle art markets, New York and California.[52] Typically, these statutes make the dealer strictly liable for loss of or damage to consigned works; require dealers to pay artists' shares of sales proceeds promptly; ensure that artists' works cannot be used to satisfy claims of dealers' creditors; and otherwise impose standards of care regarding sales proceeds and works of art. A few benefits from some of these statutes are as follows. If a work is lost, damaged, or destroyed for any reason, even for reasons beyond the dealer's control, the dealer is liable even if not negligent and often responsible to the artist for the fair market value of the work rather than merely wholesale price. When a dealer declares bankruptcy, the bankruptcy court cannot consider the artist's consigned work as a part of the bankruptcy estate. The artist must often be paid his share of the sales proceeds before the dealer is paid. Consigned works and sales proceeds are often considered trust property, imposing increased obligations on the dealer who is considered a 'trustee'. Unfortunately, wherever these statutes are not in effect, artists consigning their works are vulnerable to losing them or losing sales proceeds.

49. *See*, e.g., *Granz v. Harris*, 198 F.2d 585 (2d Cir. 1952).
50. *See*, e.g., California Penal Code Sect. 536a.
51. Ariz.Rev.Stat.Ann. Sects. 44–1771 to 44–1778; Ark.Stat.Ann. Sects. 68–1806 to 68–1811; Cal. Civ. Code Sects. 1738 & 1738.5 to 1738.9; Colo.Rev.Stat. Sects. 6–15–101 to 6–15–104; Conn.Gen.Stat.Ann. Sects. 42–116k to 42–116m; Md.Com.Law Code Ann. Sects. 11–8A–01 to 11–8A–04; Mass.Ann.Laws ch. 104A, Sects. 1 to 6; Mich.Com.Laws Ann. Sects. 442–311 to 442–315; Minn.Stat.Ann. Sects. 324.01 to 324.10; Mo.Rev.Stat. Sects. 407.900 to 407.910; Mont.Code Ann. tit. 22, Sects. 2.501 to 2–505; N.M.Stat.Ann. Sects. 56–11–1 to 56–11–13; N.Y.Arts & Cultural Affairs Law art. 12; N.C.Gen.Stat. Sects. 25–C–1 to 25–C–5; Ohio Rev.Code Ann. Sects. 1339–71 to 1339.78; Or.Rev.Stat. Sects. 359.200 to 359.240; Tenn.Code Ann. Sects. 47–25–1001 to 47–25–1007; Tex.Occ.& Bus.Code Ann. art. 9018; Wash.Rev.Code Ann. Sects. 18.110.010 to 18.110.905; and Wis.Stat.Ann. Sects. 129.01 to 129.08.
52. *See* New York and California statutes, *supra* n. 51.

III. ASSIGNMENT OF RIGHTS TO HEIRS

The artist's copyright can be transferred to any person at any time, including the heirs, either before or after death.[53] But all transfers must be in writing as per Sect. 204 of the Copyright Act.[54] Because copyrights under U.S. law are divisible, the artist can transfer all or only parts of the copyright.[55] For instance, the artist could assign reproduction and distribution rights while withholding adaptation and display rights. If the artist dies without a will, the copyright automatically goes to the heirs under the laws of intestate succession.[56] With a will, the copyright goes to those persons who explicitly inherit it under the will or sometimes slips into the residue of the estate and goes to the residuary beneficiary.

In the absence of a will, moral rights under some state statutes automatically go to the artist's heirs[57] who may typically enforce the rights for a period of fifty years after the artist's death.[58] There is no indication under U.S. law that artists' moral rights are freely assignable. In other words, these rights are not said to be *property* rights but rather *personal* rights of the artist, and there is no indication that the artist can assign these rights while alive.[59] However, the artist can bequeath moral rights by will to either natural heirs or others.[60]

On the other hand, publicity rights, including the artist's rights to control the commercial use of his name, likeness, voice, signature or photograph, especially in connection with the sale of artworks, are usually considered transferrable *property* rights.[61] For example, under the California statute allowing these rights to be exercised after the celebrity's death, all rights can

53. 17 U.S.C. Sect. 201(d).
54. 17 U.S.C. Sect. 204.
55. 17 U.S.C. Sect. 101 defines 'transfer' as follows:
'A "transfer of copyright ownership" is an assignment, mortgage, exclusive licence, or any other conveyance, alienation, or hypothecation of a copyright or of any of the exclusive rights comprised in a copyright, whether or not it is limited in time or place of effect, but not including a non-exclusive licence.'
56. 17 U.S.C. Sect. 201(d)(1). The laws of intestate succession are set forth in the probate codes of the states and prescribe how property is passed down to the heirs in the absence of a will.
57. *See* California, Massachusetts, Pennsylvania, and New Mexico statutes, *supra* n. 2.
58. *See*, e.g., California Civil Code Sect. 987(g)(1); Massachusetts General Laws Annotated, ch. 231, Sect. 85S(g).
59. The statutes refer to 'heir', 'legatee', or 'personal representative' (e.g., executor), not to 'transferee'. *See*, e.g., California Civil Code Sect. 987(g); Massachusetts General Laws Annotated, ch. 231, Sect. 85S(g). However, the Massachusetts statute allows an artist to delegate enforcement of the rights to 'any bona fide union or other artists' organization'. *Ibid.* at subdivision (e).
60. *See*. e.g., *ibid.*
61. *See*, e.g., *Price v. Hal Roach Studios*, 400 F.Supp. 836, 844 (SDNY 1975) (the Laurel and Hardy case); *Cepeda v. Swift & Co.*, 291 F.Supp. 242 (E.D. Mo. 1968), affd., 415 F.2d 1205, 1206 (8th Cir. 1969); *Haelan Laboratories v. Topps Chewing Gum. Inc.*, 202 F.2d 866, 868 (2d Cir.), cert. denied U.S. 816 (1953).

be assigned to any person, whether or not an heir of the artist.[62] Assignment can take place at any time, before or after death. Under the California statute, if the rights are not assigned *inter vivos* or by will, they pass to the heirs under specified rules as to which heirs own and in which percentages.[63] The heirs must register their rights with the Secretary of State in order to enforce these rights fully.[64]

Under the California statute, the right to collect resale royalties survives the death of the artist for a period of twenty years.[65] While the artist is alive, the statute explicitly says that the artist may not transfer or waive the rights.[66] However, by will the artist can assign the right to resale royalties to any person, including a natural heir.

IV. CONCLUSION

American law has rarely singled out artists for special treatment. The prevailing attitude has been that if artists are to be protected, it is only for the general welfare. This attitude is best exemplified by the Constitutional clause providing authority to enact patent and copyright legislation, which reads:

> 'To promote the Progress of Science and useful Arts, by securing for limited Times To Authors and Inventors the exclusive Right to their respective Writings and Discoveries'.[67]

Promoting the arts and sciences was important, not necessarily the interests of inventors and authors.

The very first expression of the *droit moral* in the United States, the California statute which was followed elsewhere,[68] also is concerned with the public interest as well as artists' rights. As the statute says:

> 'The Legislature hereby finds and declares that the physical alteration or destruction of fine art, which is an expression of the artist's personality, is detrimental to the artist's reputation, and artists therefore have an interest in protecting their works of fine art against such alteration or destruction; and that there is also a public interest in preserving the integrity of cultural and artistic creations'.[69]

62. California Civil Code Sect. 990(b).
63. California Civil Code Sect. 990(d).
64. California Civil Code Sect. 990(f).
65. California Civil Code Sect. 986(a)(7).
66. *Ibid.* at subdivision (a). Note that the artist can assign the right to 'collect' the royalties, e.g., to a royalty collection agency.
67. U.S. Constitution Art. I. n. 8, cl. 8.
68. *See* statutes, *supra* n.15.
69. California Civil Code Sect. 987(a).

To preserve the integrity of cultural and artistic creations in the public interest, the California statutes are confined to protecting works of fine art of 'recognized quality' and 'substantial public interest'.[70]

Although the New York moral rights statutes[71] which came after the California legislation are aimed at protecting the artist's reputation, they represent even weaker protection since they do not directly forbid physical alteration, mutilation, or destruction of the artist's works.

Additionally, it took decades for the United States to ratify the Berne Convention, much of the opposition to which was caused by the Art, 6*bis* moral rights. Strong user groups in the publishing and entertainment industries had always feared moral rights laws, and the same kind of political force in the art trade (e.g., collectors, museums and dealers) contributed to the weakened form of moral rights legislation in New York.[72] In fact, the Berne Convention was ratified without any domestic federal legislation in place and with only the supposition that existing unfair competition, defamation, and privacy laws gave protection somewhat equivalent to moral rights under Art. 6*bis*.[73]

The California resale royalty statute,[74] the first expression of the *droit de suite*, was a test of a new attitude to artists in the form of a statute specifically designed to benefit artists and their families. However, not only did this statute meet with ferocious opposition resulting in amendments which seriously weakened it, but all attempts on the national scale to enact a similar statute failed, and no other state legislation followed the California lead. In addition, even California artists are reluctant to enforce their resale royalty rights due to extreme public resistance.

The public attitude is best reflected by enforcement of the *droit moral* under state statutes. This author's experience has been that, unless the artist can show that the work is of substantial public interest, judges and juries are reluctant to disregard the old attitude that purchasers can treat their property as they wish.

In some ways the American attitude is quite a healthy one. Artists are not elevated above other citizens nor given special treatment. The artist in America does not walk on hallowed ground nor breathe a fine ether; she and her products are not treated much differently than the ordinary craftsman and his products, though the law now recognizes the value of the artist's reputation and how reputation is affected by mutilated art. However, the problem is that limited protection for artists and their works not only constrains artists but also leaves doubts as to what America will do to protect its cultural heritage, or better yet, to create a cultural heritage for future generations.

---

70. California Civil Code Sects. 987(b)(2), 989(b)(1).
71. N.Y. Arts & Cultural Affairs Law Sects. 11.01, 14.03.
72. In this light it is interesting to observe that the premier art cases have been mostly in New York, but the groundbreaking legislation started in California, perhaps explained by the strength of user groups in New York (dealers, collectors, and museums).
73. *See supra* n. 4.
74. California Civil Code Sect. 986.

Papers on Specific Aspects

Artistes, Héritiers, Musées

Jean-Marc Gutton*

I. INTRODUCTION

Le sujet est vaste, divers et délicat:

Vaste, car matière à de nombreuses réflexions qui pour nombre d'entre elles, en regard du temps qui nous est imparti, ne seront qu'effleurées.
Divers en regard des usages nationaux ou des règles de droit.
Délicat, car sensible en de nombreux points. Si certaines difficultés ne sont pas esquivées, nous avons toutefois un devoir de réserve. Sur certains points donc, nous ferons plus entendre le son de la flûte que celui du tambour.

Notre approche sera pragmatique et c'est notre expérience pratique qui nous guidera, telle que vécue à la Société des Auteurs dans les Arts Graphiques et Plastiques (ADAGP) présentement la plus représentative des artistes plasticiens et dont la mission est tout autant internationale que nationale.
Le décor est large au regard de la planète:

- Des dizaines de milliers d'artistes et héritiers.
- Plus de 10.000 musées ou collections publiques et privées dont des milliers en Europe et 4.600 aux USA.
- Des centaines de millions de visiteurs annuels.
- Des enjeux économiques énormes qui pèsent lourdement sur chacune des parties concernées.[1]

Cette approche se développera, par thème plus que par acteur.

II. LES ARTS PLASTIQUES, UN DOMAINE SPÉCIFIQUE

1. Premier constat:

- Pour qu'il y ait des oeuvres, il faut des artistes.

---

* Directeur général, Société des auteurs dans les arts graphiques et plastiques.
1. Cf. article de P. SCHEIDER, *L'Express*, 8 juin 1990.

– Pour que les oeuvres soient connues, il faut qu'elles soient montrées.
– Pour que les oeuvres soient montrées, il faut des instances d'accueil.

La première et la plus naturelle: la galerie, et secondairement des structures professionnelles diverses. La plus prestigieuse: le musée, c'est là un lieu de consécration qui assure à l'oeuvre sa notoriété et son rayonnement (lorsqu'elle est exposée, nous y reviendrons). Il est donc naturel de noter d'emblée qu'une relation logique et privilégiée s'impose: celle de l'artiste ou héritier et du musée.

2. *Second constat: une destinée spécifique de l'oeuvre plastique*

Nous l'avons dit et écrit: l'exploitation des oeuvres dans les arts plastiques s'effectue par d'autres moyens que dans les autres domaines de l'esprit pour lesquels s'appliquent en plénitude les droits patrimoniaux de l'auteur prévus par nos lois françaises. A la différence des oeuvres littéraire ou musicale, leurs formes d'exploitation restent, quant à elles, toujours accessoires. La vraie carrière de l'oeuvre ne se fait pas en effet, sous les seules formes d'exploitation prévues par le droit d'auteur dans sa dimension patrimoniale (droit de reproduction, droit de représentation, droit de suite...), qui viennent généralement avec le renom et la notoriété de l'artiste. Notre réflexion doit donc tenir compte, en premier lieu, des impératifs de carrière de l'artiste et, lorsqu'il est décédé, de la mémoire de son oeuvre.

De cette situation il découle que, si, pour la musique, le théâtre..., les droits patrimoniaux passent par la diffusion, la représentation de l'oeuvre, pour les arts plastiques, ces droits passent par le rayonnement donné à l'oeuvre, rayonnement qui en sous-tend largement la cote. Ces éléments sont donc plus importants que les dispositions prévues par la loi dans son acception générale, mais ne doivent pas occulter les droits des artistes ou héritiers.

La galerie nous l'avons dit et le musée, d'évidence, contribuent à ce rayonnement. Le nouveau visage qu'offre l'instance muséale devrait confirmer cette dimension.

III. LE FACE A FACE ARTISTE-HERITIERS-MUSEES

Il apparaît dans une première approche que ce face à face, que la nature des choses voudrait intime et privilégié, pose quelques questions de fond.

Tout rêve d'artiste est, peut-on dire, de voir son oeuvre présente, le plus tôt possible dans un ou des musées, montrée dans cette enceinte, *a fortiori* dans les plus prestigieuses.

Tout *curriculum vitae* et *a fortiori* biographie d'artiste, toute étude sur l'oeuvre signalent, en priorité, les expositions réalisées, la présence d'oeuvres dans telle ou telle instance muséographique, preuve notable de la reconnaissance de son talent. En outre, nul mieux que l'artiste lui-même n'est susceptible d'apprécier quelle instance muséographique est la plus à même de faire valoir l'intérêt supérieur de son oeuvre et d'en assurer le rayonnement.

L'artiste donc, lié à ceux qui assurent ce rayonnement, est le plus souvent prêt, dans cette perspective, à des actions bénéfiques en regard du musée: dons et legs sont les plus manifestes et les plus nombreux. Je pense à la donation Estève (Musée de Bourges) qui émeut par sa qualité et son cadre d'accueil.

Cet enrichissement des collections des musées leur évite souvent une politique d'achat coûteuse ou permet du moins à leurs commissions d'achat d'orienter ses choix pour combler les lacunes de leurs collections, et leur permet aussi d'obtenir à bon compte des 'oeuvres de jeunesse' bien souvent dispersées ou inaccessibles par la suite.

1. Première question: le destin de ces dons. Caves ou cimaises? Combien de dons non exposés?

Force est de souligner une juste inquiétude de l'artiste et le fait que, vraisemblablement, plus d'oeuvres seraient données ou léguées s'ils étaient certains que des structures existaient pour leur accueil et leur présentation, sinon permanente, du moins par intermittence. De même, de nombreux artistes sont préoccupés par la gestion *post mortem* de leur oeuvre, de leurs droits et soucieux des problèmes multiples que cela pose. D'autres artistes, insouciants du formel, peuvent n'avoir pris aucune disposition; c'est la source de bien des contestations ou revendications d'ayant droit proches ou lointains, ce, en termes intellectuel ou matériel que le phénomène art-argent ne peut qu'aviver.

2. Seconde question: dévolution de leur droit moral. Quelles personnes? Quels organismes? Qui investir?

Les successeurs légaux, les héritiers naturels, pas toujours spécialistes de l'oeuvre ou 'X' qui, en vertu d'une présomption de confiance, apparaît digne d'assurer cette mission délicate et souvent désintéressée.

3. Trosième question: dévolution de leur droit patrimonial.

Qui investir également, comment organiser la gestion de l'oeuvre au profit de l'essentiel: sa pérennité et son rayonnement.

Force est de constater que la machine muséale est lourde et que les musées n'apparaîssent pas outillés pour rendre ces services spécifiques que certains peuvent en attendre. Il y a là un manque patent.

En outre, le musée ne pouvant être mobilisable pour toutes sortes d'oeuvres, on doit admettre qu'il y a là un problème. Le musée ne peut tout engranger: dons, legs auxquels s'ajoutent des donations diverses (collectionneurs... cf. Donation D. Cordier de plus de 500 pièces...) les dations ... Sa lutte contre l'amnésie est quasi impossible. Ainsi, par exemple la présentation complète des collections du Centre Georges Pompidou par rotation de 4 mois prendrait 6 ans durant lesquels aucune autre exposition ne serait possible.

Aussi, si de telles structures d'accueil existaient ou, pour le moins, si des structures de conseil existaient:

- peut-être serait atténué ce qu'un journaliste dénonça récemment comme les abus provoqués par 'le règne des héritiers' ou les excès de certains en regard des 'chers disparus';
- peut-être serait préservée une 'stabilité' de l'oeuvre et évités certains éclatements nuisibles par partage, vente hâtive....
- peut-être serait plus étroitement maintenue une parenté nécessaire.

Si des abus existent et vous connaissez tous la plupart d'entre eux, on doit dire que divers exemples ont été corrigés par le temps, dans les faits ou par les tribunaux (surtout en matière d'authentification ou d'identification d'oeuvres). La grande majorité des héritiers et légataires ont une action bénéfique et exemplaire en regard de la mémoire de l'oeuvre: la réalisation de certains catalogues raisonnés en témoigne.

La question est de savoir si le musée pourrait inventer des structures paramuséales d'accueil qui soient appropriées et apportent, le cas échéant, la rigueur intellectuelle de ses conservateurs.

Pour référence nous citerons trois exemples:

a. Wassily Kandinsky: une expérience couronnée de succès. Legs de Nina Kandinsky au Musée National d'Art Moderne, avec la création d'une Association parallèle à cet établissement public, intimement liée à celui-ci avec pour mission le respect de l'oeuvre et le rayonnement de l'oeuvre.

Cette Association est membre de l'ADAGP qui en gère les droits patrimoniaux. Tout se passe bien. Les droits sont respectés; pour le droit moral, nous disposons de spécialistes à l'Association Kandinsky, et pour le droit patrimonial, nous faisons valoir les droits en tous lieux sans difficulté et dans le plein souci d'être bénéfiques à l'oeuvre puisqu'ils contribuent à la mission de l'Association.

D'autres legs, aux Musées Nationaux, à l'Association Paris Musées donnent tout autant satisfaction, mais ils restent des exceptions.

b. Hans Hartung constitue une autre expérience. Une Fondation a été créée avec notamment pour mission de susciter l'intérêt des musées et d'organiser diverses manifestations autour de l'oeuvre. Nous sommes en mesure de dire que, s'il y avait eu une instance d'accueil paramuséale susceptible de faire ce travail, il y aurait eu legs à cette structure et non création d'une Fondation.

c. Une succession célèbre et dont la presse a souvent parlé, mais dont nous tairons le nom nous a demandé de lui recommander un musée susceptible de constituer une instance d'accueil à même d'assurer en tous points la mémoire de l'oeuvre, le tout accompagné d'une donation, dévolution des droits... Que conseiller? Où aller? Nous nous interrogeons.

Bien d'autres exemples pourraient être cités. Nous profitons de ce colloque pour dire qu'il nous apparaît important, dans le cadre international dans lequel se situe notre réflexion, de penser à la création d'instances para-muséales, associées aux musées, à l'instar de l'exemple Kandinsky et qui permettraient aux oeuvres de ne pas tomber en jachère ou sous la responsabilité de personnes non préparées à cette mission, et assureraient le rôle de respect des intérêts de l'oeuvre qu'assurent par ailleurs, avec des bonheurs divers, certaines Fondations. Citons la Fondation Jean Dubuffet, bel exemple de réussite, mais aussi de prévoyance, car programmée par le Maître de son vivant.

IV. LE MUSEE

Les remarques précitées nous ont conduit au musée. Comment nous apparaît-il? On observe tout à la fois une grande diversité et une même finalité.

Diversité:
- renom et hiérarchie: il y a en tous pays une aristocratie des musées;
- statut ou type d'établissement: publics ou privés, semi-publics...;
- riches pour quelques uns, pauvres dans leur immense majorité; les variables sont si nombreuses.

Nous citerons un extrait d'un article de Janine Warnod:[2]

> 'Musées: tout le monde veut le sien!
> Les musées se multiplient en France: 200 chantiers sont ouverts, 71 constructions, 37 rénovations d'importance, une centaine de projets.
>
> 'Pourquoi une telle boulimie de nouveaux musées alors que la France en possède déjà plus de mille?
>
> 'Pendant longtemps, parents pauvres des villes, refuges pour conservateurs enfermés dans leurs études, dépôts pour oeuvres souvent ignorées, les musées ont été un luxe; ils sont à présent des outils culturo-économico-socio-politiques de première nécessité.
>
> 'L'Etat, les élus, les associations, les collectionneurs, les donateurs réclament des musées. Les politiciens y trouvent un faire-valoir; les héritiers d'artistes un lieu prestigieux pour la mémoire de leur parent; les touristes, qui rapportent 7 à 8% du revenu national brut, des loisirs éducatifs. Tous voudraient être prêts en 1992 pour recueillir les retombées de la création de l'Europe.

2. *Le Figaro*, 26/27 mai 1990 sur 'L'Art Moderne'.

> 'Cet engouement provoque l'afflux d'une population en quête de culture à bon marché. Les musées qui, comme les restaurants, se voient attribuer des "étoiles" dans les guides, accueillent selon les lieux des centaines de milliers de visiteurs par an.
>
> 'La demande de plus en plus pressante de tous les publics motive la construction, l'extension ou la rénovation des musées dont la vocation a changé. Aux salles d'exposition se greffent les services annexes: accueil, ventes, ateliers pédagogiques, auditorium, cafétéria, garderies d'enfants qui occupent de nouveaux espaces. Bref, les musées s' animent.'

Nous constatons:

i une prolifération des musées n'offrant pas tous un degré de compétence ou de préparation suffisants;

ii que les musées des beaux arts et tout spécialement d'art contemporain attirent de plus en plus sur eux l'attention du public, des médias, des autorités culturelles, des entreprises . . .;

iii que l'on assiste enfin à une révolution de ces instances, à un éclatement de l'espace muséal, à des situations de rupture pas toujours maîtrisées.

Le musée devient, ou cherche à devenir:

- Une entreprise culturelle.
- Un rouage essentiel de l'industrie touristique.[3]
- Un pivot de la vie culturelle des cités, voire, pour les plus célèbres, un pivot de la vie culturelle du pays dont ils relèvent au travers, notamment, de leurs grandes manifestations et de leurs échanges à un niveau international: on a parlé d'Europe des musées, cette dimension est mondiale: nombre de manifestations rétrospectives le prouve.
- Un partenaire des grandes entreprises au travers de l'émergence, récente mais forte, des phénomènes de mécénat et sponsoring qui traduisent ce que l'on appelle dès lors la fonction sociale de l'art, sa dimension d'investissement productif pour l'entreprise: là c'est Philip Morris pour Picasso – Braque au Moma, ailleurs des banques, des compagnies aériennes, des entreprises alimentaires . . . Le phénomène est mondial, le tissu des entreprises concernées très ouvert; USA, Japon ont donné l'exemple.

Le mécénat 'Arts Plastiques' en France vient, avec 27% en seconde position en termes d'investissement après la musique et la danse (34%) – Statistiques du Ministère de la Culture de 1988. L'initiative culturelle n'est plus synonyme de gratuité et, comme le souligne A. D. Perrin, dans son rapport sur le Mécénat: 'L'Art d'apparaître désintéressé présente un intérêt . . . Le Mécénat n'est pas charité . . .'.

Ainsi, s'épanouit ce concept de 'Musée Global' tel que défini au dernier Salon International des Musées et Expositions (SIME) à Paris.

---

3. Cf. *Muséart*, nouveau magazine d'invitation au voyage 'Musées'.

Ce concept structure un ensemble de composantes des plus traditionnelles (conservation c.a.d. 'protection' et présentation de leurs collections), et aux plus dynamiques, comme instrument de culture vivante (lieu d'exposition, de rencontre, de communication, de recherche et réflexion, lieu d'édition ouvert aux formes d'exploitation multiples que permettent les nouvelles technologies... etc.)

Révolution donc, mais cette sortie du ghetto pose une multiplicité de problèmes, offre bien des obstacles à franchir: en termes d'organisation, en termes humains, techniques, financiers et autres... mais là n'est pas notre propos.

Ces perspectives confèrent au musée, non seulement des contraintes mais des devoirs en regard des droits des artistes et ayant droit. Elles posent aussi la question des droits respectifs de chacun.

V. DROITS RESPECTIFS

1. Premier point

Le musée propriétaire de l'oeuvre, peut-il l'exposer librement? Les lois restent le plus souvent muettes.

On observe en l'état actuel du droit positif français et des décisions jurisprudentielles nationales et internationales que le musée propriétaire de l'oeuvre est libre de l'exposer comme il veut 'sous réserve qu'il ne porte pas atteinte au respect de l'oeuvre'.

C'est dans le même sens que Monsieur Desurmont conclut sa thèse *De l'existence d'un droit d'exposition publique indépendant du droit de propriété corporelle*. Le droit d'exposer publiquement une oeuvre d'art reste un attribut du droit de propriété corporelle et appartient au propriétaire de l'oeuvre.

2. Deuxième point

Les droits patrimoniaux. Ils seront abordés à 3 niveaux:

a. Premier niveau et en regard du droit commun français (Loi du 11 mars 1957) aux termes de l'art. 29, 'la propriété corporelle est indépendante de la propriété de l'objet matériel. Les droits patrimoniaux subsistent en la personne de l'auteur ou de ses ayant droit.'

L'art. 40 stipule en outre 'toute représentation ou reproduction intégrale ou partielle faite sans le consentement de l'auteur ou de ses ayant-cause est illicite'. En conséquence, le musée, non investi ou titulaire de ces droits, doit respecter les droits patrimoniaux de l'auteur ou de ses ayant droit.

b. Deuxième niveau: soucieuse d'équilibre, la législation française a prévu un moyen de corriger les abus de droit. L'art. 20 de la Loi de 1957 (celle de

1985 en a même renforcé les termes) déclare: 'En cas d'abus notoire dans l'usage ou le non usage du droit de divulgation ou des droits d'exploitation de la part des représentants de l'auteur décédé, le Tribunal Civil peut ordonner toute mesure appropriée', etc. Cette disposition est claire. Dans l'exercice de sa mission, l'ADAGP en rappelle régulièrement l'existence à certains de ses membres et les alerte sur les conséquences d' 'abus de comportement'. Son effet est dissuasif, là où il doit l'être, en amont, avant que la relation ne s'altère.

c. Troisième niveau: en regard du droit Conventionnel, force est de constater la diversité des lois nationales. Malgré l'existence de conventions internationales, la situation n'est pas satisfaisante. Nous devons l'aborder avec une extrême prudence; quelle application pratique en connaissons-nous et de quelle décision ou jurisprudence disposons-nous?

Il est donc souhaitable et impératif qu'intervienne une harmonisation des législations sur le droit d'auteur, ce à la lumière des grandes conventions internationales, et en particulier, de la Convention de Berne, ratifiée par 83 pays. Les différents pays de la Communauté étant signataires de Berne, les dispositions de cette Convention s'appliquent à leurs relations. Celle-ci constitue la source d'une protection moderne et ses dispositions sont unanimement considérées comme devant constituer les fondements de tout agrément international notamment:

i. En matière de droit moral
Ce droit est exercé par les personnes ou institutions auxquelles la législation nationale du pays où la protection est réclamée donne qualité. Deux attributs sont prévus: le droit au respect du nom et le droit au respect de l'oeuvre. Un attribut en est toujours absent: le droit de divulgation.

ii. En matière de droit patrimonial
Le principe consacré par la Convention est celui d'un droit exclusif de reproduction reconnu à l'artiste et ayant droit. Une limite est toutefois apportée: l'art. 9 al. 2, réserve aux législations des pays de l'Union la faculté de permettre la reproduction des dites oeuvres dans certains cas spéciaux pourvu qu'une telle exploitation ne porte pas atteinte à l'exploitation normale de l'oeuvre, ni ne cause un préjudice aux intérêts légitimes de l'auteur. A la souplesse de formulation de l'art. 9 al. 2 répondent de multiples normes et variantes des législations nationales et que nous n'énumèrerons pas.

Sans prolonger cette approche, il nous apparaît indispensable que cette harmonisation intervienne en priorité entre pays présentant un degré à peu près égal de développement économique, culturel, social:

- l'accord de Bangui par l'Organisation Africaine en constitue un exemple;
- la CEE, par le jeu d'harmonisation peut répondre à cette attente, souhaitons le au meilleur niveau, celui conjugué du respect des intérêts et droits de tous;
- les efforts d'harmonisation des Pays Scandinaves vont dans ce sens.

Il apparaît tout autant nécessaire que cette harmonisation aligne des conceptions nationales sur le droit Conventionnel pour ce qui concerne entre autres:

- les critères généraux de protection (absence de formalités, droit de propriété incorporelle du créateur etc.);
- la durée de protection (URSS: 25 ans, Espagne: 60, RFA: 70, France: singularisation par domaine et années de guerre);
- la limitation du droit d'auteur (citations et emprunts, libre reproduction, notions de 'fair use', 'fair dealing'). Celle-ci prévoit des exemptions de droits dans certains cas (catalogues d'exposition ou de vente en RFA, Autriche, Suisse, Tchécoslovaquie...); la question est importante car génératrice d'abus:
  là, c'est un musée britannique célèbre qui, sous couvert d'expositions, donne des autorisations d'exploitation à une compagnie pétrolière pour des concours...;
  là, c'est un musée nord-américain qui, sous couvert d'exposition, donne licence à une agence de commercialiser des ektachromes, etc...;
  là, c'est un musée italien qui 'blanchit' des faux en les reproduisant dans son catalogue d'expositions sans consultation du spécialiste de l'oeuvre ou des ayant droit qui, en l'espèce et conjointement, pouvaient apporter leur concours.

En conclusion, il est de l'intérêt de tous, et c'est là un intérêt commun à l'artiste, à l'héritier et au musée que les droits de propriété intellectuelle soient protégés et que les mécanismes de cette protection soient prévus. Une telle unification au moins sur les grands principes ne peut que contribuer au confort de la liaison *artiste-héritier-musée*.

VI. LA SOCIETE DE GESTION

Nous ne saurions enfin passer sous silence le rôle de la Société de Gestion qui, nous en sommes persuadés, contribue ou doit contribuer à l'épanouissement de cette relation naturelle *artiste-héritier-musée* et l'aider à fonctionner avec sérénité.

Le rôle national et international de ces sociétés présentes dans le monde entier et à but non lucratif est donc d'aider cette liaison étroite en se positionnant tout à la fois comme: un relais et lieu de dialogue unique et respectueux des intérêts des parties; un relais économique; et le garant contre tout trouble ou revendication abusive. Des avantages multiples pour tous aux plans psychologique, pratique, matériel et professionnel.

Si le cadre légal qui est le nôtre en France amène l'auteur à faire apport de ses droits à la société d'auteurs, la société ne saurait répondre à l'attente de ses membres, à la spécificité de leur activité:

- Sans laisser à l'auteur sa liberté et l'autonomie indispensables à l'épanouissement de son oeuvre.
- Sans avoir conscience que les plasticiens comme les auteurs dans les autres domaines ont des préoccupations morales d'abord, patrimoniales

ensuite et, pour certains, un désintéressement vis-à-vis de toute instance assurant le rayonnement de leur oeuvre.
- Sans situer le droit d'auteur de ses membres dans le respect de la carrière de l'oeuvre.

Ainsi la Société doit-elle faire valoir leur droit patrimonial après avoir interrogé l'artiste et là où il apparaît sans ambiguïté comme juste et équitable, là où il apparaît comme bénéfique et ne constituant pas un frein au rayonnement de l'oeuvre.

Elle ne saurait répondre à sa mission en traquant aveuglément les droits de reproduction ou en se manifestant de manière intempestive. Ainsi, pour nous, et répondant présentement à la volonté des plasticiens français, ces droits ne sauraient s'appliquer sans discernement à l'exposition des oeuvres qui, de façon privilégiée permet à l'artiste et à ses héritiers de faire connaître l'oeuvre, de la rendre accessible, d'en assurer le rayonnement, d'asseoir sa notoriété et sa mémoire (cf. notre *Etude Droit d'Exposition Mayer* 1990). Nous signalons toutefois que cette revendication a été prise en considération par le législateur et les prescripteurs dans les Pays Scandinaves et au Canada.

Toutefois, cette attention indispensable à la carrière de l'oeuvre ne saurait donner lieu à des interprétations simplistes. Ainsi, déclarer que reproduire une oeuvre est une publicité pour celle-ci, que l'artiste doit en être reconnaissant, qu'il doit renoncer à ses droits... en serait une. Toute communication d'une création, permettant au public de mieux connaître son auteur comporte une composante de promotion qui ne doit pas être considérée comme un 'don', un 'avantage' extérieur aux relations contractuelles faites à l'artiste par son partenaire mais, au contraire, comme un élément inhérent au contrat.

Si, à l'évidence, l'artiste a besoin du public, de sa reconnaissance et que priorité doit être donnée à cette reconnaissance, force est de constater que, de nos jours, ce public a tout autant besoin du créateur dont l'oeuvre l'émeut, le captive, élargit sa vision...

Les droits patrimoniaux de l'artiste plasticien, dans leur dimension – droit de reproduction, droit de représentation – doivent donc s'inscrire dans un juste équilibre entre les intérêts personnels et matériels de l'artiste, les intérêts des collectivités, des musées, dont nous avons souligné les mutations, et ceux du public...

C'est pour répondre à cet équilibre que des conventions adaptées ont été mises au point avec succès avec les instances muséographiques françaises: Musées de France, Musées Nationaux, Centre Georges Pompidou etc.

L'économie de ces conventions est simple et s'organise sur deux axes: reconnaissance de la mission privilégiée de ces instances en faveur de la création artistique et de sa diffusion, et reconnaissance de la mission de l'ADAGP de représenter et de défendre les intérêts matériels et moraux de ses membres.

En conséquence: l'instance muséographique s'engage à respecter les droits moraux et matériels de tous les auteurs dont elle utilise les oeuvres et à informer l'ADAGP de ses utilisations, et l'ADAGP s'engage à donner à l'instance toute facilité d'accès et d'utilisation des oeuvres de ses membres ce, à des conditions tout à fait préférentielles.

Après cinq années d'expérience, nous pouvons affirmer que ces conventions fonctionnent sainement, ont évité de nombreuses erreurs, sur des catalogues par exemple, et écarté bien des conflits.

Ces mécanismes conventionnels constituent, à l'usage, une solution saine à la relation *artiste-héritier-musée*, qui, nous l'avons vu à maintes reprises, et c'est notre voeu, doit, de manière indispensable, être étroite et privilégiée. En conclusion, information préalable (c'est là courtoisie et procédure aisée), respect de lois élémentaires, application de conventions saines... sont susceptibles, selon nous, de constituer les outils les plus à même de favoriser l'harmonie de la trilogie obligée: *artistes, héritiers, musées*.

Relations between Artists and their Heirs and Dealers, Galleries and Patrons

Richard Crewdson*

To prepare a legal contract between an artist and a gallery is a science. To administer that contract is an art. The dealer or gallery owner who specializes in contemporary art has to be not only a shrewd business man or woman. Great skill is also required in maintaining the well-being and the goodwill of the artist. Uncle; godfather; agony aunt; patroness; sponsor; all these epithets come to mind in trying to describe the relationship. Artists have their rights; but artists are not the best-equipped people in the world (with notable exceptions) to exercise these rights, certainly not those who are struggling to establish a reputation in the early stages of their career.

This is therefore rather a difficult subject to discuss in a purely legal context. It must also be seen against a practical background and it must be understood that whether willingly or not the dealer or gallery owner will often, if not usually, be effectively acting as the business agent for the artist. This can create conflicts of interest as indicated later in this paper.

Let us however assume that an artist and a gallery dealer decide to negotiate an agency agreement between themselves on more or less equal terms. Even then it is not enough for two strangers to meet and enter into a written contract at first sight. One of the essentials of any relationship between artist and dealer is one of trust, and this must first be established before negotiations can begin on any agreement. Assuming this has been achieved it will usually be the gallery which produces the first draft, probably following a standard form in regular use by the gallery. These agreements may vary quite substantially from dealer to dealer and jurisdiction to jurisdiction but there will be certain underlying essentials which one would expect any good agreement of this sort to deal with.

In the first place the gallery will, if possible, want a sole agency for a defined period of time. The artist may have difficulties with this, especially in the initial stages when he has been selling all over the place, and may have accepted many commissions or may wish to produce works for personal friends or relatives. The usual solution is to allow such arrangements to

* Partner, Field Fisher Waterhouse, London: Chairman, Cultural Property Committee International Bar Association (Section on General Practice).

continue in a strictly limited manner, but with the added sanction that the gallery will receive a reduced commission on all such sales even if they have nothing to do with the transaction.

The agreement will describe the territory in which exclusivity will apply. Unless the artist has many overseas connections this will usually be described as national and international.

There will then possibly be lengthy provisions about what the gallery will and will not do and what it will and will not pay for. These terms are generally the result of long and sometimes bitter experience, and galleries and dealers are usually reluctant to vary them. There will be references to promotion, advertising, exhibition and of course sale; sometimes also to publication which raises questions of copyright. The usual arrangement which accords with general legal principles is for the ownership of the copyright to remain with the artist, but the agreement with the gallery will include a licence for the gallery to publish, whether in a limited edition of reproductions (particularly in the case of signed prints each individually numbered and signed by the artist) or for the more general purpose of publication in books, catalogues or even postcards and greetings cards.

From the artist's point of view the most important clause in the agreement will be the one dealing with the sharing of profits. This must first deal with the expenses to be borne by the gallery and the agreement must make it clear whether these are to be a charge on the gross proceeds of sale after which the net profit is divided between the artist and the gallery, or whether the gallery is to meet these expenses out of its share of the profit. The basis on which the profit is shared will of course be affected by how these expenses are charged.

Some agreements deal in great detail with the method of pricing artworks; others stipulate that this is the sole prerogative of the gallery. This is naturally a matter of special concern for the artist. He or she will have an instinctive feeling as to whether the work of art is good, exceptional or merely indifferent which will influence the artist's opinion as to the value of the piece. The gallery will take a quite different view; for the gallery, pricing must depend on the reputation of the artist, the 'importance' of the work and the unwritten minimum level below which it may be uneconomic to sell the work. As the artist's reputation grows to an international dimension, the governing price level in the most lucrative market (usually the United States) will inhibit sales at lower prices elsewhere in the world. This can in some situations severely restrict the artist's sales globally, sometimes causing hardship; an example of the conflict of interest between artist and dealer referred to earlier.

In some countries the artist is not merely contracted to supply works of art. He also has to do the performing sea-lion act as well (I use the expression advisedly because no one has seen a performing sea-lion which is not enjoying the act as much as the audience). If personal appearances, talks, chat-shows and other forms of publicity help to sell paintings, they must be mutually beneficial and deserve ardent encouragement. It is only the fact that the artist contracts to perform to order which is perhaps slightly repugnant.

The longer a relationship continues between artist and gallery the closer this relationship becomes and the more intimately connected with the artist's portfolio and reputation the gallery will be. Bust-ups are however not uncommon. The 'artistic temperament' is not an imaginary concept, and many artists for good and bad reasons lose faith in the gallery or dealer with whom they have contracted. Even if they remain faithful and committed, it is to be expected that they will complain and grumble loud and often about the relationship to their nearest and dearest. Heirs are therefore often sensitive and full of suspicions and the gallery (which will usually have taken the precaution of inserting into the contract a provision which gives them rights in the event of the artist's death to continue as sole agents for a futher period of time, usually two, three or five years after the death) must expect to face criticism and a general lack of trust which may have been absent during the artist's lifetime. Once again the pacification and 're-education' of the artist's heirs is an art demanding the greatest skill and tact on the part of the gallery.

Here then is the profile of the dealer-artist relationship. It will be subject to many local variants, personal whims and fancies, and the balance of negotiating strength. But certain salient points remain and are common to most agreements.

Human relationships being what they are, things often go wrong. When they do, a written agreement may be a hindrance or a help. Sometimes the existence of such an agreement restricts the freedom of one party or another to take the case to court, either because it contains an arbitration clause or because of some other dispute procedure which has the effect of depressurizing the crisis, whatever it may be.

Artists on the whole are in any event reluctant litigants. It takes an awful lot of oil and canvas to pay the lawyers' fees. I have the impression therefore that the legislation of states that go to great lengths to protect the interests of artists achieve the very opposite effect – they actually drive artists away into other jurisdictions where the law of the jungle still applies.

This reluctance to litigate leaves the researcher with a great absence of case law on which to found any sort of generalities regarding the relationship of artists with dealers and collectors in the context of legal rights and obligations.

I shall therefore only draw from my own experience and from the limited amount of case law which has been recorded from one country in particular, not surprisingly, France.

But first let us consider one of the most outrageous pieces of vandalism of this century, or depending how you look at it, the most salutory rebuke any good honourable person can inflict on another. I refer of course to the fate of Graham Sutherland's portrait of Winston Churchill. It was commissioned by the Houses of Parliament, presented to Sir Winston on an appropriate anniversary, and never seen again! The best information indicates that Lady Churchill hated the portrait so much that she put it on a bonfire at Chartwell.

Later generations may have acclaimed the work as a masterpiece.

Currently Sutherland's work is in eclipse, as so often happens during the period of obscurity after an artist's death, but it is not likely to remain so for long. This being the case, in what jurisdictions could the artist's heirs have sued Lady Churchill for the loss of a masterpiece and the damage to the artist's reputation? I have not discovered an overwhelming positive response to this question. Only I think in the state of California, USA is there a right to claim damages. In France there may be an obligation to give notice of the intention to destroy (perhaps a little difficult when the bonfire is already lit), so that the artist can record his work before its destruction. Elsewhere the general principle that title has passed and all rights are extinguished seens to apply. The *droit moral* which broadly speaking is the right to protect and champion one's own work, into whosesoever hands it may have come, appears to be limited to sale, damage or mutilation or any other offensive act. Nothing is said expressly about destruction. Certainly at the time Lady Churchill threw the painting on the fire there was no relevant legislation in the United Kingdom.

In most countries, in practice, the umbilical chord between creator and creation is cut on first sale. It is the reputation of the earlier creations, now in free circulation, which determines what an artist or his heirs can charge for the later work. This is certainly a different scenario from the composer or author whose early works may be just as lucrative in terms of royalty as later ones, and one of the reasons why *droit de suite* is not a concept which is universally received. The other of course is the difficulty of administering it.

Droit moral is a concept more easily understood and easier to accept. The United Kingdom Copyright Act of 1988 acknowledges its validity although it expressly allows an artist to waive his or her right to it by contract, something which the Royal Academy of Arts, having campaigned so strongly for *droit moral*, then required all its candidates for the 1990 Summer Exhibition at Burlington House to do, thereby demonstrating the inevitable imbalance between the parties. Because of media reaction, the Royal Academy said that they would look at their contract again, but one wonders if they decided *not* to delete the waiver clause, would it make the slightest difference to the number of candidates for the exhibition? I think not.

So we have to look for a successful artist litigant in a battlefield where the patron or collector almost invariably dominates by sheer financial muscle. Only in France have I found cases where the artist has fought for his rights through the courts and won.

There are three interesting cases to refer to.

The first concerned the artist Bernard Buffet in the early 1960's. He agreed to decorate a refrigerator in aid of the Paris Centre for the Protection of Children and this was sold at a charity auction for FF 11,000.

Alas the buyer was an unscrupulous person who decided to recover his outlay and make a profit by breaking up the refrigerator and selling the six decorated panels (three on the door, one on top and one on each side) separately.

But that of course destroyed the integrity of the work – and of the refrigerator. Buffet had only signed one panel. He therefore obviously intended the composite work entitled *Still Life with Fruit* to retain its integrity. The Court held that the dismantling of the refrigerator was an offence against the *droit moral* of the artist. It must only be sold as an integral object.[1]

Less successful was the sculptor who constructed his sculpture from worn sleepers taken from a railway track and had it erected in a municipal park in Grenoble. Unfortunately the work of art deteriorated so rapidly that the municipality decided that it constituted a threat to public safety. The Court preferred the municipality's concern for public safety to the artist's rights.[2]

Finally the most interesting case of Dubuffet in 1977–78. Dubuffet had been commissioned to build a monument for the new headquarters of the Renault company in Boulogne. He prepared a maquette; construction of the full-scale monument began; then it stopped; then it was practically destroyed. The maquette was returned to Dubuffet, who protested about the destruction of the full-scale work. This was a really difficult case. In the two lower courts Dubuffet lost the case on the basis that it was the maquette that was his work, not the final monument and also that the contract did not oblige those commissioning the work to construct it. *A fortiori* they could destroy what had been done so far.

This argument was finally rejected by the *Cour de Cassation* which decided that the creator of a maquette after which a monumental construction is realized holds the *droit moral* in regard to the monument itself to the extent that it reflects the originality of the maquette and the artist's conception.[3]

So at the highest level, a French court decided that the artist's rights took precedence over that of the proprietor. This could have momentous consequences. Consider, for example, a case in which I have been involved on behalf of an institutional client who agreed to allow an artist to decorate a long dull wall in the institution with a mural 1200 centimetres long and about 100 centimetres high. No sooner had the mural been completed than the artist's lawyer submitted an agreement, ostensibly for a three year licence to exploit the work, but containing a hidden covenant on the part of the institution to preserve and protect the mural for the whole copyright period of the artist – that is to say his life and fifty years thereafter. As the institution was in the process of major rebuilding works this could have created a problem. Fortunately the proposal came after the work was finished, not before, and the mural was completed before the 1988 Act came into force. The agreement remains unsigned.

I would however conclude by reminding you that although our continental friends are always accusing us in London of being very slow in adopting the

---

1. Paris, 3 May 1962, D. 1962.570, note DESBOIS, JCP 1963.12989, note R. SAVATIER; Cass. 6 July 1965, Gaz. Pal. 1965.2.126.
2. *Revue Internationale du Droit d'Auteur* (RIDA) January 1977.116.
3. RIDA July 1977.191, note DESBOIS; RIDA October 1978.85; Gaz. Pal. 1978 III No. 3, note FRANCK; note RIDA April 1980.154; RIDA October 1981.201.

droit moral, we have in fact had what I regard as a more effective protection of artists' rights (if only they would use it) since time immemorial – I refer to the tort of 'passing-off' – which means, roughly speaking, attributing to someone a thing which is of inferior quality and therefore worth less than it would be if it were the genuine article.

This can work very favourably for the benefit of an artist or his heirs, as I learnt to my cost (or rather my clients') some years ago. These clients, a small gallery in West London, decided to hold a retrospective exhibition of the works of a good but not well-known painter, now deceased. They chose a particular painting of his for the cover of their catalogue, but when it was reproduced they suddenly realized it had what looked like a huge blank space in the forefront of the painting. There was an obvious human figure, but no face, just blank canvas. They could not decide whether the painting was finished or unfinished, but eventually they asked a very skilled apprentice to add a few touches to the blank space just to suggest some facial features, and, thus improved, the painting was reproduced on the cover of the catalogue.

The exhibition was opened – many people raved about this newly discovered artist, many successful sales were achieved – but the artist's widow was inconsolable. 'But Madame' said my clients, 'look what we have done for your husband's reputation!' 'But Messieurs' she replied, 'look what you have done to his painting'. And she sued. And I had to advise my clients to settle because they had passed off a mutilated painting as an original. If that isn't just as effective a *droit moral*, I don't know what is.

So to summarize my advice to collectors, individual and corporate:

If you collect in a country where *droit moral* is strong, collect something movable, preferably behind glass and if there is *droit de suite*, sell it overseas where there isn't.

If you want a monument, make sure it threatens to collapse before you get tired of it, or else make it mobile and keep it indoors.

If you must have something permanent, why not seek the advice of a lawyer who is experienced in art law first, before you sign the commission contract?

TOPIC. 4 AUCTION SALES AND CONDITIONS

LES CONDITIONS DE VENTE AUX ENCHERES

Introduction

TOPIC 4: AUCTION SALES AND CONDITIONS

The general features of the international art market and of the changes which have taken place within it in recent years, particularly those due to the establishment of the 'single market', were examined during this session. The possibility of an international harmonization of auction sales conditions and liabilities arising from the new services offered by the main international auction houses, such as financial services were also covered.

Chaired by *Prof. Pieter Sanders*, the discussion began with a dialogue between the audience and *Mr. Joe Och* (legal counsel for Sotheby's, London) and *Mr. David Allison* (legal counsel for Christie's, London) on the significance of the record prices reached by the sale of Impressionist and contemporary paintings in the last few years. Both indicated that these record prices were relative when inflation rates and currency exchange rates were taken into consideration. They also pointed out the difference between the national and the international markets.

Both considered that the most important changes have resulted from the use of new information technologies. They pointed out that private buyers are becoming more and more important and are requiring auction houses to provide new services.

It was noted that after twenty years of rapid growth, the art market is now stable. The new role played by international auction houses, particularly in regard to the provision of financial services, i.e., credit given to the purchaser or to the seller, or guaranteed sale prices for the seller of the work of art were, in their estimation, minor and exceptional aspects of the activities of auction houses, which did not alter their legal status as agents.

In the following part of the session, two lawyers, *Mr. Jan Maarten Boll* and *Mr. Van Kirk Reeves* discussed the need to supervise auction sales, taking as examples the introduction of regulation of the stock exchange and the rules of the civil law countries where an auction sale must be supervised by a public agent, i.e., a civil law notary, *commissaire-priseur* or some other representative of the public authorities (*see infra*, pp. 353–361).

They debated the question of whether the liability disclaimers set forth in auction sales conditions are too broad, particularly in view of the provision of new services by auction houses to their customers. The general discussion, based upon the replies to the Questionnaire on the scope of liability of auction houses, particularly concerning the authenticity of works of art sold or the existence of a valid deed of title, and on the legal status of auction houses in their relationship with the buyer and seller was very animated and disparate opinions were expressed. There was disagreement between representatives of different national legal systems regarding liability disclaimers. Some considered auction sales conditions limiting the liability of auction houses to be null and void under their national law. Others, conversely, held that under their national legal system, contracts between the auction house and the buyer or seller of the work of art containing such liability disclaimers would be valid. Questions were also raised regarding the role of auction houses which participate in the ownership of art galleries.

The feasibility of an international harmonization of auction sales conditions appeared uncertain particularly because of the French regulations concerning the *commissaires-priseurs* who, for example, are liable for thirty years for sales that they have organized. The differences existing between various national laws applicable to auction sales and between the characterization of the various types of contractual relationships existing between the auction house and the buyer of works of art, i.e., agency contract, services contracts, mandate contracts (*mandat*) also hinder harmonization. The implementation of various legal regimes for consumer protection to auction sales (thereby defining the buyer and seller of works of art as consumers) were discussed. The specific nature of transactions in art was highlighted, for example, in respect to the Vienna Sales Convention which excludes auction sales from its ambit.

List of Participants in Discussion

First Discussion
Pierre Lalive (Switzerland)
Fabio Brembati (Italy)
Jane Gregory Rubin (United States)
Jean-Pierre Blanc (France)
Caroline Duhamel (France)
Pierre Frier (France)
E. Alexander (Netherlands)

Second Discussion
Joe Och (United Kingdom)
Philippe Kahn (France)
Jean Chatelain (France)
J. B. Davidson (United States)
Jean Lerouste (France)
Quentin Byrne-Sutton (Switzerland)
Jean-Louis Delvolvé (France)
Dan Barr (United States)

General Report

General Report

TOPIC 4. AUCTION SALES AND CONDITIONS

Van Kirk Reeves* and Jan M. Boll**

I. THE CURRENT CONDITIONS FOR AUCTION SALES

For works of superb quality and extraordinary interest, the art market has become a single market. However, the auction houses serving this market are still governed by the rules designed for them before certain auction houses became world renown and at a time when the services they offered were more limited.

The traditional function of auction houses was to group similar merchandise in a central place where it could be examined and purchased. The auction house was seen as merely providing a publicized forum in which buyers and sellers interested in the same types of goods could gather.

The Anglo-Saxon countries have traditionally enacted few laws governing the relationship between the participants and the auction houses, leaving the parties to develop their own customs and contracts. The continental experience, however, has been to place much more emphasis on the regulation of such transactions. This reflected a commitment to State intervention in the conduct of these affairs. The present French rules governing auctioneers would appear the most structured.

In great part, the national rules developed in each country to govern its auctions appear appropriate for the vast majority of auctions, particularly those of only regional interest.

The traditional fine arts auction provides a means for sellers, including estates, to find buyers and provides a reasonable way for purchasers to acquire such objects as well as allowing dealers to obtain or dispose of stock while creating a method of evaluating similar goods whether for tax or insurance purposes.

However, today's great auction houses do not always play as passive a role as the traditional auction houses have in the past.

The concern for proper regulations for the great auction houses has arisen from the development for the present international art market. These

* Partner, Coudert Frères, Paris.
** Partner, De Brauw Blackstone Westbroek, Amsterdam.

auction houses have played a significant role in developing this market where the leading auction houses in the major centers are engaged in worldwide competition to attract the most important objects and an international clientele.

The large international auctioneers not only specialize in being knowledgeable about objects of art and their potential value and in being intermediaries in the public as well as the private sale of valuable objects, but they are increasingly becoming financial institutions, financing the sale or possession of valuable objects. There is even a tendency for auctioneers to become investors in objects they may later want to sell. Thus, the question arises whether is it necessary to protect against potential conflicts of interest between the auctioneer, on the one hand, and potential buyers and sellers, on the other hand. Similarly, there may be good reason to protect the market against abuses by the auctioneer of his specialized services and know-how, and against insider trading.

The international auction houses have been prepared to offer services beyond the traditional scope of their less dynamic brethren. So, in considering the present conditions of auction sales, there is a conflict between the parochial auctions providing a service within a small area and the great auction houses. There is also a division between the rules developed in the civil law countries with their tradition of government regulation and those developed in common law countries where the State has been less involved in ordering relations between the parties. Finally, within the common law countries there has been a traditional division between England and the United States in levels of consumer protection.

It may be ironic that nowhere in the world is there such control and regulation governing the purchase and sale of stocks and bonds as in the United States which is identified with *laissez-faire* government in many other contexts. Whether the American zeal for consumer protection will soon extend to the art market is a challenging question. In the EC jurisdictions, there is a strong tendency towards far-reaching consumer protection through new legislation (e.g., in the new Dutch Civil Code which will have the force of law from 1 January 1992) and through case law.

II. REGULATIONS THAT FRUSTRATE THE DEVELOPMENT OF AUCTIONS

The great auction houses only flourish in the principal cities of the world which act as sales centers for the transaction of art business. Each of these principal centres, New York, London, Paris, Amsterdam and Geneva, have access to the necessary entrepreneurs and professionals to run successful auction houses. But the competitive advantages that each of these centers offer, and indeed the very existence of certain of them, has arisen due to unfavourable legislation for the free exchange of objects developed by the laws of many jurisdictions.

In Italy there is a listing of a significant number of works for which an export permit would be required if a person wished to remove the work from the country. As the grant of an export permit is within the discretion of the State authorities, based on an analysis of the importance of the work as a cultural treasure for Italy, an important disincentive exists for the development of an international art market there.

Further, a natural shyness to make information available that would be of interest to tax authorities has also discouraged the development of an international art market in Italy.

If a ban on the export of certain items is utterly dissuasive, more limited regulations in countries such as France and England have not helped the development of these principal auction centres.

In France, the State is entitled to pre-empt a work at its closing bid unless the work has been brought into France on a temporary import permit. While the pre-emption gives the seller the full value of his sale, this legislation nonetheless has a chilling effect on the development of France as an international auction center. Bidders can be discouraged from attending sales where they fear they will not be able to acquire the objects they desire. As the value of significant works has increased, the dissuasive effect of these rules has grown since the buyer must organize and have available significant sums that otherwise could be available for investment and where at the end he may not be allowed to complete his purchase.

Even the English rules that allow the amount equal to the best bid to be raised over a limited period of time in an effort to keep the work in England, are mildly dissuasive in the development of London as an international art centre.

Each jurisdiction where international art auctions are offered has established its own rules that it deems necessary for the protection of its artistic and cultural heritage. Such rules are, however, in conflict with the free market economy proposed by auction houses. To the extent that such legislation is deemed excessive by buyers and sellers, it encourages a black or at least grey market with the great risks of chicanery and the damaging or destruction of works due to improper handling.

III. CONFLICTS BETWEEN BUYERS AND SELLERS

1. Can Auction Houses Avoid Liability?

The great battle that is developing between the buyers and the sellers in auctions is that buyers are seeking better title and sellers are seeking greater advantages. It is within this conflict that the rights, duties and privileges of the auction houses are under increasing scrutiny.

The auction house has traditionally sought to define its position as a mere intermediary and facilitator of the transaction between the seller and the buyer. In the simplest of regional auctions such a position can easily be justified. The auctioneer gathers up the paintings that came out of an elderly person's estate together with the paintings a family wanted to sell when they were moving to a new town and those that a married couple had to sell when they divorced and their property had to be divided. In this mythic situation we would not expect the auctioneer to check whether the husband, aside from his unkindness to his wife, might be a part-time art thief. We would not expect the auctioneer to have more than a guess as to who may have painted the paintings and none of the parties would seek to make him legally liable for his guess. We would not expect him to have more of an opinion on the work's condition than to express the possibility that the work may have been damaged during the flood of some years ago or that it appears that the work has been left in the sunlight.

In this mythic situation, the auctioneer, in announcing that the sale is the property of the elderly person's estate, the property of the family moving house and the property of the divorcing couple, is clearly acting only as an intermediary with no particular expertise or knowledge. Moreover, the local buyers may well have an informed opinion on the various sellers which is better than that of the auctioneer and the prices may reflect these views.

Early on, the civil law countries created rules to enforce more rigourous standards for the conduct of auction sales in providing that they were only to be conducted by especially responsible trained persons and that in holding such events the auctioneer would take upon himself certain responsibilities.

This legislation, while in certain cases creating a privileged class of auctioneers, can be seen as an effort to create in auctioneers parties who are disinterested professionals with certain training and responsibilities. In undertaking auction sales, they are to be impartial to the buyers and the sellers, have no interest in the transaction other than their commissions and provide certain standards as to title and authenticity. Moreover, certain remedies are available where title and authenticity are not as advertised.

When a work is listed in a French auction catalogue, the buyer is entitled to rely on the fact that he will acquire good title to the work and that the authenticity of the work is as disclosed. An easily understood rating system stipulates whether the work is from the hand of the master, or whether it was done by those close to him, or in the period in which he lived, or at least in a style which has recognizable elements to the style in which he worked. This should give the buyer great comfort, but in reality, the difficulties of proof are such that a twenty year litigation may be necessary to establish the rights of buyer and seller.

The principal difficulty lies in establishing proof as required by a court of law as to authenticity. Usually proof can only be established by experts and all that experts have to offer are opinions.

Certainly French courts have had to struggle with a work of the School of Carrache revealed as a work of Nicolas Poussin, but it is perhaps in the American courts, and particularly those of New York, that the greatest conflicts have emerged as to the rights and duties of auction houses. This conflict is ironically taking place where the tradition of little government intervention in the dealings between parties has been strong.

That New York would prove the principal litigation arena for defining the role of auction houses is not only due to the American enthusiasm for litigation, but because the myth of the regional auction house as a simple intermediary is a strong tradition even in a city with auction houses that are prepared to offer sellers a truly impressive number of services.

With buyers and sellers operating on a world wide scale, hiding their identity and opting for exotic places of business, it has become more difficult to assert rights against the other party. A painting owned by a British Virgin Islands Company whose shares are in trust and whose trustees are covered by strenuously asserted claims of confidentiality, which is sold to a Hong Kong partnership, may present daunting problems for the party that feels aggrieved against the other. At the same time, the principal auction houses have developed into important institutions with deep pockets and are established in jurisdictions with well developed legal systems. They have proven a more accessible defendant.

The search for liability against auction houses has been intensified as their expertise and authority in the market place has been more widely recognized. Today, so as to assist their customers, the principal auction houses provide substantial services. These can include reviewing the title and the authenticity of the work, its cultural and artistic importance and establishing an evaluation of the auction houses' opinion as to the price that the work would obtain in the market place. In addition, the auction houses also provide a developed system by which they will withdraw the work from the auction if the work does not reach an agreed price. More recently, the auction houses have been providing a guarantee that regardless of the vicissitudes of the marketplace the seller will obtain no less than a certain price for his work or have the work returned to him.

2. *Do Increased Services Imply Increased Responsibility?*

The range of services provided by the auction houses has become increasingly important and is used to attract sellers, but the actual form of the contractual arrangements between the parties, including the auctioneer, still appears to be closer to the regional auctions described above than that of a developed service industry seeking to care for its seller clients.

This choice may be justified if one considers that the sellers using the major auction houses are ambitious discerning collectors who have equally as good access to professional advisors, art historians and connoisseurs as the auction houses.

In addition, placing greater legal burdens on auction houses would lead them to seek protection through more rigourous due diligence which might well increase their costs.

The Americans have always felt that disclosure and investigation were the way to avoid legal responsibility. If the smoker knows that smoking is dangerous for him and in a mature and reasoned fashion accepts that this pleasure may reduce his life frame and result in illness, then it can be held that he has accepted the risk and can have no recourse in the event that the product causes him harm. In the sale of securities in the United States, this sytem has developed into a formalistic review beyond the standards of any English or Continental system and at a cost far in excess of the cost of issuing securities in Europe. Americans are rightly proud of their system and the European and Japanese markets have to some extent copied it although whether these copies are set up to protect the investors or simply to give investors the impression that the market is a rational and orderly place is not clear.

Fashioning a disclosure statement for an auction house provides a challenging semantic exercise. One questions whether greater disclosure and further defensive language will significantly aid a market known for sellers seeking to sell mules for racehorses and buyers seeking treasures for a pittance in a market with world class tricksters.

Under such circumstances, should that auction houses be held to any standard of due care or can it be maintained that they are only intermediaries who provide ancillary opinions on title, authenticity and provenance merely as a free courtesy service on which sellers are not entitled to rely?

3. *Duty of Fair Dealing*

The duty of fair dealing raises difficult questions in view of certain auction practices.

A seller is usually not prepared to let his possession go into the auction with no right to recover it if the work does not reach an acceptable price. To keep sellers from trying to rig the auction by bidding up the value of their own goods, they are forbidden to bid. However, it is possible for the seller to have an agreement with the auction house by which, if a certain price is not reached, the auction house will withdraw the work from the sale. The reserve system has been good for the development of auctions in that without it many sellers would have chosen to negotiate privately.

There has been some criticism of this system as being deceptive to buyers. Buyers do not know at what price they will be able to make purchases and so incur substantial expenses in attending auctions at which their maximum bid may be doomed by an agreement between the seller and the auctioneer made prior to the auction. Advocates of disclosed reserve prices claim that a system where the reserve price is set and known prior to the sale will avoid needless expense and frustration on the part of buyers. Still, the publishing of these prices might discourage certain of the practices of auction houses that add to the glamour and excitement of an auction. No longer could the chandeliers be bid at the beginning of a sale so as to warm up the audience. Moreover, the buyer's dream of bidding a work well below its price would appear more elusive than ever. What is the price of the excitement and glamour of an important auction and what level of showmanship should be allowed?

Further, if reserves were disclosed, sellers might resort to more intricate systems to avoid disclosing their reserve prices but protecting their rights against a successful bidder at an unacceptable price.

Still, the guarantee system makes the seller and the auction house co-ventures in giving the illusion to buyers that they may be able to possess an item at a fraction of its true value.

These issues become more difficult to resolve in light of the decision of Christie's to join Sotheby's in offering, in exceptional situations, guarantees for the receipt of (a percentage of) the reserve price. The offering of guaranteed prices gives even greater comfort to the seller than the reserve system but may create new legal responsibilities for the auction house. By giving guarantees, the auction house is either underwriting any loss that the seller may have if the work does not reach its minimal sales price or it is effectively purchasing the work for that price if the work fails to obtain that price at auction. The auction house will then either have to find a buyer by private sale or sustain the loss. Its impartiality and fairness to both buyers and sellers may be damaged by this stance and its duties arising from this position seem certain to be litigated at some point.

Such a situation is not consistent with that of the auctioneer as the impartial arbitrator between buyer and seller with no other interest than his service fee.

As the purchaser of last resort, auction houses are being challenged as to their ability to offer guaranteed prices without being in conflict with their role as appraiser of the market for the setting of reserve prices and as an appraiser of art and decorative art objects.

A recent New York case held, 'The auctioneer is the agent of the consignor... [and has] a fiduciary duty to act in the utmost good faith and in the interests of... its principal throughout their relationship.' This case was decided prior to the announcement by the auction houses that they would provide guaranteed prices but even in the absence of this new development, standards referred to by the court appear to be introducing judicial standards of professionalism far beyond that of the regional auction.[1]

The recent movement of the art market from skyrocketing optimism to skepticism if not pessimism, may have the effect of restraining the international auctioneers in their willingness to accept part of the commercial risks of their sellers and buyers and make them more hesitant to guarantee prices and to finance purchases.

4. *The Purchasers' Rights*

Within the evolution of standards for auction houses in relation to their consignors, purchasers have also sought protection and security for their purchases.

---

1. *Cristallina, S.A. v. Christie Manson & Woods International Inc.* 13 May 1986, App. Div. 1st D. New York Supreme Court.

For many years responsible dealers have offered their customers the possibility of returning works with which they are dissatisfied for any reason and receiving back their cash purchase price or receiving credit against another purchase. Such programs have been justified as being good business but in addition have the legal support of the theory that the works are sold with an express warranty. A failure of title or authenticity could be treated as a breach of this warranty requiring the rescision of the transaction. Such a position has been adopted by the French auctioneers and applies in a more limited manner to the New York Christie's and Sotheby's agreements. There are, however, limits to the auction houses' enthusiasm for such warranties. In Sotheby's standard form, the attribution of works produced prior to 1870 are not warranted as such attribution is treated as being only a matter of scholarly opinion which is subject to change.

Moreover, these agreements propose only rescision as the remedy for a dissatisfied purchaser and exclude alternative remedies such as reimbursement of lost profits. Such alternative damages would have to be computed on the basis of what the work would be worth if it had been authentic and courts have held that such calculations are too speculative to justify their adoption. But there may come a time when a court must rule on a situation where the equities are particularly on the side of the buyer. With courts feeling their way gingerly through the principal issues facing art auctions, a recent announcement by Sotheby's in New York placed greater pressure on that organization than ever to fulfill its duties of care and fair dealing.

In partnership with the Acquavella Galleries of New York, Sotheby's has purchased the inventory of the Pierre Matisse Gallery. This raises the interesting possibility that through its ownership of this stock of materials it may be treated as entering the art market for its own account. This additional arrow in its quiver will make its duty of fair dealing more challenging. In its acting as advisor to persons consigning works to it for sale, it objectively judges the market and gives its best opinion. In offering to set reserve prices it helps establish the rules of the market place. In providing financial guarantees to sellers it is prepared to put its financial resources behind its judgment of the market. Now, if this pronounced joint venture develops, the auction house may be seen as a dealer for its own account in the market. Its own desire to profit from its inventory of works may conflict with its client's wishes to obtain the best price for their works.

Sotheby's might establish 'Chinese Walls' as do the investment houses in New York so that the advisors to corporate clients do not share their view of company's prospects with those responsible for recommending securities for investors to buy, but can it be sufficiently evenhanded in undertaking its multiple responsibilities so that it will be able to fulfill its duty of utmost good faith to its consignors? What of its duties to buyers? It seems likely that the extent of its duties will be subject to judicial testing.

Still, it may be that courts will chose to treat both buyers and sellers at auction as mature individuals who realize the risks and dangers of the art market but are entranced by the prestige, the glamour and the excitement of entering the art market, not to mention the enjoyment of being possessors of some of the greatest examples of mankind's achievement and therefore not be willing to enforce strict regulations on auction houses.

National Reports

Austria

NATIONAL REPORT ON TOPIC 4. AUCTION SALES AND CONDITIONS*

Ignaz Seidl-Hohenveldern**

1. The holding of auction sales requires a licence by the administrative authorities, on the level of the *Land* concerned. The licence is required mainly to ensure the moral reliability of the auctioneer, but also his professional capability (Art. 130(VI) of the Trade Regulation Law (*Gewerbeordnung*) 1973 (TRL), last amended by Federal Law BGBl 1981/619[1] and Art. 295 TRL). The applicant for a licence to hold auction sales has to submit to the administrative authorities draft Business Operation Rules *(Geschäftsordnung)*. When the administrative authority approves these Business Operation Rules they become binding for him (Art. 299 TRL). These Rules must be posted in the auction room.

Exercising the profession without a licence or disregarding the approved Business Operation Rules will be punished by arrest up to six months or by the corresponding fine (Art. 366(1) under 2 TRL).

2. It may safely be presumed that the Business Operation Rules of the Dorotheum, the leading Austrian auction house, serve as yardstick for the administrative authorities when approving other Business Operation Rules.

The Auction Conditions of the Dorotheum, which are a condensed version of its Business Operation Rules, indicate, moreover, the amounts to be paid in addition to the highest bid as fees for the auctioneer (12%) and as turnover tax (either 10 or 20%).

In addition thereto, the Auction Order *(Feilbietungsordnung)* of 15 July 1786, JGS No. 565 is still applicable.[2] Insofar as this Order regulates the bidding procedure, it is more or less similar to the Rules mentioned above. In addition thereto, the Auction Order provides for due announcement of the auction and for measures to ensure discipline in the auction room. An auction sale is null and void (a) if the organ ordering the auction lacked authority to do so, (b) if the auction was not duly announced or (c) if the

* Editor's note: *see also* 'Austria: Introduction' in Part One.

** Professor, Institut für Völkerrecht und Internationale Beziehungen, Vienna.

1. MACHE/KINSCHER, *Gewerbeordnung* (Vienna, Manz).
2. EDELBACHER, *Verfahren ausser Streitsachen* (Vienna, Manz, 2nd edn. 1984) p. 573.

auction was not carried out in accordance with the rules. In such cases it is irrelevent whether the highest bidder acted in good faith or not. Only if none of these three situations has occurred, will the highest bidder acquire the property when the auctioneer hands over the object concerned.[3] A Decree by the Imperial Chancellory of 6 June 1838, JGS 1838/277[4] declares illicit and null and void all contracts not to bid or to bid only up to a certain amount. Whatever had been paid in order to achieve this result shall be forfeited. However, the validity of the auction may not be challenged on account of such illicit agreements.

According to Art. 7(2) of the Federal Law Prohibiting the Export of Cultural Property,[5] the Federal Monuments Office may guarantee the right of future re-export of an object of art imported to Austria in order to be sold there at an auction, unless the object had previously been smuggled out of Austria or had remained abroad in violation of the commitment to return to Austria an Austrian monument originally exported in virtue of a temporary export permit.

According to Art. 14(1) of the Business Operation Rules of the Dorotheum, the latter does not guarantee the exactitude of the evaluation and description of the objects by its experts.

Art. 31(1) of the Rules excludes any claim by the purchaser concerning the price, the nature and the state of the object after his bid has been accepted. However, these disclaimers cannot protect the Dorotheum against claims based on general civil law, e.g., error.

The auction conditions of the Dorotheum contain the list of the (almost) code words used by its experts to distinguish genuine from imitation objects.

I know of only one case of error concerning the authenticity of an object. Some years ago, a wood carver in the South Tyrol had carved a madonna in the style of the 14th century. He sold it for a modest sum as his own work to an Austrian collector of genuine medieval art. The collector put the madonna in his house. When he died, his heir, living abroad, entrusted the Dorotheum with the liquidation of his inheritance. This provenance of the madonna misled the Dorotheum's expert to certify that the madonna was a genuine 14th century object. The madonna was the star of the auction and sold for a very considerable price. This fact and a picture of the madonna were published in Austrian newspapers. The artist recognized his madonna and started the ball rolling. As it happened, everybody was co-operative. However, the purchaser could have sued the Dorotheum for error. The Dorotheum would have had to return the purchase price against the return of the madonna. The Dorotheum then could have sued the collector's heir for the return of the purchase price already paid to the heir, returning the madonna to him. Assuming that the heir had gone bankrupt in the meantime, the damage would have had to be suffered by the Dorotheum.

---

3. Supreme Court, 7 September 1949, *Jur. Blätter* 1950, p. 89.
4. KAPFER, *Allgemeines Bürgerliches Gesetzbuch* (Vienna, Manz, 15th edn. 1989) p. 755. Note to Art. 879 ABGB.
5. N. HELFGOTT, *Ausfuhrverbotsgesetz für Kulturgut* (Vienna, Manz 1987) p. 31.

I know of no instance involving the auctioning of works of art of unclear origin or ownership. Art. 367 of the Austrian General Civil Code provides that the claim of the real owner for *replevin* (repossession) does not prevail against the bona fide purchaser of a movable object when he proves that he has acquired the object at a public auction.[6]

The real owner has to prove the bad faith of the purchaser. However, in a relevant decision, involving a personal computer, the bidder was held to be in bad faith as he had been informed by the other bidders that the person, whose assets were sold by auction, had stated that the computer was not his property. The bidder was negligent. Prior to bidding, he should have contacted the person who was said to be the owner, in order to find out whether this statement was true or not.[7]

3. Austria, at present, sees no need to change its rules on auction sales, although in other fields Austria tends to follow the EC harmonization movement in order to facilitate Austria's entry into the Common Market.[8]

The need for a licence to hold auction sales does not discriminate against foreigners. Licences to exercise other professions may be granted only to Austrian citizens. However the list of these professions does not include the profession of auctioneers.[9] Licences have actually been granted to foreign auctioneers.

I assume that the requirement of a licence, as such, is a measure justified by considerations of public safety and hence – in virtue of Art. 100A (4) EC in the version of the Single European Act in conjunction with Art. 36 EC – could be maintained even in face of a proposal to harmonize by abandoning the need for licensing this trade.

6. P. L. BAECK, *The General Civil Code of Austria* (Dobbs Ferry, Oceana 1972) p. 68.
7. Supreme Court, 13 November 1979, *Jur. Blätter* 1980, pp. 589–590.
8. Cf. I. SEIDL-HOHENVELDERN, 'Les praticiens du droit face à l'Europe', Entretiens de Nanterre, *La Semaine Juridique*, Supplément 5/1989, pp. 28–33.
9. MACHE/KINSCHER, *op. cit.*, p. 137 commenting on Art. 25 TRL.

Belgique

RAPPORT NATIONAL SUR LE SUJET 4. LES CONDITIONS DE VENTE AUX ENCHERES*

Francis Bauduin**

1. En Belgique, les ventes aux enchères de biens meubles sont réglementées par la loi sur les pratiques du commerce du 14 juillet 1971 en ses arts. 44 et suivants.

Toutefois, les opérations portant sur des objets d'art ou de collection ou des antiquités en sont exclues.

Une intéressante décision judiciaire belge prononcée par le tribunal de commerce de Bruxelles le 7 octobre 1987 en matière de cessation d'actes de concurrence illicites s'est fondée sur cette loi pour admettre une vente aux enchères organisée par Sotheby's N. V. Amsterdam en Belgique.[1]

A l'instar de la France, aucune vente publique aux enchères de biens meubles ne peut se faire sans le concours d'un officier public, en l'occurrence huissier ou notaire.

Toutefois, en Belgique, le rôle des notaires et huissiers s'avère quelque peu différent de ce qui se produit en France.

Si dans les ventes forcées ou dans les ventes volontaires concernant des meubles classiques, les huissiers et notaires mènent seuls les enchères après avoir fait une étude des biens à vendre à l'image des commissaires-priseurs français, dans les ventes d'oeuvres d'art, le vendeur fait généralement appel à un intermédiaire-commerçant qui procédera à la vente: dans ce cas, la présence obligatoire d'un notaire ou d'un huissier, prévue par l'art. 226 du Code de l'enregistrement, n'implique pas la direction de la vente. Cette présence répond à un double objectif: garantir la perception des droits revenant au Trésor et assurer la loyauté et la sincérité des adjudications dans un intérêt général et d'ordre public.

Les huissiers et notaires belges sont en réalité, en l'occurrence, des témoins du bon déroulement des ventes publiques d'oeuvres d'art. Ils accomplissent une obligation légale, ils reçoivent un mandat *légal* et non conventionnel. Le vendeur – ou le directeur de la salle des ventes – fixe les

---

* Note d'Editeur: *v.* 'Belgique: Introduction', Francis HAUMONT *supra* pp. 31–38.

** Avocat, Bauduin & Dilley, Bruxelles.

1. Comm. Bruxelles (cess.) 7 octobre 1987, *Rev.dr.intell., L'ing. Cons.*, janvier-février 1988, n° 1–2, p. 48, avec une note d'observation de P. De VROEDE et G. L. BALLON, p. 53.

règles à l'avance (prix de réserve, refus de vendre, retrait de l'objet, etc.), l'officier public venant en quelque sorte 'légaliser' la procédure sous peine d'amende.

L'art 230 du Code belge de l'enregistrement dispose à cet égard qu'il est dressé procès-verbal de la vente publique par l'officier public. Chaque objet adjugé est porté immédiatement à ce procès-verbal. Ledit procès-verbal doit, en outre, contenir l'identification du vendeur et l'inscription correcte du lot.

Le caractère hybride du système constitue l'une des caractéristiques principales du droit belge: un formalisme à la française, comme nous le verrons ci-après, avec la présence obligatoire (mandat légal) d'un notaire ou d'un huissier, d'une part, et une liberté commerciale à la britannique quant à la préparation et la menée de la vente, d'autre part.

La responsabilité du notaire et d'huissier est ici relativement faible à l'opposé de celle du commissaire-priseur français qui joue le rôle d'officier public *et* d'intermédiaire.

Cette responsabilité découle essentiellement du respect d'un certain nombre de formalités:
- informer de toute vente publique d'objets mobiliers, sous peine d'une amende de 500 FB, le receveur de l'enregistrement dans le ressort duquel la vente doit être faite (art. 227 du Code de l'enregistrement);
- indiquer dans le procès-verbal différentes mentions relatives au requérant et aux personnes dont les meubles sont vendus (art. 228, vente forcée);
- établir un procès-verbal des objets vendus après chaque séance sous peine d'amende (équivalant à vingt fois le droit éludé).

Très tôt, la Cour de cassation de Belgique avait été conduite à se prononcer sur leur rôle et leurs responsabilités:

> 'La mission des notaires, huissiers (...) se borne au fait de la mise aux enchères publiques et à l'adjudication. L'officier public n'est pas tenu de poser lui-même matériellement les actes constitutifs de la vente, pourvu que les aides choisies par lui ou par le propriétaire agissent *en sa présence* et sous son *inspection*'.[2]

Néanmoins, vis-à-vis du vendeur, le notaire ou l'huissier se trouve dans la position du mandataire et il assumera à cet effet la responsabilité qui découle des arts. 1991 et suivants du Code civil.

2. Un texte type important est celui des conditions des ventes organisées au Palais des Beaux-Arts de Bruxelles. Tous les textes circulant en Belgique sont voisins, *mutatis mutandis*, de ce texte.

3. Une différence essentielle sépare le droit belge du droit français pour ce qui regarde les risques impliqués dans une vente aux enchères en ce qui

2. Cass. belge, 22 juin 1867, Pas., 1867, I, 369.

concerne l'origine de l'oeuvre et son authenticité. La Chambre nationale des commissaires-priseurs français garantit l'authenticité des objets mis en vente en fonction des mentions du catalogue et des conditions de vente alors qu'en Belgique, la présence fréquente des clauses de non-garantie d'authenticité, admises par les Cours et tribunaux belges et la doctrine juridique, anéantit en fait le recours pour erreur sur les qualités substantielles. Le paradoxe est que les ventes belges demeurent pourtant les plus réputées.

Pour se prémunir contre ces risques, les salles de vente belges prévoient une clause qui annule la garantie d'authenticité. Une des clauses classiques se retrouve dans les conditions de vente du Palais des Beaux-Arts évoquées ci-dessus: 'Il ne sera admis aucune réclamation de quelque nature que ce soit même si elle a pour objet la description au catalogue, une fois l'adjudication prononcée'.

Déjà en 1931, le tribunal de commerce de Bruxelles relevait à propos de cette clause:

> 'Il appartient ainsi à l'acheteur seul de s'assurer de l'authenticité du tableau au sujet de laquelle le vendeur ne prend aucune responsabilité. Si l'acheteur s'est trompé quant à cette authenticité, il y a erreur de jugement de sa part et non erreur sur la substance.'[3]

Les clauses de non-garantie se trouvent insérées dans les catalogues de vente à l'instar du droit anglo-saxon et elles limitent ainsi la portée des descriptions à une publication de renseignements relative aux objets mis en vente dont l'acheteur se doit de vérifier l'exactitude.

Si le but de ces clauses est d'éviter des suites juridiques incertaines, les salles de vente n'oublient pas la difficulté qu'il y a et le caractère onéreux qu'il y aurait à expertiser, puis garantir les divers objets mis en vente. La Cour d'appel de Bruxelles, le 19 février 1965 dans un arrêt significatif, rappelait:

> 'que dans la réalité d'ailleurs, l'authenticité d'un tableau présente très souvent une part non négligeable d'incertitude sans compter que la recherche de l'origine véritable, toujours coûteuse, dépend du crédit attaché au nom de l'expert qui en prend la responsabilité.'[4]

Même le dol par réticence semble être écarté par les juridictions belges. Un jugement très intéressant du tribunal de commerce de Bruxelles[5] paraît tracer des limites – discutables – entre le dol par réticence et le simple silence autorisé: au cours d'une vente publique, deux toiles du peintre V. de Saedeleer avaient été vendues. Après la vente et une expertise faite par l'acheteur, il s'avèra que les toiles étaient fausses. Devant le refus du

3. Comm. Bruxelles, 6 juillet 1931, J.C.B., 1931, p. 126; *v. aussi* Bruxelles, 17 avril 1935, J.C.B. 1935, p. 283; Comm. Bruxelles, 13 septembre 1978, J.T., 1979, p. 165.
4. Bruxelles, 19 février 1965, Pas., 1966, II, 50.
5. Comm. Bruxelles, 13 septembre 1978, J.T., 1979, p. 165.

vendeur de résilier la vente, l'acheteur intenta une action postulant l'annulation de la vente litigieuse sur base de l'erreur substantielle et du dol.

Or l'erreur est rejetée par le tribunal au vu de la présence d'une clause de non-garantie et de l'exposition préalable à la vente.

Par contre, le rejet du dol est ambigu car certaines circonstances entouraient cette vente: l'acheteur reprochait d'avoir mis en vente les deux oeuvres sans aucune expertise alors que la veille, une dénonciation anonyme taxant les deux tableaux de faux avait provoqué une descente de police. Le tribunal rétorqua que la vente avec certificat d'authenticité d'expertise n'est pas l'habitude dans les salles de vente belges ou internationales, exception faite pour le régime spécial des commissaires-priseurs français, et que les dénonciations sont monnaie courante sur le marché de l'art.

Le deuxième grief portait sur les réticences et les mensonges du vendeur qui aurait essayé de tromper l'acheteur et d'égarer la justice en refusant de déclarer l'origine des toiles, ce que, répond le tribunal, réfutent les procès-verbaux d'audition du vendeur qui démontrent la sincérité de celui-ci.

Une partie de la doctrine a regretté ce refus du tribunal d'admettre le dol par réticence.[6] Suite aux événements survenus à la veille de la vente, l'organisateur eut dû se montrer plus circonspect et, à tout le moins, avertir sa clientèle, au risque de déprécier les oeuvres. Dans les milieux de vente d'objets d'art, malgré les clauses de non-garantie d'authenticité, les usages professionnels veulent en effet que prévale toujours le principe de l'honnêteté des marchands et commissaires-priseurs. Ces usages imposent aussi que les personnes concernées aient le souci de décrire fidèlement les oeuvres d'art. Or un doute sur l'authenticité, révélé au vendeur avant la vente, constitue un élément qui aurait eu une influence non négligeable sur le prix de la vente. Au demeurant, les grandes salles de vente prévoient qu'en cas de doute sur l'authenticité de l'objet, elles se réservent le droit de le retirer illico de la vente.

Dans ce cas-ci, il y a, à tout le moins, une réticence à révéler un facteur fondamental de la vente. Nous pouvons même penser que l'attitude de l'intermédiaire était frauduleuse lorsque l'on sait qu'une des deux oeuvres lui appartenait – ce qui, en outre, aurait dû engager sa responsabilité.

4. *Harmonisation des ventes aux enchères*

Le commerce de l'art tombe sous le coup des règles générales du marché commun (C.J.C.E., arrêt du 10 décembre 1968, *Commission c. République italienne*, aff. 7/68, Rec., 1968, 617).

Ce sont des marchandises comme les autres et, en ce sens, elles profitent de tous les avantages existants relatifs à la libre circulation des marchandises: suppression des droits de douane et des taxes d'effet équivalent (arts. 9,

6. *V.* notamment, à cet égard, J. EECKHOUT, observations sous Comm. Bruxelles, 13 septembre 1978, J.T., 1979, p. 167.

12, 16, Traité CEE), suppression des restrictions quantitatives et des mesures d'effet équivalent (arts. 30 à 34 du Traité CEE) et élimination des discriminations fiscales (art. 95 CEE).

Si les oeuvres d'art bénéficient de tels avantages, elles sont soumises également à des obligations similaires à celles qui gouvernent les autres marchandises. Or pour celles-ci, il y a la libre concurrence. Ainsi le monopole des commissaires-priseurs français apparaît-il contraire aux règles du traité de Rome.

Dès la fin de 1986, la Commission de Bruxelles a préparé des dispositions qui, si elles étaient adoptées, obligeraient la France à adapter le système des ventes publiques aux enchères de telle sorte que le monopole serait abandonné au profit d'une libre concurrence entre tous les commissaires-priseurs européens.

Il semble que la date fatidique de 1993 devrait être l'ultime échéance pour consacrer ces dispositions.

En fait, les ventes aux enchères seraient harmonisées en Europe en ce sens que la libre concurrence serait la règle maîtresse à l'instar de ce qui se déroule actuellement en Grande-Bretagne. Les conditions de vente, quant à elles, seraient adaptées par chaque commissaire-priseur en fonction du marché et de la concurrence qui s'y retrouve.

Dans la même optique, la Commission Européenne a déposé une proposition de septième directive pour l'harmonisation de la t.v.a. concernant les oeuvres d'art et les biens d'occasion.

Les grandes maisons anglaises qui échappaient 'aux dispositions continentales' de certains pays européens se sont vu, dès 1986, notifier les projets de la Commission, ce qui les a fortement contrariées.

République Fédérale d'Allemagne

RAPPORT NATIONAL SUR LE SUJET 4. LES CONDITIONS DE VENTE AUX ENCHERES*

Martin Lange**

I. L'EXISTENCE DES CONDITIONS MODELES DE VENTE AUX ENCHERES D'OBJETS D'ART

En Allemagne, il n'existe pas de conditions modèles ou de guide applicables aux ventes aux enchères d'objets d'art. Par conséquent, chaque maison de vente aux enchéres peut établir ses propres conditions telles qu'elle le désire, naturellement dans les limites imposées par des lois applicables.

Mais l'art. 38 II N° 3 du Code contre les restrictions de concurrence (*Gesetz gegen Wettbewerbsbeschränkungen* (GWB)) donne la possibilité aux associations professionnelles et aux unions économiques de suggérer des recommandations concernant des conditions à ses membres. Ces recommandations qui sont non obligatoires en ce qui concerne leur nature juridique doivent être déclarées auprès du *Bundeskartellamt*. L'Association allemande des maisons d'enchères d'objets d'art (*Bundesverband Deutscher Kunstversteigerer*) a utilisé cette possibilité, a standardisé ces conditions et les a recommandées à ses membres. Le *Bundeskartellamt* a autorisé cette standardisation comme n'ayant pas d'effets restrictifs de concurrence (art. 38 II N° 1b et 2b GWB). Mais il faut souligner que cette publication du *Bundeskartellamt* ne comprend pas de décision sur la compatibilité des clauses recommandées avec les règlements de la loi sur les conditions générales (*AGB-Gesetz*).

Les clauses recommandées sont les suivantes (selon la notification au *Bundeskartellamt* N° 62/81, 05.06.1981, dans le *Bundesanzeiger*):

1. Clause rajoutée aux conditions de commande

> 'Le vendeur (celui qui fournit l'objet d'art) est responsable pour tous les vices matériels et les carences de titres juridiques attachés à l'objet d'art vendu.'

---

* Note d'Editeur: résumé en français du rapport en allemand.

** Assistant de Recherche à l'Institut du Droit des Affaires Internationales, Westfälischen Wilhelms-Universität, Münster.

2. *Clause rajoutée aux conditions de vente aux enchères*

> 'La maison aux enchères n'est pas responsable des vices et carences, dès lors qu'elle a rempli son obligation de diligence en décrivant les objets d'art vendus aux enchères. Elle a l'obligation d'informer le vendeur des réclamations sur des vices et carences de l'objet d'art présentées par l'acquéreur, dans les délais prévus par la loi, dans la mesure où il est possible de les porter à la connaissance du vendeur.'

Un code de déontologie (*Verhaltenskodex*) préparé en 1986 par l'Association allemande du commerce des objets d'art et des antiquités, a été établi pour le commerce international d'oeuvres d'art. Mais il n'a pas de force obligatoire et n'est pas intégré aux conditions de vente aux enchères. Seule une obligation morale en découle, il constitue une forme d'exhortation.

II. RISQUES JURIDIQUES POUR LA MAISON DE VENTE AUX ENCHERES

Avant d'analyser ces risques, il convient d'examiner la position juridique de la maison de vente aux enchères.

Les maisons de vente aux enchères allemandes ont choisi presque exclusivement la forme d'intermédiaires régie par l'art. 383 du Code commercial (*Handelsgesetzbuch*).[1] La maison de vente aux enchères mène les enchères en son nom propre pour le compte d'un tiers, de telle sorte qu'elle conclut un contrat de vente entre elle-même et l'adjudicataire.

Les risques juridiques auxquels une maison aux enchères est exposée peuvent se classer en deux catégories:

1. lorsqu'il apparaît que l'objet d'art mis aux enchères n'est pas décrit exactement dans le catalogue de vente ou qu'il est faux;
2. lorsqu'il est établi que l'objet d'art est un objet volé ou perdu.

La première catégorie relève de la garantie de vices matériels présentés par l'objet d'art, alors que la deuxième catégorie porte sur la garantie de l'absence de carence de titres de propriété sur l'objet vendu. Les conditions générales ont pour but, d'une part, de rationaliser les termes contractuels des nombreuses transactions, d'autre part, d'établir un partage de risques équilibré entre les intérêts des deux parties. Les maisons aux enchères étrangères établies en Allemagne doivent prendre en compte ces deux types de risques spécifiques.

---

1. Cf. THOMSEN, *Käuferschutz bei Kunstauktionen* (Bielefeld 1989) p. 14 et p. 65.

III. RECOURS DES ADJUDICATAIRES CONTRE LES MAISONS AUX ENCHERES

1. Recours basés sur l'art. 459 I du Bürgerliches Gesetzbuch (BGB)

L'acquéreur d'un objet d'art peut réclamer à la maison aux enchères le changement ou une diminution du prix (arts. 459, 460 et 462 BGB) lorsque l'opération d'achat est entachée d'un vice qui change la destination de l'objet ou sa valeur.

a. L'inauthenticité de l'objet d'art constituant un vice au sens de l'art. 459 I BGB

Un faux vendu comme l'oeuvre authentique d'un artiste est considéré par le *Bundesgerichtshof* (et avant par le *Reichsgericht*) et par l'ensemble de la doctrine comme un vice.[2] En tout cas, il faut souligner qu'il ne peut s'agir d'une opération de spéculation basée sur l'achat d'un objet d'art.[3] L'adjudicataire peut s'attendre à ce que le prix indique la provenance de l'objet d'art. Cependant, d'autres éléments du contrat de vente doivent être pris en compte: la description dans le catalogue, la signature apposée sur l'oeuvre et l'estampille; et pour contrôler s'il peut y avoir erreur sur l'objet du contrat d'achat.

b. Erreur sur la provenance (art. 459 I BGB)

L'attribution à une oeuvre d'art d'une fausse provenance est un élément entraînant la responsabilité; certains auteurs de doctrine estiment qu'il existe un vice seulement lorsque les experts considèrent que l'attribution a vraiment été inexacte, le *Reichsgericht* était d'un autre avis.

c. Autres erreurs

Outre les erreurs sur les dates de création, celles sur les données de technique artistique ou sur la restauration de l'oeuvre sont une autre source de vices pouvant engager la responsabilité de la maison de vente aux enchères. De tels vices sont aussi des vices au sens de l'art. 459 I BGB.

d. Diminution

La deuxième condition pour l'existence d'un vice de la chose au sens de l'art. 459 I BGB est une diminution de la valeur ou une diminution de

---

2. P. ex., BGH NJW 1972, 1658 *et seq.*, NJW 1975, 970 *et seq.*; RG 114, 239 *et seq.*; PALANDT-PÜTZO, *Bürgerliches Gesetzbuch, Kommentar*, 49. Auflage (München 1989) par. 459 Anm. 5 e aa.
3. LOCHER, *Das Recht der bildenden Kunst* (München 1970).

l'aptitude. Un vice de la chose existe si le vice a une influence essentielle sur la décision d'acheter ou sur le prix.

Sur la base de la constation d'un vice de la chose, l'acquéreur peut poursuivre la maison de vente aux enchères. Cependant, on peut se demander dans quelle mesure cette dernière peut exclure sa responsabilité dans des conditions générales et si une telle exclusion serait juridiquement valable.

2. *Le traitement de la garantie au sens de l'art. 459 I BGB dans les conditions générales des maisons de vente aux enchères*

Les recours à la disposition de l'acquéreur dépendent des clauses d'exclusion de la responsabilité contenues dans les conditions générales.

a. La possibilité d'une exclusion de toute responsabilité pour vice

i. Dans les conditions générales d'une maison de vente aux enchères importante, l'exclusion de la responsabilité est par exemple limitée au cas où l'objet d'art vendu aux enchères est vraiment faux. Si le caractère 'faux' de l'oeuvre est découvert cinq ans aprés la vente, l'acquéreur a le droit de le changer aux mêmes conditions que celles existant le jour de la vente. Les conditions générales de cette maison de vente aux enchères disposent aussi que cette possibilité n'existe pas si la description dans le catalogue s'accorde avec l'opinion prédominante du monde des experts au moment de la vente aux enchères.

ii. Bien que presque toutes les maisons de vente aux enchères allemandes aient choisi des clauses qui soient de façon similaire favorables aux acheteurs, d'autres maisons de vente aux enchères essaient d'exclure complètement leur responsabilité dans ces cas. C'est pourquoi, il reste à déterminer si de telles exclusions sont valides au regard de la loi sur les conditions générales (cf. art. 9 *AGB-Gesetz*). La doctrine se divise sur la question de savoir si des clauses d'exclusion peuvent être stipulées par les parties aux conditions générales. La jurisprudence a toutefois considéré que de telles clauses étaient valides (BGH, NJW 1975, 970 (971); BGH, NJW 1980, 1619 *et seq.*). Selon la jurisprudence les intérêts des parties et les risques impliqués dans la vente de voitures d'occasion sont comparables à la situation d'une maison de vente aux enchères ayant choisi la forme juridique d'un commissionnaire. Une exclusion de tout recours en garantie est possible pour les ventes de voitures d'occasion. Même si l'on ne suit pas l'interprétation du BGH et l'on traite la situation de vente et de la chose vendue différemment entre la vente de voitures d'occasion et le commerce d'objets d'art, une exclusion de la responsabilité tenant compte des conditions décrites ci-dessus reste permise car l'adjudicataire reste une institution juridique pouvant faire valoir son droit. Les clauses recommandées par l'Association allemande des maisons d'enchères d'objets d'art reconnaît à l'acheteur la possibilité d'intenter une action similaire à celle exercée contre un co-contractant par une partie qui a agi pour le compte d'un tiers en vue d'obtenir l'indemnisation des dommages subis par ce dernier (*Drittschadensliquidation*). Même s'il ne s'agit pas d'un cas classique d'application de cette institution juridique où le commissionnaire 'liquide' le dommage du commettant, l'adjudicataire peut se servir de cette institution juridique.[4] Elle doit être utilisée de la manière suivante: le commissionnaire 'liquide' le dommage de l'adjudicataire, car le dommage est causé par l'exonération légitime de la responsabilité. Mais, en appliquant l'idée générale de l'art. 281 BGB, l'adjudicataire peut intenter directement cette action contre le vendeur (celui qui fournit l'objet d'art).

iii. Malgré l'exclusion de la responsabilité dans les conditions générales, l'adjudicataire n'est pas privé de ses droits en fin de compte. Cependant, la règle fondamentale du collectionneur: *caveat emptor*,[5] ne perd pas sa validité.

b. La restriction de l'exclusion de tout recours en garantie

Une maison aux enchères ne peut pas s'appuyer sur l'exclusion de sa responsabilité sans restriction. Bien que cette exclusion de la responsabilité soit fixée dans les conditions générales, une maison aux enchères ne peut pas les appliquer, par exemple si les doutes sur l'inauthenticité d'un objet d'art résultent de circonstances évidentes. Dans ce cas, une exclusion des dispositions de l'art. 462 serait sans effet légal. Mais l'obligation de diligence à la charge de la maison aux enchères n'a pas été définie de façon uniforme par la jurisprudence (BGH, NJW 1980, 1619 (1621); BGH, NJW 1975, 970 (972)). Au moins, il reste toujours à la charge de la maison de vente aux enchères l'obligation de ne pas commettre une faute lourde dans le respect de son obligation d'éclairer le client potentiel.

3. Recours basés sur l'art. 459 II BGB

a. La garantie d'une qualité substantielle

S'il existe une garantie sur la qualité substantielle de l'objet d'art vendu, l'acquéreur au surplus a droit à des dommages-intérêts compensatoires pour non-exécution du contrat. En conséquence, l'adjudicataire peut choisir entre trois possibilités: ou bien le changement du bien ou une diminution du prix (arts. 459, 460, 462) ou des dommages et intérêts (art. 463,1). Il faut comprendre par 'une qualité substantielle', les éléments de fait et de droit qui influent sur l'utilisation ou la valeur de la chose.

4. P. ex., LÖHR, *GRUR* 1976, p. 411 (414).
5. R. CUMMINGS, *Christie's guide to collecting* (Oxford 1984) p. 147.

b. La possibilité d'une exclusion de tout recours en garantie dans les conditions générales

Quand une garantie est donnée sur la qualité substantielle d'un objet d'art lors d'une vente aux enchères, ce sont les règles du BGB qui s'appliqueront dans ce cas et non celles des conditions générales. Selon l'art. 11 N° 11 *AGB-Gesetz*, une exclusion de tout recours en garantie dans les conditions générales concernant le droit à des dommages-intérêts n'est pas valide, si la maison de vente aux enchères a garanti une qualité substantielle dans le cas d'espèce visé.

c. La description d'oeuvre dans un catalogue – une garantie sur la qualité substantielle au sens juridique?

Une autre question qui se pose est celle de savoir si la description d'un objet d'art dans un catalogue peut être considérée comme une 'garantie sur la qualité substantielle'. La doctrine est partagée sur cette question: certains considèrent qu'il s'agit d'une garantie, d'autres pas. La jurisprudence se divise également sur ce point. L'auteur est de l'opinion qu'une description de l'objet d'art dans un catalogue ne peut pas être considérée comme une garantie pouvant engager la responsabilité de la maison aux enchères du fait de la spécificité du commerce de l'art. Si l'on admet que la description d'une oeuvre d'art constitue une garantie sur la qualité substantielle, l'acheteur aurait dans le cadre d'une demande de dommages-intérêts, un droit au manque à gagner selon l'art. 252 BGB. Considérant la hausse des prix énorme et le développement général des prix dans les ventes aux enchères, une telle pratique constituerait un risque incalculable pour le commerce allemand utilisant les ventes aux enchères.

d. Vice caché par la maison de vente aux enchères

L'acquéreur a un recours contre la maison de vente aux enchères, lorsque cette dernière lui a caché un vice de l'objet d'art vendu (art. 463, 2 BGB).

4. La garantie d'éviction

Selon le droit allemand, l'acquéreur d'un objet volé ou perdu ne peut généralement pas en devenir propriétaire (art. 932 BGB). Les dispositions sur l'acquéreur de bonne foi ne s'appliquent pas en de telles circonstances (v. art. 935 I BGB).

Mais en ce qui concerne une vente aux enchères, la jurisprudence envisage quand même des dispositions sur l'acquéreur de bonne foi (BGH, *der Betrieb* 1989, p. 2605). Elle exige la vérification complémentaire d'autres conditions. Ces conditions résultent de l'art. 383 III BGB: la vente aux enchères doit être publique et annoncée afin de garantir l'accès du public.

L'auteur ne partage pas la position de la jurisprudence, car le commissaire-priseur n'est pas généralement désigné par des autorités publiques (art. 34b V Code industriel, *Gewerbeordnung*). Au surplus, la jurisprudence n'a pas pris en compte la garantie du droit de propriété, telle qu'elle est établie par l'art. 14 I de la loi fondamentale (*Grundgesetz*).

C'est pourquoi, à mon avis, le vendeur de l'objet d'art a l'obligation vis-à-vis de l'acquéreur de lui fournir la possession comme la propriété de l'objet. Si cela n'est pas possible, l'acquéreur a le droit de:
1. ne pas payer le prix (s'il ne l'a pas déjà fait);
2. réclamer des dommages et intérêts.

Par ailleurs, le vendeur ne pourra pas lui demander une quelconque contre-partie, en dehors de la restitution de l'objet d'art.

5. *Uniformisation*

Une uniformisation des conditions générales de vente n'est pas envisageable dans un futur proche, non seulement en Allemagne mais *a fortiori* au niveau communautaire.

France

RAPPORT NATIONAL SUR LE SUJET 4. LES CONDITIONS DE VENTE AUX ENCHERES

Jean-Louis Delvolvé*

Interrogé sur les régimes des ventes aux enchères en France, nous constatons d'abord qu'y coexiste une réglementation passablement complexe des professions ayant le monopole des ventes aux enchères, réglementation ancienne, lourde et devant probablement être remise en cause par le marché unique européen de 1993; d'autre part, le droit de la vente d'objets d'art lui-même présente par rapport au droit commun français de la vente consensualiste, un faible particularisme.

D'où un paradoxe entre la protection qui devrait résulter du monopole des officiers publics et ministériels et l'incertitude résultant d'un droit peu contraignant et d'une jurisprudence casuistique (l'exemple célèbre de l'affaire du Poussin, exposé *infra* p. 386, sur l'erreur comme vice du consentement étant particulièrement patent).

Nous présenterons donc, en premier lieu, la réglementation des ventes aux enchères (I) et, dans un second temps, les risques impliqués dans une telle vente (II).

I. LA REGLEMENTATION DES VENTES AUX ENCHERES

La vente de meubles, en France, est soumise à un régime particulier, lorsqu'elle est effectuée 'à cri public', c'est à dire aux enchères, à prix fixe (le prix ne doit pas être modifié), ou au rabais (baisse progressive du prix). Toute chose mobilière qui se trouve dans le commerce, sauf disposition particulière, peut être vendue aux enchères publiques. Cette forme de vente publique a aujourd'hui pris une extension considérable en ce qui concerne les objets d'art. La vente publique peut être volontaire ou forcée (objets abandonnés et non réclamés, meubles donnés en gage, colis transportés dont le destinataire refuse la réception, objets appartenant à l'Etat ou à une collectivité locale...). On ne retiendra que les ventes volontaires.

Les meubles... ne peuvent être vendus publiquement et aux enchères qu'en présence et par le ministère d'officiers publics ayant qualité pour y

* Avocat au Barreau de Paris.

procéder (*loi 22 pluviôse an VII, art. 871 CGI*). Les particuliers ne peuvent donc pas s'immiscer dans les fonctions des officiers publics et procéder à leur place à une vente aux enchères publiques sous peine de nullité de la vente (Req. 11 nov. 1986 DP 97 I 486) et de sanctions pénales.

Il est à noter (*Encyclopédie Dalloz, 'office public ou ministériel'*) que l'officier public est une personne (physique ou morale) titulaire de l'investiture du Gouvernement. Les charges sont en nombre limité et leurs titulaires exercent un monopole. En pratique les officiers publics sont indépendants du Gouvernement qui renouvelle toujours la charge du successeur, mais dépendants de leur Ordre professionnel. En outre le successeur doit acheter l'office à son titulaire.

Cinq corporations d'officiers ministériels ont le monopole de la vente de meubles aux enchères: les courtiers de commerce (que l'on écartera d'emblée parce qu'ils sont exclusivement compétents pour procéder aux ventes volontaires en gros et de certaines marchandises déterminées), les notaires, les huissiers, les greffiers et les commissaires-priseurs.

Les commissaires-priseurs sont les intervenants les plus usuels, spécialement en matière de vente d'objets d'art. Ils opèrent seuls ou avec l'assistance d'un expert et, le cas échéant, d'un crieur. Leur profession est régie par un certain nombre de textes:
- loi du 27 ventôse au IX
- ordonnance du 2 novembre 1945 (JCP 45 III 10.21.652)
- décret du 21 novembre 1956 – tarifs (JCP 56 III 21 652)
- décret 9 juin 1975 (JCP 75 III 42 939).

Les commissaires-priseurs ont un monopole exclusif à Paris. Ailleurs, le privilège n'est exclusif que dans la commune de leur établissement; en dehors, ils entrent en concurrence avec les notaires, les huissiers et les autres commissaires-priseurs. Les notaires, huissiers et greffiers ont également des domaines exclusifs (p. ex. ventes de fonds de commerce pour les notaires) mais qui ne concernent pas le commerce de l'art et peuvent entrer en concurrence avec les commissaires-priseurs dans les conditions ci-dessus.

Enfin, il existe un régime spécial pour les ventes administratives où interviennent certains fonctionnaires ou employés de l'Administration.

Pour ce qui est des objets, échappent au monopole du commissaire-priseur les meubles incorporels, les meubles par anticipation, les immeubles par destination et les marchandises neuves en gros. La vente aux enchères volontaire des marchandises neuves au détail, quant à elle, est interdite. Sauf cas exceptionnels, ces catégories ne comportent pas d'objets d'art.

Une fois déterminé l'intermédiaire compétent, les parties ont la liberté de désigner un ou deux officiers ministériels de leur choix.

Les officiers publics désignés ont également un droit de prisée (c'est à dire d'estimation). L'assistance d'un expert est souvent requise, notamment en matière d'objets d'art: les experts sont inscrits sur une liste dressée chaque année par le bureau de la Cour de Cassation au niveau national, ou sur une liste dressée par chaque Cour d'appel (*loi du 28 juin 1971 et décret du 31 décembre 1974*).

Quant aux formalités préalables, les ventes publiques d'objet d'arts, mais aussi d'archives, doivent donner lieu à une déclaration au Ministère de la Culture par l'officier public afin de permettre l'exercice effectif du droit de préemption (*v. infra*). Quand la vente publique est volontaire, les vendeurs sont libres d'organiser ou non, une publicité préalable.

La mise en vente, elle-même, est organisée librement par l'officier vendeur quant à l'ordre de vente des objets, le mode de mise à prix (fixe ou à réduire). L'officier ministériel a toujours droit à un honoraire spécial de mandat en plus de sa rémunération pour le droit de prisée. La vente se fait au plus offrant. Le transfert de propriété se fait par le prononcé de l'adjudication et sa mention au procès-verbal.

Pour ce qui est des oeuvres d'art, l'Etat peut exercer un droit de préemption par l'effet duquel il se trouve subrogé à l'adjudicataire. L'intention de préempter donne lieu à une déclaration remise entre les mains de l'officier public qui dirige l'adjudication, dans les quinze jours de la vente. Le Ministre est avisé quinze jours avant la vente avec toutes les indications utiles concernant l'objet vendu (ce qui se fait habituellement par l'envoi du catalogue qui tient lieu de déclaration). Ce droit de préemption a été institué par la loi de Finances du 31 décembre 1921 qui, dans son art. 86, donne une énumération très large de ce qu'elle entend par objet d'art puisqu'il s'agit des 'curiosités, antiquités, livres anciens et tous objets de collection, de peintures, aquarelles, pastels, dessins, sculpture originale et de tapisseries anciennes'.

Le procès-verbal dressé est un acte authentique. Les effets de l'adjudication sont ceux du droit commun de la vente. En outre, la matière relève d'une façon générale du droit commun de la vente (arts. 1582 et suivants du Code civil), consensuel et souple mais qui, en matière de vente d'objets d'art où l'origine et l'authenticité de l'oeuvre peuvent être déterminantes, crée parfois une incertitude fâcheuse.

II. LES RISQUES DANS UNE VENTE AUX ENCHERES

Comme tout contrat, la vente aux enchères d'objets d'art peut être annulée pour vice du consentement (art. 1109 Code civil) et spécialement pour erreur sur la substance (art. 1110 Code civil). Ce n'est pas un risque propre à ce type de contrat. Cependant, ce risque est accru dans la mesure où l'authentification de l'objet est souvent difficile, d'où l'intervention d'un expert (*v. supra*).

L'erreur sur la substance est elle-même une notion délicate à cerner et ce d'autant plus qu'il s'agit d'une oeuvre d'art. Comprise à l'origine de manière objective, la notion recouvre aujourd'hui celle de 'qualité substantielle'. Tout dépend alors de la volonté des parties, exprimée ou non. L'erreur doit être considérée comme portant sur la substance même de la chose, lorsqu'elle est de telle nature que, sans elle, une des parties n'aurait pas contracté (civ. 28.01.1913 S 13 I 487). L'authenticité d'une oeuvre peut être une qualité substantielle de la vente dont le défaut entraînerait la nullité, si les parties en sont convenues, c'est à dire si elle est entrée dans le 'champ contractuel'.

Aussi bien la pratique va-t-elle habituellement utiliser une terminologie d'usage permettant de distinguer selon le degré de certitude quant à l'authenticité; les mentions que l'on trouve dans les catalogues sont les suivantes:

1. Oeuvre de x: ce qui est de x n'est pas de y; si l'oeuvre s'avère n'être pas de x lui-même, la vente sera annulable.
2. Oeuvre signée de x: seule l'authenticité de la signature est déterminante; l'oeuvre signée par x peut être d'un autre (un élève par exemple).
3. Oeuvre attribuée à x: ce qui est attribué à x pourrait être attribué à un autre; seul le fait que l'oeuvre ait été effectivement attribuée à x est déterminant.
4. Oeuvre de l'atelier de x: l'oeuvre n'est pas de x, quoiqu'il ait pu y participer, mais nécessairement d'un élève ou d'un contemporain. L'époque, plus que l'auteur, est déterminante.
5. Oeuvre de l'école de x: l'oeuvre ne peut pas être de x mais d'un ou plusieurs auteurs assez typiquement influencés par lui et inspirés de sa manière pour constituer avec lui une école bien déterminée. L'époque est à nouveau déterminante. Dans le même genre d'idée, on a commencé récemment à utiliser la formule: oeuvre d'un 'suiveur de x'; l'expression semble être la traduction de son équivalent anglais en usage à Londres ou à New-York ('a follower').
6. Oeuvre du genre de x: l'oeuvre peut être de n'importe qui et réalisée n'importe quand.

On voit donc que, pour ce qui est des conditions de vente, l'intervention de l'expert permet de diminuer le risque d'erreur; et que, pour ce qui est de la pratique, la précision de la description au catalogue permet de caractériser au plus juste l'intention commune des parties quant au degré d'authenticité voulu.

Ces mesures ne suffisent cependant pas à chasser l'aléa d'une part et à éviter le contentieux d'autre part.

Une des affaires les plus célèbres en ce domaine est celle dite du Poussin ayant opposé les vendeurs d'un tableau à la Réunion des Musées Nationaux (Cass. 1ère Civ. 22.2.1978 D 78 p. 601, C.A. d'Amiens 1.2.1982 JCP 82 II n° 19916, Cass. 1ère Civ. 13.12.1983 D 84 p. 340, C.A. de Versailles 7.1.1987 D 87 p. 485). En l'espèce, les vendeurs savaient posséder un tableau de Poussin et souhaitaient le vendre aux enchères; l'expert de la vente les dissuada de cette attribution et le tableau fut mis en vente comme étant simplement de l'école des Carrache.

Le tableau étant vendu pour un prix modique, l'Etat exerça son droit de préemption et le musée du Louvre, fort heureux de cette acquisition, s'empressa de faire savoir qu'il avait acheté un authentique Poussin, et l'exposa comme tel.

Après un contentieux de plus de vingt ans, les vendeurs ont obtenu la nullité de la vente au motif que la vente s'était faite sur la base d'une erreur sur la substance de l'oeuvre, l'accord des volontés étant intevenu sur un tableau de l'école des Carrache, alors qu'il s'agissait bien d'un Poussin: en tous cas, il avait suffi aux yeux des magistrats de la Cour de Cassation qu'il existât une possibilité sérieuse que le tableau fût de Poussin pour que la vente fût annulable dès lors que l'attribution fausse à l'école des Carrache excluait, à elle seule, une telle possibilité.

La longueur de ce contentieux, quoiqu'exceptionnelle, caractérise suffisamment les difficultés et les risques existant dans les ventes aux enchères d'objets d'art. Mais la leçon qu'on peut en tirer est la suivante: pour éviter le risque d'annulation, il faut mais il suffit de décrire l'oeuvre offerte à la vente en précisant les éléments de certitude ou d'incertitude qu'on peut raisonnablement concevoir à son sujet au moment de la transaction. La vente du Poussin aurait problablement été à l'abri de l'action en nullité si le commissaire-priseur ou l'expert avait pris la précaution d'indiquer: 'Ecole des Carrache – Selon une tradition familiale, le tableau pourrait avoir été fait par Poussin'.

D'une manière générale, commissaire-priseur et expert doivent donc agir avec prudence et rédiger leurs catalogues avec le plus grand soin.

En conclusion, on est en droit de se demander ce que va changer le marché unique de 1993 à tout cela. A l'heure actuelle, aucune certitude n'existe sinon que, bien évidemment, ce n'est que l'organisation des professions du marché de l'art qui sera affectée et non le droit de la vente lui-même.

Cependant, et sous réserve de confirmation ou d'infirmation ultérieure, quelques conjectures sont raisonnablement possibles à l'heure actuelle. Ainsi, si on ne sait pas quel serait son domaine exact, étant donné que ses concurrents étrangers sont commerçants, la profession de commissaire-priseur serait maintenue. Les conditions d'accès, l'organisation ordinale seraient conservées. En revanche, toute idée de monopole devrait être abandonnée.

En fait, il semble que ce soit plus la confrontation commerciale directe avec la concurrence étrangère considérable qui doive modifier le marché de l'art français. Il est intéressant de noter que le chiffre d'affaires réalisé à l'Hôtel Drouot en 1988 a été de 2,8 milliards de francs contre 3,2 milliards de dollars, soit environ 19,2 milliards de francs, pour Sotheby's et Christie's (chiffres cités par le mensuel *Dynasteur* de novembre 1989).

The Netherlands

NATIONAL REPORT ON TOPIC 4. AUCTION SALES AND CONDITIONS

Jan M. Boll*

I. ARE AUCTION SALES CONDITIONS REGULATED?

From the perspective of the legal regime in the Netherlands, this question has two elements: (1) are there public regulations which specifically apply to the institutional, organizational aspects of sales by auction and (2) are there such regulations relating to the conditions of purchase and sale by auction?

1. Institutional Regulations

Under the Act on the Official Supervision at Public Auctions (*Wet ambtelijk toezicht bij openbare verkopingen* of 15 December 1971, S. 748, the 'Act') generally, a civil law notary (*notaris*) or a bailiff (*deurwaarder*) must be in attendance at public sales of movable goods.[1]

Notaries and bailiffs are state appointed although self-employed.

An auctioneer who disregards this requirement commits an offence which is punishable by imprisonment for a maximum period of six months and/or a fine of up to Dfl. 25,000 (*Wet Economische Delicten 1950*, Art. 1 under 4, and Art. 6 under 4).

The Court of Appeal of The Hague in its judgment of 16 March 1978 (*Nederlandse Jurisprudentie* (NJ) 1978, 631) ruled that the Act requires supervision by a notary or bailiff in order to bring about the 'technically correct and reliable procedure of sales of movable goods by auction'.

The Act does not specify the duties and responsibilities of the notary/bailiff

---

* Partner, De Brauw Blackstone Westbroek, Amsterdam.

1. Similarly any public sale of mortgaged immovables has to be made under the supervision of 'a public officer' (Art. 1255 Civil Code). The Code of Civil Procedure (Arts. 508 to 537j) contains various requirements in connection with the publicity for the auctioning of real property by way of execution pursuant to an attachment, the dual bidding procedure thereat (the traditional system of the 'Dutch' auction of bidding-up first and then starting again with a price which lowers till accepted by a bidder, a system which nowadays hardly ever is applied at auctions of movable goods and therefore will not be discussed herein), specific conditions of sale and some of the implications of allotment.

in respect of his supervision of the auction. The purpose of the presence of such an official is to secure that the rules of conduct to which the auction is subject will be properly followed. The notary/bailiff is deemed to be a custodian of good conduct. Accordingly, he should refuse his services if the auctioneer violates rules and regulations of public policy, e.g., provisions of the Decree regulating the establishment of auctioneers (*Vestigingsbesluit Veilinghoudersbedrijf*, 1967) or restrictions for opening hours of businesses (under the *Winkelsluitingswet*). Guidelines on the responsibilities of bailiffs at auctions are given in a circular letter of 6 January 1972 (No. 103P 872) from the Ministry of Justice addressed to all bailiffs. Notaries also follow these directives when they supervise auctions.

The circular letter requires the bailiff to prevent the public from being misled. He has to refuse his services if the auctioneer violates general standards of honesty and decency. The bailiff should verify the general information contained in the auctioneer's publicity for the sale in order that the public is not misinformed about, e.g., the subject of the sale, its location, its time and its accessibility and the applicability of general terms and conditions. The letter also instructs the bailiff to guard against improper practices at auction such as fake bidding by or on behalf of the seller, sale of stolen goods, undisclosed reserves etc. The 1972 circular letter refers to examples given in earlier similar letters of 8 January 1930 and 10 June 1933. Some of these examples however seem out of date in view of the present state of the auction business in the Netherlands.[2] In so far as art auctions are concerned much has changed for the better as a result of the internationalization of business and the harmonization of the standards and practices applied by the large international auction houses in their main places of business.

At auction, the notary/bailiff's obligations as custodian of good conduct entail, amongst others, that he should interfere in the bidding process if he observes that bids are overlooked or if fake bids are used to drive up the price artificially and he then may cancel such bids. He should ascertain that the final bid is properly allocated and that the amount of the final bid with identification of the buyer by number or otherwise, is correctly registered in the auctioneer's book. During the auction he may thus cancel a particular sale and require the item to be resold there.[3]

The usually effective remedy which the notary/bailiff has against the

2. The circular letter, e.g., ordered bailiffs to take care that the holding of an auction does not violate the *Drank-en Horecawet* (Act on the Sale of Alcoholic Drinks), but in its judgment of 29 February 1972 (No. 66221) the Supreme Court ruled that the aforementioned Act did not forbid auctions being held in places where alcoholic drinks are sold, like hotels.
3. Sometimes specific powers and duties for the notary/bailiff are contained in the sales conditions of individual auction houses. The conditions of the *Venduehuis* of The Hague empower the supervising notary to settle any disputes during the auction and to approve any decisions by the auctioneer to split or combine lots, or to change their order. Most Dutch auctioneers, however, state in their conditions of sale that during the auction the acting auctioneer has the sole discretion to settle and decide any disputes regarding each lot.

auctioneer if misconduct persists is the threat of withdrawing and thus frustrating the holding or continuation of a particular auction.

Notwithstanding the custodian function of the notary/bailiff, the auctioneer has the full responsibility for the organization of the auction in all its aspects and for the proper compliance with the conditions of sale. There is as yet no published case law about notarial or bailiff's civil liability for damage caused by inadequate supervision. Under Art. 3:370(b) New Civil Code, the State and the notary are each liable for any damages occuring as a result of non-compliance with the requirements of Art. 3:370 relating to the payment of creditors in case of the sale of real estate by means of public auction.

Although in principle notaries and bailiffs are obliged to provide their services when they are requested to supervise an auction, they may refuse for a proper reason, e.g., if the auctioneer does not enable them to abide by their professional rules. Accordingly, the Court of Appeal of The Hague in its aforementioned judgment of 16 March 1978 refused to order a notary to provide his services in a situation where the Association of The Hague Notaries, of which the notary was a member, did not give him the required permission to supervise because the auctioneer was unwilling to hold the auction at the Association's auction premises (the *Venduehuis*) in order to avoid to have to pay the fee for such use.

Although there is no general requirement that auctions are to be held in the Dutch language, local authorities may so require. Even without such official requirement the notary/bailiff should ascertain that in any event for those who participate in the auction the conditions are available in a Dutch language version. The Dutch offshoots of the international houses usually hold their auctions in English and publish in their catalogues the Dutch text of their conditions of business in the applicable version, together with an English translation thereof.

By circular letter of 27 February 1974 to all bailiffs, the Minister of Justice informed the bailiffs that the Act does not permit bailiffs and notaries to combine the supervision and the organization of a particular auction. At the auctions they supervise, the bailiffs and notaries may not act as a party or intermediary in respect of any contract of purchase and sale nor may they act as auctioneers there.

The fees of notaries and bailiffs for their attendance at an auction are subject to control by the Ministry of Economic Affairs. In 1990, the minimum and maximum *per diem* tariffs varied for bailiffs from Dfl. 160.00 to Dfl. 1,098.00 and for notaries from Dfl. 171.00 to Dfl. 1,138.00, subject to the turnover at auction.

2. The Conditions of Purchase and Sale

There are no provisions in the law of the Netherlands which specifically regulate the substance of the conditions of purchase and sale by auction of movable goods. In respect of the public sale of movables which are subject to execution under a pledge for security (*pand*), Art. 1201(1) of the Civil

Code provides that the auctioning thereof has to be public (*in het openbaar*), in accordance with local customs (*plaatselijke gewoonten*) and in accordance with the usual conditions (*gebruikelijke condities*).

In this context it may be noted that under the law of the Netherlands (Art. 1375 Civil Code) the parties to a contract are subject to what is customary (*het gebruik*) if the parties have not agreed otherwise and neither written law nor the unwritten principles of fairness (*goede trouw*) regulate the contents of their respective obligations. Even for fine art auctions local customs still play a role, e.g., in the interpretation of outdated though customary wording in standard terms and conditions (example: the sale is *zonder actie of refactie*, without any recourse to the seller).

In applying the conditions of sale, the auctioneer must take the (unwritten, jurisprudence formed) principles of fairness and good faith into account. He, furthermore, has the duty to act with such diligence (*zorgvuldigheid* – another common law, essentially jurisprudence formed concept) as is required in society in respect of the legitimate interests of other people; not doing so would constitute a tort under Art. 1401 Civil Code.

The judiciary may, according to a judgment of the The Hague Court of Appeal of 27 November 1987 (*Kort Geding Kort* 1988, 1109), be it only by way of marginal review (*marginale toetsing*), intervene in cases of obvious, arbitrary violation of such principles.[4]

Under general principles of Dutch private international law, auctions held within the Netherlands, as well as the transactions of purchase and sale resulting therefrom, are subject to domestic law of the Netherlands, also in the event the seller and/or the buyer are non-residents.

The conditions of auction of the main fine art auctioneers in the Netherlands contain an applicable law and jurisdiction provision referring to the law and the courts of the Netherlands. The United Nations Convention on the International Sale of Goods (Vienna 1980), which has been signed but not yet ratified by the Netherlands, provides in Art. 2 under b. that it does not apply to sales by auction.[5] The 1986 Hague Convention on the Law Applicable to Contracts for the International Sale of Goods (not yet in force) however, provides in Art. 9 that, failing a choice by the parties, or to the extent that such choice is prohibited, the law of the jurisdiction where the auction takes place shall apply.

4. In this case the court ruled that the auctioneer, by not giving the arguments of his refusal on the spot, had not arbitrarily or in violation of the public character of the auction refused to accept a bid of a person who in the past had been too late in settling his payment obligations for lots allocated to him.
5. The Amsterdam Court of Appeal in its judgment of 25 April 1985 (NJ 1986, 557) ruled in a dispute regarding the proper forum, in connection with an auction held in the Federal Republic of Germany, which according to its conditions of sale was subject to the law of the Netherlands, that such choice of law would only be effective – and not in violation of Art. 17 EEC Execution Treaty – if it can be established that the buyer has clearly accepted and agreed to the applicability of the law of the Netherlands.

II. CONDITIONS OF SALE AND THE AUCTIONING OF OBJECTS WITH UNCLEAR ORIGIN OF OWNERSHIP

1. Agency

The two main areas where conditions of sale deal with 'unclear origin or ownership' are the auctioning of lost or stolen property and the sale of goods which lack authenticity or, in other words, do not in essence conform to the description in the catalogue.

Under present law (Art. 637 Civil Code), the purchaser at auction who in good faith bought a stolen movable good is – by way of exception to what normally in such situation would apply – protected against the owner in that the purchaser is only obliged to return the object if the owner reimburses the purchase price. Subsequent acquirers of the object, however, do not similarly benefit from this, be it limited, ancient statutory protection for public auctions and markets. Under new Art. 3:86(3) under *a* of the New Civil Code, which shall be effective in respect of auctions held from 1 January 1993 onwards, the opposite arrangement will apply: no protection for a buyer at auction against a reclaiming owner of a stolen or lost movable object if it is auctioned within three years after its possession was lost.

Before discussing the remedies available to a buyer of a work of art which turns out to be 'non-authentic', it should be noted that Dutch law distinguishes two types of agency (*vertegenwoordiging*): the intermediary either acts in his own name (*middellijke vertegenwoordiging*), or he acts in the name of someone else (*onmiddellijke vertegenwoordiging*).

When the intermediary acts in his own name, but for the account of someone else, he establishes a contract between himself and the person with whom he acts. An example of such intermediary is the commission-agent, defined in Art. 76 Commercial Code as a person who makes it his business to enter into agreements in his own name for the account of a principal who owes him a commission fee. On the face of it this provision seems to apply to the auctioneer. The consequence of this form of agency would, however, be that the buyer and the seller in principle have no direct rights and obligations towards each other (Art. 78 Commercial Code). Were this type of agency to apply to the auctioneer, it would imply that the buyer can in connection with defects in title or status of a sold object only take legal action against the auctioneer and not against his principal, the seller not being a party to the purchase contract.[6]

When, on the other hand, an intermediary acts in the name of a principal, the acts of the intermediary are in principle attributed to the person he represents provided he acts in accordance with the terms of the principal's

6. ASSER-VAN DER GRINTEN I, *Vertegenwoordiging*, 7th edn, (1990) p. 86.

power of attorney. If such power of attorney is lacking or not complied with, the acts of the intermediary will still be attributed to the principal if the buyer in good faith on the basis of statements or actions of the principal held that the intermediary acted on the basis of a proper power of attorney.

It should be noted that for the purposes of the applicable form of agency, it is not necessary to disclose the seller's identity at the time of the sale. The intermediary may act in the name of someone he will identify later (*nader te noemen volmachtgever* – Art. 3:67(1) New Civil Code). Such intermediary must, however, when requested, identify the person he represents within a reasonable, though short period of time. If the intermediary does not disclose the name of his principal, he will be considered to have made the contract in his own name and for his own account (Art. 3:67(2) New Civil Code).

Clearly, the auctioneer who does not want to be deemed to have acted in his own name and to assume the seller's responsibility towards the buyer, has no alternative but to disclose the name of the seller which obviously may entail commercial and sometimes legal problems if the seller has implicitly or explicitly reserved the right to remain anonymous.

Although the names of sellers are not usually published in catalogues, most auction houses in the Netherlands in practice operate as if they have opted for the regime of *onmiddellijke vertegenwoordiging* and want to be deemed to act in the name of the seller.[7] Accordingly at the fall of the hammer a direct contract of purchase and sale between the seller and the buyer is established.

There is no unanimity amongst scholars regarding the legal basis of the transfer of title upon a buyer who bought from an intermediary: does the buyer acquire title directly from the seller, or rather from the intermediary?

The difference is of essence, e.g., in the event of bankruptcy of the auctioneer after the sale but before the actual transfer of title by the acutioneer to the buyer.[8] If the auctioneer acts in the name of the seller, he is deemed to 'hold' the goods on behalf of the seller. The auctioneer has an implied proxy to deliver the item to the buyer, who thus acquires the property directly from the seller.

2. *Unclear Origin of the Work of Art*

Under present law, the buyer of a work of art which has an unclear origin in that it turns out to be 'non-authentic', has, in principle, at least three forms

7. Of the sales conditions reviewed for these purposes, only those of the *Venduehuis* explicitly state that acceptance of a bid establishes a sales agreement between the buyer and the seller. Christie's Amsterdam B.V.'s conditions state that it 'acts as agent only', which implies the same provided Christie's indeed discloses the name of the seller which it for reasons of confidentiality may opt not to do.
8. Under Dutch law the final bid does not in itself constitute a transfer of title but only creates the seller's and/or the auctionner's obligation to provide title, the transfer of which generally is effected by delivery of the object to the buyer.

of remedy. The buyer can try to annul the sale on the basis of breach of contract, he may also be able to take action on the basis of a specific provision in the Civil Code relating to 'hidden defects' (*verborgen gebreken*) or he may opt for rescission of the contract on the basis of error in substance (*dwaling*).

a. Breach of contract

If explicitly or implicitly, by way of the form of the description of the object in the catalogue or otherwise, the authenticity of an object is guaranteed, and after the sale it turns out to be 'false' (in the light of such guarantee), the buyer can in principle require the annulment of the contract of sale and claim damages which may include full compensation for any reasonable loss of profit.

b. Hidden defects

Under present law, which will not be incorporated in the New Civil Code, the seller of an object is responsible for any 'hidden defect' thereof, which makes the object inappropriate – or less appropriate – for its 'use' or which jeopardizes its use in such manner that the buyer – had he known about the defect – would not have bought the object at all, or not for the same price (Art. 1540 Civil Code). The seller, however, is in this legal context not responsible for any defects which the buyer could have discovered himself and as a consequence knew or should have known (Art. 1541 Civil Code).

If the buyer actually knew about the defect, it was no longer hidden, even though normally a person in such circumstances would not have been aware thereof (HR 19–2–1915, NJ 1915, 910). In order to determine whether the buyer 'should have known' the criterion is whether a reasonable buyer exercising normal attentiveness should have recognized the hidden defect.[9]

If the buyer sues on the basis of a – material – 'hidden defect', he has the choice:

(i) to return the object to the seller and restitution of the purchase price (*actio redhibitoria)*;
(ii) to keep the object and receive part of the purchase price by way of compensation for loss in value of the object (*actio quanti minoris*).[10]

9. Sometimes it may successfully be argued that the buyer of a valuable item had the 'precontractual' obligation to specifically consult the auctioneer or an outside expert and that in not having done this he cannot in good faith make any claim. The seller and the auctioneer in situations of an extensive description and a high valuation of the object in a catalogue, will not normally be able to require such consultation. See CASTERMANS, 'Dwaling bij kunstkoop' *BW Jaarkrant* (1989) citing *Contractenrecht II* (BLEI WEISSMAN) nr. 513.
10. Art. 1544 Civil Code, however, provides that the seller who knew about the defect is liable to compensate the buyer for all costs, interest and damages. *See* ASSER-VAN DER GRINTEN, *op cit.*, p. 67.

Clearly in this context again the question comes up who legally is to be considered the buyer's ultimate contractual counterpart at auction: the auctioneer or the 'real' seller.

If the auctioneer acts in his own name, he will be responsible towards the buyer for hidden defects and may subsequently have recourse against his principal if its conditions make the seller guarantee the absence of hidden defects. The auctioneer shall normally not have such recourse if based on his general expertise, he should have been aware of the defect unless the seller knew of the defect but refrained from disclosing it.

Generally knowledge of the auctioneer is deemed to be knowledge of the seller.

If the auction house acted in the name of the seller, the seller is directly responsible towards the buyer. In case the auctioneer knew or should have known about the defect, whilst the seller did not, the auctioneer in principle is liable to the buyer for damages if the object is indeed delivered as authentic. The auctioneer, even after the sale, has the right not to deliver if he is in reasonable doubt about the object's authenticity. Accordingly the President of the Amsterdam District Court in an as yet unpublished judgment of 12 July 1990, KG 90/1227 KK, ruled that a seller was not entitled to attach the accounts of the auctioneer in a situation where the seller refused permission to take external expertise to establish the authenticity of a picture auctioned as a genuine Odilon Redon.

Often, legal action based on hidden defects is of no avail to disappointed buyers at auction because it is not practicable to establish what is deemed to be the 'use' of a non-authentic work of art.

A buyer of a non-authentic work of art would argue that its non-authenticity diminishes its monetary value but that under Dutch law does not necessarily affect its usability (e.g., a 'false' painting remains a painting and can still be used for decorative purposes).

c. Error in substance

An agreement can be annulled because of error in substance (Art. 1358 Civil Code). For annulment the following conditions must be met:

- the error must be in 'qualities' or 'circumstances' of the object which the person in error considered essential for the sale (other than the buyer's own private expectations about the future like expected price developments);[11]
- the seller and in particular the auctioneer knew or should have known the qualities and/or circumstances essential to the potential buyers (or to the particular buyer if specific information had been requested prior to a sale).

11. In the words of the New Civil Code: 'without the error the contract would not have been made', Art. 6:228(1) under *a*, New Civil Code. An essential quality could, e.g., be the fact that the work was made by a specific artist or belonged to a certain 'school' or period; an essential circumstance could be the fact that the work had been part of a specific collection.

Even when these conditions are met, a sale cannot be annuled in case of an error in substance which is deemed to be for the account and for the risk of the party in error (Art. 6:228(2) New Civil Code).

An error may have to be for the risk of the erring party if the nature of the particular agreement or the standards in society so require. Generally one party to a contract should not become the victim of the carelessness, inexperience, imprudence or stupidity of the other.[12]

There should generally be no annulment of the sale if the party in error is to blame for the error.[13]

If a sale is the result of incorrect information by the seller or the auctioneer, the lack of investigation by the buyer normally will not be held against him. Art. 6:228(1) under *a* New Civil Code provides that a contract can be annuled if the error is caused by information provided by the other party, unless that party reasonably could have assumed that the agreement would have been concluded irrespective whether or not that information had been given. The same applies similarly where a party has remained silent whilst he should have spoken.

Error in substance by the seller will generally be for the risk of the seller. The Supreme Court ruled in HR 19–6–1959, NJ 1960, 59 *Kantharos van Stevensweert* that the sole fact that an antique silver mug turned out to have a quality which the seller did not know and did not have to be aware of at the moment of sale (*in casu a greater value*), is in itself not a good legal basis for a claim to annul the sale on the basis of error in substance. The Court however indicated that other, additional circumstances might have justified annulment of the sale, e.g., when the buyer could, and according to the norms of good faith should, have informed the seller about the quality of the item.

IV. HOW DO AUCTION HOUSES PRESENTLY DEAL WITH THESE RISKS AND WHAT DEVELOPMENTS MAY BE EXPECTED?

Presently, the law of the Netherlands generally does not prevent the auctioneer from disclaiming in his conditions any liability for 'hidden defects' or for damage caused by error in substance. Such disclaimers, however, as a result of jurisprudential developments may turn out to be of little avail to the auctioneer if it is deemed to be against the concept of good faith for a professional or expert to rely on a general disclaimer.

12. *See* ASSER-HARTKAMP II, 8th edn. (1989) p. 169.
13. An auctioneer 'privately' bought a drawing which both he and the seller believed to be by Jan van Goyen. When it turned out to be a reproduction, the auctioneer did not have a claim against the seller. The court considered that the auctioneer – an art expert – could reasonably be expected to have sufficiently investigated the work before buying. The fact that the painting had belonged to the estate of a known art collector and that the frame had to be removed in order to check the authenticity were not considered valid reasons for not investigating the work, District Court Amsterdam 7–3–1973, NJ 1974, 93 (*Paul Brandt* case).

Under the New Civil Code (Art. 7:6(1)) in cases of a 'consumer sale',[14] the seller generally cannot to the detriment of the buyer exclude or restrict the buyer's rights and claims in the event of shortcomings in the object and the performance of his obligations.

A restrictive clause in general sales conditions can be disregarded or annulled taking into account the nature and content of the purchase agreement, the way in which the general conditions were made applicable, the identifiable interest of each of the parties and all further relevant circumstances. If the other party is a consumer, the code assumes the unreasonableness of a condition which substantially limits the obligations of the seller in respect of what the buyer could reasonably expect without such a clause on the basis of otherwise applicable law (Art. 6:237 under *b*). The as yet unsolved question is whether the 'non-authenticity' of the work constitutes a 'short-coming in the obligations of the seller'.

New Art. 7:17 provides that an object that has been sold does not conform to what has been agreed if it does not have the characteristics which the buyer on the basis of the purchase agreement could have resonably expected. The buyer may expect that the object possesses the qualities which are necessary for its normal use, but what is the 'normal use' of a work of art still has to be established in jurisprudence. Generally one may assume that a buyer is entitled to expect that an object conforms to its description in the catalogue. Possibly the (national/international) reputation of the auctioneer and his action house has repercussions in this respect.[15]

Whilst the impact of the New Civil Code on auctions and conditions of business applied there is still uncertain, developments in the art market have broadened the differences between the two types of auction houses. On the one hand, there still are the traditional, locally operating, auctioneers who sell anything from bicycles to fine art and act basically as facilitators of the transaction between seller and buyer. On the other hand, there is the increased economic importance of the auction houses which – due to increased competition in the market and the desire to attract clients – have widened their range of services beyond the traditional scope, employ experts in many fields and accordingly have greater responsibility to provide in their catalogues a proper description of the objects to be auctioned.

The sophisticated auctioneer fulfils a more independent role than his traditional colleague, which entails from a legal point of view increased responsibility toward sellers, buyers and the public and hence the

14. *A 'consumer sale'*: A sale of movable goods by a seller acting in the course of a business or profession to a buyer who is a person not acting in the course of a business or profession (7:6). If the item is sold by a representative of the seller and such representative is acting in the course of a business or profession, the sale is assumed to be a consumer sale, unless the buyer knew at the moment of the sale that the seller was a private person.
15. The Amsterdam Court of Appeal has stated that an *art dealer* does not have a general obligation to guarantee that the work of art he sells has a market value of more or less the purchase price (Amsterdam Court of Appeal, 24–11–1983, NJ 1984, 794).

auctioneer's liability not as a representative but *qualitate qua* for, e.g., lack of proper description, proper expertise and care.

Furthermore whilst in the past sales conditions differed from auction house to auction house and from country to country, nowadays the international auction houses and their clients increasingly want uniformity of conditions of auction and their application in the various jurisdictions where the same house operates. The tendency of international auctioneers to harmonize their conditions is hindered by differences in their applicability and interpretation as a consequence of the various local regulations and legal systems which do not treat similarly liability disclaimers and consumer protection law. Perhaps the ICC could fulfil a role in stimulating the harmonization of the sales conditions and fine art auction practices in various jurisdictions by providing model texts and guidelines.

Spain

NATIONAL REPORT ON TOPIC 4. AUCTION SALES AND CONDITIONS*

Miguel Virgós Soriano**

There are several regulations in Spain for different kinds of auctions: Decree of 18 June 1948 on 'official auction halls'; Arts. 2048–2055 Code of Civil Procedure; and Decree 2930/1972 on private cultural foundations, annex I, Arts. 1–50. None of them is directly applicable to common auctions, although some of their solutions may be applicable by analogy. Common auctions are basically regulated by means of general conditions. The special 26/1984 Consumer Protection Act (and in the future a proposed law on general conditions) imposes limits on the auctioneer, in addition to those derived from the general rules on contracts.

From the point of view of the auctioneer, auctioning works of art of unclear origin or ownership may imply civil liability towards the buyer. A duty of care is imposed on the auctioneer to exercise due diligence and skill (see Art. 1101 Civil Code, Arts. 244 and 255 Commercial Code and Art. 10 of the 1984 Consumer Protection Act. The degree of diligence due by the auctioneer will be that of a good businessman in his particular specialty, not merely the diligence of an ordinary person.[1] In some extreme and improbable cases – auction of stolen or smuggled objects, with knowledge of it – the auctioneer may be prosecuted under penal law.

From the point of view of the *buyer*, Art. 464 II Civil Code will normally be applied to decide disputes of ownership, for example, whether *a non domino acquisition* is possible or not, etc. The interpretation of this article is very controversial. The Supreme Court has been following a romanistic interpretation. Art. 464 II contains a special rule for public sales, applicable to auctions, and the *verus dominus* cannot vindicate the object that he lost or was illegally deprived of without reimbursing the price to the buyer.

---

* Editor's note: *see also* 'Spain: Introduction' by B. CREMADES in Part One.

** Associate Professor, Facultad de Derecho, Universidad Autónoma de Madrid.

1. *See.* J. ALFARO, 'La subasta de obras de arte', *Revista de Derecho Mercantil* (Madrid 1986) pp. 99–189.

Suisse

RAPPORT NATIONAL SUR LE SUJET 4. LES CONDITIONS DE VENTE AUX ENCHERES

Quentin Byrne-Sutton* et Marc-André Renold*

I. INTRODUCTION

Il est devenu presque banal de parler de l'incroyable expansion que connaît le marché de l'art et notamment en Suisse. Nous laisserons à d'autres le soin d'exposer les chiffres dont la presse quotidienne fait régulièrement état et qui prouvent non seulement l'essor de la valeur individuelle de certains objets d'art vendus sur le marché suisse, mais aussi la croissance extraordinaire du chiffre d'affaire de ceux qui participent à ce marché.[1]

Zurich et Genève sont devenus d'importants centres internationaux de ventes aux enchères pratiquées en majeure partie par les grandes maisons de vente, mais les ventes organisées par un certain nombre de galeries à Bâle, Berne et Lucerne sont également prisées par les connaisseurs, de même que celles qu'organisent un certain nombre d'huissiers judiciaires pour leur propre compte.

Il est inévitable que cette croissance des ventes aux enchères engendre une augmentation des questions juridiques qu'elles soulèvent. A cela s'ajoute la relative complexité des transactions elles-même à l'occasion desquelles interviennent une série de personnes dont il n'est pas inutile, à titre préliminaire, de rappeler les rôles respectifs.

Quoique la procédure dans laquelle se déroulent les ventes aux enchères puisse varier d'un Canton suisse à l'autre, celles-ci se déroulent très généralement sous la surveillance d'un *officier public*, huissier judiciaire à Genève, *Gemeindeammann* à Zurich, *Steigerungsbehörde* à Lucerne. Le rôle de cet officier public se limite, contrairement à celui du commissaire-priseur français, à la surveillance du bon déroulement de la vente, autrement dit à la police de l'audience, sans qu'il n'assume, sous réserve d'un certain nombre d'exceptions, une responsabilité sur la qualité des objets mis en vente, par exemple leur authenticité.

L'organisation proprement dite de la vente, à savoir toutes les opérations

---

* Avocat, Baker & McKenzie, Genève.

1. *V.* notamment au sujet de Genève l'enquête réalisée par DOSSIERS PUBLICS. *Ventes aux enchères: les chefs du succès*, Genève, No° 62 (nov–déc 1988) pp. 24 *et seq*.

préliminaires telles la publicité, la mise au point d'un éventuel catalogue, l'exposition publique des objets, ainsi que la vente elle-même et toutes les opérations postérieures à celle-ci, est toujours plus souvent le fait d'une maison de vente spécialisée. Ce sont les experts ou directeurs de la maison qui effectuent la criée des enchères et adjugent les objets mis en vente au plus offrant.

Lorsqu'une maison de vente organise une vente aux enchères, elle a souvent un rôle d'intermédiaire, ce qui pourrait faire penser qu'elle n'encourt aucune responsabilité contractuelle à l'égard de l'acheteur, le contrat de vente se nouant exclusivement entre le vendeur et l'acheteur de l'objet d'art. Tel n'est cependant pas le cas et il suffit à cet égard de lire les conditions générales de vente des principales maisons de vente pour voir qu'elles cherchent à délimiter leur propre responsabilité, indiquant que le risque d'être tenu responsable est effectivement ressenti.[2]

L'objet du présent rapport est précisément d'examiner en droit suisse dans quelle mesure la responsabilité d'une maison de vente peut dans certaines hypothèses être engagée à l'égard de l'acheteur d'une oeuvre d'art. La compréhension de cette éventuelle responsabilité nécessite toutefois deux opérations préliminaires: un bref examen des sources du droit suisse dans le domaine des ventes aux enchères (II), ainsi que la qualification juridique des rapports se nouant entre la maison de vente, l'acheteur et le vendeur (III). Nous limitant à la seule responsabilité contractuelle, à l'exclusion de la responsabilité pour acte illicite, nous examinerons l'une des principales causes possibles de responsabilité: la vente aux enchères d'une oeuvre d'art inauthentique (IV).

II. LES SOURCES DE LA REGLEMENTATION DES VENTES AUX ENCHERES EN DROIT SUISSE

Une vente aux enchères ayant lieu en Suisse sera en principe entièrement soumise au droit suisse. En effet, les législations cantonales de droit public s'appliquent aux ventes se déroulant sur le territoire du Canton,[3] tandis que

---

2. Nous nous sommes appuyés, pour le présent rapport, sur un certain nombre de textes de conditions générales publiées à l'occasion de ventes aux enchères ayant eu lieu récemment en Suisse. Il s'agit des ventes suivantes: vente du 16 mai 1990 organisée à Genève par *Christie's* (Objets Russes et Fabergé); vente du 14 novembre 1989 organisée à Genève par *Sotheby's* (Néo-Classical and Empire Porcelain); vente du 14 novembre 1989 organisée à Genève par *Phillips* (Important Jewels, European Silver and Objects of Vertu); vente du 7 au 13 mars 1990 organisée à Zurich par la Galerie *Koller*; vente du 21 avril 1990 organisée à Bâle par *Habsburg, Feldman* (Importantes montres de poche, montres-bracelets et pendules). Les références faites plus loin à des conditions générales de vente se rapportent exclusivement à celles publiées à l'occasion de ces cinq ventes.

3. Les législations cantonales se prononcent rarement expressément sur leur champ d'application spatial, mais leur but étant d'assurer le bon déroulement des enchères dans l'intérêt public du Canton, il est indiscutable qu'elles s'appliquent aux ventes se déroulant dans le Canton. Il s'agit de 'dispositions impératives du droit suisse' au sens de l'art. 18 de la Loi fédérale de droit international privé (LDIP), du 18 décembre 1987, RS 291.

le droit privé fédéral réglementant les relations contractuelles est le plus souvent applicable par le biais de clauses d'élection de droit figurant dans les conditions générales de vente.[4]

A supposer que le droit suisse soit applicable, il y a lieu de faire un certain nombre de précisions sur les différentes règles entrant en ligne de compte à l'occasion d'une vente aux enchères et en particulier sur celles qui ont trait aux garanties relatives aux défauts que peut avoir l'objet vendu.

1. Contrat de vente aux enchères

Le contrat de vente aux enchères est réglementé aux arts. 229 à 236 du Code des Obligations du 30 mars 1911 (CO). Ces dispositions se rapportent pour la plupart aux enchères publiques volontaires. Cependant, ces quelques articles ne traitent que de manière partielle les questions particulières soulevées par la vente aux enchères, notamment celles de la conclusion du contrat (arts. 229 al. 2 et 3, 231 et 232), du paiement par l'adjudicataire (art. 233), du transfert de la propriété (art. 235), des manoeuvres frauduleuses pouvant fausser le libre jeu des enchères (art. 230) et de la garantie (art. 234 al. 3).

A propos de la garantie l'art. 234 al. 3 CO stipule que:

> 'Dans les ventes publiques et volontaires, le vendeur est tenu de la même garantie que dans les ventes ordinaires; il peut toutefois, par des conditions de vente dûment publiées, s'affranchir de toute garantie autre que celle dérivant de son dol'.

Cette disposition fait référence à deux autres sources importantes de réglementations applicables lors de ventes aux enchères: le droit du contrat de vente ordinaire d'une part et les conditions générales de vente d'autre part.

2. Contrat de vente

Le contrat de vente, régi par les arts. 184 *et seq.* CO, institue deux types de garanties qui lient le vendeur sauf clause contractuelle contraire: la garantie en cas d'éviction, qui a trait aux droits que peuvent avoir des tiers sur l'objet vendu (arts. 192 à 196 CO), et la garantie en raison des défauts de la chose, qui se rapporte aux qualités de l'objet promises par le vendeur ou à ses vices cachés (arts. 197 à 210 CO). Cette dernière garantie est essentielle dans

4. Sauf exceptions qui ne nous intéressent pas ici, l'élection de droit est admise en droit international privé suisse des contrats (art. 116 LDIP). La question est plus complexe dans le cas, peu fréquent en pratique, d'une vente ayant lieu sans élection de droit, car le droit applicable dépendra alors de la qualification et de la détermination de la prestation caractéristique des différents contrats en cause (art. 117 *et seq.* LDIP). *V.* à ce sujet l'arrêt du Tribunal fédéral ATF 112 II 337 = ASDI 1988 504 (note. F. VISCHER).

notre domaine, puisque la jurisprudence considère que les dispositions relatives à la garantie des défauts s'appliquent à la vente d'une oeuvre inauthentique.[5]

Précisons aussi que, sur le plan des sources de la réglementation de la vente aux enchères, le Tribunal fédéral, dans une jurisprudence constante, considère que d'autres moyens, tirés des dispositions générales du CO, peuvent être invoqués alternativement à ceux relatifs à la garantie du vendeur. Il s'agit essentiellement en matière de vente de faux des règles sur les vices du consentement, et notamment l'erreur (arts. 23 *et seq*. CO).[6] Enfin, il faut encore préciser que la vente n'est pas le seul contrat susceptible d'entrer en ligne de compte puisque, comme nous aurons l'occasion de le voir, divers contrats de services faisant également l'objet de règles spéciales du CO sont conclus à l'occasion d'une vente aux enchères.

3. *Conditions générales de vente*

Les conditions générales de vente, auxquelles fait aussi expressément référence l'art. 234 al. 3 CO, sont également une importante source de droits et d'obligations pour les participants à une vente aux enchères. Le droit du contrat de vente aux enchères, celui du contrat de vente ordinaire, ainsi que celui des contrats de services étant en grande partie de nature dispositive, les parties peuvent aménager leurs relations contractuelles comme elles l'entendent. Cette possibilité est expressément prévue en matière de garantie dans la vente aux enchères à l'art. 234 al. 3 CO, puisqu'il y est dit que le vendeur peut s'exonérer de la garantie prévue par la loi, sauf en cas de dol, autrement dit de tromperie, de sa part (l'art. 199 CO prévoit d'ailleurs une solution similaire pour le contrat de vente ordinaire). Toutes les maisons de vente actives en Suisse font largement usage de cette possibilité et limitent dans leurs conditions générales de vente la responsabilité du vendeur en cas d'inauthenticite' ou autre défaut des objets vendus.[7]

---

5. *V*. l'important arrêt *Van Gogh*, ATF 82 II 411 = JdT 1957 I 182. B. DUTOIT, 'La responsabilité du vendeur dans le commerce de l'art en droit privé suisse et à la lumière du droit comparé', *International Sales of Works of Art/La Vente Internationale des Oeuvres d'Art* (Institute of International Business Law and Practice – International Chamber of Commerce/Faculté de Droit, Université de Genève 1988) pp. 86 *et seq*.
6. *V*. l'arrêt *Van Gogh* précité n. 5, ainsi que les divers autres arrêts cités *infra* n. 44.
7. *V*. les textes des conditions générales de vente cités *supra* n. 2 et en particulier les arts. 7 et 9 des conditions générales de Christie's:

   '(7) Christie's agit exclusivement pour le compte du vendeur; elle et le vendeur n'assument aucune responsabilité pour les défauts éventuels d'un lot, pas plus qu'elle ne garantie l'exactitude d'aucune déclaration relative à l'auteur, l'origine, la date, l'âge, l'attribution, l'authenticité, la provenance, le poids ou l'état matériel d'un lot. Aucune personne employée par Christie's n'est autorisée à donner une garantie à cet égard.'

   '(9) En dérogation aux présentes conditions de vente, si un acquéreur retourne un objet acheté dans un délai d'un an, avec la preuve qu'il s'agit d'une falsification, la vente sera annulée et le prix remboursé à l'acheteur, pour autant que l'objet soit resté dans le même état qu'au moment de la vente.'

   V. également les arts. 2 et 25 des conditions générales de Sotheby's, les arts. 5 et 6 de celles de la Galerie Koller, l'art. 2 de celles de Phillips et l'art. 4 de celles d'Habsburg, Feldman.

Relevons toutefois que la rédaction de conditions générales n'est pas entièrement libre. En effet, ces textes peuvent donner lieu à des abus étant donnè la position privilégiée dans laquelle se trouve l'auteur des conditions générales face à son cocontractant qui n'a en général pas la possibilité d'en discuter le contenu, voire simplement d'en prendre connaissance. Si la Suisse n'a pas adopté de législation spécifique sur le droit des conditions générales, l'on trouve cependant à leur sujet en droit suisse un certain nombre de règles éparses, d'origine législative ou jurisprudentielle. Tel est le cas déjà de l'art. 234 al. 3 CO lui-même qui exige que les conditions de vente aux enchères soient 'dûment publiées', ou encore de l'art. 8 de la nouvelle loi contre la concurrence déloyale qui réprime les conditions générales abusives.[8] La jurisprudence fédérale a également développé une série de principes relatifs à l'interprétation et à la validité de certains clauses contenues dans les conditions générales.[9]

4. Droit public cantonal

Le droit public cantonal, dernière source de réglementations applicables aux ventes aux enchères, contient non seulement des règles sur le déroulement des ventes, mais aussi d'importantes règles relatives aux conditions générales de vente et aux limites qu'elles peuvent contenir quant à la garantie du vendeur. L'art. 236 CO autorise expressément les cantons à adopter des dispositions complémentaires en matière d'enchères publiques, ce que la plupart d'entre eux ont fait.[10] Ces réglementations ont pour objet principal d'assurer dans l'intérêt public un déroulement correct et loyal des ventes aux enchères, raison pour laquelle elles prévoient généralement la présence d'un officier public.[11]

Si l'on prend l'exemple de la loi genevoise du 24 juin 1983 sur les ventes volontaires aux enchères publiques et de son règlement d'application,[12] outre les dispositions sur le déroulement des ventes, d'importantes règles sont posées sur les exclusions de garantie du vendeur. Celui-ci peut certes exclure sa garantie, mais cela ne peut être fait dans les conditions générales que si la clause est suffisamment claire, qu'elle est mise en relief dans le

8. Loi fédérale contre la concurrence déloyale du 19 décembre 1986, en vigueur depuis le ler mars mars 1988, RS 241.
9. C'est ainsi que la jurisprudence refuse de donner effet à certaines clauses dites 'insolites' auxquelles le cocontractant ne pouvait pas s'attendre lors de la conclusion du contrat. *V.* P. GAUCH, W. SCHLUEP, P. TERCIER, *Partie générale du droit des obligations*, 2e éd., Tome I (Zurich 1982) pp. 148 *et seq.*, NN 785 *et seq.*
10. Tel est le cas des principaux Cantons où ont lieu des ventes aux enchères d'importance, tels Bâle, Berne, Genève, Lucerne et Zurich. *V.* R. RUOSS, *Scheingebote an Kunstauktionen*, (Thèse Zurich 1984) p. 32.
11. Selon la loi genevoise sur les ventes aux enchères, citée à la prochaine note, l'huissier exerce la 'police des enchères' et doit à ce titre veiller à ce que 'le libre jeu des enchères ne soit en aucun cas entravé ou faussé' (art. 17).
12. Entrés en vigueur le 1er janvier 1984. Recueil des lois genevoises, I/3/16 et I/3/16,5.

texte de façon à frapper l'attention du lecteur et lue par l'huissier avant le début des enchères et affichée pendant celles-ci dans la salle de vente (art. 7 de la loi et 8 du règlement).

Tel est donc, sommairement esquissé, l'ensemble des règles, tant fédérales que cantonales, qui viennent réglementer une vente aux enchères se déroulant en Suisse.

III. QUALIFICATION DES RAPPORTS JURIDIQUES LIANT LE VENDEUR, LA MAISON DE VENTE ET L'ACHETEUR D'UNE OEUVRE D'ART

Une question importante qui a une grande influence sur le régime de la responsabilité de la maison de vente est celle de la qualification des relations juridiques liant les parties participant à une vente aux enchères, à savoir le vendeur, la maison de vente et l'acheteur.

1. En droit actuel

a. La relation entre l'acheteur et le vendeur

La relation entre l'acheteur et le vendeur de l'oeuvre d'art n'offre pas en principe de difficultés particulières de qualification: dès l'adjudication au plus offrant un contrat de vente aux enchères est conclu entre eux, contrat dont les grandes lignes ont été exposées au chapitre précédent et qui a pour effet de transférer la propriété de l'oeuvre d'art du vendeur, en principe propriétaire de l'objet, à l'acheteur. Les conditions générales de vente définissent un certain nombre des modalités de ce contrat de vente.

L'acheteur est généralement présent dans la salle, à moins qu'il se soit fait représenter ou qu'il ait, par une pratique de plus en plus courante, fait parvenir un ordre d'achat à l'huissier ou au crieur. Quant au *vendeur*, il est le plus souvent représenté par la maison de vente, dans un cadre contractuel dont nous allons voir qu'il est délicat à qualifier, mais il arrive aussi que la maison de vente soit propriétaire de certains des objets vendus, cas dans lequel il n'y a à l'évidence aucun problème de représentation.[13]

---

13. V. RUOSS, *op. cit.*, p. 63 et O. WEBER-CAFLISCH, *Faux et ... défauts dans la vente d'objets d'art* (Genève 1980) p. 75.

b. La relation entre le vendeur et la maison de vente

Lorsqu'un vendeur demande à une maison de vente de vendre un objet pour lui, il conclut avec elle un contrat de service très proche du *mandat* (art. 394) *et seq.* CO).[14] Le droit suisse des obligations contient un certain nombre de mandats spéciaux ou de contrats apparentés au mandat pouvant à priori entrer en considération pour la qualification juridique des relations vendeur – maison de vente, à savoir le contrat d'agence (art. 418a *et seq.* CO), le contrat de commission (art. 425 *et seq.* CO) et le contrat de courtage (art. 412 *et seq.* CO). Afin de cerner plus précisément le type de contrat généralement en cause, il convient d'examiner le contenu des contrats individuels passés entre les vendeurs et les maisons de vente, à la lumière aussi des conditions générales de vente qui font souvent référence aux contrats individuels.

i. Quoique les termes retenus dans les conditions générales et les contrats passés par écrit entre le vendeur et la maison de vente retiennent parfois le terme *d'agence*,[15] il est douteux que l'on puisse considérer ce contrat comme un contrat d'agence, car celui-ci implique une relation d'une certaine durée.[16] Or, les rapports entre la maison de vente et la personne qui désire vendre une oeuvre d'art, ou même une série d'oeuvres d'art, ne se rapportent en principe qu'à cette vente et n'ont par conséquent pas un caractère durable.
ii. Il est par contre possible, quoique cela soit rarement le cas en Suisse, que cette relation relève du contrat de *commission*. Dans le contrat de commission, le commissionnaire, soit dans notre cas la maison de vente, se charge *en son propre nom*, mais pour le compte du commettant, soit le propriétaire de l'oeuvre d'art, de conclure un contrat de vente moyennant commission (art. 425 CO). Puisque dans cette hypothèse la maison de vente agit en son propre nom, elle apparaîtra à l'égard de l'acheteur comme le *vendeur* de l'objet d'art. Il s'agit d'un cas de

---

14. D'après l'art. 394 CO le mandat est un contrat selon lequel le mandataire s'engage 'à gérer l'affaire dont il s'est chargé ou à rendre les services qu'il a promis'. *V.* ATF 112 II 337 (340); WEBER-CAFLISCH, *ibid.* Le préambule des conditions générales de Habsburg, Feldman (version en français) dit expressément que la maison de vente agit en tant que mandataire.
15. *V.* p. ex. l'art. 1.3 des conditions générales de Habsburg, Feldman selon lequel:
    'Les ventes ont lieu en francs suisses et sans autres garanties que celles prévues dans les présentes conditions de vente. Habsburg, Feldman agissant en tant qu'agent ainsi que le vendeur ne sauraient en aucun cas être tenus pour responsables d'un défaut ou d'une détérioration des lots de même que le l'exactitude des indications concernant l'auteur, l'origine, l'époque, l'âge, l'attribution, l'authenticité, la provenance, le poids ou l'état d'un objet. De même, aucune personne employée par Habsburg, Feldman n'a autorité de donner quelque garantie que ce soit.'

    Le terme d'agence est également retenu dans le contrat type individuel ('contrat d'acceptation') proposé par Christie's au vendeur.
16. L'art. 418a CO qui définit le contrat d'agence parle d'un engagement 'à titre permanent'. *V.* P. TERCIER, *La partie spéciale du Code des obligations* (Zurich 1988) p. 412.

représentation dite *indirecte*.[17] Une telle relation contractuelle est par exemple souvent celle retenue en République fédérale d'Allemagne.[18]

Qu'en est-il en Suisse? Il apparaît au contraire que, dans la plupart des cas, les grandes maisons de vente n'entendent pas agir en leur propre nom et insistent généralement sur leur rôle d'intermédiaires.[19] Elles agissent donc en principe comme des représentants *directs*, le contrat de vente prenant effet entre le vendeur, représenté par la maison de vente, et l'acheteur.[20]

iii. Reste à déterminer dans quel cadre contractuel cette représentation se noue. L'hypothèse généralement avancée est celle du contrat de *courtage* selon lequel le courtier est chargé, moyennant une commission, de servir d'intermédiaire pour la négociation d'un contrat (art. 412 CO).[21] Le rôle d'une maison de vente, qui semble bien être de mettre en contact contre rémunération un acheteur et un vendeur dans le cadre d'une vente aux enchères, paraît à première vue bien correspondre à celui du courtier. La seule difficulté est qu'en principe le courtier n'a pas en tant que tel le pouvoir de conclure un contrat au nom de son mandant.[22] La doctrine propose donc de considérer qu'au contrat de courtage vient s'ajouter le mandat particulier de conclure le contrat de vente au nom du vendeur moyennant le respect de certaines conditions, notamment celle de ne vendre qu'à partir d'un prix minimum (la 'réserve'),[23] tandis que le Tribunal fédéral suisse parle d'un 'contrat analogue au mandat'.[24]

Par conséquent en droit suisse il y a lieu de considérer la maison de vente comme un courtier du vendeur rémunéré par une commission prélevée sur le montant du prix de vente atteint, mais disposant au surplus du pouvoir d'agir comme représentant *direct* du vendeur pour la conclusion du contrat de vente aux enchères.[25] Ce contrat mixte fait souvent l'objet d'un contrat individuel écrit passé entre la maison de vente et chaque vendeur, et certaines dispositions des conditions générales de vente s'y rapportent également.

---

17. *V.* TERCIER, *op. cit.*, p. 419; GAUCH, SCHLUEP, TERCIER, *op. cit.*, pp. 196 *et seq.*, N 1062.
18. *V.* H. HANISCH, 'Aspects juridiques du commerce international de l'art en République Fédérale d'Allemagne', *International Sales of Works of Art/La Vente Internationale d'Oeuvres d'Art*, pp. 157 *et seq.*, 178; H. HEINBUCH, 'Aktuelle Rechtsfragen des Kunsthandels in der Bundesrepublik Deutschland', *ibid.*, pp. 195 *et seq.*, 209.
19. *V.* p. ex. l'art. 14 des conditions générales de la Galerie Koller, l'art. 11 de celles de Phillips et le préambule de celles de Habsburg, Feldman. *V. aussi* WEBER-CAFLISCH, *op. cit.*, p. 74 *et seq.* et RUOSS, *op. cit.*, p. 46.
20. *V.* RUOSS, *op. cit.*, p. 41. L'examen des contrats que les maisons de vente concluent avec les vendeurs confirme ce point de vue.
21. *V.* dans ce sens RUOSS, *op. cit.*, p. 46 et les auteurs cités.
22. *V.* TERCIER, *op. cit.*, p. 407, N. 3150 et la jurisprudence citée.
23. *V.* RUOSS, *op. cit.*, p. 46 et les auteurs qu'il cite à la n. 74.
24. *V.* l'ATF 112 II 337 (JdeT 1987 I, 170).
25. Le montant de la commission due varie entre 10 et 18% selon les maisons de vente et le prix de vente atteint.

c. La relation entre l'acheteur et la maison de vente

La relation entre l'acheteur et la maison de vente dépend en grande partie de ce qui vient d'être dit. En effet, dans la mesure où la maison de vente agit comme représentant direct du vendeur, le *contrat de vente* aux enchères est en fait conclu entre l'acheteur et le vendeur. Il n'y a par conséquent pas de contrat de vente entre l'acheteur et la maison de vente, celle-ci n'agissant pas pour son propre compte, comme c'est le cas en droit allemand (la maison de vente agissant alors comme représentant indirect du vendeur). Quelle est alors en droit suisse la nature de la relation juridique entre l'acheteur et la maison de vente?

En même temps que l'objet est adjugé à l'acheteur le plus offrant, autrement dit à la conclusion du contrat de vente par la maison de vente pour le compte du vendeur, il est possible de considérer qu'il se noue une autre relation contractuelle liant cette fois l'acheteur et la maison de vente. Ce contrat serait en quelque sorte le pendant du courtage existant entre le vendeur et la maison de vente et pourrait lui aussi être considéré comme proche du *contrat de courtage*, mais conclu cette fois pendant les enchères entre l'acheteur et la maison de vente.[26] L'enchérisseur le plus offrant accepte l'offre qui lui est faite par la maison de vente de le mettre en rapport avec le vendeur, afin de conclure une vente, ceci contre paiement d'une commission. Cette relation fait aussi généralement l'objet d'un certain nombre de dispositions expressé dans les conditions générales de vente.[27]

2. *Evolution possible*

La qualification d'un contrat est fondée en premier lieu sur la volonté des parties relative à l'organisation de leurs relations juridiques, cette volonté étant notamment exprimée par les termes et le contenu d'un éventuel contrat écrit. C'est par conséquent sur cette base surtout que nous avons examiné la qualification généralement admise en Suisse à l'heure actuelle, s'agissant des relations juridiques entre le vendeur, la maison de vente et l'acheteur.

Cela dit, la volonté des parties n'est pas toujours entièrement commune, ni parfaitement cristallisée, tandis que les circonstances entourant la conclusion et l'exécution d'un contrat peuvent apparaître en partielle contradiction avec le sens juridique usuel des termes employés dans le contrat. La question se pose alors de savoir si, suite à la mutation profonde du marché de la vente aux enchères de certains objets d'art et au rôle nouveau et multiforme joué

26. *V.* RUOSS, *op. cit.*, pp. 66 *et seq.*
27. *V.* p. ex. les dispositions relatives à la commission due par l'acheteur à la maison de vente. commission qui varie entre 7 et 15% selon les maisons de vente et le prix de vente atteint. Cf.l'art. 18 des conditions générales de vente de Sotheby's, l'art. 3 de celles de Christie's, l'art. 2 de celles de la Galerie Koller, l'art. 1 de celles de Phillips et l'art. 3.3 de celles de Habsburg, Feldman.

par les grandes maisons de vente, la qualification de la position juridique de ces dernières ne risque pas de changer à l'avenir.[28] En effet, la frontière entre la qualité de représentant direct qui agit au nom et pour le compte d'un tiers et celle de représentant indirect, qui vend pour le compte d'autrui mais en son propre nom, devient plus difficile à tracer lorsque l'intermédiaire entreprend un mandat à facettes multiples en offrant des services variés. Il peut alors être délicat de déterminer le rôle exact de l'intermédiaire et de distinguer ce qui relève de sa propre responsabilité ou plutôt de celle de son mandant.

Or, dans le contexte des grandes ventes actuelles, il y a toute une série de circonstances nouvelles qui, prises ensemble, pourraient influencer la qualification des relations se nouant entre le vendeur, la maison de vente et l'acheteur, du moins certains de leurs aspects. En effet, les maisons de vente mettent non seulement à disposition des services d'expertise, mais offrent également différents types de garanties financières, aux vendeurs ou aux acheteurs. Ces prestations ont pris récemment des formes diverses comprenant notamment des prêts aux vendeurs et acheteurs ainsi que des garanties de prix de vente minimum aux vendeurs. Une autre circonstance importante est la réputation acquise des grandes maisons, que les vendeurs et acheteurs peuvent percevoir comme un gage particulier de sérieux des services rendus et de qualité des objets vendus, ce qui peut d'ailleurs aussi influencer la valeur (la cote) et le 'pedigree' des objets mis en vente.

Dans ces conditions, la maison de vente peut non seulement perdre une partie de sa 'neutralité', puisque son intérêt propre à vendre les objets augmente, mais peut également être ressentie comme offrant une garantie personnelle de qualité de l'objet (relative p. ex. à la valeur d'estimation pour le vendeur[29] et à l'authenticité pour l'acheteur). Si une telle conception était admise, l'on peut imaginer qu'une maison de vente soit parfois considérée comme solidairement responsable, à côté du vendeur, d'une garantie de qualité implicite vis-à-vis de l'acheteur. C'est d'ailleurs peut-être en partie à cause de cette ambiguïté croissante de leur position que les maisons de vente ressentent la nécessité d'exclure expressément leur responsabilité dans leur conditions générales de vente, cela malgré l'adoption d'une position de simple représentant selon les termes du contrat passé avec le vendeur.

IV. LA RESPONSABILITE DE LA MAISON DE VENTE VIS-A-VIS DE L'ACHETEUR D'UN FAUX

Acheter une oeuvre d'art comporte un certain nombre de risques, en particulier celui d'acheter un faux. Le droit de la vente contient diverses règles permettant de protéger l'acheteur d'un bien, qu'il s'agisse d'ailleurs

---

28. *V.* à ce sujet, en droit américain, le très intéressant rapport général de MM. Van Kirk REEVES et Jan M. BOLL, *supra* pp. 353–361.
29. *V.* p. ex. au sujet de la responsabilité d'une maison de vente pour une erreur d'estimation liée à une expertise imprécise, l'ATF 112 99 347.

d'une oeuvre d'art ou d'un autre bien mobilier. Ces dispositions sont principalement celles relatives à la garantie en raison des défauts de la chose vendue (art. 197 *et seq*. CO), dispositions qui sont applicables au contrat de vente aux enchères selon l'art. 234 al. 3 CO. A supposer réalisées les conditions de l'action en garantie, l'acheteur d'un faux pourra faire valoir ses droits à l'encontre du vendeur, ce qui impliquera en général la résolution du contrat de vente et par conséquent la restitution des prestations effectuées.

Qu'en est-il à l'égard de la maison de vente? La réponse à cette question implique de rechercher quels peuvent être les fondements de la responsabilité de la maison de vente, puis d'examiner les moyens, action en garantie et invalidation pour erreur, que peut éventuellement faire valoir l'acheteur d'un faux face à la maison de vente.

1. Les fondements de la responsabilité éventuelle de la maison de vente

Dès l'adjudication la maison de vente est liée à l'acheteur par ce que nous avons défini comme un contrat analogue au courtage, la vente elle-même étant conclue avec le vendeur représenté par la maison de vente. L'obligation de la maison de vente en tant que 'courtier' se limite à faire en sorte que le contrat de vente puisse être conclu, ce qu'elle réalise en organisant la vente aux enchères. Selon cette qualification du rapport juridique, elle n'a en revanche, à l'égard de l'acheteur, aucune obligation liée à la conclusion ou à l'exécution du contrat de vente et donc en principe aucune obligation de garantie.[30] Tout au plus peut-on considérer que le courtier a une obligation de fidélité à l'égard de son mandant qui implique de collaborer en cas de difficulté dans l'exécution du contrat dont il a rendu la conclusion possible, par exemple en lui indiquant l'identité du vendeur afin qu'il puisse le cas échéant se retourner contre lui en cas de défaut.[31]

La question se pose alors de savoir pourquoi les conditions de vente de la plupart des maisons de vente contiennent des clauses relatives à la garantie de l'objet vendu, soit en excluant toute garantie,[32] soit plus souvent en la

---

30. *V.* TERCIER, *op. cit.*, p. 408, NN 3158 *et seq.*
31. *V.* RUOSS, *op. cit.*, pp. 69 *et seq.*
32. *V.* les arts. 2 et 11 des conditions générales de vente de Phillips:
    '(2) PHILLIPS SON & NEALE, S.A. ci-après désigné PHILLIPS, décline toute responsabilité en ce qui concerne l'âge, l'origine, l'état ou la qualité des pièces. Phillips Son & Neale ne donne absolument pas de garantie quant à la qualité des métaux précieux contenus dans chacun des articles en vente; les acheteurs doivent s'assurer eux-mêmes de la composition de ces métaux. Toute déclaration faite à cet égard, soit imprimée dans le catalogue, soit donnée oralement, ne constitue qu'une indication. Les objets sont vendus dans l'état ou ils se trouvent au moment de l'adjudication. Les acheteurs ont la possibilité, au cours de l'exposition précédant la vente, de se renseigner sur l'état et la valeur des collections. Cependant toute responsabilité est refusée.
    '(11) PHILLIPS agit pour le compte du vendeur. Elle n'assume pas plus que le vendeur, aucune responsabilité pour les défauts éventuels d'un lot. Pas plus qu'elle ne garantit l'exactitude d'aucune déclaration relative à la description, origine, date, âge, etc... Aucune personne employée par PHILLIPS n'est autorisée à donner une garantie à cet égard.'

limitant aux seuls 'faux intentionnels' (*deliberate forgery*).[33]

Il y a à cela sans doute plusieurs raisons. La première est que la garantie ou son exclusion contenues dans les conditions générales sont d'abord celles du vendeur représenté par la maison de vente, et non pas celles de la maison de vente elle-même. Rappelons à cet effet que les conditions générales de vente visent aussi à réglementer les relations entre l'acheteur et le vendeur, et non seulement celles qui lient l'acheteur à la maison de vente.[34]

La seconde raison est que la maison de vente elle-même peut, dans un certain nombre d'hypothèses spécifiques, être le vendeur des oeuvres d'art mis en vente sans qu'il n'existe aucune relation de représentation directe. Tel est le cas si la maison de vente vend des objets dont elle est elle-même propriétaire ou encore si ses relations avec le vendeur impliquent un rapport de représentation indirecte, par exemple parce que les parties ont choisi de conclure un contrat de commission au lieu d'un simple mandat de représentation.[35]

La troisième raison expliquant la présence de clauses de garantie dans les conditions générales est peut-être un désir d'éviter une certaine insécurité juridique. En effet, même s'il apparaît qu'en règle générale la maison de vente agit en tant que représentant direct du vendeur, il n'est pas exclu qu'elle puisse *à posteriori* en cas de litige être considéré comme ayant agi comme représentant indirect de celui-ci (le contrat de vente prenant alors

33. *V.* l'art. 25 des conditions générales de vente de Sotheby's selon lequel:
'a) Si dans les trois semaines qui suivent la vente d'un lot quelconque, l'adjudicataire notifie par écrit à Sotheby's que le lot vendu est un "faux intentionnel" et qu'il le retourne à Sotheby's dans le même état où il se trouvait au moment de la vente et s'il est établi que le lot vendu est un "faux intentionnel", Sotheby's annulera la vente et remboursera le montant encaissé par eux ou rachètera le lot pour le même montant.
'b) Un "faux intentionnel" signifie une imitation faite avec l'intention d'induire en erreur en ce qui concerne l'auteur, l'origine, la date, l'âge, la période, la culture ou la source qui n'est pas décrite comme telle dans la description du catalogue et qui, à la date de la vente, avait une valeur nettement inférieure à celle qu'elle aurait dû avoir si elle avait été conforme à la description en question.
'c) Bien que ledit lot rentre dans la définition de "faux intentionnel" mentionné au paragraphe b) ci-dessus, l'adjudicataire ne pourra revendiquer aucun droit se basant sur les termes de cette condition lorsque:
- la description portée au catalogue à la date de la vente était conforme à l'opinion généralement admise des experts ou spécialistes, ou
- s'il est possible d'établir que le lot en question est un faux intentionnel seulement aux moyens de procédés scientifiques qui ne sont généralement acceptés qu'après la publication du catalogue.
'd) Les droits résultant de cette condition ne seront pas cessibles et resteront acquis exclusivement à l'acheteur, c'est-à-dire à la personne seule au nom de qui la facture originaire a été faite par Sotheby's pour le lot vendu.'
V. également l'art. 9 des conditions générales de Christie's, l'art. 5 de celles de la Galerie Koller, l'art. 4 de celles de Habsburg, Feldman.
34. *V.* III *1*.a et III. *1*.b.
35. Ces hypothèses se présentent occasionnellement dans la pratique des ventes aux enchères en Suisse. *V.* RUOSS, *op. cit.*, p. 63.

directement naissance entre l'acheteur et la maison de vente), avec pour conséquence que cette dernière serait tenue à la garantie.[36]

Enfin, il reste que les relations entre l'acheteur et la maison de vente sont soumises à la liberté contractuelle et rien ne semble empêcher la maison de vente de s'engager à une certaine garantie (celle qu'elle donne en matière de 'faux intentionnel'), même si cette garantie n'est pas imposée par la loi à celui qui agit en tant que représentant direct.

Pour toutes ces raisons, l'on comprend que figurent dans les conditions de vente des dispositions relatives à la garantie dont peut répondre la maison de vente, et en particulier dans le cas de la vente d'un faux.

2. *Les conditions de l'action en garantie de l'acheteur*

A supposer que l'on soit dans l'une des hypothèses dans lesquelles la maison de vente peut être tenue responsable pour la vente d'un faux, il faut encore que soient remplies les conditions permettant une action en garantie de l'acheteur en raison des défauts de la chose vendue, action qui tendra en général à la résolution du contrat de vente.[37] En l'absence d'une réglementation particulière dans les conditions générales de vente, ce qui est rare, ce seront les dispositions supplétives du CO qui détermineront à quelles conditions l'acheteur peut rendre la maison de vente responsable.

D'après le Tribunal fédéral,[38] critiqué par certains,[39] l'achat d'un faux revient à l'achat d'une oeuvre d'art défectueuse (un *peius*), plutôt qu'à l'achat d'autre chose que ce que l'acheteur voulait (un *aliud*). Ce sont alors, selon le Tribunal fédéral, les dispositions sur l'action en garantie des défauts de la chose vendue (art. 197 *et seq.* CO) qui sont applicables. Cette action est soumise, dans l'intérêt de la sécurité des affaires, à un certain nombre de conditions assez strictes: obligation de l'acheteur, sous peine de déchéance, de vérifier la chose rapidement et d'aviser le vendeur immédiatement en cas de découverte d'un défaut (art. 201 CO), court délai de prescription d'un an (art. 210 CO), etc.[40]

Les conditions générales de ventes aux enchères modifient le régime légal ordinaire, soit en excluant totalement toute responsabilité du vendeur et de

36. *V.* à ce sujet les remarques faites plus haut dans le texte à propos de l'évolution possible de la qualification de la position des maisons de vente, ainsi que le rapport de MM. Van Kirk REEVES et Jan M. BOLL, précité n. 28.
37. Outre cette action dite 'rédhibitoire', le droit de la vente donne à l'acheteur d'un objet affecté d'un défaut l'action 'minutoire' qui permet d'obtenir une indemnité pour la moins-value (art. 205 al. 1 CO). En cas de vente d'un faux c'est généralement l'action rédhibitoire que fera valoir l'acheteur.
38. *V.* p. ex. l'arrêt de principe relatif à la vente d'un faux *Van Gogh*, ATF 82 II 411 = JdT 1957 I 82.
39. WEBER-CAFLISCH, *op. cit.*, pp. 53 *et seq.*; DUTOIT, *op. cit.*, pp. 87 *et seq.*
40. Sur ces conditions *v.* en général TERCIER, *op. cit.*, pp. 38 *et seq.*, NN 275 *et seq.* et en particulier pour la vente d'oeuvres d'art DUTOIT, *op. cit.*, pp. 86 *et seq.* et WEBER-CAFLISCH, *op. cit.*, pp. 83 *et seq.*

la maison de vente en cas de faux,[41] soit, plus fréquemment semble-t-il, en limitant leur responsabilité au cas de la vente d'un 'faux intentionnel', celui-ci étant défini comme 'une imitation faite avec l'intention d'induire en erreur en ce qui concerne l'auteur, l'origine, la date, l'âge, la période, la culture ou la source' de l'objet d'art.[42] Les mêmes disposition des conditions générales de vente apportent encore d'importantes restrictions à cette notion de faux, puisque n'est pas accepté comme étant inauthentique le faux dont la description dans le catalogue était conforme à l'opinion généralement admise par les experts à l'époque de la vente, ni celui dont l'inauthenticité a été prouvée par des moyens scientifiques inconnus à l'époque de la vente. Si l'on ajoute à cela que les délais de garantie sont souvent assez courts, l'on comprend que l'acheteur n'est que peu protégé par de telles dispositions.[43] La question se pose donc de savoir si l'acheteur bénéficie d'autres moyens d'annuler la vente d'un faux.

3. *La possibilité d'invoquer l'erreur essentielle*

Le droit suisse dispose d'un autre moyen de protéger les intérêts de l'acheteur d'une oeuvre d'art: l'invalidation du contrat pour erreur essentielle. Dans une jurisprudence constante,[44] critiquée par une part importante de la doctrine,[45] le Tribunal fédéral considère que l'acheteur peut invoquer *alternativement* l'action en garantie des défauts (art. 197 *et seq.* CO) et l'invalidation pour erreur essentielle (art. 23 *et seq.* CO). Cela a surtout une importance pour l'acheteur lorsqu'il ne peut pas invoquer la garantie pour les défauts parce que les conditions n'en sont pas réalisées, notamment parce que le court délai de prescription de cette action est échu.

Pour qu'un cocontractant puisse invoquer son erreur, ce qui amènera à une invalidation du contrat, il faut que celle-ci soit *essentielle*. L'erreur sur les motifs du contrat n'est en principe pas essentielle (art. 24 al. 2 CO), sauf dans le cas prévu à l'art. 24 al. 1 ch. 4 CO selon lequel l'erreur est essentielle lorsqu'elle

41. *V.* l'art. 11 des conditions générales de Phillips reproduit *supra* n. 32.
42. Art. 25 a) des conditions générales de vente de Sotheby's (le texte de cet article est intégralement reproduit *supra* n. 33). Les conditions de vente de Habsburg, Feldman (art. 4) contiennent une définition similaire. *V. aussi* l'art. 5 des conditions générales de la Galerie Koller.
43. Pour les ventes dont les conditions générales sont ici examinées le délai était d'un an chez Christie's (art. 9), de trois semaines chez Sotheby's (art. 25), de trois semaines chez Koller pour les pierres précieuses et de deux ans pour les autres objets (arts. 5 et 6), de cinq ans chez Habsburg, Feldman (art. 4).
44. *V.* en matière d'oeuvres d'art les arrêts ATF 52 II 143 (vente d'un faux tapis d'Orient '*Chah Abbaz*'), ATF 56 II 424 (vente d'un faux tableau de *Léopold Robert*), ATF 82 II 411 = JdT 1957 I 182 (vente d'un faux tableau de *Van Gogh*), ATF 102 II 96 (vente de faux *timbres-poste*) et récemment ATF 114 II 131 = JdT 1988 I 508 (vente d'un faux dessin de *Picasso*).
45. *V.* l'examen approfondi de cette doctrine dans l'arrêt '*Picasso*', ATF 114 II 131 = JdT 1988 I 508.

'porte sur des faits que la loyauté commerciale permettait à celui qui se prévaut de son erreur de considérer comme des éléments nécessaires du contrat.'

La jurisprudence considère à juste titre que l'authenticité d'une oeuvre d'art est un élément nécessaire du contrat,[46] qui permet l'invalidation de la vente, à supposer encore que certaines autres conditions soient réalisées, en particulier que l'erreur porte sur des éléments qui sont subjectivement essentiels pour l'acheteur et qu'il soit objectivement justifié de les considérer comme tels.[47] Il est par conséquent peu probable que dans un cas où le vendeur renonce expressément à garantir l'authenticité, l'acheteur puisse ensuite affirmer avoir été dans l'erreur en ignorant que l'oeuvre était un faux.[48]

Les effets principaux de l'erreur essentielle sont les suivants. La partie qui était dans l'erreur peut invalider le contrat dans l'année qui suit la découverte de son erreur (art. 31 CO). Les prestations faites seront à restituer sur la base des règles sur l'enrichissement illégitime (art. 62 *et seq.* CO). La question se pose de savoir quels sont les délais de prescription de l'action en restitution du prix payé, l'erreur sur l'authenticité d'un objet d'art pouvant être découverte très longtemps après son acquisition. Le Tribunal fédéral, dans son récent arrêt *Picasso*, a répondu à cette importante question de la manière suivante: en application de l'art. 67 CO, l'action en restitution du prix payé de l'acheteur se prescrit dans l'année qui suit la découverte de son erreur et dans tous les cas dans les dix ans qui suivent la *conclusion* du contrat.[49] Autrement dit l'acheteur qui découvre l'inauthenticité de l'oeuvre d'art plus de dix ans après l'avoir achetée, même s'il peut encore invalider le contrat en invoquant son erreur, ne pourra en tous les cas plus réclamer au vendeur la restitution du prix payé.[50]

Relevons enfin que l'action en invalidation du contrat de vente, même s'il s'agit d'une vente aux enchères, doit être dirigée contre le vendeur. La maison de vente ne sera donc pas directement concernée par l'invalidation du contrat de vente lorsqu'elle a agi en tant qu'intermédiaire. Cela dit, l'invalidation pour erreur ne lui sera pas indifférente dans un certain nombre d'hypothèses: d'une part lorsqu'elle vend en son propre nom dans les cas décrits plus haut et, d'autre part, lorsque le vendeur s'est fondé, pour déterminer la qualité de l'objet vendu, sur une expertise de la maison de vente. Dans ce dernier cas, il n'est pas exclu, une fois la vente annulée à

---

46. *V.* p. ex. l'arrêt *Van Gogh*, ATF 82 II 411 = JdT 1957 I 182 et plus récemment l'arrêt *Picasso* ATF 114 II 139 = JdT 1988 I 508.
47. Pour un examen détaillé des conditions de ce type d'erreur, dite erreur de base (*Grundlagenirrtum*) *v.* GAUCH, SCHLUEP, TERCIER, *op. cit.*, pp. 104 *et seq.*, NN 549 *et seq.* Pour l'erreur dans la vente d'objets d'art, *v.* DUTOIT *op. cit.*, pp. 84 *et seq.* et WEBER-CAFLISCH, *op. cit.*, pp. 97 *et seq.*
48. *V.* DUTOIT, *op. cit.*, p. 85; TERCIER, *op. cit.*, p. 51, n° 387.
49. ATF 114 II 131, 141–144 = JdT 1988 I 508, 516–518.
50. Cette interprétation du point de départ du délai absolu de la prescription est critiquée par P. PIOTET, 'A propos de l'arrêt "Picasso": Annulation pour vice de la volonté et prescription de l'action en répétition de l'indu', JdT 1988 I 519.

cause de l'inauthenticité de l'oeuvre vendue, que le vendeur se retourne contre la maison de vente en faisant valoir le dommage qu'il a subi du fait de l'expertise erronée.[51] Mais cela nous engage sur la voie de la responsabilité de l'expert qui n'est pas l'objet du présent rapport.

V. CONCLUSION

En Suisse les ventes aux enchères restent, à part l'intervention de quelques dispositions impératives, dominées par le principe de la liberté contractuelle. C'est à dire l'importance des contrats individuels conclus entre les maisons de vente et les vendeurs, ainsi que des conditions générales de vente. En effet, ces textes sont la source de la majeure partie des droits et obligations des parties et ce sont sur eux que l'on s'appuie pour définir le rôle respectif que joue chaque participant à la relation juridique triangulaire assez complexe qu'est la vente aux enchères. L'on ne saurait donc assez recommander, dans l'intérêt de la sécurité du droit, une rédaction claire et précise de ces textes, ce qui évitera d'inutiles surprises aux diverses parties en cause, notamment lorsque l'objet vendu se révèle par la suite être un faux. Cette clarté sera d'autant plus importante à l'avenir que le rôle joué par les grandes maisons de vente ne cesse d'évoluer vers une participation plus 'directe' aux ventes qu'elles organisent. Dans ce contexte, l'on relèvera enfin que le fait que les même maisons de vente organisent des ventes aux enchères dans de multiples pays, requiert sans doute de porter une attention accrue à l'harmonisation des conditions générales de vente tout en respectant les concepts et la terminologie du droit des différents lieux où se déroulent les ventes.

---

51. *V.* au sujet de là responsabilité envers le *vendeur* de la maison de vente comme expert (estimation d'une lampe de *Gallé*) ATF 112 II 347 = JdT 1987 I 28. D'ailleurs, avec l'évolution importante des conditions dans lesquelles se déroulent les grandes ventes actuelles, il n'est pas entièrement exclu que la maison de vente soit parfois considérée comme ayant donné à l'acheteur une garantie implicite de qualité ou d'authenticité engageant la responsabilité de celle-ci.

TOPIC 5. INTERNATIONAL TEMPORARY EXHIBITIONS AND INSURANCE

L'ASSURANCE DES EXPOSITIONS TEMPORAIRES INTERNATIONALES

Introduction

TOPIC 5: INTERNATIONAL TEMPORARY EXHIBITIONS AND INSURANCE

Under the chairmanship of *Prof. Jean Chatelain*, persons active in the field of organizing international temporary exhibitions presented their points of view and studied various issues raised by the organization of such events, particularly with regard to insurance questions.* *Mr. Jean Louis Chauchat* explained the concerns of an insurer *vis-à-vis* State guarantees and emphasized the lack of dialogue between insurance companies and public authorities (*see infra*, pp. 425–430). *Ms. Beverly Wolff* gave her point of view as a museum legal counsel and proposed the adoption of an international treaty for the unification of conditions of coverage by governmental indemnification insurance (*see infra*, pp. 445–448). She also pointed out the need to improve co-operation between lenders of works of art and organizers of international temporary exhibitions. *Mr. Hans-Ewald Schneider* discussed questions of transportation, as well as the customs and safety issues related to the organization of international temporary exhibitions (*see infra*, pp 449–454). He expressed concerns about the plans of the European Commission to add specific administrative requirements for customs documentation in 1993, which would increase the bureaucratic formalities to be applied to the exportation of works of art.

All of the speakers were concerned about the impact of the increase in prices of works of art on the price of insurance premiums, and more generally, on costs involved in the organization of international exhibitions. Certain speakers were unhappy with lenders' policies requiring that their own insurance company insure the works of art that they loan, as in their view, such policies increase the cost of insurance. Others pointed out that certain insurance companies do not obtain enough information about the works of art they insure. Finally, a piece of general advice was given: do not organize international temporary exhibitions which could involve too many risks to the works of art to be exhibited.

List of Participants in Discussion

H. F. Heerkens Thijssen (Netherlands)
Patrick O'Keefe (Australia)
P. Marx (Germany)
S. Follender Grossfeld (Netherlands)

* For a comprehensive analysis of the insurance of works of art, *see International Sales of Works of Art/La Vente Internationale d'Oeuvres d'Art*, ICC Institute, ed. (ICC Publishing/Kluwer, Paris/Deventer 1990) Chapter V.

General Report

Rapport Général

SUJET 5. L'ASSURANCE DES EXPOSITIONS TEMPORAIRES INTERNATIONALES

Jean Louis Chauchat*

L'assurance n'est pas un poste isolé dans le budget d'une exposition, en effet, ce n'est qu'un maillon d'une longue chaîne qui comprend la compétence des organisateurs, la prévention, la protection, la sécurité et enfin l'assurance.

C'est donc tous les maillons de la chaîne qui doivent être soigneusement calculés et attentivement surveillés; si par malheur un maillon cède par faute humaine ou par le fait de Dieu, l'assurance intervient pour remplacer par une indemnité convenable le dommage subi si tant est qu'en matière d'oeuvres d'art il soit possible de procéder à son remplacement puisqu'il peut, dans certains cas, s'agir d'oeuvre unique et irremplaçable.

Avant d'aborder les problèmes évoqués dans cette intervention, citons quelques exemples des valeurs atteintes ces derniers temps par des oeuvres d'art en vente publique sachant que les plus belles et les plus rares se trouvent dans les collections des musées.

Van Gogh	Les Iris	FF 323.000.000
Van Gogh	Les Tournesols	FF 239.000.000
Picasso	Les Noces de Pierrette	FF 300.000.000

I. DEFINITION DE L'ASSURANCE

L'assurance est une forme de mutualité qui permet grâce aux primes recueillies auprès d'assurés exposés à un même risque d'indemniser celui ou ceux qui par malheur subiront un dommage; plus les assurés sont nombreux et mieux ils sont répartis, meilleur sera le risque, c'est le cas par exemple pour l'assurance automobile, c'est moins vrai pour des expositions artistiques où l'on constate de très fortes concentrations de valeurs sous un faible volume dans un même endroit, salle de musée ou moyen de transport.

* Président du Conseil d'Administration, Société d'Assurance Seine et Rhône, Paris.

II. DEFINITION DU RISQUE

Pour permettre de déterminer le risque et calculer la prime, il y a lieu tout d'abord de le définir ainsi que les différentes protections et sécurités qu'il présente: personnalité de l'assuré organisateur d'une exposition, s'agit-il d'un musée d'Etat, d'un musée privé, d'une société commerciale, d'un particulier?

En fonction de cette situation, de la pratique que peut avoir telle ou telle des catégories précitées pour l'organisation d'une exposition, il est évident que le coût de l'assurance pourra varier sensiblement puisque par exemple un musée d'Etat aura des moyens d'intervention ou de pression sur divers organismes officiels que ne pourra obtenir aussi facilement un simple particulier; de même une longue expérience joue un grand rôle pour la mise au point des différentes dispositions ou décisions qu'il y lieu de prendre.

1. Lieux de séjour

Les expositions sont généralement présentées dans des musées d'Etat dont les caractéristiques sont connues mais qui doivent faire l'objet d'une analyse précise et continue dans le temps aussi bien pour les moyens de protection incendie dont les systèmes d'extinction par gaz ou eau doivent être étudiés pour éviter, en cas de déclenchement, tous risques de détérioration des oeuvres en fonction de leur réaction propre à tel ou tel produit.

De même les systèmes d'alarme doivent permettre en cas d'effraction ou de tentative d'effraction d'alerter non seulement la cellule de gardiennage sur place mais également par télé-surveillance des équipes extérieures susceptibles d'intervenir très rapidement; on a constaté récemment, ici même en Hollande et également en France que le déclenchement de la télé-surveillance était trop éloigné du point sensible à surveiller permettant ainsi aux agresseurs de disposer d'un temps nécessaire à l'enlèvement des objets qu'ils convoitaient.

Un risque dont il y a lieu de tenir compte est le risque d'explosion qui, par l'effet de souffle dans un espace restreint, peut entraîner des dommages très graves sur des toiles cependant relativement éloignées du point d'impact.

Enfin, il est prudent, compte tenu des valeurs considérables atteintes par certaines oeuvres, de réfléchir à l'approche et à la circulation de visiteurs de plus en plus nombreux.

2. Déplacements

Le déplacement des oeuvres comporte un certain nombre d'opérations délicates et dont l'organisateur n'a pas, comme pour le séjour, la maîtrise complète autrement que par une sélection très rigoureuse des entreprises sous-traitantes. Il s'agit d'abord de procéder à l'emballage des oeuvres et du transport à l'intérieur du pays organisateur puis, lorsqu'il s'agit d'exposition itinérante dans plusieurs pays, des opérations de transit et de douane avec les formalités administratives souvent complexes qui s'y rapportent. Dans la majorité des cas, ces opérations sont confiées à des entreprises spécialisées et entraînées mais il est indispensable de vérifier que celles-ci appliquent sans aucune défaillance les mesures de prévention, de sécurité et de cumuls de valeurs que préconisent et imposent les assureurs.

C'est ainsi que notre Société a eu connaissance d'un sinistre important – vol d'un camion – où alors que la capacité du camion était limitée par l'assureur à 10.000.000 de FF, il a été constaté qu'un lot de même valeur avait été chargé dans ce même véhicule pour le compte d'un autre organisateur doublant ainsi les valeurs transportées; en cas de vol – bien renseigné – l'opération était plus intéressante, en cas d'incendie ou d'accident du camion la mise à l'abri de 10 tableaux est relativement plus aisée que 20 ou 30 tableaux.

L'emballage est une opération délicate effectuée par les musées eux-mêmes ou confiée à des entreprises spécialisées qui elles aussi – mais ce n'est pas toujours facile – devraient tenir compte des exigences normales et raisonnables des assureurs en n'accumulant pas dans leurs locaux à l'insu des donneurs d'ordres des lots de diverses provenances multipliant ainsi les risques de cumul de valeurs. S'il s'agit d'un emballage spécialement adapté à telle ou telle oeuvre particulièrement sensible, il est important que les consignes données pour la réexpédition soient d'une extrême précision et d'une grande fermeté dans leur application afin qu'au réemballage de l'oeuvre dans le pays qui a accueilli l'exposition; la mise en place dans les caisses soit faite à l'identique de celle conçue pour le départ; la solution la plus prudente étant de prévoir, pour le retour, le déplacement du spécialiste qui a conçu l'emballage.

Les opérations de transit et de passage en douane, sous réserve des précautions prévues, ne présentent pas de difficultés majeures car dans la majorité des cas, elles sont effectuées en présence de conservateurs et souvent dans les locaux même du musée.

3. *Transports*

Le choix du moyen de transport dépend bien entendu des circonstances: le transport à l'intérieur d'un pays européen ou entre pays européens (CE) s'effectuera souvent par véhicule routier, par avion ou quelquefois par chemin de fer; pour les voyages outre-mer, il s'agira évidemment de transports aériens.

Quel mode choisir? Quel est le plus sûr? D'après les statistiques disponibles, nous trouvons dans l'ordre de la meilleure sécurité et au niveau de la fréquence: l'avion, le chemin de fer, puis la route. Toutefois au niveau de l'importance du sinistre l'accident d'avion entraînera généralement une perte totale, rare pour la route si le véhicule est convoyé et très rare pour le chemin de fer. Il faut remarquer qu'en matière de transport aérien les risques d'incidents se produisent lors des décollages ou atterrissages permettant peut-être d'en conclure qu'il est préférable de prévoir un seul gros porteur transportant des valeurs très importantes plutôt que plusieurs appareils transportant des valeurs moins élevées.

Compte tenu du risque de perte totale, la question n'est pas tranchée mais les assureurs et les dispositions des garanties gouvernementales proposées par certains Etats limitent toujours le maximum par moyen de transport.

Le transport par chemin de fer, s'il présente quelques difficultés au niveau de l'organisation apparaît comme très sûr puisqu'il n'a pas à tenir compte, pendant les périodes hivernales, des conditions météorologiques trés préjudiciables au transport routier. Le transport routier, s'il est très souple, implique néanmoins des contraintes en cas d'interruption non prévue, panne ou transbordement rapide du chargement dans des conditions qui peuvent être très précaires. Là aussi, il y a lieu de fractionner les valeurs des chargements pour maintenir un niveau raisonnable par véhicule en fonction des circonstances.

Les opérations de déplacement étant ainsi brièvement définies, le problème de la surveillance de l'ensemble reste primordial et si dans la plupart des cas l'assureur souhaite la présence pendant les déplacements d'un conservateur du musée susceptible d'intervenir au plus haut niveau en cas d'incident, il est souvent prévu, pour les transports terrestres, une escorte armée accompagnant le ou les convois mais qui entraîne des problèmes d'Etats lorsqu'il s'agit de franchir des frontières.

A ce sujet, l'Office Central de Répression des Vols d'Objets d'Art (OCRVOA), l'organisme qui dépend du Ministère de l'Intérieur Français, a mis au point un protocole avec la plupart des pays Européens permettant l'organisation d'une chaîne non interrompue d'escorte 'multinationale' évitant ainsi des ruptures de surveillance au moment du passage des frontières.

III. MODE DE GARANTIE D'ASSURANCE

La garantie d'assurance doit être souscrite par l'organisateur pour le compte des autres participants et des différents intermédiaires (transporteurs, emballeurs, transitaires, etc.) suivant la formule dite 'clou à clou' depuis l'enlèvement chez le prêteur, l'emballage, le transport, le séjour jusqu'au retour au prêteur auxquels s'ajoutent bien entendu lorsqu'il s'agit d'exposition itinérante présentée dans plusieurs musées, toutes les opérations identiques entre les musées participants.

La garantie proposée par les compagnies d'assurance spécialisées couvre tous les risques: incendie, vol, disparition, accidents ou détériorations y compris comme dans certains pays: la France, les catastrophes naturelles (Loi de 1982) ou l'Espagne (*Consortio*) à l'exception des risques de guerre et assimilés. Sont également couverts mais dans certains contrats seulement les risques de dépréciation d'une oeuvre à la suite d'un dommage partiel garanti par le contrat. Il est donc de première importance qu'une constatation de l'état de l'oeuvre soit effectuée lors de la prise en charge au départ chez le prêteur puis lors de chaque transfert entre deux musées, ainsi que les consignes à observer pour la bonne conservation de l'oeuvre. Enfin, la valeur doit être déterminée avec beaucoup de précision entre le prêteur et l'emprunteur puisque cette valeur servira de base pour tous les calculs ultérieurs.

Deux formules sont habituellement pratiquées en cette matière:

- La valeur déclarée dans le contrat d'assurance où le prêteur indique la valeur à laquelle il évalue l'oeuvre qu'il prête, est la formule qui entraîne souvent au moment du sinistre l'obligation de la faire fixer par expert et, il faut le dire, un certain climat de contestation préjudiciable à un règlement rapide de l'indemnité.
- La valeur agréée par les parties sur laquelle le prêteur, l'emprunteur et l'assureur se mettent d'accord – dès là réalisation du prêt – est la valeur de l'oeuvre qui servira de base contractuelle au cas où surviendrait un accident, évitant ainsi toute contestation.

Cette dernière formule est celle qui la plupart du temps est retenue par les musées dont les conservateurs possèdent les connaissances suffisantes pour apprécier les valeurs compte tenu de l'évolution du marché et de la qualité de l'oeuvre en question.

IV. TARIFICATION

La tarification dépend de tous les éléments qui entrent en jeu pour l'organisation d'une exposition:

- Le bâtiment, sa construction, sa protection incendie et vol.
- Le gardiennage, la télé-surveillance, la proximité des services de secours et de police.
- Les mesures de conservation, hygrométrie, éclairement.
- La durée de l'exposition et des différentes étapes s'il s'agit d'une exposition itinérante.
- Les modes de transports, leur qualité, les conditions de convoyage.
- Les étapes intermédiaires, emballeurs, transitaires, leur qualité, la durée du passage chez chacun d'eux.
- Le nombre d'oeuvres, leur matière, leur état, leur valeur unitaire, les conditions particulières d'exposition exigées.
- Les valeurs maximum par transport.

De l'examen de ces différents éléments dépend le taux de la prime appliquée en tenant compte du fait que la prime concernant les opérations de transports est beaucoup plus élevée, compte tenu des risques fréquents de détériorations, que celle appliquée pour le séjour, les oeuvres étant, pendant cette période, en position statique et exposées à des risques mieux contrôlés par les organisateurs eux-mêmes.

V. SINISTRES

Si, par malheur, un incident survient, les assureurs se trouvent confrontés à un problème simple: indemniser vite et bien la victime. Qui est la victime? On constate souvent au moment de règler que les assureurs s'inquiètent du titre de propriété afin de verser l'indemnité au légitime propriétaire et éventuellement obtenir la cession des droits de ce dernier permettant d'exercer un recours contre un tiers responsable ou obtenir la restitution de l'oeuvre s'il s'agit d'un vol.

C'est dans ce dernier cas un point particulièrement délicat car qui en devient propriétaire: l'assureur qui a réglé ou bien le propriétaire conserve-t-il des droits? En France, si les oeuvres appartiennent à l'Etat, elles sont d'après la loi inaliénables, et doivent donc lui être restituées. Mais comme le souligne le Professeur Chatelain, si par exemple Mona Lisa disparaissait et était retrouvée dans un pays voisin, la loi française ne s'appliquerait pas dans le pays en question et la restitution ne pourrait – sauf intervention au plus haut niveau – intervenir que dans les conditions du droit commun, l'acheteur de bonne foi étant considéré la plupart du temps comme légitime propriétaire.

S'il s'agit d'une oeuvre prêtée par un particulier ou même par un musée, l'identification du propriétaire réel – non pas celle du détenteur ou du prêteur – est quelquefois difficile, il peut s'agir d'un dépôt, d'un prêt de musée à musée, etc., situation rendant complexe la recherche du propriétaire légal pouvant céder ses droits aux assureurs et leur donner quitus de l'indemnité.

En matière de vol, il est d'une extrême importance que la diffusion des informations – photos, descriptifs – soit faite dans des délais très courts par les organisations officielles: OCRVON, police judiciaire, gendarmerie, douane, Interpol ou professionnelles: commissaires-priseurs, négociants, presse spécialisée. L'assureur prend généralement en charge les frais nécessités pour la recherche des objets dérobés.

S'il s'agit d'un accident survenu à l'oeuvre assurée, le prêteur et l'assureur se mettent d'accord pour désigner un expert chargé de suivre les opérations de restauration et de fixer le montant de la dépréciation subie par l'oeuvre à la suite de l'accident; c'est en général un poste difficile à chiffrer et qui peut entraîner un arbitrage par un tiers expert.

National Reports

Austria

NATIONAL REPORT ON TOPIC 5. INTERNATIONAL TEMPORARY EXHIBITIONS AND INSURANCE*

Ignaz Seidl-Hohenveldern**

1.–2. The main difficulties faced by the principal organizer of an international temporary exhibition are timely planning (loans can be obtained only if requested a year in advance) and adoption of all measures to ensure the conservation and safety of the exhibitions. According to Art. 7(2) of the Federal Law Prohibiting the Export of Cultural Property,[1] the Federal Monuments Office may guarantee the right of future re-export of an object of art brought into Austria temporarily for the purpose of an exhibition, unless the object previously had been smuggled out of Austria or had remained abroad in violation of a commitment to return it to Austria.

3. In general, the organizer of an exhibition will have to bear all costs for the objects on loan, including freight and insurance. Cultural Agreements usually provide that the lending museum pays for the transport and insurance of the object as well as for the accompanying personnel on the way to and from the exhibition, while the organizer shall bear the local costs (rent of exhibition rooms, guards, publicity, catalogue, sojourn and living expenses of accompanying personnel). The same arrangements prevailed until two years ago for exhibitions arranged within the framework of the Council of Europe's Council of Cultural Co-operation (CDCC). As the lending museums will have to bear their charges out of their relatively small budgets, museums were hesitant to lend under these conditions. Two years ago the CDCC proposed that the European Cultural Fund, financially supported by all its members, shall bear these costs. Austria has not yet agreed to this arrangement.

4. Cultural Agreements Concluded by Austria

Multilateral
  Council of Europe 19 December 1954, BGBl 1958/80
Bilateral (quoting only the latest version or amendment)
  Belgium BGBl 1953/35

---

* Editor's note: *see also* 'Austria: Introduction' in Part One.

** Professor, Institut für Völkerrecht und Internationale Beziehungen, Vienna.

1. N. HELFGOTT, *Ausfuhrverbotsgesetz für Kulturgut* (Vienna, Manz 1987) p. 31.

Bulgaria BGBl 1987/545
Egypt BGBl 1987/412
Finland BGBl 1979/213
France BGBl 1947/220
German Democratic Republic BGBl 1985/310
Hungary BGBl 1977/519
Indonesia BGBl 1976/271
Italy BGBl 1954/270
Luxembourg BGBl 1986/588
Mexico BGBl 1975/611
Norway BGBl 1986/18
Poland BGBl 1987/448
Portugal BGBl 1984/230
Romania BGBl 1974/122
Spain BGBl 1976/480
United Kingdom BGBl 1953/60
USSR BGBl 1987/429
Yugoslavia BGBl 1980/479

Not all Cultural Agreements contain such detailed rules on exhibitions as, e.g., the Agreement with Egypt or the new draft Agreement with Hungary which provides also that restorations may only be made with the agreement of the lender and that the lender will deliver information material to establish the catalogue. Such information is due three months before the opening of the exhibition.

F. R. Germany

NATIONAL REPORT ON TOPIC 5. INTERNATIONAL TEMPORARY EXHIBITIONS AND INSURANCE*

Ludger Bischop**

I. GENERAL OBSERVATIONS

All of the German museums organize temporary exhibitions. They always try to organize specific exhibitions alongside the exhibition of their permanent collections. The difficulties which can arise from the organization of temporary exhibitions are more of a 'factual' than 'legal' nature.

II. DIFFERENT STAGES FOR THE ORGANIZATION OF A TEMPORARY EXHIBITION

The first step is to establish a list of the pieces to be presented at the temporary exhibition around a specific theme or artistic trend. Thus it is necessary to contact the various owners of the pieces around the world to convince them to loan their works of art. This phase is very often difficult. The organizer must propose good insurance conditions in order to convince the owner of works of art to send them to the place where the exhibition will be held.

III. INSURANCE

Besides the transport costs, the costs for insurance constitute the most important part of the costs incurred in the organization of a temporary exhibition. The organizer takes out insurance to cover the risk of damage which could occur between the moment when the object leaves its place of origin until it is returned. The prices for such insurance coverage have increased very substantially during the last year due to the record prices reached in auction sales.

---

* Editor's note: this Report is an English language summary of the German language 'National Report on Topics 5'.

** Research Assistant, Institute for International Business Law, Westfälischen Wilhems-Universität, Münster.

IV. SPECIAL ISSUES

When an organizer of a temporary exhibition wants to include a work of art from an Eastern European country in the exhibition, one specific difficulty must be overcome. In Eastern European countries, all works of art are State-owned. However, they may have been owned before the war by private persons who are now resident in the F. R. Germany; these private persons can claim the ownership of these works of art before the courts of F.R. Germany whose case law is in favour of these private persons. Museums in Eastern European countries try to avoid such situations by the conclusion of a contract under which the Western organizer guarantees the return of the work of art in question. The problem is to evaluate if such a contract is valid in the F.R. Germany, due to court decisions which allowed the recovery by the F.R. Germany resident of the works of art originating from the Eastern European countries on the basis that the expropriation by the Eastern European State infringes the F.R. German public policy.

France

RAPPORT NATIONAL SUR LE SUJET 5. L'ASSURANCE DES EXPOSITIONS TEMPORAIRES INTERNATIONALES

Jean Chatelain*

L'assurance des objets prêtés aux expositions temporaires est une forme particulière de l'assurance des oeuvres d'art en général, et celle-ci n'est à son tour qu'une branche de l'assurance des biens (par opposition aux assurances de personnes). Elle est donc gouvernée par les règles générales qui régissent ces catégories plus vastes, complétées par les modalités spéciales qui résultent de ses particularités propres.

I. LE PRINCIPE 'INDEMNITAIRE'

Puisqu'il s'agit d'assurances de biens, elle est dominée par le principe essentiel de ce type d'assurances; le principe 'indemnitaire'. Il signifie que l'indemnité accordée à l'assuré en cas de sinistre ne peut pas excéder le montant du préjudice réellement subi ou encore que l'assurance des biens ne peut jamais aboutir à faire réaliser à l'assuré un bénéfice.

II. DIFFICULTES D'APPLICATION

Ce principe tant fondamental qu'il soit, soulève des difficultés d'application dans le cas particulier des oeuvres d'art ou autres biens culturels. La valeur de ceux-ci est souvent difficile à déterminer avec précision puisqu'il ne s'agit pas – du moins chaque fois qu'il s'agit d'objets de qualité – de biens courants dont les prix peuvent être aisément déterminés par des catalogues, des 'cotes' généralement admises pour des objets identiques.

Sans s'arrêter au cas des polices multirisques qui couvrent indistinctement tous les biens meubles ou immeubles possédés par le souscripteur manifestement inadaptées au cas des objets de quelque importance, on voit donc se multiplier des formules d'assurances spéciales couvrant les objets 'précieux'. Elles ont pour caractéristiques de préciser dès le moment de la souscription la nature ou même la liste des objets assurés; et avec plus ou moins de précision, leur valeur. Celle-ci peut être fixée de deux manières.

* Professeur, Université de Paris I Panthéon-Sorbonne, Paris.

Dans le système de la valeur déclarée, celle-ci est fixée par l'assuré lui-même, sans expertise préalable et peut encore prêter à contestation en cas de sinistre.

Dans la système de la 'valeur agréée', cette valeur est appréciée au moment de la conclusion du contrat, par des experts agrées par les deux parties (assuré et assureur), et formellement acceptée par celles-ci. Le problème de la valeur des objets assurés est donc résolu à l'avance et clairement (il subsiste cependant une difficulté d'appréciation, lorsque le sinistre n'a pas fait disparaître totalement l'objet assuré, mais l'a simplement endommagé', car il faut alors déterminer la dépréciation qui résulte de la déteriorisation subie). Par ailleurs, le contrat n'est discuté qu'entre deux parties, l'assuré et l'assureur, ce qui rend plus aisée la conclusion de leur accord.

III. DIFFICULTES TECHNIQUES ET FINANCIERES

Ce système d'assurance en valeur agréée est la forme normale de l'assurance des objets prêtés aux expositions temporaires, mais il va présenter dans leur cas des difficultés techniques et financières.

1. Difficultés techniques

Les difficultés techniques résultent de la multiplicité des risques et des parties en cause.

En ce qui concerne les risques, le prêt aux expositions temporaires en comporte au moins deux: ceux résultant du transport, aller et retour des objets précieux, et ceux résultant de sa présentation dans un cadre inusité et en présence d'un public que les organisateurs souhaitent aussi nombreux que possible. Ces deux sources de risques peuvent être couverts par une même police ou par deux polices distinctes dont il faut donc clairement déterminer les rôles respectifs. De plus, et en raison même de l'importance des objets prêtés, les prêteurs exigeront souvent, aussi bien pour le transport que pour l'exportation elle-même, la couverture de risques très particuliers le plus souvent exclus des polices d'assurances normales (risques causés par les guerres, les révolutions, les catastrophes naturelles – dommages subis par des objets spécialement fragiles, etc.)

Ces complications se trouvent accrues par la multiplicité des contractants et parfois des contrats. Il n'y a plus en présence deux contractants mais au moins trois – l'assuré qui est le prêteur de l'objet, le souscripteur qui est l'emprunteur et l'assureur – et le plus souvent bien plus, car il y a le plus souvent une pluralité de prêteurs, qui peut engendrer à son tour une pluralité d'assureurs. En effet, le prêteur pressenti peut fixer ses conditions, et par exemple, exiger que l'assurance soit souscrite auprès d'un assureur déterminé distinct de celui auquel s'adresse habituellement l'emprunteur. Il n' y aura donc plus un contrat d'assurance, mais une juxtaposition de contrats conclus entre le même organisateur d'un côté, mais de l'autre des prêteurs différents, et par l'intermédiaire d'assureurs qui peuvent ne pas être toujours le même. On conçoit dès lors que la gestion des assurances sont pour un emprunteur une fonction importante qui peut amener à la création d'un éventuel service spécialisé et qui exige au moins le concours d'un ou plusieurs agents qualifiés. Dans la pratique, cette complexité n'apparaîtra qu'au niveau de l'emprunteur; chaque prêteur, lui, ne connaîtra qu'un partenaire, l'emprunteur, et un seul assureur. La preuve des engagements de chacun des trois sera établie par un certificat de prêt, dont chaque partenaire détiendra un exemplaire et qui devra impérativement être établi avant le départ de l'objet de son lieu d'installation habituelle.

On ajoutera enfin sans y insister davantage que toute cette organisation est rendue encore plus complexe quand l'exposition est organisée non pas par un seul organisateur dans un seul lieu, mais pour plusieurs et à des endroits différents comme c'est le cas des expositions circulantes, en deux ou plusieurs lieux successifs. Il faudra alors veiller lors de la mise au point de l'exposition, à coordonner très exactement le rôle et les responsabilités des divers organisateurs de manière à éviter des doubles assurances inutiles, ou des 'trous' entre deux assurances successives. La formule de coordination la plus efficace consiste alors à désigner un organisateur principal auquel les autres font confiance pour gérer la totalité du dossier 'assurances', à charge pour chacun d'assurer sa part du coût de l'exposition. Mais elle suppose évidemment que cet organisateur principal ait la compétence technique et l'autorité morale suffisantes pour que les autres s'en rapportent à lui.

2. *Questions financières*

Il est bien évident que le coût d'une assurance, c'est à dire le montant de la prime exigée par l'assureur, croît avec la valeur des objets assurés, et l'importance des risques couverts. Or, les expositions temporaires présentent les conditions idéales pour que ce coût soit le plus élevé possible. En effet la valeur des objets prêtés, la variété des risques couverts (dans la pratique de l'assurance de 'clou à clou', l'objet est couvert contre tous les risques 'normaux' (vol incendie, etc.) depuis son départ jusqu'à son retour, mais le prêteur peut exiger la couverture de risques exceptionnels, (guerre, etc.)) sont fixées par le prêteur qui est en position de force puisque c'est lui qu'on sollicite; et le coût de la prime est supporté par l'emprunteur. Celui-ci peut tout au plus discuter du montant de la prime s'il est en rapport avec son assureur habituel, il ne le peut même pas si le prêteur lui impose en outre le choix de son propre assureur (c'est-à-dire, jusqu'à maintenant le cas des principaux pays de l'Est européen qui imposaient le recours à des assureurs d'Etat, spécialement coûteux).

Il ne faut pas cependant exagérer ce déséquilibre entre les parties, notamment lorsqu'elles sont en rapports fréquents, comme c'est le cas des grands musées du monde. En effet il prennent vis à vis les uns des autres tantôt celui le rôle de prêteur, tantôt celui d'emprunteur si bien que celui qui serait un jour prêteur trop exigeant risquerait la fois suivante de se voir imposer à son tour des conditions sévères. Une certaine solidarité s'établit donc à ce niveau. Par contre le prêteur occasionnel, ou celui qui n'est jamais que prêteur (par exemple un musée secondaire qui n'organise pas d'expositions importantes, mais qui possède quelques pièces de grande qualité qu'il est souvent sollicité de prêter) se trouve évidemment dans une position de force.

La véritable difficulté financière en matière d'expositions temporaires résulte maintenant de la hausse constante du prix des oeuvres d'art qui s'impose à tous (certains prêteurs contribuent d'ailleurs à cette hausse en imposant des valeurs d'assurances excessives, soit pour bien manifester l'importance de leurs prêts, soit en prévision d'une vente postérieure de l'objet prêté: le certificat d'assurance, délivré par un organisateur prestigieux constituant une véritable attestation de valeur). Il est trés certain que la hausse des primes qui en résulte inexorablement amène à faire des frais d'assurances ou des pertes un des postes les plus importants des budgets d'exposition.

Il n'y a sans doute pas de remède technique véritable contre cette difficulté et ceux qu'on voit proposer sont plus apparents que réels.

Il peut s'agir ainsi de sous évaluations consenties pour des prêteurs complaisants et généreux – ce qui consiste en fait pour eux d'assurer une part des risques encourus par l'objet prêté. Il peut s'agir plus valablement en cas de partenaires qui sont fréquemment en rapport d'une répartition des échanges entre eux. Ainsi deux musées A et B qui se prêtent fréquemment des objets l'un à l'autre peuvent convenir que chacun d'eux supportera lui-même la charge de l'assurance des prêts consentis à l'autre. On fait ainsi disparaître la dualité entre prêteur qui fixe les conditions de prêt et emprunteur qui assume les charges qui en résultent. La formule est bonne mais exige des rapports fréquents, équilibrés et confiants.

Il y a surtout la garantie gouvernementale qui est l'espoir de beaucoup d'organisateurs. Au lieu que l'objet sont assuré auprès d'une compagnie d'assurances, la couverture des risques de l'exposition temporaire est prise en charge par l'Etat sur le territoire duquel l'exposition a lieu. La formule, née en Angleterre gagne peu à peu les Etats-Unis et certains autres Etats. Elle a cependant ses limites. D'une part, les prêteurs n'accepteront de garantie gouvernementale que d'Etats sérieusement gérés et qui peuvent garantir le paiement d'une indemnité en monnaie solide. D'autre part, la garantie gouvernementale n'est finalement qu'une forme déguisée de subvention étatique: l'Etat assure gratuitement les objets prêtés: il épargne ainsi aux organisateurs d'expositions la charge du paiement des primes, mais il prend en charge le paiement d'indemnités qui peuvent être considérables en cas de sinistre. C'est donc une nationalisation partielle de l'organisation des grandes expositions dont on peut s'étonner qu'une bonne part de ses fondateurs soient par ailleurs des partisans du libéralisme, très réticents à l'égard de 'l'interventionisme' étatique.

La véritable solution consisterait dans une vieille recette qu'aurait sans doute apprécié le bonhomme Franklin 'ne pas dépenser plus qu'on ne peut payer' ou 'proportionner ses dépenses à ses possibilités financières'. Sous une forme abrupte, cela conduirait à renoncer aux expositions trop coûteuses (que ce soit du fait des assurances ou de toute autre dépense), mais on se gardera bien de la formuler, car ce serait paraître retarder de deux siècles et sacrifier la culture à la finance. On dira plus simplement qu'il serait peut être temps, devant les excès du marché de l'art, que les grands musées du monde qui disposent, au total d'une bonne part du patrimoine mondial le plus prestigieux, se mettent d'accord entre eux, qui ont les mêmes finalités culturelles, pour organiser en commun des expositions assurées par des formules plus originales ou plus autonomes que l'assurance commerciale ou la garantie gouvernementale.

3. Questions juridiques

On n'en mentionnera qu'une: certains contrats d'assurances contre le vol ou la perte prévoient qu'au cas où l'objet serait retrouvé après que l'indemnité accordée à la victime de la perte ou du vol lui ait été effectivement versée, l'assuré aura deux solutions: soit reprendre l'objet retrouvé et bien entendu restituer l'indemnité qu'il avait reçue; soit conserver l'indemnité et renoncer à l'objet qui devient la propriété de l'assureur (clause de délaissement); cette clause n'est admise que pour les objets n'appartenant pas aux collections publiques dans les pays tels que la France où de tels objets sont inaliénables. L'application de cette clause aménerait à aliéner l'objet.

Papers on Specific Aspects

Indemnity and Immunity from Seizure

Beverly M. Wolff*

For many museums, including The Museum of Modern Art, the cost of insurance has become a major problem in exhibition planning. Over the past several years, with each new auction, one can see, not surprisingly, correlative increases in lenders' valuations of work. With the increases in valuation in art, the availability of governmental indemnity, in lieu of basic insurance, is essential to a museum.

For The Museum of Modern Art, if governmental indemnification were not available, it would probably not be able to undertake certain exhibitions or could do so only with substantial additional underwriting from sponsors. Covering a typical large exhibition without United States indemnity would cost the Museum from one hundred thousand to one or two million dollars. Fortunately, no major exhibition has ever been denied United States indemnity. However, even with it, the excess insurance required, since the indemnity only covers up to 125,000,000 dollars per exhibition and 1.2 million dollars per object and since lenders sometimes will not agree to be covered by it or express other special needs, still causes the Museum's insurance costs for a major exhibition to be high – up to ten to fifty percent of the entire exhibition's cost or from a few hundred thousand to a million dollars, depending on the size of the exhibition and works involved. For example, a recent major exhibition at the Museum cost over 500,000 dollars in excess insurance.

Since it is not tenable to expect a lender to an exhibition to bear the risk of loss, lowering insurance costs would seem to be an almost insurmountable feat. This is true unless there is a broader move toward government indemnity and unless the level of insurance provided through indemnities is greater. It would also be helpful to have better co-operation between the institution co-ordinating the exhibition and the lending institution with respect to acceptance of indemnity.

* Secretary and General Counsel, The Museum of Modern Art, New York.

I. NEED FOR MORE COUNTRIES TO ADOPT INDEMNITY AND/OR BROADER STATUTES

Clearly, there is a need for more countries to adopt indemnity statutes and to adopt broader statutes. Relatively few countries have statutes; I am aware of only ten countries which currently have indemnity statutes. Also, as far as I am aware, at this time, and since 1985, only the United States indemnity provides for coverage for an exhibition *both* while in that country and while on tour in other countries. On this foreign coverage, preference is given to exhibitions where indemnification will be shared with foreign institutions, or exhibitions in countries where no indemnification exists.

If international exchange of exhibitions is to continue, it is essential that countries that do not have an indemnity statute consider adopting one, and that those that do, consider extending coverage to traveling exhibitions. My sense of this area, and I have held this view for sometime, even before the value of art increased so dramatically, is that the museum community and public would be best served by an international treaty on indemnification not unlike Berne is to copyright. Such a treaty might, among other things, require all countries who are signatories to:

1. Have a statute, preferably based on a 'model statute' which satisfies a number of requirements, including a specific level of coverage, international coverage, and with uniform exclusions (for example, no war risk exclusion as now exists in Britain and Denmark).
2. Provide for reciprocal acceptance of the other countries indemnification on loans out to the country. It has been urged that for this to work the coverage provided by each country would have to be virtually identical.
3. Provide the organizing institution with a choice of its own statute *or* the lender's statute, or provide for joint coverage or co-insurance under two statutes. With respect to 'joint coverage', if co-insurance and joint liability is not possible, then perhaps one policy should be able to be used for excess coverage. Note that currently United States indemnity only provides primary coverage.
4. Provide for a secured fund, bond, or other guarantee of the program.

I believe that such a treaty would be effective in helping to secure and maintain governmental indemnity, even in those countries which currently have a statute, the thought being that it would add incentive to continued coverage at appropriate levels. I recognize that it could be politically difficult to accomplish a treaty which would be satisfactory to many countries and to write one which would satisfy the insurance lobby. Such an effort would only follow very serious planning. I am hoping that the International Council of Museums, which is creating a legal committee, might create a subcommittee that would focus on how best to accomplish such a treaty.

Second, as I briefly noted earlier, there needs to be more co-operation between institutions in resolving insurance/indemnity problems. This is true not just because many loans come from museums but because institutional lenders often set the trend with respect to insurance/indemnification regarding loans from private individuals from a particular country. Let me exemplify this need for co-operation with several situations which have occurred involving the Museum and institutions of other countries:

1. A lender institution refused to accept United States indemnification, required that its country's indemnification or private insurance be accepted instead, but also required the Museum, pursuant to the loan agreement, to indemnify and hold the lender harmless for any loss not covered by said insurance or indemnity. This is a rather untenable request.
2. Another situation which occurs is that the lender of major works requests a fee for its loans above and beyond the cost of insurance, shipping and/or other expenses. Such a fee not only does not help to engender a feeling of co-operation with respect to cultural exchange, but it is also problematic for a United States institution because, in order to qualify for United States indemnification, the United States institution must demonstrate that the exhibition was not-for-profit. Often the indemnification office requests a copy of any contracts, and does ask detailed questions about expenses and/or fees.
3. A lender institution wishes the Museum to insure through its indemnity, but does not provide a copy of the idemnification provisions, which are not otherwise published.
4. A borrower of many works for an exhibition wishes to self-insure through its government without any formal statute or indemnity program. Query as to whether such a government self-insurance can be an adequate guarantee in the event of loss. If United States indemnity is not available because a United States museum is not organizing or travelling the exhibition, a better approach would be either to insist that the borrower hold insurance through the lender's regular broker or another, or that an arrangement be structured creating an exchange of exhibitions, with each institution fully insuring their own exhibition.

II. IMMUNITY FROM SEIZURE

Unrelated to indemnity, another area of concern, where I believe international legislation is required, is the area of judicial immunity from seizure, since the possible legal expense and loss through seizure is not covered by insurance. Very few countries have immunity from seizure statutes, even though, with growing concern for loss of cultural patrimony – the possibility of seizure is becoming greater. Those which do, usually except from seizure works on loan to a cultural institution. This is an area, unlike insurance or indemnification, where a governmental guarantee might be more viable, if appropriately authorized. As for indemnity, however, a statute is advisable. I think progress with immunity statutes would also be best served with a treaty which would require a reciprocal law in order for a lender to take advantage of the law of the borrowing country.

III. SUMMARY

I would like to encourage movement toward better statutory relief for museum exhibitions in both areas addressed. I could, in fact, imagine both indemnification and immunity from seizure being treated under the same international convention. Insurance has become a disproportionate portion of an exhibition budget – monies could be better spent on more visible aspects of the programs which would better benefit the public.

Transport Costs – Licences, Customs and Taxes – Safety – Insurance

Hans-Ewald Schneider*

This report deals mainly with exhibitions in museums, so that art dealers are only given secondary consideration.

I. TRANSPORT COSTS

Here it is necessary to distinguish between the situation in England and the United States, on the one hand, and continental Europe and Japan on the other hand, where there are fundamental differences in the organizational structure of art exhibitions.

Museums in England and the United States have registrars, a profession which does not exist or is rare in this scope in the other countries. The registrar selects, co-ordinates, controls and budgets the necessary service companies required for an art exhibition.

In Europe, and particularly in Germany, this task is performed by specialist companies. The degree of service required by the customers differs from case to case and extreme cases can include functions, which I would like to list as follows:

1. Establishing contact with possible lenders in the name of the museum.
2. Photographing the objects and stipulating the packing.
3. Compiling all lists and documents necessary for the exhibition, particularly customs lists, insurance lists, shipment lists, etc.
4. Manufacturing the packing, bearing in mind the concept: route → goods = packing.
5. Nail-to-nail insurance of the entire exhibition, including insurance consulting.
6. Organization of matters for the courier including hotel, air and train reservations.
7. Transport and storage.
8. Applications to the local police or to private security forces for securing the transport route.

---

* Director, Hasenkamp, Cologne.

9. Unpacking and installation (hanging the exhibits).
10. Co-ordination of the exhibition architecture with the individual exhibits, e.g., checking the ceiling load-carrying ability for particularly heavy exhibits (Serra).
11. Provision of showcases and podiums, and of captions in several languages.
12. Organization of the opening event.
13. Provision of a qualified art historian for drawing up a catalogue.
14. Mediation of exhibitions for other interested museums.

In other words, when you look at the list of services performed, a forwarding company such as Hasenkamp in this particular case is no longer simply a forwarding company but rather a service company which has acquired more and more functions in the world of exhibition projects.

The functions listed above of course include the maximum range of services which we perform today. The price naturally also depends on the extent to which these services are required. For large exhibitions where we are required to perform the above named functions, the price will amount to between DM 2,000.00 and DM 5,000.00 per exhibit including insurance, whereas for smaller exhibitions where considerably fewer service tasks are to be performed, the price can under certain circumstances be between DM 200.00 to DM 300.00 per exhibit.

These are of course only rough figures: more precise prices can only be named on the basis of precise details. Today it is also necessary to provide the customer with a so-called stand-by calculation. In other words, the customer must be informed about special aspects of the lenders, which might involve higher costs than those originally presumed, in order to avoid exceeding the budget. This procedure requires a great deal of experience and precise detailed information on the whole material; only a very limited number of companies are capable of performing this task.

At this point I would like to note that the costs are subject to change not only as a result of lenders' wishes as regards packing and mode of transport; the costs for transport in particular are being increasingly influenced by special conditions imposed by the insuring companies.

However, it can be seen that insurance premiums can be reduced by observing certain minimum requirements as far as packing and safety are concerned.

II. IMPORT/EXPORT, CUSTOMS, FISCAL PROBLEMS

Throughout the world and particularly in Europe, there are great differences and constant changes in the regulations concerning import and export licences for the transfer of works of art.

Up to now, the European Community has not been capable of drawing up uniform regulations for free transfer of works of art. I do not think that there is much point in me elaborating on the currently valid customs and fiscal formalities for each country. The list may even be out of date by tomorrow. As a general rule, it can be said that the Netherlands and Scandinavia have the most generous formalities as far as customs, taxes and licences are concerned.

On the other hand, these countries have an absolute ban on trading with materials from endangered species (ivory, etc.). Some of the other European countries have highly complicated customs and tax formalities; take Italy, for example, where there are differences even from one region to the next. We can only hope that by 1993 the EC Commission in Brussels will have imposed a uniform ruling here.

There are also different formalities from one country to the next as far as the export of so-called 'National Treasures' is concerned. Here again, in Germany there are practically no problems in exporting works of art of national significance. In France (Louvre commission), Italy and Spain, highly complicated and expensive procedures must be completed for exporting works of art even only for limited periods for temporary exhibitions.

The whole range of the problems confronting us today as far as customs, taxes, licences and permits are concerned, became only too clear at a congress under the title *Art sans frontiers* which took place last autumn in the Villa Vigoni at Lake Como in Italy. Italian officials in the persons of Professor Sesinni, chief of the *Subra intendencia de bene culturale* (a government department which takes the decisions to issue permits and licences, or otherwise!) together with a commander of the art carabinieri, Emilio Napolitano, explained how they see their task in the present day, and which approval procedures, regulations, penalties, punishments and enforcement methods are used.

For the first time, it was officially announced that five thousand special carabinieri, who are subordinated to the army, have taken over control of works of art in Italy to prevent these works from leaving the country illegally.

One overall problem is the fact that in Germany, there are only five hundred and one works of art listed in the Federal Register as works of cultural significance which should be prevented from leaving the country. In Italy, France and Spain, theoretically every work of art could appear in a list of this kind. The European authorities will be faced with the problem of harmonizing these fundamentally different opinions to the whole question of free transfer of art.

However, initial draft regulations reveal that we are more likely to be confronted with a bureaucratic catastrophe, instead of simplification.

There is an urge to insist that every export application for every work of art should be accompanied by a declaration approving of the export from the country of origin. It is suggested that every work of art be accompanied by a 'file' which is to be deposited with the EC authorities; on the basis of the 'file', an identification sheet will be drawn up with room for the decisions from every Member State. (Who will pay the court costs when the rival national bureaucracies block each other's moves? Court bailiffs, notaries and museum directors are supposed to help check the identity of every work of art.)

Finally, paragraph 59 of the draft regulations from Brussels requires all art in Europe to be documented in the form of a European register. In other words, at every frontier a customs official can check through a central computer to see whether the goods on the truck or in the car are national works of art meriting protection from one or other Member State.

This just goes to show that the already highly complicated customs, licence and permit formalities in Europe will only grow worse in 1993, if this comes to pass; this will create enormous problems for free cultural exchange, boosting the costs astronomically.

III. SAFETY DURING TRANSPORT

The greatest insecurity is of course concealed in the human factor. A company working in this field is fundamentally dependent on outstanding, loyal and impeccable (i.e. no police record) personnel. Companies working in this field can not be built up overnight, but require many years of cautious development work in personnel matters.

In addition, it is also important for all storage facilities and warehouses to be equipped with internationally recognized alarm and safety systems for fire, burglary/theft, etc.

Here it should be noted that there should be no reference to art transports in the lettering on the trucks: advertising should be dispensed with here! The same applies to the inquiries we regularly receive from journalists who would like to be informed about the details of the transports schedules and insurance values. It is advisable to reject such inquiries in a friendly but firm manner.

There are of course other aspects to ensuring the safety of the exhibits: take for example the climatic conditions of the transport. Temperature and humidity in particular, but also vibrations and shocks must be kept within certain limited tolerances. Such influences must be kept under control at all time and be recorded in accompanying documents. Constant improvement of the transport conditions is necessary, as there are constant changes in knowledge, know-how and in the materials provided.

IV. INSURANCE

I would now like to turn my attention to those aspects which for legal reasons have become very important for the forwarding company or transport agent in recent years. The art market and all involved in it have undergone drastic changes in recent years so that enterprise liability for those who deal with art must under certain circumstances be subject to reconsideration.

What was the situation like fifteen to twenty years ago?

Just think about the equipment used by the forwarding agents, about the insured sums, about the number of exhibitions and the number of persons involved in putting an exhibition together and bearing joint responsibility. There was not the same time pressure that there is today, and all those involved were more or less aware of their own responsibility. In addition, only a fraction of the number of art galleries existed. The technical aspects and equipment have become much more complicated and improved. Insurance sums have meanwhile reached astronomical values.

The number of exhibitions has risen rapidly, to be explained among others by the fact that the art market has become increasingly public and, for example in Germany, has today become a real economic factor with an annual turnover of approximately one-and-a-half to two-and-a-half billion US dollars.

In addition, there is the large number of new museums and art galleries, together with the growing interest of broad sections of the population in the art scene. On the other hand, the group of people involved has undergone radical change. In earlier times, we were involved with exhibitions which were lent out by museums, or the presentation of old family collections: today, the situation is quite different. Of course, we still have plenty of loans from museum to museum, but a new type of collector is coming increasingly to the fore. The new group of collectors corresponds to the general spirit of our times: they collect for a completely different, definitely legitimate aspect, i.e., for the creation of capital.

This means that works of art are now principally considered as capital investments, which is reflected in the commercially based exhibitions which are taking place all around the world. For legitimate reasons, this particular group of collectors has a completely different attitude towards any potential damage to the works of art involved.

The damage is first and foremost not to a work of art but to a capital investment, so that the damage itself is considered from a financial point of view. Business is increasingly international; features such as place of jurisdiction and national law have gained new importance. Juridicial subtleties have started to play a greater role in loan deals. This also applies to contracts concluded between two museums, or between a museum and a lender. In view of this development, all those involved with works of art must take even greater care.

As you all know, the large number of travelling exhibitions places a certain strain on the works of art. Any possible signs of fatigue or damage caused by the qualities of materials will in future possibly be blamed on the organizer of the events.

The insurance companies today are taking on absolute top ranking risks while premium rates are on the decline.

The insurance sums, some of which are very high, do in fact incorporate the liability and not what we have agreed with the customer. The forwarding agent knows that above a certain damage sum, the 'ability' of every customer 'to suffer' ceases. In other words, in the event of damage of a certain magnitude, it's up to lawyers. These lawyers will attempt to break the forwarding agent's liability under all circumstances, in order to create a different legal situation.

I shall refrain from examining individual national and international liability bases and limitations, as these are subject to current legislation and can already be out of date tomorrow. Here is one important question though: is each specific transport liability contract (liability restriction) legally secured when loss in the magnitude of a million occurs?

If a German forwarding company arranges on behalf of a museum in Amsterdam to transport a loan from Paris, and if the exhibition organizer in Amsterdam adopts the insurance conditions of the lender in Paris, the German forwarding agent does not necessarily know all the details of these insurance conditions for his specific case. He relies on his own national legislation, and in the event of damage he could under certain circumstances be confronted with a situation where a French court attempts to invalidate the liability limits by clever tactical moves. This means that in this market segment, most companies use the limited liability personal company corporate form such as GmbH's for their art departments which are responsible for drawing up contracts with customers.

The entire German art insurance market, for example, has an income from premium contributions of only thirty to forty million DM. When compared to the sums transported by us, this is a ridiculous contribution for the insurance industry as a whole. In co-operation with the Dutch company, Gerlach, our company has been responsible for transport of the currently running exhibition 'Vincent van Gogh'. We have received a letter from the organizer in which he informs us that the maximum value of works of art being transported in one truck may not exceed the sum of three hundred million guilders. To the relief of all involved, spectacular damage has not been incurred up to now. If this should still occur, the situations for all participants will radically change.

What are the consequences of all these problems for those companies which are required to perform the tasks I listed at the beginning?

1. It is important to stipulate firmly the national legislation and national liability limits, in other words the contracting partners must clearly understand the liability limit and accept this by signature.
2. The service company must attempt to obtain access to the insurance contracts concluded by the organizer with an insurance company. Attempts should be made that these contracts be drawn up in such a way as to exclude any forms of recourse on the organizing company.

I would like to close with the words of Karl Valentin, who said: 'Art is beautiful, but it entails a lot of work.'

Concluding Remarks

Concluding Remarks

TEXT AND SUBTEXT IN THE INTERNATIONAL ART TRADE

John Henry Merryman*

One way to bring this Symposium to a conclusion is to sum up what the distinguished speakers have said and attempt a synthesis that encapsulates what we have achieved here. That clearly is impossible; the topics discussed are too numerous and the speakers' perspectives too various to permit a coherent summary and synthesis.

As an alternative strategy one can seek to penetrate beneath the texts that have been presented to us, to expose the subtext of values and assumptions that guide and limit our thinking about the international movement of works of art. There is such a subtext; it is a set of ideas that coalesced in the first half of the nineteenth century, was popularized by Byron and other English and German Romantics and was nurtured by the exaggerated nationalism of that time. It continues to dominate our thinking about the international trade in art today. We can call this subtext 'romantic nationalism'. I shall suggest that the subtext, and the slogans and clichés that it has supplied to our discourse, cannot stand critical examination and should be replaced, and I shall propose the elements of a preferable way of thinking about and making policy for works of art and other cultural treasures.

First, a brief look at the more prominent ways in which the subtext distorts the international dialogue.[1] Driven by the subtext, the literature is liberally salted with prejudicial terms like 'patrimony', 'repatriation' and 'heritage', and the discourse is confused and obscured by chronic misuse of 'protection'. Well meaning partisans use such terms to cloak romance as reason and advocacy as scholarship.

For example: *Patrimony, Repatriation and Heritage*. To assert that an object is part of the cultural 'patrimony' of Peru or Greece or Indonesia implies, since Byron, that it has a *patria*, a homeland, a nation to which, and in which, it belongs.[2] If found abroad it should, accordingly, be

---

* Sweitzer Professor of Law, Emeritus, Stanford Law School, Stanford, California.

1. For a fuller discussion, *see* my 'The Retention of Cultural Property', 21 *University of California at Davis Law Review* (1988) p. 477 *et seq*.
2. For a fuller discussion of Byronism, *see* my 'Thinking about the Elgin Marbles', 83 *Michigan Law Review* (1985) p. 1880 *et seq*.

'repatriated', returned to the national territory. It is not surprising that source nations have found this relic of 19th century romantic nationalism congenial. It is less easy to understand how it could have been transformed into an unquestioned premise in much of the international dialogue, and even in some of the scholarship, on cultural property. Left unchallenged, it paralyzes argument. To suggest that an object is part of a nation's cultural 'heritage' often has a similar paralytic effect.

At bottom is a confusion of ideas. Accurate information about the sources and nature of cultural objects is one thing: for example, it is right and important that the Mona Lisa be known for what it is and where it came from. In the Louvre, it is properly identified as painted in Italy by an Italian artist of extraordinary genius. It is in this sense 'Italian'. But to move from this position to the conclusion that the Mona Lisa 'belongs' in Italy is to leave a logical gap that terms like 'patrimony' and 'heritage' cannot bridge. There may indeed be good reasons why some objects should remain in their nations of origin and why others found abroad should be returned, but there may also be good reasons why they should not. The assertion of a general right of 'repatriation' is not a reason; it is an assertion that, if left unexamined, assures that reason will not come into play. That is why such terms as cultural 'object' and cultural 'property' – neither term is ideal, but the English language lacks a better equivalent for *beni culturali* – are preferable; they do not assume the answer to the question.

Protection. It is clear that we want to: (1) preserve cultural objects against physical damage; (2) preserve information that would be lost by undocumented removal from its context and (3) preserve the integrity of complex objects by preventing their dismemberment (e.g., removing elements from a Mayan temple or separating the panels of an alterpiece). 'Protection' is an acceptable term for such cases (though one might better use 'preservation' – of things, of information, of integrity). But when the purpose merely is to prevent the export of an object – for example an easel painting or a coin collection – and export offers no significant threat to these values, as often is the case, then 'protection' is merely a euphemism for 'retention'.

The practice of collapsing these quite different questions into one under the 'protection' heading is endemic among enthusiasts for the international enforcement of national export controls. Their usage has crept into a variety of international instruments. Naked retentionism, fueled by cultural nationalism, thus is legitimated by misuse of the otherwise honourable term 'protection'. It will not to do protest that retention equals protection. In some cases it may, but in other cases retention would be, and has been, more dangerous to cultural property than export. It is important to distinguish such cases, but lumping them together under the 'protection' heading conceals the fact that there is something to distinguish. Since there is no necessary relation between the retention and the protection of cultural objects, we would do better to respect that fact and use 'retention' when that is what we are really talking about.

Let us now consider five works of art that have enjoyed substantial international publicity in the recent past. They illustrate both the power of the romantic nationalism subtext and the need for a new level of dialogue about the international movement of works of art.

The five works are: 1. Van Gogh, 'Irises'. 2. The Elgin Marbles. 3. Canova, 'The Three Graces'. 4. Artist unknown, the 'Afo-A-Kom'. 5. Poussin, 'The Holy Family on the Steps'.

Irises evokes the figure of the neglected genius, the lonely, socially marginal artist who creates works of such extraordinary power and beauty that they become cultural monuments. We are reminded that Van Gogh never sold a picture during his turbulent life and that he died a desperate death by his own hand, unknown and unappreciated. In popular culture, he has become a romantic figure, a character from *La Bohème*. But the world has changed. Today, artists in their thirties are multimillionaires with international markets and retrospective exhibitions in major museums. There are no geniuses starving in garrets; the scouting system of dealers, collectors, critics and curators, all avid for the newest and best in art, is too efficient. Artists of genuine talent and achievement are quickly identified and amply rewarded.

This lovely painting also reminds us of the increasingly significant role played by dealers and auctioneers, that is, the international art market, in the distribution and redistribution of works of art and other cultural objects throughout the world. This picture was consigned by an American collector to Sotheby's in New York, where it was sold, at an enormous price, to Alan Bond, an Australian tycoon. As things turned out, Mr. Bond's reach exceeded his grasp, and the painting was sold again. It now resides in the Getty Museum in Malibu, but it could as easily have gone to Tokyo or Stockholm or Basel or Cologne.

Observe that there was no legal barrier to its removal from the United States. If Alan Bond had paid what he bid for it, Van Gogh's Irises would now be in Australia. Even works by American masters like Jackson Pollock, which the subtext would lead us to characterize as part of America's 'cultural patrimony' or 'heritage', may freely be exported, without any formality, no export permit or other official permission required. This is in marked contrast to the situation in much of the rest of the world, where the subtext dictates that works claimed as part of the 'national cultural patrimony' or 'heritage' be kept within the national territory and, if abroad, should be 'repatriated'.

The Elgin Marbles. The history of removal of these sculptures from the Parthenon in Athens is familiar to all, and the demand for their return to Athens was recently renewed by Melina Mercouri when she was Greek Minister of Culture. Minister Mercouri made virtuoso use of the subtext, building her campaign on the groundwork effectively laid a century and a half ago by Byron and other Romantics. What failed to receive adequate emphasis, however, was the fact that the Elgin Marbles in the British Museum are better preserved than the sculptures that were left on the Parthenon. Although if offends cultural nationalists that these great works of the spirit remain in London, the world's cultural heritage is richer because they are there. They have been better *preserved* as a result of their removal from the Acropolis.

Removal of the Marbles from the temple had other effects, however, among which is a loss of integrity. The Acropolis and the sculptures together formed a complex work. Removal of the sculptures destroyed the relationship between the parts, depriving the sculptures, and the temple, of the power and beauty – the artistic truth – of the integral work. The loss of integrity also led to a loss of historical truth, of information about and insight into the human past that the integral structure could provide. Truth thus calls for restoration of the integrity of sculptures and structure. (That could of course be accomplished by moving the temple to London, but then the integrity of the Acropolis would be lost; if integrity is our guide, the Marbles must return to Athens.)

The interest in preservation, however, makes any such proposal unacceptable, since the smog of contemporary Athens ferociously erodes the marble of which the sculptures, and the Parthenon itself, are made. That is why many of the remaining sculptures on the Acropolis, including the Caryatids on the Erechtheion, have had to be taken indoors and replaced with reproductions. The sculptures, if returned to Athens, would be placed indoors, in a museum. The call for return of the Elgin Marbles is not a call to restore the integrity of the Parthenon, it is a call to move the Marbles from a museum in London to a museum in Athens.

The Three Graces, recently sold to a foreign buyer, is a sculpture by Canova originally commissioned for a specific site at a great house in England. The British government has taken unusual measures (short of paying for it) to keep the sculpture from leaving the country. Why? The subtext would respond that The Three Graces is a part of the nation's cultural patrimony that must be 'protected' against 'loss'. A better argument would be that the sculpture is 'site-specific', made for and installed in a particular site with which it is integrated, much as the Elgin Marbles were integrated with the Parthenon. Removal of The Three Graces from their original site would falsify both the sculpture and the setting; truth would again be impaired. Observe, however, that the regard for truth would keep the sculpture at its original site, while the subtext merely opposes its removal from the national territory.

The *Afo-A-Kom*, a beaded wooden figure of religious/communal importance to the Kom tribe in Cameroon, mysteriously appeared on the art market in New York and, after eloquent pleas by Cameroon officials in Washington, was ceremonially returned to the Kom. This moving statement by a Cameroon official set the tone of the discussion:

> 'It is beyond money, beyond value. It is the heart of the Kom, what unifies the tribe, the spirit of the nation, what holds us together.'

These words suggest something different from and more compelling than cultural nationalism: a belief that the presence of the object is essential to the welfare, perhaps even the continued existence, of the tribe. Such attribution of magical qualities to objects, a practice common among many religions – consider the importance of relics and effigies in Christianity and Buddhism – is different from cultural nationalism. Access to the object, its physical presence, seems truly necessary because (1) the culture that gave the object its cultural significance is still alive and (2) the object is actively employed by them for the religious or ceremonial or communal purposes for which it was made. The Afo-A-Kom met these criteria. Objects associated with surviving American Indian cultures would similarly qualify, as would others from other parts of the world. Such cases are, however, relatively uncommon. The relics of earlier cultures in Egypt, Greece, China and Mexico serve no contemporary religious, ceremonial or communal function. People in those nations may place a high value on such relics for other reasons, but the use for which they were created is not one of them. The specific cultural value of such objects – for example, as testimony of the way of life of a vanished people or as great works of art of a specific time and place – is independent of their situs. In the British Museum, the Elgin Marbles are still the work of Greek sculptors taken from the Parthenon in Athens.

Poussin's Holy Family on the Steps, a painting in a private collection in France, was sold by its owner to the Cleveland Museum, whose Director took it to Cleveland without a French export permit (he had legal advice from eminent French and American counsel that no permit was legally required because the painting had long resided outside France and had only recently been acquired by its French owner, but the applicable French statutes were sufficiently ambiguous to permit a different interpretation). The French authorities, impelled by the subtext, insisted that an export permit (which would certainly have been denied) was legally required. Since the painting was not stolen, even if illegally exported, they had no basis for a legal remedy in United States courts, but they vigorously employed the means available to them; the Director of the Cleveland Museum was criminally indicted (in France) and diplomatic representations were strongly made to the United States Ambassador. Italy has recently taken a similar attitude toward the export (without a permit) of a Matisse painting and has denied permission to export a Van Gogh painting. The contrast with the American attitude toward export of great works of art described above is striking. Who is right?

According to the romantic nationalism subtext, the French and the Italians, and many others, are merely 'protecting' their 'national artistic patrimony' (though one might wonder how Matisse and Van Gogh so qualify in Italy) against 'loss'. But let us ask ourselves, using the triad of *preservation, truth and access*, whether the Poussin painting should be returned to France. *Preservation* clearly is not a concern; the painting will be at least as well protected and cared for in the Cleveland Museum as in a private collection in France. How about *truth*? None of the painting's beauty, power or value to scholars was lost by moving this framed canvas from France to Cleveland; it retains its identity and integrity, whether it is in Paris or Cleveland, or, for that matter, in Tokyo or Frankfurt. As to access, when it was in the private collection in France, how many people had access to it? Now it is in a public museum, where hundreds of thousands of people a year can see and enjoy it. Poussin's painting is far more accessible in Cleveland than it was in France.

Preservation, truth and access are independent of nationalism. They direct attention to the object, not to the nation. They focus on the work itself, on its power to enrich our lives, to give testimony about the human past, to inspire further creativity. They deal sensitively with works that should not be removed from their sites or taken from their cultures, as the discussion of the Elgin Marbles, the Three Graces and the Afo-A-Kom has shown.

The romantic nationalist subtext has outlived its utility and today serves the cause of blind retentionism. It is time to raise the dialogue to a more respectable level. Together, preservation, truth and access offer an alternative and preferable basis for policy, for ethics and for law respecting the international movement of works of art.

Annexes

Committees

HONORARY COUNCIL

Mr. B. J. Asscher, President, Amsterdam District Court
Mr. Jean Dondelinger, Member of the Commission of the European Communities
Mrs. C. W. Fock, Professor, University of Leiden
Mrs. M. H. M. F. Gardeniers-Berendsen, Former Minister of Culture, The Netherlands
Mr. A. C. Helfrich, Chairman, ICC Nederland, The Hague
Mr. Frits Hondius, Deputy Director of Legal Affairs, Council of Europe, Strasbourg; Visiting Fellow, Saint Cross College, Oxford
The Honourable J. Hugh Faulker, P. C., Former Secretary-General, International Chamber of Commerce
Mr. Pierre Lalive, Professor, Faculty of Law and Director of the Department of Private International Law, University of Geneva; Attorney at Law, Geneva; Chairman, ICC Institute of International Business Law and Practice; Chairman, Institute of International Law
Mr. Jack Lang, Ministre de la Culture, de la Communication et des Grands Travaux, France
Mr. Federico Mayor, Director General, UNESCO
Mr. Henri Mercillon, Professeur, Université de Paris I-Panthéon Sorbonne; Membre, Conseil Artistique de la Réunion des Musées Nationaux, Paris
Mr. Riccardo Monaco, Professor Emeritus, Rome University; Chairman, International Institute for the Unification of Private Law (UNIDROIT)
Mr. Jorge Semprun Maura, Minister of Culture of the Kingdom of Spain
Mr. F. O. J. Sickinghe, President, Foundation Amsterdam Promotion
Mr. J. van Slooten, President, Court of Appeal, Amsterdam
Mr. Ed van Thijn, Mayor of Amsterdam
Mr. R. S. L. M. de Vilder, President, Amsterdam Chamber of Commerce and Industry
Mr. Peter Wallenberg, President, International Chamber of Commerce; First Vice Chairman, Skandinaviska Enskilda Banken, Stockholm

BOARD OF THE FOUNDATION ICC SYMPOSIUM INTERNATIONAL ART TRADE AND LAW AMSTERDAM 1990

Mr. J. M. Boll, Chairman
Mr. H. F. Heerkens Thijssen, Secretary
Mr. J. Bevaart, Treasurer
Mr. R. W. M. Brohm
Mr. J. M. Kok
Mrs. A. E. Vels Heijn
Mr. R. W. Mouw

ADVISORY BOARD OF THE FOUNDATION ICC SYMPOSIUM INTERNATIONAL ART TRADE AND LAW AMSTERDAM 1990

Mr. W. H. Crouwel, Director, Museum Boymans van Beuningen; Professor, Erasmus University Rotterdam
Mr. R. de Leeuw, Director, Rijksmuseum Vincent van Gogh
Mr. P. Sanders, Professor Emeritus, Erasmus University Rotterdam; Former Member of the Purchasing Committees, Dutch Museums; Member of the Council of the ICC Institute of International Business Law and Practice

EXECUTIVE COMMITTEE OF THE INSTITUTE FOR INTERNATIONAL BUSINESS LAW AND PRACTICE OF THE ICC

Mr. Pierre Lalive, Chairman; Professor, Faculty of Law and Director of the Department of Private International Law, University of Geneva; Attorney at Law, Geneva; Chairman, Institute for International Law
Prince Bola Adesumbo Ajibola, Vice-Chairman; The Honourable Attorney-General of the Federation; Minister of Justice, Nigeria
Mr. Florentino P. Feliciano, Vice-Chairman; Associate Justice, Supreme Court of the Philippines
Mr. Bruno Oppetit, Director of Research; Professor, Université de Droit et d'Economie, Paris
Mrs. Martine Briat, Administrative Director
Mrs. Michèle Garzon, Assistant to the Director

Sponsors

Ministry of Welfare, Health and Cultural Affairs of The Netherlands
Municipality of Amsterdam
Amsterdam Chamber of Commerce and Industry
Christie's International
Heerkens Thijssen & Caviet
Agence de Coopération Culturelle et Technique (ACCT)
De Brauw Blackstone & Westbroek
Stibbe Blaisse & de Jong
Gerlach Art Packers and Shippers B.V.
AMRO
Perscombinatie N.V.
Royal Packaging Industries Van Leer B.V.

GPSR Compliance

The European Union's (EU) General Product Safety Regulation (GPSR) is a set of rules that requires consumer products to be safe and our obligations to ensure this.

If you have any concerns about our products, you can contact us on ProductSafety@springernature.com

In case Publisher is established outside the EU, the EU authorized representative is:

Springer Nature Customer Service Center GmbH
Europaplatz 3
69115 Heidelberg, Germany

Batch number: 10830943

Printed by Printforce, the Netherlands